IMPLEMENTING LEARNING IN THE LEAST RESTRICTIVE ENVIRONMENT

IMPLEMENTING LEARNING IN THE LEAST RESTRICTIVE ENVIRONMENT

Handicapped Children in the Mainstream

Edited by

John W. Schifani, Ed.D.

Robert M. Anderson, Ed.D.

and

Sara J. Odle, Ed.D.

Special Education and Rehabilitation
Memphis State University

University Park Press
Baltimore

UNIVERSITY PARK PRESS

International Publishers in Science, Medicine, and Education
233 East Redwood Street
Baltimore, Maryland 21202

Typeset by American Graphic Arts Corporation.
Manufactured in the United States of America by
The Maple Press Company.

Library of Congress Cataloging in Publication Data

Main entry under title:
Implementing learning in the least restrictive
environment.

Bibliography: p.
Includes index.
1. Handicapped children—Education—Addresses,
essays, lectures.   2. Mainstreaming in education—
Addresses, essays, lectures.   I. Schifani, John W.
II. Anderson, Robert Meredith.   III. Odle, Sara J.
LC4019.I48   371.9   79-28190
ISBN 0-8391-1538-5

CONTENTS

v

CONCLUSION

CONTRIBUTORS

Jo Allsop, M.Ed.
Curriculum Coordinator
Shrine School
Memphis City Schools
Memphis, Tennessee 38112

Robert M. Anderson, Ed.D.
Professor
Special Education and Rehabilitation
Memphis State University
Memphis, Tennessee 38152

Burton Blatt, Ed.D.
Dean
School of Education
Syracuse University
Syracuse, New York 13210

Bryan R. Clarke, Ph.D.
Associate Professor
Special Education
The University of British Columbia
Vancouver, British Columbia
Canada

Barbara Connolly, M.Ed.
Chief of Physical Therapy
Child Development Center
University of Tennessee
Memphis, Tennessee 38105

Gail L. Ensher, Ed.D.
Associate Professor
Special Education
Syracuse University
Syracuse, New York 13210

Barbara Galtelli, M.Ed.
Instructor
Special Education and Rehabilitation
Memphis State University
Memphis, Tennessee 38152

Bonnie B. Greer, Ph.D.
Associate Professor
Special Education and Rehabilitation
Memphis State University
Memphis, Tennessee 38152

John G. Greer, Ph.D.
Associate Professor
Special Education and Rehabilitation
Memphis State University
Memphis, Tennessee 38152

William M. Jenkins, Ed.D.
Professor
Special Education and Rehabilitation
Memphis State University
Memphis, Tennessee 38152

Susan Kelly
Doctoral Student
Special Education and Rehabilitation
Memphis State University
Memphis, Tennessee 38152

Virginia K. Laycock, Ed.D.
Assistant Professor
Elementary and Secondary Education
Clemson University
Clemson, South Carolina 29631

Perry T. Leslie, Ed.D.
Associate Professor
Special Education
The University of British Columbia
Vancouver, British Columbia
Canada

Sheldon S. Maron, Ph.D.
Assistant Professor
Special Education
Portland State University
Portland, Oregon 97207

David H. Martinez, Ed.D.
Assistant Professor
Special Education
Portland State University
Portland, Oregon 97207

Wellington L. Mock, Ed.D.
Assistant Superintendent for
    Community Services
Arlington Developmental Center
Arlington, Tennessee 38002

Sara J. Odle, Ed.D.
Assistant Professor
Special Education and Rehabilitation
Memphis State University
Memphis, Tennessee 38152

H. Lyndall Rich, Ph.D.
Associate Professor
Special Education and Rehabilitation
Memphis State University
Memphis, Tennessee 38152

John W. Schifani, Ed.D.
Professor
Special Education and Rehabilitation
Memphis State University
Memphis, Tennessee 38152

James Winschel, Ed.D.
Professor
Special Education
Syracuse University
Syracuse, New York 13210

PREFACE

A decade of mainstreaming has just ended. During this era, significant legislative acts, a series of court decisions, and widespread dissatisfaction with educational programs for handicapped children led to the prevailing philosophy of "mainstreaming," an orientation toward educational programming that has been widely implemented in the public schools only since the early 1970s. As the term implies, mainstreaming refers to the reentry of handicapped children into the regular education program. Recently, Public Law 94-142 has mandated that even severely handicapped children must be educated in "the least restrictive environment" whenever possible. Shock waves generated by PL 94-142, the Education for All Handicapped Children Act of 1975, are still reverberating in the classrooms of our public schools and universities. Today, the major thrust in education is for mainstreaming, and although there may be some serious obstacles, the question clearly is no longer whether to mainstream but rather *how* to mainstream most effectively.

The term *mainstream* itself has been difficult to define and has been used to describe a wide variety of programs and concepts that resemble one another only to a very limited degree. Recent court cases, public laws, and professional literature now advocate the term *least restrictive environment*, instead of mainstreaming. In principle, this term mandates the placement of handicapped children in regular classes unless the child's limitations are so constraining that a more protective or restricted environment is considered to be necessary. For most mildly handicapped children, therefore, the concept of mainstreaming will continue to be interpreted as education within the regular classroom, at least for a portion of the day. For more severely and multiply handicapped children, however, placement in a regular classroom, even for carefully selected activities, is generally an unrealistic expectation. A more restricted environment may be necessary. Nevertheless, the public sector has been mandated to provide appropriate services for all handicapped children, regardless of the severity of the handicap.

Most regular classroom teachers and school administrators have not been adequately prepared to cope with the curricular, management, and administrative problems associated with the inclusion of mildly handicapped children in their schools. Indeed, even many traditionally trained special class teachers and resource teachers will lack the competencies to deal effectively with the problems generated by the mandate to provide services for the severely handicapped. New challenges will continue to confront educators, parents, and pupils as significant numbers of handicapped children are channeled into the mainstream of education or, at least, into educational settings that are as "normal" as possible. Faced with rapidly shifting roles and more variable pupil populations, special educators and regular classroom teachers must now take a close look at their own teaching skills, attitudes toward differences in children, and commitment to meeting individual needs. Anyone who has attempted to teach handicapped and normal children in the same classroom knows that this is one of the most difficult tasks facing educators today. Teachers and other professionals are justifiably concerned about the critical problems confronting them as they proceed to implement PL 94-142.

It is now obvious that college and university teacher preparation programs must focus on the needs of regular classroom teachers as well as special education teachers who lack the competencies to function adequately in their new roles.

Many states, for example, now require all teacher education candidates to complete at least one course on the education of exceptional children. Most special education programs are currently engaged in developing curricula to prepare teachers of the severely handicapped.

In developing this book, we have attempted to assist in the process of orienting students and experienced practitioners to the changing philosophical and programmatic considerations pervasive in today's public schools. A broad spectrum is presented; there is a continuity of concern, from birth through adulthood. Possible consumers of the book are not only education majors; others who are future parents, service providers, employers, and taxpayers need the total picture of services for the handicapped.

From our perspective, we considered it important to provide an interface, insofar as possible, between the traditional categorical textbook organization and current attempts to develop interrelated or generic models. The rationale for this book is based, in part, upon the assumption that mildly and moderately handicapped children, particularly those traditionally labeled as mentally retarded, emotionally disturbed, and learning disabled, are more alike than they are different. The book reflects this point of view. While it is impossible at this time to eliminate categories altogether, we have attempted to focus on common learning and behavior problems of these "educationally handicapped" children from a noncategorical perspective. We believe that it is more meaningful for educators to deal with educationally relevant problems, such as information processing, language, academic, and emotional-behavioral areas, rather than with categories that evolved from a medical model. On the other hand, separate chapters have been developed to highlight the unique needs of visually, auditorially, physically, and severely and multiply handicapped children.

This book has been organized as an introductory textbook or reference for: 1) advanced undergraduate and beginning graduate students in regular and special education teacher preparation programs, 2) experienced teachers, supervisors, and administrators, 3) ancillary and related personnel, and 4) parents and nonprofessional or supportive personnel who are involved with helping to provide services for handicapped children.

The book is organized into three major parts, preceded by an introductory chapter and followed by a concluding paper. The first chapter, "Introductory Dimensions: Perspectives for Change," assists in the process of orienting students to the problems that challenge the public education of the handicapped today. This introduction is organized around the major issues and trends related to the organization and delivery of services for handicapped children.

Part I, "The Least Restrictive Environment," contains five chapters that describe the characteristics of handicapped children that interfere with learning, rather than the syndromes that lead to categorizing and placing children in classrooms also identified by category. The changing needs of the child are considered not only as to immediacy but also as part of the continuum from birth to the post-school years.

Part II, "Fundamental Strategies for Instruction," highlights ideas and suggestions for enhancing competency in informal assessment, matching learner needs with appropriate methods and materials, and expanding knowledge of instructional sequences—areas that have been neglected in most introductory textbooks. Our book differs from most existing texts in that it *does* focus on these significant areas. Our reason for incorporating this material is that introductory courses now include substantial numbers of regular education students and students from related areas of the helping professions. In many cases these students who will ultimately work with handicapped learners in some capacity will have only this introductory course to serve as an orientation. Therefore, in this section and throughout the book we have attempted to provide a broad, general overview of special education, as opposed to limiting the content to an exhaustive treatment of the characteristics of the handicapped, with the expectation that all students would continue to enroll in subsequent courses dealing with all aspects of special education. This section also illustrates how teacher attitudes toward the handicapped, toward children, and toward teaching itself create the classroom "climate" and aid or impede the learning process. The concluding chapter covers the management of undesirable classroom behaviors, undoubtedly the greatest concern of the teacher today.

Part III, "Resource and Support Systems," examines the services of disciplines other than education that will assist in meeting the needs of the handicapped. Ancillary services are now to be provided as part of the total educational plan for each individual. Our book emphasizes a multidisciplinary approach to education, contributing an understanding of the effective application of resource and support system personnel, including school psychologists, speech/language pathologists, and other ancillary professionals. The expanding policy of provision of the least restrictive environment for all handicapped persons, not just those of school age, dictates the provision of more and different community services for both the handicapped individual and his/her family.

The book goes into greater detail than many of its predecessors as to the role of the community in the provision of services other than education. This is important because the policies of normalization and deinstitutionalization will require a shift from parental responsibility to that of the community. The need for advocacy (both in litigation and in a broader service sense) is presented in depth. Parent groups and others are currently becoming involved in this effort. Moreover, federal legislation mandates an expansion of vocational rehabilitation services to include the more severely handicapped. This section of the book therefore describes available services, areas of need, and problems in provision of services and communication between service providers and users.

The concluding section discusses the "pros" and "cons" of major concepts presented in this book, e.g., mainstreaming and least restrictive environment. Implicit in the content of this book is the notion that such a philosophical orientation is not only desirable but imperative. In this conclusion, however, three authors, taking divergent points of view on the efficacy of mainstreaming approaches, discuss and debate this issue.

We would like to acknowledge, with special gratitude, the extraordinary typing skills and patience of Susan Green, Gail Davis, and Linda Jones.

IMPLEMENTING LEARNING IN THE LEAST RESTRICTIVE ENVIRONMENT

INTRODUCTORY DIMENSIONS

1
PERSPECTIVES FOR CHANGE

Robert M. Anderson, David H. Martinez, and H. Lyndall Rich

One of the most dramatic eras in the history of the education of handicapped children was launched by the courts and Congress in the late 1960s and early 1970s. The winds of change have consequently swept vast numbers of handicapped children into the mainstream of education, creating new challenges for administrators, teachers, and countless others. Confronted with rapidly changing roles, regular classroom teachers and special educators alike must now reexamine their attitudes toward differences in children and look critically at their own professional skills and competencies. In addition, the implementation of programs for all children in the least restrictive environment has far-reaching ramifications for all students in teacher education. With the placement of handicapped children in regular school situations, and the resulting variance in performance levels, learning styles, and problem areas, the need for knowledge about handicapped children is paramount.

SOME KEY CONCEPTS

Throughout this book reference is made to certain key concepts that are routinely used to discuss the education of handicapped children. For example, *mainstreaming, least restrictive environment,* and *continuum of services* appear repeatedly in the discussions of different handicapping conditions and strategies for instruction. Therefore, this introductory chapter is included to provide a guide to understand the more common concepts. However, it should also be understood that concepts have often taken on definitions through use and may not represent explanations that are universally accepted. Explanations and definitions of more specific concepts are provided within the individual chapters.

The key concepts discussed in this chapter are: 1) handicap, 2) interrelationships of handicaps, 3) incidence and prevalence, 4) special education, 5) mainstreaming, 6) least restrictive environment, and 7) continuum of services.

Handicap

Terms such as *handicapped*, *special*, and *exceptional* often have been used interchangeably to describe children who have characteristics different from those of the normal or typical school population. However, the terms are different and they convey different views of characteristics among children. While the terms *special* and *exceptional* refer to the entire population of children with different characteristics, handicapped refers to those children who possess characteristics that generally are negatively valued in our society and that interfere with a regular education experience.

Traditionally, special or exceptional children are considered to be physically, intellectually, emotionally, and socially different from the normal school population. This rather broad view of human differences could include the superior athlete, the gifted, the early maturer, and the class president. On the other hand, the physically disabled, the mentally retarded, the emotionally disturbed, and the socially maladjusted are included within these same encompassing terms. Thus, *special* and *exceptional* include both positively and negatively valued differences in human characteristics.

The focus of this book is on those individuals who are considered handicapped—children and adults who possess characteristics that are different from the normal school population, that are negatively valued, and that interfere with a normal educational experience. The handicapped subgroups considered in this book include the mentally retarded, the emotionally disturbed, the learning disabled, the physically handicapped, the visually limited, the hearing impaired, and the speech and language impaired.

Interrelationships of Handicapping Conditions

Professionals in psychology and education frequently diagnose and educate handicapped children as if a single, categorical label (e.g., mentally retarded) was an independent characteristic or syndrome, unrelated to other handicapping conditions or even normal characteristics. In truth, the existence of a single handicapping condition is rare. Instead, children identified as handicapped because of a specific set of characteristics often exhibit some characteristics of other handicapping conditions, including characteristics of normal children. For example, a visually limited child may be hyperactive, which is symptomatic of behavior disorders, yet have normal auditory reception and memory. Thus, the matter of assigning a specific handicapping label to a child is often a matter of judgment, based upon which characteristics are most pronounced at the time of diagnosis.

Currently, there is considerable disagreement over the continued use of categorical labels such as mentally retarded, emotionally disturbed, and learning disabled. Advocates of the categorical position maintain that specifically labeled handicapped children possess characteristics that are unique and are not shared by other handicapping conditions. They further maintain that specifically designed educational methods, techniques, and materials are required to adequately educate the child. Advocates of a noncategorical approach (e.g., educationally handicapped) maintain that similarities, not the uniqueness, among the handicapping conditions should be emphasized. They further maintain that methods, techniques, and materials can be adapted by most trained teachers.

Both the categorical and noncategorical advocates have convincing arguments in support of their positions. Therefore, it is practical to assume that children with categorical handicapping conditions have characteristics unique to that condition, but also have characteristics similar to those of other handicapping conditions and of the normal population.

For each handicapped child, categorically or noncategorically labeled, the degree of uniqueness and interrelatedness may be a function of the individual child or the handicapping condition. Uniqueness among mild learning, behavioral, and psychological handicaps, for example, tends to be less obvious, deviating only marginally from other handicapping conditions and from normal characteristics. On the other hand, children with more severely handicapping conditions (e.g., deaf, blind, and autistic) demonstrate relatively unique characteristics; therefore, the extent of interrelatedness is less than that of mildly handicapping conditions.

All handicapped children have some characteristics that are considered normal. However, handicapped children by the nature of their handicapping condition differ from the normal population. Among mildly handicapped children, characteristic differences are often minimized and are often shared by children with different handicapping conditions. For example, a child with learning disabilities may be able to read but, on a comprehension level, be 2 years below grade level primarily because of an inability to discriminate letters; a child diagnosed as emotionally disturbed may read 2 years below grade level, a delay primarily caused by an inability to concentrate; and a mildly retarded child may read 2 years below grade level because of limited intellectual skills. Each of these three example children possesses characteristics of normal children (ability to read), interrelated characteristics (2 years below grade level), and unique characteristics (discrimination, concentration, and intellectual skills).

Children with more severely handicapping conditions possess fewer of the characteristics of normal children and are more often unique rather than interrelated. However, even severely handicapped children must, in many ways, be treated as normal children. Their needs for love, care, and for an education, for example, are no different than they are for all children. An appropriate educational program for severely handicapped children, however, may be considerably different than that provided for normal or mildly handicapped children.

Incidence and Prevalence

The terms *incidence* and *prevalence* are used to describe the frequency or numbers of handicapped children that exist in a given population. Although the terms are often used interchangeably, their meanings are somewhat different. Specifically, *incidence* refers to the number of new cases of handicapped children identified in a given period of time (usually a year), whereas *prevalence* means the total number of existing cases (old and new) in a given population, such as the United States (Hallahan & Kauffman, 1978). If a school district initiates a project to identify new (previously unknown) physically disabled students in the district, the results would constitute an incidence rate. The incidence rate plus the numbers already known to the district would constitute the prevalence rate of physically disabled for that particular school district.

It is not possible to know the actual number of handicapped children, so most agencies have relied upon prevalence data to identify needs, plan programs, and evaluate effectiveness. Therefore, this kind of information is important to local, state, and federal education agencies to prepare budgets, train teachers, and estimate required space, materials, equipment, and other services.

In the school year 1974–1975, prevalence of handicapped children (ages birth to 19 years) was almost 8,000,000, of which only half were being served by an appropriate program. The 1974–1975 prevalence of handicapping conditions by category is presented in Table 1.

Since 1974–1975 individual state and federal legislation mandating the identification of handicapped children, and the requirement to serve these children, has undoubtedly altered the data presented in Table 1. Preliminary information indicates that the prevalence of handicapping conditions is greater than the 8,000,000 reported in 1974–1975 and that the number of handicapped children served has also increased.

Special Education

Webster's dictionary defines *special* as "distinguished by some unusual quality" and "designed for a particular purpose." The same source

Table 1. Estimated number of handicapped children served and unserved by type of handicap

	Percent of child population	1974–1975 number served (projected)	1974–1975 number unserved	Total handicapped children served and unserved	Percent served	Percent unserved
Speech impaired	3.5	1,850,000	443,000	2,293,000	81	19
Mentally retarded	2.3	1,250,000	257,000	1,507,000	83	17
Learning disabled	3.0	235,000	1,731,000	1,966,000	12	88
Emotionally disturbed	2.0	230,000	1,080,000	1,310,000	18	82
Crippled and other health impaired	0.5	235,000	93,000	328,000	72	28
Deaf	0.075	35,000	14,000	49,000	71	29
Hard of hearing	0.5	60,000	268,000	328,000	18	82
Visually handicapped	0.1	39,000	27,000	66,000	59	41
Deaf-blind and other multihandicapped	0.6	13,000	27,000	40,000	33	67

Source: U.S. Office of Education, Bureau of Education for the Handicapped, March 1975.

7

provides several definitions of *education*, one of which is "the field of study that deals mainly with methods of teaching and learning in schools." Combined, *special* and *education* essentially mean the use of specifically designed teaching and learning procedures, that are not typically used with normal children, to meet the unique needs of handicapped children.

Thus, special education may be viewed as different types of specialized educational procedures that are employed with children who have a variety of handicaps. Even though *special* is a key distinction between special education and regular education the differences are often minimal. "It should be pointed out that special education is not a total program entirely different from the education of the ordinary child. It refers only to those aspects of education that are unique and/or in addition to the instructional program for all children" (Kirk & Gallagher, 1979, pp. 12–13).

Mainstreaming

The term *mainstreaming* is a descriptive concept meaning that handicapped children should be educated in the regular classroom with normal peers whenever this is the most appropriate placement. Unfortunately, mainstreaming has often been falsely interpreted to mean that *all* handicapped children should be educated in the regular class. In reality, mainstreaming is an educational placement procedure that is primarily intended for children with mild to moderately handicapping conditions who could profit from the regular classroom experience, provided some adaptations are made to accommodate the handicapping condition.

In 1976, the Council for Exceptional Children (CEC), a national organization of special educators, described the school environment in which exceptional children (handicapped and gifted) should be educated:

> Mainstreaming is a belief which involves an educational placement procedure and process for exceptional children, based on the conviction that each such child should be educated in the least restrictive environment in which his educational and related needs can be satisfactorily provided. This concept recognizes that exceptional children have a wide range of special educational needs, varying greatly in intensity and duration; that there is a recognized continuum of educational settings which may, at a given time, be appropriate for an individual child's needs; that to the maximum extent appropriate, exceptional children should be educated with nonexceptional children; and that special classes, separate schooling, or other removal of an exceptional child from education with nonexceptional children should occur when the intensity of the child's special education and related needs is such that they cannot be satisfied in an environment including nonexceptional children, even with the provision of supplementary aids and services ("Official Actions . . . ," 1976, p. 43).

Least Restrictive Environment

This is a program placement concept that means handicapped children should be educated in environments that are as "normal" as possible. Within this framework, mainstreaming is considered the most normal, or least restrictive, placement of handicapped children. Stated another way, the handicapped child's placement should not interfere with individual freedom any more than necessary.

Until recently, verified handicapped children who were attending school were segregated from the regular school population and were educated in separate facilities, such as the special class, an institution, or at home. Consequently, handicapped children, once identified, were segregated from their normal peers and educated in more restrictive environments.

The concept of least restrictive environment does not eliminate special classes, institutions, or the home as placement possibilities. But if a child can be adequately educated in the regular class, then the child should not be placed in a resource room; if a child can be educated in the resource room, the child should not be placed in a special class; and if a child can be educated in the special class, the child should not be placed in an institution. If all of the more "normal" possibilities are exhausted, then institutional or homebound placement may constitute the least restrictive environment. Thus, the concept of least restrictive environment is not designed to place every child in the regular class (mainstreamed), but to identify a program placement that is as normal as possible.

Continuum of Services

The ability of an educational system to provide least restrictive environments depends on the availability of a continuum of services. Ideally, such a continuum would consist of numerous sequential placement possibilities, ranging from the regular class to homebound instruction. During the past decade several service continuum models have been introduced, one of which is presented in Figure 1.

This model specifies 11 different placement plans, each representing sequential steps from the most "normal" or integrated environment to the most specialized or segregated environment. For placement, the handicapped child should first be considered for placement in Plan 1. If Plan 1 will not meet the child's educational needs, then Plan 2 should be considered. If Plan 2 is not appropriate, then Plan 3 should be considered. This process is continued until the "least restrictive environment" can be determined. In short, the child should be placed in the most

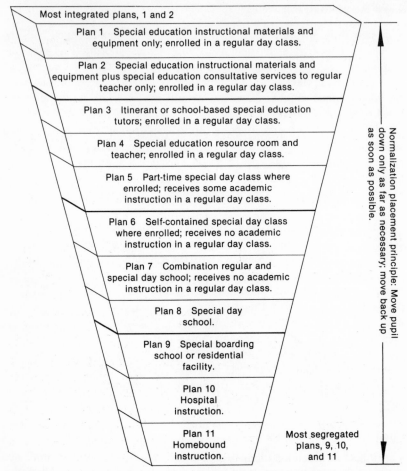

Figure 1.   A continuum of services model. (Reprinted with permission from *Exceptional Children in the Schools*, edited by L. M. Dunn, Holt, Rinehart & Winston, New York, 1973, p. 37.)

integrated plan possible. Once placed, the child should be moved toward the more integrated plans as soon as possible.

To fully implement the concepts of mainstreaming and least restrictive environment, a continuum of services, such as those presented in Figure 1, must be available within the school system. When regular class placements, special instructional materials, and consultive services are not available, then mildly handicapped children may be assigned to more segregated placements. Similarly, when segregated placements are not available, severely handicapped children may be assigned to more integrative placements. In each case the concepts of *appropriate education* and *least restrictive environment* may be violated. The availability of a full range of services will enhance the probability of providing an appropriate education for handicapped children.

A PRACTICAL JUSTIFICATION

The decade of the 1970s has witnessed a dramatic change in the educational placement of mildly and moderately handicapped children. After years, even centuries, of segregated special class, institutional, and home-bound programs, such children are now being educated more frequently in the regular classroom. With this long tradition of segregated educational placement, the value of mainstreaming as an educational placement procedure has not been completely accepted. Many teachers, administrators, and even parents have justifiably questioned the validity of mainstreaming, particularly since the educational community developed a substantial case for segregated programs just a few years ago. Consequently, both regular classroom teachers and special education teachers tend to be at a loss when asked to justify mainstreaming or to describe the benefits derived from the regular classroom placement of handicapped students. If the concept of mainstreaming is to achieve greater acceptance, teachers need to know how mainstreaming came about, why it occurred, the research that has been conducted, and the impact of mainstreaming on handicapped and nonhandicapped students.

In order to provide a practical justification for mainstreaming, this section addresses the historical, educational, and social changes that have occurred through the years, particularly in the United States. It is believed that the current attitudes and practices, educational or otherwise, have their roots in an evolving developmental process that has been tempered by experience, knowledge, and a growing social conscience concerning the dignity and worth of individuals, handicapped or nonhandicapped.

Historical Tradition

Although a detailed chronology of educational development is beyond the scope of this book, a few selected historical highlights are necessary to understand the progress made in the education of the handicapped. Kirk and Gallagher (1979) summarize four historical stages that reflect social attitudinal changes toward the handicapped.

> Historically, four stages in the development of attitudes toward the handicapped child can be recognized. First, during the pre-Christian era the

handicapped tended to be neglected and mistreated. Second, during the spread of Christianity they were protected and pitied. Third, in the eighteenth and nineteenth centuries institutions were established to provide separate education. Fourth, in the latter part of the twentieth century there has been a movement toward accepting the handicapped and integrating them into society to the fullest extent possible (p. 5).

The first historical stage, which Hewett (1974) calls the "survival" treatment of the handicapped, was characterized by the physical abandonment or even the deliberate killing of children (infanticide) who were handicapped, particularly if the handicapping condition was of an obvious physical nature. Education, therefore, placed great emphasis on physique and the training of the "mind and body," so that individuals who possessed deviant physical characteristics were ruthlessly, often permanently, excluded from participation in society.

The second historical stage, influenced by a growing religious movement, created conditions in which "the feebleminded and physically handicapped received more humanitarian care but the causes of deviant behavior were increasingly believed to be the influence of Satan himself" (Hewett, 1974, p. 18). This more humanitarian care typically took the form of custodial residential centers, such as poorhouses, where primary needs (food and shelter) were only minimally met, while education and training were nonexistent.

The third historical stage witnessed the rapid growth of specialized institutions for the handicapped. The blind, deaf, insane, and severely retarded, who were once served by custodial institutions, began to enter facilities that were programmatically designed to educate and train children with specific handicapping conditions. This specialized, segregated approach was carried over into the public school attitudes toward the handicapped. The passage of child labor and compulsory attendance laws, coupled with the movement from a rural to an urban society, resulted in public school provisions for handicapped children at about the turn of the twentieth century (Erdman & Olson, 1966). The creation of the first special classes was based on a "relief philosophy" having as its major objective the removal of handicapped children from the regular classroom since it was assumed these pupils could not cope with the prescribed academic curriculum (Hungerford, DeProspo, & Rosenzweig, 1948). Administrators and teachers generally believed handicapped children could make better progress and would be removed from social and academic pressure when grouped homogeneously. Moreover, school personnel were ill-equipped to cope with the problems generated by the inclusion of handicapped pupils.

During the middle of the twentieth century, the fourth historical stage began to take shape, that is, the movement toward totally integrating the handicapped into society as much as possible. Until the 1960s, the utilization of self-contained classes was generally accepted with minimal criticism as the most viable alternative to educating individuals who deviated considerably from the average school population. In the past two decades, however, profound societal changes have taken place which reflect a heightened awareness of the right of the individual to be different in appearance and behavior (Dunn, 1973). Along with this a change in thinking has evolved regarding the appropriateness of the traditional curricula and administrative plans provided for the handicapped. This historical evolution has culminated in an educational philosophy known as placement in the "least restrictive environment," which for the mildly handicapped is called *mainstreaming*.

A Philosophical Foundation

The historical traditions have closely paralleled the development of a philosophical foundation of education for the handicapped. Currently, the educational practices that are being advocated are a reflection of the basic philosophy inherent in the "American way of life." According to Cruickshank (1967) the following factors make America different from many other societies:

1. The democratic concept that equality of opportunity should be provided to everyone regardless of religion, race, or social standing.
2. The humanitarian ideals embodied in a heritage of Christian and Jewish tradition, ensuring the personal worth of the individual, irrespective of personal abilities or disabilities.
3. The belief that it is economically realistic to invest money in the education, care, and treatment of the handicapped early in life to minimize the amount of funds that would be required for their life time maintenance without such pre-adult expenditures.
4. The reflection of society's concern fo the "good life," the hope that through education, every individual will participate freely in the social, religious, aesthetic, and scientific aspects of his culture to the limits of his capacity (p. 45).

Historically these factors have been ignored in the education of the handicapped. All too often, classroom teachers receive information about handicapped pupils in a rather haphazard, unsystematic way. However, the importance of applying these ideals to the education of the handicapped must finally be given top priority.

Mandates for Change

The recent educational movement toward the implementations of least restrictive environments and mainstreaming was not spontaneous or accidental. Even though centuries of educational history provide evidence that handicapped children have been separated from society, each generation has witnessed changes which have progressively incorporated an integrated educational approach. Since educational practice is a reflection of the values of society, it must be assumed that the progressive humanitarian treatment of handicapped children was a function of the general increase in the social conscience of people throughout the world. But, aside from this humanitarian influence, a number of educational innovations and empirical results have contributed to a more normalized educational approach for handicapped children.

Although all the factors responsible for mainstreaming cannot be identified, there appear to have been at least three critical developments that mandated a change in the education of the handicapped. First, a number of eminent educators have discovered or developed innovative instructional techniques appropriate for handicapped children and which could be implemented in the regular classroom. Second, the increased heterogeneity of regular school populations has created the necessity for greater individualization for all children. And, third, the empirical research data comparing special class versus regular class placement of handicapped children favors mainstreaming.

Instructional Innovations with the Handicapped

Educators throughout history have risen to meet extraordinary challenges. Educators working with handicapped children are no exception. Countless individuals have discovered or developed instructional techniques for educating handicapped children which have subsequently been used or adapted to educate normal children. Table 2 identifies several of the many eminent educators responsible for influencing instructional practices with handicapped children.

Clearly, the major ideas expressed in Table 2 demonstrate that even severely handicapped children should not be condemned to a custodial existence for the remainder of their lives. Instead, these "contributions remind us that we have been traditionally too pessimistic about exceptional children and consequently find ourselves continually surprised at what we can do if we are imaginative enough to find better methods and procedures by which to stimulate them" (Kirk & Gallagher, 1979, p. 7).

In addition to the instructional innovations developed over the years, related disciplines have been contributing to the education of the handicapped. For example, technology has created a variety of teaching aids, psychology has contributed to our understanding of human differences, and medicine has physiologically enabled individuals to lead normal lives. Thus, education does not stand alone as the discipline responsible for the normalization of handicapped children.

However, as an integral part of society, education does have the responsibility for creating formal learning experiences which are

Table 2. Significant ideas influencing American special education

Initiator	Dates	Nationality	Major ideas
Jean Marc Gaspard Itard	1775–1838	French	Single-subject research can be used to develop training methods for the mentally retarded
Samuel Gridley Howe	1801–1876	American	Handicapped children can learn and should have an organized education, not just compassionate care
Edward Seguin	1812–1880	French	Mentally retarded children can learn if taught through specific sensory-motor exercises
Francis Galton	1822–1911	English	Genius tends to run in families, and its origin can be determined.
Alfred Binet	1857–1911	French	Intelligence can be measured, and it is amenable to improvement through education
Louis Braille	1809–1852	French	The blind can learn through an alternative system of communication based on a code of raised dots
Thomas Hopkins Gallaudet	1787–1851	American	Deaf children can learn to communicate by spelling and gesturing with their fingers
Alexander Graham Bell	1847–1922	American	Hearing-handicapped children can learn to speak and can use their limited hearing if it is amplified
Maria Montessori	1870–1952	Italian	Children can learn at very early ages, using concrete experiences designed around special instructional materials
Anna Freud	1895–	Austrian	The techniques of psychoanalysis can be applied to children to help their emotional problems
Lewis Terman	1877–1956	American	Intelligence tests can be used to identify gifted children who tend to maintain superiority throughout life
Alfred Strauss	1897–1957	German	Some children show unique patterns of learning disabilities that require special training and are probably due to brain injury

Source: *Educating Exceptional Children* (3rd ed.) by S. A. Kirk and J. J. Gallagher, Houghton Mifflin Co., Boston, 1979, p. 6. Reprinted by permission of the author and publisher.

15

consistent with the society it serves. Instructional innovations, supported by related disciplines, have progressively enabled schools to more effectively educate all children, handicapped and nonhandicapped. With the increased knowledge, skills, and support, education has a mandate to provide the most appropriate education possible.

Increasing Heterogeneity within the Regular Class

In the early years of this century most classroom student groups were relatively homogeneous in terms of physical characteristics, socioeconomic status, and expectations for education. Consequently, teaching procedures were remarkably similar throughout education, typically taking the form of group oriented activities, directed by an authoritarian lecturer (Anderson, Greer, & Zia, 1978). Children who did not fit this stereotypical mold were encouraged not to attend school or were excluded from formal academic educational programs. This elite and rigid concept of education, therefore, precluded the successful participation of many handicapped children.

However, as the twentieth century progressed, increasing numbers of students were enrolled in elementary and secondary schools. This massive influx of students, facilitated by attendance, labor, and discrimination legislation, reflected a new view of education as a vehicle for achieving economic goals in a society that was rapidly becoming more urban, technological, and managerial. By the mid-1950s, schools were inundated with masses of students, representing the entire spectrum of human characteristics. Unfortunately, schools were unable to completely adapt curricula, teaching procedures, materials, and the like to accommodate the wide variety of student skills, attitudes, and characteristics. Typically, students, regardless of their individuality, were required to comply with the existing programs and standards, which contained the historic remnants of an elite and rigid educational philosophy.

However, all children did not comply with this stereotypical set of educational expectations. One approach to the problem was to provide special facilities and programs for those children who were unable to "learn" compared with other children in the school. Although a pattern of institutionalization had already been implemented for children with severe problems, children with mildly handicapping conditions did not seem to "fit" in either the institution or the regular class. On the basis of this perceived educational difference, the special class was introduced on a limited scale early in this century, but grew at an alarming rate through the 1960s. In essence, the increasing use of the special class and, later, the resource room, grew as a function of increasing student heterogeneity within the regular class.

In general, the implementation of special classes and other services followed the pattern established by institutional development; that is, special classes were established for the physically and sensorially handicapped, followed by the establishment of special classes for the retarded. However, the removal of the physically, sensorially, and intellectually handicapped from the regular class did not identify all children who demonstrated learning and behavioral characteristics different from those of the so-called "average" student. Aided by development in the scientific measurement of human characteristics, a process of identifying and explaining additional variance in student characteristics was initiated. This process led to the development of a new list of educationally handicapping conditions—emotionally disturbed, learning disabled, behaviorally disordered, socially maladjusted, dyslexic, hyperkinetic, and "slow" learner, just to name some of the most frequently employed labels. This new population of children typically consisted of those with marginally different or mildly handicapping conditions.

It was during the late 1960s that many educators became concerned with the effects on children who were being labeled handicapped. Most of the critics of this labeling process maintained that children, once identified, rarely received an appropriate education, even in the special class; that the label stigmatized the child as being less competent in general; and that labels created a self-fulfilling prophecy of failure (Dunn, 1968; Johnson, 1969).

Labels have also come under attack because they reflect economic, racial, and sex bias.

> Special education is part of the arrangement for cooling out students. It has helped to erect a parallel system which permits relief of institutional guilt and humiliation stemming from the failure to achieve competence and effectiveness to the task given to it by society. Special education is helping the regular school maintain its spoiled identity when it creates special programs . . . for the 'disruptive child' and the 'slow learner,' many of whom, for some strange reason, happen to be Black and poor and live in the inner city (Johnson, 1969, p. 245).

Observation and evaluation of special class programs reveals a number of consistent characteristics among the students affected—they are black (or Spanish American), they are male, and they are poor (Rich, 1977). Although the identification of these children may be rationalized on the grounds of standardized test results, the legal and ethical uses of such tests are questionable. For example, Cruickshank (1972) noted that 73 percent of the students in one elementary school in a large city had been classified *learning disabled* after being administered group tests. One of the tests that was administered was the Stanford Achievement

Test, which Judge J. Skelly Wright in *Hobson* v. *Hansen* (1968) rejected as invalid for the purpose used. Wright held illegal the method of achievement and ability testing which was being practiced in the Washington, D.C. public schools to place children in regular and special classes, on the grounds that the tests had been standardized on white middle class students and were not accurate when applied to blacks and lower class students.

The rate of identification was also becoming a critical issue. For example, if the rate of diagnosed handicapped children over the past 45 years were projected over the next 45 years, 100 percent of all school-age children would be labeled as handicapped (see Table 3). Thus, the rapidly growing rate of identification and the proliferation of handicapping labels was beginning to affect sizeable portions of the regular classroom group.

Clearly, this stigmatized and segregated approach to the education of children with mildly handicapping conditions is inconsistent with the moral values regarding human dignity and civil rights espoused by this society. Although the labeling approach did reduce the heterogeneity within the regular classroom, it has come into conflict with values and beliefs which transcend the formal educational process. In keeping with these humanistic concerns, the mandate to education is one of reducing stigmatized and segregated education and increasing individualized programs within the regular class.

The Issue of Special Class versus Regular Class Placement

This issue remains a highly controversial topic that has not been definitively resolved. Although the professional and humanitarian viewpoints in general favor mainstreaming, the research results are contradictory and thus do not permit conclusions one way or the other. However, two specific questions have accumulated both theoretical and research support. First, severely handicapped children have not performed as well in the regular class as they have in the special class. Second, mildly handicapped students have demonstrated no difference in academic performance between regular class versus special class placement, but self-concept and social development have been enhanced by regular class placement. Thus, the least restrictive environment may be the special class for severely handicapped children, and the regular class for mildly handicapped children.

Concern by educators regarding the most appropriate class placement for mentally retarded children is not new. For example, in 1932 Bennett conducted the first of the so called "efficacy studies" comparing the effects of special and regular class placement on educating mentally retarded children. This early research reported that in educational

Table 3. Enrollment in public schools and classes, 1922–1975

Type	1922	1932	1940	1948	1952	1958	1969	1975
Mentally retarded	23,252	75,099	98,416	87,030	113,565	213,402	703,800	1,350,000
Speech defective	No data	22,735	126,146	182,308	306,747	474,643	1,122,200	2,020,000
Crippled	No data	16,166	25,784	14,510	17,813	28,355	109,000	255,000
Deaf and hard of hearing	2,911	4,434	13,478	13,959	15,867	19,199	65,200	111,000
Blind and partially seeing	No data	5,308	8,875	8,185	8,853	11,008	22,700	43,000
Special health problems	No data	24,020	27,291	19,597	11,453	21,714	Under crippled	Under crippled
Gifted	No data	1,834	3,255	20,712	22,916	52,005	No data	No data
Socially maladjusted	No data	14,354	10,477	15,340	No data	27,447	99,400	255,000
Learning disabled	No data	No data	No data	No data	No data	No data	120,000	260,000

Source: *Educating Exceptional Children* (3rd ed.), by S. A. Kirk and J. J. Gallagher, Houghton Mifflin Co., Boston, 1979, p. 10. Reprinted by permission of the author and publisher.

achievement and physical characteristics (for example, motor coordination), the performance of special class children was inferior to retarded children who remained in the regular grades.

Johnson (1962) pointed to the paradox that mentally retarded children in special classes were achieving educational goals at a slower or at the same rate as were those in regular classes. He cited studies which compared the academic achievement, social adjustment and acceptance, and postschool adjustment of mentally handicapped children in special classes and regular grades and found that no significant gains had been made by children in special classes. Blatt (1960) concluded similarly: "Notwithstanding the many obvious and valid criticisms of studies comparing special versus regular class membership, it has yet to be demonstrated that the special class offers a better school experience for retarded children than does regular class placement" (p. 54).

A number of researchers have studied the question of social position and attitudes of mildly retarded children placed in regular or special classes. The results are inconclusive and, as with the early efficacy studies, are plagued with problems of their questionable validity and reliability. Johnson's sociometric study (1950) of mentally retarded children in regular classes indicated that these children tended to be isolated and rejected. Welch (1967) studied the effects of placing mentally retarded children in part time special classes (one-half day in regular classes) and self-contained special classes. She compared the academic achievement and self-derogation of both groups and found that the children in the integrated setting made higher achievement scores and decreased in self-derogation. Meyerowitz conducted a study (1962) in which neighborhood peer relationships of educably mentally retarded children were compared with regard to special or regular class placement. In a second study Meyerowitz (1967) compared retarded children's self-perceptions on the same basis. The results of both studies indicated more self-derogation in children placed in special classes.

A more recent investigation (Budoff & Gottlieb, 1976) suggests that the effects of special class and regular class placement are complex. This study found that retarded children with IQs above 75 academically benefited from regular class placement, while children with IQs below 75 academically performed better in the special class. The same results held true for self-concept.

Finally, the special class has been condemned on the grounds that there are no appropriate models for achievement or behavior (Bandura, 1974). In other words, handicapped children who are constantly exposed to other handicapped children perpetuate that achievement level and behavior, and are not provided normal models for changing. Coleman et al. (1966) similarly concluded that children's peers are often a more important influence on achievement than the teacher or the method of instruction.

Although much of the research has been criticized for methodological reasons, the effects of the special class versus regular class placement on handicapped children are beginning to more clearly emerge. Even though the placement effect on severely handicapped children remains a question, a substantial amount of data indicates that mildly handicapped children perform significantly better in the mainstream. This latter finding is a clear mandate that every reasonable effort should be made to maintain mildly handicapped children in the regular class.

The Future

During the earlier history of education, particularly in the United States, handicapped students were typically excluded from school or were educated in programs and facilities apart from the regular school populations. However, changes in social conscience, technology, and efficacy have been responsible for a change toward the concepts of mainstreaming and least restrictive environment.

In a practical sense, this change toward the integrating of the handicapped can be justified based at least on the following developments:

1. Technological and instructional innovations have made it possible to provide more effective educational programs for the handicapped.
2. The increasing heterogeneity of the regular class population means that it is no longer feasible to continually label and segregate an infinite number of handicapped children.
3. The mounting research indicates that handicapped children perform academically and personally as well or better in the mainstream than in the special class, particularly for the mildly handicapped.

These practical justifications have only touched upon a limited number of reasons for integrating the handicapped student to the maximum extent possible. Although some disadvantages may exist, the education of the handicapped will in the future definitely be a part of the mainstream of education.

IMPLICATIONS OF LAW AND LEGISLATION

On November 29, 1975, President Gerald R. Ford signed into law Public Law 94-142, the Education for All Handicapped Children Act of 1975. The signing of this federal law was the culmination of several years of advocacy on behalf of handicapped children, related court decisions, and prior legislation. A review of the forces which collectively contributed to the enactment of PL 94-142 and a discussion of this law and its implementation will serve to highlight some of the far reaching implications.

Advocacy Groups

The impetus for improved and expanded educational provisions can be attributed to a number of forces. One of the strongest of these has been the "consumer movement" led by advocacy organizations of parents, professionals, and the handicapped themselves. These groups have sought redress through state legislatures and the courts for handicapped individuals who were being denied their rights to appropriate public education.

The largest of these interest groups is the Council for Exceptional Children (CEC), made up of educators, administrators, university teaching and research personnel, and interested citizens. Other groups represent specific exceptionalities within special education, such as the hearing impaired (Alexander Graham Bell Association) and the learning disabled (Association for Children with Learning Disabilities). Parent organizations which originally came into existence to give parents the opportunity to discuss mutual problems gradually mobilized for action. These consumer and professional organizations have militantly worked on local, state, and national levels to obliterate educational exclusion of the handicapped, to obtain government financial assistance, and to promote the acceptance of the handicapped in society by educating the public.

Court Decisions

A review of the following five court decisions illustrates how the judiciary has made a major contribution towards the recognition of handicapped children's educational rights.

Brown v. Board of Education (1954)   In 1954 the Warren Court, in an interpretation of the Fourteenth Amendment of the United States Constitution, ruled that:

> In these days it is doubtful that any child may reasonably be expected to succeed in life if he is denied the opportunity of an education. Such an opportunity, where the state has undertaken to provide it, is a right which must be made available to all on equal terms (*Brown* v. *Board of Education*, 1954, 347 U.S. 483, 74 S.Ct. 686, 98 L.Ed. 873).

Basically, this clause means that what is done to some people must be done to all. It follows that a state must not set up separate procedures and systems for dealing with different groups of people unless a justified cause for such differential treatment can be demonstrated. The 1954 Supreme Court decision has been frequently cited in litigation relative to the right of an education for handicapped children (Abeson, 1976). Clearly, the right to an education for all children, be they handicapped or otherwise, is viewed as a civil right.

Diana v. State Board of Education (1973) Several significant court decisions challenged the placement of children in classes for the mentally retarded on the basis of testing which was prejudicial to the children involved with regard to their native language, cultural background, and the population (white middle class) upon whom the tests had been standardized. In the *Diana* case, a suit was brought on behalf of nine Mexican-American students, ages 8 to 13, who came from homes in which Spanish was the major language spoken, and who had been placed in classes for the mentally retarded in Monterrey County, California. Upon retesting using bilingual measures, seven of the nine scored higher than the IQ cutoff line for mental retardation; the lowest score was only three points below the cutoff. The plaintiffs sought a class action suit on behalf of all bilingual Mexican-American children in California who were either already in classes for the mentally retarded or who were in danger of similar inappropriate placement. A stipulated agreement order signed by both parties in 1970 required that: students be tested in their primary language; that Mexican-American and Chinese students in classes for the educable mentally retarded be retested; and that children wrongly placed be given assistance to facilitate their reentry into regular classes.

Arreola v. Board of Education of Santa Ana School District (**1968**) In another California case, a suit was filed in 1968 on behalf of the Mexican-American parents of the Santa Ana School District asking for an injunction against the district's classes for the educable mentally retarded on the grounds that the psychological examinations required prior to placement were unconstitutional since adequate evaluation techniques had not been used for children from different cultural and language backgrounds, and because parents had been denied the right of a hearing to refute evidence for placement. In addition, the suit sought to force the district to grant hearings on all children currently in such placements to allow for the chance to remove the stigma of the label "mentally retarded" from school records of such pupils.

A similar decision to the *Diana* and *Arreola* cases involved litigation on behalf of six black elementary students in the San Francisco Unified School District (*Larry P. v. Riles*, 1972). The plaintiffs claimed that they had been inappropriately classified as retarded according to culturally biased intellectual tests.

PARC v. *Commonwealth of Pennsylvania* (**1972**)   In 1971 the Pennsylvania Association for Retarded Children (PARC) on behalf of the parents of 13 retarded children, brought action in the U.S. District Court for the Eastern District of Pennsylvania against the State of Pennsylvania for nonprovision of free appropriate education for their children and other retarded children of the state. The court decided in this landmark case that:

> Having undertaken to provide a free public education to all of its children including its exceptional children, the Commonwealth of Pennsylvania may not deny any mentally retarded child access to a free public program of education and training. This is the Commonwealth's obligation to place each mentally retarded child in a free public program of education and training appropriate to the child's capacity (Lippman & Goldberg, 1973, p. 31).

Mills v. *Board of Education* (**1972**)   Following the *PARC* decision, a similar ruling was made regarding the rights of not only mentally retarded children, but of all children with handicapping conditions. In *Mills* v. *Board of Education*, the parents and guardians of seven handicapped children brought suit against the Washington, D.C. Board of Education, the Department of Human Services, and the mayor for failure to provide all children with free public education. U.S. District Court Judge Joseph Waddy ordered the defendants to provide the plaintiffs with publicly supported education within a month; to produce a list within the same time period showing other children similarly not served.

Action was again brought by the plaintiffs later in 1972 when the defendants had not complied with the order. Judge Waddy ordered the implementation of the proposed judgment and issued a decree providing a declaration of the constitutional right of all children, whether handicapped or not, to free public education, and a declaration that all children so excluded were being denied rights of due process and equal protection under the law.

The court decisions rendered made a significant contribution to guaranteeing educational rights for the nation's handicapped children and fueled the movement for justice. The movement so generated addressed the handicapped child's right to due process and equal protection, to providing children with not just any educational program, but with quality education appropriate to their individual needs, all taking precedence to bureaucratic and professional needs and limitations.

Prior Legislation

Prior to the enactment of PL 94-142, there were several legislative acts which addressed the need to provide equal opportunities for handicapped citizens including adults and children. The most noteworthy of this legislation were PL 93-112, the Vocational Rehabilitation Act of 1973 (Section 504), and PL 93-380, the Education of the Handicapped Amendments of 1974. Section 504 of the Vocational Rehabilitation Act is the basic civil rights provision terminating discrimination against handicapped citizens (Ballard, 1977). The Education of the Handicapped Amendments of 1974 required states, for the purpose of receiving federal financial aid, to adopt full service goals and priority to unserved handicapped children and to adopt evaluation-placement safeguards (Abeson, 1976).

Public Law 94-142

The Education for all Handicapped Children Act of 1975 ensures a right to an education, a right to nondiscriminatory evaluation, a right to an appropriate education, and a right to due process of law (Abeson & Zettel, 1977). It is interesting to note that previous court decisions and legislation provided the basis for the rights mandated by PL 94-142. A brief discussion of each of the four major components serves to highlight major provisions of this landmark and heralded legislation.

Right to an Education All handicapped children are entitled to a free education. Handicapped children are defined as mentally retarded, hard of hearing, deaf, speech impaired, visually handicapped, seriously emotionally disturbed, orthopedically impaired or other health impaired, or children with specific learning disabilities. PL 94-142 is addressed only to those children who by reason of their handicap need special education and related services. It is also acknowledged that not every child possessing a handicap will require special education and related services. By September 1, 1980, all states and their corresponding local school districts must provide a free and appropriate education for all handicapped children ages 3 to 21. However, a free and appropriate education is not required in the 3 to 5 and 18 to 21 age ranges when such a requirement is inconsistent with state law or practice or inconsistent with court orders.

Right to an Appropriate Education PL 94-142 requires that an individualized education program (IEP) be written for each handicapped child to reflect instructional objectives. The IEP must also indicate which special education and related services will be provided for the handicapped child. Each individualized education program must include the child's present level of functioning, and also reflect a statement of annual goals. Educators, parents, and when appropriate, the child, must participate in developing the educational program. The IEP must be reviewed at least annually, although pupil progress towards the instructional objectives should be monitored as often as is necessary. Procedures must also ensure, to the fullest extent possible, that handicapped children be educated with their nonhandicapped classmates. Education for handicapped children in a nonmainstreamed setting (i.e., special classes) is only authorized when the children's handicap is such that education in regular classes with the use of supplementary aids and services cannot be achieved satisfactorily. This provision requiring, when possible, education with nonhandicapped peers is one aspect of being educated in the least restrictive environment. However, being educated with nonhandicapping peers could in itself be most restrictive if the handicapped child requires, by nature of his handicap, intensive instruction and/or other related services available only in more segregated service models (e.g., separate classes, residential schools).

Right to Nondiscriminatory Testing   Procedural safeguards must be maintained in order to ensure that testing and related materials utilized for evaluation and placement of handicapped children will be selected and administered so as not to be racially or culturally discriminatory. The law also mandates that no single testing or evaluation procedure shall be the sole criterion for determining an appropriate educational program for a handicapped child.

Right to Due Process of Law   Parents and guardians of handicapped children are to be extended the opportunity to examine all relevant records with respect to identification, evaluation, and educational placement. Parents or guardians may obtain an independent educational evaluation if they believe a fair assessment has not been rendered. Parents also have the right to an impartial due process hearing if they are dissatisfied with the educational program being provided their handicapped child. The hearings must be conducted by one not employed by or otherwise involved with the agency responsible for the child's education.

It is evident that handicapped children may no longer be denied a free and appropriate education and be the recipients of arbitrary and capricious educational decision making. The implementation of PL 94-142 will undoubtedly encounter problems and generate issues in need of resolution. However, those charged with the responsibility of educating all children must band together and meet the challenges required to ensure the success of Public Law 94-142.

Implementation

Several legal issues have arisen out of the Education for All Handicapped Children Act of 1975. Kowal and Walker (1978) have identified six major categories of litigation in which the courts have ruled or are in the process of rendering judgments. The six major categories are free appropriate public education, placement in the least restrictive environment, placement at no cost to the parents, due process procedures, discipline/expulsion, and exhaustion of administrative remedies. A trend has been established in that the courts have rendered judgments generally in favor of the plaintiffs. The courts may be expected to continue to adjudicate cases brought before them under PL 94-142.

Each state educational agency is required by PL 94-142 to undertake monitoring and evaluation of all public agencies (i.e., local school districts) which are required to respond to the law. Representative of the states monitoring and evaluation responsibility is the Oregon Department of Education (1979) which has developed a comprehensive inventory designed to facilitate the collection of required process data and comparative data relating individualized education programs (IEPs) to services. The Oregon Department of Education has made a commitment to assisting local school districts in providing effective services to handicapped children as reflected in the following four thrusts:

1. All districts (not just those receiving federal 94-142 funds) will be provided with copies of the PL 94-142 Inventory.
2. Regional meetings will be held to communicate with district personnel prior to the on site visits.
3. Monitoring will assess district response to the law, but will also assess district needs for assistance in improving the response.
4. On site visitors will be professional Oregon Department of Education staff or professionals provided by contract with the University of Oregon. In the Oregon plan data will be derived by reviewing administrative records, interviewing district and/or school administrators, examining individual student files randomly selected for each category of disability, interviewing a sample of teachers, and interviewing a sample of parents or guardians. Confidentiality of individual student records will be maintained in accordance with established law.

In addition to litigation and implementation procedures at the state and local school district levels, PL 94-142 has impact on teachers, especially classroom teachers who will be asked to accommodate some handicapped children when mainstreaming is considered the least restrictive environment. Classroom teachers have traditionally worked with some handicapped children, especially when support services were generally unavailable. Increased numbers of regular classroom teachers may be expected to work with handicapped children on at least a part time basis. Classroom teachers may also be expected to assume a major role in the formulation of an individualized education program (IEP) especially in those instances when they will participate in a mainstreaming effort.

School districts will, of necessity, generate the leadership and expertise required in developing a viable inservice education program not only for teachers but for parents and administrators as well. PL 94-142 requires that each state establish an advisory panel to monitor the implementation of the law. Classroom teachers should have representation on this advisory council in order to provide input on progress and/or needed conceptualizations and changes in practice.

EFFECTIVE INSTRUCTIONAL ALTERNATIVES

In order for regular classroom teachers to provide quality educational services for handicapped pupils, they must know what resources and assistance are available to them. Within the context of mainstreaming it is important for teachers to understand the extent to which they can rely on the following delivery system models:

1. The Resource Teacher Model
2. The Diagnostic-Prescriptive Teacher Model
3. The Consultant Teacher Model

Each delivery system model allows the special education teacher, in cooperation with the regular classroom teacher, to extend his/her skills and training into the classroom in order to meet the needs of handicapped pupils. Although the three models may overlap in purpose and function, they do differ as to whether instruction is to be provided directly to handicapped pupils by the special educator or indirectly by the special educator through the regular classroom teacher. An examination of the three service delivery models highlights some basic differences that have emerged.

The Resource Teacher Model

In the resource teacher model (ESC, 1975; Jenkins & Mayhall, 1973; Reger, 1973) handicapped students maintain continuous enrollment in the regular classroom but are scheduled for a portion of a school day into a resource room. While in the resource room the pupils receive individual and/or small group instruction until educational difficulties have been substantially reduced. It is possible that some referred pupils would need the resource room support for 1 or 2 years before being academically and behaviorally ready to maintain full time enrollment in the regular classroom.

Pupils are grouped in a resource room according to educational needs rather than the disability labels (i.e., mentally retarded) which once characterized traditional self-contained classrooms. The resource room teacher tests children to identify skills to be targeted for instruction, and develops appropriate objectives, strategies, and methods that correspond to pupils' needs. The resource room teacher, often with the assistance of an instructional aide, provides direct instruction to students referred to the resource room. The individual and/or group instruction is usually provided in, though not necessarily limited to, the basic skill areas. In a resource room an instructional group could possibly include cerebral palsied, emotionally disturbed, mentally retarded, and learning disabled students.

In cooperation with the regular classroom teacher, the resource room teacher may adapt materials that the handicapped student will use in the regular classroom. The resource teacher also assists the classroom teacher in the development of materials and educational plans, and suggests commercially available instructional materials. The number of handicapped students served in the resource room may range from 5 to 50 and varies depending on the eligibility criteria and educational policies formulated at the local school district level. The handicapped pupil may be referred to the resource room by the regular classroom teacher. However, care must be taken to adhere to the procedures and safeguards mandated in PL 94-142.

Perhaps one of the most difficult problems to be resolved in the resource room teacher model is the matter of scheduling. When during any given day should a child receive instruction in the resource room? Which regular classroom activities will a student miss while attending the resource room? What are the consequences of attending the resource room while one's peers in the regular classroom are participating in recreational activities such as music, art, and physical education? It is not always possible to schedule a student into a resource room for reading instruction when the student's classmates are receiving reading in the regular classroom or for mathematics when the student's classmates are receiving instruction in mathematics. It is of course possible, and perhaps in some cases even desirable, for a handicapped student to receive instruction in the same basic skill area from both the regular classroom and resource room teachers. The scheduling problem that may arise can be resolved when the classroom and resource room teachers plan cooperatively. Any delivery system for rendering service to handicapped students is greatly enhanced when it is characterized by a spirit of coordination, cooperation, and communication.

The Diagnostic-Prescriptive Teacher Model

Traditionally, diagnostic services for handicapped pupils were conducted by outside agencies or through psychological services within a school district itself. Often these support service personnel were more than one step removed from the educational setting from which a handicapped pupil was referred. Consequently, a gap emerged in attempting to translate the diagnostic and psychological reports into educationally relevant information. In a partial response to this problem, the diagnostic-prescriptive model was developed. The model allowed services to be brought into a school, services which had been primarily available from outside sources (ESC, 1975).

The diagnostic classroom, which is equipped with diagnostic and a variety of instructional materials, is a major component of the diagnostic-prescriptive teacher model. Unlike the resource room where a pupil may attend for a year or more, a pupil is referred to the diagnostic classroom for a period not generally to exceed 2 consecutive months. The diagnostic-prescriptive teacher interacts with the pupil in order to identify learning needs and skills to be targeted for instruction, and to determine which instructional techniques and materials are appropriate and will contribute to an optimal learning environment. After the diagnostic-prescriptive teacher has obtained sufficient diagnostic data and information relative to the effectiveness of specific instructional strategies, an individual prescription is written. The diagnostic-prescriptive teacher reviews the prescription with the regular classroom teacher and assists the teacher who will implement the prescription in the regular classroom setting. In effect, the diagnostic-prescriptive teacher is to determine, after an 8-week period of interaction, which approaches work best with a handicapped pupil and to share this information with the regular classroom teacher. The regular classroom teacher will ultimately assume the responsibility for a handicapped student's educational program. As in the resource teacher model, the diagnostic-prescriptive teacher model provides service within a school and requires coordination and cooperation between the special educator and the classroom teacher.

Prouty and McGarry (1972) present a fairly comprehensive discussion of 10 basic steps characteristic of the diagnostic-prescriptive teacher model. The steps are summarized as follows:

1. *Referral*   The classroom teacher initiates referral and summarizes the nature of the problem.
2. *Observation*   The diagnostic-prescriptive teacher observes the referred pupil in the regular classroom.
3. *Referral Conference*   The classroom and diagnostic-prescriptive teachers discuss mutual roles and responsibilities and schedule the referred pupil into the diagnostic classroom.

4. *Diagnostic Teaching*   The diagnostic-prescriptive teacher conducts individual and/or group instruction to determine successful techniques and materials.

5. *Educational Prescription*   The diagnostic-prescriptive teacher prepares a report which contains specific techniques and materials to be recommended to the classroom teacher.

6. *Prescription Conference*   The classroom and diagnostic-prescriptive teacher review and discuss the prescription, determine mutually agreed upon modifications and select a time for demonstration by the diagnostic-prescriptive teacher.

7. *Demonstration*   The diagnostic-prescriptive teacher assumes instructional responsibility for the referring teacher's class and demonstrates segments of the prescription in a total class environment.

8. *Short Term Follow-Up*   The diagnostic-prescriptive teacher visits the classroom teacher to offer suggestions, provide encouragement, and if appropriate, provide demonstrations.

9. *Referring Teacher*   The classroom teacher completes an evaluation form 30 days after receiving prescription and provides an updated pupil progress report.

10. *Long Term Follow-Up*   The diagnostic-prescriptive teacher conducts periodic checks with the classroom teacher until support services are no longer required.

The Consultant Teacher Model

Unlike the resource and diagnostic-prescriptive teacher models, the consultant teacher model does not require handicapped pupils to be removed from the regular classroom. One of the basic assumptions of the consultant teacher model is that the regular classroom teacher is accountable for the acquisition of skills by handicapped students and may, with consultant assistance, provide successful learning experiences for handicapped pupils (ESC, 1975). Long before support services became generally available in the 1960s and 1970s, the classroom teacher was expected to assume the responsibility for instruction of all pupils, be they handicapped or otherwise. Classroom teachers found themselves struggling daily, attempting to meet the needs of handicapped pupils. The ascendancy of the special education movement afforded the classroom teacher the opportunity to have these "problem" pupils removed from the regular classroom and taught by specially trained personnel. The consultant teacher model, utilizing the educational technology developed in the last decade, suggests that there is no need to remove the majority of handicapped students if classroom teachers have been effectively trained in special education techniques.

Fox, Egner, Paolucci, Perelman, & McKenzie (1972) discussed some of the major components of one consultant teacher model that appears to reflect the technology associated with behavior analysis. Some of the major components of the consultant teacher model are:

1. The consultant teacher trains the classroom teacher in classroom measurement systems that will assess referred target behaviors. The target behaviors must be well defined, measurable, and observable. An example of a referred target behavior would be the ability to compute sums through five at the rate of three problems correct per minute.

2. The classroom teacher is asked to determine the minimum acceptable performance expected of a pupil within a particular class (grade) at a given point in the school year. An example would be that every pupil would be able to compute sums through five at a minimum rate of 50 problems correct per minute.

3. The classroom and consultant teachers jointly determine the instructional objective to be attained by the referred pupil. An example would be for the pupil to attain 20 correct problems per minute within a week after intervention by the classroom teacher.

4. Teaching/learning procedures to be implemented by the regular classroom teacher are developed with the assistance of the consultant teacher.

5. The classroom teacher is trained to measure a pupil's progress toward an instructional objective. The teaching/learning procedures outlined in step four are judged to be effective if the referred pupil is making adequate progress towards the instructional objective.

Which Model to Select?

The resource teacher model, diagnostic-prescriptive teacher model, and the consultant teacher model can provide effective instructional alternatives for mainstreamed handicapped students. Selection of the model to be employed will depend on the needs of the pupils to be served and the facilities, as well as the resources and personnel available within a local school setting. Each school staff must assess its individual program needs, philosophy, and commitment to the mainstreaming concept. At the present time, there is little research evidence to support adopting one service model over another (Miller & Sabatino, 1978). Table 4 provides comparative information on the three major delivery systems that have emerged to serve handicapped pupils.

SOME CAUTIONS AND CONSTRAINTS

Even with the support of the resource personnel described in the preceding section, teaching handicapped and normal children together in the same classroom is undoubtedly one of the greatest challenges facing educators today. Teachers and other educators are justifiably concerned about the serious problems confronting them as they work to implement PL 94-142. Paradoxically, many of these problems have not been generated by the provisions of the law itself; they are, rather, problems that have long plagued public school education and educators (Massie, 1978):

1. Overcrowded classrooms
2. Rigid, overcrowded teaching schedules
3. Inadequate facilities
4. Student testing and evaluation procedures that are racially and culturally discriminatory and that tell more about a child's handicaps than about a child's abilities
5. Inadequate preservice and inservice education programs to help teachers work more effectively with all children

The National Education Association, recognizing that mainstreaming may be doomed to failure unless these problems and constraints are neutralized, recently supported NEA Resolution 77-33: Education for all Handicapped Children. In essence, this resolution states that "The National Education Association supports a free appropriate public education for all handicapped students in a least restrictive environment which is determined by maximum teacher involvement." However, the Association recognizes that to implement Public Law 94-142 effectively:

a. A favorable learning experience must be created both for handicapped and nonhandicapped students.
b. Regular and special education teachers, administrators, and parents must share in planning and implementation for the disabled.
c. All staff must be adequately prepared for their roles through inservice training and retraining.
d. All students must be adequately prepared for the program.
e. The appropriateness of educational methods, materials, and supportive services must be determined in cooperation with classroom teachers.
f. The classroom teacher(s) must have an appeal procedure regarding the implementation of the program, especially in terms of student placement.
g. Modifications must be made in class size, using a weighted formula, scheduling, and curriculum design to accommodate program demands.
h. There must be a systematic evaluation and reporting of program developments using a plan which recognizes individual differences.

Table 4. Comparison of resource, diagnostic-prescriptive, and consultant teacher models

	Resource teacher	Diagnostic-prescriptive teacher	Consultant teacher
Special educator			
1. Role	1. Provides direct instruction to handicapped pupils; assists classroom teacher in materials selection and development.	1. Determines effective methods and materials for handicapped pupil; prepares educational prescription and trains classroom teacher for prescription implementation.	1. Trains classroom teacher in instructional and behavioral management technology; models teaching behaviors.
2. Space requirements	2. Resource room with a regular elementary/secondary building.	2. Diagnostic classroom in regular elementary/secondary building.	2. Regular classroom setting only.
3. Materials-equipment	3. Variety of instructional materials for basic skill needs; audio visual aids for direct instruction and/or independent pupil learning activities.	3. Variety of instructional materials in order to identify effective curriculum intervention techniques.	3. Employs regular classroom materials when appropriate and suggests materials available outside classroom.
Classroom teacher			
1. Role	1. Maintains handicapped pupil in regular classroom on part time basis; adapts instructional materials to be used by handicapped pupil.	1. Maintains handicapped pupil in regular classroom through use of educational prescription.	1. Contributes to decision on instructional objectives; maintains periodic records on handicapped pupil's progress towards instructional objectives; provides direct instruction to handicapped pupil

2. Type of assistance from special educator	2. Curricular suggestions; full or partial responsibility for basic skill instruction.	2. Educational prescription developed by diagnostic prescriptive teacher-demonstration on how to employ prescription.	2. Training in instructional and behavioral management technology.
Handicapped pupils 1. Number served	1. Varies	1. Varies	1. Varies
2. Scheduling	2. Pupil removed from class for short or long periods of time; pupil participates in reg. class on part time basis.	2. Pupil removed from regular class for short periods of time up to 2 months; pupil participation in regular class on part time basis during 2 month interim; then full time.	2. Pupil remains in regular class; Pupil participates in regular class full time.
3. Referral	3. By classroom teachers and other professionals.	3. By classroom teachers and other professionals.	3. By classroom teachers
Cooperative planning time	1. Desirable but difficult to schedule if resource room teacher has heavy instructional load.	1. Essential component	1. Essential component

i. Adequate funding must be provided and then used exclusively for this program.
j. The classroom teacher(s) must have a major role in determining individual educational programs and should become members of school assessment teams.
k. Adequate released time must be made available for teachers so that they can carry out the increased demands upon them.
l. Staff must not be reduced.
m. Additional benefits negotiated for handicapped students through local collective bargaining agreements must be honored.
n. Communication must be maintained among all involved parties.
o. All teachers must be made aware of their right of dissent concerning the appropriate program for a student, including the right to have the dissenting opinion recorded.
p. Individual educational programs should provide appropriate services for the handicapped students and not be used as criteria for the evaluation of the teacher. (Ryor, 1977, p. 25).

The National Educational Association's recommendations are representative of the concerns held by regular educators as mainstreaming moves from the conceptual to the implementation phase. The recommendations suggest needed reconceptualizations, new directions, and changes in practice if the letter and spirit of PL 94-142 are to become an integral part of American education. Among the many directions which have been generated by the impact of PL 94-142 are the overlapping but evolving roles of teacher education, attitudinal factors, and the evaluation of mainstreaming efforts. Each of these three major roles has the potential of contributing to the success or failure of mainstreaming handicapped children.

Teacher Education

Redden and Blackhurst (1978) have identified 32 competency statements or behaviors required of elementary teachers to effectively teach mildly handicapped pupils who are integrated with regular students in a mainstreamed classroom setting. The 32 competency statements reflect the following six categories of teacher performance:

1. Develop orientation strategies for mainstream entry
2. Assess needs and set goals
3. Plan teaching strategies and use of resources
4. Implement teaching strategies and use resources
5. Facilitate learning
6. Evaluate learning

Competency statements are useful, especially when generated with the assistance of elementary and secondary classroom teachers, because they serve to delineate top priority objects for preservice and inservice teacher education. However, there are barriers that must be overcome within teacher training in order for teachers to acquire the skills necessary for teaching mainstreamed children. Until recently, general educators have had little or no reason for requiring special education training as classroom teachers were not generally required to teach children with learning problems (West & Bates, 1977). It has been observed that efforts to include such training in preservice regular education have been generally resisted (Martin, 1974). The resistance on the part of some general educators to the incorporation of special education training is understandable when viewed from their vantage point. The preservice regular education program is already crowded with university requirements, and there is concern over extending the required curriculum.

The separation of teacher education into regular and special education sections has contributed to the belief that their functions have differed. Such an administrative division was undoubtedly reinforced by the time-honored beliefs that variant and typical children were to be separated and that these children would require regular or special education teachers, trained by regular or special education teacher education programs. It would appear that both regular and special education orientations have inadvertently contributed to the dichotomy which has existed in the teacher training process. More than ever before ongoing dialogue is needed between regular and special education personnel in order to resolve the problems and issues inherited from being separated as to function, role, and responsibility. Certainly, no one discipline has a monopoly on truth. One must assume the position that both disciplines will recognize their common bond of serving children and will generate the educational leadership required to equip teachers with needed training at the preservice and inservice levels.

Traditionally, the teacher training process has been primarily concerned with the cognitive aspects of educational methodology. It has, however, been suggested that the problems to be encountered in mainstreaming handicapped children lie not in teacher competence but in teacher attitude (Reger, 1973). An examination of the role of attitude will reveal a second major contributing factor to the success or failure of mainstreaming handicapped children.

Attitudinal Factors

Mainstreaming has the potential for increasing positive interactions between handicapped and nonhandicapped students, between handicapped students and classroom teachers, between classroom and special education teachers, as well as between school administrators, parents, and the general public. For positive interactions to occur at all levels, attitudinal obstacles must be understood and ameliorated. The attitudinal dimension is exceedingly complex, involving real or imagined fears, anxieties, and the possibility for overt rejection of handicapped children not only from their nonhandicapped peers but from various adult populations within the professional staff. It is imperative that the sources of attitudinal obstacles be identified, defined, and addressed through a comprehensive, well planned program of attitude change. Zawadski (1974) has identified four general areas of regular education teacher's attitudes and concerns that need to be addressed through comprehensive and cooperative planning:

1. Classroom behavior of handicapped children
    Inappropriate behavior (i.e., conduct, short attention span)
    Emotional problems (i.e., negative self-image)
    Problems related to physical defects and/or health problems
    (i.e., poor bowel/bladder control, gross/fine motor coordination)
2. Problems related to instruction
    Concerns related to curriculum (i.e., content, materials, supplies)
    Organizing for instruction (i.e., scheduling, class size)
    Unfair grading policy
3. Negative attitudes of the handicapped
    Negative behavior of nonhandicapped peers (i.e., rejection)
4. Professional concern
    Lack of regular teacher preparation
    Negative attitudes of adults toward handicapped children in class
    Inadequate assessment of handicapped student's achievement
    Lack of supportive services
    Concerns about safety for the handicapped and nonhandicapped
    Teacher liability

One of the writers, formerly an elementary classroom teacher in the early 1960s when support services were not yet generally available, can recall a poignant event that illustrates the necessity for addressing the role of attitude in the acceptance or rejection of handicapped children by their nonhandicapped classmates. A cerebral palsied sixth grade student, who spoke haltingly and walked with a shuffle, was the target of ridicule, teasing, and verbal abuse. According to sociometric data obtained in early October of the school year, the handicapped student was a social isolate. This writer, concerned for the affective welfare of the handicapped pupil and the evolving negative attitudes of several of the nonhandicapped students, decided to intervene. The cerebral palsied student was sent on an errand within the school for approximately 30 minutes while the remaining 29 students participated in an open discussion with the teacher concerning the cerebral palsied student's physical handicaps. The nonhandicapped children volunteered the information that the handicapped student had been ridiculed for years because it was generally believed that the student was responsible for the speech and motor difficulties. The classroom teacher suggested that the student had been handicapped since birth and was not responsible for the difficulties exhibited. According to several of the nonhandicapped students, no teacher or adult had spoken frankly concerning the nature of the handicapped student's condition and they indicated regret for their past behaviors. Though one may question, in retrospect, the propriety of sending the handicapped student on an errand in order to discuss the problem, it is interesting to note that the number of positive social contacts accelerated between the nonhandicapped and handicapped student while the number of negative comments decelerated dramatically. One may only speculate as to the benefits that would have derived had these children been prepared educationally on the nature of handicapping conditions and provided with opportunities to develop positive attitudes towards their handicapped classmates. Certainly, much of our hope for mainstreaming lies in the social and emotional realms.

Although the roles of teacher education and attitude are vital to the success of the mainstreaming movement, it is the evaluation of mainstreaming efforts that will ultimately resolve issues and provide data as to the effectiveness of mainstreaming programs.

Evaluation of Mainstreaming Efforts

Jones, Gottlieb, Guskin, and Yoshida (1978) have identified five variables that, when evaluated, will provide data on the effectiveness of educational intervention efforts. A brief review of each of the five variables will serve as a point of departure for those concerned with probing the efficacy of mainstreaming efforts.

Instructional Time   One question that remains to be resolved is whether the amount of time handicapped children spend in a mainstreamed setting has any effect on their academic or nonacademic status. There is some evidence that the amount of time has little or no effect on a handicapped child's social status (Gottlieb, Note 1; Gottlieb & Baker, Note 2). However, there appears to be some relationship between the amount of time involved in academic activity and academic achievement (Cohen, 1971; Martinez, Note 3). An investigation into the nature of instructional activities for handicapped children may be more revealing than the quantity of time per se.

Instructional Integration   In order for a handicapped child to be mainstreamed for instructional purposes it is essential that there be a match between the instructional needs of the handicapped child and those of the group to which he/she has been assigned. Such a match is more readily attained when the regular classroom teacher allows for differentiated instruction and/or intraclass groupings. Where such differentiation exists, instructional integration will be greatly facilitated. Direct observation of instructional activities, coupled with a description of a handicapped child's present level of skill mastery, will reveal whether the handicapped student's instructional needs match or are compatible with the instruction available for nonhandicapped classmates.

Stating Goals and Objectives   In order to ensure that a mainstreamed student will be taught relevant skills, it is imperative that instructional objectives be developed which are well defined and within the evolving expertise of the regular classroom teacher. Otherwise, the handicapped pupil's achievement is left to chance factors which may result only in incidental learning. The individualized education program (IEP) mandated by PL 94-142 requires short term and long term objectives for handicapped children. An examination of individualized education programs will indicate whether or not rigorous standards have been employed in preparing instructional objectives.

Teacher Willingness to Accommodate   The extent to which regular classroom teachers vary their task presentations and adapt instructional materials is an indication of commitment to accommodate the mainstreamed student. There is a direct relationship between a handicapped child's daily performance and the extent to which a classroom teacher personalizes a child's program. However, if inadequate pupil progress is observed, it would be counterproductive to fault the child and/or the classroom teacher. Rather, support personnel must make a concerted effort to offer further assistance and provide direction for needed program changes. The responsibility for a mainstreamed handicapped child's progress must, of necessity, be a shared one.

Monitoring Pupil Progress   Evidence must be obtained that the mainstreamed student is making satisfactory progress toward the academic and nonacademic objectives targeted for intervention. Alternatives to standardized testing should be selected to provide continuous measurement of pupil progress. Classroom teachers, with the assistance of support personnel, may be required to employ measurement systems that are compatible with and workable in a regular classroom setting.

Martin (1974) comments on the promise of mainstreaming by stating that, "We must seek the truth and we must tolerate and welcome the pain such a careful search will bring to us. It will not be easy in developing mainstreaming, but we cannot sweep the problems under the rug" (p. 153). The cautions and constraints discussed herein should serve to challenge, not discourage, those charged with providing optimal learning environments for all children.

CONCLUSION

It has been estimated that about 45 percent of all handicapped children in the United States are not receiving educational services (National Advisory Committee, 1976). In view of this figure, the national commitment to serve every handicapped child in the manner expressed in the Education for All Handicapped Children Act of 1975 dramatically ushers in a new era in education for the handicapped. This dramatic departure from the past can be illustrated by a comparison with the 1919 decision of the Wisconsin Supreme Court that a mentally normal, blind child could be barred from school since his/her handicap had a "depressing and nauseating effect" on teachers and children (Hensley, 1973, p. 3).

As recently as 1948, according to the U.S. Office of Education, only 12 percent of all handicapped children were receiving special services. Yet, in spite of all the progress that has been made, parents, educators, and public officials face as great a challenge today as was ever faced by earlier educators of the handicapped. A recent survey of the public school students in the United States by the Department of Health, Education, and Welfare (1976) reported some surprising educational disparities and pointed out some special needs. The survey shows that nationally 6.15 percent of all black students are placed in special education, while 3.19 percent of nonminority children are so placed; that 4.55 percent of children in the South are assigned to special education categories, as compared to 3.2 percent in the West and 3.5 percent in the Northeast.

A considerable amount of progress has been made in providing the handicapped with their right to appropriate quality educational opportunities, but a good deal still remains to be done. The National Advisory Council for the Handicapped in its 1976 report refers to this challenge as "the unfinished revolution." Certainly the ultimate goal toward which we are all working is the acceptance of the handicapped on the basis of their personal human qualities rather than on their exceptionalities. Since that is the case, the trend toward placement in the least restrictive environment and the elimination of labeling in favor of functional categories are movements in the right direction. These trends will be combined in the future with the momentum achieved in the past two decades toward:

Increased funding

Greater diversity in age and type of handicap of the population being served

Guaranteeing the constitutional rights of the handicapped in the courts

A widespread implementation of the concept of accountability

The more generalized application of educational technology in programs for the handicapped

Improved preparation of personnel for educating and training the handicapped

Developing new educational strategies and materials for the handicapped

Research to determine the cause of and means to prevent handicapping conditions; early diagnostic procedures to identify handicaps and to permit early treatment to ameliorate their effects; the most effective programming and instructional procedures for the handicapped

If this movement which brought the handicapped from "charity to rights" in the past 200 years continues at its current rate and direction, then we can be assured that the future will take them from "rights to acceptance" on the basis of their worth as human beings.

REFERENCES

Abeson, A. Legal forces and pressures. In R. L. Jones (Ed.), *Mainstreaming and the minority child*. Reston, Va.: The Council for Exceptional Children, 1976.

Abeson, A., & Zettel, J. The end of the quiet revolution: The education for all handicapped children act of 1975. *Exceptional Children*, 1977, *44*, 114–128.

Anderson, R. M., Greer, J. G., & Zia, B. Perspectives and overview. In R. M. Anderson, J. G. Greer, & S. J. Odle (Eds.), *Individualizing educational materials for special children in the mainstream*. Baltimore: University Park Press, 1978.

Arreola v. Board of Education of Santa Ana School District, 160–577 (1968).

Ballard, J. *Public law 94-142 and section 504: Understanding what they are and are not*. Reston, Va.: The Council for Exceptional Children, 1977.

Bandura, A. Analysis of modeling processes. In H. F. Clarizio, R. C. Craig, & W. A. Mehrens (Eds.), *Contemporary issues in educational psychology* (2nd ed.). Boston: Allyn and Bacon, Inc., 1974.

Bennett, A. *A comparative study of subnormal children in the elementary grades*. New York: Teachers College, Columbia University, Bureau of Publications, 1932.

Blatt, B. Some persistently recurring assumptions concerning the mentally subnormal. *Training School Bulletin*, 1960, *57*, 48–59.

Brown v. Board of Education, 347 U.S. 483, 74 S. Ct. 686 (1954).

Budoff, M., & Gottlieb, J. Special-class EMR children mainstreamed: A study of an aptitude (learning potential) X treatment interaction. *American Journal of Mental Deficiency*, 1976, *81*, 1–11.

Cohen, S. A. Dyspedagogia as a cause of reading retardation: Definition and treatment. In B. Bateman (Ed.), *Learning disorders* (Vol. 4). Seattle: Special Child Publications, 1971.

Coleman, J. S., Campbell, E. Q., Hobson, C. J., McPartland, J., Mood, A. M., Weinfeld, F. D., & York, R. L. *Equality of educational opportunity*. Washington, D.C.: U.S. Government Printing Office, 1966.

Council for Exceptional Children, *Official actions of the Delegate Assembly*, Chicago, 1976.

Cruickshank, W. M. Current educational practices with exceptional children. In W. M. Cruickshank & G. O. Johnson (Eds.), *Education of exceptional children and youth* (2nd ed.). Englewood Cliffs, N.J.: Prentice-Hall, 1967.

Cruickshank, W. M. Some issues facing the field of learning disabilities. *Journal of Learning Disabilities*, 1972, *5*, 5–13.

Department of Health, Education and Welfare. *The condition of education: A statistical report on the condition of education in the United States*. Washington, D.C.: U.S. Government Printing Office, 1976.

Diana v. *State Board of Education*, C-70 37 R.F.P. (Jan. 7, 1970 and June 18, 1973).

Dunn, L. M. Special education for the mildly retarded—Is much of it justifiable? *Exceptional Children*, 1968, *35*, 5–22.

Dunn, L. M. (Ed.). *Exceptional children in the schools: Special education in transition* (2nd ed.). New York: Holt, Rinehart, and Winston, Inc., 1973.

Education Service Center. *Teacher training program: Special education delivery system models*. Austin, Texas: Region XIII Education Service Center, 1975.

Erdman, R. L., & Olson, J. L. Relationships between educational programs for the mentally retarded and culturally deprived. *Mental Retardation Abstracts*, 1966, *3*, 311–318.

Fox, W., Egner, A. N., Paolucci, P. E., Perelman, P. F., & McKenzie, F. M. An introduction to a regular classroom approach to special education. In E. Deno (Ed.), *Instructional alternatives for exceptional children*. Reston, Va.: Council for Exceptional Children, 1972.

Hallahan, D. P., & Kauffman, J. M. *Exceptional children: Introduction to special education*. Englewood Cliffs, N.J.: Prentice-Hall, 1978.

Hensley, G. Special education: No longer handicapped. *Compact*, 1973, *7*, 3–5.

Hewett, F. M. *Education of exceptional learners*. Boston: Allyn and Bacon, 1974.

Hobson v. *Hansen*, 393 U.S. 801, 89 S. Ct. 40, 21 L. Ed. 2d 85 (1968).

Hungerford, R., DeProspo, C., & Rosenzweig, L. *Philosophy of occupational education*. New York: The Association for the New York City Teachers of Special Education, 1948.

Jenkins, J., & Mayhall, W. Describing resource teacher programs. *Exceptional Children*, 1973, *40*, 35–36.

Johnson, G. O. A study of the social position of mentally handicapped children in regular grades. *American Journal of Mental Deficiency*, 1950, *55*, 60–89.

Johnson, G. O. Special education for the handicapped: A paradox. *Exceptional Children*, 1962, *29*, 62–69.

Johnson, J. J. Special education and the inner city: A challenge for the future or another means for cooling the mark out? *The Journal of Special Education*, 1969, *3*, 241–251.

Jones, R. L., Gottlieb, J., Guskin, S., & Yoshida, R. K. Evaluating mainstreaming programs: Models, caveats, considerations, and guidelines. *Exceptional Children*, 1978, *44*, 588–601.

Kirk, S. A., & Gallagher, J. J. *Educating exceptional children* (3rd ed.). Boston: Houghton Mifflin Co., 1979.

Kowal, S. A., & Walker, L. T. *Education of the handicapped litigation brought under P.L. 94-142 and section 504*. Washington, D.C.: The Georgetown University, 1978.

Larry, P. v. *Riles*, Civil Action No. 6-71-2270 343 F. Supp. 1036 (N.D. Calif., 1972).

Lippman, L., & Goldberg, I. *Right to education: Anatomy of the Pennsylvania case and its implications for exceptional children*. New York: Columbia University Teacher's College Press, 1973.

Martin, E. W. Some thoughts on mainstreaming. *Exceptional Children*, 1974, *41*, 150–153.

Massie, D. Update on education of the handicapped. *Today's Education*, 1978, *67* (3), 60–62, 73.

Meyerowitz, J. H. Self derogations in young retardates and special class placement. *Child Development*, 1962, *33*, 443–451.

Meyerowitz, J. H. Peer groups and special classes. *Mental Retardation*, 1967, *5*, 23–26.

Miller, T., & Sabatino, D. An evaluation of the teacher consultant model as an approach to mainstreaming. *Exceptional Children*, 1978, *45*, 86–91.

Mills v. *Board of Education of the District of Columbia*, 348 F. Supp. 866 (D.D.C., 1972).

National Advisory Committee on the Handicapped. *The unfinished revolution: Education for the handicapped, 1976 annual report*. Washington, D.C.: Department of Health, Education, and Welfare, U.S. Office of Education, 1976.

Oregon Department of Education. *The P.L. 94–142 inventory: An introduction.* Salem, Ore.: Oregon Department of Education, 1979.

Pennsylvania Association for Retarded Children v. Commonwealth of Pennsylvania, F. Supp. 279 (E.D. Pa. Order Injunction and Consent Agreement, 1972).

Prouty, R., & McGarry, F. The diagnostic-prescriptive teacher. In E. Deno (Ed.), *Instructional alternatives for exceptional children*. Reston, Va.: Council for Exceptional Children, 1972.

Public Law 93–112, *Vocational Rehabilitation Act of 1973*, Section 504, July 26, 1973.

Public Law 93–380, *Education of the Handicapped Amendments of 1974*, August 21, 1974.

Public Law 94–142, *Education for All Handicapped Children Act*, November 29, 1975.

Redden, M. R., & Blackhurst, A. W. Mainstreaming competency specifications for elementary teachers. *Exceptional Children*, 1978, *44*, 615–617.

Reger, R. What is a resource room? *Journal of Learning Disabilities*, 1973, *10*, 609–614.

Rich, H. L. Behavior disorders and school: A case of sexism and racial bias. *Behavioral Disorders*, 1977, *2*, 201–204.

Ryor, J. Integrating the handicapped. *Today's Education*, 1977, *66* (3), 24–26.

U.S. Office of Education. *Estimated number of handicapped children in the United States*. Washington, D.C.: Bureau of Education for the Handicapped, 1975.

Welch, E. A. The effects of segregated and partially integrated school programs on self concept and academic achievement of educable mentally retarded children. *Exceptional Children*, 1967, *34*, 93–100.

West, T. L., & Bates, P. The implications of mainstreaming for teacher education. In P. Bates, T. West, & R. Schmerl (Eds.), *Mainstreaming: Problems, potentials, and perspective*. Minneapolis: National Support Systems, University of Minnesota, 1977.

Zawadski, R. F. A study of what regular classroom teachers consider deterrents to teaching educable mentally retarded children in regular classes. *Dissertation Abstracts International*, 1974, *35* (1), 292-A.

REFERENCE NOTES

1. Gottlieb, J. *Predictors of social status among mainstreamed mentally retarded pupils.* Paper presented at annual meeting of American Association on Mental Deficiency, Portland, Ore. 1975.
2. Gottlieb, J., & Baker, J. L. *The relationship between amount of time integrated and the sociometric status of retarded children.* Paper presented at annual meeting of American Education Research Association, Washington, D.C., 1975.
3. Martinez, D. H. *A comparison of the behavior, during reading instruction, of teachers of high and low achieving first grade classes.* Unpublished doctoral dissertation, University of Oregon, 1973.

Part 1

THE LEAST RESTRICTIVE ENVIRONMENT

Editorial Introduction

It is increasingly clear that most mildly and moderately handicapped children, especially youngsters labeled as learning disabled, mentally retarded, and emotionally disturbed, often have similar, educationally relevant deficits. Such children comprise the largest group of handicapped individuals. Educators now recognize that it is more meaningful to focus on the strengths and weaknesses of each unique child rather than on medical subcategories such as mental retardation. Chapter 2, therefore, presents an interrelated orientation to teaching mildly and moderately handicapped children. Recognizing that disability categories are now so deeply ingrained in our educational system that it is impossible to eliminate them entirely, this chapter also provides an understanding of the traditional categorical system still in use. The major intent of the chapter, however, is to examine common learning and behavior problems from a noncategorical perspective.

As the severity of handicapping conditions increases, the likelihood of successful integration into the mainstream of school and society decreases. At the lowest end of the continuum of exceptionality are the severely and profoundly handicapped. Historically "warehoused" in unbelievably dehumanizing environments, these neglected citizens are finally being welcomed into the human race by a previously complacent but recently awakened society. Chapter 3, again attempting to strike a balance between categorical and noncategorical approaches, provides a general frame of reference necessary for an understanding of the challenge that the severely and profoundly handicapped now present to public education.

Because of the unique needs and problems of visually, auditorially, and physically handicapped individuals, the final three chapters of this section are organized according to these disability categories.

Chapter 4, emphasizing that the education of children with crippling conditions and chronic health problems has received relatively little attention in the past, takes a look at new developments in the field and the disabled children for whom they are designed. Included in this extremely heterogeneous population are children with cerebral palsy, spina bifida, muscular dystrophy, spinal cord injury, asthma, arthritis, cancer, cardiac conditions, diabetes, and epilepsy.

Chapter 5 focuses on the visually handicapped, a group that includes a wide range of visual abilities, ranging from total absence of sight to high levels of functional vision. When vision is reduced or absent, alternatives are necessary for the attainment of skills and competencies normally acquired through the visual mode. This chapter describes such compensatory alternatives as special materials, devices, teaching techniques, and various delivery systems.

Finally, Chapter 6 discusses the major components relating to the education of hearing impaired pupils, perhaps the oldest and most controversial area of special education. The authors describe the way in which auditory signals are processed and an overview of procedures for hearing testing is presented. In addition, this chapter summarizes the various teaching methodologies used with the hearing impaired as well as the educational programs and facilities necessary for the habilitation of this small but important sector of impaired citizens.

2
ENVIRONMENTAL ALTERNATIVES FOR THE MILDLY AND MODERATELY HANDICAPPED

Virginia K. Laycock

In the average classroom, there will be several students with learning or adjustment problems sufficiently serious for them to be identified as mildly to moderately handicapped. According to estimates by the United States Office of Education (1975), one would expect to find approximately two of these students in the typical group of 30 children. More liberal estimates (Kelly, Bullock, & Dykes, 1977; Lerner, 1976; Morse, 1975) suggest that there may be as many as 12 children with learning and behavioral handicaps in the class. It is impossible to draw a profile of the representative handicapped child, for these individuals do not share a simple set of characteristics. Overall, they are more like than unlike their normal peers. Each one has his/her own unique strengths and weaknesses. The one characteristic common to all mildly and moderately handicapped children is a failure to perform well in school.

Outside of the classroom, mild handicaps may go undetected. In the preschool years, many of these children display such slight developmental difficulties that parents do not suspect any real problems. It is not until the child enters school and cannot meet age or grade expectations that a disability is actually identified. Because the difficulties of the mildly handicapped center primarily on school performance, this group is often referred to as *educationally handicapped*. The provision of appropriate academic remediation and/or behavioral intervention in the early years can correct, or at least ameliorate, the problems of the mildly handi-

51

capped. Most of these individuals attain career and marital adjustment in their adult lives.

As the severity of problems increases, the chances for successful integration into the mainstream of school and society decrease. Whereas mild handicaps are usually not identified until school entry, moderate handicaps are typically apparent at birth or in early childhood. In some cases, there is physical involvement making the handicap more visible. In nearly every case, developmental progress is sufficiently delayed in motor, language, cognitive, or social areas to warrant parental concern during the preschool years. The nature of these children's needs necessitates special education during their school careers. They can participate in the mainstream but to a more limited extent than the mildly handicapped. Achieving independence in adult life is also more difficult for the moderately handicapped. Most of these individuals will need support and supervision throughout their lives.

THE CATEGORICAL APPROACH

Individuals described as mildly or moderately handicapped in this chapter have traditionally been labeled as *mentally retarded, learning disabled,* or *emotionally disturbed.* Although these clinical terms have evolved over time and remain in use today, there are numerous problems inherent in the categorical approach. Reliance on such terms leads to a false sense of security. It should be acknowledged from the start that there is a lack of agreement on the exact nature of these conditions and the terminology to be employed. Yet educators and other professionals tend to use the labels as though their meanings were clearly understood and accepted. The mere proliferation of labels testifies to the fact that not everyone is speaking the same jargon. Over 90 different terms have been used just to describe children with learning disabilities (Faas, 1976).

The difficulties in arriving at generally accepted terminology and definitions may stem from the number of professional groups involved in the field. Physicians, psychiatrists, psychologists, sociologists, optometrists, speech clinicians, educators, and other specialists are concerned with treating the handicapped. Different theoretical perspectives result in terms and definitions with different emphases. Professionals with a medical or biophysical foundation tend to be cause oriented. Behavioralists deal only with observable manifestations. Those approaching the issues from a sociological or ecological perspective focus upon the interactions of the individual with his/her environment. Educators tend to define handicaps in terms of need for special services in the schools. When the same problems are examined from such differing points of view, the outcome is, unfortunately, lists of labels and definitions which often complicate rather than facilitate communication.

A further danger of a strict categorical approach is that it implies a homogeneity within categories which does not exist. The term *mental retardation*, for example, is currently applied to hundreds of different syndromes. Likewise, *learning disabilities* and *emotional disturbance* are generic or global terms covering a variety of specific problems. It is misleading to use the labels as though all children within the category exhibit common attributes.

In addition to variance within categories, there is also overlap between categories. Human beings cannot be pigeon-holed as neatly as the definitions would lead us to believe. Differential diagnosis, determining what an individual's handicap is and is not, can be difficult to accomplish. Current evaluative techniques lack the precision necessary to make fine distinctions regarding certain disorders. Many times, for example, it is hard to pinpoint whether a child's learning problems stem from deficits in intelligence or in perceptual processing skills. Is the child mentally retarded or learning disabled? In many other cases, both learning and behavior problems are observed. And what does one call a child who is performing in the retarded range on IQ tests, exhibiting signs of processing disorders, and displaying deviant behaviors? Definitions frequently refer to primary and secondary conditions. When the problems of children are highly complex and interrelated, however, efforts to isolate the primary handicap are time consuming and often futile. The child's needs are most real and must be dealt with regardless of the label applied. Preoccupation with categories can easily cloud the diagnostic process, leading educators to be more concerned with what the child *is* than with what he/she can and cannot *do* at the present time. The ultimate purpose of evaluation must be to identify specific needs, not to tag the student as mentally retarded, learning disabled, or emotionally disturbed.

A final argument against the categorical approach involves instructional methodology. Perhaps the efforts to classify might be justified if there were clear categorical implications for teaching. At present, however, there are not. Similar delivery systems are advocated in the schools for all types of educational handicaps. Recommendations for placement are typically made on the basis of severity of the child's problems, not on the basis of the label applied. Furthermore, instructional strategies and materials are multicategorical. They are more geared to the levels and learning styles of the students than to any general exceptionality. As Hallahan and Kauffman (1976) point out:

> Everything else being equal, the emotionally disturbed hyperactive child with a figure-ground reversal problem, the learning disabled hyperactive child with a figure-ground reversal problem, and the educable mentally retarded hyperactive child with a figure-ground reversal problem will all be taught in the same manner. The behaviors exhibited, and not the diagnostic category in which the child has been placed, are the critical variables on which the teaching strategy should hinge (p. 35).

That categories should not dictate the nature or extent of special services is clearly the intent of PL 94-142. Throughout the law, the emphasis is on meeting individual needs. There can be no packaged plans for the retarded, the learning disabled, or the emotionally disturbed. Individualized education programs (IEPs) are to be developed for each child in recognition of present strengths and weaknesses.

Given this mandate to provide the least restrictive program for each handicapped child, there is greater need than ever to move beyond a strict categorical approach. Educators must become proficient in identifying and providing for a wider range of individual differences.

Although labels can and must be de-emphasized, it is impossible at this time to do away with them altogether. They are simply too ingrained in our educational system. A recent national survey (Garrett & Brazil, 1979) revealed that all but two states, Massachusetts and South Dakota, continue to use traditional or similar categories for estimating, identifying, and educating exceptional children. The majority of states still certify special education teachers for specific categories as well. The traditional labels also remain prominent in research literature where they are used to characterize populations under study. This is perhaps their most important contribution, for it is only through quality research that there is hope of identifying empirical anchors or "marker variables" to clarify and operationalize existing definitions (Keogh, Major, Reid, Gandara, & Omori, 1978).

As long as the categorical system is still in use, teachers and administrators must be knowledgeable of the traditional areas of exceptionality. In the next three sections of this chapter, therefore, representative definitions of mental retardation, learning disabilities, and emotional disturbance are presented. The remainder of the chapter examines common learning and behavior problems from a noncategorical perspective.

Mental Retardation

Historically, definitions of mental retardation focused upon an individual's reduced capacity for learning. As understanding of retardation has increased, definitions have been revised to include emphasis on social as well as intellectual competence. The widely accepted definition of the American Association on Mental Deficiency (AAMD) reflects the current conceptualization:

> Mental retardation refers to significantly subaverage general intellectual functioning existing concurrently with deficits in adaptive behavior, and manifested during the developmental period (Grossman, 1973, p. 11).

In this definition, there are four major elements of concern: present functioning, intelligence, adaptive behavior, and the developmental period. The following discussion deals with each of these elements and how it contributes to the concept of mental retardation.

Present Functioning   The terminology chosen for the AAMD definition reflects a definite emphasis on present performance. There is no reference to causality, nor is mental retardation defined as a disease. Furthermore, there is no implication that retardation is a permanent condition. According to the definition, the term *mental retardation* applies only to an individual's current "functioning" and "behavior." It is possible, therefore, that the term *mental retardation* could describe a person's performance at one time in his/her life but not at another.

Subaverage Intelligence   A second major component of the definition of mental retardation refers to "significantly subaverage general intellectual functioning." This means that an individual's overall cognitive skills are not as well developed as one would expect for his/her age. His performance is more typical of a younger child.

Measuring intelligence and deciding what constitutes significantly subaverage performance are necessary tasks for operationalizing this part of the definition. At present, standardized intelligence tests are the best tools available for assessing general cognitive abilities. Although IQ tests are not without their limitations, they are usually the most efficient means of gathering the normative data required.

The distribution of scores from each test's standardization sample provides the basis for determining what is average versus subaverage performance. With the 1973 AAMD definition, a score must be more than two standard deviations below the mean IQ of 100 before it is considered *significantly* subaverage. This means that a person must score in the lower 2.27 percent of the distribution for his/her performance to be classified as retarded.

According to the classification scheme endorsed by AAMD, IQ scores roughly between 55 and 70 are in the mildly retarded range. Scores of 40 to 54 fall in the moderately retarded range. The end-points of these levels will vary slightly depending on the particular intelligence test that is used.

Educators tend to employ a different classification system. The term *educable mental retardation* is applied to the range between 50 and 75. *Trainable mental retardation* refers to scores between 25 and 49. Note that the educational classification encompasses a broader range of scores than the AAMD system. The educable level extends several points above the two standard deviation limit recommended by AAMD. In other words, a person scoring in the low 70s on an IQ test might be labeled *educably retarded*, although he/she would not be considered retarded according to the AAMD guidelines. The trainable mentally retarded range extends below the AAMD moderate range, overlapping with its severely retarded range.

These two classification schemes serve to illustrate the variance in terminology and criteria for categorization. Due to the complex nature of human intelligence and resulting difficulties in measuring it, there are no absolute standards for judging whether, and to what degree, an individual's behavior is retarded.

Adaptive Deficits   Subaverage intellectual ability is a necessary but not a sufficient criterion for mental retardation. As the AAMD definition specifies, a person must demonstrate simultaneous deficiencies in intellectual and adaptive skills before the problem should be identified as retardation. A person should never be labeled solely on the basis of a low IQ score. The ability to function within the total environment must also be taken into account.

Many people who test within the retarded range are able to adjust quite normally to the demands of living in their own communities. Although they may lack the specific competencies tapped by standardized intelligence tests, they have acquired the knowledge and experience necessary to get along in the real world. The behaviors demanded in the schools and on IQ tests reflect white, middle class values for the most part, which may be very different from the values of a child's home community. The term *mentally retarded* is not meant to apply to those individuals who, for ethnic or economic reasons, test poorly but are adequately functioning in their daily living situations.

Age, as well as cultural background, must be taken into consideration when assessing adaptive behavior. Grossman (1973) clarifies the meaning of adaptive functioning in the AAMD definition by identifying major skills of concern at each stage of development. During infancy and early childhood, sensorimotor, communication, self-help, and socialization skills are involved. Adaptive tasks for middle childhood through early adolescence include basic academic and daily living skills, applied reasoning, and social judgment. In late adolescence and adulthood adaptive behaviors are primarily vocational and social in nature. By definition, a retarded individual fails to develop the age-appropriate skills. In both intellectual and adaptive areas, his/her performance is similar to that of a younger child.

Developmental Origin   The current definition of mental retardation stipulates that the performance deficits are manifested during the developmental period. Although there are no rigid limits, the developmental period usually refers to the years between birth and age 18. This criterion is included in the AAMD definition in an attempt to distinguish mental retardation from other conditions having similar behavioral indicators, such as organic brain syndrome, which might appear later in life.

Summary   *Mental retardation* is a term that describes the present functioning of an individual. The label implies nothing about the cause or the permanence of the condition. In both intellectual and adaptive areas, the retarded individual is performing at developmental levels significantly below his/her chronological age. In order to differentiate retardation from other conditions, the diagnosis is reserved for problems arising during the developmental period from birth through age 18.

Prevalence of Mental Retardation   The United States Office of Education (1975) estimates that 2.3 percent of the population between birth and age 19 is mentally retarded. With respect to the total population, a 3 percent figure is generally accepted (Ehlers, Krishef, & Prothero, 1977; Luckey & Neuman, 1976). The vast majority, approximately 89 percent, of the retarded population or 2.7 percent of the total population are mildly retarded. About 6 percent of the retarded or 0.2 percent of the total population are identified as moderately retarded.

Learning Disabilities

The rise of the field of learning disabilities has been both rapid and controversial. The Federal Register of November 29, 1976 summarized many of the issues in noting that a clear definition of learning disabilities is not possible due to the complexity of each specific learning disability, the shortage of adequate research data identifying common characteristics, and the lack of appropriate diagnostic instruments (p. 52,404). As a result, numerous definitions have been proposed and *learning disabilities* has become rather a "catch-all" category in many schools.

In light of these difficulties, it is not realistic to cite one definition as generally accepted. Instead, three different definitions are provided and common elements are examined.

The definition formulated by the National Advisory Committee on Handicapped Children (1968) is the one included in current federal guidelines:

Children with specific learning disabilities exhibit a disorder in one or more of the basic psychological processes involved in understanding and using spoken or written language. These may be manifested in disorders of listening, thinking, talking, reading, writing, spelling, or arithmetic. They include conditions which have been referred to as perceptual handicaps, brain injury, minimal brain dysfunction, dyslexia, developmental aphasia, etc. They do not include learning problems which are due primarily to visual, hearing, or motor handicaps, to mental retardation, emotional disturbance, or to environmental disadvantage (p. 4).

Bateman's (1965) definition is also frequently quoted. Children with learning disabilities:

manifest an educationally significant discrepancy between their estimated intellectual potential and actual level of performance related to basic disorders in the learning processes, which may or may not be accompanied by demonstrable central nervous system dysfunction, and which are not secondary to generalized mental retardation, educational or cultural deprivation, severe emotional disturbance, or sensory loss (p. 220).

In 1975, a National Project on the Classification of Exceptional Children composed the following:

Specific learning disability, as defined here, refers to those children of any age who demonstrate a substantial deficiency in a particular aspect of academic achievement because of perceptual or perceptual-motor handicaps, regardless of etiology or other contributing factors. The term *perceptual* as used here relates to those mental (neurological) processes through which the child acquires his basic alphabets of sounds and forms (Wepman, Cruickshank, Deutsch, Morency, & Strother, 1975, p. 306).

Although each of these definitions expresses a slightly different view of learning disabilities, three common key points emerge: a learning disability involves a specific rather than a general disability, it stems from underlying processing disorders, and it does not result from any other primary handicapping condition.

Specific Disabilities Whereas mental retardation refers to sub-average general functioning, learning disabilities involve performance deficits in limited and specific areas. Overall, the learning disabled child has average or above average intellectual ability. He/she functions very adequately in many respects. In certain specific areas, however, the learning disabled child fails to achieve up to his/her potential. As Bateman (1965) points out, there is a significant discrepancy between estimated ability and actual achievement. This notion of pronounced discrepancy or uneven development is basic to current conceptions of learning disabilities.

A child's significant learning problems might be observed in one or more of the basic skill areas. Part of the difficulty in defining learning disabilities has been due to its heterogeneity, since the handicap manifests itself in many different forms. No single problem is the hallmark of a learning disability. Each child exhibits his/her own configuration of abilities and disabilities among language, reading, writing, spelling, and math skills.

Processing Disorders   The three definitions being examined reflect the view that learning disabilities are the outward manifestations of inadequate information processing. References are made to disorders in "psychological processes," "learning processes," and "mental processes." There is uncertainty regarding the exact nature of those functions that intervene between the reception of stimuli and the execution of a response. It is generally believed that such skills as attention, perception, organization and concept formation, memory, and motor coordination are involved. A learning disability results from a breakdown or inefficiency somewhere along this underlying sequence of events.

The relationship between learning disabilities and central nervous system dysfunction has yet to be clarified. In certain cases, it is possible to find medical evidence of brain damage or disorder. In the vast majority of cases, however, the reasons for the processing deficiencies remain unknown. Each of the definitions carefully implies that there may be central nervous system involvement, but that this is not a necessary condition for the existence of a learning disability. The focus is clearly on processing disorders as the immediate source of learning disabilities.

Primary Handicap   A third important component of the definitions is an emphasis on learning disability as the primary handicapping condition. Bateman's definition and the definition by the National Advisory Committee on Handicapped Children both end with exclusion clauses indicating what learning disabilities are not. The learning disabled individual is basically intact. His/her learning problems are not the direct result of physical, mental, or emotional disorders, or cultural deprivation.

This is not to say that an environmentally disadvantaged child cannot be learning disabled, or that a learning disability cannot occur together with retardation or emotional disturbance. The key is the reference to "primary" disability. If the problems observed can be more simply explained, then a child should not be identified as learning disabled. When a student has a hearing acuity loss, for example, he/she should not be diagnosed as having an auditory processing disability. The severely deprived child who has not experienced adequate opportunities for learning may very well manifest academic difficulties, but should he/she be considered learning disabled?

The more recent definition by the Classification Committee attempts to ease the dilemma of exclusive diagnosis by focusing the decision on the presence or absence of processing disorders. If the child is experiencing academic deficiencies *because of* perceptual or perceptual-motor handicaps, then he/she should be considered learning disabled. There may be other contributing factors, but processing disorders should be the primary explanation for specific learning disabilities.

Summary   Although there is no single, agreed-upon definition of learning disabilities at the present time, an examination of three representative definitions revealed several central concepts. First, the learning disabled child is characterized by specific rather than general disabilities. An uneven pattern of development is apparent in which the child achieves well in some areas but falls far short of potential in others. Specific learning disabilities may be recognized in language or basic academic skills. A second critical component in definitions of learning disabilities is a processing disorder. The child's difficulties are viewed as the direct result of deficiencies in one or more of the underlying skills required for processing information. Finally, the diagnosis of learning disability should be reserved for those cases in which there exists no other, more direct explanation for the observed difficulties.

Prevalence of Learning Disabilities   Given existing problems in arriving at a workable definition, it is not surprising that there are wide discrepancies in prevalence figures. The United States Office of Education (1975) reports that 3 percent of the children from birth to 19 years of age are learning disabled. Several reviews (Faas, 1976; Lerner, 1976; McIntosh & Dunn, 1973) have noted that prevalence estimates range from 1 percent to 30 percent of the school-age population. Without more precise operational criteria for identification, the actual frequency of learning disabilities is unknown.

Learning disabilities do seem to occur more often in males. Three to ten times more boys than girls are identified as learning disabled (Faas, 1976; Meyen, 1978). The exact reasons for this discrepancy have not been determined.

Emotional Disturbance

Definitional controversies have raged in the field of emotional disturbance much as they have in the field of learning disabilities. Once again, the influences of different conceptual models and the shortage of adequate measurement techniques have made it difficult to arrive at generally accepted criteria. Additional complications in defining emotional disturbance stem from the very nature of the variables concerned. When all human individuals experience the same range of emotions and are capable of the same behaviors, it is hard to say at what point these emotions and behaviors should be considered extreme or deviant. Judgments are necessarily affected by the hypothetical standard of normalcy applied, cultural and situational expectations, and the personal biases of the observer. Defining emotional and behavioral disorders is, then, no simple matter.

A frequently cited definition and the one that is employed by the U.S. Office of Education was developed by Bower and Lambert (1971). It states that an emotionally disturbed or behaviorally disordered child exhibits:

> a moderate to marked reduction in behavioral freedom, which in turn reduces his ability to function effectively in learning or working with others. In the classroom, this loss of freedom affects the child's educative and social experiences, and results in noticeable susceptibility to one or more of these five patterns of behavior:
>
> (a) an inability to learn which cannot be adequately explained by intellectual, sensory, neurophysiological, or general health factors;
>
> (b) an inability to build or maintain satisfactory interpersonal relationships with peers or teachers;
>
> (c) inappropriate or immature types of behavior or feelings under normal conditions;
>
> (d) a general pervasive mood of unhappiness or depression;
>
> (e) a tendency to develop physical symptoms, such as speech problems, pains, or fears, associated with personal or school problems (pp. 142–143).

Algozzine, Schmid, and Conners (1978) analyzed numerous definitions and extracted four major components in the concept of emotional disturbance: alternative placements, behavioral deviations, behavioral interference, and exclusive etiology. They incorporated these elements into the following definition:

> The emotionally disturbed child is the student who, after receiving supportive educational assistance and counseling services available to all students, still exhibits persistent and consistent severe to very severe behavioral disabilities which interfere with productive learning processes. This is the student whose inability to achieve adequate academic progress and/or satisfactory interpersonal relationships cannot be attributed primarily to physical, sensory, or intellectual deficits (p. 49).

The four components identified by Algozzine, Schmid, and Conners are used as the framework for the description of emotional disturbance which follows.

Alternate Placements   Not all definitions contain this type of clause. Algozzine and his associates included it in their definition to highlight the importance of experiential factors. Most behavior problems can be alleviated through adjustments in the regular program. Teachers, principals, guidance counselors, and other individuals are available to help students who are experiencing normal developmental difficulties or reactions to stress. The term *emotional disturbance* should apply only to more serious problems which have not responded to the customary interventions.

Behavioral Deviations   This element of the definitions pertains to the "persistent and consistent severe to very severe behavioral disabilities" (Algozzine, Schmid, & Conners, 1978). Behavioral deviations must be observed before an individual can be considered emotionally disturbed. Unfortunately, there can be no standard criteria for judging deviance. Behaviors can vary in terms of both quantity and quality. In some instances, the deviation is a matter of degree. An individual may fail to perform a certain behavior as frequently as he/she should, or a person may engage in a behavior excessively. Qualitative distinctions are made concerning the nature of observed behaviors. A particular response may be inappropriate or in violation of the expectations for the situation.

Some common manifestations of emotional disturbance are listed in the Bowers and Lambert definition, including inappropriate behaviors or feelings, pervasive moods of unhappiness or depression, and demonstrations of physical symptoms, pains, and fears.

Behavioral Interference   It is possible for an individual to engage in deviant behavior without creating any problems for himself/herself or anyone else. In such a case, the designation *emotionally disturbed* is not warranted. A third condition in the definitions is that the observed behavior must be a significant deterrent to academic or social development. The Algozzine definition states that the behavioral disabilities "interfere with productive learning processes." Bowers refers to "an inability to learn," and "an inability to build or maintain satisfactory interpersonal relationships."

The notion of behavioral interference has been applied not only to detrimental effects on the child's own adjustment, but also to infringements on the lives of others (Kirk, 1972; Pate, 1963). When a child's behavior disrupts the family or the class, there is additional evidence of emotional disturbance.

Exclusive Etiology   A fourth component of definitions of emotional disturbance deals with the exclusion or elimination of other explanations for the behavior problems observed. Both definitions under consideration specify that the difficulties of the emotionally disturbed cannot be attributed to any physical, sensory, or intellectual deficits.

As in the case of learning disabilities, this does not imply that an emotional disorder cannot overlap with other conditions. It simply means that the label *emotionally disturbed* should not be applied if another primary handicap could be responsible for the observed behavioral deviations and interferences.

Summary   Four key elements identified by Algozzine, Schmid, and Conners were used as a framework for examining the concept of emotional disturbance. An emotionally disturbed child is one who does not respond favorably to the regular educational program and the supportive services provided to all students. The individual exhibits chronic behavioral or emotional problems. Specific behaviors are judged deviant because they seem inappropriate to the observer either in nature or in degree. These behaviors must also be disturbing; that is, the emotions or behaviors are seriously interfering with the child's own academic or social development or the adjustment of others. Finally, emotional disturbance should be the diagnosis only when no other primary handicapping condition is applicable.

Prevalence of Emotional Disturbance   Depending on the particular definition and criteria used, the prevalence of emotional and behavioral disorders may range from a low of 0.05 percent (Schultz, Hershoren, Manton, & Henderson, 1971) to nearly 20 percent of the school-age population (Kelly, Bullock, & Dykes, 1977). The U.S. Office of Education (1975) cites a 2 percent figure for the birth to 19 age group. More consistent estimates will be possible only when definitions are clarified and diagnostic procedures refined.

At present, boys outnumber girls six or seven to one in classes for the emotionally disturbed (Reinert, 1976). Reinert suggests that boys are more inclined to display the acting-out, aggressive behaviors which lead to special education placements.

CHARACTERISTIC INTERFERENCES

Definitions of mental retardation, learning disabilities, and emotional disturbance have been presented to acquaint the reader with the traditional categories of exceptionality. The limitations of a categorical system have been acknowledged. This section of the chapter, therefore, does not link problems to particular categories, but attempts to describe common difficulties of the mildly and moderately handicapped.

No one child will exhibit all of these characteristics. Moreover, there is no single characteristic that occurs with all mild and moderate handicaps. Every individual will display a unique pattern of strengths and weaknesses. It is the specific and severe weaknesses that create interferences to learning or adjustment in school.

In deciding what constitutes a significant interference, at least four factors should be considered: the age of the child, the environmental demands, the intensity, and the persistency of the behavior.

Age is an important determinant since many of the behaviors described will be recognized as typical of certain stages of development. Young children are expected to experience these problems because they have not yet acquired the skills necessary for mature performance. A problem should only be considered a handicap if it continues to be observed well beyond the age at which it is normally resolved.

The demands of the environment should also be examined before any judgments are made concerning exceptionality. Many times, a child is not able to perform because the task itself is inappropriate. It may be above the student's developmental level, for example, or poorly structured and presented, or unreasonable in length. For whatever reasons, the problem is inherent in the situation. It is not the child who is at fault. Only when an individual fails to fulfill realistic expectations does the possibility of a handicap exist.

Once it has been ascertained that a child should be performing adequately given his/her age and the demands of the situation, the intensity and persistency of the problem must be determined. All individuals exhibit difficulties on occasion. The distinction between a problem and a handicap is a matter of degree and chronicity. If the behavior of concern occurs to an extreme, and if it is observed in various situations over time, then it has become a significant interference.

Given these qualifiers, many of the types of problems experienced by the mildly and moderately handicapped are described in the following discussion. Each form of interference is defined, and several examples are provided to illustrate related behaviors. Major implications for teaching are then discussed in terms of environmental adjustments that may be made to accommodate the handicapped student in the classroom.

Processing Interferences

Virtually all sensory, perceptual, and cognitive functioning can be envisioned as human information processing. An individual is continually interacting with the environment by receiving and responding to stimulation. Effective processing hinges upon proficiency in attention, perception, organization and concept formation, memory, and motor skills. A breakdown anywhere along this chain of events can result in inadequate performance. Many of the problems of the mildly and moderately handicapped stem from deficient processing skills.

Attention Deficits　In order for processing to take place, a person must actively attend to a specific subset of incoming stimulation. Selective attention thus involves the ability to direct and sustain focus on significant information while tuning out extraneous stimuli. Problems with selective attention have been viewed as major determinants of the impaired functioning of the handicapped (Bryan & Bryan, 1975; Douglas, 1974).

Attention disorders are of two basic types—distractibility and perseveration. The distractible child has difficulty directing attention purposefully. He/she may be unable to focus attention initially, as in the case of the student who misses out on instructions because he/she is gazing around the room while the teacher is speaking. This type of child is often referred to as a "daydreamer." Other distractible students are able to focus at first but shift their attention too rapidly. This student is frequently described by teachers as having a "short attention span," or spending a great deal of time "off-task." When students are highly distractible, they often fail to complete their work or make many mistakes along the way.

Perseveration may initially seem unrelated to distractibility, but it too involves an inability to direct attention at will. Whereas the distractible child is drawn off-task easily, one who perseverates has difficulty terminating the task to go on to another. He/she continues to perform a response beyond the point at which it is appropriate. A primary student, for example, may perseverate in writing a row of cursive *l*'s and end up covering the entire page. Similarly, an older student may perseverate in choosing the alternative *c* too frequently on a multiple choice test. In these examples, the learners seem to have trouble "switching gears" or directing their attention to the next bit of information.

Implications for Teaching   Students who lack attention skills will have trouble doing quality work unless adjustments are made. The teacher may help the distractible child by positioning him/her to minimize interferences. The student may be seated in the first row close to the teacher, for instance, so that there is little between them that could be a distraction.

Distractible individuals usually require interesting and appealing tasks to keep them involved. Activities that require active participation and frequent responding by the learner are preferred. The teacher should also attempt to shape attending skills by reinforcing desired behaviors. As an illustration, when the teacher notices Mark writing in his workbook as directed, she could praise him for working so attentively. By starting with brief tasks and frequent changes of activity, the teacher can gradually shape the learner's behavior until he/she is able to attend for more reasonable periods of time.

A student who tends to perseverate will need to be told the limits of a task clearly on the front end. The teacher should specify the exact number of items to be done and the time allotted. The student may need several reminders as he/she nears the end of the lesson. Whenever a teacher discovers the child is perseverating on a response, it is advisable to gently but firmly interrupt.

Perceptual Disabilities   Perception refers to the process of refining and interpreting raw data received through the senses. Through perception, an individual is able to deal meaningfully with incoming stimulation. Whereas sensation involves innate abilities, perceptual skills must be learned. Some of the major competencies to be developed include figure-ground perception, discrimination, constancy, and closure. Educators are primarily concerned with skills in the visual and auditory modalities, although tactual-kinesthetic skills are also utilized for instruction.

Figure-ground perception refers to the ability to sort out relevant aspects from a stimulus field. A learner with visual figure-ground difficulties, for example, may be unable to read efficiently from a standard printed page, because he/she has trouble focusing on single words in a given line. The print seems to blend together and he frequently loses his place. Similarly, a student with auditory figure-ground weaknesses might be unable to follow a conversation in the lunchroom. The student cannot select what the speaker is saying from the background noise.

Discrimination is the ability to note likenesses and differences among stimuli. The learner must be able to compare items on the basis of their prominent features. Matching shapes, telling whether two sounds are the same or different, and sorting objects by texture are all classic examples of discrimination activities. Confusing similar letters and words either in speech or in print is a common discrimination problem which interferes with reading and spelling.

Constancy is another important perceptual ability in that it enables a person to recognize stimuli as the same even though the nonessential properties may vary. One must learn, for instance, that an A is an A regardless of the size, color, or context in which it is printed. It is the basic form that is critical. Likewise, a child must learn to recognize sounds and words as they are heard, although they are never pronounced identically by different speakers in different settings.

The perceptual skill of detecting a given stimulus when it is presented in incomplete form is called closure. In everyday conversations or classroom discussions, a person is at a disadvantage if he/she cannot catch words that are slightly mumbled by a speaker or masked by background noise. Children with visual closure difficulties are often slow to recognize picture puzzles or dot-to-dot figures. Others may have trouble decoding words on "fuzzy" dittoed handouts, even though the majority of readers are not bothered by minor omissions.

In addition to the skills considered here, numerous other perceptual abilities contribute to information processing. Perceptual handicaps may vary in complexity as well as severity. With some children, the deficit is fairly well defined. Evidence may point to an auditory discrimination problem, for example. At other times, a pattern may be apparent, such as a generalized weakness in a particular modality. In still other cases, no pattern is apparent and the learner demonstrates several seemingly unrelated deficiencies.

Implications for Teaching   It might seem that children who display perceptual deficits would need perceptual remediation before they could take advantage of academic learning opportunities. Such a belief has been widespread in the field of special education. Recent research, however, has led to a reexamination of the role of perceptual training. Overall, evidence has failed to indicate a significant relationship between perceptual and academic skills (Colarusso, Martin, & Hartung, 1975; Hammill & Larsen, 1974a; Hammill & Larsen, 1974b). Furthermore, the remediation of perceptual skills has not produced direct improvement in academic performance (Hallahan & Cruickshank, 1973; Myers & Hammill, 1976). Based on the evidence available at this time, Hammill (1978) cautions teachers "to implement [perceptual training] programs on a remedial basis only in those few cases where improvement in perception is the goal and to consider even these efforts as being highly experimental" (p. 372).

If direct perceptual training is not the answer, what can be done to alleviate the problems of the perceptually disabled in the classroom? One approach is to capitalize on a child's strengths. Teachers can gear instruction to the intact modalities and skills. When a child has auditory processing problems, for example, he/she may profit from having visual sources of information within a lesson. On the other hand, auditory explanations often help to structure a presentation for a visually handicapped child. When children are handicapped in both the visual and auditory channels, the teacher must often enlist support from the tactual and kinesthetic systems.

Weaknesses can be further accommodated through the use of other adaptive techniques dictated by the learner's particular needs. A student with figure-ground difficulties, for instance, may be at a great disadvantage when asked to do a page of 25 crowded multiplication problems. By spreading out the problems and giving the child just a few per page, the teacher may find that he/she is able to complete the 25 items successfully. Similar adjustments are possible for many other perceptual needs.

Cueing is a particularly useful adaptive strategy. It involves increasing the prominence of certain aspects of the task in order to direct the learner to the desired response. Color coding is a form of cueing frequently used to help the visually disabled child focus on the important information. Confusing words that contain the same letters, such as *was* and *saw*, is a case in point. Most children who miscall these words fail to recognize that the position of the letters is the critical basis for discrimination. Underlining the first letter in green will accentuate the distinction and may help the student to read these words correctly. Cues must be acknowledged as props or assists. They can greatly facilitate learning but must always be phased out so that the student is gradually able to perform the task without the additional cues.

Organization and Concept Formation Problems   Once information is received from the environment, it must be screened and classified before the individual can act upon it. The basic tools for organizing and adapting to incoming data are concepts. "The concept is an expression of a rule by which diversity is brought together and thereby reduced" (Sigel, 1975, p. 67). Concepts function as categorizers, allowing an individual to cope with a wealth of information.

The development of concepts is a complex process. As a child interacts with the world, he/she graduates from a state of being under the influence of incoming stimulation to more advanced states in which he/she can impose order on his/her experiences. The level of conceptualization attained may be limited by such factors as mental retardation, brain damage, emotional disturbance, and cultural environment (Athey & Rubadeau, 1970; Sigel, 1975).

Various problems may be apparent in concept formation. At times, the learner may fail to recognize commonalities linking objects together. When asked how an orange and a banana are alike, the child may respond that they are not alike at all. Other problems involve the level of abstraction attained. An older student who sees only functional similarities ("you can eat them both") and misses the overall classification (fruit) displays immature concepts.

In many cases, the student has acquired a concept, but it is a faulty or incorrect one. For example, multidigit subtraction problems may be worked by always subtracting the smaller from the larger digit, regardless of which is on top. It is not uncommon for the mildly and moderately handicapped also to have trouble transferring or generalizing concepts. Perhaps a student can add equations in vertical form but is unable to deal with the symbols in horizontal form.

Implications for Teaching   Stages of cognitive development should be taken into account in the planning of curriculum and instruction. Cognitive growth cannot be forced, but it can be facilitated through the right types of experiences. If a teacher can recognize a child's level of functioning, appropriate tasks and materials can be provided to enhance the learner's development. As Wolinsky (1970) points out, "the importance lies in realizing that change does take place, that children can understand things at certain times, and that the period of full realization does not spring spontaneously at a moment's urgency, but rather is built up through the experiential world of the young child" (p. 154).

The handicapped child is likely to be performing at a cognitive level lower than that of classmates. He/she may be unable to grasp concepts presented in abstract form, but is capable of learning when it is approached in more concrete and structured ways.

Typically, students with concept formation problems have not profited much from incidental learning. They tend not to "pick things up on their own" as well as their peers. It follows that a disorganized, haphazard lesson will not do for these students. Considering their needs, a very systematic and well sequenced approach is in order. Additionally, the child's ability to organize and to form concepts will be aided by methods which emphasize problem-solving processes rather than rote learning.

Memory Deficits   Successful information processing and learning depend greatly on one's ability to remember. Those with memory deficits are unable to store and retrieve information efficiently. They do not seem to retain skills that have been presented.

Some children evidence problems in short term recall. They may be unable to follow directions, to acquire sight vocabulary in reading, or to recite number facts. Memory problems are also apparent when children demonstrate little retention over time. Certain students can perform a skill one day but seem to have forgotten it the next.

The critical difference between those with effective and ineffective memories appears to be the use of mnemonic strategies. Young and developmentally immature children tend not to employ spontaneous strategies for organizing and remembering material (Brown, 1974; Stevenson, 1975).

Implications for Teaching   When learners have not developed efficient memory techniques on their own, it may be possible to teach them better ways of remembering. Frequently, older as well as younger students do not really know how to study material. They can be encouraged to rehearse information as one aid to recall. Many seem to skip or rush through this important step. Verbalizing to oneself while practicing is often helpful.

Another mnemonic strategy is imagery. Students can be led to re-visualize or to develop a mental picture of the material under study. Clustering on the basis of similarities may also facilitate retention of lists or groups of items.

Presentations may have to be streamlined at first for children with memory problems. It is important for them to learn one concept well before the next is introduced. Long and complicated directions are to be avoided. When several assignments must be given at once, it is helpful to have the necessary instructions written down for the students' reference.

Many of the techniques used to improve attending skills will also improve memory. More effective learning generally results in more effective retention.

Motor Disabilities   For some children, the execution of the motor response presents the greatest deterrent to successful performance. Although these individuals are not physically handicapped, they have difficulty with gross and/or fine motor skills. Children with gross motor problems have trouble coordinating their large muscles to move their bodies efficiently. These children are often described as "awkward" or "clumsy." Some have difficulty with basic movement patterns such as walking and running. An unusual or perhaps a dysrhythmic gait may be noted. Other children may have trouble maintaining their balance. Still others may frequently bump into things and seem to lack awareness of where their bodies are in space.

Such problems in bilateral coordination, balance, rhythm, and body awareness may be accentuated when a child attempts to perform more complex motor activities like skipping, jumping, throwing, and catching. Students with poor gross motor skills are at a great disadvantage in recreational and sports events. Their lack of proficiency can lead to ridicule and rejection by their peers.

Fine motor disabilities involve a lack of precision in tasks requiring the small muscles. Most often, manual dexterity is the primary concern. Children with problems in this area may be unable to button their clothes, string beads, cut with scissors, or turn pages of a book.

Eye-hand coordination is also a prerequisite for tracing, copying, and writing. Fine motor disabilities may be apparent in awkward pencil grip, jerky letter formation, or an inability to stay within the lines. Some students labor over fine motor tasks as if each movement must be consciously directed. As a result, they tend to work very slowly and become easily fatigued.

Instructional Implications   Physical education can be a vital part of the curriculum for children with motor disabilities. By means of a carefully sequenced program, these students can acquire many of the gross motor skills that were not developed naturally in early childhood. As students learn to use their bodies more efficiently, they usually become less conspicuous to their peers and are better able to join in recreational activities.

Fine motor skills relate more directly to classroom performance. If a child's lack of fine motor control is detected in preschool, it may be easier to provide the many manipulative activities that are needed. Building with blocks, placing pegs in a container, sewing cards, and doing puzzles are but a few of the customary preschool tasks that help to refine fine motor and eye-hand coordination skills. Many of these same readiness activities will be necessary with early elementary children who are still unable to handle scissors and pencils with ease. Special care must be taken with the left-handed child so that he/she is not confused by receiving all instructions from a right-handed point of view.

When a student demonstrates sufficient control for beginning formal handwriting instruction, it is important for the teacher to stress good habits from the start. Correct posture, paper position, and pencil grip are essential. Many tracing and copying exercises should precede independent writing. Students with more serious fine motor deficits may need to use adaptive devices, such as plastic pencil grips or paper with embossed lines.

Teachers should determine what are reasonable handwriting goals for their students who have fine motor handicaps. Rather than striving for "pretty" handwriting, a more realistic goal may be functional skills. Writing should be as efficient as possible for the student and as legible as possible for the reader. Many older students will continue to print because they have not mastered cursive. As long as students print adequately, it is doubtful whether the time and effort should be spent to teach cursive writing in the upper grades.

Student's fine motor difficulties should be taken into account when giving assignments. Long copying or writing exercises may be hard to justify. In most cases, the same objectives can be achieved in another way which would be less of a struggle for the learner.

Language Interferences

"Language is a system of verbal symbols used for human communication" (Wallace & McLaughlin, 1975, p. 131). Language represents one of man's highest attainments as it is an extremely complex function. Because language performance depends on many prerequisite abilities, the mildly and moderately handicapped often exhibit language disorders. Limitations in intelligence, auditory processing, emotional adjustment, and experiential background can adversely affect language development (Hallahan & Kauffman, 1978; Lerner, 1976; Smith, 1974; Smith, Neisworth, & Greer, 1978). The likelihood of language disorders increases with the severity of these handicaps.

Linguists have identified five major components of any language: phonology, morphology, syntax, semantics, and intonation. All five components are involved in the comprehension and production of language. Language disorders can occur in any one or more of these areas. Phonology refers to the system of speech sounds, while morphology is concerned with the system of meaningful units. The combination of words and phrases into sentences involves syntax, the grammar system of a language. The semantic system is related to the development of vocabulary. Intonation pertains to the sound patterns used in speaking words and sentences.

Language disorders are also classified in terms of inner, receptive, and expressive difficulties. Inner language disorders involve problems in organizing and associating experiences in order to form verbal concepts. It is generally believed that disorders of this type are the most serious and difficult to remediate. If language is viewed as one particular form of information processing, then inner language is but another term for organization and concept formation. The previous description of these problems and implications is, therefore, applicable to inner language disorders as well. Receptive and expressive language disorders are reviewed below.

Receptive Language Disorders Significant difficulties in comprehending oral language are called receptive language disorders. Mild and moderate language handicaps can take many forms. Some children have trouble with the phonological aspects. They may be unable to make fine discriminations among speech sounds, and consequently, they confuse words that are similar. Other students have difficulty with morphological rules, failing to comprehend certain markers that change the meaning of a sentence. "He walks," "he walked," and "he will walk" all mean the same thing to a child who does not know what the tense markers imply. Similarly, children may not grasp plurality, comparisons, or possession indicated by different morphological units.

Many receptive language disorders involving the semantic system center upon problems in comprehending word meanings. The mildly and moderately disabled may have limited vocabularies for their ages. As a result, they may lose out on information presented in class or miss the point of a conversation. A confused facial expression or an inappropriate response is a typical clue that a student has not understood a verbal message. Abstract words and words with multiple meanings may be especially difficult for these students to master. Since riddles and jokes usually capitalize upon multiple meanings and absurdities in context, these children may be slow to "get the punchline."

Syntax interferes with comprehension for some children. They may understand straightforward, declarative sentences, but they may be unable to decode more complex sentence structures. The passive form is often confusing for them. When hearing the statement "Jamie was kicked by Kim," for example, they may be unsure about which child actually did the kicking. Connective and relative clauses may also be misinterpreted. When a teacher says, "After spelling we will go out to recess," there may be certain children who expect to leave right away. Sentence length can also affect comprehension. Many students may be unable to follow long or complicated instructions.

Implications for Teaching   The language problems of the mildly and moderately handicapped will often require direct remedial services of a speech/language clinician. When this is advised, the classroom teacher should work closely with the specialist to support and reinforce target skills.

Specific attention must also be given to the child's needs within the language arts curriculum. Instructional activities can be designed to develop and refine particular listening skills. Johnson and Myklebust (1967) suggest that the material used should always be meaningful. Whole words and sentences, rather than isolated sounds and nonsense syllables, should be incorporated into drills. Instruction should procede from the simple and familiar to the more complex. When new vocabulary words or sentence structures are introduced, their meanings should be conveyed as concretely as possible. Many listening activities and games should be used to strengthen receptive language skills.

Since language permeates all areas of curriculum, the teacher will need to adjust the oral language used in other instructional presentations to insure that the child with receptive disabilities has access to information. Verbal explanations and instructions will have to be streamlined. Children often get bogged down in the amount of verbiage that is used. Direct, concise statements reduce this interference. Likewise, complex sentence structures are to be avoided. As a precaution, the teacher may develop the practice of repeating instructions in paraphrased form. This may serve to clarify any confusions with particular words or structures. The teacher may also want to check quietly with certain students after directions are given to be certain that they know what they are to do.

When new or specialized vocabulary words are used in the content areas, care must be taken that these are fully explained and related to familiar experiences. Concrete materials and pictorial illustrations are valuable aids for teaching new verbal concepts.

A climate of acceptance within the classroom is vital. The student with a receptive language disorder must be made to feel comfortable and encouraged to question the teacher or a designated peer whenever oral information is unclear.

Expressive Language Disorders   Children with expressive language disorders have difficulties with the production of oral language. Typically, these individuals understand language, and they do not have any physical problems with speech mechanisms. Still, they are unable to express themselves effectively using verbal symbols.

The most common type of language disorder involves problems in the articulation of speech sounds or phonemes. Individual children display their own characteristic errors. They may tend to omit, substitute, or distort sounds. Only certain sounds or blends are affected, and the position of these sounds within words may also influence pronunciation.

Some mildly and moderately handicapped individuals have difficulties in the semantic area. Limited speaking vocabularies may interfere with their ability to communicate. The word-finding problems of other children seem to stem mainly from retrieval difficulties. They may have used a particular word at one time, but they are unable to come up with it in the immediate situation. When faced with this dilemma, the student may resort to a general referent, such as "that thing," or implore the listener, "you know." He/she may try to convey the concept by gesturing or by giving an operational definition. A child who cannot think of the word for paste, for instance, may end up asking for the "stickum stuff."

Problems with morphology are also observed among the mildly and moderately handicapped. They may omit necessary morphemes or use them incorrectly. A classic example involves the lack of subject-verb agreement as in the statement, "She bring her lunch." Auxiliary verbs, such as the verb *to be*, are often misused. Other children have trouble with tense. They may leave off the necessary endings from verbs ("He talk yesterday") or add the *ed* suffix to irregular verbs ("He bringed it"). Considering the complexity of our morphological system, it is not surprising that children with learning handicaps have difficulty applying the rules correctly.

The teacher should be aware of the distinction between language disorders and language differences such as dialectual speech. The culturally disadvantaged, the bilingual, or any speaker of nonstandard English may be language deficient with respect to phonology and morphology. Acquisition of syntactic maturity may be impeded by this bilingual interference. This should be taken into consideration before attributing the problem to mental retardation or learning disability.

Syntax can present a major obstacle to communication. Some students may use only single words or short combinations in speaking. Others may attempt to use complete sentences but combine the words in the wrong order. Often, grammatical problems interfere when the child is transforming the basic statement into more complex sentence forms. A speaker may be unable to phrase a question adequately, for example. He/she may rearrange the words incorrectly or may try to avoid the issue by questioning only through voice inflection. At times, children use disjointed speech. They may intersperse phrases, clauses, and sentences in such a way that the message is rendered incomprehensible.

Finally, certain children have difficulty with intonation patterns. Their voices may be artificially high or low in pitch. Misplacement of accent in particular words may give their speech an unusual, almost foreign ring. Juncture, the placement of pauses, may also be inappropriate. In some cases, students display so little intonation that they seem to speak in a monotone.

Implications for Teaching   The services of a speech/language clinician may again be warranted for many expressive language disorders. This individual can serve as a consultant to the classroom teacher, providing suggestions appropriate for specific problems.

Overall, students with expressive language disabilities will need a classroom program which is conducive to language development. A key aspect of the program is the teacher who serves as a model of appropriate language. Teachers, therefore, must be conscious of their own language usage, realizing that children can learn both correct or incorrect patterns of speech through imitation. Teachers should also model an attitude of acceptance regarding expressive language. The very children who need to expand and practice their verbal skills are often the most timid about speaking in front of teachers or peers. They may be fearful of criticism and ridicule. If the teacher listens attentively and honors contributions from all students, then the children themselves are likely to be more tolerant of language differences.

Children with expressive limitations will need many opportunities to communicate in the classroom in order to improve their skills. In many classes, students are seldom permitted to verbalize. Although the language of the teacher can create a rich environment for learning, the students must be given ample time to practice their own oral skills. Language stimulation activities should become a regular part of the curriculum. In addition to formal and informal discussions, show-and-tell, and language games, simulations of real life situations may be helpful. Students can develop language skills for using the telephone, requesting assistance from a store clerk, or interviewing for a job. Correct language skills during these activities are to be continually reinforced.

As skills become more refined, Smith (1974) suggests that teachers assume a more direct role in helping students to organize their thoughts toward more logical and parsimonious communication (p. 195). Teachers can assist them in generalizing skills acquired through language arts activities by encouraging and reinforcing appropriate expressive language throughout the school day.

Academic Interferences

The "trademark" of mild and moderate handicaps is poor academic achievement. In basic skill areas, these children fail to perform up to age and grade expectations. Considering the many skills which are prerequisites for academic learning, it is not surprising that the different problems of the handicapped tend to converge in the subject matter areas. Nearly every kind of limitation has an adverse effect on academic achievement. Students with deficits in intelligence, in processing skills, or in language abilities are likely to be at a disadvantage in every area of the curriculum. Emotional problems also interfere with academic progress.

In reality, however, not all academic failures are attributable to student handicaps. Many learning problems result directly from deficiencies in the educational system. These are sometimes referred to as *teaching disabilities*. Reynolds and Birch (1977) go so far as to say that "The great bulk of learning and behavior problems appears traceable to initial instruction which did not attend well enough to a close match between what the pupil needed and what was being taught" (p. 347).

For whatever reasons, mildly and moderately handicapped children perform poorly in the classroom. Some students experience difficulty in only one major area, while others have trouble in every subject. Achievement problems also differ in severity. Several case examples may illustrate some of the variance observed in academic disabilities.

1. Sam is a fifth grade student with average intelligence. Although he is working on grade level in math, his reading and spelling skills are on an early second grade instructional level.
2. Connie is a 15 year old girl in the ninth grade. According to several measures, she is functioning in the low average range of intelligence. Connie has significant difficulties in all of the basic tool subjects. Her current instructional level in reading is 3.5, in spelling 4.0, and in math 4.9.
3. Clarence is an 8 year old who has experienced numerous adjustment problems in his first two grades in school. Despite above average intelligence, he is about one year behind in his math achievement.
4. Kathy's IQ falls in the mildly retarded range. She is 10 years old and in the fourth grade, but is performing on a second grade level in basic skill areas.
5. Joan is a moderately retarded 19 year old. She is able to recognize a few sight words in reading. Her math skills consist of counting to 20, naming and writing numerals to 10, and identifying coins.

Each student's unique difficulties will dictate the nature and extent of special education services and/or regular classroom adaptations.

Implications for Teaching Once it is recognized that a student is functioning significantly below expectations in one or more subject areas, an individualized program is in order. Never should a child be given assignments clearly beyond his/her capabilities under the erroneous assumption that "if he's (she's) in this grade, he (she) should be doing this work."

A classroom teacher can identify the student's own instructional level and specific skill deficits through observation and informal assessment. If more formal testing is desired, assistance may be obtained from a resource teacher, evaluator, reading specialist, or other ancillary personnel. After the student's needs are clarified, instructional objectives and materials should be geared to the child's level and learning style.

A further implication is that classroom teachers must be willing and able to utilize alternative teaching methods. Although the basal or developmental program may be effective for the majority of students in a class, it is not appropriate for the handicapped child or he/she would not be falling behind. It follows that something different must be provided for the child with special needs. Educators are now realizing that there are many different ways to learn to read, to write, and to compute. The best method is the one that works for a particular student. Teachers cannot be locked in to one approach but must develop more flexible repertoires of instructional skills.

While attempts are being made to remediate specific academic disabilities, care should be taken that the student is not unjustly penalized in other subject areas. Students with reading problems, for example, may be unable to use their textbooks in the content areas of science and social studies. When the learner is capable of understanding the concepts involved, it is unfair to deny the learner access to the information. Alternatives must be provided. Perhaps the material could be covered by the teacher in lecture form, or read to the student by a peer, or presented through lower level textbooks, filmstrips, or tapes. Provisions must also be made for testing the reading disabled student so that knowledge of the subject and not reading skills are being evaluated.

Similarly, an expressive disability should not interfere with achievements in other subjects. Most often, students with spelling and written expressive disabilities are affected in this respect. The student who cannot write an essay may be able to give an oral report on the same topic. One who is unable to spell and write short answers on a test can perhaps score adequately on multiple choice items. It is important, therefore, for the teacher to focus on the critical skills being taught and tested in order to prevent the learner's problems in one area from contaminating progress in all other subjects.

Emotional and Behavioral Interferences

The problems described in this section pertain to the student's personal and social adjustment. Some of these difficulties limit academic achievement, while others affect his/her relationships with adults or other children. In some cases, these behaviors seem to be the source of the child's problems in school. Many other times, the emotional and behavioral disturbances seem to be the outgrowth or the result of earlier difficulties.

Activity Level Disturbances   Recent studies have found that both quantity and quality of movement influence judgments of activity level disturbances. It is important to consider to what extent the child's behavior is goal-directed, organized, and conforming to expectations for the situation as well as the actual amount of movement (Douglas, 1974). Hyperactivity, then, refers to a pattern of behavior which is both excessive and inappropriate for the situation. In turn, hypoactivity involves a pattern of movement which is insufficient to fulfill demands of the situation.

The term *hyperactivity* has frequently been abused. It is probable that many children have been so labeled when performance expectations or environmental conditions were actually at fault. The term itself has become global and misleading, making it more important than ever to de-emphasize the label and to focus on specific behaviors observed.

Excessive and inappropriate activity can occur in many forms. Overly mobile children who frequently get out of their seats to wander about the classroom are usually the most disturbing to teachers. Other students may stay in one place but seem to be constantly fidgiting—wiggling, turning, tapping, scratching, waving, and so forth. Incessant talking may also be a type of hyperactivity. When children are in almost constant motion, they may be unable to get their work done. Moreover, their behavior can be a source of distraction to others.

Hypoactivity is less frequently a problem, in all probability because it draws less attention to itself. Children with low energy levels tend to work very slowly. They are usually quiet and not easily excitable. They often choose not to become involved in activities. Teachers may describe these students as "low key." They seldom create any problems for the class. The major concern is that they are losing out on many learning and social opportunities.

Implications for Teaching   There has been a great deal of confusion and controversy about the treatment of activity level disturbances. In recent years, drug therapies, diet therapies, and other biophysical interventions have received increased attention. Although reports of successful uses of chemotherapy and diet therapy abound, there is insufficient research evidence to conclude the actual effectiveness and desirability of these practices (Gearheart, 1977; Haring & Bateman, 1977; Shea, 1978). They may be useful in treating certain types of children, but it is doubtful that any single approach, either medical or educational, will be a panacea for problems as multifaceted as hyper- and hypoactivity. Even when students respond favorably to medical treatments, certain instructional adaptations will still be necessary in the classroom. The teacher can also contribute to the treatment process by providing physicians with accurate information about student performance for diagnostic and monitoring purposes.

Two educational practices often recommended for children with inappropriate activity levels also deserve comment. The belief that an especially strict teacher can make a child "shape up" is ill-founded. While these students may need definite and consistent limits, it is unlikely that they can be forced into conformity through a punitive approach. The suggestion of having the hyperactive child "run off his (her) energy" is also ill-advised. Fatigue symptoms seem to be only another source of stimulation for the hyperactive child (Blanco, 1972), and the child may be even less able to inhibit his/her behavior when tired.

Since there is no real evidence that a reduction in activity level results in improved learning (Douglas, 1974), a reasonable goal may be to redirect the movement into appropriate behaviors. Stimulating tasks that require a high degree of learner involvement may engage the child productively, at least for short periods of time. Frequent activity changes may be necessary. The hypoactive child often responds well to this same approach.

Task involvement and learning also improve with the provision of continuous reinforcement of correct responses (Bryan & Bryan, 1975; Douglas, 1974). It would be highly difficult for a teacher in a regular classroom to give one child continuous feedback. The use of a peer tutor or programmed materials and devices may be helpful in this respect.

Impulsivity Many mildly and moderately handicapped individuals have difficulty controlling their impulses. When faced with uncertain situations, they tend to respond quickly without evaluating alternative solutions. Impulsivity appears to be a fairly pervasive characteristic. Kagan and Kogan (1970) have found that an individual's tendency to display rapid decision making is stable over time and generalizes to many different tasks. The danger of impulsivity lies in the commission of errors. Impulsive children make more mistakes, academically and socially, than children who demonstrate slower response times.

In academic work, an impulsive student will make many, seemingly careless mistakes. When asked to respond orally, for example, the child may take wild guesses. Teachers sometimes describe this behavior as "answer grabbing." The impulsive child is also at a disadvantage socially. Because the child does not consider the consequences before acting, the child may inflict self-injury or harm others unintentionally. A child may chase a ball into the street without even glancing for cars. It is not uncommon for the impulsive student to strike out either physically or verbally when angry. He/she simply does not stop to think. Similarly, the impulsive adult may hurt someone else's feelings by blurting out the first reactions that come to mind. Tact is hardly compatible with impulsivity.

Kagan and Kogan (1970) interpret impulsivity as a motive to appear competent. Other data has suggested that failure experiences are extremely disrupting to these individuals (Douglas, 1974).

Implications for Teaching   A highly pressured environment is likely to aggravate problems of impulsivity. These students might best be helped through an instructional program that is geared toward success. In addition, they can be taught more reflective styles of behaving.

Modeling is one approach with promise. The teacher who demonstrates careful and deliberate problem-solving tactics may influence the behavior of impulsive students. Children can also be encouraged directly to slow down and to consider the alternatives before taking action. In learning situations, students have been taught to use private speech successfully as a self-monitoring technique (Palkes, Stewart, & Kahana, 1968). By continually reminding themselves to stop and think, students may be able to modify their own behaviors. It is also advantageous for teachers to reinforce observed instances of reflective responding.

Advocates of the psychoeducational approach contend that self-control can be taught in much the same manner as cognitive skills. Affective education activities, such as those suggested by Fagan, Long, and Stevens (1975) in their self-control curriculum, may help children learn to regulate their impulses and to express their feelings in more socially accepted ways.

Dependency   An overly dependent individual tends to rely on others rather than attempt to do things independently. This pattern is not uncommon among the mildly and moderately handicapped. Although they do have legitimate difficulties with certain tasks, they may easily generalize their limitations to the point that adult assistance and reassurance is required excessively.

Dependent behaviors can be observed at all ages. Young children often cling to a parent or teacher instead of venturing out into the group.

Other children seem to be forever saying, "Help me. I can't do this by myself." Dependency is evident in older students who check too frequently with the teacher as they are doing their assignments.

Gardner (1978) explains that children with developmental difficulties are likely to learn patterns of dependency as a result of the actual problems they encounter in trying to fulfill age and situational expectations, and the tendencies of adults and other children to provide too much assistance. "Stated differently, children are taught by others to be excessively dependent" (p. 359).

Implications for Teaching Once the problem is recognized, the cycle of dependency can be interrupted. If children learn to be dependent, they can also learn to be independent. Clarizio and McCoy (1976) refer to the process of teaching independence as "systematic weaning" (p. 44). It requires an environment in which reasonable expectations are established and enforced.

The student cannot be thrown on his/her own abruptly. Failure serves only to confirm the child's feelings of incompetence. Initially, the student must be asked to perform only those behaviors that are clearly within his/her capabilities. Assistance must be withheld, but liberal reinforcement should be applied whenever the student makes an attempt independently. If demands can be adjusted accordingly, the student can experience the success that is vital for building self-confidence and independence.

Great patience and control are required to change the behavior of the overly dependent individual. It is extremely hard for most adults not to intervene when children plead for help. It requires additional restraint to watch tasks being done in sloppy or inefficient form. Dependent students must be allowed to make their own mistakes, however, in order for them to learn how much they are capable of doing on their own. Properly sequenced experiences can help them to increase their skills and their independence.

Poor Self-Concept Many children with learning and adjustment problems demonstrate low self-esteem. Their actions and verbal remarks reveal consistently negative feelings about themselves. Some of these students continually belittle themselves. They may make outright statements, such as, "I'm no good. I never do anything right." Others engage in self-directed namecalling, referring to themselves as "dummy," "retarded," or "crazy." Still others are unable to accept a compliment from anyone without countering with a negative response.

In many instances, individuals do not make the verbal comments, but they communicate similar messages through their behavior. They may refuse to attempt assignments where there is the slightest risk of failure. They may voluntarily exclude themselves from recreational and social activities. Some of these students view themselves as unattractive, and therefore expend little effort in grooming themselves for school. By all indications, they seem to have given up on themselves.

Although the origins of poor self-concept are not fully understood, it is believed that self-concept is learned through actual experiences and the reactions of others. There is a correlation between academic achievement and expressions of self-worth, such that those who are performing more successfully in school display more positive self-concepts (Purkey, 1970).

Implications for Teaching   Children with poor self-concepts need to be convinced that they are worthwhile human beings who can, in fact, do many things well. Helping students to adopt this view of themselves is no easy matter. Canfield and Wells (1976) offer these five principles for enhancing self-concept:

1. It is possible to change self-concepts and it is possible for teachers to affect the changes—either way, both positively and negatively.
2. It isn't easy. Changes take place slowly over a long period of time.
3. Efforts that aim at more central beliefs have greater impact on the student even though they are harder to change.
4. Peripheral experiences are helpful.
5. Relating successes or strengths to one another is helpful (p. 4).

Since the problems of the mildly and moderately handicapped center on school performance, the logical place to begin reversing the negative cycle is in the classroom. These students need an instructional program which allows them to succeed and to receive positive feedback on their performances.

Withdrawal   While some educationally handicapped students adopt a dependent style and others express negative attitudes about themselves, withdrawn children cope with their feelings of inadequacy by simply not interacting with people in potentially uncomfortable situations. They avoid social contact and devote their attention to objects or to themselves instead.

Some withdrawn children are excessively shy. A child may hang his/her head, turn away, or become unusually quiet when meeting new people. Another child may stand alone on the playground day after day, even though other children are talking and playing in groups nearby. At times, these students appear preoccupied, playing with a toy, rocking rhythmically, or staring into space. Teachers may describe a child of this type as "in his (her) own little world."

Withdrawn children are sometimes hesitant to talk, even when directly addressed. A student may shake his/her head or give an "I don't know" response. Others may speak when spoken to but refrain from initiating any conversations.

Wallace and McLaughlin (1975) state that withdrawing behaviors may originate from an inability to succeed, the memory of previous failures, and a history of inappropriate reinforcement for remaining quiet.

Implications for Teaching   The withdrawn student cannot be forced to participate in class activities. Any pressure to take part is likely to promote further withdrawal. Efforts to involve the child must be gentle and gradual. Reinert (1976) suggests that withdrawn children need opportunities to work and play alongside others and to interact with materials and classroom pets before they are asked to become actively involved with other people.

Helping the withdrawn child to interact more comfortably is thus a shaping process. Attempts to integrate the student into class activities should begin in the child's strongest areas. Risk of failure must be minimized so that the student's initial ventures will be successful. With support and encouragement, a child can slowly progress from being on the fringe of a class to being a more involved member.

Disruptive and Aggressive Behaviors   The problems of greatest concern to teachers are usually disruptive and aggressive behaviors. These not only interfere with the student's own progress but infringe upon the rights of others as well. Any physical or verbal behaviors that intrude upon the activities of another individual or group are disruptive in nature. In the classroom, these outbursts interrupt the teaching-learning process.

Common verbal disruptions include whistling, making noises, calling out, laughing, teasing, and using profanity. Nonverbal disruptions often take the form of banging objects, finger snapping, clapping, clowning, and moving about the room. Teachers frequently label these behaviors as "acting out." They are definitely attention seeking.

Aggressive actions are a form of disruption but with more serious intent. Shea (1978) defines aggression as hostile physical or verbal actions against self or others to harm or create fear (p. 45). Verbal aggression may involve threatening, cursing, namecalling, or arguing. Physical aggression may be observed as hitting, kicking, pinching, biting, pushing, scratching, or throwing objects. Although disruptive and verbally aggressive behaviors can cause great disturbances in the classroom, with physical aggression the possibility of bodily harm is always imminent.

A well known interpretation of these behaviors has been that all aggression is the result of frustration (Dollard, Doob, Miller, Mowrer, & Sears, 1939). When an individual is cut off from attaining immediate goals, he/she is likely to strike out. While this frustration-aggression hypothesis seems applicable to the plight of the educationally handicapped, learning theory offers a second explanation for observed disruption and aggression. Children learn many of these behaviors through modeling. Thereafter, the patterns are maintained and even strengthened through reinforcement (Bandura, 1973). The exact reinforcers will differ. In most cases, the attention of teachers and peers is sufficient reward, even when that attention comes in the form of scolding, criticism, or ridicule. Other students continue to be aggressive or disruptive because it gets them their own way in the situation.

Implications for Teaching Whether one accepts the frustration-aggression hypothesis or the learning theory explanation, it is apparent that children who act out are not adequately reaching their goals and reaping rewards within the system. As a result, they may become frustrated and strike out, or they invent other ways of getting attention. It follows that the best approach may be a preventive one. If all children can be granted a fair chance to achieve through a productive instructional program, then the disruptive and aggressive incidents can be greatly reduced.

It is unrealistic to think that these behaviors can be decreased quickly or eliminated entirely. For many students, disruption and aggression are well established styles of behavior. In cases of annoying but not intolerable behaviors, the systematic withholding of attention may be enough to reduce the frequency of the episodes. Ignoring is obviously not appropriate at any time when physical safety is in question.

Hallahan and Kauffman (1978) summarize additional guidelines for teaching children to be less obnoxious as follows:

> it appears that the most helpful teaching techniques include providing examples (models) of nonaggressive responses to aggression-provoking circumstances, helping the child rehearse or role-play nonaggressive behavior, providing reinforcement (e.g., praise or other rewards) for nonaggressive behavior, preventing the child from obtaining positive consequences for aggression, and punishing aggression in ways that involve as little counteraggression as possible (e.g., using "time out" or brief social isolation as a consequence of aggressive acts rather than spanking, yelling, etc.) (p. 199).

Managing disruption and aggression thus requires a very controlled environment. The teacher must be continually conscious of the effects of modeling and reinforcement. If problems are not approached systematically, disciplinary efforts can have the effect of perpetuating the very behaviors that they seek to eliminate.

SPECIAL EDUCATIONAL SERVICES

The preceding survey has focused on ways that the mildly and moderately handicapped deviate from their peers in processing, language, academic, and social-emotional areas. Because of these differences, special educational provisions are necessary. The problems of the educationally handicapped, however, are not so severe or far-reaching that they require a totally separate school experience. These children have much in common with their age-mates and, therefore, belong in the mainstream. Special education for the mildly and moderately handicapped must be delivered in ways that provide for their unique needs but also allow them to participate in the regular program to the fullest extent possible. For most of these students, the least restrictive environment will be in the upper levels of the service continuum presented in Chapter 1.

There can be no rigid criteria for deciding what constitutes appropriate placements for these students. PL 94-142 mandates that this decision be made for each child by the committee responsible for developing the child's individualized education program (IEP). After considering the student's present levels of performance and specifying instructional goals in the areas of concern, the team is to recommend whatever educational services are necessary to help the child attain the designated goals. The nature, level, and scope of the individualized goals are the best indicators of the type and amount of special educational services that are warranted.

Nature of Goals

According to federal guidelines, the IEP is to address any unique needs of the student in academic achievement, social adaptation, prevocational and vocational skills, psychomotor skills, and self-help skills. Mildly and moderately handicapped students may not exhibit deficiencies in all of these areas. Specially designed instruction is required only in those areas of development in which their needs are significantly different from those of their chronological peers.

In setting goals for a student's program, the team has to identify needs and determine which skills are most important for the child at this stage and in later stages of life. An individual's academic record, interests, and future goals must be taken into account when weighing the relative importance of academic, social, and career needs (Goodman, 1978). As a member of the decision-making committee, the student should participate as actively as possible in setting these priorities.

The individualized goals established serve as the preliminary basis for making placement decisions. To whatever extent the student's individualized goals correspond with the goals of the ongoing curriculum, the child can be served in the regular classroom. The closer the correspondence, the better the chances for successful mainstreaming. Special educational services will have to assume responsibility for any goals that are apart from the regular curriculum.

Several case examples will illustrate possible disparities between student needs and regular educational provisions.

1. A 7-year-old girl with a language disorder has a serious problem with auditory discrimination. Distinguishing initial, medial, and final sounds has been designated a priority in her IEP. Direct training in auditory perception is not a regular component of the second grade curriculum.

2. A 13-year-old boy in middle school is experiencing adjustment problems. One of the long range goals for his IEP states that he will be able to evaluate choices of actions in terms of probable consequences. The required affective education activities are not available in his sixth grade program.

3. A 15-year-old girl with a reading disability intends to pursue a college education. In addition to functional reading skills, she will need compensatory strategies for acquiring information. The committee, therefore, specified goals in reading and in adaptive study skills. Neither of these are dealt with in the tenth grade departmentalized program.

In each of these examples, the existing curriculum does not adequately address the needs of the student. The skills of concern are not taught in the regular classroom. In each case, some form of special education will be necessary to bridge the gap between the regular and the individualized educational program.

Level of Goals

A second basis for decision making concerns the functional or instructional level of the student. The handicapped student, by definition, is performing below chronological and grade expectations in certain areas. Most of the basic skill areas are direct components of the regular developmental curriculum at the various age levels. It is up to the committee to decide when a deficit is sufficiently severe that it cannot reasonably be provided for in the regular classroom.

For example, a certain child in the fifth grade has great difficulty in reading. One of the major goals for his IEP is that he will be able to answer literal comprehension questions after reading paragraphs on the early second grade level. Since reading comprehension skills are taught in the fifth grade, special education would not be justified strictly on the basis of unique goals. The level of the student's skills, however, may be a deciding factor. To what extent can the pupil's program be individualized within the regular classroom? Can the teacher adequately provide for a student who is reading 3 years below grade level? These are the questions to be resolved by the IEP team. The classroom teacher, as a member of the committee, should have a great deal of input at this time.

The composition of the class in question ought to be a major determinant. If there are a number of students in the class who are reading several levels below the norm, then it is not unrealistic for the teacher to individualize for this pupil as well. On the other hand, this particular child may be far below everyone else in the class. As a team, the parents, child, teachers, and administrator must judge whether the individual's needs can be met in the regular program *with reasonable accommodations*. When the level of functioning differs so greatly from other students that quality individualization is unlikely within the regular classroom, then special education is in order.

Scope of Goals

The scope or breadth of individualized goals is a third factor to be considered in assigning special services. The handicaps of some children are manifested in only a few specific areas. Others have limitations in nearly every facet of development. Obviously, these students should be receiving varying degrees of special education.

When special services are justified on the bases of the level and nature of individualized goals, and the goals are narrow in scope, then resource may be the appropriate alternative. It is doubtful that resource services will suffice, however, when the special objectives are far-reaching. The team must decide how many different goals can feasibly be addressed in just a few class periods per day in a resource room. When a child needs more comprehensive services, special class placement should be considered. The student should be mainstreamed for any specific periods during the day when he/she might successfully participate in the regular program. The guiding principle is that each child should be in as normal a situation as the child can handle with necessary supportive services. Forcing a child to spend most of the day in a regular classroom when there is no appropriate program is inexcusable and can hardly be justified as the least restrictive environment.

The diversity of needs among the mildly and moderately handicapped necessitates a full continuum of services. Regular teachers with the support of consultants can adequately provide for many of these students. Others will need direct remediation in limited basic areas and can be appropriately served through a resource model with careful coordination between the regular and special programs. A certain number of the moderately handicapped will need special classes for some portion of their school careers. Deciding where a student might best be served is always a difficult judgment. The chances of delivering an appropriate program are improved when team decisions are derived from the nature, level, and scope of individualized educational goals.

SUMMARY

The mildly and moderately handicapped comprise the largest group of exceptional individuals. Overall, these students are not so different from their normal peers. The one characteristic that sets them apart is a failure to do well in school.

The mildly and moderately handicapped are often subcategorized as mentally retarded, learning disabled, and emotionally disturbed. Despite the fallacies of a strict categorical approach, it is ingrained in our present system. For this reason, educators must be familiar with accepted definitions and central concepts of mental retardation, learning disabilities, and emotional disturbance.

It is more meaningful for educators to deal with specific needs of the handicapped rather than with categories. Educationally relevant problems often occur in information processing, language, academic, and emotional-behavioral areas. These difficulties interfere with students' achievement or social adjustment. The survey of problems and implications for teaching included in this chapter is not intended to be exhaustive but simply representative of the range of possible difficulties and corresponding classroom adjustments.

Serving the mildly and moderately handicapped in the schools requires a flexible delivery system. The majority of these children will be able to participate successfully in the regular program for at least a portion of the school day. The exact type and amount of special educational services provided should vary in accordance with the nature, number, and level of the individualized goals determined for each child.

REFERENCES

Algozzine, B., Schmid, R., & Conners, B. Toward an acceptable definition of emotional disturbance. *Behavior Disorders*, 1978, *4*, 48–52.

Athey, I. J., & Rubadeau, D. O. *Educational implications of Piaget's theory.* Waltham, Mass.: Xerox College Publishing, 1970.

Bandura, A. *Aggression: A social learning analysis.* Englewood Cliffs, N.J.: Prentice Hall, 1973.

Bateman, B. An educator's view of a diagnostic approach to learning disorders. In J. Hellmuth (Ed.), *Learning disorders* (Vol. 1). Seattle: Special Child Publications, 1965.

Blanco, R. *Prescriptions for children with learning and adjustment problems.* Springfield, Ill.: Charles C Thomas, 1972.

Bower, E., & Lambert, N. In-school screening of children with emotional handicaps. In N. Long, W. Morse, & R. Newman (Eds.), *Conflict in the Classroom.* Belmont, Cal.: Wadsworth, 1971.

Brown, A. L. The role of strategic memory in retardate memory. In N. R. Ellis (Ed.), *International review of research in mental retardation* (Vol. 7). New York: Academic Press, 1974.

Bryan, T. H., & Bryan, J. H. *Understanding learning disabilities.* New York: Alfred Publishing Co., 1975.

Canfield, J., & Wells, H. C. *100 ways to enhance self-concept in the classroom.* Englewood Cliffs, N.J.: Prentice Hall, 1976.

Clarizio, H. F., & McCoy, G. F. *Behavior disorders in children* (2nd ed.). New York: Thomas Y. Crowell, 1976.

Colarusso, R. P., Martin, H., & Hartung, J. Specific visual perceptual skills as long-term predictors of academic success. *Journal of Learning Disabilities,* 1975, *8*, 52–56.

Dollard, J., Doob, L., Miller, N., Mowrer, O., & Sears, R. *Frustration and aggression.* New Haven: Yale University Press, 1939.

Douglas, V. I. Sustained attention and impulse control: Implications for the handicapped. In C. E. Sherrick, et al (Eds.), *Psychology of the handicapped child.* Washington, D.C.: U.S. Department of Health, Education, & Welfare, 1974.

Ehlers, W. H., Krishef, C. H., & Prothero, J. C. *An introduction to mental retardation.* Columbus, Oh.: Charles E. Merrill, 1977.

Faas, L. A. *Learning disabilities: A competency based approach.* Boston: Houghton Mifflin, 1976.

Fagan, S. A., Long, N. J., & Stevens, D. J. *Teaching children self-control.* Columbus, Oh.: Charles E. Merrill, 1975.

Federal Register, Monday, November 29, 1976, *41,* 52404–52407.

Gardner, W. I. *Children with learning and behavior problems: A behavior management approach.* Boston: Allyn and Bacon, 1978.

Garrett, J. E., & Brazil, N. Categories used for the identification and education of exceptional children. *Exceptional Children,* 1979, *45,* 291–292.

Gearheart, B. R. *Learning disabilities: Educational strategies* (2nd ed.). St. Louis: C. V. Mosby, 1977.

Goodman, L. Academics for handicapped students in our secondary schools—where do we begin? In J. B. Jordan (Ed.), *Exceptional students in secondary schools.* Reston, Va.: Council for Exceptional Children, 1978.

Grossman, H. J. (Ed.). *Manual on terminology and classification of mental retardation, 1973 revision.* Washington, D.C.: American Association on Mental Deficiency, 1973.

Hallahan, D. P., & Cruickshank, W. M. *Psychological foundations of learning disabilities.* Englewood Cliffs, N. J.: Prentice Hall, 1973.

Hallahan, D. P., & Kauffman, J. M. *Introduction to learning disabilities: A psycho-behavioral approach.* Englewood Cliffs, N.J.: Prentice Hall, 1976.

Hallahan, D. P., & Kauffman, J. M. *Exceptional children: An introduction to special education.* Englewood Cliffs, N.J.: Prentice Hall, 1978.

Hammill, D. D. Assessing and training perceptual motor skills. In D. D. Hammill & N. R. Bartel (Eds.), *Teaching children with learning and behavior problems* (2nd ed.). Boston: Allyn and Bacon, 1978.

Hammill, D. D., & Larsen, S. The effectiveness of psycholinguistic training. *Exceptional Children*, 1974, *41*, 5–15.(a)

Hammill, D. D., & Larsen, S. C. The relationship of selected auditory perception skills and reading ability. *Journal of Learning Disabilities*, 1974, *7*, 429–435.(b)

Haring, N. G., & Bateman, B. *Teaching the learning disabled child*. Englewood Cliffs, N.J.: Prentice Hall, 1977.

Johnson, D. J., & Myklebust, H. R. *Learning disabilities: Educational principles and practices*. New York: Grune & Stratton, 1967.

Kagan, J., & Kogan, N. Individuality and cognitive performance. In P. H. Mussen (Ed.), *Manual of child psychology* (3rd ed., Vol. 1). New York: John Wiley & Sons, 1970.

Kelly, T. J., Bullock, L. M., & Dykes, M. K. Behavior disorders: Teachers' perceptions. *Exceptional Children*, 1977, *43*, 316–318.

Keogh, B. K., Major, S. M., Reid, H. P., Gandara, P., & Omori, H. Marker variables: A search for comparability and generalizability in the field of learning disabilities. *Learning Disabilities Quarterly*, 1978, *1*(3), 5–11.

Kirk, S. *Educating exceptional children* (2nd ed). Boston: Houghton Mifflin, 1972.

Lerner, J. W. *Children with learning disabilities* (2nd ed.). Boston: Houghton Mifflin, 1976.

Luckey, R. E., & Neuman, R. Practices in estimating mental retardation prevalence. *Mental Retardation*, 1976, *14*(11), 16–18.

McIntosh, D. K., & Dunn, L. M. Children with major specific learning disabilities. In L. M. Dunn (Ed.), *Exceptional children in the schools* (2nd ed). New York: Holt, Rinehart & Winston, 1973.

Meyen, E. L. *Exceptional children and youth*. Denver: Love Publishing Company, 1978.

Morse, W. C. The education of socially maladjusted and emotionally disturbed children. In W. M. Cruickshank & G. O. Johnson (Eds.), *Education of exceptional children and youth* (3rd ed). Englewood Cliffs, N.J.: Prentice Hall, 1975.

Myers, P. I., & Hammill, D. D. *Methods for learning disorders*. New York: John Wiley & Sons, 1976.

National Advisory Committee on Handicapped Children. *Special education for handicapped children, first annual report*. Washington, D.C.: U.S. Department of Health, Education, & Welfare, 1968.

Palkes, H., Stewart, W., & Kahana, B. Porteus Maze performance of hyperactive boys after training in self-directed verbal commands. *Child Development*, 1968, *39*, 817–826.

Pate, J. Emotionally disturbed and socially maladjusted children. In L. M. Dunn (Ed.), *Exceptional children in the schools*. New York: Holt, Rinehart, & Winston, 1963.

Purkey, W. W. *Self-concept and school achievement*. Englewood Cliffs, N.J.: Prentice Hall, 1970.

Reinert, H. R. *Children in conflict: Educational strategies for emotionally disturbed and behaviorally disordered*. St. Louis: C. V. Mosby, 1976.

Reynolds, M. C., & Birch, J. W. *Teaching exceptional children in all America's schools*. Reston, Va.: Council for Exceptional Children, 1977.

Schultz, E. W., Hershoren, A., Manton, A. B., & Henderson, R. A. Special education for the emotionally disturbed. *Exceptional Children*, 1971, *38*, 313–319.

Shea, T. M. *Teaching children and youth with behavior disorders.* St. Louis: C. V. Mosby, 1978.

Sigel, I. Concept formation. In J. J. Gallagher (Ed.), *The application of child development research to exceptional children.* Reston, Va.: Council for Exceptional Children, 1975.

Smith, R. M. *Clinical teaching: Methods of instruction for the retarded.* New York: McGraw Hill, 1974.

Smith, R. M., Neisworth, J. T., & Greer, J. G. Classification and individuality. In J. T. Neisworth & R. M. Smith (Eds.), *Retardation: Issues, assessment, and intervention.* New York: McGraw Hill, 1978.

Stevenson, H. A. Learning. In J. J. Gallagher (Ed.), *The application of child development research to exceptional children.* Reston, Va.: Council for Exceptional Children, 1975.

U.S. Office of Education. *Estimated number of handicapped children in the United States 1974–75.* Washington, D.C.: U.S. Department of Health, Education, & Welfare, 1975.

Wallace, G., & McLaughlin, J. A. *Learning disabilities: Concepts and characteristics.* Columbus, Oh.: Charles E. Merrill, 1975.

Wepman, J. M., Cruickshank, W. M., Deutsch, C. P., Morency, A., & Strother, C. R. Learning disabilities. In N. Hobbs (Ed.), *Issues in the classification of children* (Vol. 1). San Francisco: Jossey-Bass, 1975.

Wolinsky, G. F. Piaget and the psychology of thought: Some implications for teaching the retarded. In I. J. Athey & D. O. Rubadeau (Eds.), *Educational implications of Piaget's theory.* Waltham, Mass.: Xerox College Publishing, 1970.

3

ENVIRONMENTAL ALTERNATIVES FOR THE SEVERELY AND PROFOUNDLY HANDICAPPED

Robert M. Anderson, John G. Greer, and Wellington L. Mock

This chapter is about children and adults who fall within the lowest ranges of intelligence and adaptive behavior. Classified as severely and profoundly handicapped, these individuals, until recently, had a bleak outlook for a reasonable social adjustment. Usually housed in the impersonal, isolated, back wards of institutions, these outcasts of humanity have historically existed in unbelievably dehumanizing circumstances. Even today, their status is sometimes deplorable. As recently as 1973, a member of the Pennsylvania Association for Retarded Children described the state institution at Pennhurst in the following way:

> Large numbers of retarded persons have been herded together to live as animals in a barn, complete with stench. Many are forced into slave labor conditions; deprived of privacy, affection, morality; suffering the indignities of nakedness, beatings, sexual assaults and exposure. Some are doped out of reality with chemical restraints while others are physically deformed by the mechanical ones. Many are sitting aimlessly without motivations, incentives, hope or programs (Lippman & Goldberg, 1973, p. 17).

Despite the shocking conditions at Pennhurst, as reported above, and similar inhumane conditions that existed and, in some cases, continue to exist in other facilities, the pendulum is now swinging dramatically

Part of this chapter was adapted from material published in R. M. Anderson and J. C. Greer, *Educating the Severely and Profoundly Retarded*, Baltimore: University Park Press, 1976.

toward the improvement of services for the severely and profoundly handicapped.

IDENTIFYING THE SEVERELY HANDICAPPED

Who are these individuals who have been so neglected? What has recently awakened society to their plight? In what direction must we go to find solutions that will correct the injustices of the past and adequately provide for a more normal existence? While comprehensive answers are obviously beyond the scope of this chapter, the discussions included are designed to provide the general frame of reference necessary for an understanding of the challenge that the severely handicapped now represent to special educators.

A Proposed Definition

Despite increased interest in and commitment to severely handicapped people, no single, inclusive definition at present delimits this population. Baker (1979) has reviewed the recent literature and analyzed the problems of defining the severely handicapped. Acknowledging the constraints inherent in attempting to adequately identify these individuals, she proposed the following definition:

> The severely handicapped individual is one whose ability to provide for his or her own basic life-sustaining and safety needs is so limited, relative to the proficiency expected on the basis of chronological age, that it could pose a serious threat to his or her survival (Baker, 1979, p. 60).

This definition of the severely handicapped serves as a point of departure for this chapter. As used here, it incorporates the characteristics typically included to describe *severely* and *profoundly* handicapped persons.

Common Characteristics

The severely and profoundly handicapped represent a very heterogeneous population. They vary tremendously in terms of the physical stigmata and behavioral handicaps they manifest. This is reflected in the numerous labels that have been used in the past to describe these children. Terms like *custodial, autistic, psychotic, schizophrenic, subtrainable, vegetables,* and *severely emotionally disturbed* all can be found in the literature concerned with the severely handicapped. Despite the ambiguity of these labels, and the variation in the population they purportedly describe, there are four generalizations that can be made. First of all, most severely and profoundly handicapped children manifest some type of gross physical abnormality or neurological involvement. Among other complications, sensorimotor deficits, minimally controlled seizures, and lowered resistance to disease frequently result.

The second generalization concerns the typical level of functioning that is attained by this population. At present there are divergent viewpoints regarding the prognosis and perceived limitations of severely and profoundly handicapped individuals. These points of view were debated in a series of articles in *Exceptional Children* (Burton & Hirshoren, 1979a; Burton & Hirshoren, 1979b; Sontag, Certo, & Button, 1979). While the prognosis is continually improving with advances in our educational sophistication, there are nevertheless competencies that they normally do not achieve. Children in this category seldom care for themselves in any way. They often must be dressed, fed, and toileted by others, even as adults. Meaningful communication, if any, is frequently restricted to nonverbal gesturing and physical contact. Although the issues related to prognosis are still being debated, it is likely that many will remain dependent throughout their lifetimes.

Third, a large proportion of severely and profoundly handicapped individuals have multiple disabilities with associated handicaps. There are almost unlimited combinations of multiple disabilities—hearing impairment and mental retardation; visual impairment and cerebral palsy; deafness, blindness, and crippling conditions. As Wolf and Anderson (1969) have suggested, the number and complexity of such conditions could proliferate endlessly. The more severe or profound the handicap, the greater likelihood that there are accompanying handicapping conditions. Dunn (1973) states that ". . . it would appear that only half of the handicapped children have one educationally significant disability; another quarter have two; and the other quarter have three or more." Obviously this fact will have a very pervasive effect on all aspects of working with this population (i.e., assessment, treatment, and training).

Finally, the prevalence of these individuals in education will probably increase due to litigation, legislation, and the field of medicine. Court cases concerning "right to education" and "right to treatment," with consequent laws enacted to protect the rights of these individuals, have forced society's recognition of them. Many individuals, who formerly spent lifetimes in basements, attics, and back wards of institutions, have suddenly been thrust into society for habilitation and education. As a result of the increased use of drugs, new strains of viruses, and environmental pollution, the potential for prenatal damage (resulting in severe and profound handicaps) is greater than before. Also, postnatal poisonings, accidents, and diseases will continue to occasionally cause severe or profound consequences. Finally, technological advances in medicine are keeping many of these individuals alive much longer than in the past.

Currently, it is impossible to estimate precisely the prevalence of individuals falling under the classification of severely and profoundly handicapped. Since the inception of services for the handicapped in the United States, the countless surveys that have attempted to establish prevalence estimates have resulted in widely different findings. Problems related to definition, geographic region, inadequacy of assessment instruments, sampling techniques, and divergent populations have complicated attempts to obtain accurate prevalence figures.

The limitation of space in this chapter does not allow for a discussion of each possible cluster of severe and profound disabilities. Instead, the following section focuses on only one disability category, the severely and profoundly retarded. It is a population typified by the four previously mentioned generalizations and one that has received increasing attention over the past several years. The problems associated with the severely and profoundly retarded, inasmuch as this heterogeneous group includes combinations of all other disabilities, are illustrative of many of the problems encountered by children and adults variously labeled and categorized according to other standard disability groupings.

SEVERELY AND PROFOUNDLY RETARDED

Definition and Classification

Professional personnel representing a wide spectrum of disciplines have traditionally defined mental retardation relative to their own professional frames of reference; hence no single definition of mental retardation has ever been satisfactory or suitable to all who work with the mentally retarded. Since numerous textbooks have dealt in detail with this and related issues, the various points of view in defining mental retardation are mentioned only briefly in this chapter.

Robinson and Robinson (1965, 1976) present an excellent review of traditional definitions of mental retardation. In general, past definitions have focused on capacity to learn, knowledge possessed, social adaptation, and personal adjustment. While the controversies that center on definition are significant to the education of children whose intellectual handicaps are relatively mild, severely and profoundly retarded children, most of whom have substantial organic involvement, will be defined as retarded no matter what criteria are used. Therefore, in defining this population, it is of small consequence to debate the criteria of classification. Of more significance is the understanding that the ultimate level at which one functions is the product of the interaction of many hereditary and environmental factors and that this level can be modified by appropriate intervention (Begab, 1973). The concept of potential for change in behavior, in even the most severely disabled, has gained widespread acceptance in recent years, and is reflected in the definition of mental retardation as stated by the American Association on Mental Deficiency. This definition, briefly examined in this section, serves as a point of departure for defining the severely and profoundly retarded.

The American Association on Mental Deficiency (AAMD) has published a series of six manuals on terminology and classification. The most recent manual (Grossman, 1973) presents a comprehensive review of the revised definition of mental retardation. While the dual requirement of impairment in both measured intelligence and adaptive behavior has been retained, this definition reflects a number of significant changes. As revised, the definition reads:

> Mental retardation refers to significantly subaverage general intellectual functioning existing concurrently with deficits in adaptive behavior, and manifested during the developmental period (Grossman, 1973, p. 5).

Intellectual functioning is separated into four levels of mental retardation. Translated into intelligence quotient (IQ) values, the corresponding levels of mental retardation and IQ ranges for three frequently used intelligence tests are illustrated in the manual (Grossman, 1973, p. 18) as in Table 1.

As can be seen, the term *significantly subaverage* refers to performance that is two or more standard deviations below the mean of the tests. The previously used borderline category has been deleted.

The upper age limit of the *developmental period*, another important concept in the AAMD definition, is set at 18 years and serves to distinguish mental retardation from other disorders of human behavior.

Table 1. AAMD classification of mental retardation by obtained intelligence quotient

Levels	Stanford-Binet and Cattell (s.d. 16)	Wechsler Scales (s.d. 15)
Mild	68–52	69–55
Moderate	51–36	54–40
Severe	35–20	39–25 (extrapolated)
Profound	19 and below	24 and below (extrapolated)

Source: *Manual on Terminology and Classification in Mental Retardation* edited by Herbert J. Grossman, American Association on Mental Deficiency, Washington, D.C., 1973, p. 18. Reprinted by permission of the author and publisher.

The third significant term, *adaptive behavior*, is defined as the effectiveness or degree with which the individual meets the standards of personal independence expected of his age and cultural group (Grossman, 1973, p. 11). Since these expectations vary for different age groups, deficits in adaptive behavior will vary at different ages. For example, deficits in adaptive behavior during infancy and early childhood might be manifested by lags in sensorimotor skill development and delays in speech. For an adolescent, on the other hand, self-help and socialization skills may provide a more accurate estimate of his/her general ability to adapt.

The AAMD manual presents a series of tables that illustrate patterns of adaptive behavior ranging from infancy and early childhood through adulthood. While space does not permit the inclusion of all the tables, Table 2 illustrates the highest level of adaptive behavior function-

Table 2.   Illustrations of highest level of adaptive behavior functioning

Age and level indicated	Behavior functioning
6 years (mild) 9 years (moderate) 12 years and above (severe)	Independent functioning: Feeds self with spoon or fork, may spill some; puts on clothing but needs help with small button and jacket zippers; tries to bathe self but needs help; can wash and dry hands but not very efficiently; partially toilet trained but may have accidents.
15 years and above (profound)	Physical: May hop or skip; may climb steps with alternating feet; rides tricycle (or bicycle over 8 years); may climb trees or jungle gym; play dance games; may throw ball and hit target.
	Communication: May have speaking vocabulary of over 300 words and use grammatically correct sentences; if non-verbal, may use many gestures to communicate needs; understands simple verbal communications including directions and questions ("Put it on the shelf." "Where do you live?"); some speech may be indistinct sometimes; may recognize advertising words and signs (ice cream, STOP, EXIT, MEN, LADIES); relates experiences in simple language.
	Social: Participates in group activities and simple group games; interacts with others in simple play (store, house) and expressive activities (art and dance).

Source: *Manual on Terminology and Classification in Mental Retardation* edited by Herbert J. Grossman, American Association on Mental Deficiency, Washington, D.C., 1973, p. 29. Reprinted by permission of the author and publisher.

ing generally expected at the ages and levels of retardation indicated in the left margin (Grossman, 1973, p. 29).

An extensive medical classification system designed to classify groups according to etiology is also included in the AAMD manual. This system, which provides descriptive symptoms of clinical conditions, views mental retardation as a manifestation of some underlying disease process or medical condition (Grossman, 1973). The biomedical system is used primarily by physicians for diagnostic purposes and it encompasses: 1) infections and intoxications, 2) trauma or physical agents, 3) metabolism and nutrition, 4) gross brain dysfunction, 5) unknown prenatal influence, 6) chromosomal abnormalities, 7) gestational disorders, 8) following psychiatric disorder, 9) environmental influences, and 10) other conditions.

While the severely and profoundly retarded suffer from many of these medical problems, a classification system based on such factors is very limited in educational utility. Therefore, the AAMD definition focuses on behavioral performance without reference to etiology. Mental retardation describes current behavior and does not imply prognosis. As defined and interpreted by this definition, an individual may meet the criteria of mental retardation at one time and not at another. The manual states, and we concur, that prognosis is related more to factors such as associated conditions, motivation, treatment, and training opportunities than to mental retardation itself. We must recognize, however, that even under the most optimal circumstances, severely and profoundly retarded individuals cannot be habilitated to nonretarded status.

A Historical Perspective

Throughout the centuries of history it is safe to say that many, if not most, of the individuals that we today label as severely and profoundly handicapped died or were put to death at a very early age. Prior to the last 200 years, the general attitude of acceptance and the idea of training (or educating) these individuals simply did not exist. In the earlier period (from the beginning of human existence until the eighteenth century) the rigors of the environment and the predominance of negative attitudes toward the handicapped in general made the life span of the severely and profoundly handicapped very short. All handicapped during this earlier period were, ". . . destroyed, tortured, exorcised, sterilized, ignored, exiled, exploited and even considered divine" (Hewett, 1977, p. 12). From the eighteenth century until now, amazing strides have been made in the education and training of all handicapped, and especially in the area of retardation.

In the early nineteenth century, two physicians were especially notable for their work with the retarded. Jean Itard's work with Victor ("The

Wild Boy of Aveyron") and Edward Seguin's methodology of training the retarded represent two initial attempts in what we know now as "special education." Their work created a worldwide hope that the "idiocy" problem had been solved. Because they expected to cure the retarded through training, Itard, Seguin, and many others felt they had failed when this was not accomplished. From an educational viewpoint, however, both men were incredibly successful and their work is still a valuable pedagogy for "special educators."

Prior to 1850, very little was done for the mentally retarded in the United States. In 1650, Maryland became the first colony to pass a law that allowed for the appointment of guardians for feebleminded children. In some cases the feebleminded, along with other deviants, were auctioned to the highest bidder, who could use them for manual labor in return for caring for them. In 1793, Kentucky was the first state to pass a "pauper idiot law," which allowed remuneration to families with feebleminded individuals. Residential arrangements prior to 1850 did not include remediation or rehabilitation. The feebleminded were merely placed in alms houses, jails, or insane asylums (Baumeister & Butterfield, 1970).

The period from 1850 to 1880 was one of considerable progress, largely through the efforts of Edward Seguin, Samuel Howe, and others. Seguin's contributions to the establishment of training schools for the feebleminded extended beyond his actual participation in the founding of schools in Massachusetts, New York, Ohio, Connecticut, and Pennsylvania; his writing provided the inspiration and philosophy upon which these training institutions were founded. He stated that, ". . . the mental defective, regardless of the reasons for his backwardness, is entitled to be treated with dignity, warmth, and kindness and with the best skills and resources available" (Baumeister & Butterfield, 1970). Dr. Samuel Howe was chosen to head a commission to look into the condition of the idiots in Massachusetts. Upon Howe's recommendation, the Massachusetts legislature authorized the first training school for idiots in 1848. In addition to state authorized schools, many private schools were established and these pioneers felt that through education and training, the mental defective could be made to live a more normal life. Wolfensberger (1976) labels this era (1850–1880) a period when an attempt was made to "make the deviant less deviant" (p. 48).

The institutions of this period were quite successful in achieving many of their goals and did return many to the community. While these successes may be viewed as uncontrived, some of the reports of their successes can be considered somewhat exaggerated. This was due to attempts to win over a skeptical public and an often recalcitrant state legislature. However, these claims eventually undermined their intended purpose and contributed to a feeling of hopelessness that came into vogue during the last two decades of the nineteenth century. It seems that many of the early founders' peers, as well as some who reflect back on this era, ". . . had misunderstood the objectives of the pioneers in expecting complete and rapid cures in large numbers, and interpreted any lesser accomplishments as tantamount to failure" (Wolfensberger, 1976, p. 51). With this perceived failure, ideologies changed between 1870 and 1880. Developmental attitudes were replaced by pity.

Toward the end of the nineteenth century, there was a general aversion to deviancy of all forms. This, coupled with the accumulation of nonrehabilitated residents, gradually changed the training "school" to an "asylum." The idea now was to offer the mentally deviant person "benevolent shelter."

By 1875 several states had begun to plan and build the large, diversified institutions that we see today. The utilization of these large institutions led to three dangerous (and ultimately disastrous) trends: 1) isolation, 2) enlargement, and 3) economization (Wolfensberger, 1976). The trend toward isolation dictated that institutions should be far away from population centers and this led to suspicion and fear of the mentally retarded on the part of the normal population. In order to group the mentally deficient together, "so he could associate with his own kind," the institution had to be enlarged from small, homelike facilities to large, dormitorylike arrangements. The trend toward labor and economization is characterized by Pennsylvania, which in 1887 passed an act that increased the number of state supported residents and reduced the per capita expenditure from $200 to $175 per year. The higher grade imbecile was used to help the institution run more economically by farming and taking care of lower grade defectives.

This transition period (1870–1890) gave way to one of the worst periods for the mentally retarded. The idea now was to "protect society from the deviant"—the mentally deficient became a "menace" to society. Wolfensberger, in quoting Fernald (1915), identifies four causal factors associated with this period. The first was the widespread use of mental tests that pointed out the extent of feeblemindedness. Secondly, studies of family histories of the feebleminded confirmed the fear that feeblemindedness was hereditary. In addition, extensive surveys, studies, and inquiries purported that feeblemindedness was an important factor in all sorts of social evil and disease (delinquency, vagrancy, venereal disease, crime, immorality, and so forth). Finally, because of the aforementioned factors, the estimates of the extent and prevalence of feeblemindedness were greatly increased. As these factors were comprehended by society, the treatment of the mentally retarded became so inhumane or dehumanizing that one author stated that their treatment was very similar to the Germans' treatment of the Jews in World War II (Nirje, 1969a). During this period (1880–1895), the retarded woman was regarded as the most dangerous: "It is certain that the feebleminded girl or woman in the city rarely escapes the sexual experiences that too often result in the birth of more defectives and degenerates" (Fernald, 1912, in Wolfensberger, 1976, p. 56). Furthermore, ". . . their children are apt to be mentally defective, with more or less pronounced animal instincts, diseased and depraved, a curse and menace to the community (Bullard, 1910, in Wolfensberger, 1969, p. 103). Around 1895, Connecticut passed House Bill 681, the first of the preventive marriage laws. These laws were enacted because "the feebleminded woman who marries is twice as prolific as the normal woman" (Fernald, 1912, in Wolfensberger, 1976, p. 56).

The ineffectiveness of these marriage laws spawned preventive sterilization laws. It was stated that, ". . . greater liberty, therefore greater happiness to the individual (will accrue by) . . . invoking the aid of surgical interference . . ." (Barr, 1902, in Wolfensberger, 1969, p. 111). The absurdity to which this line of thinking was carried is ably noted by Wolfensberger (1969):

> An apparently widely held view was stated by Taylor (1898), who reasoned that if procreation was rendered impossible by surgery, there would be no further value in preserving the sexual instinct of the retardate. Since much harm was seen to result in the cultivation or even retention of this instinct, Taylor recommended that it would be just as well '. . . to remove the organs which the sufferers are unfit to exercise normally, and for which they are the worse in the unnatural cultivation and use' (p. 81). Thus, for males, castration was widely preferred over vasectomy (Cave, 1911; Van Wagenen, 1914). In one stroke, it not only accomplished sterilization; it also eliminated 'sexual debaucheries' (Cave) and masturbation (Van Wagenen), and perhaps even improved 'the singing voice' (Barr, 1905) and diminished epileptic seizures (Barr, 1904). Sometimes, castration was performed '. . . after every other means . . .' as a '. . . cure for masturbation,' even without the perceived need for sterilization (Reports from States, 1895, p. 348). By 1914, sterilization was used not only for eugenic but also for penal reasons, sometimes in addition to a prison sentence. The courts upheld this measure as constituting neither cruel nor unusual punishment for certain crimes (Van Wagenen). In cases where vasectomy was performed, retardates did 'not require an anesthetic since all that is required is to cut the vas deferens' (Risley, 1905, p. 97) (p. 111).

When mating and sterilization laws failed to alleviate the perceived menace, only segregation or "strict sexual quarantine" (as Fernald called it in 1915), prevailed as the answer. Not only were the feebleminded to be removed from society, but the sexes from each other. In fact, Barr suggested that the federal government create one or more reservations to encompass all the feebleminded on the same basis as another group of deviants, the Indians: "The national government has provided for the mute, the Negro, and the Indian—then, why not for this branch of the population increasing as rapidly as they, and becoming yearly more inimical to national prosperity" (1897, in Wolfensberger, 1976, p. 61).

By now it is quite evident that society not only had placed the mentally retarded in the status of a serious deviant, but because retardation was considered incurable, he was not to be rehabilitated. Therefore, the retarded were merely stored until death and this is what Wolfensberger refers to as "inexpensive warehousing." Beds were lined up side by side and head to foot; so close in many cases that one had to walk from bed to bed to move about the room. In addition, during this period the retarded were exploited to the limit of their capacities and sometimes beyond:

> They should be under such conditions that many of them shall not cost the taxpayer anything . . . the state must . . . say to them, 'We will take care of you: you shall be happy and well cared for and clean and useful; but you shall labor and earn your bread in the sweat of your face according to the divine command.' That is what should be done with the whole class of degenerates, just so far as it is possible to do it (Johnson, 1901, in Wolfensberger, 1976, p. 64).

Between 1908 and 1920 the rationales had run out. Studies of community adjustment during this period began to dispute the fact that the retarded were a menace to the community and the idea that segregation would stem the tide of the retarded was proven false. Follow-up studies of retardates released from institutions prompted Fernald to say, "We have begun to recognize that there are good morons and bad morons" (1919, in Wolfensberger, 1976, p. 68). A depressing aspect of these events is that even though scientific evidence and common sense have proven how wrong the institutional policies to 1925 had been, the momentum gained over a 30 year period (approximately 1885–1915) has left us with a situation that is almost impossible to reverse. As Wolfensberger (1976) states:

> We cannot understand the institution, as we know it, with all its objectionable features, unless we realize whence it came. I propose that essentially, many of our institutions, to this very day, operate in the spirit of 1925 when inexpensive segregation of a scarcely human retardate was seen as the only feasible alternative to combat a social menace. I am not proposing that this view is still held; I am proposing that most institutions function as if this view were still held (p. 69).

In closing this section, the reader is reminded that the above quote is still true. While the situations in institutions across the United States have improved to a great extent through the impetus of litigation and legislation, there is still a long way to go before we will be rid of dehumanizing conditions in institutions. To illustrate, one should note the "Forest Haven" (Brockett, 1978) and "Pineland" (Gettings, 1978) institutions, and their current problems. Jack Anderson, in his syndicated column, has written of today's institutions:

> These are often nothing more than human warehouses; a few can be classified as snake pits. They have pleasant names like Applecreek, Forest Haven, Rosewood, Sonoma. But they are more like concentration camps, where society quietly hides away its mental misfits until they die (1978).

It is because of the above conditions that the principle of normalization has become the answer, possibly, to these intolerable situations.

Normalization

Providing the best possible services for the severely and profoundly retarded must begin with the contemporary "principle of normalization," which dictates that society provide services and facilities that allow the individual to live in as normal a manner as possible. Based on a philosophical position that had its inception in the Scandinavian countries (Baroff, 1974; Nirje, 1969b; Wolfensberger, 1972), the concept of normalization emphasizes the right of the retarded citizen to live in a family environment or, at least, in his home community. Even in cases in which the severity of the retardation dictates institutionalization, the living conditions are expected to approximate the patterns of mainstream society.

When one stops to define normalization, it is so simple that one could say that it borders on the naive: ". . . to let the mentally subnormal obtain an existence as close to normal as possible" (N. E. Bank Millelsen, in Nirje, 1970). Situations that are normal are certainly *not* found in most large institutions for the mentally retarded. Therefore, normalization infers doing away with large, diversified mental institutions which euphemistically have been called "schools," "farms," "colonies," "hospitals," and "homes."

Normalization extends beyond architectural or structural considerations; it is actually a philosophy or principle that makes ". . . available to the mentally subnormal patterns and conditions of everyday life which are as close as possible to the norms and patterns of the mainstream of society, . . . consequently it should serve as a guide for medical, educational, psychological, social and political work in this field" (Nirje, 1970). To expand, normalization means that a mentally subnormal person should have the opportunity to experience the normal rhythm of the day, the week, the seasons, and the years. It allows for a self-identity, bisexual contacts, the problems of everyday living and normal living facilities—all these within the context of the individuals' specific handicap (Nirje, 1970). Also, as Gunzburg states: ". . . it suggests simply that subnormal people who are given 'normal' opportunities for living, for experiencing, for choosing, for shouldering responsibilities, for work- ing, will be encouraged and stimulated to function on a higher level of competence than if they are deprived of these opportunities" (1970).

The refreshing aspect of normalization is that it refocuses services to the person. Where in the past, services or patterns of dealing with the mentally subnormal have been for the entertainment of others (the court jester or fool), the convenience of society (isolated asylums), or the con- venience of staff (the medical model of treatment and architectural considerations), society is beginning to recognize the mentally subnormal as a human being. One is often reminded that positive results do not accrue from a particular method as much as from the quality of the human relationship. While normalization is very much person centered, the principle and its advocates are not so naive as to think that it will be a cure-all for those labeled subnormal. "The benefits which each person enjoys will depend on the degree of his handicap, his competence and maturity, as well as the need for training activities and availability of services" (Nirje, 1970).

Gearheart and Litton (1975, p. 12), recognizing that serious attempts at normalization will involve some degree of calculated risk, suggest that the following statements might provide a starting point for more thought and consideration with respect to the implications of this concept:

1. Almost all services for the retarded provided at the community level
2. Educational and training programs integrated to a much greater extent with programs for "normal" individuals
3. Residential facilities in small units resembling homes
4. Adult retarded in much more daily contact with normal adults
5. More total involvement with a bisexual world
6. Work stations alongside work stations for nonretarded individuals

Clearly, the degree of normalization that can ultimately be realized will depend on a number of factors. First of all, efforts to implement this principle must be based on a sound estimate of the capabilities and characteristics of each handicapped individual. Second, the current attitudes and misconceptions that typify the public's understanding of the severely retarded must be replaced by a more enlightened conception. Finally, a continuum of services and programs must be made available to accommodate all the divergent habilitative and placement needs of the severely and profoundly retarded.

This latter factor, a continuum of services for the retarded, implies an array of services that has both vertical and horizontal dimensions. As described by Baroff (1974), the horizontal level refers to the need of services from more than one community agency at any given time, e.g., "the preschool-age child might be living in a foster home, attending a child development center, receiving medical care for a retardation-related physical disability, and participating in a community-sponsored summer day camp program" (p. 122). (See Chapter 13, Table 8, p. 448.)

The vertical dimension of the continuum includes the need for services at each stage of development from infancy to adulthood. Nursery and day care centers for severely handicapped preschoolers would be a necessity. For school-age children, a substantial array of community services, staffed by practitioners representing a variety of habilitative disciplines, must be provided to satisfy their educational, medical, and recreational needs. At the adult level, opportunities for employment and meaningful social interaction will be required. The provision of these basic programs, as well as supportive services like crisis centers, respite facilities, and counseling services, will enable many parents and relatives to avoid the desperate decision to institutionalize.

Litigation

The precedent established by several recent court cases and the impetus supplied by other litigation that focused on the denial of civil rights for handicapped children is now being reflected in the mandate to develop programs for the severely and profoundly retarded. While these developments on behalf of the handicapped are generally associated with the 1970s, their roots stem from decades of neglect and inadequate services. In addition, compulsory school attendance laws, the movement from a rural to an urban society, the public disenchantment with special classes and labels for categorizing handicapped children, and the inadequacy of techniques and evaluative instruments used as a basis for special class placement have all contributed to the changes now taking place. A review of these events was presented in Chapter 1. Therefore, only those events that most directly affect the severely and profoundly handicapped are summarized in this section.

Of paramount importance was the landmark legal case in Pennsylvania, described in detail by Lippman and Goldberg (1973) and summarized in Chapter 1. Perhaps Gallagher's recent review of Lippman and Goldberg's book most aptly summarizes the major implications of what has come to be known as the Pennsylvania "Right to Education" case. Gallagher pointed out that the implication of full service to retarded children would not be without problems and that the task was not completed with the rendering of the judicial action. He stated that:

The cries of agonized school administrators that they had neither the funds, nor the personnel, nor the facilities to provide the kinds of services that the court was requiring are old stories to those who have struggled to get better programs for handicapped children (Gallagher, 1973, p. 218).

Following the judgment and a subsequent needs assessment, 11,000 children in Pennsylvania were identified as having no educational services. Nevertheless, according to Lippman and Goldberg, the court rejected arguments related to lack of funds, personnel, and facilities and referred to the philosophy as stated by a spokesman for the Council for Exceptional Children:

> If, in fact, the state does not have sufficient funds to educate all of its children, the handicapped youngster must take his share of the cut with the others . . . but do not expect the exceptional child to bear the whole burden of the state's financial difficulty, Mr. Governor and Mr. Legislator. He will suffer his share of the burden—but, by order of the federal courts, he will no longer carry the whole burden (Lippman & Goldberg, 1973, pp. 64–65).

Sontag, Burke, and York (1973) have discussed the implications of another court decision that they consider to be of even greater significance for the severely handicapped. The *Mills* v. *Board of Education of the District of Columbia* (1972) case expanded the implications of the Pennsylvania case to all handicapped children, not just those labeled mentally retarded.

Finally, Public Law 94-142 has *mandated* the nationwide provision of special education and related services to all handicapped children, *regardless of the severity of their handicap.* This provision is discussed in detail in Chapter 1.

These events, then, reflect a strong movement in American education to hold the public schools of the nation accountable for providing quality education for all children, regardless of educational problems. Consequently, for many handicapped children, the responsibility is being interpreted as education within the regular classroom (Davis, 1973). While this interpretation is undoubtedly valid for many children with educational problems, it is not generalizable to all. It is self-evident that the severity of the handicapping conditions of some children will preclude placement in regular classes. There is no doubt, however, that we must respond to the mandate to provide an appropriate free education to all children, even the severely and profoundly retarded. All children in the nation, regardless of level of functioning, will have access to an education in the least restrictive environment and, consequently, the issue now centers on how we can provide the best possible developmental services to the lowest functioning individuals in our society.

PROBLEMS AND TRENDS IN PROGRAM DEVELOPMENT

This section summarizes the problems and needs of those professionals now faced with the challenge of providing quality educational programs for handicapped children. Caught between court-ordered deadlines and financial restrictions, responsible persons still must quickly find acceptable solutions for a wide range of problems, including not only instructional matters, but also complicating factors like transportation, medical services, cooperation with nonschool agencies, and community resistance or misunderstanding. While the professional literature in this area has previously been limited, a growing body of information is now available. A number of issues and problems have been identified. Summarized as follows, these issues delineate the task that lies ahead for professionals and laymen committed to adequate and effective programs for the severely and profoundly handicapped.

Meaningful Assessment

Severely and profoundly handicapped children differ tremendously in terms of intellectual functioning and adaptive behavior. Their educational needs are likewise very different. Diagnostic labels and traditional approaches to training therefore provide little or no help in developing a strong, effective instructional program. Alternative strategies for assessment must be identified and employed if the goal of normalization is ever to be realized.

Since there is little instructional validity in using labels and IQ scores, educators must focus on skills or competencies that each child does or does not have. Starting with this direct measurement of relevant behavioral dimensions, they must subsequently determine, on a frequent basis, whether or not the child is getting the desired skills and progressing in the program. The resultant feedback to the teacher is necessary for responsive programs in which modifications can quickly be made to encourage and facilitate learning.

Sound Instructional Programs

Severely handicapped children frequently differ from those with milder handicaps in a number of important instructional dimensions. Such factors as imitation, generalization, and retention must therefore be carefully considered in the design of instructional materials, as well as in the planning of lesson sequences and in the selection of learning activities. The current dearth of commercially produced materials or programs places a premium on competencies that will allow individual teachers to complete task analyses of instructional objectives and develop homemade materials with which to accomplish them.

The following important principles underlie the development of sound educational programs:

1. Severely and profoundly handicapped children need intensive training to develop *sensorimotor skills*. A variety of methods have been used in this area. Such supportive personnel as physical and occupational therapists play a significant role in implementing sensorimotor training programs.

2. While *self-care skills* are learned by most children during early childhood, severely and profoundly handicapped individuals must be given these skills through systematic instruction and training. In some cases, the time and effort required to accomplish these self-care objectives is extensive. Attempts are being made, however, to develop procedures that can be used to teach skills to groups of severely handicapped children. In any case, every effort must be made to prepare these children with the skills necessary for a more independent existence.

3. If the severely and profoundly handicapped are now to be served by public school systems, the development of their *functional language skills* must be given great emphasis. This is true for several reasons. First, any approximation of normalization is largely dependent on the presence of language. Second, the development of this ability will facilitate the attainment of many other educational objectives. Finally, if and when verbal control can replace overt physical prompting by teachers or attendants, staff time can be more efficiently used to encourage higher levels of functioning.

4. Severely and profoundly handicapped children and adults often engage in behavior that is annoying, disturbing, and even frightening to other persons. The literature is replete with descriptions of *maladaptive behaviors* exhibited in the seclusion of institutional settings, ranging from the smearing of feces and masturbation to a variety of aggressive and/or self-destructive behaviors.

Although current evidence as to the effect of the various intervention attempts used to reduce such maladaptive behaviors is inconclusive, a number of behavior modification programs have had very good results. It is imperative that such programs be utilized.

In line with these principles, Luckey and Addison (1974) have presented a table (Table 3) that outlines suggested areas of program emphasis. In the past these skill areas have not been considered to be within the domain of the public schools.

Considering the serious learning, behavioral, and medical problems that characterize this population, it is clear that a wide range of adminis-

Table 3. Suggested areas of program emphasis for profoundly retarded persons

Preschool age	School age	Adults
Sensorimotor Stimulation a. stimulating sight, hearing, touch, smell, and muscular response b. enriching environment and encouraging exploration of interesting and attractive surroundings	**Sensorimotor Development** a. identifying shapes, colors, sizes, locations, and distances b. identifying sound patterns, locations, tonal qualities, rhythms c. identifying textures, weights, shapes, sizes, temperatures d. identifying familiar, aversive and pleasant odors	**Sensorimotor Integration** a. sorting, transferring, inserting, pulling, folding b. responding to music activities, signals, warnings c. making personal choices and selections d. discriminating sizes, weights, colors, distances, locations, odors, temperatures, etc.
Physical Development a. body positioning b. passive exercising c. rolling, creeping and crawling d. balancing head and trunk e. using hands purposefully f. standing practice g. training for mobility	**Physical Mobility and Coordination** a. practicing ambulation b. overcoming obstacles; walking on ramps and stairs, running, skipping, jumping, balancing, climbing c. using playground equipment d. participating in track and field events	**Physical Dexterity and Recreation** a. riding vehicles; participating in gymnastic-like activities and track and field events b. marking with pencil; cutting with scissors; stringing beads; pasting; and assembling c. swimming and water play d. using community parks, playgrounds, and other recreational resources

Pre-Self Care

a. taking nourishment from bottle and spoon; drinking from cup and finger feeding
b. passive dressing; accommodating body to dressing; partially removing clothing
c. passive bathing; handling soap and washcloth; participating in drying
d. passive placement on toilet; toilet regulating

Language Stimulation

a. increasing attention to sounds
b. encouraging vocalization
c. responding to verbal and non-verbal requests
d. identifying objects

Interpersonal Response

a. recognizing familiar persons
b. requesting attention from others
c. occupying self for brief periods
d. manipulating toys or other objects

Self-Care Development

a. self-feeding with spoon and cup; eating varied diet; behaving appropriately while dining
b. removing garments; dressing and undressing with supervision; buttoning, zipping, and snapping
c. drying hands and face; partially bathing
d. toilet scheduling; indicating need to eliminate; using toilet with supervision

Language Development

a. recognizing name, names of familiar objects, and body parts
b. responding to simple commands
c. imitating speech and gestures
d. using gestures, words or phases

Social Behavior

a. requesting personal attention
b. playing individually alongside other residents
c. using basic self-protective skills
d. playing cooperatively with other residents

Self-Care

a. eating varied diet in family dining situation; using eating utensils; selecting foods
b. dressing with partial assistance or supervision
c. bathing with partial assistance or supervision
d. using toilet independently with occasional supervision

Language and Speech Development

a. listening to speaker
b. using gestures, words, or phrases
c. following uncomplicated directions

Self-Direction and Work

a. using protective skills
b. sharing, taking turns, waiting for instructions
c. traveling with supervision
d. completing assigned tasks
e. participating in work activity center program

Source: "The Profoundly Retarded: A New Challenge for Public Education" by Robert E. Luckey and Max R. Addison in *Education and Training of the Mentally Retarded*, 1974, 9, 125. Reprinted by permission of the author and publisher.

trative alternatives and instructional settings must be developed to accommodate the various needs of such children.

DEVELOPMENT OF SUPPORTIVE SERVICES

Parent-Training Programs

The presence of a severely or profoundly mentally retarded child within the family constellation usually has an alarming impact upon his parents and siblings who are responsible for his care and management. Conversely, catastrophic reactions of the family members will have adverse effects on the child. Acceptance by the family contributes immeasurably to the normalization of a severely or profoundly retarded individual. Nevertheless, the tremendous emotional and financial burden that accompanies such persons often precludes this possibility. While many parents are willing to keep their severely handicapped children in the home, the lack of services and community support frequently makes this an insurmountable task. Programs must be developed to help parents better cope with their emotions, to provide the skills necessary to play a more active role in training their child, and to keep them aware of any available assistance.

Without question, parents need help in learning how to cope with the problems of their handicapped child as well as their own emotional problems which are generated by his/her presence.

More Trained Personnel

Considering the multiple learning and behavior deficiencies that characterize the severely retarded, it is evident that low student-teacher ratios are a prerequisite to success. Preservice and inservice training programs are therefore critically necessary in order to provide the personnel required. Such programs must identify the competencies needed to work with the severely retarded and prepare teachers accordingly. At the same time, every effort must be made to more effectively utilize ancillary personnel, paraprofessionals and volunteers, to assist the teachers and allow for increased flexibility and individualization in pursuing their educational objectives (see Chapter 12).

Vocational Rehabilitation Programs

Until recently, occupational opportunities for the severely and profoundly handicapped were virtually nonexistent. As a result of the legislation and litigation discussed in Chapters 1 and 14, increasing numbers of severely involved adults are requesting habilitative services and a few are now being served in organized programs (see Chapter 14).

Community Programs

Since former President Kennedy's challenge to Congress in 1963 regarding the deinstitutionalization of the retarded, numerous programs and approaches have been attempted. While many of the programs have met with failure, a few have been successful and can serve as prototypes in the development of community services for the severely and profoundly retarded (see Chapter 13).

Additional Research

The field of special education has experienced a period of rapid transition. As the focus continues to shift to the plight of the more severely handicapped youngsters, the gaps in our knowledge and expertise become painfully obvious. To develop more adequate facilities, better methods and techniques, and more appropriate instructional materials, a comprehensive research and development program must be initiated. With an emphasis on empirical validity, we can objectively identify those procedures that optimize the chances for severely retarded children to learn and develop.

Accountability

The financial commitment required to implement the various educational, occupational, and social programs needed by the severely handicapped will be extensive. To promote its continuance, those responsible for the education and care of these individuals must conduct their programs in a manner that is clearly accountable to the public. Meaningful objectives must be specified for each handicapped individual, and desired changes in his/her behavior must be demonstrated.

These trends and problems in program development reflect the dimensions of the task that now faces not only special educators but also the numerous other professionals who necessarily will be concerned with the challenge of normalization for the severely and profoundly handicapped. Although we have a very long way to go, the traditional fatalism associated with this handicapped population is now being replaced by frequent reports of success and a growing optimism. It is now clear that the severely and profoundly retarded can, with the assistance of an increasingly sophisticated educational technology, function at levels far above those commonly expected of them today.

Cooperation Among Professions and Services

The various professions and organizations concerned with the well being of the severely handicapped must join together in planning an effective communitywide program for them. Whereas the majority of these individuals will remain totally dependent throughout their lifetimes, services and programs must be made available to them in all phases of their development. To ensure the effectiveness of these efforts, open communication between professionals in education, rehabilitation, occupational therapy, physical therapy, speech pathology and audiology, recreation, and health care must prevail.

CONCLUSION

Despite the optimism and the promise of future successes, in all likelihood many severely and profoundly handicapped individuals will remain dependent on society. While this might discourage some people, we believe that for this very reason the endeavor may be one of our most important. A society's effort to help and care for those who can contribute very little in return pays dividends that far outweigh the required financial investment. Undertaking programs of the scope discussed in this chapter exemplifies our belief in the equality of opportunity for every human being. The cost required to actually live this principle seems a small price to pay if it will help us avoid the mistakes of those societies of the past in which it has been disregarded. It has only been a little more than a decade since Blatt and Kaplan (1966) dramatically documented the horrors of the institutional setting in their pictorial presentation "Christmas in Purgatory." In the introduction to this poignant collection of photographs, Blatt stated:

> Our "Christmas in Purgatory" brought us to the depths of despair. We now have a deep sorrow, one that will not abate until the American people are aware of—and do something about—the treatment of the severely mentally retarded in our state institutions (Blatt & Kaplan, 1966, p. 6).

Indeed, this exposé and other events have forced society as a whole, and special educators in particular, out of the complacency that permitted such conditions to exist.

Fortunately, Blatt's concluding prophecy has come to pass:

> It is our belief that now that our most undefensible practices have been laid bare for public scrutiny, men of good will from all walks of life and all professions will sit down at the planning table and seek solutions to the plight of our brethren (Blatt & Kaplan, 1966, p. 121).

The proof is in the content of this chapter.

REFERENCES

Anderson, J. Warehousing the retarded. *Herald Statesman*, Yonkers, N.Y., June 6, 1978.

Baker, D. B. Severely handicapped: Toward an inclusive definition. *AAESPH Review*, 1979, *4*(1), 52–65.

Baroff, G. S. Mental retardation: Nature, cause, and management. Washington, D.C.: Hemisphere Publishing Corp., 1974.

Barr, M. W. President's annual address. *Journal of Psycho-Asthenics*, 1897, *2*, 1–13.

Barr, M. W. The imperative call of our present to our future. *Journal of Psycho-Asthenics*, 1902, *7*, 5–14.

Baumeister, A. A., & Butterfield, E. C. (Eds.). *Residential facilities for the mentally retarded*. Chicago: Aldine Publishing Co., 1970.

Begab, M. J. Preface. In J. Grossman (Ed.). *Manual on terminology and classification in mental retardation*. Washington, D.C.: American Association on Mental Deficiency, 1973.

Blatt, B., & Kaplan, F. *Christmas in Purgatory: A photographic essay on mental retardation*. Boston: Allyn and Bacon, 1966.

Brockett, D. Court decreee finally dooms Forest Haven. *The Washington Star*, Washington, D.C., June 15, 1978.

Brown, L., & York, R. Developing programs for severely handicapped students: Teacher training and classroom instruction. *Focus on Exceptional Children*, 1974, *6*, 1–11.

Bullard, W. N. State care of high-grade imbecile girls. *Proceedings, National Conference on Charities and Correction*, 1910, 299–334.

Burton, T. A., & Hirshoren, A. The education of severely and profoundly retarded children: Are we sacrificing the child to the concept? *Exceptional Children*, 1979, *45*(8), 598–602.(a)

Burton, T. A., & Hirshoren, A. Some further thoughts and clarifications on the education of severely and profoundly retarded children. *Exceptional Children*, 1979, *45*(8), 618–625.(b)

Davis, M. D. Foreword. In E. Deno (Ed.), *Instructional alternatives for exceptional children*. Arlington, Va.: The Council for Exceptional Children, 1973.

Dunn, L. M. Special education for the mildly retarded: Is much of it justifiable? *Exceptional Children*, 1968, *35*, 5–24.

Dunn, L. M. *Exceptional children in the schools: Special education in transition*. New York: Holt, Rinehart & Winston, 1973.

Fernald, W. E. The burden of feeble-mindedness. *Journal of Psycho-Asthenics*, 1912, *17*, 87–111.

Fernald, W. E. What is practical in the way of prevention of mental defect? *Proceedings, National Conference on Charities and Correction*, 1915.

Fernald, W. E. State programs for the care of the mentally defective. *Journal of Psycho-Asthenics*, 1919, *24*, 114–125.

Gallagher, J. Media reviews. *Exceptional Children*, 1973, *40*, 217–219.

Gearheart, B. R., & Litton, F. W. *The trainable mentally retarded: A foundations approach*. St. Louis: The C. V. Mosby Company, 1975.

Gettings, R. M. Community standards developed in Maine. *New Directions*, 1978, *8*(7), 1.

Grossman, H. J. (Ed.). *Manual on terminology and classification in mental retardation*. Washington, D.C.: American Association on Mental Deficiency, 1973.

Gunzburg, H. G. Editorial. *Journal of Mental Subnormality*, 1970, *16*, 55–56.

Hewett, F. M., with Forness, S. R. *Education of exceptional learners* (2nd ed.). Boston: Allyn & Bacon, 1977.

Johnson, A. Discussion on care of feebleminded and epileptic. *Proceedings, National Conference on Charities and Correction*, 1901, 410–411.

Lippman, L., & Goldberg, I. *Right to education: Anatomy of Pennsylvania case and its implications for exceptional children*. New York: Columbia University Teacher's College Press, 1973.

Luckey, R., & Addison, M. The profoundly retarded: A new challenge for public education. *Education and Training of the Mentally Retarded*, 1974, *9*, 123–130.

Nirje, B. A Scandinavian visitor looks at U.S. institutions. In R. B. Kugel & W. Wolfensberger (Eds.), *Changing patterns in residential services for the mentally retarded*. Washington, D.C.: President's Committee on Mental Retardation, 1969.(a)

Nirje, B. The normalization principle and its human management implications. In R. B. Kugel & W. Wolfensberger (Eds.), *Changing patterns in residential services for the mentally retarded*. Washington, D.C.: President's Committee on Mental Retardation, 1969.(b)

Nirje, B. The normalization principle: Implications and comments. *Journal of Mental Subnormality*, 1970, *16*, 62–70.

Public Law 94-142. Education for all handicapped children act of 1975, final regulations. Washington, D.C.: U.S. Office of Education, 1977.

Robinson, N. M., & Robinson, H. B. *The mentally retarded child: A psychological approach*. New York: McGraw-Hill, 1965.

Robinson, N. M., & Robinson, H. B. *The mentally retarded child: A psychological approach* (2nd ed.). New York: McGraw-Hill, 1976.

Sontag, E., Burke, P. J., & York, R. Considerations for serving the severely handicapped in the public schools. *Education and Training of the Mentally Retarded*, 1973, *8*, 20–26.

Sontag, E., Certo, N., & Button, J. E. On a distinction between the education of the severely and profoundly handicapped and a doctrine of limitations. *Exceptional Children*, 1979, *45*(8), 604–616.

Wolf, J., & Anderson, R. *The multiply handicapped child*. Springfield, Ill.: Charles C Thomas, 1969.

Wolfensberger, W. The origin and nature of our institutional models. In R. B. Kugel & W. Wolfensberger (Eds.), *Changing patterns in residential services for the mentally retarded*. Washington, D.C.: President's Committee on Mental Retardation, 1969.

Wolfensberger, W. *The principle of normalization in human services*. Toronto: National Institute on Mental Retardation, 1972.

Wolfensberger, W. The origin and nature of our institutional models. In R. B. Kugel & A. Shearer (Eds.), *Changing patterns in residential services for the mentally retarded* (Rev. ed.). Washington, D.C.: President's Committee on Mental Retardation, 1976.

Wright, Judge J. S. *Hobsen* v. *Hansen: Court of Appeals decision on the District of Columbia's track system. Civil Action No. 82-66*. Washington, D.C.: U.S. Court of Appeals, 1967.

4
ENVIRONMENTAL ALTERNATIVES FOR THE PHYSICALLY HANDICAPPED

Bonnie B. Greer, Jo Allsop, and John G. Greer

Historically, the education of the physically disabled has received relatively little attention. Children with orthopedic and health problems were thought of first as patients, not students. They were placed in hospitals or state institutions where the primary emphasis of the services they received was on the medical treatment of their impairments. Concern for the overall development of each child, for the academic, social, and emotional fulfillment that everyone needs, was often lost in the overriding preoccupation with physical well being. This has now changed. Today, in the wake of federal legislation for the handicapped and increased public concern for this segment of our population, programs are being developed that meet the needs of the "whole child." This chapter takes a look at these new programs and the disabled children for whom they are designed.

DESCRIPTION

Children with crippling conditions and chronic health problems represent an extremely heterogeneous population. They are afflicted with a large variety of problems, including such things as cerebral palsy, spina bifida, muscular dystrophy, spinal cord injury, asthma, arthritis, cancer, cardiac conditions, diabetes, and epilepsy. Some of these handicaps are congenital problems, while others occur after birth through accidents or disease. Some can be controlled effectively and are relatively limited in their effect on the child, while others get progressively worse and can even result in death.

117

Academically, the effects on the children involved are just as varied as the physical handicaps and health problems with which they are afflicted. While some may require an extensive array of special devices and adaptive aids to learn, others may excel in school with little if any extra help. Because of the continuing demands for bed rest, medical treatment, and hospitalization, some will fall far behind their classmates. Nevertheless, others, through superior intelligence and motivation, may overcome tremendous disadvantages to reach very high standards in the classroom.

Similarly, in terms of social and personal development, the effects of such handicaps differ tremendously. While earlier studies on the adjustment of the physically handicapped have suggested certain generalizations about this group (Barker, Wright, Meyerson, & Gonick, 1953), more recent research does not support any blanket generalizations or "personality types" associated with physical handicaps (Bartel & Goshin, 1971; Newman, 1971; Telford & Sawrey, 1977). It stands to reason, however, that the physically handicapped are more likely to suffer from emotional problems of one type or another. The tremendous frustration that usually results from all of the physical, personal, and social limitations concomitant with their handicaps undoubtedly takes its toll. The degree to which each individual is able to adapt and cope with his/her disability depends heavily on the reactions of those around him/her (Bigge & O'Donnell, 1977). As one would expect, the physically handicapped have the same social and emotional needs as their peers. Acceptance and understanding from family members, friends, and the general public are critical to normal, healthy development. When this is not the case, and the reactions of others are based upon such things as fear, pity, shock, and misunderstanding, it can have a devastating effect on the disabled individual. While there is apparently no typical reaction to such societal barriers, Sirvis (1978) lists the following possible problem areas:

1. Unresolved dependence feelings which may create an excessive need for affection and attention;
2. Excessive submissiveness which actually may be covering deep seated hostility toward physical dependence on others;
3. Extreme egocentrism and inability to deal with aloneness;
4. Fantasy as compensation for feelings of inferiority and/or inadequacy;
5. Resignation to, rather than recognition of limits; and
6. Superficial conscious recognition of handicaps, with a subconscious rejection of self (p. 373).

PREVALENCE

The physically handicapped represent such a broad category, with such heterogeneous characteristics, that it is very difficult to accurately determine incidence or prevalence figures. As Telford and Sawrey (1977) point out, any estimate of the number of orthopedically handicapped children is dependent on how they are defined. Estimates based on different definitions yield very different numbers. For this reason, Fait (1972) states that it is not possible to accurately determine how many physically handicapped youngsters there are now or how many can be expected in the future in school or hospital programs.

The job of estimating the prevalence of physically handicapped children is further complicated by various recent developments which have had contradictory effects on the size of the handicapped population. Some factors, such as advances in medical treatment and prevention, have helped to eliminate or reduce some types of disabling conditions. The success of the Salk vaccine in preventing poliomyelitis is well known, and the number of post-polio youngsters served in public school programs has dropped dramatically. Medical advances have also resulted in significant decreases in numbers of children handicapped by osteomyelitis, arthritis, and tuberculosis of the bones and joints. At the same time, rapid advances in the use of prosthetic devices, combined with early treatment and correction of congenital defects, have served to remove many children from the ranks of the handicapped. Despite this progress, some health agencies have actually reported increases in physical handicaps in recent years (Wilson, 1973). There are probably several reasons for this. First, with our increasing sophistication in the medical sciences, the infant mortality rate among even the most severely handicapped has dropped tremendously. Children with multiple handicaps, who in the past would have died at birth or soon after, can now be maintained indefinitely through advanced medical treatment and care. Second, there has been a trend toward an increase in crippling accidents (Boyles & Calovini, 1960). It has been estimated by the National Safety Council (1963) that over 50,000 children are permanently disabled by accidents each year. Finally, reported increases in physical handicaps could be the result of greater efforts to identify and serve afflicted youngsters. Pressure from concerned parents and organizations like the Cerebral Palsy Association and the Easter Seal Society, as well as state and federal legislation, has helped more physically handicapped children to receive appropriate services than ever before.

Despite the apparent inability to accurately determine the prevalence of physical handicaps, the statistics reported by the U.S. Office of Education (1975) should provide the reader with at least a "ball park" estimate. They estimate that children with physical handicaps represent approximately 0.5 percent, or about 5 in 1,000, of the school age population. Based on this percentage, in 1975 there would have been 328,000 children with nonsensory physical handicaps.

PHYSICAL CHARACTERISTICS

A primary reason why children who have physical handicaps or health impairments require special services is the frequency and duration of their absences from school. This consistent disruption of the continuity in their learning creates problems for both teacher and child. It is important that the teacher understand why these absences occur and also why, although in school, on some days the child appears unable to perform even the simplest, routinely required tasks. A brief description of the physical and health conditions that affect the life of the child may somewhat further this understanding and provide some insight into the long term effects of the condition upon the child.

Neurological Impairments

The major neurological disabilities considered in this discussion are cerebral palsy, epilepsy, spina bifida, and poliomyelitis. Damage to the central nervous system, which is present in these conditions, is permanent, and the consequent paralysis or muscular dysfunction requires special educational modifications for the child in school. Often the child will lose sensation, lose voluntary control of his/her movements, or be unable to feel or move the affected parts of his/her body. Specialized equipment and teaching methods usually enable the student to effectively participate in the school program.

Cerebral Palsy   Cerebral palsy (sometimes called Little's disease) is a condition caused by brain damage and results in motor dysfunction. The most common causes are anoxia and physical trauma which damage the areas of the brain that control body movement and coordination. Although cerebral hemorrhaging, poisonings, and congenital malformations of the brain can also result in cerebral palsy, cases of genetic determinants are quite uncommon. Approximately 1.5 per 1,000 live births are cerebral palsied children (Cruickshank, 1976).

Most children with cerebral palsy have multiple handicaps. Mental retardation often accompanies this condition, with estimates ranging as high as 50 percent to 60 percent of the persons who have cerebral palsy scoring below 70 IQ. Auditory, visual, and perceptual disorders are also more common in children with cerebral palsy than in the normal population. Defective speech is probably the most commonly associated disability among cerebral palsied children, with approximately 70 percent of the population having some speech involvement (Kirk, 1972). It is easy to see why cerebral palsy is often classified as a multihandicapping condition.

In describing the characteristics of a cerebral palsied child, a diagnostic team would usually classify the condition in two ways: 1) by the limbs that are involved, and 2) by the type of neuromotor involvement. The first method of classification (by number of extremities) is used to describe all types of motor dysfunction and/or paralysis. Denhoff (1976) has estimated the approximate percentage of cerebral palsied that would fall into each of these following classes:

Hemiplegia—one side of body affected (50 percent)
Quadriplegia—all four limbs involved (15 percent to 20 percent)
Paraplegia—only legs involved (10 percent to 20 percent)
Diplegia—all limbs are affected but with greater involvement in legs (10 percent to 20 percent)
Monoplegia—one limb affected (rare)
Triplegia—three limbs affected (rare)
Double hemiplegia—all four limbs affected but one side of the body is more involved (rare)

The second classification, according to the type of neuromotor involvement, encompasses five areas: 1) spasticity, 2) athetosis, 3) ataxia, 4) rigidity, and 5) tremor. The first two (spastic and athetoid involvement) comprise approximately 75 percent to 80 percent of the cerebral palsied (Kirk & Gallagher, 1979).

Spasticity   This condition refers to involuntary contractions of the muscles which result in short, jerky movements that are uncontrolled. Approximately 40 percent to 60 percent of the cerebral palsied show characteristics of spasticity.

Athetosis   The involuntary writhing, twisting, fluctuations of movement in the athetoid child create difficulties when any purposeful movement is attempted. Athetoid children often have involvement in the fingers and wrist which makes writing extremely difficult. About 20 percent to 25 percent of the cerebral palsied children have some athetoid movements.

Ataxia   Balance and coordination are affected which makes the ataxic child unsteady and causes him/her to fall easily. Approximately 20 percent of children with cerebral palsy exhibit ataxic symptoms.

Rigidity   This type of cerebral palsy causes continuous muscle tension, thereby inhibiting movement because of the extreme stiffness in the involved limbs. This type of cerebral palsy is rare.

Tremor   The affected limb(s) or entire body moves rhythmically or vibrates uncontrollably. This type is also rare.

A child with any type of cerebral palsy may exhibit very mild involvement or may be so severely involved that extraordinary adaptations must be made to accommodate him/her in the school environment. Such things as stress, noise, and movement can have a pronounced effect even on a mildly involved child, and the teacher should be prepared for fluctuations in the child's motor ability related to these factors.

Epilepsy   Epilepsy is a convulsive disorder that can occur at any point in a person's life. Sometimes its cause can be traced to a brain lesion or tumor, but often the cause is unknown. An electroencephalogram (EEG) is used to record the brain's electrical output in an attempt to ascertain a cause for the seizures. The seizure occurs because there is a sudden abnormal discharge of electrical activity in the brain which subsequently affects the motor and sensory capabilities of the body for the duration of the seizure.

There are four major types of seizures: 1) grand mal, 2) petit mal, 3) Jacksonian, and 4) psychomotor. Grand mal and petit mal seizures, alone or in combination, are the most common. Approximately 0.5 percent of the population experience episodic convulsions.

Grand Mal   This type of major motor seizure usually develops in stages (aura, tonic, clonic, and sleep) and lasts from 2 to 6 minutes. The person often senses a particular feeling or odor that warns him of an impending seizure. This *aura* can occur immediately before the tonic stage of the seizure or may precede the convulsion by an hour or even a day. Following the aura, the person stiffens (*tonic* state) and often falls or slumps unconscious to the floor. During the convulsive *clonic* stage, the muscles of the body contract and relax involuntarily while the person may thrash around, lose bladder or bowel control, vomit, and/or breathe heavily. It is important to remove any objects nearby that might cause injury and to refrain from sticking anything in the person's mouth. As the clonic stage lessens, the person will awaken exhausted and should be allowed to rest or sleep as long as needed. In some unusual instances, the person may continue in seizure without a return to consciousness (status epilepticus). This should signal immediate medical attention.

Petit Mal   This form is a very mild seizure which often happens more frequently than a grand mal. It is characterized by a momentary loss of consciousness that may go unnoticed by the person but is viewed by another as rapid blinking, a vacant stare, dropping an object, or any other brief loss of contact in the environment. The entire seizure lasts no more than a few seconds.

Jacksonian   This is a type of focal seizure that begins with involuntary twitching in one part of the body. It often progresses throughout that side of the body or sometimes until it encompasses the entire body in a grand mal type of seizure. Adults are more apt to have this form than children.

Psychomotor   One who is experiencing a psychomotor seizure acts automatically in a trancelike motion while engaging in curious behaviors.

The individual may have facial grimaces, mumble, become violent, or move in a robotlike fashion. The duration can be several hours or even a day. After returning to normal, the person will have no recollection of the events that occurred. This type is also very uncommon in children.

Medication can greatly reduce the number and severity of seizures in an epileptic. With proper dosage and monitoring of activities, the epileptic child may function quite well in the regular classroom.

Spina Bifida   Spina bifida is a congenital defect characterized by an incomplete closure of the bony spinal column. When no neurological impairment is evident and there is no protrusion of the spinal cord, it is technically called *spina bifida occulta*. However, when there is an opening in the back along the spine and a sac containing cerebrospinal fluid without nerve tissue protrudes through the opening, the spina bifida is termed a *meningocele*. A *myelomeningocele* condition is more debilitating because by definition there is neurological involvement, often paralysis of the legs, bowel, and bladder muscles. This occurs when parts of the spinal cord are contained in the sac that protrudes through the opening in the spine and back.

Soon after birth, a large percentage of the children born with spina bifida develop hydrocephalus (an increase of the cerebrospinal fluid causing extreme pressure and consequently an enlargement of the head). This condition is also associated with increased incidence of mental retardation. Although spina bifida itself does not cause a deviation in normal intellectual functioning, if it is accompanied by hydrocephalus, meningitis, or some other congenital abnormality there is a significantly increased chance of lowered intellectual ability.

Poliomyelitis   This contagious disease, which has been largely controlled by vaccines since the original 1956 contribution by Salk, has unfortunately shown some resurgence within the past few years. Complacency has permitted many parents to ignore the need for early vaccination of their infants. The polio virus attacks the tissue in the spinal cord, often leaving the victim paralyzed for life. Although intelligence is not affected, mobility is curtailed with a resulting need for orthopedic appliances, surgery, and long term medical care.

Orthopedic Conditions

A child who is disabled because of defects in his/her bones and/or muscles is primarily thought of as orthopedically handicapped, even though other serious health impairments may become apparent in conjunction with his/her orthopedic involvement. Included in this group would be children who have muscular dystrophy, rheumatoid arthritis, and Legg-Calve-Perthes disease.

Muscular Dystrophy   The most common forms of muscular dystrophy are pseudohypertrophy (Duchenne) and facioscapulohumeral. Both are inherited and result in a progressive, wasting deterioration of the person's voluntary muscles resulting in loss of physical mobility and often total disability or early death.

Pseudohypertrophy   This type of muscular dystrophy, which afflicts males, has an early onset. Most victims display enlarged muscles in the legs, arms, and pelvic and shoulder regions about the time they begin to walk, and by early adolescence they have lost enough mobility to require a wheelchair. Death often occurs while the affected person is still a young adult.

Facioscapulohumeral   This form is not usually apparent until adolescence and affects both males and females. Progression of this form is slower, with involvement primarily confined to the upper extremities and facial muscles. Most live to middle age with the disability, while a few live normal lives and incur few symptoms.

Rheumatoid Arthritis   Rheumatoid arthritis has no known cause or cure and occurs in females more than in males. It is characterized by severe pain, brought on by inflammation and swelling in the joints and connective tissues. In many cases there is permanent damage to the affected areas with resulting physical deformities, even though 75 percent go into remission within 5 to 10 years of onset.

Legg-Calve-Perthes   This disease, although debilitating for a period of time, eventually disappears. Because of an interruption in the blood supply, the head of the femur bone dies and breaks down. Eventually this dead material is absorbed, and renewed circulation enables the bone to regenerate and again function normally. More boys than girls are affected, with 5 or 6 being the typical age at which it occurs. Treatment usually involves supporting the leg and preventing stress on the bone.

Other Health Impairments

There are numerous medical conditions that warrant attention by the teacher so that special consideration can be given to safeguarding the health of the child. Not only is there the problem of a high absentee rate at school with these conditions, but the very well-being of the child is often threatened if the condition is not carefully monitored. Some of the more common health disorders that occur in children are hemophilia, diabetes, sickle cell anemia, cystic fibrosis, and asthma. Nephrosis, rheumatic fever, and leukemia are also severe medical problems that sometimes affect children.

Hemophilia   With this inherited disorder there is a deficiency of the clotting factor which prevents the blood from coagulating properly.

Either as a result of trauma or spontaneous hemorrhaging, the person bleeds uncontrollably, and transfusions are often required when bleeding is severe. Predominantly seen in males, it is inherited from the mother by a recessive gene. The child's activities must be limited in order to minimize the possibility of injury. Spontaneous hemorrhaging into the joints causes extreme pain and sometimes a permanent crippling condition. These factors contribute to poor school attendance.

Diabetes   When the pancreas does not produce sufficient amounts of insulin, which is needed for the body to metabolize sugar, the condition is termed diabetes. With proper management of diet, insulin therapy, and appropriate amounts of activity and rest, the child can attend regular classes. Inattention to treatment or complications can result in a diabetic coma which requires immediate medical intervention. Most affected children have a family history of diabetes and a prognosis for vision loss, kidney disorder, and shortened life span (estimates range as high as 20 to 25 years shorter).

Sickle Cell Anemia   This severe blood disease is an inherited disorder that causes complications throughout the body. The normal round red blood cells are replaced by angular (sickle shaped) red blood cells which are consequently destroyed by the body since they are "abnormal." This leaves the child with only one-half to one-third as many cells to carry oxygen throughout the body. In addition, those sickle cells that are left to carry the oxygen tend to clump together in the bloodstream, cutting off blood supply and causing great pain, shock, and even death. Complications from the disease include intestinal, liver, and gallbladder involvement, blood clots, swelling of the joints, jaundice, and often result in death before the age of 20. Sickle cell anemia is found predominantly in the black race.

Cystic Fibrosis   This disorder of the exocrine glands is also an inherited condition. The exocrine glands secrete a thick mucus which clogs organs, affecting their ability to function. The most serious aspects of the disease are reflected in chronic pulmonary infections, difficulty in breathing, pneumonia, and digestive problems. The majority of affected children die from respiratory complications before reaching young adulthood.

Asthma   Although the causes of asthma are difficult to pinpoint, some combination of emotional factors and allergic reactions to foods or environmental irritants affect the child's breathing. These episodic attacks are characterized by difficulty in breathing, wheezing, and/or gasping for air due to a narrowing of the airways. Drug therapy is effective in controlling these attacks which can cause permanent neurological damage or even death as the result of a lack of oxygen.

Nephrosis This condition, also known as Bright's disease, refers to chronic kidney failure which may be a result of infection, injury, congenital malformations, or other factors. It is often accompanied by edema (swelling due to water retention) in the body. The usual age of onset ranges from 18 months to 4 years, with periods of remission occurring from time to time during the child's life.

Rheumatic Fever After a child has had a strep throat or scarlet fever, he/she is particularly susceptible to rheumatic fever. This condition involves inflammation of the joints with painful swelling and sometimes inflammation of the brain and/or heart, which can result in permanent heart damage. Extended bed rest with close medical supervision is imperative when rheumatic fever occurs.

Leukemia The most common form of childhood cancer, this group of diseases often results in death. There are various types of leukemia, all characterized by an increase of white blood cells in the body. Chemotherapy has proved to be exceptionally effective in controlling the disease, and this sometimes allows the child to live out his life with the leukemia in remission.

Obviously, with physical and health disorders as serious as those previously discussed, most children have a difficult time going through the traditional routine in a regular classroom, even if they are able to attend school on a fairly regular basis. Because of pain, medications, mobility limitations, or psychological reactions, their ability to function at grade level is often impaired, sometimes severely. Thus, a diagnosis of normal or nearly normal intelligence does not automatically mean that the child can successfully complete the traditional curriculum without the need for some special education services.

WHAT IS THE BEST ENVIRONMENT?

When considering the best possible environment for educating physically handicapped and health impaired children, it is important to assess several variables that will affect the success of the placement. These variables generally fall into two broad areas: the child's resources, and the school's resources. Although deficiencies that interfere with the child's learning potential can often be compensated for with adaptive equipment and/or methods of teaching, each of the variables must be considered to establish the extent to which the environment must be altered so that learning can occur.

The *child's resources* represent a more significant contribution to a viable educational setting than do the school facilities per se. Although a great deal can be changed within the school setting to accommodate wide ranging disabilities, there are certain fixed characteristics that the physically disabled child has that sometimes virtually dictate the adaptations and adjustments that must be made. Communication skills, physical mobility and stamina, attitude toward learning, and drive for independence are primary considerations in evaluating the child for placement. Although a child may have adequate intelligence to complete the regular school program, a severe deficiency in one of these critical areas could preclude a successful placement in the regular class.

Severe physical limitations that prevent any consistent voluntary movement, even with the head or foot, will minimize the chances for successful regular class placement; communication will necessitate extraordinary measures which many regular classroom teachers are not trained to handle. Communication is the basis of learning, and when a physiological problem results in a substantial loss of communication skills, the whole learning environment is affected. Sophisticated, often costly, adapted systems can be designed for the learner such as the Autocom (a computerized communication board) or a light beam that activates a computer to spell out a message, but these devices are usually time consuming and therefore best used in a special education class.

The nature of the physical impairment itself often demands special arrangements in the classroom to accommodate for the health needs of the child. For example, children with spina bifida will need someone to assist them in the bathroom; those with advanced muscular dystrophy will lack stamina and be unable to perform routine tasks, such as picking up a book, because of the strength required. A hemophiliac child must guard against bumps or strenuous activities that may result in hemorrhaging. In some cases it is possible for the school to provide for these needs in the regular setting. However, careful evaluation of the child may suggest a special education environment to allow for closer supervision of the health problems and a smaller pupil/teacher ratio. Again, the decision must be based upon an assessment of the child's total capabilities and the school's resources.

Probably of paramount importance to anyone's success is personal attitude and drive toward achievement of a goal. This is no less true of handicapped individuals. The family, the self-concept, the determination, and the critical experiences (surgeries, life-threatening illness) of a child directly influence his/her performance in school. Thus, a child may have seemingly insurmountable disabilities and function beautifully in the regular classroom because he/she has been able to adjust and compensate with the help of adaptive equipment. One who "obviously" belongs in a self-contained class may not need to be there at all! Conversely, a child with a terminal disease such as cancer or muscular dystrophy may ordinarily be assigned to a regular classroom, but, because of the diverse psychological ramifications involved when living with a terminal disease, the child may be totally unprepared to cope with the normal requirements of school. A child's resources *must* be assessed with an *overall* view of his functioning potential.

School resources include personnel, architectural design, materials, methods, and equipment that alter the environment so that physically impaired children can learn more easily. These adaptations can compensate for a wide range of disabilities and approximate a more normal learning environment in the school.

Personnel who are specifically trained to teach physically impaired children have not been easy to find. Most teachers of physically handicapped children have received on-the-job training but little formal education with this population. However, this is changing as more preservice and inservice training programs are offering courses to prepare teachers for this field. In addition to the special education teachers, physical therapists, occupational therapists, and speech/language clinicians are an integral part of the education program within the public school. Each works with the child's teacher to help implement the individualized educational program as well as suggest adaptive equipment and materials, positioning techniques, and communication strategies. A team approach must be utilized if an effective educational plan is to be carried out.

With the passage of Public Law 93-112, section 504, public facilities receiving federal funds (including schools) are mandated to remove architectural barriers and educate handicapped children in the "least restrictive environment." Common access areas such as bathrooms, doorways, and stairs must be usable by persons in braces, wheelchairs, or on crutches. This sometimes necessitates ramps, wider doorways, and attention to whether the door should swing in or out of the room. Library materials in the school should be stored on shelving that is waist-high or lower so that persons in wheelchairs can retrieve needed books or equipment. Such often used items as water fountains, sinks, paper towel dispensers, telephones, elevator buttons, and light switches must be placed so that they are usable by a person in a wheelchair. A short checklist, such as the one that follows, might be used to ascertain just how accessible a given school building is.

Sidewalks
    Are there curb cuts which provide access?
    Is there a width of at least 48"?
    Are they level, without irregular surfaces?
    Is there a level area of 5' × 5' if the door swings in?

Ramps
> Are handrails present (32" high)?
> Is the grade of the ramp more than a 1" rise in every 12' length?
> Does it have a non-slip surface in all types of weather?

Doors
(including elevator)
> Is there an opening of at least 32" when door is open?
> Are floors level for 5' in both directions of the door?
> Are the thresholds navigable (½")?

Floors
> Do hallways, stairs, and class areas have carpeting or some other non-slip surface?

Toilets
> Is one stall 3' wide by 4'8" deep with handrails 33" high?
> Is the toilet seat 20" high and urinals 19" from floor?
> Are sinks, towel dispensers, mirrors, etc., 36"–40" from floor?

Water fountains
> Are the controls hand operated?
> Is the spout in the front of the unit?
> Are they mounted 26"–30" from the floor?

Making the school environment accessible to the handicapped child not only fosters independence, but the very safety of the child while in the building often depends upon this barrier-free design. If doorways are too narrow or thresholds too high, the child in a wheelchair is trapped in the event of fire.

Looking at the physical design of the school is only a part of the process involved in assessing the school's resources. The classroom setting, materials, equipment, and the many accommodations and adaptations that can be facilitated by the teacher are all extremely important contributions to the child's learning environment.

The Classroom[1]

When a physically handicapped student is placed in "the least restrictive environment" or in a regular class setting, careful consideration must be given to the selection of an appropriate environment. In organizing a schoolroom to accommodate the physically handicapped student, priority must be given to the inclusion of that student in the group. Social and emotional development cannot take place in isolation.

---

[1] Parts of this discussion have been adapted from the recent book on instructional materials edited by R. M. Anderson, J. G. Greer, and S. J. Odle, *Individualizing Educational Materials for Special Children in the Mainstream*, Baltimore: University Park Press, 1978.

One asset the nonhandicapped child has in a classroom is the freedom of movement that allows the student to see all of the room, to see it from different perspectives, and to change perspectives at will. This encourages and facilitates much incidental learning and makes a student feel part of the environment. Movement is just as important, perhaps more important, for the handicapped student. In addition to changing the immediate environment, the handicapped child must avoid long periods of immobility to maintain and improve the motor function that he/she has and to prevent loss of function (Peterson & Cleveland, 1975). Furniture must be arranged with wide aisles to facilitate free and easy movement. Activities should be planned to provide a vantage point to all areas of the room at some time during the day. Furniture around which a handicapped student must maneuver should have legs that are perpendicular to the floor to prevent falls caused by stumbling over furniture legs that extend out further than the top of the furniture. Straight legs rarely interfere with the mobility of a student in a wheelchair or a student using a walker.

Furniture for the handicapped student should be sturdy, durable, and have a wide base. Often the student does not "sit down" in a chair—he "falls" onto it. Care should be taken to ensure that all furniture (bookcases, room dividers, etc.) is heavy enough that it cannot be turned over by a child falling against it.

Desks, chairs, and tables must be the proper height. Wooden ones are easily adapted by cutting off long legs to shorten them or by putting on new legs to make them higher. When purchasing new tables and desks, it is advantageous to get those with adjustable legs. Wooden tables may need the frame cut out to allow a wheelchair to roll under them. New tables or desks should have nothing under them that would interfere with wheelchairs.

A quiet corner should be provided where any student can go for special interests or for study. The cerebral palsied student who has uncontrolled movements works best from a quiet, relaxed position. A great deal of extraneous noise and confusion often results in increased random motor activity which prevents optimal learning. Large beanbags or rest mats on which students can recline are useful for specific periods of relaxation.

Provision must be made for the storage of pencils, paper, books, and similar school supplies. For children in wheelchairs, a bag can be made or purchased that can be placed over the back or arm of the chair, or a storage shelf can be provided close at hand at a height that allows the student easy access to it. For students with muscular weakness of the upper torso and arms, books should always be kept on the desk so that no lifting is necessary. Desks with pencil grooves are helpful; some desks and tables are available with material storage compartments on the side.

Crutches tend to get in the way when they are not in use. Provision should be made for crutches, and children should be trained to keep them in their proper place. Crutch holders can be fastened to either the back or side of a child's chair (see Figure 1). This makes the crutches easily accessible to the student and out of the way of others.

The physically handicapped student has less available energy than does a nonhandicapped person. In addition to a lower energy reserve, the student often must use muscles with abnormal tone to perform necessary tasks. For this reason, all adaptive methods and/or assistive devices are important from the standpoint of increased independence, educational progress, and resulting self-worth (Hardy & Cull, 1974). For example, if a child must utilize an inordinate amount of energy to maintain an upright position, he/she has little energy left to learn. Therefore, a stable, secure seating posture is mandatory.

Many items that are readily available can be used to achieve an optimal seating position. Desks and chairs with arm rests can be used with the student who has little lateral stability or who is seizure prone. If

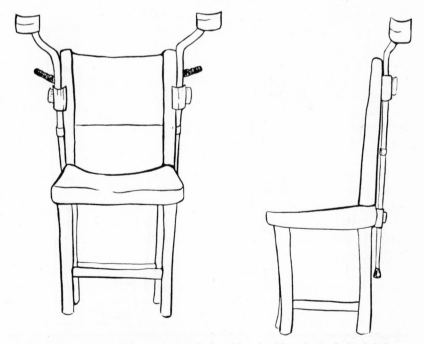

Figure 1.   Crutch holders can be attached to either the side or back of school chairs.

more stability is needed, lateral trunk supports can be built onto the back of a wooden chair that would support the trunk, particularly around the ribs (see Figure 2). Footrests, built so that the hips, knees, and ankles are placed at 90° angles or less, will often help the student who has some spasticity in the hips and legs, which tends to make the student slide forward in his/her seat. Security and comfort will be enhanced if a wedge seat is used in conjunction with the footrest. It may also be necessary to place firm foam rubber behind the student's lower back to position the learner further forward in the chair. Velcro belts at 45° angles to the hip will help hold the child securely in the chair (see Figure 3). Velcro material is particularly good for strapping purposes because it holds tightly and can be easily and quickly fastened and unfastened. Some other commercially available seating accessories are safety straps, lateral trunk supports, wedge cushions, and knee separators.

Once a practical arrangement has been worked out that accommodates the needs of the handicapped student as well as those of the teacher and other students, it should be maintained. A stable environment provides a feeling of security and enhances the probability of suc-

Figure 2. Trunk supports can be attached to school chairs to provide stability for the student, thus lessening the amount of energy required to sit upright.

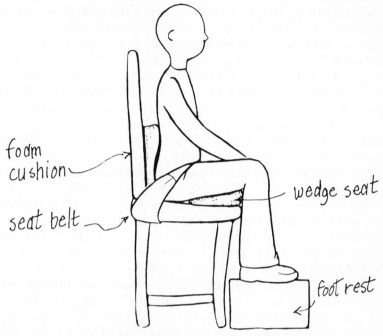

foam cushion

seat belt

wedge seat

foot rest

Figure 3.   Footrests, foam rubber, seat belts, and wedge seats provide security and comfort for disabled students. Once these are established, learning can become the primary focus.

cess (Hardy & Cull, 1974). With the student comfortably positioned in an accessible environment, learning can become the primary focus of attention.

Materials and Media   The handicapped child often appears in the classroom before the teacher has time or money available to order special assistive devices and instructional materials. Teachers should not be discouraged. Most materials can be adapted for use, and others can be made or altered using materials that are readily available.

Materials to Adapt and Construct   Paper-and-pencil tasks will be easier for students with involuntary motor movements if the paper is taped to the writing surface. The use of large paper will help because their writing will be larger and thus less difficult to read. For those students who need supplemental assistance in fine motor control, color-cued control paper that has four red and green control lines (Developmental Learning Materials (DLM) or Ideal) or "right line paper" that has raised lines to help the student stay on the lines when writing (Modern Education Corp. (MEC)) may be substituted for the large primary paper. The teacher should also realize that large pencils and pens are easier for some handicapped students to grasp. The grip can be built up by using Styrofoam hair curlers, small rubber balls, dental acrylic, or foam. In addition to these homemade adaptations, cylindrical foam padding (Sammons) and vinyl triangular pencil grips (DLM, Ideal) can be purchased. Cardboard stencils can be made that will help a child draw horizontal, vertical, and diagonal lines. These lines, when combined with circles and arcs, form the basic strokes necessary for printing and cursive writing (see Figure 4). Several companies offer grooved letters and numerals for tracing (DLM, Ideal). These assistive devices, when combined with plywood templates and double-handed training scissors (DLM), will provide maximum opportunities for the physically handicapped student to develop fine motor control.

Lap trays to fit on wheelchairs can be made from heavy plywood, and greatly aid wheelchair-bound students. The trays not only provide the best possible work surface for the students, but also contribute to their feeling of security. They can easily be cut so that they do not interfere with propelling the chair (see Figure 5).

Many children in wheelchairs who have braces need an opportunity to stand every day. This necessitates some physical support. A standing table can be constructed that will provide work surface, enabling children to continue working while they stand (see Figure 6). In fact, many students will work better on paper-and-pencil tasks because of the added leverage they get when standing. The standing table can also be adapted for chalkboard use by turning it with the gate next to the board. Students

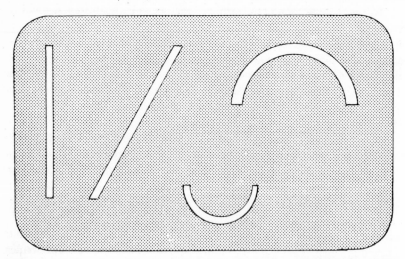

Figure 4.   Cardboard stencils are useful aids in drawing lines—a prerequisite for printing.

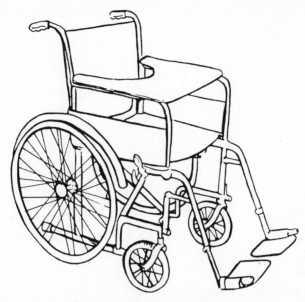

Figure 5. Wheelchairs can be converted into desks by attaching lap trays. They provide the student with security and work space.

with crutches who are braced but need added stability find this useful when working at a chalkboard. If funds are available, these standing tables may be purchased (Childcraft).

The student with a great deal of rigidity of the hips may find doing paper-and-pencil tasks on a horizontal surface an impossible assignment. A slant board can be constructed or purchased (DLM) to provide a correctly angled surface for the student and to hold pencils and keep paper in place (see Figure 7). This same slant board could also become a stand on which more handicapped students' typewriters are placed to provide enough angle so that they can see over the keys to read what they have typed.

Typewriters and Special Aids   Those students who have very little manual control for writing should be taught to use an electric typewriter. Some of these students will need a hand pointer with which to strike the keys. Wooden dowels with a rubber tip added to the end can be used for this purpose. Figure 8 shows some diagrams depicting various grasps that can be tried until the best one is found. If the grasp is not dependable, Velcro can be used to strap the device onto the hand. Students who have no useful hand control can be taught to type on an electric typewriter using a head pointer. This is a stationary piece, much like a hand pointer,

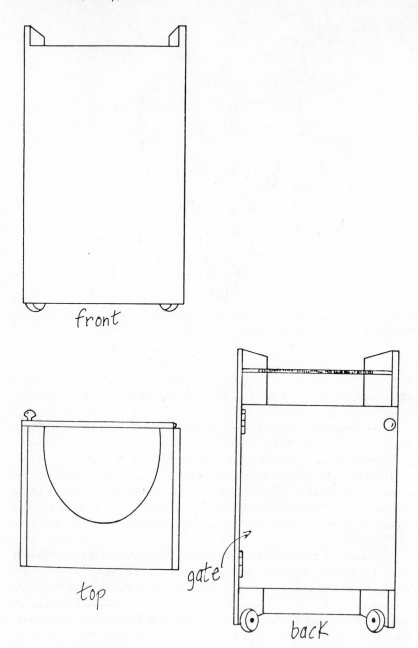

Figure 6.   Standing tables provide work space and enable many students to more successfully complete writing tasks because of the added leverage.

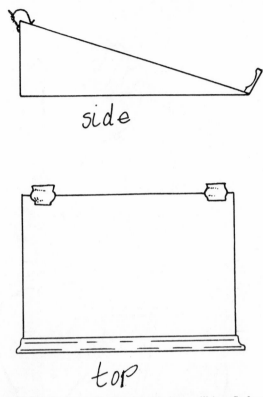

side

top

Figure 7.   If standing tables prove inadequate, students will benefit from the angled surface of a slant board. It can be used for writing or as a typewriter stand.

that is affixed to a cap that is strapped onto the child's head. The head pointer can also be used to point to and move light objects such as answer cards. The Enabler (Adaptive Therapeutic Systems) is an excellent example of a well constructed head pointer.

Special aids can be purchased to help the students who are using typewriters. Typewriter shields can be purchased that help the child with uncontrolled movements to hit the desired key. If shields are not commercially available for a particular kind of typewriter, they can be made in a metal shop from metal or plastic. Adjustable slant boards and tables can also be made or purchased. They enable the child to reach the keys with a minimum amount of strain.

Alternative Writing Methods   If an electric typewriter is not available, students may be taught to write holding a pencil in their mouth, or by holding it in their hand while bracing it with their cheek for stability.

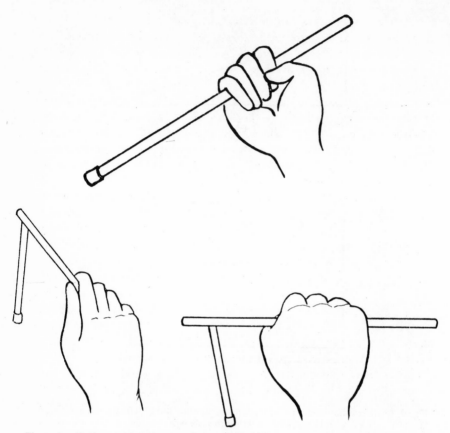

Figure 8.   Students with little manual control should be taught to type. Hand pointers can be used with various grasps to improve typing accuracy.

Some have even learned to write with their feet. The important thing to remember is that where there's a will, there's a way. Consultation with an occupational therapist is recommended if assistance is needed for these adaptations.

Adapting Books   The handling of books can also be a very difficult task for the physically handicapped. Books are often cumbersome and heavy, and handling them can consume much energy. The slant board described above can be used to hold books, but this may eliminate a writing surface for those who need it. A book holder can be constructed that can be used in conjunction with the slant board or the typewriter (see Figure 9). Many kinds of book holders are commercially available. Some companies also offer page turners for the severely involved student (Sammons, DLM).

If necessary, books can be taken apart and used a story or chapter at a time to make them less cumbersome. It is well to remember that books and materials are expendable—children are not. If the choice is between the welfare of a book and the welfare of a child, the child must come first.

Talking books can be an aid to the physically handicapped student in that they are an easy way for the student to assimilate knowledge when traditional methods prove slow and physically taxing. Teachers may write to the Library of Congress, Division for Blind and Physically Handicapped, 1291 Taylor, N.W., Washington, D.C., 20542, to inquire about how to procure these aids.

Certain adaptations can be made to make workbooks easier for the handicapped student to handle. It is always easier for the student to handle one page than it is to handle a book. Workbooks that the student has purchased may be taken apart and presented one page at a time. This will be necessary for students using typewriters. Sometimes it helps to provide a separate sheet for answering, or to recopy the workbook page to make it usable in the typewriter. If the school provides the workbooks, it may be advantageous to laminate or cover each page with clear Contact paper, so that the answers can be written with grease pencil and erased after they are evaluated and corrected. The workbook would then become a permanent and reusable instructional kit.

Teacher-Made Worksheets Teacher-made worksheets should have a limited number of activities on each sheet, should be easily readable with large, dark print, and should have ample space for the answer. Because many handicapped children have limited interaction with the environment, teacher-made games and other manipulative learning devices are of great benefit to them. Paper-and-pencil tasks often consume tremendous amounts of energy; these alternative learning

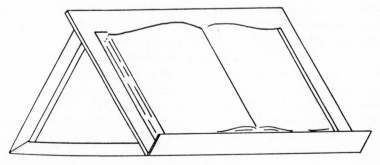

Figure 9.   Book holders, when used in conjunction with slant boards, preserve work space and save children the energy of maneuvering books.

experiences can be used as energy savers as well as good motivators. The materials should be of an appropriate size to be easily manipulated (students with poor manual control will require larger materials), and should be either laminated or covered with clear Contact paper for durability. Many cerebral palsied children drool. This and their uncontrolled movements may ruin materials that are not sturdy and durable. Commercially made instructional kits and games will also last longer if they are laminated or covered with clear Contact paper.

Children with erratic head movements often have difficulty keeping their place on a page, which ultimately affects their comprehension. For some students, it is helpful to cover a part of the page to reduce the amount of stimuli and help the student keep his/her place. Tagboard or construction paper strips clipped to a page can serve as a place keeper to assist these children, or tachistoscopes can be constructed so that the information is presented in small segments. These simple adaptations can often make the difference between independent learning with books, workbooks, and worksheets, versus time-consuming, one-to-one tutoring with these materials.

Adapting Media Materials   Certain media center materials are also easily adapted to allow independent learning by handicapped children. Even children who must use head pointers can use tape recorders with easily depressed buttons. Individual filmstrip previewers can be useful if the film is advanced by a push button. Storybooks on tape, Language Masters, and calculators may also be useful tools in the instruction of the physically handicapped child, and are timesaving devices for the teacher.

Materials for the Non-oral Child   One of the most challenging problems that may be presented to a teacher is that of the cerebral palsied child who is functionally non-oral. The functionally non-oral child may be completely non-oral, may have some potential for vocalization, or may be partially verbal. In any case, he must have a way of communicating in the classroom. Teachers need not be concerned that a supplemental communication system will completely replace any partial approach a student might have or that it might eliminate any potential for future vocalization. Studies indicate that a communication device tends to increase spontaneous vocalizations in the partially verbal, with children using their own system when possible, and using the other when theirs break down (Vanderheiden & Grilley, 1975). Because these children are difficult to work with, teachers are encouraged to seek assistance from a speech-language therapist in the school system or from another agency.

Handwriting is one alternative to oral communication. Although writing is both quick and comprehensive, a prerequisite to the printed word as an alternative means of communication is the student's ability to spell and to express himself/herself in written language. This would greatly limit the use of this means of communication for a child younger than 8 or 10 years of age (Vicker, 1974). Unfortunately, even many older handicapped children have great difficulty writing because of poor fine motor control, and therefore would find communication through this medium slow and laborious. This problem can be partially overcome by the use of a typewriter. As discussed earlier, children who have poor fine motor control can use aids such as hand-held typing sticks, mouth sticks, and head pointers. Using a typewriter would still be a slow means of communication, however, and it would be a nonportable means, restricted to the close proximity of a typewriter.

Another mode of communication for a non-oral student is finger-spelling. Its effectiveness as a communication tool depends on the person's manual dexterity and control, speed, and ability to spell. However, actual communication would be limited to those individuals who know how to read fingerspelling.

Probably the most efficient means of communication for non-oral children is the communication board. This is a piece of plastic, wood, or fiberboard that contains pictures, words, numerals, etc., that the non-oral child recognizes. When some communication is needed, the child indicates the appropriate response on the board. Communication boards can be made to fit on a student's wheelchair tray or they can be made for table use with students using crutches. The first step in the development of a communication board is to select the best means for a student to indicate the words, pictures, and so forth, that convey the thought he/she wants to communicate. The technique selected must be the one the student can use most efficiently while expending the least energy (Vanderheiden & Grilley, 1975).

The most commonly used indicating technique is the direct selection approach. This approach is used with children who have the ability to point to the item they want or to the exact word or letter on a communication board. When this is not feasible, another method must be selected.

One basic means of indication is called scanning. Scanning, in its simplest form, requires the presentation of words, pictures, or verbal questions to a child one at a time; the child then indicates *yes* when the desired message is reached. Indication of *yes* could be a smile, a nod, a look up, or some other prearranged signal. A higher level scanning device presents letters one at a time; the student indicates the letters that spell his/her message. One advantage of this approach is that it can be used with severely physically handicapped students who have useful hand control, as well as with the multiply handicapped whose cognitive capabilities limit them to responding only to spoken words or to pictures of basic objects (Vanderheiden & Grilley, 1975).

A fundamental scanning board can be made using plywood or heavy fiberboard. It should contain the alphabet as well as numerals (see Figure 10). The teacher points to each letter in turn and the student indicates when the correct letter has been reached. The teacher then starts over until the second letter is indicated. The procedure is continued until the entire message had been spelled out. The major disadvantage of this approach is that it is time consuming and therefore not practical for some classroom situations (Vanderheiden & Grilley, 1975).

The encoding approach may be more practical in the classroom where speed is a consideration. The encoding device pictured in Figure 11 can be easily constructed and, although only slightly quicker than the scanning technique, is practical for the child with very little hand control. By pointing to two numbers, the student can indicate a letter any place on the matrix. For example, if the student points first to 4 and then to 3, he/she indicates that the letter is in the fourth row and that it is in the third box.

After a means of indication has been selected, the next step in the development of a communication board is the preparation of the vocabulary itself. A picture chart may be designed for the child who is just beginning to read, but a chart containing letters, numerals, pictures, words,

Aa	Bb	Cc	Dd	Ee	Ff
Gg	Hh	Ii	Jj	Kk	Ll
Mm	Nn	Oo	Pp	Qq	Rr
Ss	Tt	Uu	Vv	Ww	Xx
Yy	Zz	1	2	3	4
5	6	7	8	9	0

Figure 10.   A fundamental scanning board. This permits severely handicapped children to communicate by spelling out messages.

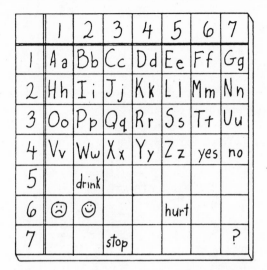

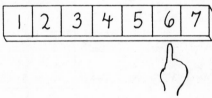

Figure 11. An encoding device with matrix. This means of communication is more practical than the scanning board because it is slightly faster.

and phrases would be more appropriate for the child who reads and spells. The teacher may find it advantageous to develop several charts. One may be appropriate for communication between the children, another may be more appropriate for communication during special interest sessions (i.e., social studies, math), and still another may be more appropriate for communication at home. In all situations, the chart should be arranged in systematic order so that it can be used efficiently by all. It has been suggested that proper names and pronouns be placed on the left and that these be followed by verbs, modifiers and/or quantifiers, object-nouns, prepositions, and words indicating time. Commonly used phrases such as "I don't know," "please," and "thank you" should be included, as well as words needed to communicate a student's special interests, numerals, and the alphabet (Vicker, 1974) (see Figure 12).

Teachers who feel a need for more detail in the development of communication board displays should refer to Vicker (1974). It contains a wealth of material, including sample displays.

	1 2 3 4 5 6 7 8 9 0		Who Why	Yester-day today
	Q W E R T Y U I O P		Where When	Tomor-row

Keyboard / symbols

1 2 3 4 5 6 7 8 9 0
Q W E R T Y U I O P
A S D F G H J K L
Z X C V B N M . , ?

start over

Question / day words

Who Why
Where When What How
Yesterday today Tomorrow
Monday Tuesday Wednesday Thursday Friday Saturday Sunday

Object words

stand-up box, class room, radio, wheel chair, glasses, Shetland, brace(s), T.V., head, food, Sheepdog, stick, Speech Station, channel, type-write, water, Music, wrestling, tasket, inside, ball, outside, pop, dining, baseball, football, comic book, pencil, juice, room, Twins, Uniden-tified, paper, milk, sun, Batman, Flying Object, Hospital, Robin, book, shirt, home, letter, camp, jacket, pants, school, bed-room, bath-room, sweater, sun room

Pronouns / names (left column)

nurse aide orderly
Mom Dad Craig
Grandma Mrs. Brown classmates
Mrs. Monson Blaze
I me
Mr. Baxter you we
your he she
my it
Yes No I don't know

Words

am eat be will / was are been would
have drink do call / had drank did
want sleep is help / slept was
need sit are tell / sat were told
go stand type listen sing can / went stood sang could
come talk fix move play -ed / came
look read break get ride -ing / broke got rode
see write lose give dress / saw wrote lost gave
watch wash find work buy / found bought

red yellow hot cold to from in out
blue green hungry thirsty up down on off
orange pink sick tired before after with of
purple brown happy sad over under for becaus
black white OK hurt fat near

not

Function words (boxed)

a and the
an
Please Thank you Excuse me

Figure 12. Sample communication display materials, 1964-1967. Reprinted with permission from *Nonoral Communication System Project, 1964-1973*, edited by Beverly Vicker. Copyright © 1974 by the University of Iowa.

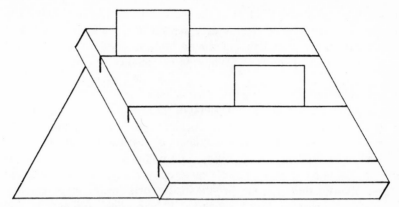

Figure 13.   Cardholders help the nonoral student respond to questions. They are easily made from wood or tagboard.

Communication is the foundation of learning. It is therefore imperative that some type of reliable communications system be established with the physically handicapped child. The non-oral student is undoubtedly the greatest challenge. Typing is often extremely tiring to these children, and the use of communication boards is sometimes impractical because of the length of instructional time involved. This problem can be circumvented by giving the student a choice of responses from which the learner selects the correct one. These responses can be presented verbally with a simple *yes/no* answer, or on cards with the student pointing to the correct response. Picture cards can be used for the nonreader, while cards with written responses can be employed for the student who reads. Card holders can be purchased or simply made. Effective holders similar to those pictured in Figure 13 can be easily constructed from wood or tagboard.

Assuming that the regular classroom teacher has support from the resource and itinerant special education personnel, the previously described adaptations in materials should assist in providing for even the severely physically handicapped child in the class. By making minimal changes in the physical environment and a few of the modifications to compensate for uncontrolled or inflexible movements and impaired communication, the teacher can smoothly continue the normal teaching/learning process.

SUMMARY

Today, in the wake of federal legislation for the physically handicapped and increased public concern, programs are being developed that meet the needs of the "whole" child in the least restrictive environment. The diverse characteristics of the children represent a challenge to teachers both from a programming standpoint and because of the physical demands of their handicaps. While some handicapped children may require an extensive array of special devices and adaptive aids, others may excel in school with little if any extra help.

Approximately 5 children in 1,000 of the school-age population have a physical handicap. Some of these handicaps are congenital, while others occur after birth through accidents or disease. Disorders such as cerebral palsy, epilepsy, spina bifida, and poliomyelitis are classified as neurological impairments. Muscular dystrophy, rheumatoid arthritis, and Legg-Calve-Perthes disease are basically orthopedic involvements. Numerous disorders such as hemophilia, diabetes, sickle cell anemia, and cystic fibrosis are severe health impairments for children.

In deciding upon the best possible learning environment for educating the physically handicapped and health impaired, it is imperative that both the child's resources and the school's resources be assessed. Although deficiencies that interfere with the child's learning potential can often be compensated for with adaptive equipment and/or methods, each of the variables must be considered to establish the extent to which the environment must be altered so that learning can occur.

Suggestions for adapting the environment and modifying instructional materials and media for physically handicapped and health-impaired children have been made. Although not intended to be a comprehensive view of adaptations, these practical ideas can be easily implemented by regular or special classroom teachers.

RESOURCES

Adaptive Therapeutic Systems, Inc.
  162 Ridge Rd.
  Madison, CT 06443
  203-245-7311

Childcraft Education Corp.
  Special Education Division
  20 Kilmer Rd., Dept. SCT 6
  Edison, NJ 08817
  800-631-5652

Developmental Learning Materials
  7440 Natchez Ave.
  Niles, IL 60648

Dick Blick
  P.O. Box 1267
  Galesburg, IL 61401
  800-447-8192

Division for the Blind and
Physically Handicapped
  The Library of Congress
  Washington, D.C. 20542

Educational Teaching Aids
  159 W. Kinzie St.
  Chicago, IL 60610
  312-644-9438

Fred Sammons, Inc.
  Box 32
  Brookfield, IL 60513

Ideal School Supply
  11000 South Lavergne Avenue
  Oak Lawn, IL 60453

J. A. Preston Corp.
71 Fifth Ave.
New York, NY 10003
800-221-2425

Kaplan School Supply Corp.
600 Jonestown Rd.
Winston-Salem, NC 27103

Modern Education Corp.
P.O. Box 721
Tulsa, OK 74101

National Audio Visual Center
National Archives and Records
Service
General Services Administration
Order Section DA
Washington, D.C. 20409
301-763-1896

Zaner Bloser
612 North Park St.
Columbus, OH 43215
614-221-5851

REFERENCES

Barker, R. G., Wright, B. A., Meyerson, L., & Gonick, M. *Adjustment to physical handicap and illness: A survey of the social psychology of physique and disability*, No. 55. (Rev. ed.), New York: Social Science Research Council, 1953.

Bartel, N. R., & Goshin, S. L. A handicap as a social phenomenon. In W. M. Cruickshank (Ed.), *Psychology of exceptional children and youth* (3rd ed.). Englewood Cliffs, N.J.: Prentice-Hall, 1971.

Bigge, J., & O'Donnell, P. *Teaching individuals with physical and multiple disabilities*. Columbus, Oh.: Charles E. Merrill, 1977.

Boyles, I. J., & Calovini, G. *Statistical report: Physically handicapped children in Illinois*. Springfield, Ill.: Office of Superintendent of Public Instruction, 1960.

Cruickshank, W. M. The problem and its scope. In W. M. Cruickshank (Ed.), *Cerebral palsy: A developmental disability* (3rd Rev. ed.). Syracuse, N.Y.: Syracuse University Press, 1976.

Denhoff, E. Medical aspects. In W. M. Cruickshank (Ed.), *Cerebral palsy: A developmental disability* (3rd Rev. ed.). Syracuse, N.Y.: Syracuse University Press, 1976.

Fait, H. F. *Special physical education*. Philadelphia: W. B. Saunders, 1972.

Hardy, R. E., & Cull, J. G. *Severe disabilities: Social and rehabilitation approaches*. Springfield, Ill.: Charles C Thomas, 1974.

Kirk, S. A. *Educating exceptional children* (2nd ed.). Boston: Houghton Mifflin Co., 1972.

Kirk, S. A., & Gallagher, J. J. *Educating exceptional children* (3rd ed.). Boston: Houghton Mifflin Co., 1979.

National Safety Council. *Accident facts*. Chicago: The National Safety Council, 1963.

Newman, J. Psychological problems of children and youth with chronic medical disorders. In W. M. Cruickshank (Ed.), *Psychology of exceptional children and youth* (3rd ed.), Englewood Cliffs, N.J.: Prentice-Hall, 1971.

Peterson, R. M., & Cleveland, J. O. *Medical problems in the classroom: An educator's guide*. Springfield, Ill.: Charles C Thomas, 1975.

Sirvis, B. The physically disabled. In E. L. Meyen (Ed.), *Exceptional children and youth: An introduction*. Denver: Love Publishing Co., 1978.

Telford, C. W., & Sawrey, J. M. *The exceptional individual* (2nd ed.), Englewood Cliffs, N.J.: Prentice-Hall, 1977.

U.S. Office of Education. 1975. *Estimated number of handicapped children in the United States*. Washington, D.C.: Bureau of Education for the Handicapped, 1975.

Vanderheiden, G. C., & Grilley, K. *Non-vocal communication techniques and aids for the severely physically handicapped*. Baltimore: University Park Press, 1975.

Vicker, B. *Nonoral communication system project, 1964–1973*. Iowa City: Campus Stores Publishers, 1974.

Wilson, M. I. Children with crippling and health disabilities. In L. M. Dunn (Ed.). *Exceptional children in the schools* (2nd ed.). New York: Holt, Rinehart & Winston, 1973.

5
ENVIRONMENTAL ALTERNATIVES FOR THE VISUALLY HANDICAPPED

Sheldon S. Maron and David H. Martinez

The sense of vision provides man with the raw data necessary for optimal growth and development. It is a remarkably adaptive and resilient system that allows for instantaneous monitoring of the environment. As a motivational source it "invites" an individual to partake of his/her surroundings.

When vision is reduced or absent, alternatives are needed for the attainment of developmental goals normally gained through the visual channel. Educationally, these alternatives will involve materials, equipment, procedures, and delivery systems. This chapter focuses on these compensatory mechanisms within the framework of the least restrictive environment for the visually handicapped child.

DESCRIPTION AND TERMINOLOGY

Who Are Blind Children?

Visually limited children represent a relatively small and heterogeneous group of exceptional individuals. Despite the label "blindness," their ability to see varies markedly, from absence of sight to high levels of functional visual ability. Hatfield's (1975) study of visually handicapped school children indicated that: 1) more than three-fourths became blind before age one, 2) the vast majority had some degree of usable vision, and 3) males outnumbered females, 54 percent to 46 percent. Hatfield's study of blind preschoolers (1972) resulted in similar findings, as well as the fact that prenatal factors were the most common cause of blindness, especially those that were genetic in origin.

Vision loss can be classified in many ways, and because of this, it is often difficult to determine or agree on how well a person can see. Measuring sharpness of distance vision (acuity) or visual fields (overall area seen by the fixed eye) often conflicts with functional visual ability—how well vision is used for the purposes of everyday life. Furthermore, the younger the child the less accurate the visual determination, and the greater the probability of visual score fluctuations. Other classification categories include binocular vision (simultaneous use of both eyes with production of a single image), near vision (e.g., for reading), color vision, and night vision. Thus, vision is a highly complex sense—its physical measurement in a doctor's office may differ from its functioning ability in the classroom, at home, or in the community. This in turn will depend on factors such as motivation, presence of additional disabilities, use of educational aids, lighting conditions, and stability of the eye problem.

The Social Security Act of 1935, which coined the term *legal blindness*, established a level of vision below which an individual could receive financial, educational, and social services. This included textbooks and other educational aids, special income tax benefits, talking book machines and discs (specially modified phonographs for recorded material), and financial aid of various kinds (Kirk, 1972). Blindness, thus defined, was a distance visual acuity of 20/200 or less in the better eye after best correction, or an acuity better than 20/200, but where the visual fields are constricted to 20 degrees or less (NSPB, 1966). An acuity of 20/200 means that at a test distance of 20 feet, a person can see what a normally sighted individual sees at a distance of 200 feet. Best correction refers to the use of eyeglasses/contact lenses or medicine/surgery or both. While written as a fraction, this visual designation should not be interpreted as such. For example, 20/40 does not indicate 50 percent of normal vision, but 85 percent visual efficiency. *Partial sight*, on the other hand, refers to a range of visual acuity better than 20/200, up to and including 20/70, after best correction.

Both legal blindness and partial vision are based on medical information, namely, distance vision and visual fields. Teachers, however, have long noted a consistent discrepancy between medical measurement and classroom functioning. For example, two children with the same visual acuity may function quite differently in school—one being a print reader and the other a braille reader.

For that reason, two more educationally descriptive terms were introduced, *visual impairment* and *blindness*. The visually impaired child is one who is capable of reading the printed word, while the blind child is a tactual reader. In this chapter, the term *blindness* refers to the absence of usable vision. Visual impairment will be used to indicate the presence of functional, residual vision. The terms *visual handicap* or *visual limitation* are broader labels, encompassing both visual impairment and blindness.

Today, print readers far outnumber braille readers. An earlier study by Jones (1961) indicated that more than four-fifths of the legally blind children sampled were print readers. There was a much greater probability of print readers attending day school programs than residential school programs (92 percent versus 51 percent). Nolan's studies (1965, 1967) showed a consistent trend toward greater use of print in both types of educational settings.

Much greater emphasis on the use and training of residual vision has been stimulated by Barraga (1964). From her work came the concept of visual efficiency, or how well an individual uses the vision he/she has. This functional definition has far more relevancy for teachers, regardless of setting or medical classification.

Where Do They Attend School?

The first recorded attempt to educate blind children occurred in Paris in 1785. A residential school, founded by Valentin Haüy, became the early model for educating the visually handicapped in the United States. The first schools in this country were residential facilities in the Northeast (The Perkins School in Massachusetts, the New York Institute, and the Overbrook School in Pennsylvania). They were structured much like the European boarding schools of their day.

Until relatively recently many of these schools segregated students on the basis of sex and/or degree of vision (separate programs/classrooms for boys and girls, the totally blind and the partially sighted). The residential school had its advantages and disadvantages. In fact, the controversy over preferential placement in residential or day school programs has been (and continues to be) argued by educators of the blind. At one time the residential school represented the only educational placement for visually handicapped children other than home training. More importantly, this educational setting has maintained trained professional staffs with specialized programs and facilities for short term or long term needs of children. On the other hand, lack of socialization opportunities with sighted peers, lack of family and community contact, and the routine of institutional life represent limitations imposed by this setting.

Over a century ago, Dr. Samuel Gridley Howe, first Director of the Perkins School for the Blind, said that blind children needed to attend the same schools as their contemporaries. Thus, the principle of mainstreaming has a long standing historical precedent in the education of the visually handicapped. To present a balanced perspective of this issue, it must be noted that educational setting should not be the primary determinant of placement. Rather, individual educational needs should assume highest priority.

Placing visually handicapped children in programs with their normally sighted peers (mainstreaming) has been the focus of heated debate in recent years. Since each child is an individual with unique needs, mainstreaming may be the most appropriate placement decision for some. For others, the residential school may be the least restrictive environment with the most appropriate program.

Day school programs did not begin until the early 1900s, and were first introduced in Cleveland, Boston, and Chicago. Several programs were modeled after the "myope schools" of England which were organized for nearsighted children. Others were termed "sight-saving" or "sight conservation" classes. They were based on the erroneous notion that one's sight would be preserved if it was not used extensively. Current research indicates that vision will not be harmed by use, given proper lighting conditions and absence of certain types of ocular pathology. In fact, it is now sound educational practice to encourage visually handicapped children to use their vision whenever possible.

Day school programs can be organized into the following five basic types (Jones and Collins, 1966):

1. *Self-contained or full time special class*   Here, visually handicapped children spend at least three-fourths of their class time. Staff and equipment are housed in this room which can be located in a regular public school or a special school.
2. *Cooperative plan*   Visually handicapped children are on the rolls of a specially trained teacher, but they receive more than one-fourth of their instruction in the regular classroom.
3. *Resource room*   A plan involving a specially trained teacher with specialized educational aids. Students report here at regularly scheduled times, but are registered with the regular class teacher. Students are trained in specific skills, such as braille, Optacon, vision stimulation, etc.
4. *Itinerant plan*   Children receive services from a specially trained teacher at regularly scheduled times. These teachers travel to the schools, and spend the majority of their time as instructors and distributors of educational aids. Some states have moved almost totally to this plan.
5. *Teacher-consultant*   Part-time itinerant teachers, in this approach, also work with school administrators, regular class teachers, and other professionals to plan comprehensive educational programs. The

regular class teacher assumes greater responsibility for programming with this plan. "This may prove to be a most efficient format, especially in rural parts of the U.S." (DeMott, 1972).

Clearly, there are a number of educational alternatives available. By the early 1970s, more than 60 percent of the visually handicapped children registered with the American Printing House for the Blind were enrolled in day school programs. Of these, itinerant teachers and resource room teachers were the most prevalent. They have supplanted the full-time special class teacher, who was more commonly seen less than a generation ago.

What Is the Least Restrictive
Environment for the Visually Handicapped Child?

Perhaps one of the most difficult components of Public Law 94-142 to operationalize is the provision requiring the educational placement of handicapped children in the least restrictive environment. The least restrictive environment provision, as applied to the visually handicapped, requires that 1) visually handicapped children be educated, when possible, with sighted children and 2) removal of visually handicapped children from the regular educational program should occur when the severity of the handicap is such that education in the regular education program cannot be achieved satisfactorily even with the use of supplementary assistance (Parks & Rousseau, 1977). It is interesting to note that programs to integrate the visually handicapped with sighted children existed as early as 1938 (Hanninen, 1975), long before the efficacy of special classes for the mildly handicapped became an issue (Dunn, 1968) and before the onset of the mainstreaming movement.

The continuum of services, previously discussed, affords alternative educational placements for visually handicapped children. However, no one type of delivery system can adequately meet the educational, social, and emotional needs of every child at each stage of his/her development. A residential program may be appropriate when a visually handicapped student is multiply handicapped, when family circumstances are not sufficiently supportive, and when parents prefer, for their own personal reasons, to have their child reside away from home (O'Brien, 1973). A resource room may be appropriate when intensive instruction is required in order to equip visually handicapped children with basic skills such as braille reading and writing, and the use of the abacus (Hanninen, 1975). An itinerant program may be appropriate when the visually handicapped child already possesses basic survival skills, is well motivated, and demonstrates emotional stability and adaptability (O'Brien, 1973). To place a visually handicapped child in an itinerant program when his/her needs require the services of a resource room is to unnecessarily restrict the opportunity to maximize the child's learning potential, emotional growth, and social development. A delivery system that is the least restrictive and appropriate for one visually handicapped child may be most restrictive for another. The consequences of only employing one delivery system for all visually handicapped children are apparent. The least restrictive environment provision of PL 94-142 is more readily attained when a school district utilizes educational alternatives for the visually handicapped and/or has access to a continuum of services. However, the existence of alternative educational placements, pursuant to mainstreaming, does not necessarily ensure the placement of visually handicapped children in the least restrictive environment. The eligibility criteria for entry into a particular service model must be well defined. Professionals, involved in making placement decisions, must be prepared to document and defend the judgments rendered. In addition, they must be able to justify the continued enrollment of a visually handicapped child in a particular integrated, educational alternative.

The determination of the least restrictive environment must, of necessity, be ultimately based on a match between the academic, social, and emotional needs of the visually handicapped child and the educational placement that best affords the opportunity for optimal development.

THE HUMAN EYE: NORMAL AND ABNORMAL FUNCTION

Normal Vision Development

Not only is the human eye a highly intricate receptor organ, but it is also capable of transmitting complex information at birth. The rate-limiting step with infants is not a decreased ability to see, but a decreased ability to process the incoming stimuli (Bower, 1966). By 3 months of age, infants can focus on objects closeup and at distances, follow moving objects, and distinguish something novel from something seen previously. No other sense provides the quality and quantity of sophisticated information that vision can, nor can any compensatory medium come close to duplicating the effectiveness of this system. Therefore, it is essential that children understand the importance of their vision, how to make the best use of it, and how to maintain proper vision care (NSPB, 1972).

From front to back, the human eye (see Figure 1) is composed of the *conjunctiva*, a thin membrane that lines the eyelids in front and reflects back to cover the *sclera*, the tough, outer protective coat of the eye. The white sclera joins with the *cornea*, a convex transparent structure that forms the outermost front portion of the eye. Beneath the sclera lies the

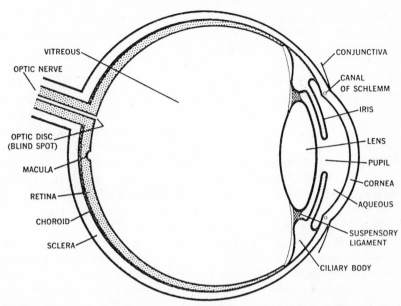

Figure 1.   Schematic section of the eye. (Reprinted with the permission of the American Optometric Association.)

choroid, a membranous layer containing numerous blood vessels serving as an ocular nutrition source. The third and deepest ocular coat is the *retina*, a double-layered, complex neurological tissue.

The *anterior chamber* lies behind the cornea, and contains the *aqueous humour*, a fluid that supplies nutrition to the cornea, aids in lens maintenance, and helps keep a constant pressure within the eye (NSPB, 1972). The aqueous fluid is produced by the *ciliary body*, and eventually drains back into the general circulation via the *Canal of Schlemm*. The *iris*, which gives the eye its characteristic color, is a circular membrane whose central opening, or *pupil*, can be regulated to allow varying degrees of light to enter.

The transparent *lens* is located behind the pupil and iris, and is held in place by the *suspensory ligament*. The *ciliary muscle*, part of the ciliary body, enables the lens to change its shape in order to maintain sharp images at varying distances. Taken together, the choroid, ciliary body, and iris form the *uveal tract*.

Behind the crystalline lens is the vitreous, which comprises the largest portion of the eye. It contains a clear, jellylike substance. The *retina* contains millions of light-sensitive cells that ultimately form the *optic nerve*. This cranial nerve connects the eye with the brain. Within the retina lies the *macula lutea*, which has within it the *fovea centralis*.

The fovea is responsible for producing man's sharpest vision. The *optic disc* or *blind spot* is that part of the retina where the optic nerve exits, and therefore is a nonfunctional receptor area.

As light rays from one's visual fields reach the eyes, they pass through the cornea and aqueous humour and are refracted or bent. They then pass through the pupil, which can dilate or constrict depending on the amount of available light. As the rays reach the lens, they are refracted again, so that a sharp image will fall on the retina, especially the fovea. The lens thickens for viewing objects close by and relaxes for viewing objects further away. This adjustment process is called *accommodation*. As light rays strike the retina (and form an inverted image), light energy is converted to electrical energy. Electrical impulses are then sent via the optic nerve to the visual cortex of the brain. Here, in the occipital lobe, the image is righted and given meaning.

Rod and cone cells are found in the retina. The rod cells are more numerous and are more commonly found in the periphery of the retina. They are especially sensitive during low levels of illumination, and aid in the perception of motion. Cone cells, which tend to cluster in the fovea, function to give sharpest vision under normal lighting conditions, and are responsible for color vision. Movement of the eye is controlled by six extraocular muscles working in synchrony, and they are innervated by a series of cranial nerves (NSPB, 1972).

The more common eye problems found in school-age children are listed in Table 1.

Behavioral Signs of Possible Vision Problems

It is essential that teachers be sensitive to behavioral changes in children, since some of them may be warning signs of possible eye pathology. The following behaviors *may* represent ocular problems:

1. Inability or reduced ability to see distant objects as clearly as before (e.g., blackboards, bulletin boards)
2. Difficulty with closeup work (reading, sewing)
3. Withdrawn, irritable, and/or aggressive behavior in recent times
4. Head and/or body tilting when doing school work
5. Frequent eye rubbing, complaints of burning, itching, or general eye pain.
6. May cover or close one eye when working. May complain of blurred vision or double vision
7. Has lost interest in detail work (e.g., map construction, special projects, art work)
8. Books held close to eyes; often accompanied by headaches, dizziness and/or nausea

Table 1. Common eye problems in school-age children

Disorder	Cause(s)	Treatment	Comments
Myopia (nearsightedness)	Eyeball too long or lens refracts light too much: focus in front of retina.	Concave (−) lenses; diverge light rays.	Usually seen in early elementary school years; cannot see objects well at far distances; may squint.
Hyperopia (farsightedness)	Eyeball too short; focus behind retina.	Convex (+) lenses; refract light to focus on retina.	May compensate without glasses, but will fatigue easily (NSPB, 1972). Dislikes closeup work.
Astigmatism	Improper curvature of the cornea.	Eyeglasses or contact lenses (cylindrical lenses).	Head and/or body tilting; dislike of closeup work; must be corrected early.
Amblyopia	Reduced acuity with no apparent ocular pathology. May be due to strabismus or refractive errors.	Patching good eye; surgery; eye exercises; eyeglasses, or a combination of the above.	Prognosis much better if treated in preschool years. 85% of cases occur before age 4 (Barker & Barmatz, 1975).
Cataract	Opacity of the crystalline lens. Can be due to rubella virus; trauma; radiation.	Surgery followed by convex lenses.	Surgery generally highly successful. Some distortion of peripheral vision.
Glaucoma	Increased intraocular pressure. May be hereditary in some.	Surgery for acute forms, medication for chronic forms.	Insidious in chronic stages, gradual vision loss with few symptoms. Peripheral vision loss in early stages.
Albinism	Hereditary defect of pigment metabolism.	Treating refractive errors and hypersensitivity of sunlight.	Control exposure to light. May see nystagmus (oscillation of the eyes).
Strabismus (crossed eyes)	Improper coordination of eye mucles.	Patching straight eye; eyeglasses; surgery; medication; muscle exercises or orthoptics (Abrahamson, 1977).	Improper alignment. Eye(s) may deviate inward, outward, up, or down. Must be corrected before age 6.
Optic nerve atrophy	Inflammations; infectious diseases; glaucoma; ingestion of toxic substances; blood vessel blockage.	Does not respond to treatment to correct pathology. Medical treatment of primary causative agent.	Condition not reversible.
Conjunctivitis	Bacteria; virus; irritating agents; environmental pollutants; trauma.	Medication (e.g., antibiotics).	Often contagious with hypersensitivity to light. Must be treated to prevent significant loss of vision.
Retrolental fibroplasia (RLF)	In most instances, excessive oxygen tension given to premature infants.	No known treatment to reverse existing pathology.	Much more common in mid-1950s and early 1960s.

9. Excessive lid closing ("squinting")
10. Blinking eyes more than usual
11. Emergence of coordination problems in the classroom or on the playground

If any of these behaviors are present, an indepth eye examination should be recommended by teachers. It is a wise practice to recommend to parents that their children receive yearly examinations even if vision screening tests indicate no problems.

Vision Screening

Vision screening is a process aimed at identifying children who *may* require eye care. Since it is not a comprehensive examination, it will not identify all children who need further attention, nor will all referred individuals need treatment (NSPB, 1972). Screening tests should be short, simple in nature, with easy to understand directions. They should be inexpensive and easy to administer to a large group by nonmedical personnel (Harley & Lawrence, 1977). As many as one out of every four children in school today may require eye care. Teachers should be sensitive to behavioral changes which could indicate eye problems and refer children for screening as soon as possible.

The National Society for the Prevention of Blindness (1972, 1969) recommends that an annual visual acuity test be given, but if that is not possible, screening be done according to the schedule in Table 2. It is critical that the following testing procedures be followed closely (Harley & Lawrence, 1977):

1. Test chart should be clean and placed at eye level (eye at level of 30 foot line).
2. Room should have proper illumination (10–30 foot candles), and be free from glare.

Table 2.   Recommended screening schedule

Grade	Age	Test	Criterion for referral
Kindergarten or first grade	5–6	Snellen E Symbol Chart (Illiterate E)	20/50 or less
Second grade	7	Snellen (or other) Letter Chart	20/40 or less
Fifth grade	10–11	Snellen (or other) Letter Chart	20/30 or less
Eighth grade	13	Snellen (or other) Letter Chart	20/30 or less
Tenth or eleventh grade	15–17	Snellen (or other) Letter Chart	20/30 or less

3. Test distance should be precisely measured (usually 20 feet, but some charts are used at 10 feet).
4. First test both eyes together, then right and left eye individually.
5. To be given credit for passing each line, the child must correctly read a majority of the letters, or if the symbol chart is used, correctly determine in what direction the E is pointing in the majority of items (see Figure 2). Very young children and/or multihandicapped children should be given some practice to make sure that they understand the directions.
6. The test administrator should carefully observe for suspect behaviors during testing (head tilting, watering eyes, etc.).
7. Eye appearance should be noted and a medical history included if possible.
8. The room must be free from distractions.
9. If the child wears eyeglasses, test with them on.

Other screening tests include the Massachusetts Vision Test (a test battery measuring acuity, muscle balance, and hyperopia) and the Pseudoisochromatic Plates (for color discrimination). The Telebinocular, OrthoRater, and Titmus Vision Tester are machines used to screen for near and distance acuity, depth perception, fusion, muscle balance, and visual fields. Faye's (1970) "House, Apple, Umbrella" symbol test, and Boyce's (1973) Home Eye Test are especially good for preschoolers and/or lower functioning children. A listing of screening test instruments is presented in Table 3.

Common Myths about Vision and the Visually Handicapped

Like most minority groups, the visually handicapped have been historically stereotyped as having certain undesirable characteristics (usually insurmountable). Vision loss has been frequently seen as the most severe disability that could befall man. On the other hand, the blind have been occasionally thought to possess special powers. Following is a list of some of the more common misconceptions about blindness and blind people.

1. *Myth*: Blind people have a better sense of hearing and/or touch than sighted people.

   Fact: Loss of vision (partial or total) in no way results in automatic sensory compensation by improvement of hearing, touch, or any other sense. Hayes (1941) reviewed a series of studies comparing blind and sighted subjects in hearing, touch, taste, and smell discriminations. These studies indicated no differences in acuity between the two groups, and

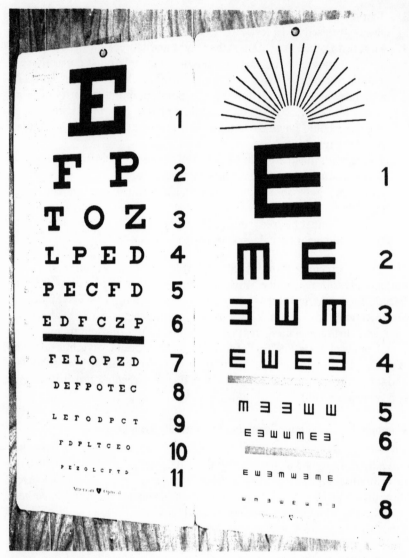

Figure 2. Snellen letter and E symbol charts for vision screening. (Reprinted from *Protection of Vision in Children*, by A. Patz and R. Hoover, 1969, courtesy of Charles C Thomas, Publisher, Springfield, Ill.)

Table 3.   Commonly used screening tests

Test	Age range	Time required	Professional required	Purpose
Optokinetic nystagmus test	Any age	5 minutes	Nonprofessional	Central visual acuity (crude); useful with newborns; presence or absence of vision.
Allen picture cards	2½ years and above	3 minutes	Nonprofessional	Central acuity useful with non-English speaking children and those unable to respond to the Illiterate E Test.
Illiterate E test	3 and above	2–4 minutes	Nonprofessional	Central visual acuity.
Snellen letters	6 and above	less than 2 minutes	Nonprofessional	Central acuity; usually administered at 20 feet.
Cover test	Any age	½ minute– 2 minutes	Nonprofessional	Muscle imbalance.
Bausch and Lomb school vision tester	5 years and older	2 minutes or more	Nonprofessional	Central acuity; hyperopia; muscle balance; near point acuity; depth perception; color discrimination.
Keystone tele-binocular	5 years and older	3 minutes	Nonprofessional	Central acuity; hyperopia; near point acuity; muscle balance; color discrimination.
Titmus screener	4 years and older	2–5 minutes	Nonprofessional	Central acuity; hyperopia; muscle balance; near point acuity; color discrimination.

Source: Adapted from "Eye Function" by J. Barker and H. Barmatz in *Pediatric Screening Tests* edited by W. Frankenburg and B. Camp, 1975, Springfield, Ill.: Charles C Thomas.

occasionally, the sighted group outperformed the blind group. Hayes concluded that any superiority on the part of the blind was due to the development of the existing senses, practice, increased use, and attentional factors.

2. *Myth*:   Blind people have superior musical abilities.

   Fact: No research is available to substantiate the above statement (Pitman, 1965). In fact, an early study by Merry (1931) found no consistent trends when evaluating performance on the Seashore Musical Talents Test. A number of blind children have become successful musical performers because of basic musical talent, practice, encouragement, and more liberal attitudes by society toward the blind in this vocational endeavor. Unfortunately, these attitudes are often absent when it comes to other, equally valued occupational choices.

3. *Myth*:   All blind people read braille.

   Fact: No compelling research exists which has linked near visual acuity with mode of reading. Many legally blind children and youth have sufficient vision to read not only large print materials, but regular print as well. Under optimum lighting conditions using appropriate corrective lenses, Sykes (1973) found that visually handicapped teenagers performed just as well with standard print as they did with large print. Since the majority of visually handicapped children have some residual vision, the printed word is a most important reading mode for many of them. Only a small percentage of the visually handicapped population are braille readers.

4. *Myth*:   Eyes will be damaged by sitting too close to the television set or movie screen.

   Fact: No damage will occur by sitting too close to a television set or movie screen. However, if watching causes aching eyes, fatigue, or headaches, this may be a sign of a refractive error, and this child should be seen by an eye specialist. Ideally, a TV viewer should sit 8 to 10 feet away, and directly in front of the screen. The room should be lit with the light source behind the viewer (Abrahamson, 1977).

5. *Myth*:   Eyeglasses make your eyes stronger.

   Fact: Eyeglasses help bend light so that a person can see better (image comes to a sharper focus on the retina). Glasses do not *cure* any underlying ocular pathology, nor can they change the intrinsic cause and progression of an eye problem.

6. *Myth*: Vision and reading are synonymous.

   Fact: Both vision and reading are functions of the brain. Reading, however, involves not only the eye, but those parts of the brain that internalize what is seen, relate what is seen to past experiences, and translate these results into a meaningful decision-making system. Print reading involves not only vision, but perceptual functioning which develops in children according to an orderly, sequential format.

7. *Myth*: Eye exercises will cure myopia, hyperopia, and astigmatism.

   Fact: Eye exercises (orthoptics) often help in muscle balance problems, other binocular vision difficulties, and attending to visual cues. The above-mentioned refractive errors are caused by the abnormal shape of the eyeball or cornea, and cannot be resolved by these exercises, especially where these eye conditions are of long standing.

8. *Myth*: Drinking alcohol and smoking can cause blindness.

   Fact: Moderate drinking of alcohol or ingestion of smoke will not harm the eyes. However, drinking methyl or wood alcohol can cause blindness by optic nerve destruction. Excessive drinking of commercial alcohol can cause double vision (diplopia) and hallucinations. There is some evidence that excessive smoking (3 to 6 packs/day or 8 to 10 cigars/day) can produce significant visual impairment (Abrahamson, 1977). Some glaucoma patients have reported alleviation of symptoms from smoking marijuana.

Sensation

The visual channel is the primary sensory pathway by which information about the world is initially determined. Visually handicapped children, therefore, need to sharpen their remaining senses to compensate for this reduction in sensory input. Hearing gives environmental clues of direction and distance, but does not provide concrete information about the intrinsic nature of objects as such (Lowenfeld, 1971). The sense of touch requires direct contact with objects, tedious "putting together of physical units" piece by piece. Furthermore, tactual limitations are imposed by complex objects, and they must be sturdy to withstand manipulation (Scholl, 1968). Visual stimuli, on the other hand, occur continuously, giving the observer "whole" pictures of reality. It is most difficult, if not impossible, to perceive tactually objects that are exceptionally large or small, in rapid motion, of extremes in temperature, or especially fragile (airplanes, bacteria, butterflies, and so forth).

Sighted people tend to ignore the tactual modality, and often even the auditory channel. Tactual observations give surface quality (rough versus smooth) and sensations of weight and temperature (Lowenfeld, 1971). While not as efficient as sight, touch does give clues regarding size, shape, and position, but with some restrictions. Hearing enables individuals to communicate verbally, and keep in direct social contact with the environment. However, sounds must be emitted for an object or person to be identified, they may be masked by other sounds, or they may be produced only intermittently. All these factors leave a blind person with potential sociocultural and cognitive restrictions. The senses of smell and taste generally provide less useful information than hearing or touch.

For the visually handicapped child, finding substitutes to compensate for the reduction of visual input poses a significant obstacle. In the area of reading, assistance can be provided by braille, Optacon, tape recordings, sighted readers, and large type. For mathematics, the abacus and Talking Calculator can replace the traditional paper-and-pencil approach. For writing, braillewriters, slates, and typewriters are used. These approaches represent but a few alternatives, and substitutes exist for the other curriculum areas as well.

Extensive, first-hand experiences with the environment are essential for the visually limited child. Replicas or models of objects should be used only when first-hand experiences are not possible. Constant verbal descriptions and explanations by parents and teachers should accompany the learning process. However, it is important that the child experience and organize the environment himself, rather than relying completely on the verbal explanations of others. Since much of what is learned arises from visual imitation, the blind child will require more practice and closer supervision by teachers, using tactual and auditory clues. Increased opportunity, encouragement, and a realistic reward system will go a long way in combatting many of these potential learning problems.

For the child with usable vision, the so-called visually impaired or low vision child, utilizing the existing visual channel is crucial. Controlled classroom lighting, free from glare, is essential. Natural lighting is preferred over artificial lighting. After a thorough vision work-up, the child will need access to low vision aids such as eyeglasses, hand held magnifiers, closed circuit television (CCTV), telescopes and projection enlargers (Hanninen, 1975). Visually impaired children do not automatically function better just because optical aids are prescribed. Training, patience, and encouragement will be required, and this takes time.

Reading aids become especially important as the volume and complexity of reading increases in the upper elementary grades. Large and regular type give the child a broader range of available reading experiences than does braille. Barraga's pioneering study (1964) indicated that visually impaired children should be trained to improve their functional vision. This was even true in visually impaired children with light perception (able to detect only the presence or absence of light). Barraga's Visual Efficiency Scale provides a profile of visual discrimination skills from which intervention strategies can be planned.

Cognitive Skills

While a loss of vision does not result in cognitive deficits per se, there is evidence that it may do so indirectly. According to Lowenfeld (1950), restrictions imposed by blindness upon such factors as ability to get about, range and variety of experiences, and control of environment could accentuate cognitive difficulties. As stated previously, the remaining senses cannot compensate totally for the role(s) normally subsumed by sight. Lack of opportunity for first-hand experiences and dependence on the verbal explanations of others can lead the blind child to seek stimulation from within. To counteract this, the child must actively explore the environment and organize his/her conceptual world. This venture must be encouraged as early as possible (Foulke, 1962b). Restrictions in concept development have important social and emotional implications as well.

Based on Piaget's theory of cognitive development in children, Stephens (1972) has noticed significant conceptual lags in visually handicapped children, despite normal IQ scores. Fraiberg (1968) has also noted that the comparable development of thought in blind and sighted children ceases midway in the first year of life, when the sighted child is able to conduct a systematic search of the environment. If the child does not see, or sees little, there is less motivation to reach for objects and people. Blindness may retard development by leading to 1) decreased sensory input, and 2) the short circuiting of a visual mechanism that not only collects data, but that may organize and unify data arriving from other sensory modalities (Warren, 1977). These factors, together with the notion that the blind child may have limited awareness of his/her impact on the environment, have led Scott (1969) to postulate that the blind child has difficulty in distinguishing his/her thoughts from the thoughts of others, or self from non-self.

However, it should be noted that some investigators believe that blindness has little effect on cognition. Hatwell (1966) found few differences between comparable groups of blind and sighted children on specific reasoning tasks, and Juurmaa (1973) found similar results on certain tasks requiring abstraction skills.

Perceptual-Motor Development

Norris, Spaulding, and Brodie (1957) found a strong relationship between motor skill proficiency and learning opportunities in blind children. In motor areas where blind children tended to perform poorly compared to seeing children (fine motor control and reaching), the authors found that the blind children had had insufficient encouragement to systematically explore and move about. Adelson and Fraiberg (1974) demonstrated that congenitally blind infants had normal postural skills, but showed a lag in self-initiated movement. Training and opportunity for motor experiences tended to reduce this developmental lag. Cratty et al. (1968) found that the congenitally blind showed more difficulty mastering the concept of laterality (left-right discriminations) than the adventitiously blind. In addition, Cratty noted that veering could be overcome by training.

Early motor experiences are essential for the visually handicapped child, as they are for all children. Free movement enables the child to learn that his/her world is an exciting place to explore. This exploration provides valuable sensory information for facilitating cognitive growth. Movement helps to structure a chaotic world, while building feelings of environmental control.

Young children often define objects in their world not by static properties, but by their motor qualities (e.g., a fence is something to be climbed). To some, movement may be the basis of learning (Van Dijk, 1968). Physical education teachers have long expressed the idea that good mental health begins with good physical health. This in turn depends on motor skill development.

Motor development helps the visually handicapped child differentiate self from non-self. It gives the child a reality-based concept of his/her body, how to control it, and the extent of the spatial relations involved. Overprotection by well meaning parents can have negative effects on the child's perceptual-motor development (Warren, 1977). The benefits accrued by encouraging free movement far outweigh a few bruises incurred by the child in self-initiated exploration. The independence thus gained will help ensure that the child's growth and development is as normal as possible.

Intelligence

Hayes (1941) was the first to measure the intelligence of blind children (as expressed by IQ tests) over long periods of time. He found that these scores were within normal limits when compared with sighted children, and that general intelligence had no relation to the age at which sight was lost. There were, however, fewer blind children in the higher IQ ranges and more in the lower IQ ranges. The Interim Hayes-Binet test has been extensively used. The verbal portion of the Wechsler Intelligence Scale for Children (WISC) is also frequently utilized, with relatively high correlation between it and the Hayes-Binet. Livingston (1958) found IQ scores for partially sighted children to be similar to sighted children.

On the WISC, Tillman (1967) compared the performance of blind and sighted children with the following results: 1) arithmetic, vocabulary, and information scores were similar, 2) blind children scored below their sighted peers in comprehension and similarities, 3) with the blind group, facts tended to be retained as isolated bits of information, and 4) sighted children tended to do better on problems requiring abstraction skills. Some prefer the WISC because of its ease of administration and its stability at the lower and higher age ranges. Other tests that have been used include the Blind Learning Aptitude Test (BLAT), a performance test requiring minimal verbal interaction, the Perkins-Binet, an adaptation of the Hayes-Binet, and the Williams Intelligence Test.

Many authors have cautioned against making comparisons between blind and sighted groups on the same intelligence test because: 1) verbal tests measure but one aspect of intelligence, 2) a blind child's verbal skills may not be indicative of general ability to learn in other developmental areas, 3) some blind children use words without sufficient experiential content (verbalisms), 4) some test items require visual imagery, thus penalizing blind children, 5) tests generally do not demonstrate high levels of predictive validity, 6) tests are often not administered in the same format or with the same time restrictions (i.e., given in braille or large type with extended administration times), 7) striking differences between the two groups at the outset militate against making comparisons, and 8) even though overall scores are similar, significant selective differences often exist within subscales (Bateman, 1965; Coveny, 1976; Goldman, 1970; Warren, 1977).

Educational Achievement

Commonly used achievement tests that have been adapted for use with visually limited children include the Stanford Achievement Test,

Metropolitan Achievement Test, Gray Oral Reading Test, and The Sequential Tests of Educational Progress (STEP). Blind children of normal intelligence with no additional disabilities will require about twice as much time to complete the tests (Lowenfeld, Abel, & Hatlen, 1969). The following results regarding educational achievement have been put forth:

1. There was no relationship between age at which sight is lost and level of educational achievement (Hayes, 1941).
2. The overall reading achievement level of partially sighted children compared favorably with that of sighted children (Bateman, 1963). However, more reading errors were found among the partially sighted group.
3. Generally, level of educational achievement among the visually handicapped tended to be within normal limits. Reading comprehension was also similar when more completion time was allowed (Kirk, 1972).

It should be noted that other studies have not totally agreed with the above findings. Therefore, teachers should interpret these findings with caution.

Social-Emotional Development

Traditionally, the visually handicapped have been viewed as marginal members of society with a low probability of becoming independent, productive citizens. To understand these negative attitudes, one should think of this group as a stereotyped minority group subject to deep-seated misconceptions concerning 1) the causes of vision loss, and 2) the ability of these individuals to compensate successfully.

Blindness is looked upon in many different ways. Parents of blind children may view it as divine punishment, a result of sexual transgression, a personal and social disgrace, and/or a result of having had venereal disease (Sommers, 1944). Some see blindness as the most incapacitating of all disabilities (Gowman, 1957). However, sighted children, especially those in the lower elementary grades, show more positive attitudes as they interact more with their blind peers (Bateman, 1962; Steinzor, 1966). Lukoff and Whiteman (1961) discovered that while a sighted person may have negative attitudes toward *blindness*, he/she may have positive attitudes toward *blind people*.

Vision is the primary provider of information by which children learn to differentiate themselves from the environment. This process begins in infancy and develops as a result of stimulating home and school environments (Scholl, 1973). Ultimately, the child is able to evaluate himself/herself as a worthy individual.

How a person feels about himself/herself is often related to how he/she is perceived by those in his/her environment. Self-evaluation or self-concept is no doubt affected by how others, especially parents, feel. Blind children, like sighted children, internalize the feelings, values, and expectations of the role models around them, often adopting them as their own. If a visually handicapped child is consistently told that he/she is not a worthy person, it is conceivable that his/her self-concept will reflect this judgment at least partially. This can lead to greater uncertainty about future competence (Jervis, 1959).

In a study by Sommers (1944) five distinct attitudes were found in parents of blind children: acceptance of the blind child and his/her handicap, denial of disability, overprotection, overt rejection, and disguised rejection. The first two were seen as being the most positive since they allowed room for healthy compensation efforts. Sommers also noted that blindness per se did not lead to adjustment problems (there is no "blind personality"). Adjustment problems were more likely to be the result of a stimulus-poor social environment. Finally, Sommers found that the adjustment of the blind child was closely related to the parents' own personal and social adjustment to life.

Conflicting information exists regarding the adjustment of visually handicapped children as compared with their sighted peers. Some investigators have found no differences (Pintner and Forlano, 1943), while others have indicated a higher incidence of maladjustment among the visually handicapped (Brieland, 1950; Petrucci, 1953).

Bauman's (1964) study indicated that: 1) residential school students showed more social and emotional maladjustment than nonresidential school students, and 2) blind adolescents had fewer adjustment problems than partially sighted adolescents (less anxiety and insecurity, fewer home adjustment problems). Imamura (1965) compared blind preschoolers with a comparable group of sighted children and found that the blind children demonstrated greater dependency. This result, as well as those in the Bauman study, *has not been consistently duplicated in the research literature.* Tait (1972) proposed that a blind child has less control over social interactions (and subsequently feels less in control of everyday events), possibly leading to more withdrawn, egocentric behavior.

Cutsforth (1951) was an early proponent of the importance of a healthy home life for the visually handicapped child, especially in the early formative years. He believed that a loss of vision necessitated a complete reorganization of one's cognitive world. Furthermore, Cutsforth said that a supportive home life would facilitate this process. Cowen, Underberg, Verillo, and Benham (1961) found that positive adjustment by blind children was closely linked to the level of understanding in the home.

Communication Skills

Studies of speech and language acquisition by the visually handicapped tend to yield conflicting results. Some have indicated that blind children do not differ in vocal skill development from sighted children (Brieland, 1950; Tillman & Williams, 1968). Where differences do exist, visually limited children tend to show more problems with sound production and quality (Warren, 1977). Language skill programs are vital for these children, especially in the preschool years. They should stress visual and auditory imitation, vocal stimulation by parents, environmental exploration, and the attachment of verbal labels to all sensory experiences.

One area of debate for some time has been the use of verbalisms by the blind. Verbalisms are words that are used without having first-hand experience with their referents (i.e., naming objects based on visual concepts). Termed *verbal unreality* by Cutsforth (1932), it was postulated that this would lead to significant educational problems in the future. Other investigators have not shared Cutsforth's alarm. Dokecki (1966) stated that word concepts for the blind without adequate sensory referents were not necessarily meaningless, and that sighted children use words in this very way. Neither Nolan (1960) nor DeMott (1972) could find substantiation for Cutsforth's results and conclusions. Warren's review (1977) of DeMott's study speculated that the blind may use words with fewer emotional overtones. This would also contribute to the idea that language programs for blind children be based on direct environmental experiences, utilizing *all* sensory data available.

Another problem area for the blind involves nonverbal communication. Frequently, communication is based on facial expression and body movement, putting the blind person at a distinct disadvantage. Apple (1972) has suggested that the blind be taught these skills. Not only would it provide an added dimension for communication, but perhaps it would lead to greater social acceptance. It is a most important topic which merits further study.

Not to be confused with verbalisms, mannerisms are ritualistic, repetitive behaviors, such as eye poking, rocking back and forth, and head tilting. These stereotypic behaviors (mistakenly called blindisms) are also seen in autistic, mentally retarded, and nonhandicapped children. There is no agreement as to the cause(s) of such activity, but some have postulated the following explanations: 1) the need for self-stimulation due to the lack of external visual stimulation (Burlingham, 1961; Cutsforth, 1951), 2) emotional stress and/or frustration prompting a return to a "safer" activity of a lower developmental age (Knight, 1972), and 3) social isolation.

If frequent enough, some mannerisms can produce medical problems, and they divert attention from more acceptable adaptive behaviors. Behavior modification strategies, such as token economies with positive reinforcers, have been used successfully to reduce mannerisms in blind children (Caetano & Kaufman, 1975; Miller & Miller, 1976).

THE ENVIRONMENT: VISUALLY LIMITED CHILDREN IN THE MAINSTREAM

Although an interest in mainstreaming the visually handicapped substantially predates PL 94–142, there is a dearth of literature on integrating the visually handicapped into the regular classroom (Keilbaugh, 1977; Peterson & Bass, 1977). Such a lack may be partly accounted for by the fact that next to the multiply handicapped, the visually handicapped constitute the smallest group of exceptionality (Hewett & Forness, 1977). Nevertheless, a review of the role of the vision teacher, classroom teacher, school administrator, and peers and parents can highlight some basic intervention strategies supporting the mainstreaming of the visually handicapped. An analysis of the possible criteria for success serves to illustrate how the efficacy of intervention efforts may be determined.

The Role of the Vision Teacher

The vision teacher, especially one who has been a regular classroom teacher, may be expected to serve as a resource to classroom teachers and school administrators, to identify the special needs of the visually handicapped, to assist with the decision making process relative to curricular and behavioral management considerations, and when appropriate, to provide direct instruction and related services to visually handicapped students. Reynolds and Birch (1977) have identified the following eight major service areas offered by the vision teachers:

1. To provide special materials, such as braille, large type and recorded materials, braillewriters, typewriters, braille slates, and magnifiers
2. To help develop proper use of special equipment, such as that listed above as well as others, such as the abacus, tactual maps, tape recorders, and records

3. To assist in the assessment of students and to make referrals for further studies, as needed
4. To monitor general progress and specific problems and needs as each student with visual handicaps proceeds through the school program
5. To participate in team planning sessions
6. To advise and counsel parents and teachers
7. To organize reader and brailling services
8. To teach students orientation and mobility skills and stimulate the use of residual vision

The vision teacher is in a position to extend valuable training and expertise into the regular classroom. Any classroom teacher who consents to participate in the mainstreaming of a visually handicapped child may rely on the support and expertise of the vision specialist regardless of the service model employed.

The Role of the Classroom Teacher

One of the most encouraging aspects of mainstreaming the visually handicapped is that minor, not major, modifications will be required in the regular educational program. A review of five aspects of integrating the visually handicapped—1) attitude, 2) orientation and mobility, 3) classroom arrangement, 4) curricular considerations, and 5) physical education and recreation—will serve to illustrate how they may be accommodated by the regular classroom teacher.

Attitude The attitude of the regular classroom teacher is exceedingly important in that his/her attitude toward the visually handicapped sets an example for sighted classmates. One of the most difficult concepts to accept is that visually handicapped children should be treated just like other students, not as if they are different or special (Hulsey, 1973; Orlansky, 1977). The tendency to "favor" the visually handicapped is undoubtedly related to a combination of compassion and a general unawareness of their capabilities. A major issue to be resolved is whether different standards of performance, especially in regard to academics, should be applied to the performance of the visually handicapped (Keilbaugh, 1977). However, there appears to be a consensus that the visually handicapped should be held to the same standard of excellence required of their sighted peers (Martin & Hoben, 1977; Orlansky, 1977). As visually handicapped children generally require more time to complete assigned tasks, it may be necessary to allow more time or to shorten assignments. However, they should be held responsible for their performance and encouraged to develop independence and self-sufficiency which are traits expected of all children in our society.

Orientation and Mobility   Although orientation and mobility skills are taught by a specialist, it may be necessary for a classroom teacher to demonstrate to the class the proper sighted guide techniques. However, many visually handicapped children who are partially sighted will not require any special assistance in relating to and maneuvering in their physical environment (Martin & Hoben, 1977). In the regular classroom, one may assist the visually handicapped locate something by providing verbal cues (e.g., left, right). However, these directional cues should be related to the child's body and not that of classmates or the classroom teacher.

Classroom Arrangement   Some minor modification may be required in order to facilitate a visually handicapped child's integration into the regular classroom. A few of the many possible modifications include:

1. A table large enough for braillewriters, recorders, and Optacon
2. A desk so that the visually handicapped may, during a listening activity, be part of a group
3. A book case large enough to hold braille and large print books
4. Folders, labeled in braille, with pockets in which to place completed assignments
5. Opportunities to explore the room and become oriented to surroundings
6. Doors should be completely shut or open in order to prevent obstacles to mobility
7. Visually handicapped children should be informed when the room has been rearranged and given opportunity to relocate room contents
8. Visually handicapped children should become familiar with fire drill procedures and be assigned a classroom buddy for possible assistance in exiting (Whitelaw 1978; Orlansky, 1977)

An examination of the preceding modifications, relative to the arrangement and contents of the classroom and related procedures, will reveal that visually handicapped students are afforded considerations similar to those extended to their sighted classmates.

Curricular Considerations   Perhaps one of the greatest sources of concern for a regular classroom teacher is how to include the visually handicapped child in the daily instructional activities. It is possible to include a visually handicapped child in reading and mathematics groups by securing corresponding textbooks that are available in braille and/or large type. The vision teacher should be consulted as to the availability of brailled or large print textbooks. Some basic skill workbooks (reading, arithmetic, spelling) are available in both braille and large print. When supplementary instructional materials are unavailable, the vision teacher may be asked to transcribe them for the visually handicapped child. For the partially sighted child it may be necessary to use the darkest dittoes with spacing, contrast, and boldness more relevant than the size of print. Several educational periodicals (e.g., *My Weekly Reader*) are available in braille. Partially sighted children, through the use of low vision aids, may prefer to use instructional materials with regular sized print.

The visually handicapped child will profit from direct individual and/or group instruction. It may be necessary, perhaps even desirable, to vary the instructional format to include oral as well as written responses. The chalkboard may be used for explanations, and when necessary, a blind child can braille words, numerals, or phrases at the moment they are required. It may be necessary for a classmate to repeat an explanation to a visually handicapped child, although one must guard against encouraging dependency. When necessary, a vision teacher can braille an assignment; a copy of a teacher's assignment may be provided to a partially sighted child (Martin & Hoben, 1977). The visually handicapped child can profit from films, educational TV, and the use of overhead projections by participating in listening and oral discussion activities.

Maintaining the visually handicapped child's attention is no more of a task than it is for sighted classmates. However, since eye contact with a visually handicapped child may be difficult to achieve, one may need to encourage on-task behavior through touch or hearing. It may also be necessary to identify visually handicapped children by name when calling on them to respond or providing verbal praise. Providing immediate feedback and/or reinforcement for a visually handicapped student's written work presents a problem if the work has been brailled. The visually handicapped child must wait until the work can be corrected by the vision teacher. However, Whitelaw (1978) suggests that classroom teachers consider enrolling in a short course on beginning braille. In this way, the regular classroom teacher may provide immediate feedback as to the quality of the written assignments and record such comments as good work, keep it up, wow, and similar praise which is generally available to one's sighted peers. Being able to provide immediate feedback greatly enhances the visually handicapped student's acquisition of skills and contributes to the interpersonal relationship between the classroom teacher and the visually handicapped member of the class.

The visually handicapped child can be successfully integrated into the regular classroom. The classroom teacher and the vision teacher must plan together so that the visually handicapped student may become an active participant in the educational mainstream.

Physical Education and Recreation   The visually handicapped student, given the opportunity and minor adaptations, may be expected to participate in a variety of physical education and recreational activities. Among the activities that should be extended to the visually handicapped are wrestling, canoeing, skiing, swimming, roller skating, ice skating, dribbling a basketball, and bicycling (tandem). The trampoline, with a bell placed underneath the center to aid in orientation, is a popular recreational activity, as is playing catch with audible balls. The safety precautions provided for and explained to sighted children should also be shared with the visually handicapped. With the ascendancy of interest in the use of leisure time, the visually handicapped should participate in activities with their sighted peers.

The extent to which the visually handicapped may participate in the educational mainstream is directly related to the opportunities afforded them. The classroom teacher, in cooperation with the vision teacher, may accommodate the visually handicapped into the regular classroom with minor modifications that will have a major impact on the total development of the visually handicapped as well as their sighted classmates.

The Role of the School Administrator

In order to facilitate the mainstreaming process, the support and leadership of the building principal is critical. Beery (1972) reported that positive changes in educational services are likely to occur when principals possess knowledge of handicapped children and their educational needs. In essence, the building principal has the power to make a major contribution to the success or failure of the mainstreaming process. As with classroom teachers, school administrators' attitudes remain a basic issue. Some administrators may resist mainstreaming, not out of antagonism but because of a general concern that the visually handicapped student may be unable to compete academically, is prone to safety hazards, and may encounter difficulty in participating in courses that require special equipment characteristic of industrial arts and home economics (Hulsey, 1973). However, minor adaptations in the equipment required in specialized subject areas allow the visually handicapped to participate and attain levels of proficiency previously attainable only by sighted students (Dillman & Maloney, 1977).

Scholl (1968) discussed the role of the school administrator as it relates to the visually handicapped student. Some of the suggestions made were:

1. Work with the vision teacher to provide appropriate housing and storage facilities required for the service model to be employed

2. Encourage the vision teacher to participate in staff meetings and in regular inservice education programs so that the vision teacher is considered an integral part of the total professional staff
3. Interpret the special program to parents of nonhandicapped children
4. Assert leadership in providing that regular classroom teachers become informed about the nature of visual handicaps
5. Become informed as to local, state, and regional resources available for the visually handicapped students

Enlisting the support of the building principal will greatly enhance the mainstreaming efforts for the visually handicapped and other handicapped children.

The Role of Peers

Although the roles of the vision teacher, classroom teacher, and school administrator contribute to the academic, social, and emotional well being of the visually handicapped child, the role of the child's classmates should not be underestimated. The benefits derived from having a visually handicapped student as a regular class member extend to his/her sighted classmates as well.

In a regular classroom study reported by Scheffers (1977), it was found that fourth grade children substantially increased their knowledge of blindness and improved their attitude toward blindness after participating in a 20 lesson unit on blindness. The inclusion of visually handicapped children in a regular classroom affords an excellent opportunity to observe behavior and attitude change in the visually handicapped as well as in their sighted classmates. A visually handicapped student's classmates may be given the opportunity to:

1. Share classroom duties and responsibilities with the handicapped student (e.g., feeding pets)
2. Encourage the visually handicapped child to develop acceptable social behaviors (e.g., looking at the person with whom he/she is speaking and listening)
3. Become a buddy for emergency situations (e.g., fire drill)
4. Assist in carrying braillers and/or books
5. Read directions used in leisure time games and activities
6. Repeat teacher directions to visually handicapped child when necessary
7. Learn to differentiate between needed assistance and oversolicitous behavior
8. Participate with the visually handicapped child in physical education and recreational activities

9. Ask questions related to the visually handicapped
10. Encourage the visually handicapped child to develop independent orientation and mobility skills, although some assistance may be needed

The children enrolled in the regular classroom may mirror the behavior of the classroom teacher toward the visually handicapped student. The role of peers in the development of a child's academic, social, and emotional characteristics is no more or less important for the visually handicapped than for sighted classmates. The acceptance or rejection of a visually handicapped child is undoubtedly influenced by the same factors affecting the acceptance or rejection of sighted classmates (Martin & Hoben, 1977).

The Role of Parents

Within the last 15 years parents have demonstrated that they can serve in an effective advocacy role for their handicapped children. Parents have been instrumental in presenting the case for improved services to school boards and government agencies (Scott, Jan, & Freeman, 1977). With the advent of PL 94-142, parents have been given the opportunity to approve the individualized education program and to monitor a child's progress. McNair & Smith (1977) suggested the following activities which allow parents to monitor the implementation of the individualized education program:

1. Examine the child's work that is brought home
2. Call the teacher and/or arrange for a visit to the classroom
3. While visiting, determine if the handicapped student is allowed to actively participate in classroom activities
4. Ascertain if teacher's expectations afford the child the opportunity to participate
5. Determine if the child is happy and looks forward to attending the regular classroom setting
6. Obtain evidence that the handicapped student is progressing adequately towards the short term objectives

Apart from the parents' role in monitoring the implementation of a visually handicapped student's individualized education program, parental involvement may also be rendered by:

1. Listening to child read and maintaining a list of errors to be reported to the regular classroom and vision teachers
2. Providing assistance in orientation and mobility

3. Darkening lines in workbooks and duplicated materials that employ regular sized print
4. Learning to sight-read braille, or when possible, getting print versions of the braille books
5. Making braille copies of the visually handicapped children's favorite books and/or stories
6. Reading to the blind and partially sighted directly or through taped recordings
7. Encouraging the blind or partially sighted child to participate in family and neighborhood physical education activities
8. Providing intellectual, social, and emotional stimulation and support afforded sighted siblings

The role of parents in the education of their visually handicapped children need not be relegated to a secondary position; in the mainstreaming process their assistance is essential in creating a maximal learning environment.

Criteria for Success

To the extent that the vision and classroom teachers, administrators, peers, and parents contribute to the mainstreaming effort, each generates information that allows one to form judgments as to the success or failure of the integration of the visually handicapped child into the regular classroom.

Perhaps the greatest source of information is the regular classroom teacher who interacts with the visually handicapped child on a daily basis and is therefore in a position to provide evidence as to academic, social, and emotional adjustment. The classroom teacher may provide data indicating whether or not the visually handicapped child is completing assignments that meet acceptable proficiency standards, meeting performance criteria on informal tests in the basic skills, developing appropriate social behaviors such as initiating contacts with peers, developing a positive self-concept through the use of attitude scales, and participating in class discussions either by responding to questions posed or volunteering relevant comments.

The classroom teacher is also in a position to provide information concerning the adjustment of the nonhandicapped classmates. Observational data may be obtained showing the degree to which social interactions are extended to the visually handicapped child. The degree to which sighted peers cooperate with the mainstreamed child in physical education and recreational activities also provides subjective and objective data on the social and emotional climate of the educational setting. A concern held by some general educators is that the inclusion of a visually handicapped child in the regular classroom may have a negative effect on the academic achievement of the nonhandicapped class members. The classroom teacher is in a position to resolve this issue by monitoring general pupil progress and making changes if necessary.

Teacher behavior during direct instruction and independent student activities is a major source of information on the success or failure of the mainstreaming effort. Does the classroom teacher afford the visually handicapped child the opportunity to respond during instructional sessions? If so, how often? To what extent is the visually handicapped child given verbal praise and reinforcement for oral and/or written performance? In what manner does the classroom teacher demonstrate a willingness to accommodate the visually handicapped child relative to curricular considerations and the physical arrangement of the classroom? The classroom teachers' behavior reflects their commitment to the mainstream of a visually handicapped child.

The school administrator's performance may also be a helpful source of information for determining the degree of administrative support for mainstreaming the visually handicapped. How has the building principal exercised leadership in bringing about inservice education for regular classroom teachers and promoting understanding of the visually handicapped to the parents of nonhandicapped children? In what manner has the school administrator attended to the space, instructional materials, and equipment needs of the vision and regular classroom teacher? Does an analysis of the class attendance record of the visually handicapped child indicate an attendance rate equal to those of sighted classmates? Each of these questions generates information on the degree of support of administrative personnel to the mainstreaming effort.

The vision teacher and parents of the visually handicapped are also valuable sources of information. The vision teacher, in cooperation with the classroom teacher, can assist in monitoring pupil achievement through criterion-referenced and normative (standardized tests) testing. The vision teacher, responsible for the beginning skills acquisition, must ascertain if he/she has been effective in teaching basic survival skills which will allow a visually handicapped child to profit from classroom instruction. Parents of the visually handicapped may provide useful information about the child's perception of educational progress in the academic, social, and emotional realms.

Each of the preceding sources of information may provide data on the success or failure of the mainstreaming effort. Ultimately, the criteria for success must be based on whether or not the visually handicapped child is making adequate progress commensurate with his/her sighted classmates. Where adequate progress is documented, the intervention efforts may be considered successful. Where performance is less than desirable, an analysis of each variable contributing to the mainstreaming effort will reveal areas in need of modification and suggest where appropriate changes should be made.

Problems may be encountered in the mainstreaming of the visually handicapped child. However, the problems may be resolved through the collective efforts of all concerned. Being patient with the educational process is no more or less a consideration for visually handicapped students than it is for their sighted classmates.

EDUCATION OF BLIND CHILDREN: CURRICULAR MODIFICATIONS AND SPECIALIZED EQUIPMENT

School Readiness

Visually handicapped preschoolers, just like their sighted peers, need opportunities and experiences that will enable them to reach developmental potential. Lowenfeld (1973) lists these needs as: 1) first-hand or concrete experiences with people, objects, and situations, 2) unifying experiences whereby piecemeal sensory clues are organized and integrated into meaningful wholes, and 3) opportunities for learning by doing. Early sensory stimulation at home is vital. All infants require fondling and a consistent show of affection. Their world should be filled with meaningful sounds. They need an enriched environment where they are challenged sensorially, intellectually, and emotionally. Parents should work closely with preschool specialists so that the environment can be structured to meet these needs. Such an intensive early program will pay educational dividends in the future.

Prior to, and usually contingent upon, school entrance, visually handicapped children must become proficient in daily living skills. Feeding, grooming, and toilet training can be learned without too many anxious moments if parents give ample opportunity for imitation, exploration, and practice. Verbal explanations should be used at every available opportunity. A meaningful reward system is a necessity for a skill learned well. Care must be taken to ensure that the child is *ready* to perform a task. When teaching, it is advisable to do the task with the child (coactively). This is especially true at the outset of instruction.

Visually handicapped children need to know as early as possible that appropriate dressing and grooming are skills highly valued in society. With sufficient practice and repetition these children can master activities of daily living when their peers do.

All individuals, handicapped or not, must learn to live in a world of people. Socialization skills begin at birth with maternal contact. Absence of eye contact, physical contact, and negative reactions by the family to the inactivity of the newborn often occur. This produces a vicious cycle whereby the visually handicapped infant becomes the recipient of increasing social isolation (Scholl, 1973). Physical closeness and recognition of familiar sounds can help develop the social function of selective smiling, which is often delayed.

The visually limited child is more likely to be separated from his/her mother. This may be due to the nature of his/her eye condition or the lack of sensory input due to the visual disability itself. Reactions to separation can lead to serious emotional problems on the part of both the parents and the child (Colonna, 1968; Fraiberg, 1972). Parents must have access to professional counseling help, not just at times of crisis, but as a preventive measure when first learning about the child's visual disability.

As the child grows, the influence of siblings, peers, and teachers takes on an increasingly important role. Many of these individuals become role models and set standards of acceptable social behavior. Scholl (1973) has pointed out that the visually handicapped child must be accepted first within the family unit. Only then can the child gain acceptance within the adolescent peer group. Parental overprotection, which is all too common, must be reduced to the point where the child can proceed with self-initiated social contact. Social growth for the visually handicapped child requires experiences with individuals unlike himself/herself.

Listening, Reading, and Writing

Hearing plays a major role in both speech and reading development. Listening involves more than simply hearing; it encompasses auditory attending and gives meaning to spoken language. For the visually handicapped child, developing listening skills is critical and should serve as a primary focus in early educational training. It has been estimated that two-thirds of class time is spent by students listening to their teacher (Hanninen, 1975). It is most important that visually limited children have their hearing evaluated at least annually.

Differences in reading rates via listening, touch, and sight become more pronounced by the time a child reaches high school. At this time, touch readers (using a raised dot system known as braille) read about 70 words per minute and listeners to tape-recorded material average about 175 words per minute, while sighted students read print at about 250 words per minute (Hanninen, 1975).

Listening skills are affected by many factors such as reader interest and motivation, the type of material (literary versus scientific materials), familiarity with material, attention level, vocal quality of the speaker, environmental noise, and quality of sound reproduction. Studies that have compared comprehension ability via listening and braille tended to show no differences. However, listening required one-third of the time that braille did (Morris, 1966; Nolan, 1963).

Attempts have been made to accelerate the spoken message, without decreasing the quality of speech or listening comprehension. Foulke (1962a) showed that when a random time sampling procedure was used where tiny message segments were clipped, presentation rate was increased without distortion. This method, called speech compression, increased the presentation rate by 50 percent. Comprehension was maintained through 275 words per minute. Despite its advantages, speech compression has not been as widely used as was initially anticipated.

Another way of presenting recorded material is through the use of talking book machines and discs. This device is a modified phonograph that plays talking book records or discs which have been recorded at slower speeds to store more information. Machines and discs are available free on extended loan through the Library of Congress and the regional library programs.

Touch reading via braille involves a system of raised dots in a six position cell, with two columns of three dots each (see Figure 3). Devised by Louis Braille, and not significantly changed since its creation (despite heated debate), 63 dot combinations represent letters, partwords, whole words, and punctuation symbols. Currently, Braille Grade 2 (using space-saving contractions) is taught to blind children, rather than Braille Grade 1 (each word spelled out fully). The braille code has a literary form, mathematical system (Nemeth Code), and musical notation system.

Braille is written with a slate and stylus (see Figure 4), or more commonly, with a braillewriter (see Figure 5). Braille does have a number of

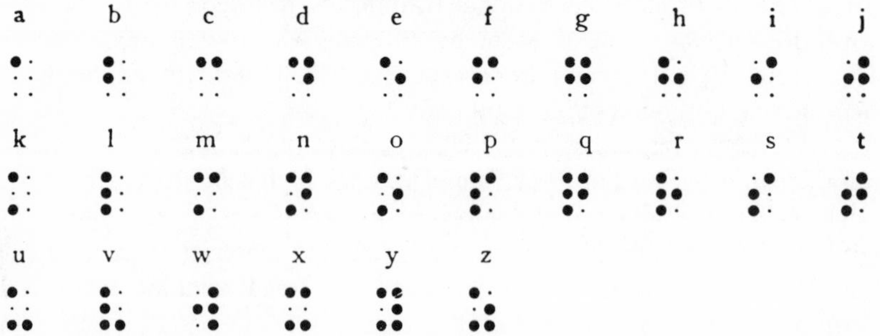

Figure 3.   Standard English braille alphabet.

Figure 4.   Braille slates and styli. (Courtesy of the American Printing House for the Blind.)

Figure 5.   Perkins braillewriter. (Courtesy of the American Printing House for the Blind.)

limitations, namely, slower reading speed, bulkiness, multiple meanings for a single dot configuration, high cost, and occasional lack of availability. However, it still remains a time-tested, useful communication tool for some blind individuals. Determining braille reading readiness is an important concern for teachers, and the Roughness Discrimination Test (Nolan and Morris, 1965) may be used for this purpose.

A newer tactile reading device is the Optacon (see Figure 6). Developed by Telesensory Systems, Inc., it consists of a miniature camera that captures the image of the printed word. An ensuing electrical signal is converted to mechanical movement by a series of vibrating rods. These rods create a tactual sensation on the finger that closely resembles its print analog. While reading rates with the Optacon are generally slower, it nevertheless affords the blind person a degree of privacy and independence (e.g., reading mail, job vacancies) less attainable previously.

For many partially sighted and legally blind children, the printed word is the reading mode of choice (see Figure 7). Some students use large type books, which are most commonly produced in 18 points (a

Figure 6.   Child using the Optacon. (Courtesy of Telesensory Systems Inc.)

8 Point Type

Few parents realize that during the progress of these diseases the eyes of
the patient may develop serious ulcers or other dangerous conditions,which,
unless skilfully treated, may leave a white film over the "sight" of the eye

10 Point Type

Few parents realize that during the progress of these diseases the eyes of the patient may develop serious ulcers or
other dangerous conditions, which, unless skilfully treated,

12 Point Type

Few parents realize that during the progress of these
diseases the eyes of the patient may develop serious
ulcers or other dangerous conditions, which, unless

14 Point Type

Few parents realize that during the progress of these diseases the eyes of the patient

18 Point Type

Few parents realize that during
the progress of these diseases the

24 Point Type

Few parents realize that
during the progress of these

30 Point Type

Few parents realize
that during the prog-

Figure 7.   Examples of regular and large type set in Caslon Boldface type.

designation of type size). This print size is also routinely used in the reading books of the first three elementary school grades. Large type is very costly and many texts are unavailable in this size. This magnified print can be used as another useful reading tool, and it should be remembered that there are many different "types of type." For example, serif type tends to be easier to read than sans-serif type of the same size (Nolan, 1959).

Regular print books are produced in 10 point type. As greater reading demands are placed on children, books are printed in this size for economical and space-saving reasons. With proper lighting and optical aids, many visually impaired children can read regular print. This approach should be tried before adopting large print selections. In the future, print material may be automatically read by computer controlled reading machines. With this device, print material is converted to a verbal message using synthesized speech. Its implications for the blind are most exciting.

The largest publisher of textbooks in print and braille is the American Printing House for the Blind (APH). Each year the United States Congress allocates funds to APH for this purpose. Each school district annually determines the number of legally blind children and youth on their roles and sends this list to APH. An expenditure of funds for educational materials is calculated for each child by dividing the total allocation by the number of legally blind children registered. Educational materials can then be ordered on a quota system account.

Mathematics

Mathematical symbols and formats can be transcribed into braille using the Nemeth Code of Braille Mathematics and Scientific Notation. Formatting can be done with a braillewriter or slate and stylus. Until relatively recently, mental arithmetic served as the most common method of calculation, but this proved to be difficult as problems became more complex. The Cranmer Abacus (see Figure 8), a modification of the Japanese Abacus, has helped alleviate this problem. Lightweight, portable, inexpensive, and easy to use, the abacus has given blind individuals greater accessibility to the world of mathematics. The abacus may be purchased in a larger version for those with motor problems and/or so that younger children can move the beads in each column with greater ease. The manipulation of the beads requires fine motor control, and mathematical readiness testing should include this developmental area. Calculator frames with braille symbols, such as the Cubarithm and Taylor Slate, are less commonly used now.

Figure 8.   The Cramer abacus. (Courtesy of the American Printing House for the Blind.)

An electronic device, the Speech Plus Calculator (see Figure 9), will undoubtedly open even greater vistas in this field. Manufactured by Telesensory Systems, Inc., it can be manipulated easily with one hand. It not only gives a verbal readout via synthesized speech, but can perform several complex mathematical functions. In a short time its popularity has grown greatly; it can be purchased from the American Printing House (APH) on quota accounts.

Mathematical tools in print and braille, as well as measuring instruments and tactual models, can be purchased from APH and the American Foundation for the Blind (AFB). APH publishes a Tangible Aids Catalog and AFB publishes an Aids and Appliances Catalog.

Orientation and Mobility

Earlier it was stated that the inability to get about was one of the major restrictions imposed by blindness. Many feel that free movement is an absolutely necessary prerequisite for the development of social, cognitive, and communication skills. To some, movement may be the basis of learning (Kephart, 1971; Van Dijk, 1968). Orientation refers to the ability to localize oneself in relationship to the environment, whereas mobility refers to movement from one position to another.

Establishment of proper mobility skills should occur long before school entrance. Prerequisite abilities include: good listening skills, especially sound localization; tactual discrimination skills; proper body image and body control (coordination); kinesthetic skills; and utilization of all other senses (Suterko, 1973). Motivation is another crucial factor, as

Figure 9.   Student using the talking calculator. (Courtesy of Telesensory Systems, Inc.)

visually handicapped individuals must appreciate early that mobility skills will give them a level of independence that will help them realize their educational and vocational potential.

Numerous techniques exist for facilitating movement by a blind individual. These are: 1) use of a sighted person (sighted guide), 2) dog guide, 3) use of the long or Hoover Cane, and 4) electronic devices, such as the Laser Cane and Kay Device.

While orientation and mobility training began with adults, especially war blinded adults, increasing interest has focused on its importance with children. It is not an end in itself but a vehicle for the achievement of competence and independence. As such, it should assume an important role in the curriculum of blind children.

Closely related to this topic is the phenomenon of object or obstacle perception. This refers to the ability to perceive objects without the aid of sight. After much study, it was determined that this skill was based on the perception of auditory clues (changes in pitch) from the environment (Cotzin & Dallenbach, 1950; Supa, Cotzin, & Dallenbach, 1944). With practice, it can be developed by both sighted and blind individuals.

Physical Education, Recreation, and Leisure Activities

Sometimes, visually handicapped children are denied access to physical education programs because of the mistaken belief that they are less capable of handling the rigors of these activities. Actually, these children need such a program *more* than their sighted peers! Physical education is essential not only for physical health and stamina, but as a success factor in academic pursuits. It is almost axiomatic that good mental health begins with good physical health. Recreation programs can provide skills for helping manage leisure time, which has increased significantly in modern society.

Resource room teachers of mainstreamed children should try to coordinate programs with physical education teachers and regular classroom teachers (Napier, 1973). During and afterschool recreation programs may include dancing, track and field events, crafts, swimming, music, and skating, to name a few. Most, if not all, should include sighted children. Encouraging the development of hobbies and special interests will also help children use their leisure time more effectively. Changing negative attitudes of the public toward the visually handicapped is more likely to occur as a result of competency than by any other single factor. Skills in physical education, recreation, and management of leisure time should assume a high priority in any program.

Low Vision Aids

For some visually handicapped children, low vision aids have significant educational and vocational implications. Teachers must carefully consider a number of factors, such as reading speed, fatigue, closeness to reading material, motivation, and cosmetic appearance, before recommending the use of a low vision aid. Low vision aids generally magnify the image, thus reducing the dependency on large print materials (Harley and Lawrence, 1977). Certain eye conditions, however, such as those where central visual acuity is impaired, do not respond as well to magnification.

Common low vision aids are (Faye, 1970; Harley and Lawrence, 1977):

1. Eyeglasses (with and without modifications): Jeweler's loupes and bifocals are helpful for near vision, and telescopic spectacles improve distance acuity. Eyeglasses and loupes do not reduce visual fields as much as the other aids and the cost is relatively low. Bifocals may not be tolerated well, and will require close supervision for possible adjustment problems. Like all convex lenses, the greater the strength, the greater the magnification, and the more constricted the field of vision.

2. Hand held magnifiers: Advantages include portability, low cost, and adjustability of reading distances, but field of view is decreased.

3. Closed circuit television (CCTV): Material is magnified and shown on a TV screen (e.g., Visualtek, Apollo Laser). Good contrast, brightness, and high levels of magnification can be achieved. Success will require training, and the cost is high.

4. Projection magnification (e.g., Optiscope): Image is projected on a screen. Limited magnification and poor contrast have been noted.

5. Telescopes: Hand held or mounted in spectacles (see 1 above). Available in monocular and binocular types. Permits compensation for distance viewing. Again, higher magnification constricts field of view significantly.

Low vision aids by themselves will not suddenly produce significant gains in educational achievement. This requires an adjustment period, practice, and proper maintenance of equipment. Cosmetic factors, especially during adolescence, must be carefully considered. Where peer pressures are high, any "different appearance" may have many social and emotional implications. Successful use of these devices depends greatly on a well coordinated program involving the eye specialist, parents, teacher(s), and student.

Sources of educational materials, library services, low vision aids, and educational research are listed below (see Table 4). For a more detailed listing of services and agencies, see American Foundation for the Blind (1978).

CURRENT AND FUTURE ISSUES AFFECTING VISUALLY LIMITED CHILDREN

Prevocational and Vocational Needs

The unemployment rate among the visually handicapped is rather high (Scholl, Bauman, & Crissey, 1969), and this rate tends to increase during

Table 4.   Available resources and agencies serving the visually handicapped

Service provided	Agency
Educational materials	American Printing House for the Blind (APH) Howe Press (HP) Recordings for the Blind (RB) Science for the Blind (SB)
Library services (Braille, talking book machines and discs, tape recordings, and periodicals)	Library of Congress and the regional libraries for the blind and physically handicapped
Nation-wide agencies	American Association of Workers for the Blind (AAWB) American Foundation for the Blind (AFB)
Education	APH
Rehabilitation	Association for the Education of the Visually Handicapped (AEVH)
Research	National Society for the Prevention of Blindness (NSPB) Hadley School for the Blind (HSB)
Periodicals—Braille	APH Colvernook Printing House for the Blind (CPH) National Braille Press (NBP)
Periodicals—Tape recordings	SB; HSB
Periodicals—Talking book machines	APH; AFB; NBP
Large type	APH; NBP; National Aid to the Visually Handicapped, Inc.; Stanwix House; also check other major publishing houses. Large type typewriters are available from IBM, Smith-Corona, and other major producers.
Reading aids	AFB; APH; SB

periods of economic stress. As with minority groups in general, the visually handicapped are often the victims of job discrimination. To combat this successfully, a comprehensive and realistic vocational program needs to be formulated.

An effective program requires close cooperation among the student, his/her parents, and the school or rehabilitation counselor. The cornerstone of such an approach should stress independence, self-reliance, and achievement motivation. Prerequisites for success include: good orientation and mobility skills, opportunities for diversified, community-based training (part time employment and/or work-study jobs, social service agency training programs), and a vocational counselor who is knowledgeable about the current job market and its implications for the visually handicapped.

Training should begin early in mastering job skills and preparing for the world of work. Just as with all job seekers, an appropriate vocational assessment is needed for an appropriate selection of careers. Individuals need to develop physical and mental stamina, an understanding of meeting deadlines and time requirements, an ability to manage their finances, and facility with organization of their leisure time. Current federal legislation has played a major role in helping handicapped individuals find opportunities in the competitive marketplace. It should be noted, however, that not all the visually handicapped will have sufficient skills for competitive employment, and may require job placement in sheltered settings. Whatever the option, teachers should play a major role in the preparation process.

Sex Education

Human sexuality and sex education are topics that unfortunately receive less than adequate attention in many homes and schools. Sex role learning is heavily dependent on vision and visual imitation. It is not surprising then to see how problems could arise in a person with partial or total loss of vision (especially if congenital). Overprotective parents and limited opportunities for peer interaction can intensify this problem (Scholl, 1973).

The need for sexual expression does not differ greatly whether a person is handicapped or not. The needs to give and receive affection, to be close to someone else, and to be comforted are shared by everyone (Trippe, 1975). The blind individual learns early that his/her dependence on touch meets with disapproval when learning about sex in this way. Limited access to graphic materials also blocks another avenue of learning. Finally, reliance on replicas of human anatomy generally provide limited tactual value.

Teachers and parents should work toward enabling visually limited children to have opportunities for understanding human sexuality through self-awareness. This translates to a broader interpretation of sex as something we are rather than something we do (Spungin, 1975). From birth, the visually handicapped infant needs to feel secure, loved, and encouraged to show affection. He/she must adopt a more activist posture for social interaction. Trippe (1975) has proposed that sexual behavior be based on self-respect, respect for others, a knowledge of socially appropriate behavior, and open dialogue with others. As such, this expanded view of sex education requires greater attention from teachers and parents.

Rapidly Changing Subgroups

Within the past decade, some of the leading causes of blindness have changed, as have medical and educational philosophies of intervention. This has resulted in a change in the characteristics of groups of visually handicapped children that teachers are called upon to serve. Rather than the child with retrolental fibroplasia so commonly seen in the mid 1950s and early 1960s, different etiologies have emerged.

Services are required for many more multihandicapped blind children than ever before. Special education legislation, medical advances, and a more positive educational outlook has made this so. The visually handicapped child with additional disabilities represents a rapidly increasing percentage of the overall population. Due to a number of educational options available, these youngsters are being served in both residential and day school programs. The deaf-blind have been the focus of increased interest and support, especially since the outbreak of the rubella epidemic in 1963–1965.

The second group being found in increasing numbers involves those with residual vision, the so-called "low vision" individual. The preponderance of visually handicapped children being educated today have some degree of residual vision. Teachers need to have a strong preparation base in vision stimulation, use of low vision aids, and techniques of vision screening. No artificial system that attempts to compensate for functions subsumed by the eyes can come close to their adaptiveness and effectiveness. It behooves teachers to maximize a child's visual potential.

The third and largest group is composed of those of middle age and older. The most common causes of visual impairment and blindness tend to strike individuals in this age group (e.g., diabetes, cataracts, glaucoma). With people living longer today, this group will continue to have a larger number of blind people than any other.

SUMMARY

The term *visual handicap* includes a wide range of visual abilities, from total absence of sight to high levels of functional vision. The imposition of a visual disability can and often does affect many aspects of human growth and development, but many compensatory avenues are available to parents and teachers. There is no such thing as a "blind personality," nor does blindness per se indicate any specific educational disability.

Visually handicapped children are *children first* and can be best understood by looking at their similarities to *all* children. As members of a minority group, they are subject to many of the same stereotypes and discriminatory policies. The goal for teachers of visually handicapped children is to provide the skills necessary for competence and self-fulfillment within the least restrictive environment. Many alternative delivery systems exist for this purpose, and individual needs will dictate the appropriate selection of educational strategies.

REFERENCES

Abrahamson, I. *Know your eyes: An introductory text for medical personnel.* New York: R. E. Krieger Publishing Co., 1977.

Adelson, E., & Fraiberg, S. Gross motor development in infants blind from birth. *Child Development*, 1974, *45*, 114–126.

American Foundation for the Blind. *Directory of agencies serving the visually handicapped in the United States* (20th ed.). New York: AFB, 1978.

Apple, M. Kinesic training for blind persons: A vital means of communication. *New Outlook for the Blind*, 1972, *66*, 201–208.

Barker, J., & Barmatz, H. Eye function. In W. Frankenburg & B. Camp (Eds.), *Pediatric screening tests*. Springfield, Ill.: Charles C Thomas, 1975.

Barraga, N. *Increased visual behavior in low vision children.* New York: American Foundation for the Blind, 1964.

Bateman, B. Sighted children's perceptions of blind children's abilities. *Exceptional Children*, 1962, *29*, 42–46.

Bateman, B. *Reading and psycholinguistic processes of partially seeing children.* Washington, D.C.: Council for Exceptional Children, 1963.

Bateman, B. Psychological evaluation of blind children. *New Outlook for the Blind*, 1965, *59*, 193–196.

Bauman, M. Adjustment to blindness. *International Journal for the Education of the Blind*, 1964, *13*, 101–106.

Beery, K. *Models for mainstreaming.* San Rafael, Cal.: Dimensions Publishing Co., 1972.

Bower, T. The visual world of infants. *Scientific American*, 1966, 80–92.

Boyce, V. The home eye test program. *Sight-Saving Review*, 1973, *43*, 43–48.

Brieland, D. A comparative study of the speech of blind and sighted children. *Speech Monographs*, 1950, *17*, 99–103.

Burlingham, D. Some notes on the development of the blind. *Psychoanalytic Study of the Child*, 1961, *16*, 121–145.

Caetano, A., & Kaufman, J. Reduction of rocking mannerisms in two blind children. *Education of the Visually Handicapped*, 1975, 7, 101–105.

Colonna, A. A blind child goes to the hospital. *Psychoanalytic Study of the Child*, 1968, *23*, 391–422.

Cotzin, M., & Dallenbach, K. "Facial vision": The role of pitch and loudness in the perception of obstacles by the blind. *American Journal of Psychology*, 1950, *63*, 485–515.

Coveny, T. Standardized tests for visually handicapped children: A review of research. *New Outlook for the Blind*, 1976, *70*, 232–236.

Cowen, E., Underberg, R., Verillo, R., & Benham, F. *Adjustment to visual disability in adolescence.* New York: American Foundation for the Blind, 1961.

Cratty, B., Peterson, C., Harris, J., & Shoner, R. The development of perceptual motor abilities in blind children and adolescents. *New Outlook for the Blind*, 1968, *62*, 111–117.

Cutsforth, T. The unreality of words to the blind. *Teachers Forum*, 1932, *4*, 86–89.

Cutsforth, T. *The blind in school and society*. New York: American Foundation for the Blind, 1951.

DeMott, R. Verbalism and affective meaning for blind, severely visually impaired, and normally sighted children. *New Outlook for the Blind*, 1972, *66*, 1–8.

Dillman, C., & Maloney, F. *Mainstreaming the handicapped in vocational education*. Palo Alto, Cal.: American Institutes for Research, 1977.

Dokecki, P. Verbalism and the blind: A critical review of the concept and the literature. *Exceptional Children*, 1966, *32*, 525–530.

Dunn, L. Special education for the mildly retarded—is much of it justifiable? *Exceptional Children*, 1968, *35*, 5–22.

Faye, E. *The low vision patient*. New York: Grune and Stratton, 1970.

Foulke, E. The comprehension of rapid speech by the blind. *Exceptional Children*, 1962, *29*, 134–141. (a)

Foulke, E. The role of experience in the formation of concept. *International Journal for the Education of the Blind*, 1962, *12*, 1–6. (b)

Fraiberg, S. Parallel and divergent patterns in blind and sighted infants. *Psychoanalytic Study of the Child*, 1968, *23*, 264–300.

Fraiberg, S. Separation crisis in two blind children. *Psychoanalytic Study of the Child*, 1972, *26*, 355–371.

Goldman, H. Psychological testing of blind children. *Research Bulletin*, American Foundation for the Blind, 1970, *21*, 77–90.

Gowman, A. *The war blind in American social structure*. New York: American Foundation for the Blind, 1957.

Hanninen, K. *Teaching the visually handicapped*. Columbus, Oh.: Charles E. Merrill Publishing Co., 1975.

Harley, R., & Lawrence, G. *Visual impairment in the schools*. Springfield, Ill.: Charles C Thomas, 1977.

Hatfield, E. Blindness in infants and young children. *Sight-Saving Review*, 1972, *42*,(2), 69–89.

Hatfield, E. Why are they blind? *Sight-Saving Review*, 1975, *45*,(1), 3–22.

Hatwell, Y. *Privation sensiorielle et intelligence*. Paris: Presses Universitaires de France, 1966.

Hayes, S. *Contributions to a psychology of blindness*. New York: American Foundation for the Blind, 1941.

Hewett, F., & Forness, S. *Education of exceptional learners* (2nd ed.). Boston: Allyn and Bacon, 1977.

Hulsey, S. Liberating the blind student. *American Education*, 1973, *9*, 18–22.

Imamura, S. *Mother and blind child*. Research Series, no. 14, American Foundation for the Blind, 1965.

Jervis, F. A comparison of self-concepts of blind and sighted children. In C. Davis (Ed.), *Guidance programs for blind children*. Watertown, Mass.: Perkins Institute for the Blind, 1959.

Jones, J. *Blind children, degree of vision, mode of reading*. Bulletin 24. Washington, D.C.: U.S. Office of Education, 1961.

Jones, J., & Collins, K. *Educational programs for visually handicapped children.* Washington, D.C.: U.S. Government Printing Office, 1966.

Juurmaa, J. Transposition in mental space manipulation: A theoretical analysis. *Research Bulletin,* American Foundation for the Blind, 1973, *26,* 87-134.

Keilbaugh, W. Attitudes of classroom teachers toward their visually handicapped students. *Journal of Visual Impairment and Blindness,* 1977, *71,* 430-434.

Kephart, N. *The slow learner in the classroom* (2nd ed.). Columbus, Oh.: Charles E. Merrill, 1971.

Kirk, S. *Educating exceptional children.* Boston: Houghton Mifflin, Co., 1972.

Knight, J. Mannerisms in the congenitally blind child. *New Outlook for the Blind,* 1972, *66,* 297-302.

Livingston, J. Evaluation of enlarged test form used with the partially seeing. *Sight-Saving Review,* 1958, 37-39.

Lowenfeld, B. Psychological foundation of special methods in teaching blind children. In P. Zahl (Ed.), *Blindness.* Princeton, N.J.: Princeton University Press, 1950.

Lowenfeld, B. Psychological problems of children with impaired vision. In W. Cruickshank (Ed.), *Psychology of exceptional children and youth* (3rd ed.). Englewood Cliffs, N.J., 1971.

Lowenfeld, B. Psychological considerations. In B. Lowenfeld (Ed.), *The visually handicapped child in school.* New York: John Day Co., 1973.

Lowenfeld, B., Abel, G., & Hatlen, P. *Blind children learn to read.* Springfield, Illinois: Charles C Thomas, 1969.

Lukoff, I., & Whiteman, M. Attitudes toward blindness—some preliminary findings. *New Outlook for the Blind,* 1961, *55,* 39-44.

McNair, D., and Smith, B. *Seeing the i.e.p. through the eye of a parent.* Eugene, Ore.: Center on Human Development, University of Oregon, 1977.

Martin, G., and Hoben, M. *Supporting visually impaired students in the mainstream.* Reston, Va.: Council for Exceptional Children, 1977.

Merry, R. Adapting the Seashore Talent Tests for use with blind pupils. *The Teachers Forum,* 1931, *30,* 15-19.

Miller, B., & Miller, W. Extinguishing "blindisms": A paradigm for intervention. *Education of the Visually Handicapped,* 1976, *8,* 6-15.

Morris, J. Relative efficiency of reading and listening for braille and large type readers. Washington, D.C.: *48th Biennial Conference Report,* American Association of Instructors of the Blind, 1966, 65-70.

Napier, G. Special subject adjustments and skills. In B. Lowenfeld (Ed.), *The visually handicapped child in school.* New York: John Day Co., 1973.

National Society for the Prevention of Blindness. *N.S.P.B. fact book: Estimated statistics on blindness and visual problems.* New York: NSPB Inc., 1966.

National Society for the Prevention of Blindness. *Visual screening in schools.* Publication No. 257. New York: NSPB Inc., 1969.

National Society for the Prevention of Blindness. *Teaching about vision.* New York: NSPB, Inc., 1972.

Nolan, C. Readability of large types: A study of type size and type styles. *International Journal for the Education of the Blind,* 1959, *9,* 41-44.

Nolan, C. On the unreality of words to the blind. *New Outlook for the Blind,* 1960, *54,* 100-102.

Nolan, C. Reading and listening in learning by the blind. *Exceptional Children,* 1963, *29,* 313-316.

Nolan, C. Blind children: Degree of vision, mode of reading: A 1963 replication. *New Outlook for the Blind*, 1965, *59*, 233-238.

Nolan, C., & Morris, J. Development and validation of the roughness discrimination test. *International Journal for the Education of the Blind*, 1965, *15*, 1-6.

Norris, M., Spaulding, P., & Brodie, F. *Blindness in children*. Chicago: University of Chicago Press, 1957.

O'Brien, R. The integrated resource room for the visually handicapped. *New Outlook for the Blind*, 1973, *67*, 363-368.

Orlansky, M. *Mainstreaming the visually impaired child*. Austin, Tex.: Learning Concepts, 1977.

Parks, A., & Rousseau, M. *The public law supporting mainstreaming*. Austin, Tex.: Learning Concepts, 1977.

Patz, A., & Hoover, R. *Protection of vision in children*. Springfield, Ill., Charles C Thomas, 1969.

Peterson, R., & Bass, K. *Mainstreaming: A working bibliography* (3rd ed.). Minneapolis: University of Minnesota, 1977.

Petrucci, D. The blind child and his adjustment. *New Outlook for the Blind*, 1953, *47*, 240-246.

Pintner, R., & Forlano, G. Personality tests of partially sighted children. *Journal of Applied Psychology*, 1943, *27*, 283-287.

Pitman, D. The musical ability of blind children. *Research Bulletin* American Foundation for the Blind, 1965, *11*, 63-79.

Reynolds, M., & Birch, J. *Teaching exceptional children in all America's schools*. Reston, Va.: Council for Exceptional Children, 1977.

Scheffers, W. Sighted children learn about blindness. *Journal of Visual Impairment and Blindness*, 1977, *77*, 258-261.

Scholl, G. *The principal works with the visually impaired*. Washington, D.C.: Council for Exceptional Children, 1968.

Scholl, G. Understanding and meeting developmental needs. In B. Lowenfeld (Ed.), *The visually handicapped child in school*. New York: John Day Co., 1973.

Scholl, G., Bauman, M., & Crissey, M. *A study of the vocational success of groups of the visually handicapped: Final report*. Ann Arbor, Mich.: University of Michigan, 1969.

Scott, E., Jan, J., & Freeman, R. *Can't your child see?* Baltimore: University Park Press, 1977.

Scott, R. The socialization of blind children. In D. Goslin (Ed.), *Handbook of socialization theory and research*. Chicago: Rand McNally, 1969.

Sommers, V. *The influence of parental attitudes and social environment on the personality development of the adolescent blind*. New York: American Foundation for the Blind, 1944.

Spungin, S. Sex education for the visually handicapped. In E. Foulke (Ed.), *Sex education for the visually impaired*. Reston, Va.: Council for Exceptional Children, 1975.

Steinzor, L. School peers of visually handicapped children. *New Outlook for the Blind*, 1966, *60*, 312-314.

Stephens, B. Cognitive processes in the visually impaired. *Education of the Visually Handicapped*, 1972, *4*, 106-111.

Supa, M., Cotzin, M., & Dallenbach, K. "Facial vision": The perception of obstacles by the blind. *American Journal of Psychology*, 1944, *57*, 133-183.

Suterko, S. Life adjustment. In B. Lowenfeld (Ed.), *The Visually Handicapped Child in School.* New York: John Day Co., 1973.

Sykes, K. A comparison of the effectiveness of standard print and large print in facilitating the reading skills of visually impaired students. *Education of the Visually Handicapped,* 1973, *3,* 97–106.

Tait, P. The implications of play as it relates to the emotional development of the blind child. *Education of the Visually Handicapped,* 1972, *4,* 52–54.

Tillman, M. The performance of blind and sighted children on the Wechsler inteligence scale for children. *International Journal for the Education of the Blind,* 1967, pp. 65–74; 106–112.

Tillman, M., & Williams, C. Associative characteristics of blind and sighted children to selected form classes. *International Journal for the Education of the Blind,* 1968, *18,* 23–40.

Trippe, M. Sexuality and disability. In E. Foulke (Ed.), *Sex education for the visually impaired.* Reston, Va.: Council for Exceptional Children, 1975.

Van Dijk, J. *Movement and communication with rubella children.* Presentation at the National Association for Deaf/Blind and Rubella Children, May, 1968.

Warren, D. *Blindness and early childhood development.* New York: American Foundation for the Blind, 1977.

Whitelaw, N. Mainstreaming a blind child—one classroom teacher's experience. *Journal of Visual Impairment and Blindness,* 1978, *72,* 153–154.

6
ENVIRONMENTAL ALTERNATIVES FOR THE HEARING HANDICAPPED

Bryan Clarke and Perry Leslie

Hearing impaired children have varying degrees of difficulty acquiring a language naturally and automatically. Any inability to utilize their potential communicative abilities to the maximum will stand as a barrier between them and the full realization of their academic, social, and cognitive potentials. The more impoverished their language and resultant lack of communication skills, the more their academic, social, vocational, and behavioral development is restricted. The educational process that provides hearing impaired children with the opportunity to acquire language is difficult and laborious, but has from the beginning attracted many gifted and dedicated teachers.

Education of the hearing impaired is the oldest and most controversial area of special education. Almost from the time of the first teacher of the deaf—Pedro Ponce de Leon (1520–1584), a Benedictine monk who tutored deaf children of Spanish nobility—the field has been embroiled in an unremitting controversy over methodology.

Without minimizing the importance of earlier educators of the deaf, two teachers stand out for their contribution to methods of teaching hearing impaired children. The first was Abbé Charles Michel de l'Epée (1712–1789) who formulated the French or manual system of language instruction through the use of fingerspelling and formal signs. The second teacher was Samuel Heinicke (1729–1790), who in the same era developed a method that spurned the use of fingers and hands and used instead speechreading and speech to educate deaf students.

Both men were very much aware of the educational dichotomy that resulted from their methodological stances on communication. The letters they exchanged leave no doubt of the heat generated by this dissidence. Even today in North America there are separate journals and separate organizations to serve professionals and parents depending upon which methodology they espouse. The protagonists in this sustained polemic have generally harbored points of view that are largely if not totally immersed in emotions. This emotional contingency is perhaps the most serious deterrent to progress in education of the deaf. Only when it is realized that there is no one method that meets the needs of all hearing impaired children and their parents will we be able to come to grips with the generic problem of establishing a fail-safe hierarchy of methods that will ensure for each child the opportunity to demonstrate his/her capacities and to develop them without a serious loss of time through extended use of inappropriate strategies.

If this controversy were not enough, there is incontrovertible evidence that our educational efforts have not been very successful. The Babbidge report (1965), produced by a national committee sponsored by the U.S. Department of Health, Education, and Welfare, warned that "the American people have no reason to be satisfied with their limited success in educating deaf children and preparing them for full participation in society." The committee claimed that, except for advances in medical technology and increased sophistication in audiology, psychology, and linguistics, education of the deaf is almost exactly where it was more than 150 years ago when the first public school—the American Asylum for the Deaf—was opened in Hartford, Connecticut.

A further indictment comes from Moores (1978), who sees "an endless stream of children pouring out of programs for the deaf unable to read at the fifth grade level, unable to write a simple sentence, unable to speechread anything but the most common expressions, and unable to speak in a manner understandable to any but the immediate family" (p. 2). The plethora of research evidence confirming this educational circumstance can hardly be controverted.

Difficulties with standard English usage, auditory signal systems, and other obstacles the hearing impaired face in life impose severe constraints on the hearing impaired. However, it is well documented (Schein & Delk, 1974) that as adults they comprise a vital, well adjusted, concerned segment of society, and are highly respected by anyone who makes the necessary and sufficient effort to become an acquaintance or colleague. Although many are underemployed, their rate of unemployment is low and they are productive in the labor force. They are law abiding and have better driving records with respect to both violations and accidents than their hearing peers. There is a very high percentage of intermarriage among the hearing impaired but the a priori expectation on the birth of a child to deaf parents is that its hearing will be normal.

Deaf parents are so successful in raising their hearing children, many of whom have become eminent in a variety of professional fields, that it is most surprising we have not turned to them for assistance in formulating the factors which contribute to successful parenthood.

Attempts by the hearing impaired to acquaint normally hearing persons with deafness and to overcome its negative stereotypes are gradually gaining ground. In the not too distant future equity and justice may prevail for those whom Best (1943) has called "the most misunderstood among the sons of man" (p. 1).

LABELS AND DEFINITIONS

The numerous educational definitions and classifications that deal with hearing impairment testify to the inability of administrators and teachers alike to reach a consensus on terminology. Ambiguity in dialogue, even between professionals, is due to the fact that the same terms are often used to refer both to the auditory deficit and to its effects. A common example arises with the use of the term *hearing loss*. Many professionals still refer to a child as having a hearing loss of say 65–70 dB. This is not correct. It comes about because the ASA standards of 1951 and 1952 required the intensity dial on the audiometer to be labeled '*hearing loss*.' However, the newer revision of standards (ANSI, 1970) recommended the term *hearing threshold level* (HTL) so that *hearing loss* could correctly be reserved for the general condition of hearing impairment or the process that causes it. Further confusions also arise when dealing with children, because the deficits and their effects must often be interpreted predictively in a developmental context.

Hearing impairment means not only loss of auditory sensitivity but also what Davis and Silverman (1978) have called *dysacusis*. Loss of sensitivity is readily measured and covers a continuum from a mild intermittent loss of auditory acuity to an irreversible and almost total, if not complete, loss of hearing. Dysacusis covers other important dimensions of hearing, which may range from malfunction of the sense organ (e.g., poor discrimination for amplified speech) to abnormal function of the brain (e.g., auditory agnosia).

There is no hard and fast distinction between a disability and a handicap, and in the past the term *hearing impaired* has unfortunately been used as a synonym for both of these concepts. The handicap of deafness is the degree to which a person's overall function is limited by the disability or the extent to which a disadvantage renders success more difficult. Whether the disability constitutes a handicap for an individual child and, if so, to what extent, will depend on a variety of factors. The effects of the disability stem primarily from organic correlates which include the physiological impairment (structural deficits or damage), abnormalities in auditory function (sensitivity and dysacusis), and other structural conditions (brain, central nervous system, vision, and so forth), and are evidenced in the behavioral and developmental areas of language acquisition and communication. When the dynamic interaction of sociocultural factors, including value systems, expectations, and prejudices, are added, the final effects are encapsulated in cognition, social development, and academic achievement. Thus the relationship between disability and a handicap is very difficult to disentangle. But what is not hard to conceptualize is that under one set of circumstances a particular child with a hearing impairment may be handicapped, whereas under different conditions the same child may not be as handicapped. When seen in this light, it is clear that the concept of handicap must not be used as an explanation but rather as a means to formulate and to implement procedures to change environmental conditions.

The report of the committee to redefine the terms *deaf* and *hard of hearing* for educational purposes (Frisina, 1975) recommended that the term *deaf* be used only as a modifier and not as a noun and that *deafness* be the preferred term in reference to hearing disability. They also suggested use of the generic term *hearing impaired* to include both *deaf* and *hard of hearing* persons. It is important to bear in mind that neither of these terms is, in any significant measure, indicative of the handicap involved. To describe someone as hearing impaired conveys nothing of the educational help or provision that is required.

The committee's report, which was adopted by the Conference of Executives of American Schools for the Deaf, differentiates between a deaf and a hard of hearing person as follows:

A *deaf* person is one whose hearing disability precludes successful processing of linguistic information through audition, with or without a hearing aid.

A *hard of hearing* person is one who, generally with the use of a hearing aid, has residual hearing sufficient to enable successful processing of linguistic information through audition.

Prelingual deafness is deafness present at birth or occurring early in life at an age prior to the development of speech and language.

Postlingual deafness is deafness occurring at an age following the development of speech and language. (*American Annals of the Deaf*, 1975, *120*, 509–510.)

In addition the committee specified the following hearing threshold levels of classification, based on the average pure tone threshold for 500, 1,000, and 2,000 Hz in the better ear.

Mild, 26–54 dB. Students in this category generally do not require special class placement but usually require special speech and hearing assistance.

Moderate, 55–69 dB. These students occasionally require special class placement and generally require special speech, hearing, and language assistance.

Severe, 70–89 dB. Those in this category generally require special class or special school placement; they usually require speech, hearing, language, and educational assistance.

Profound, 90 dB and above. These students generally require special school placement for speech, hearing, language, and educational assistance. (*American Annals of the Deaf,* 1975, *120,* 511.)

Although the new definitions reflect a greater educational orientation than previously and contain a warning that the classifications are not directly related to hearing sensitivity, the necessary distinction between sensitivity and auditory function is not made. The emphasis on prediction of educational placement from hearing threshold level is not sound. The parameters of any classification system for educational services must be based on needs of individual children. Accepting hearing threshold levels as criteria is as futile as using IQ measures to categorize educable mentally retarded and trainable mentally retarded children.

Within the hard of hearing category, there is not any direct relationship between the handicap in educational terms and the degree of permanence of a disability. A hearing impairment that may be only temporary can, while it lasts, have significant educational implications. An intermittent hearing loss, which becomes more severe at certain times, may for relatively short periods be so handicapping to a child in school that necessary help in the form of special equipment and teaching techniques will be required. Moreover, the implications of a disability vary at different stages of development. An impairment that is temporary and that may be responsive to treatment will affect an older child's comprehension of linguistic information far less seriously than a younger child whose vocabulary, syntax, and skill at processing receptive language are less well developed. With "deaf" children the age at onset is critical, particularly in relation to language development. The greater the child's competency in language skills before the onset of the loss, the greater advantage he/she has.

The danger in using any system that classifies children is in adhering too rigidly to the definitions with too little cognizance of the lack of precision used in identifying and measuring the phenomena that modify their performances. Too often the label *hearing-impaired* is written so large that it obscures the true identity of the child who is forced to wear it. The relationship between hearing sensitivity and the normal spontaneous development of language in a child, with other general relationships, helps determine the emphasis in various educational programs and the appropriate placement of a hearing impaired child within these programs.

Investigations have attempted to clarify the relationship of various factors with hearing impairment, but there is so much variation that it is impossible to draw a single composite picture of the hearing impaired child. Indeed, it is unnecessary. Definitions are delimiting and potentially dangerous. If each hearing impaired child is assessed individually by the best methods available, there should be no need of classification systems for educational purposes; we can save definitions for those occasions when legislation or legal precedents and funding formulas demand their use.

THE AUDITORY SYSTEM

Auditory Mechanism

The hearing mechanism consists of three parts—the outer, middle, and inner ear. In the process of hearing, sound waves arrive at the ear as variations in air pressure. These sound waves travel down the external auditory canal to the tympanic membrane (eardrum), which moves in response to changes in air pressure. The ossicular chain of the malleus, incus, and stapes in the middle ear conducts the vibrations of the eardrum almost completely without distortions but with increased power to the oval window over which lies the footplate of the stapes. The difference in relative surface areas of the larger drum and smaller oval window results in an increase in transmitted pressure at the oval window. This increased power is essential when moving from air—a lighter conducting medium—to the heavier fluid (perilymph) of the inner ear. The Eustachian tube in the middle ear provides drainage as well as equalizing pressure (see Figure 1).

The cochlea (in the inner ear) is the most important organ for hearing. Lying below the vestibular mechanism, this tubular organ is shaped like a snail shell. It contains the parts necessary to convert the mechanical energy of the middle ear into electrical potential in the inner ear. The inside of the spiral cochlea contains a horizontal partition producing two parallel circular spiral staircases (scala vestibuli and scala tympani) which contain perilymph. A third wedgeshaped compartment lying between the two scalae is the cochlear duct, separated from the scala

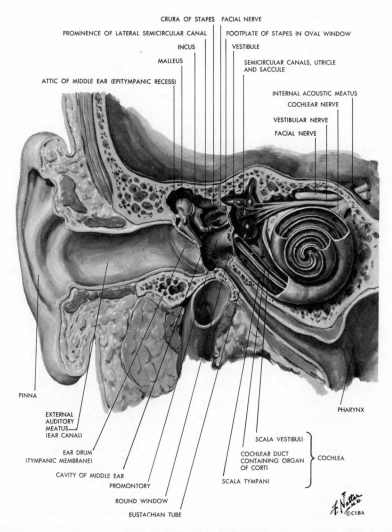

CRURA OF STAPES   FACIAL NERVE

PROMINENCE OF LATERAL SEMICIRCULAR CANAL

FOOTPLATE OF STAPES IN OVAL WINDOW

INCUS

VESTIBULE

MALLEUS

SEMICIRCULAR CANALS, UTRICLE AND SACCULE

ATTIC OF MIDDLE EAR (EPITYMPANIC RECESS)

INTERNAL ACOUSTIC MEATUS

COCHLEAR NERVE

VESTIBULAR NERVE

FACIAL NERVE

PINNA

PHARYNX

EXTERNAL AUDITORY MEATUS (EAR CANAL)

SCALA VESTIBULI

EAR DRUM (TYMPANIC MEMBRANE)

COCHLEAR DUCT CONTAINING ORGAN OF CORTI

COCHLEA

CAVITY OF MIDDLE EAR

PROMONTORY

SCALA TYMPANI

ROUND WINDOW

EUSTACHIAN TUBE

Figure 1.   A cross-section of the ear showing the pathway of sound reception. (Reproduced with permission from *Clinical Symposia*, illustrated by Frank H. Netter, M.D., copyright © 1970 C.I.B.A. Pharmaceutical Co., Division of CIBA-GEIGY Corp. All rights reserved.)

vestibuli by Reissner's membrane, and from the scala tympani by the basilar membrane. This duct is filled with endolymph, and, although separated from the scalae by the closure at the helicotrema, it is connected to the vestibular mechanism (three semicircular canals) responsible for the sense of balance.

When the stapes of the middle ear pushes in the oval window, this sends a wave through the perilymph of the scala vestibuli and into the perilymph of the scala tympani, pushing out the round window. As the wave moves through the scala vestibuli, the vibrations are also transmitted through Reissner's membrane. Low frequency sounds create slow waves in the cochlear fluid which activate nerve fibers farthest from the middle ear. High frequency sounds create rapid waves that activate only those closer to where the middle ear ossicles are connected to the cochlea. In some types of hearing impairment, fibers that normally detect high frequency tones are partly or completely destroyed, while other fibers remain intact. This not uncommon condition results in a high frequency hearing loss (see Figure 3). The movement of Reissner's membrane causes the endolymph fluid in the cochlear duct to flow against the basilar membrane. At this point the vibrations of the basilar membrane and the organ of Corti will cause a shearing movement on the hair cells attached to the tectorial membrane. The energy, which so far has been mechanical, is transformed into electrical (nerve) impulses that stimulate the fibres of the eighth nerve, giving rise to action potentials responsible for nerve transmission to the brain (see Figure 2).

Types of Hearing Loss

The above brief description of the ear and its functions indicates that the ear canal and the middle ear structure serve to conduct sound waves to the cochlea. Hearing impairment due to faults in the components of this system, such as atresia (absence or malformation of normal structure), wax blocking the canal, damage to the drum, or infections, disease, or damage in the middle ear, is termed a conductive loss. Such faults generally are amenable to medical and surgical intervention and the hearing loss is reversible. This does not mean, however, that disorders associated with the outer and middle ear will not at times cause substantive educational problems.

Severe hearing impairments are associated with the inner ear and are called sensori-neural losses. Anatomical abnormalities of the inner ear may be endogenous (genetic) or exogenous (when a prenatal or postnatal environmental factor is claimed as a cause of deafness), as in viral infections (measles, mumps), bacterial infection (encephalitis, meningitis), anoxia, injury, prenatal infection (maternal rubella), side effects of ototoxic antibiotics, or excessive noise.

When both a conductive and a sensori-neural impairment are present, the result is a mixed hearing loss or a sensori-neural loss with a conductive overlay. The conductive element may again be alleviated by medical intervention.

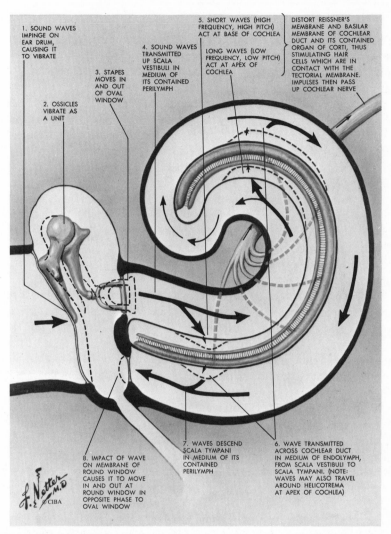

1. SOUND WAVES IMPINGE ON EAR DRUM, CAUSING IT TO VIBRATE

2. OSSICLES VIBRATE AS A UNIT

3. STAPES MOVES IN AND OUT OF OVAL WINDOW

4. SOUND WAVES TRANSMITTED UP SCALA VESTIBULI IN MEDIUM OF ITS CONTAINED PERILYMPH

5. SHORT WAVES (HIGH FREQUENCY, HIGH PITCH) ACT AT BASE OF COCHLEA

LONG WAVES (LOW FREQUENCY, LOW PITCH) ACT AT APEX OF COCHLEA

DISTORT REISSNER'S MEMBRANE AND BASILAR MEMBRANE OF COCHLEAR DUCT AND ITS CONTAINED ORGAN OF CORTI, THUS STIMULATING HAIR CELLS WHICH ARE IN CONTACT WITH THE TECTORIAL MEMBRANE. IMPULSES THEN PASS UP COCHLEAR NERVE

8. IMPACT OF WAVE ON MEMBRANE OF ROUND WINDOW CAUSES IT TO MOVE IN AND OUT AT ROUND WINDOW IN OPPOSITE PHASE TO OVAL WINDOW

7. WAVES DESCEND SCALA TYMPANI IN MEDIUM OF ITS CONTAINED PERILYMPH

6. WAVE TRANSMITTED ACROSS COCHLEAR DUCT IN MEDIUM OF ENDOLYMPH, FROM SCALA VESTIBULI TO SCALA TYMPANI. (NOTE: WAVES MAY ALSO TRAVEL AROUND HELICOTREMA AT APEX OF COCHLEA)

Figure 2. A cross-section of the cochlea. (Reproduced with permission from *Clinical Symposia*, illustrated by Frank H. Netter, M.D., copyright © 1970 C.I.B.A. Pharmaceutical Co., Division of CIBA-GEIGY Corp. All rights reserved.)

MEASUREMENT OF HEARING

Pure Tone Audiometry

To determine whether an impairment is conductive, sensori-neural, or mixed, tests are available to measure the hearing threshold level (HTL), i.e., the level at which a sound is heard at least 50 percent of the time. The most common method is by pure tone audiometry, which is designed to establish responses to air conduction and bone conduction. Pure tone audiometers are designed to produce tones of various frequencies at different intensities. Frequency is measured in Hertz (Hz), i.e., the number of simple harmonic vibrations per second which give rise to the tone. It is the physical measurement of what we call pitch. The normal range of hearing is from about 30 to 30,000 Hz but testing generally encompasses only those frequencies important for speech reception, i.e., 125 to 8,000 Hz. Intensity is measured in decibels (dB). The psychological correlate of intensity is loudness. Zero dB level or audiometric zero is the average threshold of hearing for normal listeners. The normal range is from 0 to about 115 dB, above which are the successive thresholds of discomfort, tickle, and pain. The dB scale is logarithmic and not linear. A sound at 80 dB is not twice as intense as a sound at 40 dB but in fact 10,000 times greater. Average speech levels at a distance of about two meters is approximately 60 dB.

The procedure for testing a subject's sensitivity to pure tones is relatively simple. Typically, the audiologist delivers in a systematic way a variety of tones through earphones to each ear in turn, until it is established at what level of intensity (dB) the subject can detect each of the octave frequencies from 125 to 8,000 Hz. The hearing threshhold level (HTL) at each of these frequencies is marked on the audiogram (see Figure 3).

The average HTL is obtained by adding the losses of acuity in the better ear at 500, 1000, and 2,000 Hz and dividing by three. In Figure 3 the average HTL in the left ear is 50 dB. To determine how much amplification a hearing aid provides, aided thresholds can be obtained by testing while the hearing aid is worn. The audiogram by itself is generally a poor predictor of how well a child will learn through hearing. Children with identical or very similar audiograms frequently have quite different capacities for utilizing their residual hearing.

Testing can be carried out by air conduction or by bone conduction. In air conduction the tones were conveyed by earphones through the air-filled canal and middle ear to the cochlea. In bone conduction sound is transmitted through a vibrator which, when placed on the skull at the midline of the forehead or the mastoid process, conveys these vibrations directly to the cochlea (Hirsh, 1952). If normal responses are obtained with bone conduction, there is no cochlear deficit and the loss is conductive, i.e., the impairment is in the middle or external ear. If, however, the responses to bone conduction testing are elevated beyond normal limits, the impairment is either partially or wholly sensori-neural in origin. With

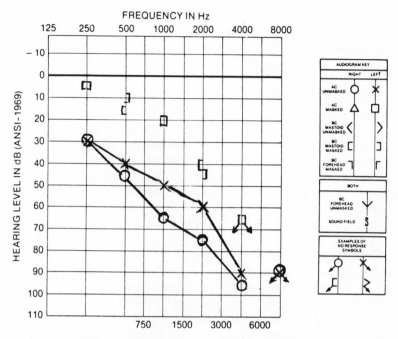

Figure 3. Pure tone audiogram showing a bilateral high frequency loss. The air bone gap is indicative of a mixed hearing loss.

a mixed loss, bone conduction thresholds, although elevated, are not as great as those obtained by air conduction. This shows up as an air bone "gap" on the audiogram (see Figure 3). Results of air conduction (AC) testing are shown on the audiogram by the symbols X (for the left ear) and O (for the right ear). Bone conduction (BC) responses are recorded as shown in Figure 3.

Impedance Audiometry

This is one of several sophisticated tests which employ total stimuli through which involuntary responses are obtained and recorded. The electroacoustic impedance technique is based on the principle that sound pressure level is a function of closed cavity volume. If sound waves impinge on an eardrum that is stiff or heavy, a high amount of energy is reflected back along the canal and can be measured. In this case we can say the system has a low compliance or poor mobility and has high impedance (resists motion). On the other hand, if the drum is flaccid or loose only a small amount of energy will be reflected back. This system has high compliance or a good deal of mobility and has low impedance (very little resistance to motion). Impedance audiometry is tested by securely seating in the ear canal a probe that contains three miniaturized channels. One delivers a tone (usually 220 Hz) to the ear, another leads to a microphone that picks up the quantity of sound reflected from the eardrum, and the third is connected to an air pump. Changes in the amount of sound pressure reflected from the drum, as air pressure is increased or decreased, are recorded on a graph called a tympanogram. Different tympanographic patterns are indicative of various middle ear pathologies (Jerger, 1970). This clinical testing is valuable in resolving doubts as to the causes and nature of hearing impairments. The impedance technique is also used in tests of static compliance and acoustic reflex threshold. Results of the three tests are considered together to reduce the limitations which each test has when used singly. A more detailed description of these procedures is found in Northern and Downs (1978).

Electrophysiological Tests of Hearing

These tests are used in major hearing clinics and in research. Equipment expense, technical problems, and time-consuming procedures make routine use of such procedures impractical, but such tests provide definite and useful information in difficult cases. They can be used with very young children, or when mental retardation, autism, or multiple handicapping conditions make the use of other forms of audiometry impossible.

Speech Tests of Hearing

Speech sounds are complex in nature, and speech discrimination ability cannot generally be predicted from pure tone threshold measurements. Hence, speech hearing tests are used to provide necessary information for the selection of appropriate hearing aids and for evaluating the use the child makes of his/her residual hearing. So-called speech reception thresholds are obtained by presenting spondaic words (i.e., having two equally stressed syllables such as *birthday* or *cowboy*) to each ear separately and determining the level at which 50 percent of the words are understood. Scores obtained when a listener is asked to repeat monosyllabic phonetically balanced words are called discrimination scores. With very young severely impaired children who generally have too little command of language and speech to articulate, identify, or comprehend test words, speech tests can seldom be reliably administered. For school-age hearing impaired children the Word Intelligibility by Picture Identification Test (Ross & Lerman, 1970) has been found useful in obtaining discrimination scores.

HEARING AIDS

Although primitive but systematic procedures for the utilization of residual hearing have been in existence since the eighteenth century (Bender, 1960), it was the advent of the electronic hearing aid, not yet 80 years old, and the subsequent growth in electroacoustic technology (Ling, 1971) that has had a marked methodological effect in education of the hearing impaired.

A variety of works describe the educational possibilities and limitations associated with hearing aid use among children (Clarke & Rogers, in press; Pollack, 1975), and the educational utilization of residual hearing even with very young children has been formulated (Pollack, 1970). Because it has been demonstrated that severe and even profound childhood deafness does not preclude the use of amplification in the classroom and as a part of everyday function, hearing aids have become an integral part of both oral-aural and total communication programs.

Basic to the concept of amplification is a realistic understanding of what a hearing aid can and cannot do to help the child. No hearing aid will enable a hearing impaired student to function normally in all situations—nor will it even compensate completely for the hearing loss. Some limits are imposed by damage to the ear, others by the nature of speech sounds, and others by the input/output limitations of the hearing aid.

A hearing aid is an amplifying system with the primary function of making sounds louder. The hearing aid consists basically of a microphone that picks up sound wave vibrations from the air and converts them to electrical impulses or signals. The amplifier, which is powered by a battery, increases the electrical strength of the signals and a speaker or receiver reconverts the electrical signals back into sound waves and directs them through an earmold which is fitted in the ear canal. Usually the aid is fitted with a volume and a tone control. A telephone coil which enables the listener to amplify electromagnetic signals directly from the telephone is also available. Solid state electronic devices have greatly reduced the size of these instruments and their power source so that generally they have more cosmetic appeal than formerly.

Classification   There are many different types of hearing aids and they vary in size, cost, and efficiency. The various kinds range from individual wearable hearing aids to group auditory training units that can be used by a number of students at the same time.

One system of classification is the location where the aid is worn, either on the torso (body-type aid) or at ear level. Body-type aids are now durable, small in size, and lightweight, with external controls that are easy to adjust. The advantages of using sturdy yet compact body aids with children younger than school age still outweigh the disadvantages (Northern & Downs, 1978).

Ear-level aids include behind-the-ear models, eyeglass models and all-in-the-ear models. These types of hearing aids are becoming increasingly popular with the advent of greater gain and saturation sound pressure level from the miniaturized amplifier. This type of aid does not amplify clothing rub, is less conspicuous, and is ideally located at the more natural level of the head. These instruments, particularly behind-the-ear models, have been successfully fitted with children as young as 3 years.

The other method of classification, monaural or binaural, concerns the number of ears provided with amplification. Although some manufacturers house two complete hearing aids in one case to provide binaural hearing, generally binaural fitting is accomplished with two separate hearing aid units of the same make and type. A Y-cord hearing aid supplies an electrical signal to two receivers, one in each ear, from a single body aid. This is called bilateral and not binaural hearing.

There has been much controversy concerning the benefits of the binaural over the monaural system (Briskey, 1978) but now it is generally accepted that the principal advantage afforded by binaural aids is the improvement of speech discrimination in the presence of background noise. This is due to the microphones, shielded by the head, giving improved time-intensity parameters to the wanted signal (speech). The best candidates for binaural fitting are children with a bilateral symmetrical hearing loss but it has become standard therapy for most cases of bilateral hearing loss (Jordan, Griesen, & Bentzen, 1967).

Group auditory trainers are usually found in school situations in which it is desirable to provide amplification for a class or group of students. Because they do not need to be small enough to wear, group trainers usually provide better sound quality. For a long time the hardwire version confined the movement of both children and teacher because their headphones and microphones needed to be plugged into the system. Today, radio FM systems are used which allow for greater mobility but the quality of amplification of FM can present a problem at high frequencies (Ling, 1975). Different FM channels are allocated to each system to avoid interference.

Fitting When the hearing impaired child has receptive and expressive language, speech hearing tests with and without hearing aids can be given to help select an appropriate aid. With a nonverbal child, aided awareness thresholds measured with speech, pure tones, or narrowband noise are sometimes used to establish the effective gain of an aid. To fit an aid correctly to a very young child, the audiologist will also need information concerning maximum power output and frequency response of the aid, and all the time and patience he/she can summon (Pollack, 1975). Ross (1975) maintains that

> the proper selection and use of amplification is the single most effective tool available to us in our remedial efforts with young hearing impaired children. I would not minimize the importance of parent-counseling or any type of therapeutic endeavour; these will often set limits to the success of our efforts. Auditory amplification, however, is the only therapeutic tool specifically focused on the problem—the hearing loss itself. It is after all, the hearing loss that is the responsible agent for observed speech, language and educational deviancies. The effective exploitation of residual hearing will minimize these developmental deviancies and ensure the maximum effectiveness of other therapeutic endeavours (p. 239).

Innovative researchers have also attempted to transform acoustic stimuli into other sensory modalities such as vibrotactile stimulation (Boothroyd, 1972) or visual displays (Potter, Kopp, & Green, 1947). Others have used aids that transpose the acoustic properties of the signal into different auditory patterns more likely to be heard by the child (Ling, 1968), but none of these events has proved highly successful (Clarke, Kendall, & Leslie, 1978).

EDUCATIONAL PHILOSOPHIES

Reduced efficiency of the auditory system has great effect upon the development of language and communication skills. Concerns related to the development of proficiency in these areas lead professionals to the use of varied intervention strategies. These strategies or communication methodologies derive from the influences of two major philosophies associated with the education of hearing impaired children.

The oral and total communication philosophies have been presented in the literature as *oral philosophy:*

> speech is recognized by society as the universal mode of communication: . . . deaf children who develop speech communication proficiency during early childhood ultimately have more options open to them for education and fuller participation in society than those who do not develop speech communication skills (Flint, 1975).

and *total communication philosophy:*

> the right of a deaf child to learn to use all forms of communication to develop language competence. This includes the full spectrum of child devised gestures, speech, formal signs, fingerspelling, speech-reading, reading, and writing. To every deaf child should also be provided the opportunity to learn to use any remnant of residual hearing he may have by

employing the best possible electronic equipment for amplified sound (Denton, 1969).

The major difference in philosophies is that total communication philosophy provides for communication utilizing oral and manual systems while the oral philosophy does not provide for use of a standard or formalized manual system of communication.

While the term *total communication* has been associated with the philosophy only since the late 1960s, the communication methodologies associated with it and those associated with the oral philosophy have been in use for centuries (Clarke, 1972). These methodologies vary in application within philosophies.

Oral Methods

The oral philosophy may result in communication methodology that is unisensory or multisensory in nature. Unisensory approaches are identified in the literature as auditory/oral or aural/oral. Educational interventions using this methodology place strong emphasis on use of amplification and development of communication skills through use of residual hearing (Pollack, 1970; Grammatico, 1975). Stress is placed upon auditory reception of speech pattern as "residual audition must be regarded as potentially the most important [receptive modality] because it is the only one directly capable of appreciating the primary characteristics of communicative speech, which are acoustic" (Ling, 1976, p. 22). Auditory/oral programs may use visual inputs as secondary resources but information presented in an auditory/visual mode is subsequently auditorially reinforced whenever possible.

Multisensory oral programs are best described as employing visual/oral methodologies. Visual/oral methodologies encourage the use of residual hearing but presentation of information most often involves a student's visual and auditory attention. In this manner the student is encouraged to speechread (lipread) and listen. As in all methodologies, use of amplification is stressed. Students unable to comprehend particular spoken elements may use a combination of visual, auditory, and tactile receptions to gain clarity. Once elements are understood the visual-auditory reception is reinforced so that, in future, the student will be able to receive a message without use of tactile reception. Cued speech, a variant visual/oral methodology, was developed by Cornett (1967) to

> reduce the ambiguity inherent in speechreading . . . certain hand positions and hand configurations are used to distinguish between speech sounds that look alike on the lips [e.g., bat, mat, pat] . . . no hand position or configuration uniquely specifies a phoneme; hence, continuous, simultaneous attention to the lips of the speaker is demanded (Ling, 1976, p. 97).

This is not identified as a manual system since the hand signals carry no meaning without the accompanying speech signal. This approach is, therefore, classified as a visual/oral methodology. In summary, the oral methodologies have as a central focus the development of receptive and expressive oral communication skills. These ends may be approached through auditory, visual-auditory, or visual-auditory-tactile receptive channels. The majority of oral programs in North America would be classified as visual/oral, with a very few using cued speech. A small number of auditory/oral programs are in operation throughout the continent.

Total Communication Methods

The total communication philosophy leads to communication methodology that is multisensory in nature. Visual/oral methodologies described above are used in combination with manual systems. The simultaneous presentation of information using oral and manual modes is known as the simultaneous or the combined method. The simultaneous method generally refers to the combination of the oral method plus signs and fingerspelling. Whenever possible, signs representing complete words or ideas are employed in the simultaneous method. Fingerspelling (spelling words letter by letter, using a manual representation of the English alphabet) is used when a sign does not exist for a particular word or idea. A variant of this approach is identified as the Rochester method. This method involves the simultaneous presentation of information through fingerspelling and oral modes.

Most total communication programs utilize a simultaneous methodology involving oral plus sign and fingerspelling systems, but the use of differing sign language systems results in varied applications of this methodology. Ameslan (an acronym for American Sign Language) is a language in its own right, with no spoken or written vocabulary, but having a separate syntax. In attempts to overcome the differences between sign and English there has been a growth of pedagogical systems that purport to code English in sign. The most common are *Seeing Essential English* (Anthony, 1971), *Signing Exact English* (Gustason, Pfetzing, Zawolkow, & Norris, 1972), *Linguistics of Visible English* (Wampler, 1972), and *Signed English* (Bornstein, 1974). Some fears have been expressed that the impending debate concerning appropriate sign systems will be more internecine than the oral-manual controversy.

A recent survey (Jordan, Gustason, & Rosen, 1976) shows what appears to be a sweeping change in the frequency of use of these methods. Although fewer than half the programs contacted responded to the questionnaires, it is somewhat significant that almost six out of every seven returns indicated a change from oral to total communication methodology. Since no one has yet clearly demonstrated that it is always possible to select reliably the method that will work best for a particular hearing impaired child, it is hoped that the current trend is more than a simplistic solution to a complex problem and one that is based on more than wishful thinking. It may be worth considering that a combination of all methods is tantamount to providing a smorgasbord from which the child is asked to make his/her own selection of communication skills. It seems that only the future will decide whether total communication is the appropriate tool for a breakthrough in the education of hearing impaired children. Although the method is not new, it is doubtful whether in the past proponents have given equal emphasis to both its oral-aural and manual components.

PSYCHOSOCIAL CORRELATES

Intelligence

The effect of a hearing impairment upon intelligence has been a topic of study for many years. Moores (1978) has described these studies as reflective of three stages.

Stage I, The Deaf as Inferior: Pintner
As a culmination of his own decades of research in deafness, Pintner (Pintner, Eisenson, & Stanton, 1941) reviewed and summarized all available data on the intelligence of the deaf. Although the results of different investigations frequently were confusing and even contradictory, Pintner concluded that deaf children were inferior in intelligence. He set the average retardation at 10 IQ points as compared to hearing norms. He reported a relatively small variation across different types of tests (1941, pp. 216–228), listing mean IQs for deaf children of 88 on the Draw-a-Man Test, 91 on performance tests, and 86 on drawing-on-paper tests. In each case the hearing norm was 100.

Stage II, The Deaf as Concrete: Myklebust
Reviewing work done from the time of Pintner's summary, Myklebust (1953, p. 351) concluded that the evidence indicated deaf children were not generally inferior in intelligence. However, Myklebust qualified his stand by arguing that even if deaf children were quantitatively (in terms of IQ points) equal to the hearing, they were not necessarily qualitatively equal. He went on to claim that the qualitative aspects of the perceptual and conceptual functioning of deaf individuals, and their reasoning, seemed to be different. Myklebust concluded that it was difficult for the deaf child to function in 'as broad and in as subtle and abstract a manner as the hearing child.'

Stage III, The Deaf as Intellectually Normal: Rosenstein and Vernon
In a review of the literature of perception, cognition, and language in deaf children, Rosenstein (1961) remarked on the lack of agreement on terminology. He noted (p. 276) for example, that the label abstract ability

has been used to refer to a visual memory task, a test of nonverbal reasoning by analogy, and an arithmetic reasoning task. In other contexts the same tasks have been assigned different labels; for example, a figure-ground relations test was interpreted by one writer as representing a perceptual ability and by another as representing a conceptual ability (p. 276).

Rosenstein reviewed several studies conducted with deaf subjects and reported that no differences could be found between deaf and hearing subjects in conceptual performance when the linguistic factors presented were within the language experience of the samples of deaf children. He concluded that the sphere of abstract thought is not closed to the deaf. In a survey of the literature on language and cognition, Furth (1964) reached essentially similar conclusions and reasoned that the poorer performance of deaf individuals on some tasks may be explained parsimoniously either by lack of general experience that is no longer manifest by adulthood or by specific task conditions that favor linguistic habits (pp. 130–131).

Results of studies of intelligence of hearing impaired persons are obviously limited by the instrumentation used. Levine (1974) conducted a survey of test instruments used for psychological assessment of hearing impaired persons. The results of her survey indicated a strong preference for performance test instruments. Hearing impairment usually results in English language development irregularities and it is, therefore, not surprising that many psychologists prefer performance or nonverbal tests as instruments for measuring intelligence.

Most intelligence tests used with hearing impaired persons are instruments developed for and standardized on a hearing population. Interpretation of the results of these tests are, therefore, often suspect. The most recent attempt to standardize an intelligence test on a hearing impaired population was conducted under the aegis of the Office of Demographic Studies, Washington, D.C. The researchers selected the WISC-R performance scale as it is most frequently used with hearing impaired persons. This performance scale was administered to 1,228 deaf children with the results reflecting the following:

> deaf children performed similarly to hearing children on all performance subtests except Coding and Picture Arrangement; deaf children, particularly young, low-scoring deaf children, performed significantly below their hearing peers on these subtests (Anderson & Sisco, 1977, pp. 6–7).

The authors make no mention of standardization of administration procedures. Varied communication methodologies associated with administration procedures very likely introduce a language component into the testing, thereby confounding the attempt to measure intelligence through performance testing.

It is likely that the results of the Anderson and Sisco study (1977) are low estimates of the intelligence of the hearing impaired school population, as the sample drawn for purposes of standardization was predominantly from state schools for the deaf and large day schools for the deaf. These programs tend to have a higher percentage of multiply handicapped deaf students than would be found in small day programs and in integrated settings. It is likely that the inclusion of students in smaller programs and integrated settings, along with a standardization of administration and communication guidelines, would result in a normal distribution of intelligence in the hearing impaired population.

While it is widely accepted that use of verbal scales in measuring intelligence of a hearing impaired person may adversely affect IQ results, it is also recognized that hearing impaired students functioning in a regular classroom setting need considerable verbal skill in order to perform successfully in that environment. In order to aid in the assessment of students being considered for placement in regular classes, verbal scales of intelligence tests are often used. Persons using results of these tests are more interested in the overall verbal ability than the verbal IQ of the student. A hearing impaired student scoring at or above average on a verbal intelligence test is usually recognized as a student having above average intelligence.

Emotional/Behavioral Problems

Hearing impaired students in appropriate educational placements will most likely exhibit satisfactory academic and social behaviors. Students who are unable to perform to expected levels are often identified by teachers as having poor academic records or as exhibiting emotional/behavior problems. These students may be in need of educational placement review. Academic performance is discussed later in this chapter. Emotional/behavioral problems may be related to family and other factors not discussed here. The intent is not to minimize the importance of these factors; rather, it is to focus on the variables present within the educational setting.

Emotional/behavioral problems may derive from inter- and/or intrapersonal conficts. The gregarious nature of human beings suggests that social acceptance should be an important factor in student adjustments. Sociometric studies by Elser (1959), Force (1956) and Perry and Johnson (1965) suggest that hearing impaired students as a group are not as socially accepted as their normally hearing peers in regular classroom settings.

Kennedy and Bruininks (1974) and McCauley, Bruininks and Kennedy (1976) found no significant differences between hearing and hearing impaired groups in regular classroom settings. Elser (1959), Kennedy and

Bruininks (1974), and Perry and Johnson (1965) found that severely to profoundly impaired students were more readily accepted than less impaired students. Attempts to isolate variables associated with acceptance have led to speculation that sympathy (Perry & Johnson, 1965), preschool intervention (Kennedy & Bruininks, 1974), and presence or absence of hearing aids (Force, 1956; Shears & Jensema, 1969) may be factors. The literature describing social acceptance of hearing impaired students by hearing students in regular class settings is inconclusive. Sociometric studies examining peer acceptance variables within a school for the deaf do not appear in the literature.

Teacher-reported information provided annually to the Office of Demographic Studies, Gallaudet College, includes reports of hearing impaired students considered to have "educationally significant emotional/behavioral problems." Jensema and Trybus (1975) examined the relationship of reported emotional/behavioral problems to selected demographic variables. These results reflect students attending residential school for the deaf, day school for the deaf, full-time special education, part-time special education, itinerant program, resource room, speech and hearing clinic, parent-child program, residential school for multiply handicapped, and program for the multiply handicapped. The data were examined for relationships between emotional/behavioral problems and sex, ethnic background, birth year, age at onset of hearing loss, degree of hearing loss, number of reported causes of hearing loss, specific causes of hearing loss, number of additional handicaps, and specific additional handicaps.

Slightly fewer than 44,000 hearing impaired students were included in the survey and emotional/behavioral problems were reported for 2,320 males (9.8 percent) and for 1,118 females (5.6 percent). "These sex differences were in accord with the general expectations of the mental health professions that in the case of children a substantially higher proportion of males than females will be referred for treatment" (Jensema & Trybus, 1975 p. 2). Emotional/behavioral problems reported for males were highest for those born in 1958–1959 and 1964–1965. "These, of course, were the years of rubella epidemics, and the data support the statement of Vernon (1967) that maternal rubella, in addition to causing hearing losses in infants, can also cause brain damage which may later manifest itself in emotional/behavioral disorders" (p. 4).

The percent distribution of reported emotional/behavioral problems for selected program types is presented in Table 1. It is of interest to note that percentages of reported emotional/behavioral problems are higher for males in full-time and part-time special education programs than for males in schools for the deaf.

Table 1. Percent distribution of emotional/behavioral problems in educational programs for the hearing impaired

Program type	Male (%)	Female (%)
Residential school for the deaf	8.8	5.3
Day school for the deaf	8.0	4.8
Full-time special education	12.6	6.4
Part-time special education	10.2	5.2
Itinerant program	6.2	3.4

Source: *Reported Emotional/Behavioral Problems Among Hearing Impaired Students in Special Educational Programs* by C. Jensema and R. Trybus, Gallaudet College Office of Demographic Studies, Washington, D.C., 1975, p. 3.

A summary indicates that the "greatest differences in rates of reporting of emotional/behavioral problems are related to the student's sex (higher rates among males) and the presence or absence of other handicapping conditions (higher rates among those with other handicapping conditions)" (p. 11).

Clearly, the hearing impaired population has a higher rate of reported emotional/behavioral disturbance than the hearing population (Goulder & Trybus, 1977; Jensema & Trybus, 1975). In an attempt to examine emotionally/behaviorally disturbed children's actions, Goulder and Trybus (1977) studied the identified population in three residential schools for the deaf. Results indicated that these students were:

> educationally unmotivated, physically aggressive toward peers, disruptive in the classroom, and withdrawn from others.
>
> Further, hearing impaired children who have other handicapping conditions are characterized as withdrawn, anxious, and as having exceptional difficulty with academic achievement. It appears that the behavioral effects of other handicapping conditions, while clearly atypical, are clearly different from the effects of emotional/behavioral disturbances on classroom behavior, so that the two influences operate independently and additively (p. 28).

Emotional/behavioral problems may derive from a number of sources, and this broad label may reflect varied behaviors. Rather than identifying these students as members of a deviant subgroup of hearing impaired children, professionals are challenged to develop "conditions necessary for the development of a healthy, whole, well-integrated person" (Moores, 1978, p. 140).

Adjustment Patterns

The effects of hearing impairment upon mental health of individuals are as variant as severity and types of losses encountered. A description of major types of adjustment patterns has been presented by Meyerson (1963).

Meyerson's first adjustment pattern describes hearing impaired persons as being most comfortable with other hearing impaired individuals. This "world of impaired hearing" is predominately a positive environment while the "world of normal hearing" is considered predominantly negative.

> The amount of overlap or commonality with the life space of the normally hearing is slight. The valence of the overlap is simultaneously positive and negative. It is positive because some areas . . . cannot often be restricted to the psychological world of impaired hearing. It is negative because a situation open equally to hearers and impaired hearers often requires the impaired hearer to function at a disadvantage. . . . It is not surprising that many deaf individuals perceive safety in a small and restricted but well organized world (p. 146–147).

This type of adjustment

> is often called 'withdrawal' and condemned as undesirable by practically all except those who practice it. . . . Withdrawal is not necessarily an undesirable or maladjusted reaction. In many cases it is appropriate and realistic. In some degree it decreases the opportunities for varied satisfactions and gratifications. However, it also solves the problem of antagonistic overlapping role situations (p. 149).

Meyerson's second adjustment pattern describes hearing impaired persons as rejecting the "world of impaired hearing" and aspiring to the "world of the normally hearing."

The hearing impaired person

> desires to do exactly the same things as the normally hearing and in exactly the same way. . . . however, the ability and social barriers to participation in the world of the normally hearing are strong (p. 147).

> In adjustment pattern two there are also positive and negative aspects. On the one hand, the psychological world may be larger and better differentiated. On the other hand, the person may be uncertain about the boundaries of his world, about the group to which he belongs, and about his status in the world of the normally hearing. This pattern is often considered 'best' by the normally hearing (p. 152).

The hearing impaired person

> will frequently be placed in new psychological situations in which his tool loss [hearing] will hinder him from structuring the unknown regions. He will frequently have to deny his own perceptions in favor of the perceptions of others who have better tools . . . Frustration, tension, and conflict in high degree are inevitable. In brief, while he may make a more or less effective adjustment to normally hearing society, he will be more or less disorganized

and maladjusted as a person. . . . [This] point should not be misinterpreted.
. . . The values of maladjustment to self must be weighed against the values
of maladjustment to society with the person himself as the judge
(p. 157–158).

Meyerson's third adjustment pattern describes hearing impaired
persons as recognizing "the large area of commonality that exists
between those who have normal hearing. Such a person perceives himself
as one who shares many behavioral areas with others." For selected
activities where hearing does not have a bearing upon performance, the
hearing impaired person "may feel as able to participate . . . as normally
hearing individuals."

> Other activities which require hearing can be entered by different methods.
> A lecture can be listened to, translated into signs, or written down. The
> same goal can be reached by a variety of methods.
>
> The special activities in the psychological world of impaired hearing are
> accepted also as additional regions for rich and fruitful living (p. 147).
>
> The person is easily able to say, 'I have impaired hearing.' He does not
> devalue himself or his group. Differences can be neutral. He sees the value
> of 'hearing behavior' as an asset, but 'impaired hearing behavior' does not
> affect the worth of the person. If he is placed at a disadvantage in a nor-
> mally hearing world it is because of the difficulty of the task and not the
> incompetence of the person. He, therefore, does not blame himself or feel
> guilt and shame. Because he is cognitively clear about this, his behavior is
> flexible and not bound by anxiety. He can cognitively guide his behavior in a
> conscious, goal-directed, and voluntary way and describe what he is doing to
> others. At one stroke he frees himself from ambiguous group memberships
> and their conflicting group demands (p. 165).

It has been suggested that each adjustment pattern has merit and should
be considered appropriate for some hearing impaired individuals. It is
also worthy of note that hearing and hearing impaired adults make
choices as to life-style after some considerable input from the home and
school environments. These choices may be rationally made if school and
home environments are providing the supports leading toward healthy
mental adjustments to hearing loss.

Educational placement options should be considered in light of the
students' academic and social needs. Obviously, some educational placements are more closely aligned with one of the adjustment patterns
described than with another. Questions must be asked of the compati-
bility of academic and social needs of a hearing impaired student with a
given educational placement option.

Residential and day schools for the deaf generally provide environments that limit interaction with hearing peers (Evans, 1975; Ross, 1978).
Self-contained special programs in regular school settings generally

provide a restricted academic environment and an opportunity for social interactions with hearing peers. Such opportunities are not often utilized, and the overall effect is to have social interactions restricted to the hearing impaired population within the school. These educational options may be viewed as encouraging adjustment described in Pattern One.

Part-time special education and resource programs generally provide environments facilitating interactions with hearing and hearing impaired peers. These program options may be considered most supportive of adjustments described in Pattern Three.

Fully integrated and itinerant support programs usually provide environments facilitating interactions with hearing peers and minimal opportunity exists for interaction with hearing impaired peers. Placement in this program option often supports adjustments described in Pattern Two.

Academic Achievement

Assessment of achievement performances of hearing impaired students presents difficulties similar to those discussed in the earlier section of this chapter dealing with assessment of intelligence. Attempts to measure performances utilizing standardized instruments result in the use of tests designed for and normed on hearing populations. These tests presume English linguistic competence that is usually not present in a hearing impaired population. Results of the use of these tests must be cautiously interpreted. Hearing impaired students' performances are often lower than results for hearing students of similar age. These lower performances may reflect the hearing impaired child's difficulty with the English language rather than knowledge of specifics being tested. At the same time it may be argued that performances by hearing impaired students on standardized reading tests may reflect an overestimate of their English language skills since most standardized tests give "students a choice of responses usually restricted to one grammatical category and they might artificially raise estimates of reading ability in that all answers would be at least grammatically correct" (Moores, 1978, p. 250).

There have been many studies of achievement in the hearing impaired population. The largest studies have been conducted by the Office of Demographic Studies at Gallaudet College in Washington, D.C. This office undertook to gather "national data on the achievement levels of hearing impaired students as well as . . . a deliberate research effort to determine the appropriateness and suitability of standard achievement tests" for this population (Di Francesca, 1972, p. 1).

The Stanford Achievement Tests were selected for use in these national studies of the hearing impaired population. The test battery has been modified in that a screening test is administered to determine appropriate battery level assignment rather than assigning levels according to age or grade placement as is done with the hearing population. This initial screening is intended to place a student in a battery level that would minimize the effects of restricted facility with the English language. The effects are by no means eradicated, as is demonstrated by results of the studies.

The Stanford Achievement Tests were administered to 16,908 students in the spring of 1971.

> The results show that in the first 1 to 3 years of their education, hearing impaired students perform slightly better in reading areas than in other subjects. This appears to reflect the great emphasis given beginning students in vocabulary and basic reading ability. At about the middle of the second grade level the academic areas of arithmetic, spelling and language mechanics, such as punctuation, capitalization etc., begin to surpass reading comprehension. The trend for higher performance in non-verbal and low verbal academic areas continues through all student age groups.
>
> For the most part, students do poorest in reading comprehension ability and best on those low verbal areas such as arithmetic. This may result from a language deficit whereby students can most effectively study academic material which does not require a high reading level.
>
> The effect of hearing loss level on achievement was also studied. Aside from the Word Study Skills sub-test, hearing loss affects reading comprehension most directly. Students with the most severe hearing losses performed poorer on reading tests than did others with less severe hearing losses.
>
> The reverse of this occurs for the low verbal academic areas. Students with greater hearing losses perform better in mathematics and in areas where reading is not required for achievement. This trend is present for the entire range of student ages but becomes less decisive for those older students who are exceptionally high achievers   (Di Francesca, 1972, p. 41).

While hearing impaired students performed best on arithmetic computation subtests, it must be pointed out that the weighted grade equivalent score for 19-year-olds was 6.73 and that the weighted grade equivalent for 19-year-olds on the paragraph meaning subtest was 4.36. Obviously, the effects of hearing impairment upon achievement performances as measured by standarized tests remain a major concern for educators.

Speech

The development of hearing impaired students' expressive speech skills is an integral part of educational programs whether these programs utilize oral or total communication methodologies. While numerous studies have examined specific aspects of speech production, there have been few studies of the overall effect of speech training. The largest published study to date examined the rated speech intelligibility of 978 hearing impaired children (Jensema, Karchmer, & Trybus, 1978). Teachers were asked to rate "the degree to which the speech of each student would be understood by the average person unfamiliar with that individual child" (p. 1). Results indicated that there were no overall differences among age groups in speech intelligibility.

> This does not imply that speech intelligibility can never be improved, given training of appropriate quality, duration, and intensity. It simply indicates overall results of current practice as reported . . . The extent of the child's hearing loss bears a major relationship to the speech intelligibility rating received. . . . Rated speech intelligibility is uniformly high for the groups of students with less than 70 dB loss; more than 80% of these students are rated as speaking intelligibly or very intelligibly. Beyond the 70 dB point, there appears to be an abrupt downward shift in intelligibility ratings (Jensema, Karchmer, & Trybus, 1978, p. 2).

Comparisons of results of recent studies "with those obtained in similar studies some 40 years ago suggests that there has been no improvement in standards despite the technological advances which have been made and the knowledge relating to speech which has emerged during this period" (Ling, 1976, p. 6).

Ling (1976) has observed that high standards of speech production can be achieved through informed, systematic, and sustained effort and that there "is considerable evidence that speech teaching efforts have, in general, rarely merited these three adjectives" (p. 9).

Ling (1976) examined "the problems underlying the acquisition of speech by children with various degrees of hearing impairment and suggest[ed] an approach through which increasingly effective speech communication skills may be established" (p. 1). He offered a comprehensive and systematic model for hearing impaired children's speech development. It is encumbent upon specialist teacher training programs and teachers of the hearing impaired in service to utilize such a model in attempts to improve the speech intelligibility of hearing impaired students.

Language

Numerous references throughout this chapter indicate that hearing impaired children experience difficulty in acquiring English language proficiency. Cooper and Rosenstein (1966) summarized studies investigating the language performances of hearing impaired children. The analyses generally reported comparisons of hearing impaired and hearing children on such language variables as productivity (sentence length or average number of words per sentence), complexity (subordination index), flexibility (type-token ratio or number of different words divided by the total number of words), distribution of parts of speech, and correctness (error classifications).

> The fact that the written language of deaf children when compared to that of hearing children is found to contain shorter and simpler sentences, to display a different distribution of form classes, to appear more stereotyped and to exhibit more numerous errors may be interesting. But these results have not proved immediately useful to teachers who are faced with the development of language or the remediation of language deficits with hearing impaired children (Clarke, Rogers, & Booth, 1979, p. 4).

More recent studies (Montanelli & Quigley, 1974; Power, Note 1; Quigley, Smith, & Wilbur, 1973; Quigley, Wilbur, & Montanelli, 1974; Russell, Quigley, & Power, 1976) have employed transformational-generative grammar models to examine "rules" children used to process sentences. These studies demonstrate that transformational models enable more precise investigation of differing aspects of syntax than was possible when using traditional grammar models. The studies confirm that hearing impaired children's interpretation of written English and generation of structures is heavily influenced by their familiarity with the simple-active-declarative form.

Attempts to develop English language facility have generally reflected two basic approaches. The first is known as the natural method, also called the synthetic or maternal reflective method (Van Uden, 1970). This approach encourages the development of language through modeling and discussions emanating from "natural" situations. The approach would encourage use of teacher models and student utterances as they should naturally occur in discussion related to any given topic. The approach does not involve a formal structure or developmental sequence of language skills but does recognize the performance levels (receptive and expressive) of the student. The major treatment of this approach has been described by Groht (1958).

The second approach is the structured method, also known as the analytic or formal method. As the name implies, a structured, developmental sequence of English language skills may be associated with this approach. While there have been numerous structured systems developed over the years, the most commonly used system has been the *Fitzgerald Key* (Fitzgerald, 1929).

The Key is a traditional grammar approach that provides the child with labeled categories (initially, *who, what,* and *where*) and the student is encouraged to practice generating sentences using correct word order. Development of skills is specified in Fitzgerald's publications.

Most recent developments in English language instructional strategies utilize transformational-generative theories of language development (Kretschmer & Kretschmer, 1978; Streng, 1972; Streng, Kretschmer, & Kretschmer, 1978). These recent texts hold much promise as they include considerations of semantic components of the language.

Educational interventions over the past 50 years have met with relatively little, if any, success in improving hearing impaired students' English language performances. Emerging models utilizing morphologic, syntactic, and semantic components of English offer potential for improving strategies that may result in the desired incremental growth.

EDUCATIONAL PROGRAMS

Education of the deaf and regular education have in the past coexisted within the educational enterprise with little or no significant degree of overlap. Indeed, the label *deaf* may have served as a warning to regular teachers that the problems of this group were too difficult to be solved by the public school system. Although hearing impaired children in Europe were placed in public schools more than 150 years ago, with anything but satisfactory results (Bender, 1960), traditionally the majority of North American students have attended residential schools. Since World War II, however, there has been a rapid rise in the number of public school programs and a growing tendency of residential schools to educate increasing numbers of day pupils. Over the same period there have been changing characteristics in school populations. Due to medical advances, more preverbal deaf children (deafened before the acquisition of language) and more multiply handicapped deaf children than ever before are now in the school system.

In 1979 in the United States there were 16,356 deaf students, or 35.1 percent of the total, enrolled in residential schools; 7,779 or 15.2 percent attended day schools; 10,017 or 21.5 percent were in full-time classes in local public schools; and 12,386 or 26.6 percent were in itinerant programs, resource rooms, or other part-time special education classrooms. There were more males (54.2 percent) than females, and 14,503 or 28.3 percent had one or more additional handicaps. All told, there are approximately 700 different programs providing some kind of special educational services to more than 51,000 deaf students (see Table 2).

It is also interesting to note the distribution of hearing loss categories within the various programs. This distribution has been relatively stable in surveys conducted over the last 5 years (Karchmer, Milone, & Wolk, 1979). Although the numbers are occasionally augmented as a result of cyclical epidemics (particularly rubella), enrollment figures

Table 2. Frequency and percentage distribution of the school-age hearing impaired population in the United States for hearing threshold level by different educational programs (N = 46,538[a])

Hearing threshold level	Residential school	Day school	Full-time special ed.[b]	Part-time programs[c]
< 70 dB	1,619 (3.5%)	1,525 (3.3%)	2,935 (6.3%)	8,162 (17.5%)
71–90 dB	4,367 (9.4%)	2,054 (4.4%)	2,875 (6.2%)	2,168 (4.7%)
> 91 dB	10,370 (22.2%)	4,200 (9.1%)	4,207 (9.0%)	2,056 (4.4%)
Total	16,356 (35.1%)	7,779 (16.8%)	10,017 (21.5%)	12,386 (26.6%)

Collated from Karchmer, Milone, & Wolk (1979).

[a] Includes only those students for whom audiometric data were available.

[b] Full-time special education classes in local public schools.

[c] Itinerant programs, resource rooms, and other part-time special education programs.

place the incidence of deafness at about 1 per 1,000 in the school-age population.

There is also a large number of children who do not hear normally and who have been called "our forgotten children" (Davis, 1977). Traditionally these children have been educated in schools for the deaf when the hearing loss was acute or in regular schools when the hearing loss was less severe. Neither kind of programming is actually addressed to their special needs. It is difficult to estimate their numbers, but Ross (1977) conservatively estimates the hard of hearing population at about 15 to 30 times greater than that of the deaf, with an incidence which may be as high as 30 per 1,000 school children or a probability of one or more hard of hearing children in every school in the country. These children may be found in all grade levels of public school (many without special services), in clinics and private tutoring situations, in special classes (often for emotional, neurological, or language disabled children), in residential and or day schools for the deaf or in classes or institutions for the retarded. One of the most urgent tasks confronting us is to seek out and identify hard of hearing children and to examine carefully whether the educational delivery system is appropriate to their needs.

In addition, it is of paramount importance that educational programs for hearing impaired children begin at an early age. While children with normal hearing develop language informally from many sources, hearing impaired children must acquire language through a systematic program of training. Educators of the deaf emphasize beginning training in communication skills as early as possible, either in the home or in an educational setting. If such a program is not initiated early, the resulting language handicap can be especially debilitating.

The importance of early language stimulation cannot be overemphasized. Early integration of the hearing impaired also brings significant benefits by breaking down social barriers and stereotypes, not only among the young but among their parents as well. Early education programs generally consist of mixed ages and sizes and are oriented to more individualized handling than are grade schools, but the program must be carefully evaluated to ensure provision of adequate and appropriate training at this very critical stage of language development.

Various types of programs are available and although terminology may vary at the local level, seven broad basic classifications can be made as follows:

1. *Residential school*   These facilities, originally for educating and accommodating hearing impaired students, now generally accept day pupils and are frequently called residential-day programs. They may be either public or private and they may serve students in an age range of about 3 to 21. The programs are often divided into a nursery or kindergarten unit, a lower school, a middle school and an upper school, which may be further divided into academic and vocational departments. Generally, they have a relatively large population of about 300 or more students. Most of the private residential schools use the aural-oral method, with the public residential schools traditionally using oral methods from kindergarten through middle school, and manual methods in the senior classes. Today the pattern is changing as many of these schools adopt a Total Communication philosophy.

2. *Day schools*   These are similar to residential schools except that the students reside at home. Usually they are located in large metropolitan areas.

3. *Self-contained classes*   These classes are located in regular elementary or secondary schools but, although they are contiguous with classes for the normally hearing students, the hearing impaired students are separated into their own self-contained programs.

4. *Part-time integration programs*   In these programs, hearing impaired students are assigned to their own special classes but spend part of the day with normally hearing students in regular classes. The ratio of special/regular class time and the subject areas that are integrated or segregated are determined on an individual basis. Generally these programs are oral but the Holcomb plan in Dela-

ware (Holcomb & Corbett, 1977) shows that with tutor-interpreters the plan can work with Total Communication.

5. *Resource centers or partial segregation programs* These programs set apart a room with a trained teacher of the deaf in the regular school, for the purpose of giving the hearing impaired student in a regular class tutorial assistance on a scheduled basis wherever it is needed.

6. *Itinerant programs* In these programs specialist teachers visit hearing impaired students enrolled in a regular class. The amount of time varies from daily through monthly and will depend on the special educational needs of the individual student. These programs are organized at preschool, elementary, junior, and senior high school levels.

7. *Postsecondary programs* Education after high school can take place in:
   a. Regular junior colleges, vocational, or technical programs, with or without help of itinerant specialist teachers or tutor-interpreters.
   b. Colleges for the hearing impaired, e.g., Gallaudet College for the Deaf in Washington, D.C., or The National Technical Institute for the Deaf in Rochester, New York. In the latter, students take courses along with hearing peers with the aid of notetakers and/or interpreters.
   c. Junior colleges and vocational and technical schools where provisions are made for including hearing impaired students by providing at the school the special services they need. A listing of college and career programs for deaf students is available (Rawlings, Trybus, & Biser, 1978).

At the turn of the century, the deaf and general populations were at a parity with respect to the percentage of persons who attended college. In the next 50 years rates for the general population increased greatly, while those for the deaf remained fairly constant. Due to vigorous action in the 1960s, the proportion of deaf students attending postsecondary programs has risen, but is only one-third that of the general population.

Models of Mainstreaming

Traditionally, severely and profoundly deaf children have been educated in segregated facilities—which were, in fact, the earliest facilities for exceptional children. The literature is replete with descriptions of various integration models for deaf and hard of hearing students. Löwe's (1972) typology, summarized below, reflects the continuum of services, which ranges from full integration to complete segregation:

Full Integration

Level 1: Hearing-impaired children in regular classes

These children are able to get along with regular class accommodation without supportive therapy, provided they are well equipped with hearing aids and their teachers know their handicap.

Level 2: Hearing-impaired children in regular classes

These children are also provided with hearing aids. They can still master the normal curriculum of a regular class. In addition they need transitory or permanent supplementary instructional services like auditory training, speech reading training, speech therapy, etc.

Level 3: Hearing-impaired children in regular classes

These children need regularly, in addition to the supplementary instructional services already mentioned, a few hours of remedial instruction. Also a certain modification in materials and procedures offered by the regular classroom teacher is needed.

Partial Integration

Level 4: Hearing-impaired children in special classes attached to an ordinary school.

These children need part-time special class education. They are still able to be instructed with normally hearing children in certain subjects.

Level 5: Hearing-impaired children in special classes attached to an ordinary school

These children are taught with normally hearing children only in subjects like art and physical education.

Partial Segregation

Level 6: Hearing-impaired children in special day schools

These children receive full-time specialized instruction in separate facilities and programs. They return home every day and spend part of their spare time with normally hearing children.

Level 7: Hearing-impaired children in special residential schools

These children receive full-time specialized instruction in separate facilities and programs and return home only once a week or less. They spend only part, if any, of their out-of-school time in contact with normally hearing children.

Full Segregation

Level 8: Hearing-impaired children in special programs for multiply handicapped children (not including the severely mentally defective)

Owing to additional handicaps (visual impairments, physical handicaps etc.) these children cannot be instructed within an integrated program and need full-time special education. Their opportunities to have contact with ordinary children are much reduced.

Level 9: Hearing-impaired children in special programs for the mentally retarded

These children need full-time special care in a residential situation and training for an occupation in a sheltered workshop.

The Warnock report (1978), in looking at types of integration in the United Kingdom, distinguished three main forms that are not discrete but overlapping and representative of progressive stages of association. These forms are:

1. *Locational*—where special classes, units or programs are set up in special schools
2. *Social*—where hearing impaired children attending a special program eat, play, and consort with normally hearing children
3. *Functional*—where hearing impaired children join part-time or full-time the regular classes of a school and make a full contribution to the activity of the school

Each element of the triad has a separate validity, but together they are seen not only as a framework for planning and organization but also as a means for evaluating program effectiveness.

Reich, Hambleton, and Klein (1975), disenchanted with incomplete descriptions of mainstreaming models, specified eight dimensions that would enable a more precise identification of what is happening in a program. The dimensions are summarized as follows:

1. *Level*:   Integration can involve preschoolers, elementary children, or students at the secondary or post secondary level.
2. *Degree*:   At one extreme is complete segregation, i.e., a special school unattached to a regular school; next is partial segregation where the child's main attachment is to a special school or unit, but in which he or she spends some time with regular students; the next level is partial integration. There the child's main attachment is to a regular class, but some specialized help is provided in a group setting outside of that class. Finally there is full integration in which the child's association is with normally hearing peers in a regular school or class.
3. *Range*:   Assuming that there is some integration, its range will at one end of this continuum be purely social—here contact between hearing impaired and normally hearing children only occurs outside

of the classroom. Usually it is of an informal nature (e.g., recess, lunch, busing). The next level is integration for practical subjects (e.g., home economics, shop, or physical education). In such cases social integration would usually also occur. At the other end of the scale is academic integration in which the child takes his/her main academic work with hearing peers.

4. *Unit*: The level indicates whether the hearing impaired child is integrated individually or with a number of other hearing impaired students.

5. *Specialization*: This refers to the type of special resource persons available. It varies from trained teachers of the deaf to generalists or ancillary professionals (e.g., tutors, psychologists, speech therapists).

6. *Availability*: In some cases special services are episodic (provided to child and/or teacher on an occasional basis) and, in others periodic. The frequency of periodic contact may vary, for example, from monthly to daily visits. Finally, continuing contact occurs when the specialist is present full-time within the school or continually available for consultation or tutoring.

7. *Focus*: All three levels of availability (above) may differ in their focus. The major activity may be to help the regular teacher to understand and plan better for the hearing impaired child in the class; or it may be to help the child directly or finally to provide both these services in varying proportions of time.

8. *Type*: If the focus of help is the child, the type of services may be: a) advising (giving counsel and encouragement to the hearing impaired child, in order that he can cope with the teacher of, and the pupils in the regular class), b) tutoring (giving additional help in specific subjects), c) language training (including any attempts to build language skills including speech, speechreading, auditory training, etc.), or d) interpreting (oral and or manual interpreting and note-taking).

The advantages of the Reich et al. paradigm is that it can be easily and readily applied to point up quickly the differences in the programs that would otherwise appear to be congruent. It also provides an excellent schema not only for determining very precisely the delivery system available but also for identifying the particular service that may be dictated by the needs of an individual hearing impaired child.

There are numerous position papers and a random set of research studies that address themselves to how well or how poorly hearing impaired children succeed in mainstream settings, but decision makers must await more comprehensive empirical studies both on the relative success of various types of integration and the criteria required of a hearing impaired child for success in these programs before they can feel comfortable with their judgments. Success in these instances should not be limited to academic achievement but should also encompass psychosocial adjustment.

Thurman and Lewis (1979) proposed that when labels with negative connotations are placed on already discriminable differences, prejudices and rejection are likely to result. They therefore suggested that, in order to facilitate patterns of social integration between handicapped and nonhandicapped children, educators should begin to develop intervention strategies and modifications that address discernible differences and the emotional responses which they generate.

Equal and appropriate education, considering the uniqueness and the heterogeneity of hearing impaired students, must by nature be differential if it is to be appropriate (Vernon, 1975). Mainstreaming of hearing impaired children will therefore require hard work, careful planning, and sensitive consideration. Mere dispersal of the severe and profoundly deaf into the public school system can never be regarded as a change to an "appropriate educational environment." Before the humanistic approach to mainstreaming gets too far in advance of practical realities it could be wise to re-evaluate the role of the residential-day school. These schools have a more important part to play now than ever before. If first they integrate those pupils from their own schools for whom mainstreaming is more appropriate than traditional segregation, it would then be uneconomical for any state not to use their facilities and highly skilled personnel—administrators, teachers, audiologists, psychologists, and the like—to provide assessment, planning, and individual program evaluation for mainstreamed hearing impaired students. The school for the deaf recommends itself as the focal point from which all types of service delivery could be monitored. There are complex logistical problems related to serving widely dispersed low incidence populations. This, plus the changing characteristics of hearing impaired students (the greater incidence of prelingual and multihandicapped students), makes it unreasonable to fear that schools for the deaf have no purpose in the scheme of things.

The least restrictive environment and individualized planning will be easier to accomplish for many more hearing impaired students as all education becomes special education, i.e., as education moves more and more to individualization of the learning-teaching process and further away from grade grouping and grade leveling. Students with mild or moderate hearing threshold levels who have been mainstreamed by an accidental process of attrition or convenience will be addressed more efficiently as school programs move toward individualized education and development of individualized education programs (IEPs) for each child.

SUMMARY

Education of the hearing impaired has existed in North America for more than 150 years. While much conscientious effort has been directed toward the quality of this education, the results indicate that there is no cause for complacency. Hearing impaired adults have demonstrated responsible citizenship and steady contributions to society despite general conditions of underemployment and low overall educational standards due to their lack of facility with the English language. The challenge clearly remains for education to improve its contributions to the habilitative process.

This chapter has described major components relating to the education of hearing impaired students. No attempts have been made to list suggestions for classroom teachers as the authors' intent is to describe the current state of the art, not to provide a checklist for day-to-day activities. Too often checklists, minimal standards, or educational definitions result in simplistic solutions to complex problems.

Educators should be aware of the way in which auditory signals are processed. This chapter has included a description of basic anatomy and physiology of the auditory mechanism and a discussion of types of hearing loss associated with abnormal function in the outer, middle and/or inner ear. The reader has also been provided with an overview of basic clinical procedures for pure tone air conduction, bone conduction, impedance audiometry, and speech hearing tests.

Whenever possible diagnosis of abnormal auditory function will result in the fitting of a hearing aid. Electroacoustic amplification varies greatly in type and response characteristics. Body-level, ear-level, monaural and binaural individual aids, and group amplification systems have been distinguished.

One explanation of the prevailing standards in education of the hearing impaired is that much energy has been expended on the "methods controversy." While this debate is by no means resolved, it is generally recognized that emotion and not logic is found in polemics on the relative merit of communication methods. Two major philosophical positions have been differentiated: first, the recognition of oral communication and its orientation to provide the child with the necessary and sufficient skills to function in society, and, second, the right of the hearing impaired child to use all forms of communication in the learning process. These two basic positions result in differences which have been described. Oral methodologies may reflect unisensory (aural) or multisensory (visual/oral) approaches, with the latter encouraging development of speech reception through audition and speechreading with the addition, in a few programs, of cued speech to differentiate between speech sounds that have similar visual patterns. Total communication employs a multisensory approach combining visual/aural techniques with fingerspelling and sign systems. However, there is inconsistency in the use of Ameslan and pedagogical systems that purport to code English in sign. Exclusive use of oral methods and fingerspelling, known as the Rochester method, occurs in some programs.

Discussions of deviance often inadvertently lead to stereotyping, and such is the case with hearing impairment. In an attempt to examine some effects of reduced sensitivity to sound, results of national studies relating to measures of intelligence were presented. Verbal scales are not generally used for purposes of assessing intelligence, but results of assessment using performance scales confirm that there is a normal distribution of intelligence in the hearing impaired population. Results of a national study indicated teacher-rated incidence of emotional/behavioral problems in the school-age hearing impaired population to be higher for males than for females. Examination of three hearing impaired adult adjustment patterns suggests possible relationships between school program placement and subsequent adjustment.

Studies of achievement performances were discussed. The results of national studies indicate that hearing impaired students are well below comparable age-grade performances of normally hearing students in all areas. Studies of speech and language performances indicate that little, if any, improvement has been made in these critical areas. Emerging literature holds promise for better intervention strategies in the future.

Patterns of enrollment in various program types were described. Current program types were discussed under seven broad classifications. Consideration was also given to comparison of normally hearing and hearing impaired populations attending post secondary programs.

Various models describing the range of educational placement options were examined. A simple discrete stage model (Löwe, 1972), while convenient for funding purposes, may lead to a disregard of multiple variables critical in placement considerations. A more complex model, while awkward for classification purposes, allows for accurate identification of important variables in program planning.

Educators and administrators must recognize the need for a full range of educational services and the re-evaluation of the role of the residential-day school. Development of IEPs will be more easily achieved as all education becomes special education.

REFERENCES

American National Standards Institute. *American National Standard Specifications for Audiometers, ANSI-S3.6-1969.* American National Standards Institute, Inc., New York.

Anderson, R., & Sisco, F. Standardization of the WISC-R performance scale for deaf children. Office of Demographic Studies Annual Survey of Hearing Impaired Children and Youth. Series T, No. 1. Washington, D.C.: Gallaudet College. 1977.

Anthony, D. *Seeing essential English.* Anaheim, Cal.: Anaheim School District, 1971.

Babbidge, H. S. *Education of the Deaf. A Report to the Secretary of Health, Education, and Welfare by his Advisory Committee on the Education of the Deaf.* U.S. Government Printing Office, 0-765-119, 1965.

Bender, R. *The conquest of deafness.* Cleveland: Case Western Reserve, 1960.

Best, H. *Deafness and the deaf in the United States.* New York: Macmillan, 1943.

Boothroyd, A. Sensory aids research project—Clarke School for the Deaf. In G. Fant (Ed.), *International Symposium on Speech Communication Ability and Profound Deafness, Stockholm 1970.* Washington, D.C.: Alexander Graham Bell Association for the Deaf, 1972.

Bornstein, H. Signed English: A manual approach to English language development. *Journal of Speech and Hearing Disorders,* 1974, *3*, 330–343.

Briskey, R. J. Binaural hearing aids and new innovations. In J. Katz (Ed.), *Handbook of clinical audiology* (2nd ed.). Baltimore: Williams and Wilkins, 1978.

Clarke, B. R. Total communication. *Canadian Teacher of the Deaf,* 1976, *2*(1), 22–30.

Clarke, B. R., Kendall, D. C., & Leslie, P. T. Communication systems with the hearing impaired. *Auditory and Hearing Education,* 1978, (Part 1) February and March, *4*, pp. 17–19; 33. (Part 2) April and May, *4*, pp. 6–16; 40.

Clarke, B. R., and Rogers, W. T. The relationship between personal hearing aids and selected characteristics of hearing impaired students. *Journal of Auditory Research,* in press.

Clarke, B. R., Rogers, W. T., & Booth, J. A. Use of the screening forms of the test of syntactic abilities with hearing impaired students in British Columbia: A progress report. *British Columbia Journal of Special Education,* 1979, *3*(1), 3–26.

Cooper, R. L., & Rosenstein. J. Language acquisition. In S. P. Quigley (Ed.), *Language Acquisition.* Volta Review, Monograph, 1966.

Cornett, O. R. Cued speech. *American Annals of the Deaf,* 1967, *112*, 3–13.

Davis, J. *Our forgotten children: Hard-of-hearing pupils in the schools.* Minneapolis: University of Minnesota 1977.

Davis, H., & Silverman, S. R. *Hearing and deafness.* New York: Holt, Rinehart & Winston, 1978.

Denton, D. In P. Ottinger, *Dr. David Denton: Total communication.* Deaf American, 1969, pp. 3–6.

Di Francesca, S. *Academic achievement test results of a national testing program for hearing impaired students, United States: Spring, series D. No. 9.* Washington, D.C.: Office of Demographic Studies, Gallaudet College, 1972.

Elser, R. The social position of hearing handicapped children in regular grades. *Exceptional Children,* 1959, *25,* 305–309.

Evans, D. Experiential deprivation: Unresolved factor in the impoverished socialization of deaf school children in residence. *American Annals of the Deaf,* 1975, *120*(6), 545–552.

Fitzgerald, E. *Straight language for the deaf.* Staunton, Va.: McClure Co., 1929.

Flint, R. A. G. Bell Board re-examines the association's purpose and mission. *Volta Review,* 1975, *77*(3), 152–154.

Force, D. G. Social status of physically handicapped children. *Exceptional Children,* 1956, *23,* 104–133.

Frisina, R. Report of the Ad Hoc Committee to Define Deaf and Hard of Hearing for Educational Purposes (Mimeo) For a summary of this report see American Annals of the Deaf, 1975, *120,* 509–512.

Furth, H. Research with the deaf: Implications for language and cognition. *Psychological Bulletin,* 1964, *62,* 145–162.

Goulder, T. J., & Trybus, R. *The classroom behavior of emotionally disturbed hearing impaired children. Series R, no. 3.* Washington D.C.: Gallaudet College, Office of Demographic Studies, 1977.

Grammatico, L. The development of listening skills. *Volta Review,* 1975, *77*(5), 303–308.

Groht, M. *Natural language for deaf children.* Washington, D.C.: Alexander Graham Bell Association of the Deaf, 1958.

Gustason, G., Pfetzing, D., Zawolkow, E., & Norris, C. *Signing exact English.* Rossmore, Cal.: Modern Science Press, 1972.

Hirsch, I. *The measurement of hearing.* New York: McGraw-Hill, 1952.

Holcomb, R., & Corbett Jr., E. Mainstream: The Delaware approach. *Special Education in Canada* 1977, *52*(1), 10–15.

Jensema, C., Karchmer, M., & Trybus, R. *The rated speech intelligibility of hearing impaired children: Basic relationships and a detailed analysis. Series R, no. 6.* Washington, D.C.: Gallaudet College Office of Demographic Studies, 1978.

Jensema, C. & Trybus, R. *Reported emotional/behavioural problems among hearing impaired students in special educational programs. Series R, no. 1.* Washington, D.C.: Gallaudet College Office of Demographic Studies, 1975.

Jerger, J. Clinical experience with impedance audiometry. *Archives of Otolaryngology,* 1970, *92,* 311–324.

Jordan, I. K., Gustason, G., & Rosen, R. Current communication trends at programs for the deaf. *American Annals of the Deaf,* 1976, *121,* 527–532.

Jordan, O., Griesen, O., & Bentzen, O. Treatment with binaural hearing aids. *Archives of Otolaryngology,* 1967, *85,* 319–326.

Karchmer, M., Milone, Jr., M., & Wolk, S. Educational significance of hearing loss at three levels of severity. *American Annals of the Deaf,* 1979, *124*(2), 97–109.

Kennedy, P., & Bruininks, R. Social status of hearing impaired children in regular classrooms. *Exceptional Children,* 1974, *40*(5), 336–342.

Kretschmer, R. R., & Kretschmer, L. W. *Language development and intervention with the hearing impaired.* Baltimore: University Park Press, 1978.

Leckie, D. Creating a receptive climate in the mainstream program. *Volta Review,* 1973, *75*(1), 23–27.

Levine, E. Psychological tests and practices with the deaf: A survey of the state of art. *Volta Review,* 1974, *76*(5), 298–319.

Ling, D. Three experiments of frequency transposition. *American Annals of the Deaf,* 1968, *113,* 283–294.

Ling, D. *Speech and the hearing impaired child: Theory and practice.* Washington, D.C.: The Alexander Graham Bell Association for the Deaf, 1976.

Ling, D. Conventional hearing aids: An overview. *Volta Review,* 1971, *73,* pp. 343–52; 375–377; 379; 381; 383.

Ling, D. Recent developments affecting the education of hearing impaired children. *Public Health Reviews,* 1975, *4,* 117–152.

Löwe, A. Difficulties facing the integration of hearing-impaired children into regular educational programs in the Federal Republic of Germany. *Scandinavian Audiology* (Supplementum) 1972, *2,* 9–11.

McCauley, R. W., Bruininks, R. H., & Kennedy, P. Behavioral interactions of hearing impaired children in regular classrooms. *Journal of Special Education,* 1976, *10*(3), 277–284.

Moores, D. *Educating the deaf: Psychology, principles and practices.* Boston: Houghton-Mifflin Co., 1978.

Meyerson, L. Somatopsychology of physical disabilities. In W. Cruickshank (Ed.), *Psychology of exceptional children and youth.* Englewood Cliffs, N.J.: Prentice-Hall, 1963.

Montanelli, D., & Quigley, S. *Deaf children's acquisition of negation.* Institute for Research on Exceptional Children, University of Illinois, Urbana, Ill., 1974.

Myklebust, H. Towards a new understanding of the deaf child. *American Annals of the Deaf,* 1953, *98,* 345–357.

Newby, H. *Audiology* (4th ed.). Englewood Cliffs, N.J.: Prentice-Hall, 1979.

Northern, J. L., & Downs, M. P. *Hearing in children* (2nd ed.). Baltimore: Williams and Wilkins Co., 1978.

Perry, F. R., & Johnson, I. R. The social acceptance of hearing impaired children in schools and some possible factors affecting this acceptance. *Australian Teacher of the Deaf,* 1965, *6*(1), 4–24.

Pintner, R., Eisenson, J., & Stanton, M. *The psychology of the physically handicapped.* New York: Crofts and Company, 1941.

Pollack, D. *Educational audiology for the limited hearing infant.* Springfield, Ill.: Charles C Thomas, 1970.

Pollack, M. (Ed.). *Amplification for the hearing impaired.* New York: Grune & Stratton, 1975.

Potter, R. K., Kopp, G. A., & Green, H. C. *Visible speech.* New York: Van Nostrand, 1947.

Quigley, S., Wilbur, R., & Montanelli, D. *Development of question formation in the written language of deaf students.* University of Illinois Institute for Research on Exceptional Children.

Quigley, S., Smith, N., and R. Wilbur. Comprehension of Relativized Sentences by Deaf Children. University of Illinois Institute for Research on Exceptional Children, Urbana, Ill., 1973.

Rawlings, B., Trybus, R., & Biser, J. *A guide to college/career programs for deaf students*. Washington, D.C.: Gallaudet College, 1978.

Reich, C., Hambleton, D., & Klein, B. *The integration of hearing impaired children in regular classrooms*. Ontario: Research Service, Ministry of Education, 1975.

Rosenstein, J. Perception, cognition and language in deaf children. *Exceptional Children*, 1961, *27*, 276–284.

Ross, M. Hearing aid selection for children. In M. Pollack (Ed.), *Amplification for the hearing impaired*. New York: Grune and Stratton, 1975.

Ross, M. Definitions and descriptions. In J. Davis (Ed.), *Our forgotten children: Hard-of-hearing pupils in the schools*. Minneapolis: University of Minnesota, 1977.

Ross, M. Mainstreaming: some social considerations. *Volta Review*, 1978, *80*(1), 21–30.

Ross, M., & Lerman, J. A picture identification test for hearing-impaired children. *Journal of Speech and Hearing Research*, 1970, *13*, 44–53.

Russell, W. K., Quigley, S. P., & Power D. J. *Linguistics and deaf children: Transformational syntax and its applications*. Washington, D.C.: The Alexander Graham Bell Association for the Deaf, 1976.

Schein, J. D., & Delk, M. T. *The deaf population of the United States*. Silver Springs, Md.: National Association of the Deaf, 1974.

Shears, L. N., & Jensema, C. J. Social acceptability of anomalous persons. *Exceptional Children*, 1969, *36*, 91–96.

Streng, A., Kretschmer, R., & Kretschmer, L. *Language, learning, and deafness: Theory, application, and classroom management*. New York: Grune & Stratton, 1978.

Streng, R. *Syntax, speech and hearing*. New York: Grune & Stratton, 1972.

Thurman, S. K., & Lewis, M. Children's response to differences: Some possible implications for mainstreaming. *Exceptional Children*, 1979, *45*(6), 468–470.

Van Uden, A. M. J. *A world of language for deaf children. Part 1: Basic principles. A maternal reflective method*. Rotterdam: Rotterdam University Press, 1970.

Vernon, M. Characteristics associated with post-rubella deaf children: Psychological, educational, and physical. *Volta Review*, 1967, *69*, 176–185.

Vernon, M. Integration or mainstreaming. *American Annals of the Deaf*, 1975, *120*, 15–16.

Wampler, D. *Linguistics of visible English*. Santa Rosa, Cal., 1972.

Warnock, H. M. (Chairman) *Special educational needs: report of the committee of enquiry into the education of handicapped children and young people*. London: Her Majesty's Stationary Office, 1978.

REFERENCE NOTES

1. Power, D. *Deaf children's acquisition of the passive voice*. Unpublished doctoral dissertation, University of Illinois, 1971.

Part II

FUNDAMENTAL STRATEGIES FOR INSTRUCTION

Editorial Introduction

The chapters included in Part II provide an orientation to systematic programming for handicapped children. They cover formal and informal assessment, teaching techniques and materials, classroom climate, and the management of undesirable behaviors.

The first chapter in this section describes the individualized education plan required by the Education for All Handicapped Children Act of 1975. This plan is the basis for the appropriate placement and effective education of the handicapped child. Elements of the plan are described, and possible problems in its development and implementation are identified. The succeeding chapters in this section are designed to aid the classroom teacher in development of the individual instructional plan which arises from the individualized education program (IEP).

Chapter 8 covers the all-important process of diagnostic assessment as it relates to individualized instructional programming. As this chapter points out, educational diagnosis is meaningless unless it results in accurate specification of functional levels, skills and behaviors of concern, and learning style. The role of the classroom teacher is emphasized in formal and informal criterion-referenced testing, direct observation, and diagnostic prescriptive teaching.

Chapter 9 provides a basic approach to teaching that can serve as a guide for instructional decision making when planning for each handicapped child in his particular learning environment. The suggested approach is systematic and includes continuous measurement of learner performance. Generally referred to as diagnostic prescriptive teaching and originally developed for use in special education, the approach can be used effectively to individualize within regular classrooms.

The classroom teacher often fails to recognize the importance of the classroom learning climate on the behavior and achievement of pupils. Chapter 10 is based on the belief that an appropriate classroom learning climate will enhance the teacher's ability to provide better instruction, reduce discipline problems, and enable greater individualized learning for both handicapped and nonhandicapped learners. The author of this chapter discusses three climate influences: the teacher, the students, and the curriculum.

The concluding chapter centers on the management of undesirable classroom behaviors. The management of inappropriate behavior is probably the most serious problem in the public schools today. A variety of techniques are introduced. The concept of individualized management is stressed—different techniques must be employed to meet the needs of students with diverse academic, psychological, and physical characteristics.

7

THE INDIVIDUALIZED EDUCATION PROGRAM (IEP)
Foundation for Appropriate and Effective Instruction

Sara J. Odle and Barbara Galtelli

The Education for All Handicapped Children Act of 1975 (PL 94–142) was designed to ensure the availability to all handicapped children of a free, appropriate education. Appropriate placement and effective education of the handicapped is ensured by the section of the act which provides that an individualized educational program (IEP) be developed for each eligible handicapped child. This section is perhaps the most important, for both student and teacher, of the six main provisions of PL 94–142. The requirement for formalization of goals, objectives, and procedures for evaluation provides a management tool designed to ensure and facilitate delivery of appropriate special education and/or related services to meet the unique needs of the handicapped student.

THE INDIVIDUALIZED EDUCATION PROGRAM

The concept of an individualized education plan is not new. "Individualization of instruction" has long been an advocated objective of the teaching profession. Nor is specification in PL 94–142 of a written individualized plan for the education of the handicapped the first requirement for such documentation. Many states had passed legislation including such provision before the passage of this mandatory federal legislation

245

(Hayes & Higgins, 1978). Provision of individualized programs has always been considered a characteristic of special education. However, development of the IEP represents a modification of past special education practices, and moves away from the traditional practice of categorical placement and programming. The handicapped child was formerly determined to be eligible for special education services on the basis of test results by which he/she was labeled "mentally retarded," "perceptually handicapped," or "emotionally disturbed." After being thus labeled, the student would be placed in a classroom for that type of disability. An individualized program within that structure then might or might not be prepared for the child. The current requirement that the IEP be written prior to placement is designed to ensure that the curriculum be adapted to meet the needs of the child rather than forcing the child to adjust to the structure of an existing curriculum.

Procedural policies set forth in guidelines for the development of the IEP provide a common format for the planning process. Although there will be variances in procedures of different state or local educational agencies, the IEP guidelines provide for consideration of all essential steps in the provision of appropriate services. The team responsible for placement of the child is guided through the requirements of the law. Communication is facilitated between those persons responsible for planning, implementing, and evaluating the program for the child. This common format thus ensures a higher quality of service provision to all children than might otherwise be provided.

Steps Preliminary to Development of the IEP

In brief, the steps leading to the point at which an IEP must be written are as follows:

1. *Referral for services*:   This may be done by the parent or guardian, the teacher, principal, doctor, or others.
2. *Preliminary diagnostic screening*:   Information is collected concerning the history of the referred student. This information may come from the child's cumulative school record and interviews with parents, teachers, and/or others who are knowledgeable about the student's educational, psychological, emotional, social, physical, and/or behavioral status. After reviewing the student's history, the decision is made by a school personnel screening team to either accept or reject the referral. If the referral is accepted, parental permission must be gained for comprehensive, multidisciplinary assessment.

3. *Comprehensive assessment*: There is no set battery of tests that must be given to every student. An assessment plan is designed based on the information found in the preliminary screening as to the child's learning needs. Assessment may be in any area or group of areas—self-help skills, readiness, perceptual capabilities, reading, language, social skills, thinking skills, behavioral patterns, prevocational skills, or vocational skills.

4. *Individualized education program* (*IEP*): The team then meets to determine the child's needs, based on all information available. If the team decides that special education services are advisable, the development and implementation of an IEP becomes necessary. PL 94–142 requires that if a student is identified before the school year begins as being in need of services, the IEP must be developed by October 1. If it is decided after the school year begins that special education services are necessary, an IEP must be developed within 30 days after the decision has been made.

Writing the IEP

The provisions of PL 94–142 identify the basic composition of the team that will develop the IEP. The following persons must be included:

1. The teacher or teachers (special and/or regular) of the child
2. A person who has responsibility for providing or supervising provision of special education services (must be someone other than the child's teacher)
3. The parent(s) or guardian of the child
4. The student, whenever appropriate

In addition, if the student is being considered for initial placement in special education, the team should include a member of the evaluation team or someone familiar with the assessment procedures used and with the results. This may be the child's teacher, the representative from special education, or other representative. Selection of other team participants will differ with the child being considered: a speech/language therapist or audiologist for the hearing impaired child, a physical therapist or occupational therapist for the physically impaired, and so forth.

The responsibility for actually writing the IEP is not federally legislated. It seems to customarily fall upon the teacher, although it is not necessarily a teacher responsibility. Teacher input is certainly desirable, since the child's teacher(s) will be translating the committed educational services in the IEP into an instructional plan. Moreover, participation in writing the IEP may help relieve teacher anxiety concerning accountability if the student does not reach specified annual goals. The law does not require such accountability of the teacher, the school system, or any other involved person. This point was clarified by the Bureau of Education for the Handicapped:

> ... to relieve concerns that the individualized program constitutes a guarantee by the public agency and the teacher that a child will progress at a specified rate. However, this section does not relieve agencies and teachers from making good faith efforts to assist the child in achieving the objectives and goals listed in the individualized education program. Further, this section does not limit a parent's right to complain and ask for revisions of the child's program, or to invoke due process procedures, if the parent feels that these efforts are not being made (Public Law 94-142, Final Regulations, 1977, Sec. 121a. 349 (Comments)).

Content of the IEP

Although specific information in the IEP will vary from child to child, the regulations outlined by PL 94-142 describe the following minimum components:

1. Statements indicating the child's present level of performance
2. Annual goals indicating anticipated progress during the year
3. Intermediate (shorter term) instructional objectives
4. A statement of the specific special education and related services to be provided, as well as the extent to which the student will participate in regular education programs
5. The projected date for initiation of services and the anticipated duration of services
6. Evaluation criteria and procedures for measuring progress toward goals, on at least an annual basis

Some state agencies may require additional information (Schrag, 1977; Turnbull, Strickland, & Brantley, 1978), such as:

1. A procedural checklist
2. The student's schedule
3. A list of committee members
4. Relevant test information
5. Health information
6. Recommendations as to appropriate methods and materials
7. Justification for placement (This may include the legal category under which the child qualifies for state or federal funding, but such "labeling" should not be used for program planning for the child.)
8. Specification by name and position of each person responsible for carrying out the objectives of the IEP

Statements Indicating Present Levels of Performance   Statements of present levels of performance will include not only academic achievement but also pertinent information in such areas as self-help, social adaptation, and prevocational or vocational skills. Much of the information used in developing these statements will have been gathered before the IEP team meets. Moreover, different people on the team will have knowledge of the child's strengths and weaknesses in various areas through their interaction with him in their professional roles. The inclusion of the child's parents as members of the team provides additional insight into the child's needs. Their involvement will also usually result in better understanding and increasing cooperation between school and home.

This basic assessment data that has been accumulated should be accurate and recent. This picture of the student's performance provides the basis for appropriate placement and for the writing of annual goals and short term objectives. Its completeness and accuracy is therefore vital.

As the team reviews this information, subject areas in which instructional need exists are identified. Weaknesses and strengths within each subject are then pinpointed. Examples of statements of present levels of performance follow:

Reads 85 percent of the Dolch Sight Words at the second grade level.
Can independently compute 3-digit addition and subtraction problems with regrouping and renaming.
Cursive handwriting is often illegible. Manuscript handwriting is adequate as to letter formation and spacing but reveals habitual reversal of *b* and *d* and inversion of *m* and *w*.
Reveals an inability to cooperate with teammates in group sports by refusing to pass the ball or remain in his position.
Can read silently on a 2.1 grade level, demonstrating good comprehension in answering oral questions concerning factual information, main idea and detail and sequencing of events. Demonstrates poor comprehension in answering questions requiring the drawing of inferences.

If there is insufficient evaluative data available to make specific statements such as these, the team should identify areas in which information is lacking and request further evaluation of those skills.

IEP teams have sometimes been provided with scores from testing done the preceding school year or even earlier, or with only standardized scores, which give no information as to specific strengths or weaknesses. Statements of current performance should be based on current information. Turnbull et al. (1978) emphasize the need for recent and accurate evaluation data:

> If the IEP committee is unable to specify behavioral statements of current performance levels for each subject and skill area or the nature of specially designed instruction, they should gather more evaluative data rather than risk developing an inappropriate IEP based on false assumptions. The accurate specification of goals and objectives is dependent upon the precise stating of current performance levels (p. 148).

Once sufficient evaluation data is compiled and interpreted, the IEP team should make every effort to use clear and concise language in stating performance levels. These statements, which indicate specific strengths and weaknesses in skill areas, will become the basis for class placement, the development of the individual implementation plan, and the selection of appropriate teaching strategies, activities, and materials.

Annual Goals Indicating Anticipated Progress During the Year Annual goals provide a basis for specifying services that the student will be receiving during the school year. These goals may be in areas of social and behavioral needs as well as in the cognitive and/or psychomotor domains. It is recommended that three or four annual goals be developed for each area; however, the number is dependent upon such variables as the student's chronological and mental age, the amount of time to be devoted to instruction leading to goal fulfillment, the priority needs of the student, and the practicality of the goals (Hudson & Graham, 1978). Priorities for these annual goals should also be established, taking into consideration the most immediate needs of the student, and being sure that prerequisite skills will be taught. These annual goals should be global but also detailed enough that they may be understood by all persons reading them. It is not enough to state that Bob will read on a 3.1 reading level. This broad area of reading should be broken down into subskills, goals written for these subskills, and the order in which these goals are to be taught indicated.

Short Term Instructional Objectives Once annual goals are identified and priorities decided upon, the team must specify the intermediate steps leading to the attainment of these goals. Most subject areas can be broken into skill sequences or task hierarchies, moving from simple to complex. This is not to say that an inflexible hierarchy exists within each skill area but that, in general, some skills are antecedent to others. The process of analysis of the task (goal) involves isolating, describing, and sequencing the steps that, when taught, will lead the student to competency and the fulfillment of the annual goal.

It is not necessary for the purposes of PL 94–142 to list each and every step of a sequence. Usually three to five objectives may represent "milestones" in an orderly progression toward the annual goal. These objectives should, however, be written in behavioral terms. The verb used to describe the desired behavior should be as clear and specific as possible. Terms like "to know," "to understand," and "to appreciate" are open to many interpretations. The teacher is given no specific means of determining when and if a skill has been taught. Action verbs such as "will list," "will solve," "will decode," and "will classify" are explicit as to what the learner will do to demonstrate that he has reached the desired goal. The desired degree of mastery, or criterion, should also be included within the behavioral objective.

Excellent guides to the writing of behavioral objectives (Mager, 1975; Popham, 1969) are available. Although PL 94-142 does not stipulate that objectives must be written in true behavioral terms, it is required that criteria and measurement techniques for determining progress toward goals be included in the IEP. Such criteria will have been included if the objective has been stated behaviorally. A well written annual goal or short term objective will be in pupil terms, be measurable or observable, be stated in specific terms, and be realistic for the student. Benefits of such written goals and objectives have been summarized: Written goals and objectives provide accountability, can motivate students, facilitate teacher-parent communication, make teacher preparation more relevant, and help focus learning activities (Hayes, 1977).

Statement of Specific Services to Be Provided   It is required that the IEP be specific in listing the special education and related services necessary to provide for the student's unique needs. The committee should specify:

1. What type of special education is necessary
2. The extent to which it is needed
3. Which environment will best provide the needed support
4. How much time will be provided
5. Who will provide the service (Turnbull et al., 1978, p. 186)

Related services such as speech therapy, physical or occupational therapy, counseling, psychological services, and so forth, are also listed, as well as the person responsible for their implementation and the amount of time to be provided for each. Documentation of services will also include the extent to which the student will remain in the regular classroom and participate in the regular education program.

Projected Dates for Initiation and Duration of Services   The time at which a service will be initiated must be specified in the IEP. In the past, children were often referred, tested, and identified as eligible for a particular program, only to remain on a waiting list for a period of months or even years. This is no longer permissible. If it is apparent that a particular service is necessary but not available, the local education agency (LEA) must find a way to provide the service, either within the school system, through agreement with other school systems, or through outside agencies.

Anticipated duration of services must also be stated. It is understood that the student may progress faster or more slowly than was expected; the statement of duration of services is an estimate only, made on the basis of the initial evaluation. Specification of implementation and completion dates for services are safeguards for ensuring placement and review of student progress. The school system also benefits from this provision, being better able to tell when openings will occur in existing programs and when services are to be available.

Appropriate Objective Criteria and Schedule for Evaluating Progress   The IEP must, by law, include "appropriate objective criteria and evaluation procedures and schedules for determining on at least an annual basis, whether the short term instructional objectives are being achieved" (*Federal Register*, p. 42491). Evaluation is necessary to ensure that progress is being made and to ascertain whether revisions in the IEP are necessary. For each goal statement, the IEP team must also state how attainment of the goal will be evaluated. If measurable behavioral goals were stated, and appropriate behavioral terminology used in stating annual goals and short term objectives, the criteria have been established. No matter what the skill involves, it can and should be evaluated objectively and observably. By specifying within the written goal exactly how the objective will be evaluated, the team leaves nothing to chance. Unless criteria are specified, the teacher may make only a subjective evaluation of student progress, or it may be difficult to determine whether the objective has been reached.

Procedures for reviewing progress must be done on at least an annual basis. This does not mean that a student must be completely reassessed each year. It does mean that the teachers and support personnel responsible for the program are to keep the IEP team informed of the student's progress. This stipulation protects the student from being continued in a program with no review as to progress or continued appropriateness of the placement. The IEP team is concerned with getting answers to the following questions:

1.   Is the educational placement still appropriate?
2.   Are the supportive personnel still necessary?
3.   Are the deficits being remediated?
4.   Are the recommended goals and procedures still viable?

Without such an evaluative component, the IEP could lose its effectiveness.

While PL 94-142 mandates only the annual review, for most effective use of the individualized program, evaluation should be on a continuous basis. Systematic, daily collection of data on an informal basis gives the teacher the immediate opportunity to change teaching methods or materials, revise objectives, or provide motivation to students and parents through the documentation of even small gains.

The Individualized Implementation Plan

The IEP becomes more specific as its development moves toward actual service delivery. The more specific level, sometimes termed the Individualized Implementation Plan (IIP) follows the development of the total service plan. Teachers and/or other school personnel are to develop and carry out this phase of the IEP. The Individualized Implementation Plan will include (Schrag, 1977):

1. More specific program objectives
2. Strategies and instructional techniques
3. Specific materials and resources
4. Criteria for achievement of implementation/instructional objectives
5. Date objectives are initiated and completed (p. 27).

Objectives in the IIP are a more specific breakdown of those objectives and goals which were more generally specified in the first level of the IEP. The short term objectives and ongoing evaluation included within the IIP provide the basis for the annual review by the IEP team of the effectiveness and appropriateness of the child's program. The three levels of the IEP (the total service plan, the implementation/instructional plan, and the annual review) are interdependent, and there is much overlap between levels of the plan. Implementers of the IIP are often involved as members of the IEP committee in preparing the total service plan. The committee has the reponsibility both for developing the plan and for its appropriate implementation. The mandatory annual review by the committee "assures that program goals and objectives are being met, that implementators are held accountable for carrying out their program responsibilities, and that any program changes will be based on the results of ongoing accumulation of data" (Schrag, 1977, p. 57).

Parents and the IEP

The specific provision in PL 94-142 that the parent should be a member of the IEP committee made clear the intent of Congress "that IEP's should decidedly reflect the observations, opinions, and desires of the parent" (Crawford, 1978, p. 5). Active and continued involvement of the parent in preparation of the IEP and in evaluation and monitoring of the child's progress is desirable. It is unfortunate that many parents do not avail themselves of this opportunity to become involved in the educational experiences of their children. There are many reasons for the seeming indifference or the unwillingness of some parents to participate in the IEP process. Each school should make a sincere effort to develop more meaningful and positive relationships with these parents.

Parents who have been involved in implementation of the IEP were recently surveyed (Yeager, 1979). This nationwide study collected data from these parents regarding their impressions of the way in which the mandates of PL 94–142 have been carried out. Responses reflected some enthusiasm and gratitude, but greater frustration, concern, and confusion. It became evident from parent comments that there is no consistency in implementation of the mandated services to the handicapped, and that much remains to be accomplished in effective provision of such services.

Areas of Concern

The individualized education program was described by the National Advisory Committee on the Handicapped (1977) as "an invaluable education tool which should be fully and unreservedly used by every school in the nation with every handicapped child." Advantages of a well written IEP are obvious. It eliminates misunderstanding and confusion, provides a needed interdisciplinary team approach, and ensures good standard teaching practices for the handicapped (Crawford, 1978). The IEP and IIP serve as an academic management system, providing the basis for daily lesson plans and an ongoing evaluation program. The IEP helps the teacher to better organize and plan, preventing a "hit-or-miss" or "trial-and-error" approach to remediation. The teacher is led to a better understanding of the child and the handicap. Implementation of the program will introduce the teacher to the necessity of identifying skills to be taught, finding the entry level of the student, and progressing from there. Such an introduction often leads to an upgrading of the quality of instruction for the entire classroom.

Guidelines differ as to what comprises a "well written" IEP. Minimum elements to be included are specifically stated in PL 94–142. However, there is no general agreement among state education agencies, intermediate educational units, local education agencies, and teacher training institutions as to its scope. In many cases, inadequate, improper, and incomplete IEPs have been provided to teachers receiving children. The report of the "placement team" of some systems is called the IEP, although it may be so general that it is of little or no value as an educational tool. Generalized, nonspecific statements that do not clearly enumerate the services to be provided and delineate the teacher's responsibilities are unsatisfactory. In other systems, however, the IEP has included overly detailed instructional strategies and even daily lesson plans. In neither instance has the IEP been appropriately developed.

Such variations in the IEP content may arise from failure to visualize the IEP as a part of the orderly *process* of providing appropriate and effective educational situations for students with differences. Failure to differentiate between levels of the process (the total service delivery plan and the implementation/instructional plan), or between the functions of the placement committee, the IEP team and the team responsible for the implementation of services may contribute to the differences in amount and specificity of content.

Teacher and administrator attitudes may present a formidable obstacle to appropriate development and implementation of the IEP. Many have negative attitudes toward mainstreaming, feeling that the handicapped should remain the sole responsibility of special education. Others will not agree that the handicapped child can and will progress, given a program that focuses upon the child's needs and provides appropriate remediation. However, the single factor causing most resentment, on the part of both regular and special education teachers, is the great amount of "paper work" necessary to comply with local, state, and federal guidelines. A great amount of information must be documented for each child, from the time of initial referral to termination of service provision. Published guidelines for writing and implementation of the IEP have included sample forms for organization of this required information. School systems have adapted these forms or developed their own to include state and local system requirements. Workshops on "Developing the IEP" have in many cases been workshops on filling out these forms, with little or no information being given on ways to determine specific needs, write behavioral objectives, choose appropriate methods and materials, and carry out ongoing assessment procedures. In some systems, emphasis seems to be on completeness of the forms rather than on effective delivery of the listed services.

Monitoring of service delivery has revealed such gross misuse as identical IEPs being written for every child in a class. Other IEPs have been written, signed, shelved, and disregarded. Such misuse or disuse of the IEP may result from ignorance of what is required, or from resentment at having to comply with the legislative requirements, but discussions with teachers reveal a much more serious cause for failure to implement an individual educational plan. The teacher already in the classroom is not trained in planning and implementing a program specifically designed to meet the needs of the individual child. In some instances the teacher has expected the child to be delivered complete with a program that requires no planning on the part of the teacher. Provision of such detailed programs for teacher implementation is not only impractical, but is undesirable. However, teachers who have "taught the textbook" do *not* know how to identify specific competencies, to determine skill sequences, and to "make the match" between objectives, methods, and materials. Training of both regular and special education teachers in such areas as developmental assessment, diagnosis of needs, and appropriate individualization of objectives and instruction is therefore crucial for the success of the mainstreaming concept. It is imperative that institutions of higher learning develop course content designed to provide such skills and knowledge. School systems must also make greater efforts to provide appropriate and effective inservice experiences for those teachers already in the classroom.

CONCLUSION

Educational specialists and teachers have been encouraged by Duffey and Fedner (1978):

> . . . to make use of and to refine the technology available to them. They are capable of measuring each student's individual progress . . . and of adjusting instruction appropriately. Miraculously, haphazard education has been successful for many children. We educators do, however, have a large population of students, especially those regarded as special, who have not been able to benefit from haphazard instruction. It is primarily these students who should receive the benefit of accurate educational diagnosis and instruction based on that assessment. (p. 250).

Virtually every public school teacher in the United States is already or soon will be involved in writing and/or implementing IEPs. The individualized education program is the foundation of appropriate placement and effective provision of services for the handicapped. Teachers must be both receptive to and competent in methods of individualized assessment, implementation, and evaluation. Unless they receive help in achieving such competency, the promise and full potential of PL 94–142 can never become a reality.

REFERENCES

Crawford, D. Parent involvement in instructional planning. *Focus on Exceptional Children*, 1978, *10*(7), 1–5.

Duffey, J. B., & Fedner, M. L. Educational diagnosis with instructional use. *Exceptional Children*, 1978, *44*(4), 246–251.

Federal Register, 42, (Aug. 23, 1977).

Hayes, J. Annual goals and short term objectives. In S. Torres (Ed.), *A primer on individualized education programs for handicapped children*. Reston, Va.: The Foundation for Exceptional Children, 1977.

Hayes, J. & Higgins, S. Issues regarding the IEP: Teachers on the front line. *Exceptional Children*, 1978, *44*(4), 267–273.

Hudson, F. G., & Graham, S. An approach to operationalizing the IEP. *Learning Disability Quarterly*, 1978, *1*, 13–32.

Mager, R. F. *Preparing instructional objectives* (2nd ed.). Belmont, Cal.: Fearon Publishers, 1975.

National Advisory Committee on the Handicapped. *Annual Report*. Washington, D.C.: United States Department of Health, Education, and Welfare, 1977.

Popham, W. J. *Instructional objectives*. Skokie, Ill.: Rand McNally, 1969.

Public Law 94-142, *Education for All Handicapped Children Act of 1975*, 94th Congress, 1st Session, 1975.

Public Law 94-142, *Education for All Handicapped Children Act of 1975, Final Regulations*. U.S. Office of Education, 1977.

Schrag, J. A. *Individualized educational programming (IEP): A child study team process*. Austin, Tex.: Learning Concepts, 1977.

Torres, S. (Ed.). *A primer on individualized education programs for handicapped children*. Reston, Va.: The Foundation for Exceptional Children, 1977.

Turnbull, A., Strickland, B., & Brantley, J. *Developing and implementing individualized education programs*. Columbus, Oh.: Charles E. Merrill, 1978.

Yeager, P. Parents speak on the IEP. *The Directive Teacher*, 1979, *2*(1), 13–14.

8
ASSESSMENT AND EVALUATION IN THE CLASSROOM

Virginia K. Laycock

In order to educate all children in the least restrictive environment, teachers are being asked to accommodate a wider range of individual differences in the classroom. Not all of the differences between handicapped students and their normal peers are instructionally significant. There are, however, certain unique characteristics of each learner that directly affect his response to educational experiences. These critical characteristics must be identified and taken into account in instructional planning.

The effectiveness of the entire process of individualized educational programming hinges upon accurate assessment or diagnosis. Unless a teacher can pinpoint exactly *what* a child needs to learn and *how* he learns most successfully, any attempt at individualization is like a shot in the dark. Chances of being on target in instructional decision making are greatly increased when reliable information about the learner is available. Educational assessment or diagnosis is, therefore, a necessary first step in individualized programming.

Diagnosis refers to the process of gathering and interpreting educationally relevant information about a particular learner. As Salvia and Ysseldyke (1978) point out, there are at least five reasons for conducting assessment: screening, placement, program planning, program evaluation, and evaluation of individual progress. Issues surrounding the many functions of educational assessment are both complex and controversial. The present chapter, therefore, considers diagnostic assessment only as it relates to individualized instructional programming. The "educationally relevant information" to be collected will provide the basis for the selection and revision of instructional objectives and teaching strategies.

An earlier version of this chapter appeared in Robert M. Anderson, John G. Greer, and Sara J. Odle (eds.), *Individualizing Educational Materials for Special Children in the Mainstream*, Baltimore: University Park Press, 1978.

THE DIAGNOSTIC PROCESS

Misconceptions and misuses of educational diagnosis abound in practice. Too often, evaluation is viewed as simply a necessary step in getting a child placed in special education. Finding out whether he/she "qualifies" becomes an end in itself. It is not uncommon for students to be administered the same pre-established battery of tests regardless of presenting problems or reasons for referral. Testing is usually administered in a single session by an evaluator who is unfamiliar to the child. The written report sent to the teacher may contain little information that was not already known. Even if it is determined that the student should receive special services, it is probable that he/she will remain in his/her regular classroom for at least a portion of the day. When the teacher has received no practical guidance for providing for this child, diagnosis has served no real purpose.

Meaningful educational assessment is far different from the situations just described. It is, first of all, goal directed. Diagnosis is conducted for the express purpose of describing an individual's learning behavior in terms that imply instructional interventions. Complete assessment should focus on gathering and organizing information about three major learning characteristics: 1) present levels of performance, 2) specific skills and behaviors of concern, and 3) learning style. These represent the desired outcomes of assessment. The exact diagnostic techniques to be used for arriving at these determinations may differ in each case, depending on the presenting problem and the information already available. The accurate description of learning behaviors with respect to performance levels, specific skills, and learning style leads directly to the selection of individualized objectives, teaching strategies, and instructional materials.

A second characteristic of good educational diagnosis is that it incorporates a variety of sources for information. Testing is indeed useful, but it is not the sole method of obtaining data. A number of other assessment techniques may also be employed. A medical examination is usually in order to identify health and acuity problems. Interviews may be conducted with the child and his/her parents to determine their perceptions of the situation. Permanent records and case histories may contribute to the understanding of a child's development and adjustment over time. Valuable information may be gathered by observing the student in his/her everyday interactions. Finally, formal, standardized tests, as well as informal, teacher-made tests, are important assessment tools. The most complete educational diagnoses draw upon many relevant sources of information.

A third requirement for meaningful educational diagnosis is that the classroom teacher play a central role in gathering and interpreting information. Assessment should be conducted within the child's everyday learning environment to the greatest extent possible, because it is under these conditions that he is asked to perform. The classroom teacher must be actively involved in the assessment process, because it is this individual who is in closest contact with the child and in the position to obtain the richest diagnostic data. In addition, it is the classroom teacher who will be ultimately responsible for implementing many aspects of the instructional program developed from the diagnosis.

The needs of the majority of students in the regular classroom can be adequately assessed by the teacher. When serious learning or behavior problems become apparent, however, the teacher may request assistance in a more intensive evaluation. Different states and school districts have defined their own referral procedures. The titles assigned to the different individuals who assist in educational diagnosis also vary. In many areas, the resource teacher, diagnostic prescriptive teacher, or psychoeducational evaluator is available within each school to work with the classroom teacher. Typically, these individuals will coordinate and conduct whatever necessary assessment cannot reasonably be accomplished in the regular classroom. School psychologists are also available within each district to confer with teachers and evaluators and to administer tests requiring specialized training and certification, such as IQ tests. A multidisciplinary approach is most helpful when a student's problems are particularly complex. Any number of specialists may be involved as needed. Pediatricians, neurologists, ophthalmologists, optometrists, speech and language clinicians, physical therapists, psychiatrists, psychologists, and guidance counselors are but a few of the professionals who might contribute to the complete diagnosis. Although there is no need to prolong the assessment process or to involve any more individuals than necessary, multifaceted problems do require the expertise of other professions whenever these might have direct bearing on the child's performance in the classroom. Educational diagnosis, then, begins in the classroom, and its end product, an individualized instructional program, must also be classroom oriented. Along the way, the teacher may consult any number of individuals who can directly contribute to the understanding of a child's learning behavior.

A final characteristic of meaningful educational assessment is that it is an ongoing process. Certainly, there must be a limit to initial diagnostic efforts. If one simply tested and observed until all desired information was known about a child, one would never reach the stage of designing an instructional program. Assessment is not an end in itself; it is, rather, the means to delivering the appropriate educational services. Initial diagnosis should be conducted until educators have achieved a working knowledge of a child's present levels of performance, related behaviors and skills, and learning style. An individualized program can then be developed. Results of the diagnosis are not infallible. Furthermore, the student's performance is subject to change over time. For these reasons, diagnosis is continually amended in light of current evidence. The teacher's daily interactions with the learner provide the best indications of his/her abilities. Assessment, therefore, should be inseparable from instruction, characterizing teaching in a diagnostic prescriptive way.

In summary, meaningful educational diagnosis differs from its less effective counterparts in several important respects. It is goal-directed, conducted specifically to describe three aspects of student performance: functional levels, skills and behaviors of concern, and learning style. The most valuable diagnostic information is drawn from a variety of sources and does not result solely from testing. Diagnosis is likely to be most relevant for instruction when the classroom teacher plays a key role in the process. Other school personnel and professionals should assist in diagnosis to whatever extent is indicated. Preliminary assessment is necessarily finite. The process of diagnosis, however, is never-ending, because it continues to pervade all teaching interactions. Assessment information is updated and revised based on daily observations of the child's performance.

In the sections that follow, each of the three areas of investigation is discussed in greater detail. It is beyond the scope of the present chapter to deal with the specific applications of the various measurement techniques. The construction, administration, and interpretation of assessment devices constitute a major study in their own rights. This chapter attempts only to describe the *types* of diagnostic information to be gathered and the *organization* of these data into a form that facilitates instructional planning.

MEASURING PRESENT PERFORMANCE LEVELS

A teacher may have only a global definition of a student's problem as assessment is begun. Because assessment progresses from the general to the highly specific, it is sometimes viewed as a process of pinpointing or "zeroing-in" on the exact difficulties. An early step in the process is the determination of performance levels. Within any area of development—motor, perceptual, language, cognitive, social, academic, etc. —there exists an orderly progression of skills. The age at which the majority of learners demonstrate specific skills is determined empirically and referred to as the norm. In reality, individual children pass through a sequence of skills at different rates. For this reason, it is helpful to measure performance levels to indicate at what stage the child is presently functioning in developmental sequences in the areas of concern.

The terms *performance level, functional level,* and *developmental level* are often used interchangeably. Age or grade equivalents are the customary means of reporting these levels. To obtain such normative data, educators must rely for the most part on formal, standardized testing. These tests have been norm-referenced so that a child's obtained score can be compared with the scores of his/her chronological peers in the standardization sample to yield an age or grade equivalent. Thus, a student who earns a developmental age of 14-2 performed comparably to children in the standardization sample who were 14 years, 2 months of age. Similarly, a derived score of 2.5 on an achievement test would indicate that the child in question performed as those in the standardized sample who were in mid-second grade.

Caution must be exercised to avoid overinterpretation of age or grade equivalents. The same derived age or grade may mean different things for different chronological ages. One should not expect a 12-year-old child with a developmental age of 6, for instance, to behave the same as a 5-year-old with a developmental age of 6. Furthermore, identical abilities are not implied even for children of the same chronological and performance ages. Age or grade equivalents merely provide an index of the child's functional level. They serve a valuable role in narrowing the range of abilities under consideration and in guiding further investigation.

Intelligence Testing

When learning problems exist, it is generally helpful to obtain an estimate of the child's overall cognitive capabilities. Information from an intelligence test that has been correctly administered, scored, and interpreted can be useful in clarifying the nature of a child's problem and in predicting school performance in the near future. In many states, an IQ test is required as one basis for judging a student's need for special services. Never should an IQ score be the sole criterion for labeling a child or assigning him/her to special education. Such abuses of intelligence testing have been opposed on educational, ethical, and legal grounds.

It is important for the teacher to understand what intelligence testing can and cannot do. Based on a comprehensive review of literature, Sattler has summarized the limitations of intelligence testing as follows:

1. The IQ is limited in predicting occupational success.
2. The IQ is limited in predicting nonacademic skills.
3. Intelligence tests do not provide measures of innate capacity.
4. Intelligence tests provide limited information about the domain of cognitive functions.
5. Intelligence tests do not measure the processes underlying the test responses.
6. Intelligence tests penalize nonconventional responses.
7. Intelligence tests may be unreliable for long range predictions (1974, p. 24).

Additional complex issues must be considered when IQ tests are used with children from minority groups, whose sociocultural experiences often differ significantly from the conventional and from the backgrounds of the children comprising the standardization sample. Until the matter of nondiscriminatory testing is resolved, extreme caution must govern any decision making based on the results of standardized testing of minority group children.

Despite the shortcomings of intelligence testing, it remains the best available means of measuring an individual's general level of functioning. It has been found to correlate highly with scholastic achievement, and it is one of the most useful predictors of the ability to profit from the types of educational experiences customarily provided in the schools. When IQ tests are used responsibly, they serve as one valuable source of information about a child's learning behavior.

Many tests are currently available that purport to assess intelligence. In most school districts, group intelligence tests are administered in designated grades, usually in conjunction with achievement tests. Although group tests may prove useful as screening devices, they are usually inadequate intelligence measures for children with learning and behavior problems. Disorders of attention, perception, reading, and handwriting can interfere with performance and produce inaccurate IQ scores. Individually administered intelligence tests are, therefore, preferred for in depth educational diagnosis.

The two individually administered tests of intelligence most commonly used are the Wechsler Intelligence Scales (1955, 1967, 1974) and the Stanford-Binet Intelligence Scale (Terman and Merrill, 1973). The administration of these tests is restricted to psychologists or evaluators who have received specialized training and licensing. Teachers in both regular and special education, however, should become sufficiently familiar with the construction, administration, and interpretation of these tests that they can utilize the information provided in reports of psychological evaluations to student advantage.

Performance Levels in Other Areas

Getting an estimate of overall cognitive functioning may be a common starting point in the assessment of children with learning problems, but it is also important to determine performance levels in specific areas of concern. According to the nature of a student's problems, any of the following might warrant investigation: gross and fine motor development, visual processing, auditory processing, language development, social-emotional development, and the basic academic skills of reading, writing, spelling, and mathematics.

Numerous assessment devices are available to assist in the measurement of performance levels. For the most part, the necessary information may be collected using either of two techniques—tests or developmental checklists.

In testing, stimuli are presented to an individual under controlled conditions to sample from the domain of behavior under consideration. The situation is structured to evoke behavior in a form that can be measured and quantified. A test is valid to the extent that responses sampled truly reflect a person's performance in the intended area.

Behavior samples also provide the basis for assessment when developmental checklists or rating scales are employed. With developmental checklists, however, it is not necessary for the child to demonstrate target behaviors under actual testing conditions. Instead, a parent, teacher, or other responsible individual reports whether the child has performed each behavior at some time in the past in his/her everyday environment.

Developmental checklists or rating scales have proved most useful in the assessment of abilities that do not readily lend themselves to testing. It is often difficult, for example, to sample the richness of an individual's language behavior under controlled testing conditions. Aspects of social and emotional adjustment may also need to be evaluated in the natural environment. Rating scales are particularly helpful in the assessment of very young children when testing is not always appropriate. Many of the tasks considered landmarks in early childhood development would be difficult to elicit under testing conditions.

An example of a developmental checklist for preschool children is provided in Figure 1. This section of the *MEMPHIS Comprehensive Developmental Scale* (Quick, Little, and Campbell, 1974) is designed for assessing personal-social abilities. The 60 skills to be sampled are

Chronological Age

Developmental Age

Raw Score

Date of Evaluation

Date of Birth

Name

PERSONAL–SOCIAL SKILLS

#	Years	Months	Pass	Fail	Skill
60	5.00	60	P	F	Plays competitive exercise games.
59			P	F	Dresses self with attempts at tying shoes.
58			P	F	Spreads with knife, partial success.
57	4.75	57	P	F	Uses play materials constructively; builds, does not tear down.
56			P	F	Dresses self except tying shoes.
55			P	F	"Picks up" some after playing with no coaxing.
54	4.50	54	P	F	Attends well for short stories.
53			P	F	Uses paper straw appropriately without damaging.
52			P	F	Washes face well.
51	4.25	51	P	F	Separates from mother easily.
50			P	F	Distinguishes front from back of clothes.
49			P	F	Completely cares for self at toilet, including cleaning and dressing.
48	4.00	48	P	F	Plays with others with minimal friction.
47			P	F	Buttons medium-sized buttons.
46			P	F	Goes on very short distance errands outside the home.
45	3.75	45	P	F	Performs for others; i.e. performs a simple rhyme or song.
44			P	F	Washes hands well.
43			P	F	Brushes teeth adequately.
42	3.50	42	P	F	Attempts help at little household tasks; i.e. sweeping, dusting.
41			P	F	Completely undresses for bedtime.
40			P	F	Removes clothing for toileting.
39			P	F	Buttons large buttons.
38	3.25	39	P	F	Performs toilet activities by self (not dressing, cleaning).
37			P	F	Plays cooperatively, interacts with others.
36	3.00	36	P	F	Puts on shoes and socks (tying not required).
35			P	F	Feeds self with little spilling, both fork and spoon.
34			P	F	Shares upon request.
33	2.75	33	P	F	Avoids simple hazards (hot stove, etc.)
32			P	F	Puts on a coat (buttoning not required).
31			P	F	Dries hands well.
30	2.50	30	P	F	Is not overly destructive with household goods, toys, etc.
29			P	F	Gets a drink unassisted from fountain or sink.
28			P	F	Sucks from a plastic straw.
27	2.25	27	P	F	Eats with fork but spills some.
26			P	F	Recognizes self in mirror.
25			P	F	Uses single words or likenesses to show wants.
24	2.00	24	P	F	Minds—does as told generally.
23			P	F	Removes coat or dress (unbuttoning not required).
22			P	F	At least asks to go to toilet—day and night.
21	1.75	21	P	F	Does not place objects on floor in mouth.
20			P	F	Eats with spoon, spilling little.
19			P	F	Voluntarily "slows down" to take naps or rest.
18	1.50	18	P	F	Plays around other children effectively.
17			P	F	Drinks from cup or glass unassisted.
16			P	F	Pulls off socks, but not necessarily shoes.
15	1.25	15	P	F	Follows simple commands or instructions.
14			P	F	Feeds self with a spoon—some spilling allowed.
13			P	F	Holds out arms to assist with clothing.
12	1.00	12	P	F	Temporarily responds to "no," "stop."
11			P	F	Cooperates with dressing—does not resist.
10			P	F	Chews food.
9	.75	9	P	F	Places food in mouth with hands.
8			P	F	Grasps small objects with thumb and index finger.
7			P	F	Desires personal attention and contact beyond just holding.
6	.50	6	P	F	Drinks from a cup or glass with assistance.
5			P	F	Occupies self with a toy for a short period of time.
4			P	F	Grasps foot or brings hand to mouth.
3	.25	3	P	F	Pulls at clothing with hands.
2			P	F	Sucking and swallowing are present.
1			P	F	Reaches for and wants to be held by familiar persons.

This scale reprinted by permission of the Author and the Publisher, Fearon Publishers, Inc., 6'Davis Drive, Belmont, Calif. 94002.

Figure 1.   An example of a developmental checklist for preschool children.

arranged in developmental order from simple to complex. One month's credit is assigned for each task the child successfully performs. A developmental age can then be calculated.

For most of the items listed, an observant parent, teacher, or guardian would be able to indicate whether a child has mastered the task in question. In instances where the adult is not certain of the child's capabilities, the situation may be structured in the attempt to elicit the desired response. In application then, the *MEMPHIS Scale* incorporates both the reporting by significant adults and the informal testing of specific skills as necessary.

The usefulness of rating scales depends directly on the reliability of the sources consulted. Those reporting may be subtly biased or simply unaware of a child's actual abilities. To reduce chances of error in diagnosis, developmental checklists are generally employed in conjunction with formal or informal testing and systematic observation. When tenuous data are verified by using these other measures, rating scales can be helpful tools in determining developmental levels.

For academic subjects, grade equivalents are usually considered more instructionally relevant than performance ages. Although developmental checklists can be used effectively, testing may be a more efficient means of determining grade equivalents. Several different subject matter areas may be sampled within a relatively short period of time by means of achievement tests. Group achievement tests are often administered to all students within a school district at established intervals. Results of such testing should be considered in educational diagnosis, but interpretation of achievement scores should take into account the possible confounding effects of a child's specific disabilities. A serious reading problem, for example, may contaminate scores on all other subtests, even those purporting to measure skills in other areas such as science or mathematics. Individually administered achievement tests are therefore advised for the more accurate identification of the performance levels of students with learning and behavior problems.

In addition to achievement tests, diagnostic tests may also be used to obtain grade equivalents. Whereas achievement tests briefly sample from several different areas at a time, diagnostic tests focus in greater detail upon a single subject. Although the major function of diagnostic tests involves the determination of specific skill deficits, the majority of diagnostic tests are also norm-referenced to provide grade equivalents as well.

Thus far, discussion has centered on assessment of a child's performance in comparison to the performance of his chronological peers to identify his level of functioning. Measuring an individual's abilities with reference to his/her age-mates represents a concern for *interindividual differences*. Of equal importance is the consideration of *intraindividual differences*. Intraindividual differences refer to the discrepancies that exist among the child's own levels of functioning across the various developmental areas. A certain amount of unevenness in development is to be expected, because all individuals are more advanced in some areas than in others. Individual profiles must be interpreted with care and with a knowledge of what constitutes significant differences. When approached in this way, analysis of intraindividual differences may reveal whether a child's deficiencies are generalized or limited to specific areas. It may also indicate relative strengths that might be used to the student's advantage.

A case study is now introduced to illustrate the application of the assessment process described. Background information about the student is first presented. Data contributing to the identification of performance levels are then summarized. This same case study is later extended within this chapter to provide examples of the organization of diagnostic data into the remaining categories—skills and behaviors of concern and learning style.

Case Example

Jason, age 13 years, 9 months, is an eighth grader experiencing many problems in the regular classroom. His teacher has become greatly concerned over his disruptive behavior and his sporadic academic performance.

Jason is a fair-skinned boy with expressive blue eyes. He is shorter than average for his age and considerably overweight.

Jason's family resides in a small community where his father is a practicing attorney. Jason's mother has a master's degree in education and teaches in a nearby elementary school. Jason has two older sisters, one of whom is away at college. The parents feel that Jason learns slowly because he lacks the necessary motivation. They would like for the school to help Jason improve his work habits.

Jason's general health is good, with no indications of vision or hearing difficulties. The pediatrician has recommended several weight reduction diets in the past, but Jason has been reluctant to cooperate. At times he complains of upset stomach and trouble with sleeping. His mother tends to attribute these problems to "nerves."

An investigation of Jason's school history revealed that no serious problems were reported in the primary grades. Jason attained B's and C's in his schoolwork. In the fourth grade, Jason's parents first became aware of his difficulties—he received unsatisfactory grades in several subjects and was also labeled as a discipline problem. Jason was promoted into fifth grade on the condition that he receive special help. A private tutor was hired to work with Jason until his grades rose to A's and B's the second semester. In sixth and seventh grades, however, he began failing in math and science. Jason was also suspended from school on three separate occasions for fighting, yelling obscenities at the teacher, and refusing to participate in class.

The results of Jason's educational assessment are summarized and presented for each area of investigation. First summarized are results from present levels of performance assessment.

On the Wechsler Intelligence Scale for Children—Revised (WISC-R), Jason obtained a Full Scale IQ of 77 ± 3. The chances that the range of scores from 74 to 80 includes his true IQ are about 68 out of 100. This indicates that, overall, Jason is functioning in the borderline range of intelligence, and at the 6th percentile with respect to children of his age in the standardization sample. Jason achieved an IQ of 91 ± 4 on the Verbal Scale, showing average ability. A Performance Scale IQ of 65 ± 5 reveals deficient performance of tasks requiring nonverbal, primarily visual-motor capabilities. The 26 point difference between Jason's Verbal and Performance IQs is significant. Although he is able to deal adequately with situations requiring language skills, his performance deteriorates when he is forced to rely on his less developed perceptual skills.

Results of the Bender Visual Motor Gestalt Test confirm Jason's difficulties in the performance areas. Jason was unable to reproduce designs adequately and attained a developmental age of 7 years, 10 months, a functional level approximately 6 years below his chronological age.

On the Wide Range Achievement Test, the following grade equivalents were obtained: Reading—7.2, Spelling—6.4, and Arithmetic—4.3. Jason's performance in all three academic areas was lower than his actual grade placement of 8.2. Jason received his lowest score in arithmetic, which is also one of the subjects he is failing in the classroom.

On an individual reading inventory used as a placement test for the school's basal reading program, Jason's instructional level was high seventh grade. His independent level was high sixth grade, and his frustrational reading level was mid-eighth grade.

IDENTIFYING SKILLS AND BEHAVIORS OF CONCERN

The measurement of functional levels was presented as a necessary first step in assessing learner characteristics. A developmental age or grade equivalent helps to narrow the range of skills under consideration. Once a child is described as having a language age of 2–6, for example, one has a general idea of his/her receptive and expressive capabilities. Likewise, a sixth grade reading level implies a certain subset of competencies. As helpful as performance levels might be, however, they cannot provide the direct bases for academic or behavioral programming. Typically, children with learning problems have acquired skills in somewhat piece-meal, nonsequential fashion. Simply knowing *where* a student is functioning in a developmental sequence does not guarantee accurate knowledge of *what* he/she can and cannot do. One has to measure specific skills.

If affective and social difficulties are evident, these too must be specifically assessed. Frequently used terms such as dependency, hyperactivity, poor self-concept, withdrawal, and aggression suggest only general behavior patterns and fail to imply what can be done for a particular child. The problem must be behaviorally defined before appropriate intervention strategies can be planned. A teacher needs to know exactly what a child *is doing* or what he/she *is not doing* that fails to meet expectations. Rather than saying that a child is aggressive, for example, the problem could be operationally defined as hitting classmates and addressing the teacher as "old lady." Instead of labeling a student withdrawn, a more useful assessment would point out that the child walks off by himself/herself on the playground, does not volunteer to participate in class activities, and does not initiate conversation with the teacher.

Once target behaviors are specified, related diagnostic information can be gathered. One can determine the extent of the problem by measuring how frequently the behavior is occurring and comparing this with the desired level. It is also helpful to identify the conditions under which the behavior is typically demonstrated.

The task at this stage of the diagnostic process is to describe problem skills and behaviors as specifically as possible, so that goals can be easily derived for instruction and intervention. The assessment tools most useful for this purpose are criterion-referenced testing and direct observation.

Criterion-Referenced Testing

Although norm-referenced devices were most useful for ascertaining performance levels, criterion-referenced devices are best suited for pinpointing exact strengths and weaknesses. In criterion-referenced testing, an individual's performance is evaluated against a preestablished criterion or standard for mastery rather than against the performance of his/her peers. Criterion-referenced measurement allows a teacher to describe a child's competency in absolute instead of relative terms. A result of such testing might be, for example, the determination that a second grade student can print 23 lower case letters correctly but misforms the letters *e*, *g*, and *y*. From a criterion-referenced reading inventory, a teacher might learn that a pupil is able to read 80% of the 220 Dolch Sight Words correctly. On the scoresheet, individual words would be marked to indicate correct or incorrect responses.

There are many criterion-referenced tests published commercially. Some are entitled "diagnostic," to emphasize the detailed analysis of skills. Formal diagnostic tests are often constructed to yield both norm- and criterion-referenced results. In selecting a particular test for use, a teacher should want the necessary skills to be thoroughly sampled through instructionally relevant tasks. Ease and efficiency in administration and scoring are also desirable attributes.

When published tests are unavailable or inappropriate, an informal, teacher-made test may be constructed to assess a child's specific abilities. Effective informal assessment for any developmental or subject matter area involves essentially the same steps. These are:

1. Locating or developing a skill sequence for the area of concern
2. Defining each skill as an observable, measurable behavior
3. Specifying the conditions for performance of each skill in terms of materials and mode of presentation
4. Establishing criteria for mastery of each skill in terms of number correct, percentage, rate, or other standard
5. Preparing stimulus materials and scoring sheets
6. Presenting designated tasks to the child
7. Recording responses
8. Evaluating performance in reference to criteria

Informal testing conducted in this manner can be a highly valuable source of diagnostic information. A test can be designed to tap the exact skills of interest, and the assessment tasks devised can be closely related to teaching tasks. In this way, results of testing can be generalized to the instructional setting with greater confidence.

Formal or informal diagnostic tests usually require more time to administer than achievement tests, because they involve a more in-depth sampling of skills. Interpretation is also done in detail. In addition to the basic determination of whether or not a student has achieved mastery of each skill, the teacher is also concerned with the nature of learning difficulties demonstrated.

By analyzing a pupil's errors, one can often detect a pattern. In some cases, a child gives the same type of wrong response consistently, suggesting that he/she has learned the skill or concept incorrectly. At other times, a student may make numerous errors with no apparent pattern, leading one to conclude that he has not yet learned any consistent association. Although the two overall scores might be similar, the response patterns have different instructional implications.

Diagnostic Observation

Although testing is a powerful tool for educational assessment, one must not underestimate the usefulness of observation. Testing and observation actually complement each other in the assessment process. When a parent or teacher has carefully observed a child in home or classroom activities, the adult can often provide accurate descriptions of his behavior. In many instances, good observation reduces the amount of testing that is necessary. It can also serve as an informal reliability check after testing is done by providing evidence to confirm or contradict the results of testing.

Observation can take many different forms. It is usually characterized in terms of the degree of structure imposed in the perceiving and recording of behaviors. The simplest, unstructured observation consists of watching behavior with no attempt to systematize or quantify the information. The chances of overlooking or forgetting important diagnostic information can be reduced by applying more methodical approaches.

Many teachers keep daily journals and record brief notes about a child's performance. Other teachers prefer to use checklists on which they simply mark or date the skills a child has demonstrated.

To avoid the loss of precision and objectivity that often results from recording in retrospect, direct observation can be conducted for chosen times and situations. Narrative recording or naturalistic observation involves writing down a behavior sequence as it is actually taking place. This type of observation is most helpful when a teacher is first defining a problem, because it provides a record of the total situation in sequence. Once specific behaviors have been targeted, other systems may prove more efficient for measuring the extent to which behaviors are demonstrated.

When behaviors of concern are discrete—that is, they have a definite beginning and end—either frequency counting or duration recording may be appropriate. Frequency counting should be used when a teacher wants to know how often a behavior is occurring. This technique is sometimes called "event recording," because one simply counts the number of times the behavioral event takes place. When a teacher is interested in finding out how much time a student spends engaged in a particular behavior, duration recording is in order. A stop watch or regular clock is used to keep a running account of the time elapsing while a student is performing the target behavior.

When behaviors are not discrete, or when several behaviors are to be measured at once, time sampling may be the preferred technique. Time sampling involves "recording the presence or absence of the behavior within short, uniform time intervals" (Sulzer and Mayer, 1972, p. 264). After these or similar systems are employed to collect baseline data for several days, the teacher has obtained a more precise description of the problem.

Case Example

The sample assessment summary is now continued with a description of Jason's specific academic skills and classroom behaviors.

It is apparent from both testing and observation that Jason demonstrates strong language abilities. His Verbal IQ on the WISC-R was significantly higher than his Performance IQ. Within the verbal areas, Jason displayed a good background of general information and could give socially acceptable solutions for practical problems. He was able to solve oral arithmetic problems adequately and could define vocabulary words well. He showed average ability in recalling a series of digits. Observations by both parents and teachers emphasize Jason's strengths in comprehending and producing oral language.

Overall, Jason's perceptual motor skills are weak. His low Performance IQ resulted from significant difficulties in completing puzzles of familiar objects, reproducing abstract block designs, and attending to details in pictures.

Visual-motor problems were evident in Jason's drawings on the Bender Gestalt. In copying the nine geometric designs, Jason tended to distort shapes and to position them incorrectly in reference to each other.

Jason's visual-motor deficits are further apparent in his handwriting. Jason continues to print rather than to write in cursive. Letters are sometimes left incomplete, and capital and lower case letters are not correctly proportioned. Inconsistent sizing and spacing render Jason's printing nearly illegible at times.

Reading is one of Jason's stronger subject areas. His ability to read and comprehend paragraphs is close to grade level, as evidenced by his score on the reading inventory. Jason often chooses to read in his free time and particularly enjoys comic books and mystery stories. When reading words in isolation, such as on the Wide Range Achievement Test, Jason tends to guess at unknown words rather than decode them systematically. His higher grade level attained on the paragraph inventory may reflect his ability to use context clues to his advantage in attacking unfamiliar words.

Jason's comprehension skills are adequate on the literal level. He has difficulty with certain more advanced skills, such as drawing conclusions and detecting cause and effect.

An informal phonics inventory supported the teacher's observations that Jason can adequately recognize and identify basic consonant and vowel patterns. He becomes confused when one sound may be represented by more than one symbol, as *c* and *s* or *ou* and *ow*. In such instances where one must rely on visual memory to recall which symbol appears in a particular word, Jason does not do well.

His visual memory difficulties also affect his spelling. Most of Jason's errors occur on phonetically irregular words where he has tried to apply phonic generalizations inappropriately. On the Wide Range Achievement Test, for example, he misspelled "nature" as "nacher." Jason also omitted some letters in longer spelling words. In testing as well as in his everyday work, Jason refused to attempt long words (over five letters) that he could not readily spell.

Math is Jason's weakest subject area. According to an informal math assessment and teacher observations, he has mastered basic addition and subtraction combinations, but occasionally reverts to counting on his fingers. Jason can demonstrate the processes involved in addition and subtraction computations, but makes many seemingly careless mistakes when asked to complete a set of these problems independently.

Jason does not know all of his multiplication facts automatically. In performing computations, he sometimes goes back to recite a table from the beginning in order to figure out a particular combination. In multiplication problems with two or more digits per term, Jason frequently errs in carrying or in aligning the partial products.

Jason demonstrates an understanding of the process of division and can complete examples with single digit divisors adequately. He tends to have trouble grouping digits correctly in the dividend. Common errors also include leaving remainders larger than divisors.

Jason's skills in applying basic money, measurement, and time concepts are satisfactory. The only Roman numerals that he recognizes consistently are I, V, and X.

Jason can add and subtract fractions with like denominators but cannot reduce fractions to lowest terms and find least common denominators.

Jason's teacher described his behavior in the classroom as "disruptive." Her anecdotal records revealed the following behavioral incidents occurring over a four-week period:

> Came to class without paper or pencil; talked constantly and refused to do his work; put his head down on his desk; walked around the room; made

faces at others; tried to cut another child's hair; glued pages of his reading book together; handcuffed his own hands behind his back; went up on the roof to get a ball and would not come down; balanced a book on his finger during reading; and tried to leave school grounds.

The following items were checked on an adaptive behavior scale as characteristic of Jason: often wastes time, moves sluggishly, does not persist with assignments even though he has the ability, and talks back to adults.

Narrative recording conducted during three 20-minute work periods suggested that disturbing behaviors, such as talking loudly to himself or rolling a pencil across the desk, tended to occur when the teacher was at the far side of the room. Peers typically responded to Jason's behavior with giggling and tattling.

A five-day check showed that Jason completed 20 percent of his written assignments in math. In other subject areas, he completed approximately 55 percent.

Time sampling was conducted for three days to assess two specific off-task behaviors during independent work periods. Target behaviors were talking aloud without permission and handling objects other than assigned instructional materials. Behaviors were recorded at 30-second intervals for 15 minutes each day. It was found that Jason was talking aloud during 35 percent of the intervals sampled. In 15 percent of the intervals, he was handling inappropriate objects.

DESCRIBING INDIVIDUAL LEARNING STYLE

The determination of functional levels and specific deficits provides the essential information for deciding *what* a child should be taught. Deciding *how* to teach him/her effectively requires a different data base. The aspect of student performance having the greatest implications for teaching method is learning style. Learning style refers to an individual's characteristic way of responding to certain variables in the instructional environment. Stated more simply, a student's learning style is the way that he/she learns best. All individuals have developed personalized techniques for acquiring and remembering information. More appropriate instructional strategies and materials can be selected for a particular child when the teacher is aware of his learning style.

There are few standardized tests that contribute meaningfully to the assessment of learning style. Educators must rely, for the most part, on their observational skills. The determination of learning style requires time. Only a few characteristics may be apparent upon completion of preliminary diagnosis. As a teacher continues to interact with a child and to observe him/her at work, the understanding of learning style becomes more complete. A teacher is apt to notice patterns emerging in student performance. The way that a learner tends to organize himself/herself for work, to study assigned material, to solve problems, and to make decisions all reveal something about his/her unique style.

Observations during individual testing may be particularly fruitful. Although the tests themselves may be measuring other abilities, the child's behavior during testing provides many clues about his/her learning style. In addition to observing a student's general approach to problems, the examiner is often able to detect the individual's bases for decision making from the types of errors that he/she makes.

Another useful application of observation occurs in diagnostic prescriptive teaching. By manipulating specific variables in the instructional program and observing the effects on student performance, the teacher can determine how he/she learns most effectively.

In describing learning style, therefore, the many forms of observation play a primary role. The nature of learning style and the lack of appropriate standardized devices make it necessary to assess this aspect of student performance in the actual instructional setting.

Dimensions of Learning Style

An individual's learning style might be characterized in numerous different ways. Significant learning handicaps, as well as learning preferences, should be identified for each exceptional student. Many of the common limitations of mildly and moderately handicapped learners have already been described in Chapter 2. Awareness of a child's special strengths and weaknesses in information processing, language, and social-emotional areas enables a teacher to design a more individualized academic program.

In addition to previous discussions of educational characteristics, six of the more common aspects of learning style are considered in this section. These include attention control, modality preference, levels of processing, reflection-impulsivity, grouping preferences, and reinforcement. It is particularly important for teachers to investigate these dimensions of learning style because they have such direct implications for the selection of instructional strategies and materials.

It is a pupil's attention skills that dictate to a great extent how time and space should be managed in the classroom. Knowledge of a student's modality preferences and levels of processing allows a teacher to provide more appropriate types of instructional input. Impulsive or reflective tendencies must be taken into account when planning the pacing of lessons and the format of instructional materials. Human resources can be used to greater advantage when grouping preferences are recognized.

Finally, an understanding of individual reinforcement needs helps a teacher to make tasks more motivating to the learner.

Each of these six dimensions of learning style is briefly defined in the following discussion. Special assessment considerations are addressed as applicable.

Attention Control   Students differ considerably in their ability to focus and sustain attention on a given task. Children with learning difficulties are generally more distractible than their peers. These children exhibit problems in filtering out extraneous stimuli in order to attend to the significant information. Because attention occurs very early in the information processing sequence, faulty attention skills can seriously impede learning.

There is no way of knowing for certain when an individual is "paying attention." Therefore, one can assess attention skills only by measuring the behavioral evidence available. One possible route is to investigate the products of attention, because it can be assumed that a person must attend in order to perform an assigned task adequately. It is the student who seldom completes assignments or who makes many errors along the way that raises concern about attention skills.

A word of caution is in order. Assessment of attention abilities can easily be confounded by other factors. A teacher should carefully examine task demands to ensure that the amount of work and the skills required are reasonable and appropriate for a given child. Once this has been checked, baseline observational data may be collected to determine the actual number of assignments or the percentage of assigned work completed acceptably.

In addition to measuring the products of attention, one can also investigate the process. Certain behaviors suggest whether or not an individual is attending. Eye contact and body orientation are two common indicators. Specific signs of task involvement, such as writing in a workbook or focusing on an open book and turning pages, may also serve as evidence of attending. Obviously, such behavioral indicators are fallible. It is possible for an individual to demonstrate eye contact or to turn pages in a book without really attending to the task. For this reason, multiple measures of attentive behaviors usually provide a more reliable indication. Most of the behaviors associated with the process of attending are continuous rather than discrete and would, therefore, lend themselves better to duration recording, interval recording, or time sampling than frequency counting.

Modality Preference   The aspect of learning style that has generated the most study and also the most controversy is modality preference. This refers to an ability to learn and retain information more efficiently when certain channels of communication are employed. Some students learn best visually, others aurally, and still others through tactual-kinesthetic means. Students who are achieving adequately may experience little difficulty in learning through less-preferred perceptual pathways. They may acquire information more easily through their stronger channel, but they are not actually deficient in any channel. Many children with learning problems, however, do have significant weaknesses in perceptual skills, to the extent that they are unable to profit from instruction directed primarily to that channel. In these instances, the identification of students' open or intact modalities becomes more critical.

Certain standardized tests designed to measure perceptual and psycholinguistic skills have been widely used for the determination of modality preference. The empirical support for this practice has proved less than satisfactory, however. It has been found that the most commonly used instruments fail to differentiate adequately between normal children and those diagnosed as learning disabled (Larsen, Rogers, & Sowell, 1976; O'Grady, 1974). Unsuccessful attempts to enhance achievement by matching instructional treatments to perceptual learning styles have been attributed to the lack of adequate assessment devices (Sabatino, Ysseldyke, & Woolston, 1973; Ysseldyke, 1973).

A more promising means of identifying learning style may be the trial lessons approach. Specific informal tests incorporating trial lessons have been proposed by Mills (1956) and Roswell and Natchez (1971) for assessing modality preferences in learning to read. In successive lessons, new words are taught using four major reading approaches: visual, phonic (auditory), combination, and multisensory (visual-auditory-tactual-kinesthetic). The student is tested for immediate and delayed recall of the words taught. By keeping the difficulty of the words, the duration of the lessons, and the time intervals between testing constant, one is able to parcel out modality effects and identify a child's learning style. Similar trial lessons have been recommended for assessing modality strengths in spelling (Westerman, 1971).

The trial lessons paradigm is highly similar to a diagnostic prescriptive teaching approach. As such, it can be applied in any subject matter area. Trial lessons and diagnostic prescriptive teaching permit the investigation of modality preference in the actual content area of concern without having to generalize from tests that were not specifically designed for this purpose.

Levels of Processing   Another aspect of learning style related to information processing concerns the levels of complexity or abstraction that can be successfully employed. Most of the theoretical models have postulated levels to represent the range of human information processing (Bown, 1972; Kirk, McCarthy, & Kirk, 1968; Meyers & Hammill, 1969;

Osgood, 1957). The most basic level deals with sensory data. Successive levels correspond to perceptual motor and habitual automatic functions. The most organized levels require highly symbolic cognitive integration.

At present, the concept of processing levels requires further clarification and empirical support. Neither assessment nor treatment procedures has been adequately developed for classroom application. The practice of characterizing a child's competence in manipulating symbols is not new, however. The traditional distinction between concrete and abstract functioning captures the essence of the current, more elaborate constructs.

A child who is very concrete in his/her thought processes depends heavily on sensory and perceptual information. To understand a concept, he/she must experience it. Slightly less concrete learners can profit from pictorial representations. At the advanced end of the continuum are students functioning at the abstract level. These learners are able to deal successfully with symbols in verbal and graphic form. Observation and diagnostic prescriptive teaching are the major tools for assessing a child's differential ability to manipulate concrete things or abstract symbols.

Reflection-Impulsivity   Through the work of Kagan and his associates, a generalized tendency has been recognized for a child to display fast or slow decision times across various kinds of tasks that contain uncertainty (Kagan & Kogan, 1970). In problem-solving situations, reflective individuals pause and evaluate the quality of a decision before responding. Impulsive children, on the other hand, are less cautious, respond more quickly, and make a greater number of errors. Bruner observed similar tendencies in children, but labeled them differently. His "conservative focusers" perform reflectively, and the "gambling focusers" are more impulsive (Bruner, Goodnow, & Austin, 1956).

A visual discrimination task devised by Kagan, "Matching Familiar Figures," has been used to identify an individual's characteristic response style. The consistency noted across different kinds of tasks suggests that an observant teacher could detect evidence of extreme reflection or impulsivity from a child's classwork by focusing on the time it takes a student to formulate a response and the number of errors made.

Grouping Preferences   In most classrooms, a number of different grouping arrangements are employed to facilitate teaching and learning. Many children function productively whether they are working in a large group, small group, a student dyad, one-to-one with the teacher, or independently. There are other pupils, however, who do not work as effectively in one or more of these modes. Describing a child's learning style on this dimension involves identifying his productive grouping patterns.

It is not unusual to find that special children need a greater degree of structure and supervision. They often learn best in teacher-directed, small group, or one-to-one situations. Peer tutoring may also be effective with many students. Children with learning and behavior problems have seldom developed the necessary skills to work independently for more than a brief period of time. A diagnostic prescriptive approach will help a teacher to identify the specific arrangements that are successful with an individual child.

Reinforcement   Reinforcement can be defined only by its effect on behavior. What serves to strengthen or maintain behavior of one individual may have far different effects on another. For this reason, it is necessary to determine the types of reinforcers that work with a particular child.

The majority of students respond favorably to certain generalized or common reinforcers, such as attention, praise, knowledge of results, and grades. These are some of the customary means of maintaining desired school behaviors. Many children with learning and behavior problems, however, do not work sufficiently for these rewards. They often need more personalized and powerful reinforcers. Tokens such as gold stars, check marks, or chips may be effective with some pupils. Others will work hard to earn special privileges. There are children who require tangible rewards, and some who will respond only to food, a primary reinforcer.

A teacher may identify effective reinforcers in a number of ways. The most direct means of finding out reward preferences is to ask the child. Interest inventories may also be used for this purpose. More reliable information, however, is obtained through observation. The way a student chooses to spend his/her free time is usually indicative of his/her real interests. Other clues from a child's behavior suggest things he/she might respond to. Prospective reinforcers must always be tested empirically. Observing and recording data are the only means of determining for certain whether the application of a particular contingency is truly reinforcing.

The schedule, as well as the type of reinforcement, is important. Most students perform adequately under conditions of partial or intermittent reinforcement. Continuous reinforcement is necessary only when new behaviors are being acquired. Exceptional children, however, often have difficulty in deferring reinforcement.

Case Example

Jason's levels of functioning and specific difficulties have been described earlier in this chapter. This final section of the assessment summary deals with Jason's learning style.

Attention Control   Jason has trouble maintaining his attention on task. At present, he is completing only about 40 percent of his assignments. He is highly distracted by other events in the room and can work more productively in a private study office. Jason often refuses to use the carrels, however.

Modality Preference   Test results, observation, and prescriptive teaching all concur that Jason has strong auditory-verbal skills. He is able to profit more from a teacher's oral explanations than from reading and studying about a concept on his own. He seems to learn best when he is allowed frequent opportunities to verbalize his understandings.

Levels of Processing   Jason seems able to deal adequately with the abstract, particularly verbal concepts.

Reflection-Impulsivity   Jason displays many impulsive tendencies. His patterns of guessing at reading words, making numerous careless errors in math, and erasing and crossing out in handwriting support this interpretation. Jason's impulsivity becomes more pronounced in testing or in other situations where he feels on the spot. When confronted with evidence of behavioral infractions, for example, his outrageous explanations reflect his style of grabbing quickly for answers.

Grouping Preferences   Jason has difficulty working constructively in a large group. His disruptive behaviors occur most frequently in this setting. Jason also performs poorly when asked to do written work on his own, but he can read or use manipulative materials independently for as long as 20 minutes, at times. Jason tends to make abusive comments when he must work in a small group with girls. He does participate adequately in teacher-directed lessons for small groups of boys, but responds most consistently to one-to-one instruction.

Reinforcement   Jason is highly responsive to social reinforcers. His disruptive behaviors in the classroom seem to be maintained by attention from his peers. Attention from the teacher, even in the form of a correction, has the effect of increasing behavior. Praise from the teacher for appropriate behavior works only if it is given at frequent intervals.

Jason's preferred reward is food. He has responded favorably to the contingency that he must complete his assignments before he can have his snack, which consist of fruit and a diet drink he brings from home. Because of Jason's weight problem, the teacher would rather not use food as a reward.

Jason does respond to activity reinforcers. Talking aloud without permission decreased 40 percent when Jason was allowed to choose a special privilege each day that his behavior improved. His preferred activities were reading comics and using the cassette recorder. Jason tires easily of the same reinforcers, however, and needs novelty.

SUMMARY

Diagnosis has been defined as an ongoing process of gathering and interpreting educationally relevant information about a particular learner.

Meaningful educational diagnosis should result in the accurate specification of functional levels, skills and behaviors of concern, and learning style. These three aspects of student performance have important implications for instructional decision making.

A number of different techniques may be employed in assessment. Norm-referenced, standardized tests contribute primarily to the determination of performance levels. Formal and informal criterion-referenced testing, direct observation, and diagnostic prescriptive teaching are the most useful tools for defining problems behaviorally and for analyzing learning style. Specific dimensions of learning style discussed in this chapter included modality preference, attention control, reflection-impulsivity, levels of processing, reinforcement, and grouping preferences.

The role of the classroom teacher is emphasized, because it is this individual who is ultimately responsible for translating assessment results into a workable instructional program. Other school personnel and professionals from related fields may be called upon to assist in the diagnostic process as needed. Preliminary diagnosis is completed when there is a sufficient data base for planning an individualized program.

Knowledge of a student's functional levels, specific skills, and behaviors of concern should enable the teacher to pinpoint instructional goals and objectives. Awareness of the child's learning style permits the more systematic selection of teaching strategies. In turn, the chosen objectives and teaching strategies provide the bases for the selection of instructional materials. Once preliminary diagnosis has contributed to the development of the initial individualized program, the system should become self-perpetuating. The program is continually refined and updated in light of current student performance.

REFERENCES

Bown, J. C. A communication model for evaluation and remediation. *Exceptional Children*, 1972, *38*, 385–394.
Bruner, J., Goodnow, J., & Austin, A. *A study in thinking*. New York: John Wiley and Sons, 1956.
Kagan, J., & Kogan, N. Individuality and cognitive performance. In P. H. Mussen (Ed.), *Carmichael's manual of child psychology* (Vol. 1). New York: John Wiley and Sons, 1970.
Kirk, S. A., McCarthy, J. P., & Kirk, W. D. *The Illinois test of psycholinguistic abilities* (Rev. ed.). Urbana, Ill.: University of Illinois Press, 1968.
Larsen, S. C., Rogers, D. & Sowell, V. The use of selected perceptual tests in differentiating between normal and learning disabled children. *Journal of Learning Disabilities*, 1976, *9*, 85–90.
Meyers, P. I., & Hammill, D. D. *Methods for learning disorders*. New York: John Wiley and Sons, 1969.

Mills, R. E. *Learning Methods Test*. 1612 E. Broward Blvd., Fort Lauderdale, Fl., 1956.

O'Grady, D. V. Psycholinguistic abilities in learning disabled, emotionally disturbed, and normal children. *Journal of Special Education*, 1974, *8*, 157–165.

Osgood, C. E. A behavioristic analysis of perception and language as cognitive phenomena. In J. S. Bruner (Ed.), *Contemporary approaches to cognition*, Cambridge, Mass.: Harvard University Press, 1957.

Quick, A. D., Little T. L., & Campbell, A. A. *Project MEMPHIS: Instruments for individual program planning and evaluation*. Belmont, Cal.: Fearon Publishers, 1974.

Roswell, F., & Natchez, G. *Reading disability: Diagnosis and treatment*. (Rev. ed.). New York: Basic Books, 1971.

Sabatino, D. A., Ysseldyke, J. E., & Woolston, J. Diagnostic-prescriptive perceptual training with mentally retarded children. *American Journal of Mental Deficiency*, 1973, *78*, 27–36.

Salvia, J., & Ysseldyke, J. E. *Assessment in special and regular education*. Boston: Houghton Mifflin Co., 1978.

Sattler, J. M. *Assessment of children's intelligence*. (Rev. ed.). Philadelphia: W. B. Saunders Co., 1974.

Sulzer, B., & Mayer, G. R. *Behavior modification procedures for school personnel*. New York: Holt, Rinehart & Winston, 1972.

Terman, L. M., & Merrill, M. A. *Stanford-Binet intelligence scale:* Manual for the third revision. Boston: Houghton Mifflin Co., 1973.

Wechsler, D. *Manual for the Wechsler adult intelligence scale*. New York: Psychological Corp., 1955.

Wechsler, D. *Manual for the Wechsler preschool and primary scale of intelligence*. New York: Psychological Corp., 1967.

Wechsler, D. *Manual for the Wechsler intelligence scale for children* (Rev. ed.). New York: Psychological Corp., 1974.

Westerman, G. *Spelling and writing dimensions*, San Rafael, Cal., 1971.

Ysseldyke, J. E. Diagnostic-prescriptive teaching: The search for aptitude-treatment interactions. In L. Mann & D. L. Sabatino (Eds.), *The first review of special education*. Philadelphia: Grune & Stratton, 1973.

9
PRESCRIPTIVE PROGRAMMING IN THE MAINSTREAM

Virginia K. Laycock

Teaching handicapped children in the regular classroom is often viewed as an overwhelming task. When students with learning problems do not respond to customary instructional procedures, teachers can easily succumb to feelings of frustration and inadequacy. Many times the child, parents, special educators, or federal mandates are blamed in turn for the dilemma of mainstreaming. In order to respond to the challenge more constructively, classroom teachers need practical techniques for shaping their instructional offerings to accommodate a wider range of individual differences.

There can be no simple, universal solutions to providing for the handicapped in the regular classroom because of the great diversity apparent in both teaching and learning styles. No single method can be effective since each situation is truly different. What teachers need is a basic approach to serve as a guide for instructional decision making when planning for each special student in his/her particular learning environment. The overall approach should be highly systematic in that it directs teachers to identify and to adjust whatever factors in the regular, ongoing program that are impeding the progress of the handicapped child. Such a system for individualizing must also include continuous measurement of learner performance, for only in this way can plans be geared toward changing student needs and teacher accountability be preserved.

The instructional approach meeting the above requirements is generally referred to as *diagnostic prescriptive teaching* (DPT). Specific versions of prescriptive teaching (Charles, 1976; Mercer, 1979; Moran, 1975; Peter, 1965) differ somewhat in the particulars of implementation,

Figures in this chapter originally appeared in earlier work by the author in Robert M. Anderson, John G. Greer, and Sara J. Odle (eds.), *Individualizing Educational Materials for Special Children in the Mainstream*, Baltimore: University Park Press, 1978.

but all are derived from a similar philosophy and all emphasize the same major steps for instructional programming. Several other systems, such as *clinical teaching* (Lerner, 1976; Smith, 1974) and *directive teaching* (Haring & Schiefelbusch, 1976; Stephens, 1977) have been popularized under different titles but are basically prescriptive in nature. Although diagnostic prescriptive teaching originally evolved for use in special education settings, it is none the less applicable to individualizing within the regular classroom.

Prescriptive teaching is best envisioned as a cycle of seven essential tasks, as illustrated in Figure 1. The initial step, diagnosis of learner needs, permits the selection of more individualized objectives, strategies, and materials in instructional planning. After the prescribed program is implemented, its effectiveness is evaluated in terms of learner performance. The original plan is then refined or new plans developed in light of current progress.

Clearly, the diagnostic prescriptive teaching approach is compatible with the requirements for individualized education programming discussed in Chapter 7. Although PL 94-142 does not employ diagnostic prescriptive terminology, the development, implementation, and evaluation of the IEP involves the same sequence of instructional tasks. Because of this parallel between comprehensive long range planning and specific, short range planning, a diagnostic prescriptive system aids the teacher in converting the annual program, the IEP, into daily individualized lessons. Each of the seven steps in prescriptive teaching as it guides the process of mainstreaming is described in this chapter.

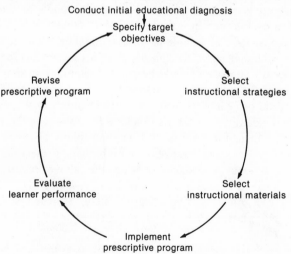

Figure 1.   The diagnostic prescriptive teaching cycle.

INITIAL DIAGNOSIS

Thorough assessment of learner characteristics is always the starting point for all further instructional planning. Because diagnosis is such a critical first step, an entire chapter (Chapter 8) has already been devoted to this topic. In addition to what has been discussed, certain points should be emphasized here specifically in relation to prescriptive teaching.

Educational diagnosis is most meaningful when it provides a working knowledge of a student's present levels of performance, strengths and weaknesses in areas of concern, and preferred styles of learning. This information is best gathered from a variety of sources, including formal and informal tests, developmental checklists, rating scales, and observation. Since the classroom teacher is with the child on a daily basis and is ultimately responsible for his/her educational program, it is vital that this individual take an active role in collecting and interpreting diagnostic data. When assessment is approached in this way, the results are likely to be more accurate and more directly relevant to instruction. The teacher is then able to make more informed decisions concerning what and how the student should be taught.

TARGET OBJECTIVES

Once learner characteristics have been adequately assessed, individualized instructional planning begins. A vital step at this point is to define *exactly* what it is that the student is expected to do in each area where he/she is experiencing difficulty. Requirements should always be clarified and stated as specifically as possible. Objectives set for the class as a whole should be examined in light of identified strengths and weaknesses of the handicapped child. It is probable that the mainstreamed student will possess the necessary prerequisites to be working toward many of the same objectives established for the regular program. In such instances, observed difficulties in achievement usually stem from *how* he/she is expected to learn rather than *what* he/she is expected to learn. The objective itself may be judged appropriate, but related teaching strategies and materials will have to be more tailored to student needs.

At other times, the teacher will decide that certain course objectives are inappropriate for the handicapped child at his/her present state of readiness. Often in basic skill areas, the student's instructional level is significantly below grade level. Special objectives suited to his/her current level of functioning will, therefore, have to be defined. It is advisable for regular classroom teachers to have on hand developmental skill sequences in reading, writing, spelling, and math to use as references when individualizing programs. Suggested resources include curriculum guides prepared by state and local agencies, scope and sequence charts from basal programs, and professional textbooks in education. It should also be helpful to confer with teachers from lower grades and to work closely with resource or consulting teachers when gearing instruction toward a much lower level.

Task Analysis

Instructing the handicapped may require a teacher to attend more closely than ever to the proper sequencing of skills. Whereas efficient learners may be able to overcome poor instruction and fill in missing links on their own, the handicapped are seldom so fortunate. They are usually doomed to fail if asked to master a skill out of sequence or to acquire a concept when learning is not carefully broken down into steps. Engelmann (1977) comments on the importance of adequately sequencing cognitive and academic tasks by saying:

> Although my associates and I have worked with thousands of children labeled "learning disabled," we have never seen a child who could not learn to read, learn arithmetic, or learn more complicated skills. Not one. The learning disability should more appropriately be labeled a teaching disability. But the learning disability will remain so long as teachers (and publishers) present demonstrations that are consistent with more than one interpretation (such as the picture on the page that always corresponds to the words and encourages the poor, naive reader to think that perhaps he is supposed to read the word by looking at the picture) or operations that are covert (such as "intuiting" the number of the set without counting) and in general violation of every principle of sequencing skills (pp. 60–61).

Although adequate skill sequences can usually be located for most academic tasks, teachers may on occasion be forced to develop an original sequence or to refine a given one into smaller units in order to facilitate learning. In such instances, the teacher must be able to construct a task analysis. Task analysis involves breaking down a target skill into component steps which are sequenced in logical, developmental order. The steps must be sufficiently fine-grained to direct both teaching and learning efforts toward the specific desired outcome.

In order to complete a task analysis of a selected skill, one should proceed as follows:

1. Define the target skill in behavioral terms. It is necessary to choose a goal that is manageable in scope and to describe it precisely. The instructional goal must always be stated as an observable skill which the *learner* is to perform. Examples of target skills defined in this way include the following: to compute single digit multiplication

facts in writing, to recite the alphabet, to bounce a ball, and to write identifying personal data on a job application form. Such statements represent responses to the critical instructional question, "What is it that the student must do?"

2. Specify prerequisites for learning the target skill. Here one is concerned with entry behaviors, those skills that a learner should already have mastered before attempting the present task. These statements describe the current functioning of the learner. It is helpful to include prerequisite assumptions in a task analysis because they limit the focus to a manageable range. Theoretically, any task analysis could be infinitely long, extending downward to the most basic human capabilities. If one begins as suggested, however, by setting specific parameters, then task analysis becomes a matter of simply closing the gap between the prerequisite skills already possessed and the target skill to be yet acquired.

3. Identify the steps leading to performance of the target skill. This is the most difficult and time-consuming aspect of task analysis. The listing of component skills must be inclusive and explicit. There is no one established method for analyzing a given task. Moyer and Dardig (1978) suggest that a teacher become familiar with a variety of procedures so that he/she may employ whichever is best suited to a particular goal and preferred style of analysis. One may analyze a given task in at least six different ways: by watching a master perform, by performing the task oneself, by working backward from the terminal behavior, by brainstorming, by successively approximating conditions for final performance, or by listing discrete behaviors that represent attainment of the desired goal (Moyer & Dardig, 1978). The latter technique, listing contributory behaviors, is most applicable in the affective domain. Given a goal such as "demonstrating a positive self-concept," for example, many subbehaviors might be identified which collectively evidence attainment of the goal.

Regardless of the method of analysis employed, teachers must ensure that every step involved in completion of the final task is described in specific behavioral terms. One way to avoid general, nonbehavioral statements (*know, understand, improve, learn,* and so forth) is to use only those verbs which denote concrete, observable actions (*write, name, point, trace,* etc.). The task analysis should clearly indicate what the learner must do to perform the target skill.

4. Check the entire task analysis for appropriate sequencing and comprehensiveness. It is important to evaluate the completed task analysis and to correct any deficiencies which become apparent. The teacher may work through the prescribed sequence on his/her own or

have it reviewed by a colleague in an attempt to locate specific weaknesses. Any steps that are not directly essential to the final task should be eliminated at this time. Particular attention should be focused on developmental sequencing. All steps should flow in logical order from the simple to the more complex. Finally, the teacher must check that all steps are approximately equal in difficulty. It is not unusual to discover that certain parts of the task have been broken down finely, while others have been dealt with in large chunks. Any gaps in the sequence must be corrected so that the listing represents a smooth progression from specified entry behaviors to the desired goal. The ultimate test of any task analysis is its applicability to the teaching-learning process. Additional revisions may be necessary if progress is not apparent.

A sample task analysis constructed according to these guidelines is presented in Table 1. This illustrates a possible sequence for advancing a learner from telling time to the hour and half hour to telling time to the quarter hour. Note that the target skill or behavior appears at the top of the table. Prerequisite or entry behaviors are listed at the bottom because these are the most basic. Between entry and target behaviors is the listing of enroute behaviors from simple (bottom) to more complex (top). Although developing a task analysis in such thorough form is a demand-

Table 1.   Sample task analysis

Target behavior	To tell time to the quarter hour given a clock with arabic numbers
	To state the time shown as both "quarter after (*hour*)" and "fifteen minutes after (*hour*)"
	To state the time shown as both "quarter to (*hour*)" and "fifteen minutes to (*hour*)"
	To equate one quarter hour with fifteen minutes by counting by five's
Enroute behaviors	To identify orally the time shown on a given clockface as "quarter after (*hour*)"
	To identify orally the time shown on a given clockface as "quarter to (*hour*)"
	To identify orally fractional parts of a clockface divided into quarters
	To say "after or past the hour" when the big hand is on the right half of the clockface
	To say "before, till, or to the hour" when the big hand is on the left hand of the clockface
Entry behaviors	To tell time to the nearest hour and half hour
	To count by fives to 60

ing process, its importance in effective teaching cannot be overemphasized.

Adapting Objectives in Content Areas

In science, social studies, and other content areas, general objectives may also have to be individualized but in a different way. In these subjects it is often the case that the handicapped child is capable of learning the concepts involved but is simply unable to complete required assignments. Difficulties in reading, oral, or written expression can seriously limit the pupil's ability to demonstrate what knowledge he/she has actually acquired. This distinction between content and the behaviors demanded for classroom performance has been recently emphasized by Cawley, Fitzmaurice, Goodstein, Lepore, Sedlak, and Althaus (1977). Students are often unfairly penalized when they, in fact, possess the necessary knowledge.

When setting objectives in content areas, therefore, the teacher must define both knowledge and performance expectations. For example, one desired outcome of a history unit might be the identification of five causes of the American Revolution. Certain students could not meet this objective if required to write a paragraph about the causes of the war, but these same students might pass if asked to name the causes orally. Whenever the form of an assignment or test interferes with a pupil's ability to communicate understanding of the subject matter, then the general objectives should be modified. It is usually possible for a teacher to set special objectives for a handicapped student without compromising the nature or the amount of information for which the student is held responsible.

Depending on their specific limitations, handicapped students may be asked to demonstrate their knowledge through different modes or at different levels of complexity. Beyond the primary grades, pupils are typically held accountable for information in written form. Many teachers adhere too rigidly to this response mode, however, When students are unable to convey their ideas in writing, demonstrations and oral explanations should be recognized as legitimate alternatives. Laurie, Buchwach, Silverman, and Zigmond (1978) urge teachers to allow disabled students such options as answering essay questions orally into a tape recorder, drawing figures, constructing models, or conducting experiments. Even when written tests are retained, the level of memory required can be adjusted to aid the handicapped child. As Laurie and her associates suggest, the same content might be tested at the recognition level through fill-in-the-blanks, or at the total recall level through written essay questions (1978, p. 69). It is important, therefore, that the teacher establish course requirements in such a way that the mainstreamed student is allowed to demonstrate his/her knowledge in the content areas without being unfairly penalized for another disability.

Setting definite course objectives is thus a critical step in instructional programming for children with special needs. Existing objectives should be carefully reviewed in consideration of the abilities and disabilities of the handicapped student. In subjects where the learner is experiencing difficulty, the teacher may decide on one of the following: 1) objectives themselves seem appropriate for the student and it is other aspects of the program which need to be changed, 2) grade level objectives are too difficult for the student and special objectives must be established for his/her instructional level, or 3) the content of the objectives is appropriate but performance requirements are not and have to be modified accordingly. The teacher who has carefully determined that what he/she is expecting the student to do is both possible and appropriate for the child at the present time has taken a major step toward individualizing instruction.

TEACHING STRATEGIES

After objectives have been clarified, the teacher must consider how particular variables in the environment contribute to performance of the desired tasks. An optimal teaching environment is one in which obstacles to learning are minimized and all conditions encourage mastery of the target skill. Although the ideal situation for every student cannot be achieved in reality, teachers must none the less strive to manage as many factors as possible to learner advantage. Instructional variables that warrant particular concern include time schedule, grouping arrangement, physical setting, mode of presentation, and reinforcement. Although instructional materials are obviously relevant and might be included in this list, they are instead considered under a separate heading because they constitute such a major part of individualized programming.

Time Schedule

Mainstreaming difficulties can sometimes be alleviated by using time more effectively. If a teacher suspects that a student's poor classwork is related either to fatigue or to restlessness, then adjustments in the daily schedule may be in order. It is not unusual to observe that certain students experience temporary slumps during the school day. They may yawn, slouch in their chairs, or even doze off for awhile. Others are exceptionally restless during certain periods. These activity level disturbances are often heightened noticeably at certain times, such as before or after lunch, or late in the school day. The child who is hungry, tired, or fidgety is less likely to do quality work, and it is better to avoid placing excessive demands on him/her at such times. Once a teacher recognizes that performance fluctuates according to a pattern, more difficult subjects and assignments can possibly be planned for the more productive periods of the day.

Not only the placement but also the duration of lessons should be considered in using time strategically. The length of time allotted for certain activities may have to be changed for the handicapped child. When students can do their work but simply cannot keep up the pace of the rest of the class, additional time might be granted for them to complete assignments. Similar concessions might be made for those pupils who rush to meet time limits and make many needless errors. If there is no class time to spare, the amount of work might be reduced to permit adequate completion within the established time frame. Having the student finish assignments at home may be helpful on occasion but is not advisable as a general practice. The child who works slowly in the classroom often labors over homework as well. Assignments can quickly pile up to an insurmountable load. With this in mind, the classroom teacher must attempt to balance the amount of work with the length of time assigned in order to encourage good performance.

Timing also plays a significant role in teaching children with attention problems. Tasks that are appropriate for the class as a whole may need to be abbreviated for the highly distractible child. When longer assignments have to be done, it is often to the child's advantage for the teacher to break the work into several brief sessions and to intersperse it with other activities.

In summary, inadequate performance of the handicapped child in the regular classroom can result from inappropriate time factors. In consideration of individual learning style, the teacher might reduce interferences by scheduling the most demanding lessons for prime periods of the school day, by permitting additional class time for completing assignments, or by presenting briefer tasks and frequent activity changes.

Grouping

Many teachers mistakenly believe that individualized instruction means one-to-one instruction. Fortunately, a teacher does not have to focus such exclusive attention in order to be individualizing. With careful grouping, other students can actually contribute to, rather than detract from, the effectiveness of the program. The key is in finding what works for a particular student in a particular subject area.

Many mainstreamed pupils appear to function satisfactorily within the customary organizational patterns of their classrooms. The size of the group does not seem to affect their performance. Other students seem to be intimidated by large groups. During presentations by the teacher, they seek to blend into the crowd. They may hesitate to raise questions when they are confused and even refrain from responding when they know the information for fear of seeming stupid in front of everyone. There are also pupils who confront too many distractions in a large group. They may be unable to pay attention to the teacher or to get their work done because they are easily drawn off-task by others.

A second common grouping arrangement that often presents problems for handicapped learners is the independent mode. Many children perform poorly because they are unable to follow directions, to structure time, or to control attention on their own. They require more supervision and teacher assistance than others in the class.

A teacher who uses only one or two grouping systems may well be forcing certain children to learn under conditions that are difficult for them. Various other grouping arrangements should be attempted, therefore, to discover more efficient ways of teaching and learning specific skills. Alternatives to the whole class and independent modes include the use of small groups, one-to-one instruction, and peer tutoring.

Small Group Instruction   Small groups may be used effectively for many different educational purposes. In reading, it is a familiar practice to group students according to instructional level. Although this does not ensure that every child is on precisely his/her own level and progressing at his/her own optimal rate, it does reduce the range of abilities sufficiently to permit the management of a basal program.

Skill development, rather than instructional level, provides a second basis for grouping students. This is a useful adjunct approach in reading, and it can also serve as the basic teaching mode in math, language arts, or other core subject areas. To use skill grouping, pupils are placed together because they need to work toward the same objectives. All those who require instruction in a particular skill, such as identifying medial vowels or converting decimals to percents, are clustered accordingly. As students master target objectives, they move on to more advanced skills and other groups.

The two approaches to small group instruction discussed thus far have brought learners together to address more homogeneous needs. It can also be advantageous to group students with heterogeneous skill and instructional levels. This technique is most applicable in the content areas as a means of handling reading deficiencies and of providing a more student-centered curriculum. To use this instructional mode, a teacher may plan the groups or allow students to divide themselves into teams according to special interests. Each group should have its share of advanced readers, average readers, and poor readers. Specific discussion questions and/or projects are assigned to each team. Through verbal interaction and the development of concrete projects, all pupils, regardless of ability level, can contribute to the group work. Heterogeneous study groups provide an excellent way for mainstreamed youngsters to become involved in cooperative efforts and to acquire basic concepts in content areas.

Individual Instruction   Teachers in the regular classroom can seldom afford the luxury of extensive one-to-one teaching. Even though the handicapped child has exceptional needs, there are always many others demanding teacher support and assistance. The little time that a teacher can devote exclusively to the mainstreamed student is precious indeed, and should be reserved for those kinds of instructional interactions that cannot be accomplished in any other mode.

When the special student is working on objectives or assignments which differ from those of the rest of the class, it is then necessary for the teacher to introduce his/her lessons individually. If these sessions are carefully planned, they need not be lengthy. Even 5 or 10 minutes of one-to-one instruction can be highly effective. It is also helpful to deal with some students individually when gathering evaluative data, providing corrective feedback, or contracting for future goals and responsibilities. Many teachers arrange to work briefly with mainstreamed pupils while the others are engaged in independent activities.

Peer Tutoring   When one-to-one instruction seems to be the desirable mode, peer tutoring may offer a valuable supplement to teacher-directed lessons. Although the practice of using children to teach other children dates historically to the one room schoolhouse, peer tutoring remains a practical and efficient means of individualizing instruction today. There is a wealth of experimental evidence to indicate that both cognitive and affective gains can be achieved by children who are tutored by their peers (Bloom, 1976; Devin-Sheehan, Feldman, & Allen, 1976; Gartner, Kohler, & Riessman, 1972; Stainback, Stainback, & Lichtward, 1975).

Peer tutoring has been attempted at all age levels and in nearly every skill area. In general, it works most effectively when teachers themselves introduce new concepts and then allow student tutors to provide the practice necessary for mastery. Many of the basic learning tasks, such as sight words, spelling words, and math facts, lend themselves well to a peer tutoring arrangement.

A tutorial system may be organized within a single classroom or on a larger scale within an entire school. Laycock and Schwartzberg (1977) outline six essential steps in setting up any peer assisted learning program: 1) selecting participants, 2) delineating responsibilities, 3) training tutors, 4) making arrangements, 5) initiating tutoring, and 6) monitoring and evaluating.

In selecting prospective tutors and tutees, desire to participate should be the primary criterion. Children who are being mainstreamed have much to gain by receiving tutorial help from other students. Just because of their difficulties, however, these handicapped children should not be denied the opportunity of helping others who are younger or lower functioning. Not only can students with learning and behavior problems tutor effectively (Brown, Fenrick, & Klemme, 1971; Conrad, 1976), but they can also profit greatly from the experience. By applying previously learned skills, the tutor often improves his/her own performance while teaching (Allen & Feldman, 1974; Bean & Luke, 1972; Hassinger & Via, 1969). Furthermore, positive changes in self-concept and behavior frequently result from the realization that one has something to offer and has been entrusted with the responsibility of tutoring someone else (Balmer, 1972; Lane, Pollack, & Sher, 1972; Wagner, 1974).

Before peer tutoring gets underway, it is essential that all those involved clearly understand their roles. Teachers must always retain responsibility for instructional programming. They are to decide what needs to be taught and the overall strategies to be employed. Tutors must agree to be responsible for their own behavior, including completing their assigned classwork and following through on tutorial commitments. The tutees must promise to cooperate with their tutors in order to receive help. It is often wise to specify all responsibilities in a written contract to be signed by all parties involved.

Tutors should not be asked to work independently with their tutees until they have been adequately prepared. The actual nature and extent of tutor training will vary, but teachers should ensure that tutors possess certain basic competencies. They should be able to praise and encourage, to correct errors constructively, to use assigned teaching materials and techniques, and to record simple data on learner performance. Some students seem to acquire these skills quite naturally, while others must be taught to do these things through careful preservice training. Depending on the number of children involved, teachers may choose to model and to reinforce the desired skills in individual tutorial sessions or to conduct a series of group training workshops. Although tutor training need not be elaborate or extensive, tutors should be given sufficient preparation to feel comfortable in tutoring and to create a positive learning experience for tutees.

Practical details concerning when and where tutoring will take place must also be resolved. In most instances, brief tutoring sessions several times per week are preferable to longer or less frequent lessons. Tutoring can occur in a variety of settings—in a corner of the classroom, the resource room, the library, or even the hallway.

As actual tutoring begins, the student helper and the teacher must work closely together. The teacher typically plans the program and the tutor implements it. The tutor should also be required to report regularly on learner progress. As the tutor gains confidence and competence, he/she may be given more freedom in planning lesson activities.

Peer tutoring must be continually monitored if it is to be effective. Teachers should periodically observe tutorial sessions. They must also check tutor reports of learner performance on a regular basis. Frequent expressions of appreciation and support for student efforts are also vital to the continued success of peer tutoring.

Although the use of peer tutoring requires a definite commitment from the teacher, it can effectively multiply the amount of instructional time available to children in the classroom. If teachers are already using a systematic approach to programming, it is a helpful and a rewarding experience to involve students in the actual delivery of instruction.

Alternate grouping arrangements thus allow a teacher to manage the human resources within the classroom more productively. Although the large group and the independent modes continue to predominate in most settings, the need to provide for children with special learning problems encourages increased use of small group instruction, one-to-one teaching, and peer tutoring.

Physical Setting

Another facet of instructional planning involves the management of physical space. The most elementary concern in this respect is, of course, the removal of all physical barriers to ensure accessibility to the physically and sensorily handicapped. Certain adaptive equipment may also be necessary to provide for these children in regular classrooms. Earlier chapters have addressed specific environmental needs of the orthopedically, the visually, and the hearing impaired. Many of the adjustments recommended for classrooms are prerequisites for instruction. The present discussion focuses upon another aspect of physical space that must be controlled during the actual teaching-learning process—the positioning of students within the classroom environment.

It is not unusual to find that the location of the handicapped student within the classroom places him/her at a disadvantage. Many times, a problem child is seated in the last desk of the last row. Teachers have also been known to move the desks of handicapped students to special spots in the front or the back of the room. Whatever the teacher intentions, such placements serve only to accentuate differences and to keep the handicapped on the fringe of the group. It is as though these children have been allowed in the classroom but are not being integrated with their peers in any real sense.

At the same time, mainstreamed students do display unique learning styles that often warrant modification of the physical environment. In making programming decisions, therefore, a teacher must attempt to provide for special learning needs in ways which do not physically isolate the mainstreamed child to any greater extent than is absolutely necessary. The notion of "least restrictive environment" should thus apply to more than just the initial placement in a room with a regular class.

Teachers who are already using classroom space more flexibly are able to accommodate exceptional children without drawing undue attention to their problems. If all students are allowed to relocate for certain activities and to position themselves as needed to get their work done, then few special arrangements will have to be made for the handicapped. In such a setting, the teacher and the students are accustomed to movement from directed-teaching areas, to activity centers, to individual desks, and even to private study offices. These options make it easier for handicapped students to have immediate access not only to instruction and social interaction but also to more quiet, controlled space whenever it becomes necessary to restrict stimulation.

In more traditional classroom settings where students are seated in their own desks for both presentations and independent work, certain adjustments may need to be made for the handicapped. Children with visual or auditory deficits need to be positioned in the front of the room close to the teacher and the chalkboard. Students who are highly distractible also need to be near the front. The less there is to intervene between the learner and the source of instruction the better.

Pupils with more severe attention difficulties may still be unable to handle the normal distractions of the classroom at times, even though they have been seated in the most desirable spot within the group. It then becomes necessary to structure the learner's space to a greater degree. Turning the student's desk around so that his/her back is toward the major distractions often serves to reduce his/her visual field sufficiently to permit completion of independent assignments. Study carrels or partitions may be used to further reduce extraneous stimuli. Once again, the teacher must be sensitive to any treatment that has the effect of setting the handicapped student apart from the rest. When study offices are utilized, therefore, it is recommended that they be made available not only to the handicapped but to any pupil who needs a more quiet, secluded place to work. As students become familiar with this arrangement, they often learn to recognize their own difficulties in concentrating and move to the study carrels voluntarily. Acceptance of the fact that all children do not learn in the same way will lead teachers and students to discover more creative and favorable uses of physical space within the classroom. (For a discussion of the physical setting and the management of interfering behavior, see Chapter 11.)

Instructional Mode

The management of temporal, spatial, and human resources sets the conditions for learning. A teacher still has to select the most suitable mode for communicating instructional information to the student. Specifically, it must be determined how the learner is to find out the correct way to perform the target skill.

Despite the sophistication of current educational technology, there are actually only a few basic strategies for direct instruction. An instructional model developed by Cawley, Fitzmaurice, Shaw, Kahn, and Bates (1978) at the University of Connecticut identifies four primary methods of providing input to learners. In teaching any particular content, a teacher has the choice of constructing it, presenting it, stating it, or graphically symbolizing it. These input options may be employed singly or in combination.

The *construct* mode involves the use of concrete demonstrations. The teacher actively manipulates materials to model the desired response. In the *present* mode, fixed visual aids or pictorial representations are displayed to illustrate the concept under study. Use of the *state* mode requires a verbal explanation from the teacher. Finally, a teacher may communicate instructions through printed words and symbols in the *graphic-symbolic* mode.

These four methods of input have been incorporated into a comprehensive mathematics program, Project MATH (Cawley et al., 1976, 1977). This program is being recognized as a model for teaching developmental or remedial curriculum through a multiple option method. It affords great flexibility in tailoring instruction to individual learning needs.

The very same options are available to any teacher designing an instructional program. Recognition of the alternatives and a willingness to try them are the chief prerequisites for applying such a system in the classroom. It is often difficult for teachers to deviate from their own preferred instructional strategies, but true individualization depends upon the adaptation of teaching styles to match student learning styles.

Two aspects of learning style are particularly relevant to the selection of instructional modes—modality preference and level of abstraction. When a student demonstrates a significant perceptual processing deficit, the intact perceptual channels then assume great importance for teaching. In general, the teacher should attempt to gear presentations to the stronger modalities. For example, a child with auditory processing disabilities would be at a tremendous disadvantage in a class where the lecture or state mode was used almost exclusively. The teacher might facilitate his/her learning by combining the oral explanations with concrete demonstrations (construct mode), illustrations (present mode), or printed outlines (graphic-symbolic mode). In contrast, a student with visual limitations will rely heavily on the verbal input (state mode). Seldom does a teacher use only one mode to teach a concept or skill. More often, a combination of input methods is employed to activate several different perceptual channels. In this way, the information is more accessible to students with a variety of learning styles.

In addition to modality preferences, teachers must consider students' abilities to deal with abstractions. Many handicapped youngsters have trouble comprehending abstract ideas or manipulating symbols. These children need more concrete instruction. The construct mode which teaches through actual manipulative experiences and the present mode which uses fixed displays and pictures are particularly appropriate for students who function at the more concrete levels. The four input options suggest a hierarchal progression of strategies from concrete aids, to pictorial representations, to oral symbols, to graphic symbols. The same content can be presented in different ways depending on the student's level of processing.

In order to individualize modes of instruction for exceptional learners, teachers should begin by identifying input methods currently employed. If it is apparent that the content of the curriculum is not being delivered effectively to some students, then additional, more appropriate modes of instruction must be utilized.

Reinforcement

The various components of teaching strategy discussed thus far have been geared specifically toward eliciting desired performance from the learner. A final strategy for consideration deals with what is to be done once the learner actually responds. It is a well known principle of learning theory that behaviors that are positively reinforced tend to be repeated. To help a student master a particular skill, therefore, it is essential that his/her efforts are reacted to in a way that encourages frequent and accurate responding.

It would be relatively simple if all pleasurable rewards chosen by teachers automatically functioned as positive reinforcers. Unfortunately, the problem is not so easily solved. Positive reinforcement must be defined solely by its effect on behavior. No matter how desirable or undesirable a consequence may seem, it is a positive reinforcer if it has the effect of strengthening or maintaining a behavior.

This operational definition of reinforcement has two critical implications for teaching. It means, first of all, that not every reward dispensed by the teacher will have the intended effect on student performance. While it is true that most pupils work hard to earn good grades and teacher approval, these generalized rewards are not enough for some children. Teachers often describe such students as "unmotivated" or having "a poor attitude." From a more behavioral point of view, the customary rewards of the educational system are simply not reinforcing for these children.

A second implication of importance is that certain consequences that a teacher intends to be negative in nature for the purpose of decreasing undesirable behaviors may, in practice, have the opposite effect. If a child continues to make the same mistake or to act inappropriately, then the teacher's reprimand has actually served as a positive reinforcer. The student has learned the wrong response in that situation.

Recognizing these difficulties related to the use of reinforcement, the teacher must carefully attend to the consequences of behaviors. What happens when a student performs correctly? What happens when a learner performs incorrectly? Once consequences are identified, the teacher can address the most relevant instructional question: is the present consequence changing behavior in the desired direction?

A frequent symptom of ineffective reinforcement is sporadic performance. The student may complete a few items correctly but make many errors on the remaining ones. On certain days, a pupil works very conscientiously, but on other days, the student is haphazard in his/her efforts. A child who is able to do the work nevertheless continually fails to complete assignments in the classroom. In all of these instances, behavior is not under control. More powerful reinforcers are needed to improve quality and consistency of performance.

It was recommended in Chapter 8 that individual reinforcement preferences be identified in the initial diagnosis of learning and behavior problems. Through direct questioning of a student, observations of the pupil in free-choice situations, and trial and error, a teacher can select likely reinforcers.

To illustrate the alternatives available in a typical classroom setting, a hierarchy of potential reinforcers is presented in Table 2. Several specific examples are noted for each type of reinforcement. Whenever the usual rewards are not effective and a more individualized system is necessary, the teacher should choose alternative reinforcers from the

Table 2. Hierarchy of potential reinforcers with classroom examples

1.	*Primary reinforcers*—	food, candy, treats, soft drinks
2.	*Concrete reinforcers*—	toys, prizes, school supplies, awards
3.	*Token reinforcers*—	points, checkmarks, stars, signatures, which can later be exchanged for other reinforcers
4.	*Activity reinforcers*—	special privileges, duties, free time, games
5.	*Social reinforcers*—	attention, praise, approval, calls and notes to parents
6.	*Knowledge of results*—	feedback on accuracy, confirmation, number or percentage correct
7.	*Intrinsic reinforcers*—	challenge of learning, sense of accomplishment

higher levels if at all possible. It is seldom necessary to use primary or even concrete reinforcers in the regular classroom. Token, activity, and social reinforcers are less artificial and less costly. Furthermore, they are easy to administer yet afford great flexibility in meeting individual needs.

A word is in order here about grading. The assignment of points and letter grades is in fact a form of token reinforcement. The letter *A* has no intrinsic value but has become reinforcing because it brings special recognition, privileges, awards, and the like. Many children with learning problems have never earned a high grade. They have instead learned that low marks are to be associated with loss of approval, ridicule, and, in some cases, even physical punishment. It is no wonder that the traditional grading systems are not motivating to many mainstreamed students.

If the grading system for a particular class can be set up so that all children have fair access to the better marks, then grades can function as more powerful, positive reinforcers. The kinds of accommodations suggested throughout this chapter will help the handicapped learner to compete more equitably for grades. The use of cumulative point totals as the basis for final grades often permits more individualization than the familiar practice of averaging. Students might also be allowed to contract for their grades, thus receiving credit for alternative or additional work.

In some cases, it is not the type of reinforcement that is inappropriate for special students but rather the timing. In the early stages of learning, a pupil needs continuous feedback about his/her performance. Learning proceeds most efficiently if every correct response is reinforced. Later, to maintain desired performance, a partial schedule is adequate. The student may be required to complete several responses before receiving reinforcement. In a regular classroom, the mainstreamed student may not be given feedback as frequently as his/her needs require.

Some handicapped children also have difficulty in delaying reinforcement. They need immediate feedback, and reinforcement becomes less effective as they are asked to wait. Through a gradual process, students can be taught to delay reinforcements for a more reasonable time.

Individualizing reinforcement is an essential part of teaching. Whenever it is apparent that a certain student is not responding to the reinforcers customarily applied in the classroom, adjustments should be made in the type and/or schedule of reinforcement. If a certain child needs more continuous and immediate feedback than a classroom teacher is directly able to provide, then this should be taken into account in other areas of planning. The problem may be alleviated somewhat through changes in grouping arrangement or instructional materials. It may be helpful, for example, to have the student work with a peer tutor or use programmed learning materials. Ways can be found to meet special needs without placing unrealistic demands on teacher time.

Summary

Several different aspects of teaching strategy have been considered as they affect special education in the regular classroom. Depending on the learning style of the student, the teacher might need to adjust time schedules, grouping arrangements, physical placements, modes of instruction, or reinforcement practices. Only minor changes will be necessary to accommodate some mildly handicapped students. Others who have more serious problems will require more extensive adaptations. The key to prescriptive programming is approaching instructional variables systematically. The factors discussed in this section are operative in virtually every classroom environment. Individualized instruction can occur effectively in the mainstream if teachers attempt to manage relevant variables to learner advantage.

INSTRUCTIONAL MATERIALS

The right instructional materials can greatly facilitate the process of individualization. They serve as the vehicles of instruction, carrying the content of the educational program directly to the learner. Given the impressive array of instructional materials currently on the market, it is sometimes difficult to keep their role in perspective. Many teachers routinely assign children to the most available or inviting commerical package, allowing the material to dictate the instructional program. In diagnostic prescriptive teaching, however, material selection is one of the later steps in planning. Only after the student's needs have been analyzed, and the teacher has decided what and how he/she should be taught can the matter of instructional materials be approached meaningfully.

Special materials are often required when objectives or teaching strategies have been modified for the mainstreamed child. Necessary materials can often be as simple as flash cards, worksheets, or educational games. In other situations, more comprehensive or elaborate aids might be used, including remedial kits, programmed devices, and the like.

Because there are so many options available, classroom teachers should have a thorough yet practical system for selecting instructional materials. A checklist, developed to assist teachers in matching material characteristics to instructional needs (Laycock, 1978), is provided in Figure 2. This scale directs teachers to rate materials on important dimensions and to choose those materials that correspond most closely to instructional priorities.

When the characteristics of a certain material correspond exactly to established needs, a score of 3 is assigned. A rating of 2 is used to indicate adequate correspondence. When features of the material do not meet instructional needs, a score of 1 is given. If several prospective materials are rated in this way and their average scores compared, the teacher is able to choose the one with the highest mean rating as the most suitable for the student's instructional program.

The 18 factors to be evaluated are clustered into the subsections entitled Instructional Specifications, Teaching Concerns, and Cost Effectiveness. Major points to be considered in each area are briefly described.

Instructional Specifications

The initial set of factors to be reviewed are those that relate to pupil characteristics and needs. Unless a prospective material teaches the desired skills in a manner appropriate to the student's learning style, it is simply not an adequate instructional tool for that program. By rating these factors first, low-scoring materials can be eliminated from further consideration.

Objectives The most basic test for suitability concerns instructional objectives. A desirable material should be compatible with program objectives not only in terms of specific skills being taught (scope) but also the order in which they are introduced (sequence).

Target Population Every instructional material has been designed for an intended group of learners. The teacher must note to what extent designated age ranges, grade levels, and other descriptive characteristics fit the child in question.

Prerequisite skills   There are entry level skills that are required to use any given material successfully. The authors have assumed that learners are coming to the material with a certain set of competencies. The teacher must decide how accurately prerequisite assumptions apply to the particular student.

Learning Modalities   Each material is set up to provide information to the learner and to elicit responses from the student. Considering the modality preferences of a given child, the teacher should evaluate the suitability of input and output demands.

Format   A number of different types of materials can be found to teach the same skills. The teacher must judge whether the specific medium (workbook, activity cards, games, filmstrips, tapes, etc.) is appropriate for the student. In addition, the desirability of the material should be rated in terms of overall quality and safety.

Pacing   The rate at which skills are introduced and the amount of practice allowed at each step must be matched to individual learning style. It should also be noted whether a material is sufficiently flexible to permit self-pacing by the learner.

Feedback Mechanisms   Considering a child's reinforcement needs, the teacher must decide whether a material provides the desired type of feedback and whether the feedback is available with sufficient frequency.

Motivating Factors   Finally, the teacher must rate the physical attractiveness of design and packaging (aesthetic appeal) and the relevancy of the content (thematic appeal) in light of the learner's interests and background experiences.

Teaching Concerns

Once materials have been matched to learner needs, the teacher is then concerned with variables related to the management of instruction. The most desirable materials should fit comfortably with the teacher's own style of instruction and patterns of classroom organization. The teacher rates five factors in terms of their application to him/her in his/her teaching situation.

Teacher Competencies   Specialized training and skills are sometimes required for effective use of a material. The teacher assigns ratings in these categories to reflect the correspondence between recommended and demonstrated competencies.

Teaching Environment   The teacher must judge how easily the prospective material could be used within the existing classroom struc-

MATCHING MATERIALS TO INSTRUCTIONAL NEEDS: A RATING SCALE

Learner: _____

Title of Instructional Material: _____

Publisher: _____

For each of the following factors, indicate to what degree material characteristics correspond to identified instructional needs by circling the appropriate number. If certain variables are not applicable, write NA in the

	Degree of Correspondence			
	High	Adequate	Low	Notes
INSTRUCTIONAL SPECIFICATIONS				
Objectives				
Scope	3	2	1	
Sequence	3	2	1	
Target Population				
Chronological Age	3	2	1	
Mental Age	3	2	1	
Grade Equivalent	3	2	1	
Other Descriptors	3	2	1	
Prerequisite Skills	3	2	1	
Learning Modalities				
Input	3	2	1	
Output	3	2	1	
Format				
Medium	3	2	1	
Quality	3	2	1	
Safety Features	3	2	1	
Pacing				
Rate	3	2	1	
Flexibility	3	2	1	
Feedback Mechanisms				
Type of Reinforcement	3	2	1	
Schedule	3	2	1	
Motivating Factors				
Aesthetic Appeal	3	2	1	
Thematic Appeal	3	2	1	

Total _____

Number of factors rated _____

Mean rating _____

continued

Figure 2.   A checklist for selecting appropriate materials.

right-hand column. Where low correspondence is observed, comment briefly on the potential for adaptation or modification in that area.

	Degree of Correspondence			
	High	Adequate	Low	Notes
TEACHING CONCERNS				
Teacher Competencies				
Training	3	2	1	
Specialized Skills	3	2	1	
Teaching Environment				
Classroom Organization	3	2	1	
Physical Requirements	3	2	1	
Teaching Aids	3	2	1	
Teachers' Guide	3	2	1	
Supplementary Resources	3	2	1	
Evaluative Criteria				
Test Items	3	2	1	
Scheduling	3	2	1	
Teacher Time				
Preparation	3	2	1	
Supervision	3	2	1	
Evaluation	3	2	1	
COST EFFECTIVENESS				
Cost				
Total Price	3	2	1	
Component Prices	3	2	1	
Replacement Parts	3	2	1	
Durability	3	2	1	
Number Served	3	2	1	
Research Data	3	2	1	
Nondiscriminatory Representation	3	2	1	

Total_____
Number of factors rated_____
Mean rating_____

ture. If any specialized equipment or facilities are required, this, too, must be taken into account.

Teaching Aids   The adequacy of the manual and other supportive resources should be evaluated in light of the teacher's own needs and expectations.

Evaluative Criteria   Many materials include evaluative components to assist teachers in the difficult task of measuring progress. The adequacy of evaluative aids should be judged in terms of the nature and number of responses sampled, and the frequency of testing within the instructional program.

Teacher Time   Knowing how much time can realistically be allotted to specific instructional tasks, the teacher should rate the appropriateness of material demands for preparation, supervision, and evaluation.

Cost Effectiveness

The remaining five factors encourage the teacher to weigh the advantages of the material against the expense involved. When several materials have been found to satisfy instructional specifications and teaching concerns, the teacher should choose the material that offers the greatest educational returns for the money. When materials are already available in the classroom or from a local media center, the first three factors in this section may not be applicable.

Cost   When a material is being considered for purchase, the prices of component and replacement parts should be investigated as well as the cost of the total package. The most desirable materials will be within budget allowances and also compare favorably in price to similar materials on the market.

Durability   After considering the cost of the material and the quality of its construction, the teacher must decide whether the material is likely to render reasonable service in return for the investment.

Number Served   Again, a relative judgment is required, this time indicating whether enough students can benefit from the material to justify the expense involved.

Research Data   Regardless of what a material purports to do or how reasonably it is priced, there should always be research evidence provided to substantiate its effectiveness. A highly desirable material will present data-based results of field testing using samples of adequate number and representation.

Nondiscriminatory Representation   A final consideration before investing in a material pertains to the portrayal of human diversity. Any material that casts a particular race or sex in a negative or stereotyped manner is to be avoided.

Summary

A rating scale has been introduced to guide the process of materials selection. Material characteristics are to be evaluated in terms of the degree of correspondence with instructional needs. Materials earning the highest mean scores on the rating scale are considered most suitable for the learner and the teacher in their given situation.

If none of the materials rated at first seem to be appropriate, the teacher has several options. He/she can attempt to locate other, more promising commercial materials, or he/she can decide to adapt a material that originally failed to meet specifications in certain areas. A final alternative is to construct a teacher-made material. The rating scale may then function as a checklist helping the teacher to design a material that conforms precisely to specifications.

PROGRAM IMPLEMENTATION

Once instructional objectives, strategies, and materials have been selected, the teacher has a complete educational plan. For a program to be of any real value, however, it must be delivered effectively to the learner. It is during this implementation stage that the personal and interactive nature of education is most apparent. The same written plan would not be carried out in identical fashion by different teachers, nor would it have the identical impact on students. Just as each pupil possesses a unique learning style, so does each educator possess a unique teaching style. Suggestions offered in this section are in no way intended to dictate conformity or to limit the richness of instructional interactions. They are simply to serve as guidelines, and, as all other recommendations in this chapter, should be personalized in practice.

An initial, obvious concern is that an instructional program should be implemented as it was written. After thorough planning has taken place, the decisions should be translated into action. In working with handicapped children, it is admittedly difficult to achieve such consistency. It is often tempting to abandon one's original plan in favor of a more spontaneous "Plan B." Nevertheless, a teacher must make every attempt to control variables in the instructional program exactly as prescribed. This is the only way to identify systematically what does and does not work to learner advantage.

Although the written plan serves mainly as a blueprint for the teacher, it can also be a meaningful reference for the student. It is often effective for the teacher to share the actual plan with the learner, discussing any individualized provisions to be made. In some instances, instructional variables are explicitly defined in contract form to represent a formal agreement between teacher and student. Even with very young children, it is important for the teacher to specify the limits of the program on the front end. Handicapped learners tend to respond well to this type of structure.

Interpersonal Factors

The teacher's attitude toward the student and the instructional program is seldom reflected on a written plan but is of great significance during the implementation phase. Children labeled as handicapped typically have histories of negative school experiences. As a result, they are often skeptical about trying something new. Many mainstreamed students also feel that teachers "don't care." A half-hearted presentation is likely, therefore, to confirm pupil's fears and to encourage low quality participation.

A teacher who is able to communicate belief in the student and enthusiasm for the lesson may make a critical difference in program effectiveness. The personalities of the individuals, the age of the student, and the nature of the lesson will determine the exact verbal and non-verbal cues employed. However the enthusiasm is conveyed, the message needs to come through very clearly to the mainstreamed student.

Another dimension of communication contributing to teacher effectiveness involves the interpretation of feedback from students. A perceptive teacher is able to detect early signs of distress. At times, a child's difficulties are verbally expressed through a question or comment. More often, the teacher must depend on facial expressions, body language, and even the absence of a response to provide clues about student involvement in the task. When these messages denote frustration, an extra word of encouragement may be in order. The child who appears confused may need to have instructions repeated in simpler language. Other signs may suggest boredom, leading the teacher to step up the pace of the lesson. These subtle exchanges serve to smooth out the rough edges of the instructional program, personalizing it even further as it is being implemented.

Transitions

In presenting a lesson to students, the beginnings and endings of activities warrant special attention. Handicapped learners often have trouble making transitions from one activity to the next. They may perseverate on the previous activity, experience a lapse of attention, or become engaged in another off-task behavior. In addition, these students may not grasp the relationship between activities, failing to see how the separate tasks fit together for a definite purpose. For these reasons, transitions within a lesson should be approached with care.

It is always advisable to focus attention of students before starting a presentation. Unless they are looking and listening, they are likely to miss important information. Attention focusers can be very simple but should be part of every teacher's repertoire. Verbal openers include such directives as "Let's get started. Everyone look up here at the chalkboard" or "Ready? Listen carefully." Nonverbal cues, such as pointing or tapping, can also help to capture attention.

As soon as students are attending, the teacher should further orient them toward the lesson by explaining how today's activity relates to the overall plan. The teacher might emphasize that the present activities are an extension of what was done yesterday. Another time, the teacher might point out that certain goals have been achieved, and the group is now moving on to something new. When lessons are introduced in this way, it helps students, particularly the handicapped, to get their bearings.

Similarly, most students like to have a sense of closure at the end of an activity. In many classrooms, the end of one task simply marks the beginning of another. Children are frequently left hanging with little sense of accomplishment. A sentence or two is all that may be required to provide closure. The statement, "You've really worked hard on punctuating these sentences. We'll learn some other uses of the comma tomorrow," draws a lesson to a close and promises the learner some continuity in his/her program.

Summary

In operationalizing the written lesson plan, a teacher must attempt to manage instructional variables as prescribed. The program may be enhanced, however, by the application of certain teaching skills during the lesson itself. A teacher who is able to present tasks enthusiastically, to capitalize on student feedback, and to make smooth transitions between activities is likely to be an asset to any instructional program.

PROGRAM EVALUATION

No matter how carefully a program is planned and implemented, it is only valid if it produces measurable gains in achievement. The sixth step in the diagnostic prescriptive cycle, therefore, is evaluation of learner performance to determine effectiveness of the instructional program. Classroom teachers are already involved in evaluation of student performance. Standardized achievement tests, teacher-made tests, and graded assignments are a few of the more familiar tools for assessing academic progress. These evaluation techniques used in the regular program provide some useful information about the effectiveness of mainstreaming as well. They fall short, however, when it comes to evaluating a diagnostic prescriptive program.

Prescriptive programming depends upon highly accurate and current data on learner performance. One cannot afford to wait 3 weeks before measuring performance on a unit test, only to discover that important concepts have been missed. Even small fluctuations in performance should not go undetected. When handicapped children are already significantly behind their peers, there is simply no time to waste. Precise, up-to-date information is required to ensure that the instructional program continues to fit changing needs.

Continuous Measurement

When instruction is to be individualized, teachers should collect data on a regular basis. Daily measurements of performance are ideal. Such a recommendation may seem unreasonable if evaluation is viewed only in the traditional sense of testing. Once it is recognized, however, that every response from the learner represents an opportunity for evaluation, continuous measurement becomes a more manageable task.

In prescriptive teaching, diagnostic evaluation is an inseparable part of instruction. The objectives themselves specify what is to be measured. Criteria for mastery should likewise be established in the plan. Evaluation then consists of measuring the quantity and/or quality of learner responses as they occur and comparing present levels of performance with pre-established standards for mastery.

If, for example, a target objective is "to spell the names of the 7 days of the week correctly in writing," then one must count and record the number of days spelled correctly. An objective calling for the learner "to solve 10 word problems requiring one-step operations of addition or subtraction with 80 percent accuracy" necessitates data in a slightly different form. One would keep track of the percentage of problems solved correctly each day. Formal tests are seldom necessary for this type of evaluation. Practice exercises included in the daily lesson can usually provide sufficient performance samples.

Graphing or charting the number of correct and incorrect responses each day is a convenient way of summarizing the data. A graph makes it easier to recognize even slight trends in performance over time. This can be very helpful in working with the handicapped since progress often occurs in small increments. A teacher is less likely to become discouraged if there is evidence of an upward trend despite the inevitable setbacks.

A graph can be reinforcing to the learner as well, particularly if the student can be actively involved in counting his/her own behaviors and plotting the points on an individual chart. Even youngsters in kindergarten and first grade have learned to chart their own performance successfully (Bates & Bates, 1971; Starlin, 1972). Not only is this highly motivating to students, but it also reduces demands on teacher time.

Error Analysis

Keeping continuous records of the number of correct and incorrect responses is a major part of the evaluative process, but there is more. Evaluation must be diagnostic in its orientation. This means that a teacher must be concerned not only with the *number* of errors but also with the *types* of errors made. It is the child's mistakes that provide clues about his/her faulty learning strategies and interfering variables in the instructional program.

Given several samples of a student's work, it is usually possible to detect patterns of difficulty. It may become apparent that the student has failed to acquire a particular concept or that the pupil is confusing it with some other concept. On a math worksheet, for example, a learner may have written a different answer each time the combination 8×3 appeared. This suggests that the student has not yet learned any consistent association. On the other hand, the child who makes the very same error each time on a certain combination has indeed formed a concept but an incorrect one. In the latter instance, the teacher will have to straighten out the pupil's misconception while teaching the correct association.

Error analysis can be applied in all subject matter areas. It requires an attempt to decipher what exactly the student is doing wrong. This is a more time consuming evaluative task than the familiar tallying of X-marks, but it has direct and important implications for teaching.

Performance Patterns

It is usually advisable to base evaluative decisions on *trends* observed in student performance over a given period of time. A single measurement should not be considered sufficient evidence of either success or failure of the instructional program. Whenever substantial modifications are introduced in a program, student performance is likely to change dramatically, for better or for worse. If a teacher reacts too quickly, the program will be changed before it has been given a chance to work. Once again, continuous measurements are helpful. They allow the teacher to recognize the adaptation period and to wait for more consistent, representative data before making judgments.

After the novelty of a new program has worn off, several different performance patterns may emerge. The most fortunate is that a student is able to perform with consistency at criterion level. The target objective has been mastered, indicating the instructional program was indeed effective for the learner.

A second trend revealed through continuous measurement shows gradual progress toward the goal. If performance is being graphed, one would observe a fairly steady rise in correct responses and a corresponding decline in the number of errors. In this instance, the program is basically appropriate. The student is profiting from it, but needs additional time and practice to achieve mastery.

A third pattern occurs when pupil performance levels out below the criterion. On a graph, this resembles a plateau. It suggests that the instructional program has advanced the learner somewhat, but it is falling short of his/her needs in certain respects. The present program is not yet individualized to the extent that it should be.

It sometimes happens that a program produces the exact opposite effect from what is intended. The student's performance does change, but in the wrong direction. Clearly the program is inappropriate because it has succeeded only in compounding the problem.

In the fifth pattern there is little or no change apparent in student performance. Points plotted on a graph may fluctuate slightly, but overall there is a rather flat effect. The instructional program appears to have no appreciable impact.

A final pattern that is often encountered reveals sporadic performance over time. A chart would show a spiking progression with sharp peaks and valleys. There is simply no consistency in the learner's performance from day to day. The program in this case is teaching the desired skills but is failing to bring behavior under control.

Summary

Only through continuous measurement and analysis of learner performance can a teacher determine the effectiveness of an instructional program. In the diagnostic prescriptive system, precise information about the student's present level of performance and the difficulties he/she is experiencing allows a teacher to adapt the program to the learner's changing needs.

PROGRAM REVISION

Diagnostic prescriptive teaching was originally presented as a cycle of programming tasks. After completing the first six steps in the sequence, a teacher has developed and tested out an individualized instructional program. Because of the complexity of decisions involved and because student needs are continually changing, the initial set of judgments may not be the most appropriate. Some modifications are usually required before an instructional program succeeds in advancing performance to mastery levels. Program revision, the seventh step in the prescriptive cycle, thus returns the teacher near the starting point to work through the process again.

In some cases, only minor refinements are needed to improve the program. At other times, major portions of the program seem inappropriate, and the teacher must almost start over in designing another. The very same factors that were considered in the original program must be reexamined for "goodness of fit." After working with the child and noting the learner's difficulties, the teacher can usually pinpoint suspect variables that should be adjusted to permit more efficient learning.

In the previous section on evaluation, six frequently observed patterns of performance were described. These same patterns are now referred to again in order to discuss their implications for program revision.

The preferred outcome of evaluation was pattern one, indicating mastery of target objectives. Revision, in this instance, consists of designing a new program to teach the next, more advanced objectives in the curriculum.

The second pattern revealed steady progress toward attainment of objectives. At this point, no actual revision is in order. If the rate of progress is judged satisfactory, the program should simply be recycled allowing the learner additional practice to improve his/her proficiency.

When performance has leveled out short of criterion for mastery, several factors should be checked for possible revision. In some cases, the teacher has set standards of performance too high for the child to attain. The learner's best performance may be at a 75 percent level. The teacher must question the need for very high criteria (90 percent to 100 percent) in any skill areas where perfect performance is not absolutely essential. It may be justified, for example, to expect students to identify all 26 letters of the alphabet correctly, but it may not be mandatory for them to attain 100 percent accuracy on pages of long division problems. If the criterion itself is unnecessarily high, it should be lowered to a more realistic level.

If the criterion does seem appropriate for the learner and the skill in question, either strategies or materials need to be changed. Mode of instruction may warrant particular attention, since it appears that the student has not received sufficient input to improve his/her performance.

The instructional program that worsens performance is indeed a matter of concern. Since so many things are going wrong, it is often difficult to identify specific variables responsible. There is a similar problem when the program is found to have no significant effect. Teachers would do well in these instances to start at the beginning and recheck each step in prescriptive programming. Even the original diagnostic data may have been inaccurate, leading the teacher to base the entire program on false assumptions. It is also possible that the objectives were poorly chosen. The learner may not have been able to benefit from the program because he/she lacked prerequisite skills. Lower level objectives may need to be defined, or the task may need to be analyzed into smaller units for instruction.

If the objectives appear suited to the student's level of readiness, then strategies and materials must be at fault. A careful review of evaluative data should provide the clues necessary to locate the specific factors impeding progress. When a program has been highly ineffectual, there are usually several different variables that must be managed in an alternative way.

The program that produces sporadic performance may not require substantial revision. It has in fact taught the learner to perform the desired response. What is lacking is consistency. In all probability, the reinforcement is not appropriate. Either the reinforcers are not strong enough, or they are not being applied with sufficient frequency to bring behavior under control. More individualized reinforcement practices should be attempted.

In summary, the final step in prescriptive programming encourages a review of all previous steps in order to improve the suitability of instruction. Certain adjustments may be needed because original decisions, based on the diagnostic data then available, did not prove advantageous to the learner. Other adjustments are required because learner needs change over time. This refining and updating of a program to correspond to the current performance of the learner is the essence of diagnostic prescriptive teaching.

CONCLUSIONS

Individualizing for special students in the mainstream requires certain adaptations in the regular program to meet unique learning needs.

Throughout this chapter a diagnostic prescriptive approach has been advocated. A thorough assessment of learner characteristics provides the information necessary to design a more personalized educational program. Knowledge of a student's current level of functioning allows a teacher to identify reasonable target objectives. An understanding of his learning style leads to the selection of appropriate instructional strategies and materials.

Once a teacher has student needs clearly defined, major dimensions of the regular developmental program must be analyzed. It is essential to determine how instructional variables are currently being managed in the classroom. When the existing program is examined in light of the needs of the handicapped, any significant discrepancies should become

Student's name:_____ Area of concern:_____
Date:_____ Class:_____

Instructional variables	Student needs	Existing program	Necessary adjustments
Objectives			
Strategies Timing			
Grouping			
Setting			
Mode of instruction			
Reinforcement			
Materials			
Implementation			
Evaluation			

Figure 3.   A DPT worksheet.

apparent. Adjustments are then necessary in whatever areas the regular program is failing to provide for the mainstreamed student.

To facilitate the application of a diagnostic prescriptive approach to mainstreaming, a worksheet is suggested in Figure 3. This chart is straightforward and brief, yet thorough in scope. Space is provided to describe learner needs and the existing program in each instructional category. This format permits direct comparison of program characteristics with student needs in all major prescriptive areas. Additional columns might be added to aid in program revision.

Seldom are learner needs so rigidly specified that only one instructional treatment can be justified. In most cases, the problem might be solved in numerous ways. Final decisions should represent an attempt to reconcile individual teaching styles with learning styles. With this approach, the seemingly overwhelming problem of mainstreaming can be reduced to specific concerns that can be dealt with constructively in the classroom.

REFERENCES

Allen, V. L., & Feldman, R. S. Learning through tutoring: Low achieving children as tutors. *Journal of Experimental Education*, 1974, *42*, 1–5.

Balmer, J. Project tutor. *Teaching Exceptional Children*, 1972, *4*, 166–175.

Bates, S., & Bates, D. F. ". . . and a child shall lead them." *Teaching Exceptional Children*, 1971, *3*, 111–113.

Bean, R., & Luke, C. As a teacher I've been learning. *Journal of Reading*, 1972, *16*, 128–132.

Bloom, S. *Peer and cross-age tutoring in the schools.* Chicago: Chicago Board of Education, District 10, 1976.

Brown, L., Fenrick, N., & Klemme, H. Trainable pupils learn to teach each other. *Teaching Exceptional Children*, 1971, *4*, 189–194.

Cawley, J. F. Curriculum: One perspective for special education. In R. D. Kneedler & S. G. Tarver (Eds.), *Changing perspectives in special education.* Columbus, Oh.: Charles E. Merrill, 1977.

Cawley, J. F., Fitzmaurice, A. M., Goodstein, H. A., Lepore, A. V., Sedlak, R., & Althaus, V. *Project MATH*, Levels I and II. Tulsa: Educational Progress Corporation, 1976.

Cawley, J. F., Fitzmaurice, A. M., Goodstein, H. A., Lepore, A. V., Sedlak, R., & Althaus, V. *Project MATH*, Levels II and III, Tulsa: Educational Progress Corporation, 1977.

Cawley, J. F., Fitzmaurice, A. M., Shaw, R. A., Kahn, H., & Bates, H. Mathematics and learning disabled youth: The upper grade levels. *Learning Disability Quarterly*, 1978, *1*(4), 37–52.

Charles, C. M. *Individualizing instruction.* St. Louis: C. V. Mosby, 1976.

Conrad, E. The effects of tutor achievement level, reinforcement training, and expectancy on peer tutoring. Tucson, Ariz.: Arizona University Center for Research and Development, 1976. (ERIC Document Reproduction Service No. ED 116 807).

Devin-Sheehan, L., Feldman, R. S., & Allen, V. L. Research on children tutoring children: A critical review. *Review of Educational Research*, 1976, *46*, 355–385.

Engelmann, S. E. Sequencing cognitive and academic tasks. In R. D. Kneedler & S. G. Tarver (Eds.), *Changing perspectives in special education*. Columbus, Oh.: Charles E. Merrill, 1977.

Gartner, A., Kohler, M. M., & Riessman, F. *Children teach children*. New York: Harper & Row, 1972.

Haring, N. G., & Schiefelbusch, R. L. *Teaching special children*. New York: McGraw-Hill, 1976.

Hassinger, J., & Via, M. How much does a tutor learn through teaching reading? *Journal of Secondary Education*, 1969, *44*, 42–46.

Lane, P., Pollack, C., & Sher, N. Remotivation of disruptive adolescents. *Journal of Reading*, 1972, *15*, 351–354.

Laurie, T. F., Buchwach, L., Silverman, R., & Zigmond, N. Teaching secondary learning disabled adolescents in the mainstream. *Learning Disability Quarterly*, 1978, *1*(4), 62–72.

Laycock, V. K. Making the match. In R. M. Anderson, J. G. Greer, & S. J. Odle (Eds.), *Individualizing educational materials for special children in the mainstream*. Baltimore: University Park Press, 1978.

Laycock, V. K., & Schwartzberg, I. M. *Mainstreaming through peer assisted learning*. Paper presented at International Convention of the Council for Exceptional Children, Atlanta, April, 1977. (ERIC Document Reproduction Service No. ED 143 150).

Lerner, J. L. *Children with learning disabilities*, (2nd ed.). Boston: Houghton Mifflin, 1976.

Mercer, C. D. *Children and adolescents with learning disabilities*. Columbus, Oh.: Charles E. Merrill, 1979.

Moran, M. R. Nine steps to the diagnostic prescriptive process in the classroom. *Focus on Exceptional Children*, 1975, *6*(9), 1–14.

Moyer, J. R., & Dardig, J. C. Practical task analysis for special educators. *Teaching Exceptional Children*, 1978, *1*(1), 16–18.

Peter, J. L. *Prescriptive teaching*. New York: McGraw-Hill, 1965.

Smith, R. M. *Clinical teaching: Methods of instruction for the retarded*. New York: McGraw-Hill, 1974.

Stainbach, W. C., Stainbach, S. B., & Lichtward, F. The research evidence regarding the student-to-student tutoring approach to individualized instruction. *Educational Technology*, 1975, *15*, 54–56.

Starlin, A. Sharing a message about curriculum with my teacher friends. In *Let's try doing something else kind of thing: Behavioral principles and the exceptional child*. Arlington, Va.: Council for Exceptional Children, 1972.

Stephens, T. M. *Teaching skills to children with learning and behavior disorders*. Columbus, Oh.: Charles E. Merrill, 1977.

Wagner, P. Children tutoring children. *Mental Retardation*, 1974, *12*(5), 52–55.

10
ESTABLISHING THE LEARNING CLIMATE

H. Lyndall Rich

If a person strolls down the hall of a typical elementary school briefly looking into each classroom along the way, a number of rather obvious differences can be observed. In one classroom, students are seated in a rather orderly fashion, watching and listening to the teacher lecturing from the front of the class. In a second classroom, the noise is much greater, clusters of students are scattered around the room, and the teacher is moving around from group to group. In a third classroom, the teacher is working on records at the desk while the students read, write, or talk individually at their own desks. In a fourth classroom, the teacher is severely admonishing a student while the rest of the classroom group watches the disciplinary process. Of course, these four exemplary classrooms represent only a small portion of an infinite number of teacher-student behaviors that can be routinely observed.

A closer look at the four classrooms will reveal even greater differences among both teachers and students. Assuming the brief observation is characteristic of each teacher's style, the four teachers represent 1) an authoritarian "information giver" who conceptualizes education as a one-way communication process, 2) a facilitator of student interaction who places priority on informality and involvement, 3) an uninvolved or laissez-faire teacher, who places emphasis on the recordkeeping aspects of classroom organization, and 4) a disciplinarian who is concerned more with the managerial aspects of teaching.

Among the students, the observed behaviors will range from motionless, quiet, obedient students to those who are active, loud, and defiant. Some will be completely involved in a lesson; others are virtually asleep. Some students always comply with teacher expectations, while others pursue their own interest regardless of the classroom situation. Most important, some students like school and succeed in learning while others, who do not like school, fail to learn.

Over the past few years a number of terms have evolved that have been used to identify, study, or describe learning climates, such as *envi-*

ronmental psychology, social psychology, therapeutic milieu, social climate, and *learning atmosphere.* Although the terms are not synonymous, they infer that the classroom learning climate includes all ". . . the surrounding conditions and influences that affect personal development" (Dale, 1972, p. 16).

Every teacher would like to have a classroom climate that is free of personal conflict, where children learn in a free and cooperative environment. However, such a climate is difficult to achieve and is often never attained by many teachers. Conflicts between children erupt, unmotivated children may waste their time, and teachers may serve primarily as behavioral censors.

During the past few years, educational issues, such as the "back to basics" movement, accountability, competency testing, discipline, and mainstreaming have been of primary concern to teachers, frequently at the expense of an appropriate classroom learning climate. So much teacher energy has been devoted to meeting individual cognitive, behavioral, and legal requirements that the classroom learning climate and its impact on the performance of both teachers and students has been ignored.

This chapter is based on the belief that an appropriate classroom learning climate will enhance the teacher's ability to provide better instruction, reduce discipline problems, and enable greater individualized learning for both handicapped and nonhandicapped children. Although the focus of this chapter is on individual teachers, handicapped students, and classroom groups, it should be recognized that both teachers and students throughout an entire school building or even an entire school system may be influenced by the leadership philosophy demonstrated by principals, superintendents, and the community in general. Often this influence is so great that it interferes with the most conscientious teacher efforts to alter the existing learning climate. For example, if the philosophy of the leadership is basically custodial, complete with a rule orientation, orderliness, and unquestioned obedience to authority, then the teacher is limited in the types of procedures that may be attempted. On the other hand, administrative leadership that recognizes the importance of learning climate and supports teachers and students by providing resources, encouragement, and understanding gives the teacher a wide range of alternatives.

Within a school system, a school, or an individual classroom, a number of behaviors and attitudes may be evidenced that are indicative of a negative school climate. Fox, Boies, Brainard, Fletcher, Huge, Martin, Maynard, Monasmith, Olivero, Schmuck, Shaheen, and Stegeman (1974) have developed a checklist of school-related problems that are symptomatic of a negative school climate:

_____ High student absenteeism
_____ High frequency of student discipline problems
_____ Weak student government
_____ Student cliques
_____ High faculty absenteeism
_____ Negative discussion in faculty lounges
_____ Crowded conditions
_____ "Lost" feeling of students because the school is too large
_____ Vandalism
_____ Student unrest
_____ Poor school spirit
_____ Poor community image of the school
_____ Faculty cliques
_____ Property theft from lockers
_____ High student dropout rate
_____ Underachieving students
_____ Low staff morale
_____ Passive students
_____ Faculty apathy
_____ Supplies and equipment unavailable when needed
_____ Students carrying guns, knives, and other weapons
_____ Poor image of the school by staff
_____ Dislike of students by faculty members
_____ Feeling among students that school has little purpose
_____ High incidence of suspensions and expulsions (pp. 2–3)

The presence of one or more of the above conditions clearly identifies the school as having a learning climate that needs immediate and direct attention. When several of the negative conditions exist, teachers and students are primarily concerned with day-to-day existence, even survival in many cases, with little attention devoted to academic learning or human needs. "It could be said that if schools continue to perpetuate an antihumane climate in which apathy, failure, punishment, and inadequate success in achieving the curriculum are characteristic, they may guarantee their own demise, and ultimately that of the American social system" (Fox et al., 1974, p. 3).

Under such negative conditions, children, particularly handicapped children, have little opportunity to succeed. If children have difficulty relating to their peers, their teachers, or the curriculum because of their physical, intellectual, or emotional handicapping condition, a negative school climate accentuates the competition between teachers and students and among students, ensuring greater degrees of failure and apathy.

The checklist serves only to identify and list school climate problems. However, many schools are positive, showing little evidence of a negative climate. The differences among schools and between negative and positive climates appear to be attributable to at least eight factors:

1. *Respect.* Students should see themselves as persons of worth, believing that they have ideas, and that those ideas are listened to and make a difference. Teachers and administrators should feel the same way. School should be a place where there are self-respecting individuals. Respect is also due to others. In a positive climate there are no put-downs.

2. *Trust.* Trust is reflected in one's confidence that others can be counted on to behave in a way that is honest. They will do what they say they will do. There is also an element of believing others will not let you down.

3. *High Morale.* People with high morale feel good about what is happening.

4. *Opportunities for Input.* Not all persons can be involved in making the important decisions. Not always can each person be as influential as he might like to be on the many aspects of the school's programs and processes that affect him. But every person cherishes the opportunity to contribute his or her ideas, and know they have been considered. A feeling of a lack of voice is counterproductive to self-esteem and deprives the school of that person's resources.

5. *Continuous Academic and Social Growth.* Each student needs to develop additional academic, social, and physical skills, knowledge, and attitudes. (Many educators have described the growth process as achieving "developmental tasks." Educators, too, desire to improve their skills, knowledge, and attitudes in regard to their particular assignments within the school district and as cooperative members of a team).

6. *Cohesiveness.* This quality is measured by the person's feeling toward the school. Members should feel a part of the school. They want to stay with it and have a chance to exert their influence on it in collaboration with others.

7. *School Renewal.* The school as an institution should develop improvement projects. It should be self-renewing in that it is growing, developing, and changing rather than following routines, repeating previously accepted procedures, and striving for conformity. If there is renewal, difference is seen as interesting, to be cherished. Diversity and pluralism are valued. New conditions are faced with poise. Adjustments are worked out as needed. The "new" is not seen as threatening, but as something to be examined, weighed, and its value or relevance determined. The school should be able to organize improvement projects rapidly and efficiently, with an absence of stress and conflict.

8. *Caring.* Every individual in the school should feel that some other person or persons are concerned about him as a human being. Each knows it will make a difference to someone else if he is happy or sad, healthy or ill. (Teachers should feel that the principal cares about them even when they make mistakes or disagree. And the principal should know that the teachers—at least most of them—understand the pressures under which he or she is working and will help if they can (Fox et al, 1974, pp. 7–9).

(The authors do not believe the factors listed above, or the other listings used to describe the school's climate, are all-inclusive. Readers may wish to delete or add items.)

Even though the eight factors are intended to create a positive climate within the school, the factors are equally important to the climate of the individual classroom. The task of establishing an appropriate learning climate in the classroom is not a simple one, nor is the responsibility clearly defined in many situations. The fact that an infinite number of variables exist that have influence on the learning climate can be an overwhelming problem for the teacher. The complex nature of the classroom climate created by individual needs, high rates of behavior, and prescribed educational objectives requires both planned and spontaneous actions and reactions on the part of the teacher. Handicapped children introduced to the regular classroom typically increase the complexity of the classroom climate.

In order to systematically discuss the establishment of an appropriate classroom learning climate, the focus of this chapter is on the separate influences of the teachers, students, and the curriculum. These three factors, above all else, are the most instrumental in establishing the classroom climate.

TEACHER INFLUENCE

There seems to be little question that the teacher is the single most critical factor in determining the classroom climate (Smith, Neisworth, & Greer, 1978). The teacher, as an adult with both the power and responsibility to educate the children assigned to the classroom, occupies a commanding and influential position. According to Mehrabian (1976), an obvious feature of schools is that ". . . a small number of people occupy positions of great dominance—persons who command resources enabling them to reward greatly or punish severely" (p. 153).

Thus, the character of the classroom learning climate is largely dependent upon the teacher's use of personal, professional, and legal influence on the students within the classroom. How a teacher exercises influence becomes a critical factor in promoting either a positive or negative climate. The direction in which teachers influence the climate appears to be dependent upon 1) the teachers' expectations of students, and 2) how the teachers exercise leadership behavior.

Teacher Expectations

The extent to which teachers reward and punish is a critical dimension of teacher influence. This complex pattern of approval and disapproval is often a function of teacher expectations and attitudes toward members of the classroom group. Unfortunately, children with handicapping conditions, children who are members of minority groups, and even children who are male may receive proportionately more punishment and fewer rewards than other children in the classroom. Although most teachers probably do not intentionally demonstrate such bias, the fact remains that teachers, in general, have a lower expectation of success for handicapped students. Such expectations may be obvious, but more often are conveyed in subtle ways. For example, a teacher may stand near the handicapped child more frequently than other students, or he/she may give the handicapped child more privileges than other students; or he/she may proclaim that a handicapped child did not perform as well as other students, but that the child did as much as could be expected. Each of these examples represents a condescending, protective attitude which, in reality, is one of low expectation for the handicapped child.

Other teachers demonstrate more obvious negative attitudes and low expectations for the handicapped. Turnbull and Schulz (1979) provide an example of a negative teacher attitude toward a handicapped student:

> Kate, a third-grader, has been classified as educable mentally retarded on the basis of formal diagnostic tests. Kate goes to the resource room for one and one-half hours every day. Her classroom teacher tends to exclude her from almost all activities on the basis that 'no child with her limited development can effectively participate in the regular classroom.' When other students in the class fail to achieve according to the teacher's expectations, the voiced threat by the teacher is, 'If you cannot do your assignments, you will have to go with Kate to work with the other EMRs in the resource room.' Both Kate and her peers get the message (p. 340).

Low teacher expectation of handicapped students is a negative value that can condemn the concept of mainstreaming and the needs of handicapped students. "A particular danger is that low expectations combined with an attitude of futility will be communicated to certain students, leading to the erosion of their confidence and motivation for school learning" (Good & Brophy, 1978, p. 100). Low expectations not only reduce school learning, but they are a signal that the teacher has "given up" on the handicapped student and has accepted the handicapping condition as an explanation and justification for failure. Clearly, low teacher expectations have a significant impact on the classroom learning climate, particularly for the handicapped student.

Teachers' Leadership Behaviors

Several studies have demonstrated that the teachers' leadership behaviors influence the behavior and performance of students. The clearest evidence of leadership effect comes from an early but classic study by

Lewin, Lippitt, and White (1939) that dealt with three distinctively different leadership styles: authoritarian, laissez-faire, and democratic. Brophy and Good (1974) provide an excellent summary of this classic study:

> Laissez-faire leadership tends to create chaos and confusion. Authoritarian leadership achieves efficient productivity but at the cost of frustration and a generally negative group atmosphere, leading to outbreaks of aggression when the leader is absent. In contrast to both of the above, democratic leadership appears to be successful in enabling groups to reach productive goals but without the cost of frustration and aggression. In fact, it seems to have the advantage of teaching the group to function more maturely, cooperatively and independently in the leader's absence as well as in his presence (p. 245).

With those results one may wonder why democratic teacher leadership style is not more prevalent in schools. Although there may be as many reasons as there are teachers, there appear to be at least two global explanations for the continued reliance upon authoritarian teacher leadership style.

Personal Growth versus Academic Achievement   Undoubtedly, most elementary teachers place high priority on children's ability to perform academically. Contrary to the rather specific conclusions reached in the Lewin, Lippitt, and White study, the controversy over the desirability of democratic versus authoritarian teacher leadership styles has continued.

In general, the research on teaching styles in education indicates that authoritarian methods are more effective when the students are to accomplish lower level cognitive objectives, such as memorizing the multiplication table, matching colors, and locating specific answers (Bennett, 1976). On the other hand, democratic methods are more effective for promoting self-discovery learning and personal adjustment (Bills, 1956). Stern (1962), in a review of studies dealing with learning environments, found that only one research report actually demonstrated that the democratic style resulted in significantly greater mastery of subject matter. McKeachie (1962) similarly concluded that students achieved lower scores on content examinations with democratic styles, which indicated a ". . . weakness, at least in achieving lower level cognitive goals" (p. 328). Stern, however, reaffirms the findings that a democratic style is associated with more positive personal adjustment.

Anderson (1959) summarized the research on democratic and authoritarian methods which emphasized differences in educational outcomes. "Democratic leadership is associated with high morale when the primary group goal is social . . . authoritarian leadership is most effective when the task is simple and concrete" (p. 204).

For elementary school children, the research results indicate that the authoritarian leadership style is preferable in assisting children in achieving lower level cognitive objectives. Such a priority is certainly within the role and scope of educational institutions, but it cannot be the singular concern of teachers. The development of an appropriate classroom climate requires that the teacher alter leadership style behaviors toward a more democratic method when the classroom objectives are more social, managerial, or interpersonal in nature.

Reduction in Environmental Complexity   Harvey, Hunt, and Schroder (1961) hypothesized that individuals, including teachers, can only assimilate so much stimuli bombardment. When their capacity was reached, they developed interpersonal techniques for coping with the situation. For teachers, this coping procedure frequently took the form of authoritarian leadership, which emphasized order, lecturing, and individually focused interaction.

Mehrabian (1976) reached a similar conclusion: "confronted with a potentially complex and unpredictable situation, teachers and school administrators foist a large number of rigid rules and regulations upon students so as to make their behavior far less varied, more uniform, and more predictable; in short, to achieve low-load (low information rate) classrooms" (p. 156).

An example of stimuli bombardment and high information load resulting in an authoritarian style is evidenced in the following anecdote:

> After a particularly difficult examination, the teacher, desiring to show the class her sense of fair-play, decided to hear reactions from students regarding their scores. Within a matter of seconds most of the students were complaining about questions, challenging answers, making excuses, and so on. What was once a quiet, orderly classroom became a mass of noise and movement. The teacher, unable to answer one question before being asked several more, backed away from the students who began to crowd around her. "Alright," she yelled, "Everyone sit down and keep quiet. If you raise your hand, I will answer one question at a time."

In the above anecdote, the environment became so loaded with stimuli that the teacher was unable to cope with the situation. Consequently, she reestablished her authoritarian style in order to reduce the information load and environmental complexity.

With 30 children per classroom, some of whom demonstrate exceptional learning and behavioral problems, it is easy to understand why teachers may have an "information overload" and attempt to reduce the classroom information rate. The frequency of interaction alone is remarkably illustrated by different leadership styles. For example, it has been estimated that teacher-student and student-student interactions occur every 5 seconds in democratically oriented classrooms and every 18 seconds in more controlled classrooms (Adams & Biddle, 1970). In a 6-hour school day, this amounts to 4,320 interactions in the democratically oriented classrooms as opposed to 1,200 interactions in the more controlled classrooms—a significant difference in information load. Unquestionably, this pervasive quality of interaction is a significant factor in establishing the classroom climate (Randhawa & Fu, 1973). Since high rates of interaction reduce teacher awareness of individual differences, the handicapped student is apt to be overlooked in the classroom (Brophy & Good, 1974). On the other hand, "... children who participate actively learn more than those who don't . . ." (Cohen, 1972, p. 444).

While the authoritarian style reduces the information rate for teachers, it also reduces the stimulation for children. "The children, in contrast, are going to feel confined and bored, and end up trying to generate arousal and pleasure by interacting amongst themselves" (Mehrabian, 1976, p. 156). Unsanctioned interaction typically leads to more authoritarian teacher behaviors, including an increase in the number of rules and disciplinary actions.

However, the frequency of interaction may not be as critical to the classroom climate as the quality of interaction. Investigations of classroom interaction patterns have yielded data that support the conclusion that the quality of the classroom climate is primarily shaped by dominating (authoritarian) behaviors, rather than nurturant or facilitating interactions. Anderson and Brewer (1946) researched two characteristic interaction patterns (dominance and social integration) and found that two of every three teacher initiated social interactions were dominant. Socially integrative interaction, on the other hand, was more likely to result when students initiated the interaction. These results led Anderson and Brewer to conclude that a "vicious cycle" was evident in teacher-student interactions. "Domination and socially integrative behavior were each . . . found to be 'circular' in their effects: as a stimulus to others, each tended to produce its like" (p. 153). Subsequent research has supported the role of dominance and the circular pattern of interaction on the classroom climate (Rich, 1979).

Both the personal growth versus academic achievement and stimuli reduction explanations for authoritarian teacher leadership styles have significant implications for establishing the classroom climate. It seems reasonably clear that no one style is appropriate for all children, personally or academically. Therefore, the exclusive reliance upon authoritarian or democratic styles will potentially create a negative classroom climate for a substantial portion of the classroom group.

Initially, it would be useful for the teacher to determine which students require authoritarian leadership and which students need democratic leadership. Handicapped children in the regular classroom may require either of the leadership styles. For example, the accomplishment of lower level objectives (knowledge, receiving, etc.) may require a more structured method, implemented by an authoritarian leadership style. A similar method and style may be required for children whose behavior is characterized as impulsive, unsocialized, or fearful, in short, children functioning on the basic personal and academic levels who are ". . . lacking important basic skills, who need direction or protection until they can acquire them" (Joyce & Harootunian, 1967, p. 95). Children functioning on the higher levels require a different leadership style. Children who are gifted, independent, or who are attempting to meet higher level objectives (analyzing, synthesizing, valuing, etc.), are best facilitated by a more "open" environment with a democratic leadership style (Rich, 1978b).

After the decision has been reached as to which leadership style would be most profitable for each child, the next step is to consider the physical classroom organization. Certainly any classroom arrangement that treated all children the same, either autocratic or democratic, would be inappropriate for some children. Thus, the establishment of classroom areas is a preferable approach: a section of row seats for providing direct group instruction (authoritarian style); small group interaction areas (democratic style); and provisions for individualized or independent learning. Recently, the trend toward learning centers (Charles, 1976) has served to alter teaching methods, provide more individualized instruction, and create a more positive classroom climate.

The use of planned methods and leadership styles appropriate to individual learner needs is critical to the classroom climate. According to Turnbull and Schulz (1979), "A key element to successful mainstreaming . . . is the creation of a positive school environment . . . in which the human differences of all students are accepted and respected" (p. 339).

STUDENT INFLUENCE

Even though the teacher is the single most critical factor in setting the tone of the classroom learning climate, the impact of the classroom student group cannot be overlooked. According to Morse (1960), "the teacher can ill afford to ignore alignments when they operate to influence learning behavior of the pupil members" (p. 230). In many classrooms, teachers demonstrate a knowledge of both group and individual student needs through the use of effective instruction, management, and personal communication. However, even in the most skillfully led classroom groups, student behaviors and attitudes may emerge that are counter-productive to an effective learning climate. The problem is escalated when teachers ignore student needs, inadvertently setting the stage for increased student influence. Under such circumstances, the teacher's influence may erode as the students assume more influence over the learning climate. Such a situation becomes a "power struggle" where the teacher becomes more concerned with control and discipline, and the students become more concerned with resisting control and exerting influence. For both the teacher and students, the classroom climate is shaped more by the motivation to independently survive, rather than the motivation to teach and to learn.

These negative classroom climates can be minimized if teachers recognize critical group characteristics and their effect upon individual students and then provide appropriate instructional leadership. The handicapped student who has been mainstreamed into the regular classroom often presents a special case of individual student relationship with an ongoing group.

Any consideration of group influence on the learning climate must include at least two significant properties—norms and cohesiveness (Schmuck, 1966). While the two group properties are interrelated, *norms* refer to a standard of behavior that is shared by the group, and *cohesiveness* refers to the degree of attractiveness and unity among group members.

Norms

The standards of behavior shared by the classroom group regulate student behavior and resist teacher influence. In varying degrees, everyone is subject to the peer group influence to conform to expectations of behavior. Even though individuals may intentionally engage in behaviors in order to gain peer approval, more often individuals may not be consciously aware of the tremendous psychological pressure that is exerted by the peer group to ensure that individuals conform to group standards and expectations of behavior. For example, what one wears, the clubs one joins, and the expressed motivation for school, teachers, and friends are shaped by group norms (Jackson, 1960). Often this pressure comes in the form of statements or gestures that convey approval or disapproval of an individual student's behavior, whether or not such behavior is productive or appropriate in the eyes of the teacher.

Teachers must be sensitive to the classroom group norms. Teachers who encourage students to violate peer norms are inviting a negative, sometimes hostile, reaction. For example, some classrooms have expectations of how often a student may speak out in class. Students who go beyond the norm and speak out more frequently than the accepted rate, particularly to the teacher, may be socially rejected and "unofficially" labeled "teacher's pet," "brain," or "Miss Know-it-all." Similarly, students who speak out less than the norm requires are usually pressured by the peer group into verbalizing, even if the questions or answers are inappropriate. Of course, the acceptable norm for speaking will vary from class to class, and from student to student. In some classes, particularly if the teacher is disliked by the most popular and powerful students, the norm may be that no student speaks out. Efforts by the teacher to encourage verbal interaction result in blank stares, shrugging shoulders, or inaudible grunts. Under such circumstances, teachers who demand interaction, without understanding the peer group norm structure, are inviting a confrontation. Such a confrontation has no winners, only losers, and the classroom climate grows steadily more negative.

Although younger children are greatly influenced by adult behaviors and expectations, with increasing age the peer group gradually becomes a stronger force. In fact, it is well documented that older children, particularly adolescents, may intentionally violate school rules or teacher expectations in order to gain or maintain peer approval (Vorrath & Brendtro, 1974). Typically, classroom groups that demonstrate a high rate of work involvement, frequently ask the teacher for guidance, and show a low tolerance for peer distractions are often the result of group norms. Similarly, such behaviors as aggression, defiance, and academic failure are an indication that classroom norms exist, but are contradictory to the expectations of the teacher and education in general.

Norms that are in opposition to a positive learning climate often go beyond the boundaries of a single classroom and are evidenced throughout an entire school, perhaps the entire community. For example, Brookover and Schneider (1975) found that the academic environments within schools, rather than individual classrooms, had an effect upon academic achievements. Two particular student norms appeared to have contributed significantly to low achievement: 1) students' belief that significant others (e.g., teachers, parents, etc.) were pessimistic regarding the students' future academic accomplishments, and 2) the students' sense of futility, lack of control, or hopelessness regarding academic accomplishment. Since approved and desired goals were considered unattainable, counter-productive group norms emerged that reinforced toughness and independence. The handicapped student introduced to such a classroom may find the situation intolerable. If the student aligns with the teacher, the group will exert pressure to conform to existing group norms; if the student aligns with the group, the teacher may perceive the behavior to be intentional resistance. In either case, the probability of success for the handicapped student is minimized. In the case of negative climates, there is rarely a middle ground; one is typically accepted or rejected.

Johnson and Bany (1970) have provided a list of student behaviors that are symptomatic of group norms associated with negative classroom learning climates.

A hostile, aggressive classroom group is one that subtly defies the teacher and often disrupts instructional activities . . .

1. Murmuring, talking, lack of attention throughout the group when tasks are presented or assigned.
2. Constant disruptions which interfere with carrying out assignments.
3. Subtle defiance, united resistance, and some evidence of solidarity within the group.
4. Overall nonconformity to generally accepted school practices.
5. Solidarity in resisting teachers' efforts, poor interpersonal relations.

A class that is dissatisfied with conditions in the classroom and frustrated because of pressure stemming from inappropriate teacher control techniques . . .

1. The group applauds disruptive behavior of one or a few individuals.
2. Defiant acts of one or two individuals are approved by group as a whole.
3. The group sometimes reacts with imitative behavior.
4. The group employs scapegoating.
5. The group promotes fights between individuals.
6. Apathetic and indifferent attitudes are shown to school tasks.
7. It is indifferent about completing tasks.
8. The group is apathetic (but exhibits little problem behavior in the classroom), aggressive, and always in trouble on the playground.
9. Members are well behaved when the teacher is present—unruly and aggressive when the teacher is away or does not constantly supervise the group.
10. Some individuals are not tolerated by group—little attempt is made to be a group.

An insecure, dependent class that has not developed a good functioning group . . .

1. The students are easily distracted when any outsider enters the room.
2. They cannot adjust to changes in routine.
3. Members are easily upset by rumors.
4. Changes in the weather upset the class.
5. Newcomers to the class may be resented (pp. 410–412).

Direct confrontation, utilizing the legal power ascribed to the teacher, usually results in disaster, increasing the hostility, frustration, or dependency. It is equally important to understand that the handicapped student introduced to classroom groups will tend to demonstrate behaviors that are consistent with group norms and therefore may be totally unrelated to the nature of the student's handicapping condition. However, the development or continuation of group norms that deter academic achievement, mental health, or social development must be altered.

The establishment of an effective classroom learning climate requires that the teacher support those group norms that are positive and develop a strategy for changing those that are negative. Interestingly, there is very little information available that tells teachers how to specifically bring about change in the classroom norm structure. This is probably due to the fact that classroom groups are individually different, forming unique social structures, so that generalizations regarding how a teacher should influence change may be inappropriate, even counterproductive.

Given this tentative and unique nature of group norms and teacher-group relationships, a number of teacher role behaviors appear to be prerequisites to the establishment of a positive climate. Smith, Neisworth, and Greer (1978) identify five teacher characteristics that are essential to a positive learning climate: 1) a *positive* attitude, 2) a *planned* instructional approach, 3) the ability to be *flexible*, 4) maintaining *consistency*, and 5) showing *understanding*. Each of the teacher characteristics is directly related to the establishment of an appropriate learning climate. A positive attitude is necessary to reduce students' sense of futility and project an attitude of optimism regarding their academic accomplishments. A planned instructional approach, including the use of IEPs, is required if, in reality, the teacher is to enable the students to learn academically. Flexibility in expectations and behavior is needed if students are to be considered individuals and not stereotypes that possess the same ability, skill, and motivation, Consistency, or reliability, is necessary if students are going to be able to accurately identify and predict the important rules and standards of the classroom. And understanding between human beings, expressed as empathy, concern, or appreciation, goes a long way in promoting the classroom climate.

Cohesiveness

The degree of group cohesiveness (attractiveness for and unity within a classroom group) has critical implications for the classroom climate. Some classroom groups appear to function as a single unit, moving smoothly from one activity to another, displaying little deviant behavior, and freely cooperating and sharing. In other classrooms it is difficult to shift activities, noise and physical intimidation are commonplace, and individual but selfish behaviors are frequent. In the first example, the group structure would appear to be attractive to the individual members, possessing a rather balanced sociometric structure, lacking significant "stars" and "scapegoats." In the second example, there is less group attractiveness, probably possessing well defined status positions or "pecking order." Schmuck (1966) found that classroom ". . . groups characterized by a nearly equal distribution of liking and influence choices in contrast to those which were distinctly hierarchical had both more cohesiveness and more positive norms concerning the goals of school" (p. 62).

This balanced social structure, or equal distribution of classroom social choices, provides one of the clearest indicators of cohesiveness. Socially balanced classroom groups have a greater capacity to attract new members (including the mainstreamed handicapped child), function more harmoniously as a unit, and create a positive learning climate. By comparison, groups that are polarized into subgroups are repeatedly plagued by interpersonal conflict. Subgroups may form along many lines; for example, race (blacks versus whites), economic status (rich versus poor), academics (bright versus slow), and social stance (popular versus isolates). The continuous competition between subgroups for social-psychological superiority typically results in a negative learning climate. Teachers may unwittingly contribute to the classroom polarization by reinforcing members of one subgroup, and punishing or ignoring members of the other. Consequently, teachers must be conscious of the distribution of grades, privileges, and responsibilities so that they do not routinely favor one subgroup over another.

Group cohesiveness has rather significant implications for handi-capped students mainstreamed into the regular classroom. Obviously, the probability of success is enhanced if the student is assigned to a cohesive classroom group. Since the attitudes of such groups are more positive toward peers, school life, the teachers, academic work, and themselves as students, the handicapped student is placed in a climate that minimizes the exceptionality and maximizes personal and academic success.

On the other hand, groups that lack cohesiveness are apt to create a survival climate. With the distinct hierarchy of power among the class members, the handicapped student is apt to be relegated to an inferior position, become a "scapegoat," or even alienated. Regardless of the normative role, the handicapped student will be more preoccupied with physical and psychological survival than with learning academically.

Teachers can be instrumental in creating a more cohesive group, thus establishing a more favorable climate.

> The teachers with more positive social climates, in contrast to the others, emphasized and were more sophisticated about classroom mental health

conditions. They also perceived more linkages between mental health and academic learning concepts than the other teachers. Teachers with more positive climates perceived their pupils' characteristics in a more differentiated manner and emphasized psychological attributes in contrast to physical characteristics more than other teachers. Teachers with positive climates appeared to converse often with a wide variety of students and to reward individual students while punishing the whole class. In contrast, teachers with more negative climates conversed often with only a few students, seldom issued reward statements, and often punished individual students publicly (Schmuck, 1966, p. 65).

Thus, the attributes of a teacher who desires to influence the normative structure of the classroom hold true for influencing the cohesiveness of the group; namely being positive, planned, flexible, consistent, and understanding. Unfortunately, as obvious as these attributes may seem, a substantial percentage of teachers choose to exercise negative, haphazard, rigid, inconsistent, and intolerant behaviors. The differences in the learning climate for these two teacher extremes is remarkable. For the handicapped student, the results will be equally remarkable in favor of the teacher who, with the group, establishes a positive learning climate.

CURRICULUM INFLUENCE

The curriculum, traditionally defined as the educational experiences planned for students, is a persistent influence on the learning climate. Unlike the variable influence exercised by different teachers and student groups, the curriculum tends to have a more long term, but subtle impact on the classroom learning climate. Although curriculum influence may not be as obvious on the immediate classroom climate, the cumulative effects on academic achievement or failure are profound. The curriculum influence on the learning climate includes both the *content* of the material to be learned by students and the *process* that is employed to facilitate that learning. Even though the content and process impact on the learning climate are discussed separately, in reality they are intricately interrelated and cannot be dichotomized. However, the individual treatment of content and process can serve to identify and describe critical curriculum factors and their effects on classroom climate, particularly as they relate to handicapped students.

Content

More and more, all students are being required to learn more information earlier in their school experience. The increasing education emphasis on the acquisition of academic knowledge has reached the point where neither teachers nor students can ignore the fact that prescribed levels of competency are required if school is to be successfully completed. To a great extent curriculum patterns and subject matter areas are predetermined by regulations and policies and, therefore, cannot be grossly altered to fit the individual needs and interests of students. Thus, the question of content is not whether students will be required to study math, reading, science, and so forth, but what content alternatives are available that will enable handicapped students to be academically successful students.

An obvious alternative is related to content relevance. Relevance refers to consistency between the content material and the characteristics of the students, at least including the students' learning style and life-style, which will increase interest, motivation, and success. If students can relate to the content and, consequently, experience success, their rate of appropriate involvement will enhance the classroom climate. On the other hand, if the content is inappropriate, boredom and frustration may evolve into active or passive behaviors that will create a negative climate.

For handicapped students, content relevance includes both cognitive and affective consistency. Although teachers have traditionally been concerned with cognitive content (i.e., intellectual and academic learning experiences), they have typically ignored the affective implications (i.e., feelings, emotions, and acceptance). This discrepancy between cognitive and affective concerns exists because the curriculum content is based on the cognitive requirements of the various subject matter disciplines rather than the affective characteristics of students (Weinstein & Fantini, 1970). For example, a teacher who requires a slow learner to read from a textbook two grade levels below that which the classroom group is using, even though it may be cognitively appropriate, totally ignores the affective needs of the student. This situation is affectively inappropriate because it negatively influences the student in several ways—it reduces self-worth, it identifies the student as different, and the content of the text may be chronologically or developmentally inappropriate.

The failure to recognize the affective impact on students is evidenced by content materials about far away lands, when some students do not understand much of their own environment; content materials about etiquette and manners, when some students are malnourished and battered; and content materials on vacation trips and whaling ships, when some students are physically or economically attached to the neighborhood streets. For many students in the regular classroom, such content materials may have affective relevance, but for many mainstreamed students the affective irrelevance is accentuated because of their environmental, physical, and/or psychological handicap or disability. Certainly, life beyond the students' immediate environment must be introduced, but to require attention, performance, and participation, and to cognitively evaluate on irrelevant content denies the feelings and experiences of some students (Rich, 1978a).

Aside from the affective emphasis, the cognitive and psychomotor relevance of content must also be considered.

> The choice of materials must also consider the input-output modalities in light of both the student's knowledge and feelings and the student's cognitive style. For example, students from lower socioeconomic environments, whose language experience is "restrictive" rather than "expressive," tend to perform poorly on materials that require verbal outputs. Similarly, deficient reading skills among many exceptional children tend to limit their interest and understanding of materials that rely heavily on written words. Therefore, poor performance may result from the negative affective feelings associated with cognitive materials that emphasize or utilize student weaknesses rather than strengths. The poor performance will be accentuated if the subject of the material is outside the realm of the learner's experience.
>
> The physical requirements of both the classroom and the materials must also be evaluated. Individual students have different skills and require varying degrees of time and space to complete activities. Whereas some children function adequately with their individual desks, other children require larger, less encumbered areas. Whereas some children have excellent motor coordination and can complete physically intricate tasks, other children have extreme difficulty drawing a line, circling an answer, or coloring a figure. Whereas some children can see the chalkboard and hear the teacher, other children need additional visual and verbal information.
>
> In the above examples, children may be able to sort shapes into the appropriate stack, but they continue to get knocked from the desk; children may know that "George" goes with "Washington," but cannot draw the connecting line; and children may know that two plus two equals four, but cannot see the problem on the board. In short, materials may be inappropriate because of environmental limitations. Such limitations create frustration, disinterest, and, ultimately, cognitive failure, resulting in a less adequate self-concept and less self-control (Rich, 1978a, p. 246).

Clearly, curriculum content influences the classroom learning climate. Unlike teacher influence and student influence, the impact of curriculum content tends to be limited to a relatively few individual students in the classroom. If the students affected do not have a positive relationship with the teacher, or are not status group members, the negative climate created by their sense of futility and lower self-esteem does not directly permeate the classroom. In such a situation, students' own private, personal climate of irrelevance will prevent success in school. On the other hand, if their sense of irrelevance is shared by other classroom students, then the effects on the classroom climate are much more obvious. The establishment of a positive classroom learning climate is facilitated by curriculum content that has relevance to students' personal characteristics, which are shaped by their life experiences and expectations. Although this concept of relevance is important for all students, it is critical for handicapped students who have been subjected to repeated and cumulative negative experiences throughout their formal education.

Process

The teaching-learning process employed by teachers to enable students to learn the required content may be more influential on the classroom climate than the content itself. The process, or *how* students learn, is as important as *what* they learn. "Educators are finding . . . that children learn different amounts of content at different rates at different times (and) that children learn by talking, doing, and teaching as well as by listening" (Turnbull & Schulz, 1979, p. 121). Clearly, the optimal process of learning math, reading or science will be different for different students, and will vary with different objectives. For example, a student who has poor auditory memory skills will be penalized if a teacher relies heavily on a lecture process; a student who is hyperactive will perform poorly when the task is sedentary; and a student who has difficulty discriminating stimuli will not perform well under highly stimulating conditions. In each of the three examples, inappropriate process procedures create a negative learning climate for the students involved.

In order to promote a positive climate for handicapped students, individualized process procedures are required. Depending on the individual student, a number of process factors must be planned and implemented to create the most effective learning experience, thus the most appropriate climate. Process factors include the students' input modality (how they receive stimuli), output modality (how they transmit what they have learned), instructional setting (the class group organization), structure (the degree of instructional freedom), and activity level (the amount of physical involvement). Table 1 graphically lists some of the process options available.

Table 1.   Available curriculum process options

Student's input modality	Student's output modality	Instructional setting	Preferred structure	Activity level
Visual	Verbal	Independent	Controlled	Passive
Auditory	(Combination)	One-to-one	(Mixed)	(Mixed)
Tactile		Small group		
Sensory	Physical	Large group	Permissive	Active

There is no one pattern of options that is appropriate for all students. Also, with different content areas and objectives, the process options may be changed to fit the student.

Fox et al. (1974) identified a number of school climate determinants that relate to the above process options. Each must be viewed in terms of amount or degree for individual students.

1. Opportunities for active learning
2. Individualized performance expectations
3. Varied learning environments
4. Flexible curriculum and extracurricular activities
5. Support and structure appropriate to learning maturity
6. Rules cooperatively determined
7. Varied reward system (pp. 73–81).

Each of the above climate determinants, if employed individually, will enhance the climate, making ". . . it possible to work productively toward important goals, such as academic learning, social development, and curriculum improvement" (Fox et al., 1974, p. 1).

The role of curriculum process on the classroom climate is closely related to teacher leadership style, which was discussed early in this chapter. For the most part it is difficult to separate these influences on the classroom climate. How a teacher perceives leadership responsibility and student learning will be reflected in the classroom setting. Nor can teacher leadership behaviors and curriculum influence be separated from the influence exercised by the student group. Each of these three influences is evidenced in the primary classroom structure. According to Johnson and Johnson (1975), three distinctive forms of group structure exist: cooperative, competitive, and individualistic. "Cooperative goal structure exists when students perceive that they can obtain their own goals if, and only if, the other students with whom they work can obtain their goals. A competitive goal structure exists when students feel that they can obtain their own goals only if other students fail to obtain their goals. Individualistic goal structures occur when a student's achievement goals are unrelated to the achievement goals of other students" (Good & Brophy, 1978, p. 301).

These three forms of structure can only exist with the support of a consistent leadership style and curriculum processes. In terms of handicapped students the cooperative and individualistic structures provide the most appropriate learning climates. The competitive structure which limits the number of students who can succeed, thus receive rewards, typically places the handicapped student at an educational disadvantage. If learning is perceived as a cooperative or individual effort, then the success of handicapped students will be enhanced; if learning is perceived as a competitive effort, handicapped students will develop a sense of futility. In the former, a positive climate will have been created for the handicapped learner.

SUMMARY

This chapter has emphasized the importance of the classroom learning climate on the behavior and achievement of both handicapped and nonhandicapped students. Three climate influences were discussed: the teacher, the students, and the curriculum.

The teacher, with expectations of the handicapped and through the use of stereotypic leadership styles, has the most significant impact on the climate. Many teachers use an authoritarian approach to promote academic achievement and reduce the complexity of the classroom environment. Although such a style may be appropriate for some students and some objectives, it is suggested that alternative leadership styles be employed that will encompass a greater variety of student learning characteristics, including student affective concerns.

Student influence was discussed in terms of two group characteristics: norms and cohesiveness. Both the group standards of behavior (norms) and degree of attractiveness (cohesiveness) are instrumental in shaping the classroom climate. It is essential that teachers recognize these group influences, and, when they create a negative climate, intervene by being positive, planned, flexible, consistent, and understanding.

Finally, the curriculum influence was discussed in terms of content and process. A positive climate is dependent upon the development of relevant content alternatives supported by a process that recognizes individual learner characteristics.

Throughout the chapter, it has been stressed that handicapped students, as well as other students in the regular classroom, require an appropriate classroom learning climate. Teacher leadership styles, group influence, and curricular experiences need to facilitate the unique characteristics of the handicapped student. Although the ongoing climate may be sufficient in many cases, frequently adaptations are required if the classroom learning climate is to promote and encourage a successful school experience.

REFERENCES

Adams, R., & Biddle, B. *Realities of teaching*. New York: Holt, Rinehart & Winston, 1970.

Anderson, H. H., & Brewer, J. E. Studies of teachers' classroom personalities, II: Effects of teachers' dominative and socially integrative contacts on children's classroom behavior. *Psychological Monographs, 8*, 1946.

Anderson, R. C. Learning in discussions: A resume of the authoritarian-democratic studies. *Harvard Educational Review*, 1959, *29*(3), 201–215.

Bennett, N. *Teaching styles and pupil progress.* Cambridge, Mass.: Harvard University Press, 1976.

Bills, R. E. Personality changes during student centered teaching. *Journal of Educational Research*, 1956, *50*, 121–126.

Brookover, W. B., & Schneider, J. M. Academic environments and elementary school achievement. *Journal of Research and Development in Education*, 1975, *9*, 83–91.

Brophy, J. E., & Good, T. L. *Teacher-student relationships: Causes and consequences.* New York: Holt, Rinehart & Winston, 1974.

Charles, C. M. *Individualizing instruction.* St. Louis: C. V. Mosby, 1976.

Cohen, E. G. Sociology and the classroom: Setting the conditions for teacher-student interaction. *Review of Educational Research*, 1972, *42*, 441–452.

Dale, E. *Building a learner environment.* Bloomington, Ind.: Phi Delta Kappa, 1972.

Fox, R. S., Boies, H. E., Brainard, E., Fletcher, E., Huge, J. S., Martin, C. L., Maynard, W., Monasmith, J., Olivero, J., Schmuck, R., Shaheen, T. A., & Stegeman, W. H. *School climate improvement: A challenge to school administrators.* Bloomington, Ind.: Phi Delta Kappa, 1974.

Good, T. L., & Brophy, J. E. *Looking in classrooms.* New York: Harper & Row, 1978.

Harvey, O. J., Hunt, D. E., & Schroder, H. M. *Conceptual systems and personality organization.* New York: John Wiley & Sons, 1961.

Jackson, J. M. Structural characteristics of norms. In N. B. Henry (Ed.), *The dynamics of instructional groups.* Chicago: National Society for the Study of Education, 1960.

Johnson, D., & Johnson, R. *Learning together and alone: Cooperation, competition and individualization.* Englewood Cliffs, N.J.: Prentice-Hall, 1975.

Johnson, L. V., & Bany, M. A. *Classroom management: Theory and skill training.* New York: Macmillan, 1970.

Joyce, B., & Harootunian, B. *The structure of teaching.* Chicago: Science Research Associates, 1967.

Lewin, K., Lippitt, R., & White, R. K. Patterns of aggressive behavior in experimentally created social climates. *Journal of Social Psychology*, 1939, *10*, 271–299.

McKeachie, W. J. Procedures and techniques of teaching: A survey of experimental studies. In N. Sanford, (Ed.), *The American college: A psychological and social interpretation of the higher learning.* New York: Wiley & Sons, 1962.

Mehrabian, A. *Public places and private spaces.* New York: Basic Books Inc., 1976.

Morse, W. C. Diagnosing and guiding relationships between group and individual class members. In N. B. Henry (Ed.), *The dynamics of instructional groups.* Chicago: National Society for the Study of Education, 1960.

Randhawa, B., & Fu, L. Assessment and effect of some classroom environment variables. *Review of Educational Research*, 1973, *43*, 303–321.

Rich, H. L. Affective concerns in the utilization of instructional materials. In R. M. Anderson, J. G. Greer, & S. J. Odle (Eds.), *Individualizing educational materials for special children in the mainstream*. Baltimore: University Park Press, 1978. (a)

Rich, H. L. A matching model for educating the emotionally disturbed and behaviorally disordered. *Focus on Exceptional Children*, 1978, *10* (Whole No. 3). (b)

Rich, H. L. Classroom interaction patterns among teachers and emotionally disturbed children. *The Exceptional Child*, 1979, *26*, 34–40.

Schmuck, R. Some aspects of classroom social climate. *Psychology in the Schools*, 1966, *3*, 59–65.

Smith, R. M., Neisworth, J. T., & Greer, J. G. *Evaluating educational environment*. Columbus, Oh.: Charles E. Merrill, 1978.

Stern, G. C. Environments for learning. In N. Sanford (Ed.), *The American college: A psychological and social interpretation of the higher learning*. New York: Wiley & Sons, 1962.

Turnbull, A. P., & Schulz, J. B. *Mainstreaming handicapped students: A guide for the classroom teacher*. Boston: Allyn & Bacon, 1979.

Vorrath, H. H., & Brendtro, L. K. *Positive peer culture*. Chicago: Aldine Publishing Co., 1974.

Weinstein, G., & Fantini, M. D. *Toward humanistic education: A curriculum of affect*. New York: Praeger Publishers, 1970.

11
MANAGING INTERFERING BEHAVIOR

H. Lyndall Rich

The management of interfering behavior has been a persistent and critical concern of classroom teachers. No educational issue or problem has created more discussion, frustration, or irritation among teachers than the need to manage educationally interfering behavior among individual students or the classroom group. Numerous hours and enormous energy have been expended by teachers in an effort to create and maintain a positive learning environment in the classroom. The time and energy that have been devoted to classroom behavior management have consumed an inordinate amount of teacher attention, thus reducing the teacher's instructional responsibility and minimizing the students' learning experiences. In addition to the physical and emotional drain on teachers, the frequent teacher focus on interfering behavior is a primary factor that has contributed to the failure of many students to achieve educational objectives.

To a great extent, the current managerial dilemma is a consequence of rather traditional and rigid educational practices and expectations that have remained relatively stable in the presence of scientific, technological, and social change. Historically, teachers have been well trained to transmit academic information to large groups of students who were considered to be very much alike. Within such an academic and teacher-centered approach an orderly, passive learning environment was usually required. Classroom control, therefore, was primarily dependent on students' willingness to submit to authoritarian demands and expectations. Students who failed to comply with the prevailing standards were reprimanded, punished, or otherwise "disciplined." Thus, the classroom has historically represented an external control model in which student conformity to standards of conduct was rewarded and disruptive interference was categorically punished through adult intervention.

However, disruptive behavior is not the only source of interfering behavior. Often students provide their own internal source of interference through extreme forms of withdrawal, daydreaming, and apathy. Even though a student does not disrupt the classroom, teachers have a responsibility to intervene and bring the student back to the reality of learning. This precautionary note is included because disruptive behavior is highly visible, demanding and even provoking, thus consuming an inordinate amount of teacher attention. Consequently, teachers tend to ignore or omit managerial techniques for the more behaviorally compliant students even though the students may be engaging in intrapersonally interfering behaviors.

This managerial situation has been accentuated during the past few years by the introduction of exceptional students to the regular classroom. Even though individual exceptional students, in general, are no more or less difficult to manage than "normal" students, at least two critical conditions underscore the need to develop more effective management procedures. First, the fact that exceptional students are being mainstreamed has created a more complex and divergent student population in the regular classroom, increasing the usual range of student needs and characteristics. As a result, the typical classroom may include students from a variety of socioeconomic backgrounds, functioning on different academic and intellectual levels, possessing a broad range of physical and sensory traits, and evidencing an assortment of psychological and behavioral conditions. For example, the regular classroom may contain a large contingent of "normal" students, as well as some students who are mildly to moderately retarded, learning disabled, physically impaired, visually or auditorially limited, behaviorally disordered, and/or emotionally disturbed. It is unlikely that such a composite of individual students will respond appropriately and uniformly to the repetitive use of a relatively few authority oriented management procedures that are associated with most classrooms.

Second, many exceptional children require managerial techniques that take into consideration the uniqueness of their handicapping conditions. For example, verbal threats, such as "Sit down and keep quiet or I'll send you to the principal," may have little effect on a student who is hyperactive or hearing impaired; the teacher's physical closeness, rearranging the classroom, or positive reinforcement may be preferable. Similarly, techniques such as corporal punishment, extra work, and restricted movement, all of which are punitive in nature, may not take into account a student's intellectual level, degree of mental health, or ability to understand and perform in accordance with teacher expectations.

With the increasing range and uniqueness of student needs and characteristics included within the regular classroom, teachers can no longer rely on the traditional authoritarian methods of behavior management. Even though some students accept the classroom procedures and respond appropriately to external control, other students do not recognize the value of school, the ascribed authority of educators, or do not possess the skills necessary to respond appropriately. This mixture of traditional expectations and diversified students has resulted in inappropriate management procedures that tend to be overly severe, negative, and self-defeating, forcing a confrontation between teacher and student. To avoid these "bad" disciplinary procedures and to effectively manage interfering behavior demonstrated by a wide variety of exceptional students, the teacher should be equipped with a comprehensive repertoire of managerial techniques.

The management of interfering behavior refers to corrective interventions on the part of teachers that are intended to prevent or appropriately change student behaviors that are considered incompatible with the accomplishment of educational objectives in the classroom. The managerial techniques discussed in this chapter do not ascribe to a single theoretical approach but draw from a number of theories, including biophysical, behavioral, dynamic, sociological, and ecological (Rhodes & Tracy, 1972). For discussion purposes, managerial techniques have been grouped into the following categories: 1) general principles of management, 2) surface management, 3) interpersonal management, 4) instructional management, 5) environmental management, and 6) group management. These six categories do not include all of the available managerial techniques, nor do they imply success unless they are individually and appropriately employed.

GENERAL PRINCIPLES OF MANAGEMENT

The successful utilization of specific management techniques will be increased if a number of guiding principles are recognized. Although these principles do not constitute a unitary model of all the available techniques and concerns, they are frequently reported as prerequisites to direct behavior intervention in the literature and by experienced teachers (Long, Morse, & Newman, 1976).

Knowledge of Individual Students

Even though teachers may have command of a variety of management techniques, the techniques will be of limited assistance unless the teacher also has substantial knowledge of individual students. Although a "trial-

and-error" strategy may be appropriate in a limited number of circumstances, the probability of increasing management effectiveness is enhanced by the utilization of techniques that are appropriate for the individual. Matching the appropriate technique with the individual student requires that the teacher be aware of individual academic, psychological, and physical characteristics. Academically, the teacher needs knowledge of the student's functional level, modality strengths and weaknesses, motivational level, and interests in the various subject areas. Psychologically, the teacher needs to be aware of frustration levels, self-concept, degree of acceptance, and attitudes toward the teacher, peers, and education. And physically, the teacher needs to know the individual's strengths and limitations, and the impact of physiological differences on academic and psychological performance.

Practical differences in individuals include students who are behaviorally disordered, for example, who require techniques that are quite different than those needed for students who have low self-esteem. Whereas the former may benefit from structure, the latter typically respond to positive reinforcement. Students from deprived, as opposed to enriched, backgrounds may respond differently to the same technique. For example, reactions may be quite different to a teacher's appeal for academic performance, the use of tangible rewards, or acceptance of authority. Similarly, students who are auditorially impaired or who lack verbal skills may respond more favorably to physical and visual techniques than to verbal intervention. The degree of self-control, achievement, motivation, and environmental experiences of individual students also may result in the differential success of various intervention procedures. In short, the management of interfering behaviors should be as individualized as the academic program that has been designed for the individual student.

Tolerance of Selected Behaviors

Teachers should not manage each and every "deviant" behavior in the classroom. In fact, some "deviant" behaviors are not maladaptive at all but constitute individual responses to the learning environment. Behaviors that are a function of individual differences should be tolerated, not managed through teacher intervention. According to Long and Newman (1961), tolerating behavior includes such individualized concepts as "learner's leeway," "behavior that reflects a developmental state," and "behavior that is symptomatic of a disease." Each of the three concepts dictates the need for teachers to recognize the variability in human behavior.

Learner's leeway simply reflects the teacher's belief that students perform in accordance with their individual characteristics. Certainly not all children will complete the same number of math problems in the same amount of time, with the same degree of accuracy; nor will they drink the same amount of water from the hall fountain; nor can they physiologically remain still for identical periods of time. Therefore, the teacher should expect individual differences in behavior and provide some leeway in the expression of those differences.

Although most children and adolescents go through the same developmental stages, they do not accomplish the developmental milestones at the same time or at the same rate. High levels of motor activity, for example, are more evident among primary-age children, but show a steady decrease as children get older (Rich, 1978c). Similarly, boys are generally more motor active than girls. Impulsiveness, "lying," "tattling," and grooming are examples of other behaviors which may only reflect a developmental stage. If the interfering behaviors are developmental in nature, then maturation is the most effective intervention technique.

Behavior that is symptomatic of a disease is a critical concern when working with exceptional students. Loud vocal noises emitted by hearing impaired students, the inability of a student with cerebral palsy to remain still while in line, or a learning disabled student's confusion about classroom organization and time orientation are only a few obvious examples of symptomatic behavior. Behaviors that are not under the conscious control of the student should be tolerated. However, toleration does not imply a lack of educational programming. It does imply a degree of futility that will be experienced if direct management is attempted.

Focus on Specific Behaviors

Vague, general statements, such as "He's lazy," "He never does what I tell him," or "She's a disruptive child," convey little meaning and are behaviorally inappropriate. Attempting to manage behaviors so globally described does not provide the information necessary to focus on a manageable behavior. Similarly, a teacher who attempts to intervene with numerous behaviors, both important and trivial ones, is spreading intervention so thin it is doubtful that any technique will be successful.

Unfortunately, some teachers have so many rules of conduct that neither the teacher nor students are aware of them all and certainly there is no consistency in enforcing them all. Classroom rules should be clear, specific, and limited to a relative few. Each behavioral rule should contribute to the effective maintenance of the learning environment. Rules to regulate behaviors that personally annoy the teacher but that have no visible impact on the learning environment should be avoided.

Some students may engage in a series of disruptive behaviors on occasion. For example, a student may arrive late, slam the door, engage another student in conversation, stumble over the trash can, drop a book, and finally be seated rather loudly and clumsily. The teacher may similarly use a series of verbal interventions: "You're late . . . don't slam the door . . . no talking . . . watch where you're walking . . . pick up that book . . . sit quietly, please!" Although this example may not reflect a typical classroom scene, certainly elements of the sequence occur daily. In the example, the teacher's attempted management was ineffective for a number of reasons. A primary reason, however, was that the teacher attempted to manage each and every deviant behavior that occurred within a few seconds. The teacher's effectiveness could have been increased if a single behavior had been selected. In this case, "being on time" should have been the teacher's focus since the subsequent behaviors would have been unimportant if the class had not started.

Since it is impossible to manage every deviant behavior, it is important to select specific behaviors that have the greatest threatening, disruptive, or interfering effect. Without a focusing perspective the teacher is forced into the role of disciplinarian rather than instructional leader.

Develop a Variety of Techniques

Many teachers repeatedly use relatively few intervention techniques, whether or not the techniques are successful. Sending students to the principal, raising one's voice, telling students to sit down or be quiet, and giving them the "evil eye" are techniques used routinely in most classrooms. With some students such obvious procedures may be effective, but for most students the techniques have become so commonplace and undifferentiating that they are ineffective. Teachers who rely on stereotypic techniques often unconsciously convey to the students whether or not they are serious about intervention. Students may know that a particular teacher will not intervene until he/she is standing, or not until the teacher's voice reaches a certain decibel level, or not until students verbally challenge his/her authority. Students usually know when, where, how, and with whom teachers will intervene, and the students have developed stereotypic responses to neutralize anticipated patterns of teacher behavior.

Based on the teacher's knowledge of the students and the desire to intervene with a specific behavior, any number of possible techniques may be attempted until success is experienced. Success with a technique does not imply that it will continue to produce the same results—students change, the activities change, the environment changes—making it necessary to develop other techniques.

Reward Appropriate Behavior First

Deviant behavior, particularly behavior that is disruptive in nature, tends to distract both teacher and students so that the learning environment is destroyed or, at least, temporarily altered. Extreme motor activity, student arguments, and loud obnoxious noises tend to interfere with the teacher's instructional responsibilities and create a contagious distraction within the classroom group. Such disruptive behaviors have a distracting quality that creates negative teacher attention and intervention. To continually intervene with certain types of inappropriate behavior creates an atmosphere of negativism. Such responses also provide attention for the deviant, while the student who is performing appropriately goes unnoticed. Therefore, a systematic plan of rewarding appropriate behavior—students who are sitting still, completing their work, and remaining quiet—would serve a more positive function. Students who are disruptive for attention would learn that appropriate behavior is rewarded.

The most disruptive student performs appropriately at times. Even though a student may be out of his/her seat 50 minutes an hour, there are 10 minutes per hour the student is demonstrating inseat behavior. For every examination, homework assignment, or project, the disruptive student has performed something correctly—correctly completing one problem, putting his/her name on the paper, or just turning something in to the teacher. Such performance, as minimal as it may be, should not go unnoticed. In short, "catch the children being good" (Tinsley & Ora, 1970) and reinforce the behavior.

Deal with the Present

Reminders of past problems serve no purpose other than to kindle feelings of failure or resentment. Teacher statements such as "This is the third time you've been late," "You did the same thing last week," or "How many times have I had to tell you" are direct signals to the student that the teacher will continue to use past behaviors to evaluate current performance. As problems occur they should be dealt with "here and now," without bringing past problems into the discussion. Certainly, all problems will not be managed successfully, but focusing on current behavior affords the opportunity for change. Past behavior, on the other hand, is a record of behavior that cannot be altered.

Management for Learning

Most students are willing to accept a teacher's authority and knowledge with reference to academic instruction. However, teacher intervention within the personal realm is viewed with skepticism by many students. Whether or not students eat all their lunch, wash their hands, button their coat, or cut their hair are areas that have created the most serious conflicts between teachers and students (Geer, 1968). Certainly there are enough educationally related managerial issues without bringing in personal issues that will only compound the management problems. If changes in personal behaviors are considered necessary for the adjustment of the student in the social-vocational world beyond school, then such issues should be pursued through a course of study, rather than by the individual values and spontaneous judgment of the teacher.

Prevent Rather Than Intervene

Most teachers know in what situations and under what circumstances a student becomes a management problem. Therefore, it seems pointless to subject a student to a condition that will cause the student to get into difficulty and cause the teacher to intervene. A more educationally and mentally sound procedure would be to prevent the problem by moving to the student, providing an interesting activity, restructuring the environment, or utilizing other techniques suggested in this chapter. Once a deviant behavior has developed, the energy and resources necessary to effectively intervene are much greater than those necessary to prevent the behavior.

When to Intervene

Classroom teachers obviously have a wide variety of expectations regarding the appropriateness of student behaviors. Whereas some teachers encourage student movement, verbalization, and exploration, other teachers intervene with the same behaviors. Some teachers intervene more frequently if the principal is near the classroom, when the classroom temperature is uncomfortable, or during the middle of the week. Certainly intervention is conducted by human teachers with human feelings and will always reflect a degree of idiosyncratic behavior. However, intervention should not be totally dependent upon the personal or spontaneous whim of the teacher.

To provide some consistency among teachers, Long and Newman (1961) have developed a set of criteria to guide teachers in knowing when to intervene:

1. Reality dangers: Adults are usually more reality-oriented than children and have had more practice predicting the consequences of certain acts.

If children are playing with matches so that it looks as if they might injure themselves, then the teacher moves in and stops the behavior.

2. Psychological protection: Just as the adult protects the child from being physically hurt, he also should protect the child from psychological injury. If a group of boys is ganging up on a child, or scapegoating him, or using derogatory racial nicknames, then the teacher should intervene. The teacher does not support or condone this behavior and the values it reflects.

3. Protection against too much excitement: Sometimes a teacher intervenes in order to avoid the development of too much excitement, anxiety, and guilt in children. For example, if a game is getting out of hand and continues another 10 minutes, the children may lose control, mess up, and feel very unhappy about their behavior later. Once again, the teacher should intervene to stop this cycle from developing.

4. Protection of property: This is almost too obvious to mention, but sometimes it is easy to overlook. Children are not allowed to destroy or damage the school property, equipment, or building. When the teacher sees this, he moves in quickly and stops it. But at no time does he give the impression so common in our society that property is more important than people. Protecting property protects people.

5. Protection of an on-going program: Once a class is motivated in a particular task and the children have an investment in its outcome, it is not fair to have it ruined by one child who is having some difficulty. In this case, the teacher intervenes and asks this child to leave or to move next to him in order to ensure that the enjoyment, satisfaction, and learning of the group is unimpaired.

6. Protection against negative contagion: When a teacher is aware that tension is mounting in the classroom and a child with high social power begins tapping his desk with his pencil, the teacher might ask him to stop in order to prevent this behavior from spreading to the other students and disrupting the entire lesson.

7. Highlighting a value area of school policy: There are times when teacher interferes in some behavior not because it is dangerous or disturbing but because he wishes to illustrate a school policy or rule which may lie slightly below the surface of the behavior. For example, he might want to illustrate why it is impossible for everyone to be first in line, or to point out how a misunderstanding develops when there is no intent to lie or to distort a situation. The focus is on poor communication.

8. Avoiding conflict with the outside world: The outside world in school can mean neighboring classrooms or the public. It is certainly justifiable to expect more control on the part of your children when they are attending an assembly or are on a trip than when they are in their classroom.

9. Protecting a teacher's inner comfort: Inner comfort is not the first thing to be considered by a teacher. If it is, he is in the wrong profession. For example, if a certain type of behavior makes a teacher feel exceptionally uncomfortable, the behavior may not need to be totally inhibited, but the teacher may have to learn to be more comfortable with it, whether he likes it or not (pp. 51–52).

These general principles of management have been presented as prerequisites for effective intervention with student behaviors. The managerial techniques employed by the teacher will be most effective if the following questions can be answered positively:

1. Do I have sufficient knowledge of the student to be able to reasonably predict the outcome of a particular intervention?
2. Do the behaviors exceed the conditions for individual learning, developmental stages, or pathology?
3. Have I selected specific behaviors with which to intervene?
4. Have I rewarded the student when the student demonstrated appropriate behavior?
5. Do I plan to ignore past problems and focus on the current behaviors?
6. Does the behavior interfere with the learning environment, rather than cause personal teacher irritation?
7. Have measures been taken to prevent the inappropriate behavior?
8. Does the behavior constitute a physical or psychological threat to the student or others?

If the answers to the above questions are yes, then intervention with deviant behavior can be facilitated with the following variety of management techniques.

SURFACE MANAGEMENT

"Surface management may be defined as dealing with overt behavior that needs to be regulated immediately without regard to underlying causes or motives" (Fagan & Hill, 1977, p. 209). Surface techniques, therefore, are only temporary or "stop-gap" methods that are designed to eliminate infrequent deviant behavior and restore the learning environment. When teachers are responsible for large groups of students it is not always possible to look for underlying causes; instead, immediate action is required. Fights, destruction of property, loss of behavioral control, and violent disruption of the learning environment are examples of behavior that require immediate teacher intervention. However, if such behaviors continue to recur, then more permanent and well designed solutions should be considered.

The surface techniques described in this section are a composite of intervention procedures reported in the literature (Gnagey, 1965; Long, Morse, & Newman, 1976, Redl & Wineman, 1957). Teachers will recognize many of the techniques from their own personal classroom experience. Other teachers may have used some of the techniques without any conscious awareness that they were doing so, or of their effect on students. At any rate, a list of surface management techniques is presented as a tool for teachers to enlarge the variety of techniques available to them and to increase awareness of their purposes and potential effects.

Ignoring Behavior

Many deviant behaviors are spontaneous and occur infrequently, usually motivated by some extraordinary classroom event. The cancellation of a field trip, a fire drill practice, or the introduction of a new pet animal to the classroom are examples of incidents that spark highly contagious disruptive behavior, but which typically subsides after a brief period of time. The best intervention technique under such circumstances is not to directly intervene, but to ignore the behavior.

On other occasions, however, student behavior may be more purposeful, designed to "test" the teacher or solicit attention, even if such attention may be negative in nature. If the teacher is perceived to be the target of the deviance, thereby making the teacher the rewarding agent, planned ignoring of student behavior can produce a positive behavioral change.

Teachers must be careful in the use of planned ignoring. Before employing this technique the teacher must be certain that the behavior is one that can be ignored, that the teacher (not the peer group) is the reinforcer, and that nonreinforcement will produce the desired change. This technique does have the advantages of being unobtrusive, limiting contagion, and permitting the teacher to remain with the instructional activities.

Signal Intervention

The use of physical cues is one of the most frequent forms of intervention currently employed by teachers. A variety of body postures, hand movements, and facial expressions are routinely used to convey approval and disapproval of student behavior. Smiles, winks, and a pat on the back are used to convey approval; frowns, throat clearing, and finger snapping are used to deter behavior. Although signals can be effective during the initial stage of deviance, their usefulness is limited after deviance has moved into advanced stages of behavior and emotions.

The frequent use of signals among teachers is partially responsible for their limited effectiveness. Unfortunately, signals are used indiscriminately in situations where other forms of intervention would be more appropriate. However, because of the relative ease of signal intervention, i.e., quick and effortless, signals remain a routine intervention technique.

If signal intervention is to remain a useful technique, more creative uses must be developed. Special, individualized signals can be designed to communicate with selected students. The signals can be as simple and subtle as tugging the ear, touching the nose, or pulling out a handkerchief. Personal signals are successful if the student knows that the signal is a unique message between teacher and student. Such a technique also has the advantage of remaining a "secret" and does not identify the student in the presence of peers, thus eliminating a potential confrontation.

Entire classrooms can also participate in the development of signals whereby students become managers of deviant behaviors. For example, the class may decide to use the "peace sign" if the noise in the classroom becomes so loud that it is distracting. Any student or the teacher could raise the "peace sign"; when observed every individual in the class would imitate the signal behavior until the class was quiet. This example was actually witnessed in a class of emotionally disturbed children and the results were amazing—contagion in a positive direction.

Closeness Control

Many students, particularly younger elementary-age children, need the physical presence of an adult to aid them in controlling impulsive, anxious, and even "forgetful" feelings and emotions. Without this physical assurance, negative feelings and emotions stimulate behaviors that may be unacceptable in the classroom. Even after interfering behaviors are evidenced, movement of the teacher toward the student is typically associated with reduced deviance. However, such movement must be interpreted by the student as concern and reassurance and not closeness to punish.

Older students also respond favorably to teacher movement in the classroom. Again, the movement must be associated with positive concern, academically or emotionally, and not a "spying technique" to catch students doing something that violates classroom rules. Often teacher movement does little more than remind students that they are off-task, which is sufficient to reduce deviance in many situations.

Teachers who are "glued" to a small area of the classroom (e.g., behind a desk, in front of the chalkboard, or near a relatively few students) tend to have the highest rates of deviance among those students who are the greatest distance from the teacher. In such instances, intervention usually takes the form of verbal directions or reprimands shouted across the classroom. Such techniques often do more to destroy the classroom learning environment than the student deviant behavior. Classroom movement, or closeness control, could be used to reduce the frequency of "interfering" teacher intervention.

Hurdle Help

This technique combines well with closeness control since it requires individual tutoring to help a student overcome an academic roadblock. This individual hurdle help can be an effective intervention technique when students need only minimal information to get them functioning appropriately. For example, a student may not have understood the teacher's directions and, therefore, is not involved in the lesson. "Instead of asking for help and exposing himself to the teacher's wrath for not paying attention . . ., the child is likely to establish contact with neighbors, find some interesting trinket in his pocket, or draw on his desk" (Long & Newman, 1961, p. 56). Providing the student with directions would get the student back on task, eliminating the deviant behavior. The concept of hurdle help as an intervention technique is thus designed to help the student "hurdle" frustrating obstacles within an academic setting.

Teacher Interest

Student performance on various academic tasks often wanes because of a lack of motivation or interest in the particular activity. Typically, the lack of motivation is accompanied by nonperformance, followed by boredom or restlessness. It is in this latter stage that students begin to engage in behaviors that disrupt the classroom.

Before the boredom or restlessness develops into behaviors that are difficult to manage, the teacher should demonstrate interest in the student's assignment or performance. Verbal cues, such as "That's an important assignment you're doing," or "You have a difficult assignment, but I'm sure you can do it," can serve to motivate the student. Teacher interest is a particularly effective technique for students who have a tendency to seek approval from adults.

Removing Temptations

Classrooms are usually filled with a variety of objects that are designed to enhance learning: globes, bulletin boards, games and the like. Most students can handle the variety of stimuli that bombards the classroom, even though most of the stimuli may be totally unrelated to the current lesson. However, some students, particularly those who are hyperactive, learning disabled, or impulsive, have difficulty separating the relevant from the irrelevant stimuli. The globe may be more attractive than the math assignment; the baseball on the teacher's desk may be more enticing than the reading assignment; or the student's new lunch box may be more visually alluring than the spelling words. In each case an environmental stimulus, unrelated to the lesson, becomes a visual temptation.

Teacher intervention, in the form of stimuli reduction, is required for those students who are inclined to be tempted by visual or verbal distractions. The most effective procedure is to remove the temptation—place the globe, the ball, or the lunch box out of sight. Of course, it is not possible, perhaps not desirable, to remove all irrelevant stimulation. Observation, however, may reveal that some students are more inclined to be distracted by specific objects. In these situations, the removal of temptation would help the student focus attention on the lesson and reduce task avoidance behavior.

Altering Instructional Methods

Often students are satiated with a repetitive task or a routine instructional method. Examples of repetitive methods include answering every question box in a text, completing a specified number of math problems each day, and limiting the instructional method to lecturing or reading. These stereotypic, monotonous, and repetitive approaches tend to create an attitude of indifference toward learning and negative feelings toward the teacher.

Teacher intervention in this context is related to the teacher's willingness to alter the instructional methods and/or requirements. Using a wider variety of input-output procedures may prevent satiation, increase interest, and, consequently, reduce deviant behavior. For the previous examples of repetition, methodological changes can include using a blend of verbal and written responses, devising a math program that emphasizes utilization rather than paper-and-pencil practice, and organizing exploratory discussion sessions as a substitute for lecturing. After all ". . . the task is not so much to teach children as to provide the conditions under which learning can take place" (Long, Morse, & Newman, 1976, p. 313).

Routine Structure

While some students are bored with the routine of a classroom, other students thrive on the predictive quality of structure. Students who have failed to develop basic trust in themselves, others, or their environment are psychologically threatened by confusion, spontaneity, and unstructured situations. When the classroom setting is unpredictable, these students express their fear and anxiety through withdrawal, hyperactivity, crying, and other behaviors that interfere with their learning.

Unstructured situations are created by many classroom conditions; for example, when teachers change their minds or make exceptions to selected rules or behaviors, when free-time activities or active games are introduced, and when the class schedule is interrupted by announcements, special events, or even a substitute teacher. Structure, at least initially, is a preferable intervention technique when students need the security of predictability. A stringent schedule of sequential activities accompanied by teacher consistency and punctuality, and permanent resources (desk, books, etc.) may reduce student apprehension and thus intervene with deviant behavior.

Rule Reminders

When emotions are high or events in the classroom generate excitement, students are prone to forget classroom rules. A teacher should be aware of the fact that the escalation of confusion and potent feelings may eventually erupt into behaviors that will require direct intervention. Before that point, however, it is suggested that the teacher remind the group or individual students of rules that are about to be violated. "Remember, you must remain in your seat" or "The rule is 'keep your hands to yourself'" should be announced as reminders before such violations occur. Signal interference or closeness control may serve the same function as a verbal reminder.

A rule reminder is a minimal intervention technique designed to prevent deviance and the need for more dramatic intervention. Just as speed limit signs are posted along the highway to remind drivers of the legal speed, rule reminders are announced by the teacher so that students are cognizant of behavioral limitations. In fact, teachers should routinely remind students of important classroom rules, even when the students are on-task and such violations are not anticipated. These reminders reinforce classroom behavior, provide predictable structure, and convey the message that classroom rules are important.

Positive Removal

There are times when students lose control and become a threat to themselves or others. A frequent disciplinary procedure to control threatening behaviors has been to exclude students from the classroom by sending them to the hall or the principal's office. In less severe cases, some teachers have developed procedures for isolating students in the classroom by using special "time-out" areas. In each case, isolation has a degree of merit, if isolation or exclusion is used as the last available measure to protect people or property.

However, the issue here is to make the removal of a student as positive as possible by avoiding the purely punitive aspect of exclusion. The teacher's interpretation of the isolation process can be a positive intervention technique. For example, the teacher could verbally interpret the action as a helping action:

> "I'm sending you to the hall, because you are going to hurt someone including yourself. I can't permit that. I don't want you or anyone else hurt. When you've settled down, you can come back."

or,

> "People are trying to learn in here and you won't let them. So, I'm sending you outside. When you think you can help people to learn, I'd like to have you back in the classroom."

For both examples, the teacher is excluding the student, but the verbal messages convey the need to help, not punish. Consequently, the student's re-entry into the classroom is based on behaviors or expectations that promote a more positive relationship.

The surface management techniques discussed in this section were presented as tools to assist the teacher in maintaining a learning environment in the classroom. Since the presentation did not follow a comprehensive model, there were both duplications and omissions. In fact, surface techniques not covered have probably occurred to the reader, perhaps techniques you have used in the classroom.

Before concluding this section, two points need to be emphasized. First, surface management techniques should be as individualized as the academic program. Whereas some students may respond appropriately to a specific intervention technique, other students may become more deviant. Thus a knowledge of the individual student and a variety of intervention techniques available to the teacher will increase the probability of successful management. Second, surface management techniques are only temporary solutions to behavioral problems. If deviant behaviors occur frequently, then other intervention techniques must be considered. In addition, some deviant behaviors require techniques that are designed to intervene with the causes of behavior, rather than externally manage surface behavior.

Because of the limitations of surface management, other intervention techniques are explored in the chapter. Within the classroom a number of critical factors contribute to the deviance of students and, therefore, must be altered if appropriate behavior is to be increased. The critical classroom factors include interpersonal, environmental, instructional, and group sources of deviancy and management.

INTERPERSONAL MANAGEMENT

Interpersonal management refers to psychological or affective techniques that involve both the teacher and the student. Affective techniques, as opposed to academic or behavioral controls, focus on those phases of the classroom experience that are concerned with feelings, emotions, and acceptance (Krathwohl, Bloom, & Masia, 1956). It is well known that students' psychological-affective states, including anxiety, frustration, rejection, and helplessness, are precipitators of deviant or disruptive behaviors. Therefore, "tuning in" to the student's affective state and responding interpersonally can facilitate more positive mental health and reduce the frequency and intensity of inappropriate classroom behavior.

Even though teachers have long known that students' academic, behavioral, and psychological-affective performance cannot be separated, there remains a tendency in education to promote academics, control behavior, and ignore feelings and emotions (Rich, 1978a). This emphasis on academic and behavioral performance partially exists because of the traditional subject-oriented curricular designs and large instructional group responsibility (Weinstein & Fantini, 1970). Interpersonal management requires some alteration in the traditional patterns and beliefs, and emphasizes the need for personal interaction between teacher and student.

The personal characteristics of the teacher, rather than the size of the group, grade level, or knowledge of the academic discipline, are more significant in the effective use of interpersonal management techniques. Obviously, a teacher who is exclusively concerned with teaching material content and maintaining strict order is less prone to exercise interpersonal intervention. For those students who require structure, academic-behavioral teaching priorities may be appropriate. However, there are students who need understanding, warmth, and even psychological support from teachers.

Hamachek (1969) has identified five teacher characteristics that facilitate the interpersonal teacher-student dimension:

1. They seem to have generally more positive views of others—students, colleagues, and administrators.
2. They do not seem to be as prone to view others as critical, attacking people with ulterior motives; rather they are seen as potentially friendly and worthy in their own right.
3. They have a more favorable view of democratic classroom procedures.
4. They seem to have the ability and capacity to see things as they seem to others—i.e., the ability to see things from the other person's point of view.
5. They do not seem to see students as persons "you do things to" but rather as individuals capable of doing for themselves once they feel trusted, respected, and valued (p. 343).

Given that many teachers possess these characteristics, there are a number of interpersonal techniques that may be used to manage interfering behavior. However, the employment of interpersonal techniques is also dependent on the rapport the teacher has established with individual students. Rapport, in this context, refers to a positive teacher-student relationship, based upon the students' perceptions of the teacher as a caring, fair, courteous, friendly, and trustworthy person (Howard, 1972). Although the use of interpersonal management may serve to build a positive relationship, initial attempts to use these intervention techniques may be relatively unsuccessful in reducing interfering behavior if positive rapport does not exist. The greatest deterrent to interpersonal management occurs when students accurately perceive their teacher as an insensitive task-master or censor of behavior, who is only "going through the motions" of caring.

Everyone, normal or exceptional, experiences unpleasant and intolerable feelings that make it difficult to function appropriately in the classroom. Typically, large groups of students assembled in schools and classrooms create settings for crises that precipitate negative feelings. Behavioral incidents, or crises, that can precipitate strong feelings and emotions include: student-student crises (e.g., threats, teasing, or separation); student-teacher crises (e.g., forgetting homework, "talking back," or violating a rule); and internal crises (e.g., disappointment, mistakes, or inadequacy). Each of these crises may foster so much anxiety or anger that the student is unable to function in the classroom. In turn, these feelings and emotions may motivate deviant behavior that must be managed in order to preserve the learning environment and protect the students.

In order to effectively intervene with deviant behavior among students, strong negative feelings must be positively reduced. For the teacher described by Hamachek (1969), there are a number of interpersonal techniques that may be appropriate for individual students.

Listening to Feelings

This intervention technique requires two basic ingredients—interest and time. On the simplest level, listening to feelings is being physically available to a student at a time when the student needs to vent emotions that are about to explode. Sitting close, leaning forward, providing eye-to-eye contact, and showing understanding by nodding or smiling can provide the body language necessary to convey a personal interest in the student.

This passive listening technique does not approve or condemn the circumstances that precipitated the feelings, but it does indicate teacher interest in the student's problem. This sympatic communication can be used to "drain off" the strong feelings which would otherwise result in deviant behavior (Redl, 1959). In times of crisis, many people are comforted by the fact that a sympathetic ear is available and that feelings do not have to be dealt with alone—students are no different.

Responding to Feelings

This interpersonal interference technique goes beyond the passive listening to feelings, adding the dimension of teacher response. To facilitate communication the teacher becomes an active listener, accurately interpreting the meaning of the message sent by the student and responding in a way that reflects the student's feelings.

"In active listening, then, the receiver (teacher) tries to understand what it is the sender (student) is feeling or what the message means. Then he puts his understanding into his own words . . . and feeds it back for the sender's verification. The receiver (teacher) *does not* send a message of his own—such as an evaluation, opinion, advice, logic, analysis, or question. He sends back *only what he feels the sender's message meant*—nothing more, nothing less" (Gordon, 1970, p. 53).

The technique of responding to feelings requires that the teacher ". . . discerns the overt as well as the covert or disguised behavior of another person" (Gazda, Asbury, Balzer, Childers, Desselle, & Walters, 1973, p. 39). This is particularly important since the verbal message may not convey what the student is feeling. For example, a student who has failed an exam may feel inadequate unless the failure is projected to the teacher by saying, "You said this part of the book wouldn't be required on the exam." Similarly, a student who feels threatened by a peer may want protection, but says, "I don't feel well today; I don't want to go out to recess." Or a student who is not selected to be on a team may elect to reduce the pain by saying, "I really didn't care about being on the team anyway." Each of these examples of verbal messages carries an entirely different meaning than the feeling behind it.

Teacher responses to feelings should reflect the feelings, not the overt message. For the three examples, teacher responses should be something like: "You're saying that it hurts when you don't do well on an exam," "We all need someone to help us when we are afraid," and "It really hurts when we are left out." These examples are based on the teacher's knowledge of the student, an empathic understanding of the problem, and a desire to help the student. Although the three responses may seem trite, they are certainly more facilitative than: "I specifically said that the entire chapter would be on the exam," "You weren't ill ten minutes ago," and "Then why did you try out for the team?"

Effective responding techniques can reduce the probability of deviant behavior by demonstrating teacher understanding of the student's personal crisis. Strong feelings and emotions that are not reduced, but are increased by responses that condemn, question, or emphasize the negative, often explode into crises that require extraordinary amounts of time and energy.

Maintaining Communication

In times of crises, students often retreat into a solitary world, not communicating with either peers or the teacher. Attempts to identify the problem or find a solution are negated by the fact that the student is nonverbal and nonresponsive. However, if teachers involve the student in some form of communication, it can prevent the next level of retreat (Redl, 1959).

A student accused of theft, cheating, or related behaviors may choose this regressive course of action as the least painful, particularly if a student lacks the skills necessary for adequate self-protection. Efforts on the part of the teacher to "grill" the student, point out the unacceptable behavior, or even encourage more appropriate behavior typically fall on deaf ears and motivate the student to increase the personal-emotional distance from the teacher.

Maintaining communication requires that the teacher involve the student in conversation completely unrelated to the situation that motivated the crisis. In short, find a psychologically comfortable area in which the student can relax the defenses and engage in appropriate behavior. If the crisis involved peers, then the teacher may want to provide the student a solitary learning responsibility; if the teacher was the source of the crisis, then peer group activities may be more appropriate; or if stealing or cheating was the accusation, then communication involving baseball, dancing, or hobbies may be areas of renewed communication. Even though the teacher may not be able to deal directly with the issue, it is necessary to maintain contact with the student by involving the student in an area or activity that is psychologically safe. At a later time, when communication has been re-established, the teacher may elect to deal with the original crisis.

Emphasizing Natural Consequences

Many traditional teacher-student disciplinary interactions are based on threats of punishment for noncompliant student behavior. Failing grades, suspension, moral devaluation, and even corporal punishment are common consequences which are administered by teachers for failure to respond appropriately to classroom rules or teacher expectations. However, these examples are not natural consequences, but are forms of punishment that may only occur in school related environments.

Natural consequences, in the context of interpersonal management, are those negative experiences that logically and functionally occur as a result of behavior. A failing grade is not a natural consequence if a student does not study. The natural consequence is that the student will not learn the information necessary for a vocation. Similarly, fighting physically hurts; the inability to get along with peers causes loneliness; and resentment of authority leads to limited job opportunities.

Many students do not understand the relationship between their behaviors and the natural consequences. Greater emphasis on life situations and adjustment, particularly for older students, is more meaningful since they may perceive school as an irrelevant obstacle in the path to adulthood. The motivation to perform more effectively will be increased for those students who understand that adult success is partially based on correct behavior, but not necessarily related to teacher expectations.

Increasing Verbal Skills

Educational institutions tend to be highly verbal settings where teachers talk a great deal and students are expected to communicate appropriately with both teachers and peers. Many students, however, are physically oriented, lacking the verbal skills necessary to communicate their needs and wishes. This physical orientation is especially common among younger students and students who have experienced restrictive language patterns in their home and community life-styles. If a second grade boy likes a girl, rather than saying, "I like you," he may knock her books to the ground, inviting a chase. A friendly tap on the shoulder, a shy glance to the floor, and touching, in general, are physical expressions of affection. Similarly, unverbalized anger may erupt into fighting, cursing, or hyperactivity. Often these indirect, but deviant, behaviors are the result of insufficient verbal skills necessary to convey feelings, resolve differences, or obtain needs.

The management of behaviors precipitated by inadequate verbal skills therefore requires the development of appropriate verbal skills. To successfully implement this intervention technique, teachers need to provide students with more opportunities to communicate, explore feelings, and identify ways of expressing needs. Such a program of verbal skill development will require that teachers talk less and students talk more. If teachers continue to tell students what they did wrong, why they did it, and what's going to be done about it, then students will have limited opportunities to interact or understand their own feelings, behaviors, and consequences. Currently, there is an inverse relationship between student talk and chronological age in elementary school (Karlin & Berger, 1972; Rich, 1978c). In short, as students grow older they talk less and teachers talk more. In terms of teacher-student interaction, this regressive development needs to be reversed. Teachers must also become effective listeners.

Although the interpersonal management techniques reported in this section do not constitute an exhaustive list, the techniques are believed to be important in facilitating adjustment in the classroom. Prerequisites for interpersonal management, such as trust, acceptance, and understanding, were not discussed at length because they reflect personal teacher characteristics rather than management techniques per se. However, the presence of positive personal characteristics is related to both the desire and effectiveness of interpersonal techniques.

It is important to remember that interpersonal management is basically a personal learning experience for the student, rather than a disciplinary action. The process of interpersonal teacher-student interaction should emphasize an understanding of feelings and emotions, and how they are translated into inappropriate behavior. The management of behavior therefore involves the development of skills necessary to express feelings and emotions in a more acceptable manner.

INSTRUCTIONAL MANAGEMENT

How a teacher teaches makes a difference. Not only are instructional methods related to student achievement, but they are associated with the rate of deviant behavior as well. Student achievement, time at task, attitude toward school, and behavior form a "syndrome" of characteristics that tend to be inseparable. Therefore, teaching behaviors that promote achievement also tend to reduce deviant behavior. The opposite is also true: teaching behaviors that do not promote achievement, involvement, or positive attitudes are also associated with higher rates of deviant behavior.

Because of the instructional relationship between student behavior and other educational factors, this section discusses several critical instructional techniques that are associated with teaching effectiveness. Although teaching is a complex variety of multidimensional functions that must be considered in totality for an accurate assessment of teaching, there are several instructional techniques that are reported to reduce or increase student interfering behaviors. The management techniques identified for discussion in this section include teacher instructional behaviors that 1) provide clarity, 2) affect movement, and 3) convey expectations. Most of the research and literature on these aspects of instruction have focused on normal student populations; however, there is substantial information to support the belief that special students in the regular class would be similarly affected.

Instructional Clarity

In an effort to quickly bring about behavioral and academic compliance, teachers frequently use vague references to deviant behavior and nonacademic performance. General statements, such as "Stop that!",

"What is the class supposed to be doing?", and "What did I say yesterday?", tend to produce anxiety, create distractions, and generate confusion. Students who are on-task and are behaviorally compliant shift their attention to the teacher's intervention; students who were the intended target of the intervention are often oblivious since they were not clearly identified in the communication. Typically such vagueness creates more deviance than it reduces.

Instructional clarity could eliminate the unnecessary side effects. Directed statements, such as "George, stop kicking the chair," "Class, you are to be working your math problems," and "Talking is not permitted during quiet time," provide more clarity by specifically identifying expected behaviors.

Academic behaviors are also affected by teacher clarity. Bush, Kennedy, and Cruickshank (1977) found that teacher clarity involves ". . . explaining concepts and directions in a manner which is understandable and at a pace which is appropriate" (p. 10). Examples of teacher clarity in this context include taking sufficient time to explain concepts and tasks and emphasizing difficult problems and ideas. A second dimension of clarity includes the teacher's use of frequent demonstrations, examples, and illustrations.

Failure to provide clear communication regarding behaviors and academic tasks creates deviance. Compliant students become distracted witnesses to the intervention, and deviant students lack the information necessary to perform appropriately. Conversely, instructional clarity provides specific information to both the compliant and deviant students, conveys a clear message of teacher expectations, and prepares students to more satisfactorily complete academic tasks.

Instructional Movement

The transition from one activity to another is critical to behavioral intervention. For example, the shift from math to reading, from individual activities to group projects or from recess to the classroom are transition times that are highly susceptible to the development of deviant behavior. The success with which the teacher can terminate an old activity and initiate a new one is related to the frequency of interfering behavior.

According to Kounin (1967), a smooth transition between activities increases the teacher's managerial success. On the other hand, deviance increases when the transition reflects "jerkiness." This latter transition problem is created by "(a) dangles (initiating an activity without immediate follow through); (b) flip-flops (stopping an old activity and initiating a new one and then engaging in an action such as a question about the old one); (c) thrusts (bursting in with the initiation of a new activity without engaging in any action to ascertain the target group's readiness to receive the induction)" (Kounin, 1967, p. 226).

Clearly, students with learning and behavioral problems are adversely affected by jerky types of instructional movements. This transition problem is often fostered by the fact that many teachers use individual key students to determine the group's readiness to shift activities. Unfortunately, the brighter, more compliant students are used by the teacher as a cue to alter activities; the special student is rarely considered in a large group of regular students. However, to reduce deviance the teacher must employ smooth instructional movement techniques that consider individual readiness for the transition.

Instructional Expectations

Even though many teachers maintain that they treat all their students "the same," that is, with impartiality and equality, the evidence does not support this claim. For example, Rosenthal and Jacobson (1968) report a strong relationship between teacher perceptions of students and students' success in the classroom. When teachers perceived students positively, those students were more successful; when teachers perceived students negatively, those students were less successful. However, the degree of student success is not a function of teacher perception, but of teacher behaviors that are consistent with those perceptions. Teachers respond differently toward different students. This difference in teacher responses may account for a great deal of the success and failure of individual students.

Certainly, differences in the instructional process may be minimal, but they do exist. Brophy and Good (1974) have collected and synthesized data that support the position that teachers translate different expectations into instructional differences.

1. Waiting Less Time for Lows to Answer: Teachers have been observed to provide more time for high achieving students to respond than for low achieving students. The determinants of this behavior could include excessive sympathy for the student, teacher anxiety, and lack of probing skills, among others. As with the other variables that appear below, the determinants of such behavior are largely unknown.

2. Staying with Lows in Failure Situations: In addition to waiting less time for lows to begin their response, teachers in replicated studies have been found to respond to lows' (more so than highs') incorrect answers by giving them the answer or calling on another student to answer the question. High achieving students in failure situations are much more likely to have the teacher repeat the question, provide a clue, or ask them a new question. Thus teachers have been found to accept mediocre performance from lows but to work with and demand better performance from highs.

3. Rewarding Inappropriate Behavior of Lows: In some studies teachers have been found to praise marginal or inaccurate student responses. Praising inappropriate substantive responses (as opposed to perseverance, and so on) when the children's peers know the answer may only dramatize the academic weakness of such students.

4. Criticizing Lows More Frequently than Highs: Somewhat at odds with the above findings is that in some studies teachers have been found to criticize lows proportionately more frequently than highs when they provide wrong answers. This is indeed a strong finding, for it suggests that lows' expression of risk taking behavior and general initiative is being discouraged. One would expect that lows might receive more negative feedback (but not necessarily criticism) simply because they emit more wrong answers. But the analyses alluded to here were controlled for the frequency of wrong answers and found that on a percentage basis lows were more likely to be criticized than highs. It is possible that the quality of lows' responses may have been lower, but criticism for a serious attempt to respond is an inappropriate strategy in any case. The seeming discrepancy between variables three and four may reside in differing teacher personalities. Teachers who praise inappropriate answers from lows may be mired in sympathy for these students, whereas hypercritical teachers may be irritated at them for delaying the class and/or providing evidence that the teaching has not been completely successful.

5. Praising Lows Less Frequently than Highs: Also in contrast to (3) above, some research has shown that when lows provide correct answers they are less likely to be praised than highs even though they provide fewer correct responses. The situation is clear for lows in certain classes. If they respond, they are more likely to be criticized and less likely to be praised; thus, the safest strategy is to remain silent, because here the teacher is likely to call on someone else.

6. Not Giving Feedback to Public Responses of Lows: Teachers in some studies have been found to respond to lows' answers (especially correct answers) by calling on another student to respond. Failure to confirm their answers seems undesirable in that these students more than other students may be less sure about the adequacy of their response.

7. Paying Less Attention to Lows: Studies have shown that teachers attend more closely to highs (and, as we noted above, provide more feedback). Some data exist to suggest that teachers smile more often and maintain greater eye contact with highs than lows. Studies also show that teachers miss many opportunities to reinforce lows simply because they do not attend to their behavior. Such studies provide support for part of Rosenthal and Jacobson's original explanation of the Pygmalion results: positive expectations increase a student's salience and his opportunity for appropriate reinforcement.

8. Calling on Lows Less Often: Relatedly, teachers have been found to call on high achieving students more frequently than low achieving students. Although much of the difference can be explained by student differences, the data show that few teachers compensate for these student differences. The difference in public participation becomes more sharply differentiated with increases in grade level.

9. Differing Interaction Patterns of Highs and Lows: Interestingly, contact patterns between teachers and lows are different in elementary and secondary classrooms. In elementary classrooms highs dominate public response opportunities, but highs and lows receive roughly the same number of private teacher contacts. In secondary classrooms highs become even more dominant in public settings, but lows begin to receive more private contacts with the teacher. Perhaps at this level private conferences with teachers are a sign of inadequacy, especially if the teacher does not initiate private contacts with highs.

10. Seating Lows Farther from the Teacher: Studies have suggested that when students are grouped randomly within classrooms, undesirable discrepancies in teacher behavior between high and low achievers are less likely. Perhaps this is because lows are sitting next to highly salient or "liked" students so that teachers are more likely to notice them and to maximize treatment of them as individual learners. Seating pattern studies have sometimes found that lows tend to be placed away from the teacher (creating a physical barrier). Random placement seems to reduce the physical isolation of lows and the development of sharp status differences among peers.

11. Demanding Less from Lows: Several studies have suggested that this is a relevant variable. It can be seen as an extension of the more focused "giving up" variable discussed above. This is a broader concept suggesting such activities as giving these students easier tests (and letting the students know it) or simply not asking the student to do academic work. Also, sometimes if a low achieving student masters the elementary aspects of a unit he may be neglected until the elementary aspects of the next unit are dealt with. Teachers set different mastery levels for students. At times, however, being less demanding may be appropriate if initial low demands are coupled with systematic efforts to improve performance (pp. 330–333).

The differences in expectations that Brophy and Good (1974) have translated into instructional and communication practices have a number of implications for both behavior management and special students in the mainstream. If special students are considered "lows" in the regular class and teacher communication is consistent with many of the 11 differences listed, special students will be less successful and they will constitute behavior problems. In addition, the differences in teacher instructional behavior violate most of the intervention principles discussed. For example, there is less tolerance of behaviors, more criticism and less praise, and fewer opportunities for interpersonal management. Individually, teachers need to be aware of the differences in their instructional expectations, and consciously and intentionally communicate with students in terms of an educational and managerial plan based upon knowledge of individual students.

Teacher Style
The characteristic manner in which the teacher fulfills the classroom leadership role in an educational environment is referred to as a teaching

style. For example, teaching style may be characterized by lecturing, directing, question-and-answer sessions, or independent study. Since the teacher is singularly the most important manager of interfering behavior, the style employed is a significant factor in instructional management. Although teacher style may constitute innumerable variables and constructs, the simplest conception represents a continuum of teacher-centered to child-centered behaviors. Terms synonomous with "centered-ness" include authoritarian, direct, and structured, on one extreme, while democratic, indirect, and reflective represent the other extreme. Regard-less of the terms, the ". . . continuum involves the extent to which the teacher makes decisions for the child" (Kauffman & Lewis, 1974, p. 281).

The extent to which the teacher controls or makes decisions for students can serve as an effective instructional intervention technique. Since different students require different amounts of control, the objec-tive of instructional management is to match the degree of teacher con-trol with student needs for control. Typically, students functioning on lower developmental levels, evidenced by hyperactive, withdrawn, or dependent behavior, require a more controlling teacher than do students who are functioning on higher developmental levels. Table 1 illustrates the "matched" relationship between the optimal level of teacher control and different student behaviors (Rich, 1978b).

The relationship illustrated in Table 1 must be considered a hypothetical match, particularly since behaviors may not be representa-tive of developmental needs for individual students. However, given that the general construct is valid, then instructional intervention in the form of teacher style should be appropriately matched to the functional developmental level of students. This match will prevent, certainly

Table 1. Relationship between percentage of teacher style control and student developmental behaviors

Percent of teacher control	Student developmental behaviors
100	
90 ⟷	unsocialized
80 ⟷	hyperactive
70 ⟷	withdrawn
60 ⟷	compulsive
50 ⟷	dependent
40 ⟷	negativistic
30 ⟷	aggressive
20 ⟷	assertive
10 ⟷	independent
0	

reduce, the frequency of deviant behavior. Teacher styles that are inconsistent with student behaviors may serve to create more interfering behavior, thus requiring additional intervention procedures.

Instructional management is a critical intervention technique. Appropriate teacher clarity, movement, expectations, and style not only reduce deviant behavior but also enable students to achieve academic objectives more effectively. Furthermore, well conceived instructional procedures serve as preventive measures, thereby reducing the time and energy necessary to intervene with deviant behavior apart from the teacher's primary educational role.

ENVIRONMENTAL MANAGEMENT

Physical classroom characteristics have been an overlooked dimension of behavior management. Although teachers are aware that classroom factors such as room size, temperature variations, and general decor do affect learning and behavior (Drew, 1971), there is little evidence that the physical environment by itself directly causes appropriate or deviant behavior. Therefore, the emphasis on environmental management will be that ". . . physical settings have their own properties which place constraints on some behavior and facilitate, if not require, others" (Proshansky, 1974, p. 553).

Even though teachers should be able to justify the physical arrangement of the classroom, many teachers do not recognize ". . . which aspects of learning and social behavior should be expected to change as a function of the particular environmental design . . ." (Cruickshank & Quay, 1970, p. 265). One way of evaluating the environmental design is to study both the *symbolic* meaning and the *pragmatic* function of the physical classroom arrangement and what the arrangement communicates to students and teachers (Proshansky & Wolfe, 1974). Symbolic meaning refers to the psychological expectation of behavior, while the pragmatic function refers to the actual effectiveness of the environment in supporting or reducing specific behaviors.

For the purpose of discussing both the symbolic and pragmatic implications of environmental management, two different examples of classroom physical arrangements are considered—traditional and informal. Figure 1 illustrates the physical arrangements of the two classrooms.

Certainly the traditional and informal classrooms, as presented, represent only a portion of the possible classroom arrangements that are currently in use. However, the two examples do constitute, with minor variations, arrangements that are the most frequently employed instructional-managerial designs.

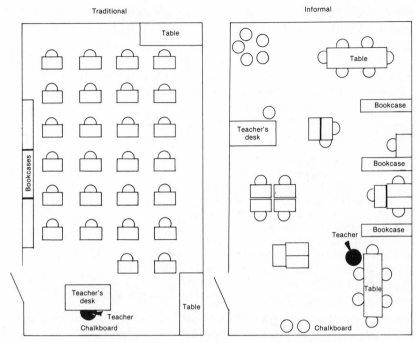

Figure 1.   Physical arrangement of "traditional" and "informal" classrooms.

Symbolic Meaning

Traditional Classrooms   This more formal design, often referred to as a teacher-centered environment, has been the basic model of classroom arrangement for several centuries. The typical arrangement consists of several rows of student seat-desks, one behind the other, facing the front of the room where the teacher's desk and chalkboard are located. The teacher's primary work station, near the desk, enables the teacher to control the flow of traffic in and out of the classroom, speak directly to students, and maintain visual supervision of the entire group.

This standardized classroom design psychologically emphasizes expected patterns of behavior on the part of teachers and students alike. These expectations include the exercise of authoritative control, a lecture method of instruction, the passive use of space, and the presumed homogeneity of students. "The location of the teacher's desk in the traditional room not only communicate(s) the isolated role of the teacher; it also physically place(s) that space off limits for the use by the children" (Proshansky & Wolfe, 1974, p. 559).

The uniformity and position of the students' seating arrangement suggests educational conformity, passive learning, and an orderly standard of behavior. The lack of variability in student work space implies that all students require the same spatial area regardless of the task, perceptual-motor abilities, or psychological needs. Because students face the teacher and not each other, the instructional format is predetermined to consist primarily of teacher lecturing, directing, and questioning; the physical arrangement does not facilitate student communication with anyone other than the teacher.

A student poem reflects one attitude regarding the traditional classroom arrangement:

> . . . It was funny about school.
> He sat in a square brown desk
> like all the other square brown desks
> and he thought it would be red.
> And his room was a square brown room
> like all the other rooms.
> And it was tight and close. And stiff.
> He hated to hold the pencil and chalk,
> with his arm stiff and his feet flat on the floor, stiff,
> with the teacher watching and watching . . .
>   (Schultz, Heuchert, & Stampf, 1973, p. vi).

In summary, the symbolic meaning of the traditional classroom emphasizes controlled behavior and unilateral communication that is directed and supervised by the teacher. The physical separation of teacher and students reinforces the authoritative role of the teacher and increases the social distance, precluding interpersonal management. The confined, standard student seating arrangement requires passive, isolated learning within the context of reduced motor activity, limited exploratory behavior, and restricted student-student interaction.

Informal Classrooms   The informal classroom arrangement, which approximates an open-space or child-centered environment, conveys a different symbolic meaning than that of the traditional classroom. A visual overview of the informal classroom reveals a nonuniform arrangement of student work areas, a variety of work-size surfaces, and both individual and small group activity settings. The teacher's physical position in the classroom is not well defined; nor does the teacher's desk constitute a physical or psychological barrier.

The informal arrangement precludes a lecture method of instruction because the teacher does not occupy a commanding position that is directly visible to all students. Similarly, many students are out of the visual range of the teacher. The lack of reciprocal face-to-face contact requires that task objectives and/or activities be different for individuals and small groups. Thus, the teacher functions in the role of facilitator, rather than a director or controller.

Noise, movement, and general activity are expected behaviors since the physical arrangement is predicated on the assumptions of involvement, flexibility, interaction, and individualized programming. Different work surfaces, spatial allowances, and activity settings symbolically suggest that individual differences are accommodated, at least in terms of the physical task requirements and motor needs.

In summary, the informal classroom ". . . is not a single homogenous space cube; rather it is a network of interconnected and varied micro-environments" (Sommer, 1977, p. 175). Individualized activities, teacher movement and facilitation, and the variety of spatial arrangements add up to a classroom with a great amount of noise, verbal interaction, and physical mobility. The informal classroom is partially predicated on the assumption that an individualized physical environment will reduce environmental constraints that impede student performance.

Pragmatic Functions

The management of interfering behavior can be assisted by a physical classroom arrangement that is consistent with the teacher's instructional-managerial style and the characteristics of the students. No one arrangement is universally preferable—the best arrangement is one that is effective for the individuals involved. Both the traditional and informal classrooms have managerial advantages and disadvantages.

The traditional arrangement was designed as an orderly, lecture type environment. Therefore, if the teacher's style is one of maintaining control and of lecturing, then the straight rows of desks are more preferable than random clusters of students (Sommer, 1977). On the other hand, the informal arrangement is designed to implement more individualized, self-directed learning. An interpersonal, facilitating teacher style is more consistent with this latter environmental arrangement.

It is important to note, however, that the teacher's style and preference is only one factor in the determination of physical arrangements. Any decision to use a particular arrangement must account for and accomodate the needs of the students who occupy the learning environment. It is this critical relationship between teacher style and student needs that should be used to determine the most appropriate classroom arrangement. These interacting conditions require that the teacher determine ". . . the physical relationship between the child and the teacher, the physical and visual needs of the child, and all other similar factors which may have an effect on physical structure" (Cruickshank & Quay, 1970, p. 264).

Differences in the physical and spatial needs are typified by Fitt's (1974) description of two students:

Johnny and Susy enter the classroom together. Susy waves expansively at the teacher, throws her sweater vaguely in the direction of her locker, and charges into the room waving frantically at her friend who is already at work across the room. She sprawls at her desk, spreading her arms out onto the two adjoining desks. Meanwhile, Johnny has moved to his locker and has carefully folded his sweater and placed it in one corner of his locker. He walks to his desk with his arms held closely to his sides and sits down, drawing his feet under his chair and stacking his books and papers carefully in the center of his desk (p. 618).

Johnny's physical and spatial needs are obviously more limited than those of Susy. Whereas Johnny may function well in the traditional classroom arrangement, Susy's physical expression would be disruptive and generally inappropriate in the same classroom. In all probability the most conscientious surface, interpersonal, and instructional managerial techniques would be unsuccessful with Susy, unless the physical environment was arranged to meet her needs.

Johnny, on the other hand, may constitute a behavior problem in the informal classroom, particularly if his spatial needs are indicative of related psychological needs for consistency and predictability. The symbolic assumption of openness, movement, and independence may be so psychologically traumatizing that Johnny will be unable to function effectively and may intrapersonally withdraw or attack the informal environment.

Of the management techniques discussed in this chapter, some are more functionally appropriate for the traditional classroom, while others are more compatible with the informal arrangement. For example, it is generally assumed that the hyperactive child should be in close proximity to the teacher and work under conditions relatively free of unnecessary stimulation (Fairchild, 1975). These intervention procedures could best be accomplished in the traditional classroom where teacher mobility and environmental stimulation are more limited. The traditional design also enables hearing impaired students to ". . . see the teacher's face for speech reading development . . . " and aid a student with a mobility handicap ". . . to anticipate obstacles, traffic, and new spatial areas" (Cruickshank & Quay, 1970, p. 263). The use of teacher signal intervention, rule reminders, and routine structuring are also more practical in the traditional class.

The informal arrangement, accompanied by high teacher mobility, has the advantage of personalizing intervention without drawing attention to the student in question. Certainly it is easier to tolerate selected behaviors when students are not expected to conform to an established pattern of passive behavior. Ignoring behavior, spontaneous closeness control, and individual tutoring are similarly consistent with both the symbolic and pragmatic functions of the informal class. Interpersonal management can be conducted within the classroom, and does not require waiting for an appropriate time or going out into the hallway as one might expect in the traditional classroom.

Certainly no one classroom arrangement will adequately deal with every instructional-managerial concern. Each classroom is designed with specific objectives, styles, and behaviors in mind; those that are inconsistent with the environmental design will be less than successful. One answer may be to use a combination of both arrangements—a segment of the class assigned to individual seat desks while the other students are working independently or in small groups. Whatever classroom arrangement is used, it should not be based on historical precedents but on a knowledge of the students, including their physical, academic, and psychological needs, and the instructional-managerial philosophy of the teacher.

GROUP MANAGEMENT

Whenever deviant behavior occurs in the classroom the teacher must decide whether to intervene with individual students or consider the entire group. Of the two choices, this chapter has emphasized teacher management of interfering behavior demonstrated by individual students. This was an intentional focus since the purpose of this chapter is to assist teachers in managing special students in the regular classroom.

The management of individual students, however, has at least two primary limitations. First, individual intervention may create a negative "ripple effect," that is, result in unintended but inappropriate teacher influence on nondeviant students (Kounin, 1970). Visible teacher intervention techniques tend to reduce the task-appropriate behavior of students witnessing the intervention, thereby shifting the classroom emphasis from learning to management. Second, deviant behavior may be a function of group norms, rather than individual interfering behavior. Thus, deviance may be a role behavior acquired by an individual student, but one that is expected and supported by the group as a whole.

If mainstreaming is to be effective, teachers must be cognizant of the fact that special students are also members of the classroom group. Although students may occupy the same physical space and are legally present to learn a prescribed curriculum, they will have a variety of needs, skills, behaviors, and values which can prevent the class from becoming an effectively functioning educational group. Students who defy the teacher, act as the class clown, or are "lazy" and unconcerned are typically demonstrating role behaviors that have group support. Even though these behaviors are not indicative of academically successful students, nor are they ". . . desirable in the teacher's set of values, some peer recognition of what ever kind may be better than no recognition at all" (Smith, 1959, p. 11). This failure to comply with teacher expectations is partially attributable to the fact that students in general, but particularly older students, are more concerned with peer expectations and not those of the teacher, or even parents.

The classroom group sanctions those behaviors that are consistent with the norms of the group, and the group condemns those behaviors that are not. Although the teacher is exclusively responsible for awarding grades and granting privileges, ". . . it is quite possible for students who have a high degree of social acceptance to influence the distribution of public praise and approval among class members" (Jensen, 1960, p. 107). This is particularly evident among members of smaller subgroups who have developed an identity and goals independent of the total group and the stated purposes of the educational program.

The effective use of group management first requires that the teacher identify classroom behaviors which are symptomatic of group problems. Toward this end, Johnson and Bany (1970) have classified group behavior problems in terms of distinguishing characteristics (Table 2).

Problems that are inherent in the group will not be effectively managed by intervening with individual students. Many students may deliberately demonstrate deviant behaviors in order to maintain a group role, inviting teacher intervention that will serve to accentuate the desired role. For example, a student considered a subgroup leader may challenge the teacher's authority and even welcome punishment in order to reaffirm peer group leadership status. Special students in the regular classroom constitute an unusual group problem. Often, their special problems are used as a negative source of group identification and status. Students identified as retarded, aggressive, and learning disabled may engage in behaviors that are consistent with their group-recognized roles as a "dummy," "tough," and "clumsy." Direct and individual teacher intervention with the students involved typically serves to reinforce these role behaviors.

The group and teacher maintenance of such deviant roles, although productive for group status, are counter-productive in terms of personal development and academic achievement. Therefore, management that considers the total classroom group must be implemented. A prerequisite to group management is the teacher's willingness to involve the group in open communication and share some of the power typically allocated to teachers. In short, teachers must develop an atmosphere of understand-

Table 2.   Classroom management problems in terms of behavioral descriptions

Distinguishing characteristics	Behavior descriptions
1. Lack of unity	The class lacks unity and conflicts occur between individuals and subgroups as: when groups split; argumentative over competitive situations such as games; boys against girls; when groups split by cliques, minority groups; when group takes sides on issues or breaks into subgroups; when hostility and conflict constantly arise among members and create an unpleasant atmosphere.
2. Nonadherence to behavioral standards and work procedures	The class responds with noisy, talkative, disorderly behavior to situations which have established standards for behaving, as: when group is entering or leaving room or changing activities; lining up; cleaning up; going to auditorium; when group is working in ability groups; engaging in committee work; when group is completing study assignments; receiving assignments; correcting papers; handling work materials; when group is engaged in discussion, sharing, planning.
3. Negative reactions to individual	The class becomes vocal or actively hostile toward one or more class members, as: when group does not accept individuals and derides, ignores, or ridicules children who are different; when group reacts negatively to members who deviate from group code; to those who thwart group's progress; or when a member's behavior upsets or puzzles members of the class.
4. Class approval of misbehavior	The class approves and supports individuals, as: when they talk out of turn; act in ways which disrupt the normal work procedures; engage in clowning or rebellious activities.

continued

Table 2.   (*Continued*)

Distinguishing characteristics	Behavior descriptions
5. Easily distracted; prone to work stoppage and imitative behavior	The group reacts with upset, excited, or disorderly behavior to interruptions, distractions, or constant grievances, as: when group is interrupted by monitors, visitors, a change in weather; when members constantly have grievances relating to others, lessons, rules, policies or practices they believe are unfair; and when settlements are demanded before work proceeds.
6. Low morale and hostile, resistant, or aggressive reactions	The class members engage in subtle hostile, aggressive behavior which creates slowdowns and work stoppages, as: when materials are misplaced, pencils break, chairs upset; when books, money, lunches are temporarily lost; when there are constant requests for assignments to be repeated and explained; when children constantly complain about behavior of others, with no apparent loss of friendship; when children accuse authority figures of unfair practices and delay classwork by making claims.
7. Inability to adjust to environmental change	The class reacts inappropriately to such situations, as: when a substitute takes over; when normal routines are changed; when new members transfer into the class; when stress situations cause inappropriate reactions.

Source: *Classroom Management: Theory and Skill Training* by L. V. Johnson and M. A. Bany, Collier-MacMillan Ltd., London, 1970, pp. 46–47.

ing and cooperation, rather than one of control and competition (Vorrath & Brendtro, 1974).

The best techniques for managing group behavior are those that are based on cooperative and participatory practices. These practices include:

1. Guiding group toward examination of behavior.
2. Creating in group an awareness of the problem.
3. Helping group clarify problem.

4. Guiding group in diagnosis of the problem.
5. Helping group establish goals and intentions of actions.
6. Helping group improve techniques for resolving conflicts and solving problems (Johnson & Bany, 1970, p. 106).

Effective group management is based on the teacher's awareness of the group's psychosocial structure, an accurate assessment of individual behaviors within the group, and a willingness to involve the group in understanding and resolving the problems. Group management, then, is assisting the group in identifying problems and issues that have negative influence on classroom performance, helping the group decide upon solutions and strategies for resolving problems, and facilitating the group in dealing with their own problems. This approach requires that the teacher be open, communicative, and democratic within the context of a problem-solving philosophy.

SUMMARY

This chapter has been devoted to the management of interfering behavior that occurs within the classroom. Throughout the chapter it has been stressed that a variety of management techniques are required if teachers expect to maintain an effective learning environment. Whereas some students may respond appropriately to surface techniques, others may require a more interpersonal approach. Similarly, some students may adjust to individual techniques, while others may be fulfilling group expectations that require group management. Different instructional procedures and environmental designs also have different managerial effects on different students.

The success of any managerial technique is determined by the teacher's knowledge of the student and the employment of a technique that is appropriate to the academic, psychological, and physical characteristics of the student. Management should be as individualized as the academic program—no two students learn the exact same thing from the same instruction, nor do they respond the same way to the same management. This concept of individualized management is particularly important for the exceptional student in the mainstream since the student may have unique characteristics that are not appropriate for the traditional types of teacher intervention.

REFERENCES

Brophy, J. E., & Good, T. L. *Teacher-student relationships: Causes and consequences.* New York: Holt, Rinehart & Winston, 1974.

Bush, A. J., Kennedy, J. J., & Cruickshank, D. R. *An empirical investigation of teacher clarity.* Paper presented at the annual meeting of the American Educational Research Association, New York, April, 1977.

Cruickshank, W. M., & Quay, H. C. Learning and physical environment: The necessity for research and research design. *Exceptional Children,* 1970, *37,* 261–268.

Drew, C. J. Research on the psychological-behavioral effects of the physical environment. *Review of Educational Research,* 1971, *41,* 447–465.

Fagan, S. A., & Hill, J. *Behavior management.* Washington, D.C.: Psychoeducational Resources, 1977.

Fairchild, T. N. *Managing the hyperactive child in the classroom.* Austin, Tex.: Learning Concepts, 1975.

Fitt, S. The individual and his environment. *School Review,* 1974, *82,* 617–620.

Gazda, G. M., Asbury, F. R., Balzer, F. J., Childers, W. C., Desselle, R. E., & Walters, R. P. *Human relations development.* Boston: Allyn & Bacon, 1973.

Geer, B. Teaching. *International Encyclopedia of the Social Sciences.* New York: MacMillan, 1968.

Gnagey, W. J. *Controlling classroom misbehavior.* Washington, D.C.: National Education Association, 1965.

Gordon, T. *Parent effectiveness training.* New York: Peter H. Wyden, Inc., 1970.

Hamachek, D. Characteristics of good teachers and implications for teacher education. *Phi Delta Kappan,* 1969, *50,* 341–345.

Howard, A. W. Discipline is caring. *Today's Education,* 1972, *61,* 52–53.

Jensen, G. The sociopsychological structure of the instructional group. In N. B. Henry (Ed.), *The Dynamics of Instructional Groups.* Chicago: The National Society for the Study of Education, 1960.

Johnson, L. V., & Bany, M. A. *Classroom management: Theory and skill training.* London: Collier-Macmillan Limited, 1970.

Karlin, M. S., & Berger, R. *Discipline and the disruptive child.* West Nyack, N.Y.: Parker Publishing Co., 1972.

Kauffman, J. M., & Lewis, C. D. *Teaching children with behavior disorders: Personal perspectives.* Columbus, Oh.: Charles E. Merrill, 1974.

Kounin, J. S. An analysis of teachers' managerial techniques. *Psychology in the Schools,* 1967, *4,* 221–227.

Kounin, J. S. *Discipline and group management in classrooms.* New York: Holt, Rinehart, & Winston, 1970.

Krathwohl, D. R., Bloom, B. S., & Masia, B. B. *Taxonomy of educational objectives, handbook II: Affective domain.* New York: David McKay Co., 1956.

Long, N. J., Morse, W. C., & Newman, R. G. *Conflict in the classroom* (3rd ed.). Belmont, Cal.: Wadsworth Publishing Co., 1976.

Long, N. J., & Newman, R. G. The teacher's handling of children in conflict. *Bulletin of the School of Education.* Bloomington, Ind.: Indiana University, 1961.

Marshall, H. H. *Positive discipline and classroom interaction.* Springfield, Ill.: Charles C Thomas, 1972.

Phillips, E. L., Wiener, D. N., & Haring, N. G. *Discipline, achievement, and mental health.* Englewood Cliffs, N.J.: Prentice-Hall, 1960.

Proshansky, E., & Wolfe, M. The physical setting and open education. *School Review,* 1974, *82,* 557–574.

Proshansky, H. M. Theoretical issues in environmental psychology. *School Review*, 1974, *82*, 541–556.

Redl, F. The concept of the life space interview. *American Journal of Orthopsychiatry*, 1959, *29*, 1–18.

Redl, F., & Wineman, D. *The aggressive child*. Glencoe, Ill.: Free Press, 1957.

Rhodes, W. C., & Tracy, M. L. (Eds.). *A study of child variance, Vol. II: Interventions*. Ann Arbor, Mich.: The University of Michigan, 1972.

Rich, H. L. Affective concerns in the utilization of instructional materials. In R. M. Anderson, J. G. Greer, & S. J. Odle (Eds.), *Individualizing educational materials for special children in the mainstream*. Baltimore: University Park Press, 1978. (a)

Rich, H. L. A model for educating the emotionally disturbed and behaviorally disordered. *Focus on Exceptional Children*, 1978, *10* (3), 1–11. (b)

Rich, H. L. Teacher's perceptions of motor activity and related behaviors. *Exceptional Children*, 1978, *45*, 210–211. (c)

Rosenthal, R., & Jacobson, L. *Pygmalion in the classroom*. New York: Holt, Rinehart & Winston, 1968.

Schultz, E. W., Heuchert, C., & Stampf, S. M. *Pain and joy in school*. Champaign, Ill.: Research Press, 1973.

Smith, L. M. *Group processes in elementary and secondary schools*. Washington, D.C.: National Education Association, 1959.

Sommer, R. Classroom layout. *Theory into practice*, 1977, *16*, 174–175.

Tinsley, D. G., & Ora, J. P. Catch the child being good. *Today's Education*, 1970, *59*, 24–25.

Vorrath, H. H., & Brendtro, L. K. *Positive peer culture*. Chicago: Aldine, 1974.

Weinstein, G., & Fantini, M. D. *Toward humanistic education: A curriculum of affect*. New York: Praeger Publishers, 1970.

Part III

RESOURCE AND SUPPORT SYSTEMS

Editorial Introduction

The final part of this book includes three chapters that describe the all-important contributions of education-related disciplines, practitioners, and community services that help to meet the needs of handicapped individuals. Preceding chapters have focused primarily on teachers and classroom activities; this section emphasizes tasks and responsibilities other than teacher-oriented academic instruction that enhance or support the education of the handicapped. Inasmuch as ancillary services have been mandated as part of the education plan for each individual, this section emphasizes a multidisciplinary approach.

Chapter 12 describes the rapidly changing roles of the supportive personnel to whom educators may turn for help in providing a comprehensive continuum of services for the handicapped. This chapter summarizes the issues now challenging the various related disciplines such as school psychology and physical therapy as they work toward providing improved services for the handicapped.

The policies of normalization and deinstitutionalization require a shift from parental responsibility to that of the community. Chapter 13 goes into detail as to the role of the community in the provision of services other than education. Parent groups and others are currently becoming intensively involved in these community efforts, based on a growing realization of the need for advocacy, both in litigation and in a broader service sense.

The goal of appropriate vocational and avocational training for the handicapped can only be attained through the cooperative efforts of the family, regular and special education, agencies involved with the handicapped, and business and industry. The concluding chapter, therefore, describes the available services, areas of need, and problems in provision of services, keeping in mind the recent federal legislation mandating an expansion of vocational rehabilitation services to include the more severely handicapped.

12
RELATED SERVICES IN THE SCHOOLS

Barbara Connolly, Sara J. Odle, and Robert M. Anderson

The concepts of mainstreaming and least restrictive environment require that skilled ancillary personnel be available to assist the classroom teacher in meeting the needs of handicapped children in educational settings. For the purpose of this chapter, these ancillary or "related" services are defined as services, such as speech therapy, social work, and psychological services, which support educational programs and practices. While previous chapters focused primarily on teachers and classroom activities, this chapter emphasizes those professional responsibilities, other than teacher-oriented academic instruction, that are undertaken to ameliorate problems or in other ways support the education of handicapped children. Placement of these significant support services within a single chapter should not be interpreted as minimizing the value of their contributions to the education of the handicapped. Obviously, classroom teachers require a wide array of supportive professional resources, including both direct and indirect services, if the classroom program is to be effectively individualized. Frequent reference is made throughout this volume as to the part played by various professions and support service personnel in the provision of appropriate services to the handicapped.

Both state and federal legislation mandate public school provision of the gamut of services necessary to adequately educate handicapped children. Most public school systems, however, do not presently include all of these programs. Programs of related services now existing, moreover, are often inadequate, hampered by financial problems and other constraints that have long afflicted public school education, and sometimes staffed by individuals who do not have the training or experience to handle this new population of students. Many of these practitioners are presently as inadequately prepared and equipped to work with the handicapped in mainstream contexts as are the educators who are already bearing the brunt of this problem. Quite clearly, mainstreaming practices have significant implications for training of service delivery personnel, as well as for teacher use of such services.

Schools must make optimum use of psychologists, nurses, occupational and physical therapists, counselors, social workers, speech and language therapists and pathologists, audiologists, paraprofessionals, volunteers, and others if desired goals are to be achieved. Because of the closer working relationship with related service personnel made necessary because of mainstreaming, teachers and administrators must become knowledgeable about the roles and functions of each of the professions or services involved. This chapter, therefore, assists by describing the rapidly changing roles and contributions of the supportive personnel to which educators must turn for help in providing a total continuum of services for the handicapped. In addition, the chapter summarizes some of the trends and issues now challenging the various support disciplines and the schools as they attempt to provide an interface between the needs of the children and the available services.

SPEECH/LANGUAGE PATHOLOGY AND AUDIOLOGY

The American Speech-Language-Hearing Association (ASHA) defines these professions as follows:

> The professions of Speech-Language Pathology and Audiology are concerned with the study of human communication and its disorders. Professionals are devoted to the study and management of disorders, normal development, and cultural-ethnic influences in human communication. They provide clinical services for children and adults and conduct related basic and applied research.
>
> Speech-Language Pathologists concern themselves primarily with speech and language disorders; audiologists are concerned with hearing disorders. Nevertheless, these disorders are so interrelated that professional competency requires familiarity with all. Such terms as *speech correctionist* and *speech and hearing therapist* have been used to identify the workers in these professions. However, the American Speech and Hearing Association recommends the use of *Speech-Language Pathologist* (or Speech Clinician) and *Audiologist*. (ASHA, Note 2, p. 2).

High professional standards for certification of speech-language pathologists and audiologists are maintained by ASHA. The clinician certified by ASHA will have had at least master's level training, and will have demonstrated competency in clinical skills under close supervision (Perkins, 1971). After certification, the speech-language pathologist or audiologist may serve in a number of settings, including medical rehabilitation centers, vocational rehabilitation centers, community speech and hearing centers, hospitals, health departments, and public and private school systems. The mandates of PL 94-142 have made it imperative that services to the handicapped be expanded, thus greatly increasing the demand for school-based services.

Service Under PL 94-142

Dublinske and Healey (1978) provided a listing of services needed for identification and remediation of children with speech and language disorders:

> Speech-language pathology as defined in PL 94-142 includes:
> 1. identification of children with speech or language disorders.
> 2. diagnosis and appraisal of specific speech or language disorders.
> 3. referral for medical or other professional attention necessary for the habilitation of speech or language disorders.
> 4. provision of speech and language services for the habilitation or prevention of communicative disorders.
> 5. counseling and guidance of parents, children, and teachers regarding speech and language disorders.
>
> Audiology services include:
> 1. identification of children with hearing loss.
> 2. determination of the range, nature, and degree of hearing loss including referral for medical or other professional attention for the habilitation of hearing.
> 3. provision of habilitative activities such as language habilitation, auditory training, speechreading, hearing evaluation, and speech conversation.
> 4. creation and administration of programs for prevention of hearing loss.
> 5. counseling and guidance of pupils, parents, and teachers regarding hearing loss.
> 6. determination of the child's need for group and individual amplification, selection, and fitting an appropriate aid and evaluating the effectiveness of amplification (p. 191).

To meet the intent of PL 94-142, local education agencies must now provide these assessment and intervention services in the areas of speech-language pathology and audiology. According to the legislation, such services may be defined as either special education or as a related service. There appears to be some confusion about these definitions and their implications. Dublinske and Healey made this distinction:

> It is important to understand that, within the interpretation of these definitions, speech-language pathology and audiology are included under both "special education" and "related services." For example, if a child's primary handicap is speech or language impairment and the only specially designed instruction the child receives to meet his or her unique needs is speech-language pathology service, then the service is considered to be "special education." When the child's primary disability is considered to be a

handicap such as mental retardation, any speech-language pathology and audiology services provided to support the child while enrolled in a special class for the mentally retarded, for instance, are considered a "related service" (p. 191).

According to Dublinske and Healey, it is critical that speech-language pathology and audiology not be defined *only* as a related service because of possible problems related to program funding. This is an area of concern to the profession. Program administrators will need to consult state and federal guidelines regarding provision of speech-language and audiology services.

History and Early Trends

Few services for individuals with language, speech, or hearing disorders existed in America prior to the twentieth century. Earlier, provision of services to these handicapped in Europe had come about through the interest of the medical profession. In America, however, the disciplines of speech, psychology, and education led in the development of such services. Some public school systems initiated the provision of speech and hearing services in the 1920s. During this same period, university programs were developed for the preparation of clinicians in speech-language pathology and audiology, and the organization which was later to become the prestigious American Speech-Language-Hearing Association (ASHA) was founded.

The need for speech and hearing services in the schools was documented in 1931 by the results of a national school survey to determine the extent of such needs (West, 1966). This survey was one of the important outcomes of the 1930 White House Conference on Child Health and Protection, a major milestone in this nation's concern with the care of children. In the next decade, hearing, speech, and language training programs became an important part of rehabilitation services to veterans of World War II. Important advances in research, teaching techniques, and communication systems were made during this period.

During the 1950s and 1960s, a number of states recognized the needs of the communicatively handicapped, and passed legislation specifically directed at serving these needs. Federal legislation provided increased funding for training audiologists and speech-language pathologists. By the 1960s, approximately 4,500 speech clinicians were employed in the public schools. The clinicians' primary functions were to provide diagnostic and therapeutic services to children with handicaps (Wilson, 1961). However, mentally retarded children did not often receive services. The rationale for this exclusion was that the limited availability of services dictated their provision to those children with the most potential.

Apparent discrimination against other groups was pointed out by Nichols (1966), who stated that proportionately fewer children of minority groups received speech and hearing services even though the incidence of defects seemed higher among them. Very little investigation into treatment and remediation of speech problems of the cerebral palsied, mentally retarded, or children with delayed speech or language development was being reported during this period. In the school systems, the major role of the speech clinician was to carry out screening programs for speech and hearing problems, and to provide remediation in voice and articulation problems.

Growing Demand for Services

Ten percent of the American people suffer from some form of communication problem, according to an estimate by the National Institute of Neurological and Communicative Disorders and Stroke. The number of adults with speech and language disability as a result of stroke or cancer is increasing. While reliable statistics on the number of adults with speech and hearing problems are not available, the prevalence of communication problems among children can be more easily established. Table 1 gives the approximate percentages of school-age children with serious problems.

Several factors other than the mandatory legislation have contributed to the growing demand for speech-language services. The public has become more aware of the effects of early deprivation on language and speech development, and of other factors which influence the need for diagnostie and remedial programs. Expanded Medicare and Medicaid coverage of speech and hearing services has placed such help within reach of many who previously could not afford these services.

Table 1.   Approximate percentages of school age children with speech problems

Problem	Percentage of children with serious problem
Articulation	3.0
Stuttering	0.8
Voice	0.2
Cleft palate speech	0.1
Cerebral palsy speech	0.1
Retarded speech development	0.3
Speech problem related to hearing loss	0.5

Source: Adapted from the American Speech and Hearing Association and Bureau of Education for the Handicapped data, 1972 estimate (Lundeen, 1972, p. 158).

Progress toward meeting the increased need for professionals in the field of communication services was made possible by passage in 1973 of PL 94-484, the Health Professions Educational Assistance Act, which provided funds for grants and contracts in speech-language pathology and audiology. Training in the profession is now being offered in more than 300 colleges and universities in the United States, with more than 6,000 master's degree graduates each year (ASHA, Note 2).

The Speech Clinician in the School

The speech clinician in the public schools will be concerned with problems other than oral speech defects. For some children, the clinician's emphasis will be on vocabulary building, language concepts, and syntax. For a more severely handicapped child, the immediate and ultimate goal may be the acquisition of functional, needs-communicating words (Van Hattum, 1978). The roles of the speech clinician include those of clinician, consultant, counselor, and member of an educational team. As a clinician, the therapist provides assessment, diagnosis, and evaluation of each child's speech, language, and/or hearing disorder. Following evaluation, a program must be designed that is appropriate for the child. In particular, the clinician must be aware of the intellectual range of the child and work within his/her range of abilities.

The role of consultant is assuming more importance for the speech clinician in the public schools. The classroom teacher may need information on normal speech and language development and on identification of children who should be referred for assessment. The clinician can also assist the teacher by suggesting activities to facilitate language development and speech production, both for the class as a whole and for individual children needing such stimulation or remediation. In the area of special education, the teacher may need help in determining the relationship between the child's verbal communication disorders and overall learning problems. Speech and language problems are associated with many other handicapping conditions, so the speech clinician will often be included as a member of the team planning a child's individualized education program (IEP).

Eisenson and Ogilvie (1977) stated that the speech clinician must have the ability to

1. Identify accurately and efficiently those individuals who exhibit disorders of speech, language and/or hearing
2. Plan a program of remediation for each individual
3. Carry through this program effectively, modifying the speech and language behaviors of these children

4. Evaluate in an organized fashion the effectiveness of the program
5. Plan and supervise the activities of the aide or aides that the school assigns
6. Serve as a resource teacher for the classroom teacher for stimulating language development and for the learning disabilities specialist in the prevention and intervention of language disorders
7. Interpret a child's speech problems for his parents
8. Function usefully as a member of the learning disabilities team and to determine the nature, etiology and severity of the specific handicaps of those children with language handicaps
9. Program one's own continual professional growth through association activities, attendance at summer schools and additional reading
10. Distinguish between language differences such as dialectual speech and language disorders
11. Measure results of one's own speech, language and/or hearing strategies in the treatment of these disorders
12. Measure data collected from the program against the published data (p. 36)

Speech Clinician–Classroom Teacher Relationships

Children with speech and language problems will benefit greatly from the establishment of a close working relationship between the speech clinician and the classroom teacher. The speech clinician has the responsibility for providing information to the teacher about a specific child's problems, the objectives of treatment, and ways in which the teacher can provide positive support and reinforcement for the remediation program being initiated by the clinician. The speech clinician and the classroom teacher also have mutual concerns for the general improvement and refinement of speech skills of all children, including development of vocabulary, syntaxical skills, and increase of oral output. The teacher can profit from consultation with the clinician about appropriate activities for the stimulation of speech and language in the classroom.

Referrals of children for assessment by the school-based speech clinician are usually initiated by the teacher, who should be able to recognize problems which require referral. Provision by the clinician of guidelines for referral, with examples of the types of speech and language problems, can aid the teacher in making appropriate referrals.

The teacher should also have some knowledge of the normal development of speech and of the various speech and language disorders. Such knowledge is an important prerequisite for the systematic teaching of children with learning disorders and for the general improvement of communication skills in the classroom.

Garber (1969) summarized the role of the classroom teacher of speech and hearing impaired children:

1. Accept the child and help his classmates accept him.
2. Make sure that the classroom invites communication.
3. Foster good relationships among the children.
4. Be cooperative.
5. Take the necessary steps to make his own speech and voice worthy of imitation.
6. Hear accurately the speech errors his children make.
7. Have accurate knowledge of how the sounds of our speech are produced.
8. Create a good speech environment for speech and language improvement.
9. Be cognizant of the values of speech and hearing services.
10. Be able to identify students in his class who need the speech clinician service.
11. Understand normal speech and language development and concepts.
12. Be well informed on how to incorporate the objectives of the speech and language program with the objectives of the regular classroom curricula (p. 68).

The Changing Role of the Speech Clinician

Children in the public schools who need speech services have traditionally been served by an itinerant speech therapist or clinician, each child typically receiving a 30 minute lesson twice a week. The clinician's case load and travel schedule has interfered with desired communication between the classroom teacher and clinician. Speech therapy scheduling now seems to be moving toward provision of services based on the extent of the child's needs as well as on availability of the clinician's time (Meyen, 1978). The changing role of the speech therapist was described by Hallahan and Kauffman (1978):

> In years past, many or most of the cases seen by clinicians in public schools were children with mild articulation problems were quick to respond to therapy. However, the current trend is toward having clinicians in public schools serve fewer children and work more intensively with those children who are more severely handicapped. More and more, the role of the clinician is that of a thoroughly trained resource person who can serve the more severely handicapped children while at the same time directing and assisting regular and special education teachers and professional aides in carrying out corrective programs for children with mild handicaps. Many children with mild and moderate speech and language disorders will be found in regular classrooms. Most children who have severe or profound disabilities (e.g., those considered severely or profoundly retarded or disturbed), if they attend the public schools, will be placed in special classes. The speech clinician may be expected to serve as a resource person regardless of where the children are placed in the schools for which he or she has responsibility (pp. 266–267).

The speech-language pathology and audiology professions are rapidly developing in provision of services, in training of personnel, and in the area of research. Areas that are seen by Lilly (1979) as receiving special emphasis during the next decade include 1) an increase in service to the severely and profoundly handicapped, emphasizing communication rather than speech, 2) concern with the communication problems of the elderly, 3) interdisciplinary cooperation to improve services in special education, and 4) an increased availability of speech services.

SCHOOL PSYCHOLOGY

Traditional Role

The development of school psychology is closely related to the development of special education. As early as 1871, special classes were developed for children who were unable to perform in the regular classroom. The children were usually selected for these special classes by someone who had a knowledge of child development and who was able to identify special children. However, the discipline of school psychology was not identified until 1896, when a paper proposing a scheme of practical work in psychology was presented to the American Psychological Association (Fein, 1974). One justification for the inclusion of psychologists in the schools was that they were needed in the selection of children for the special education classes. Another strong argument was the development during that period of testing instruments for children, including the adapted Binet Scales (Herron, Green, Guild, Smith, & Kantor, 1970). Even with these strong reasons for the use of psychologists in the schools, the first official school psychologist in the United States was not employed until 1915. Interestingly, Dr. Arnold L. Gesell, who later authored a number of well known books on child development, was this first school psychologist.

By 1938, 35 states were providing services through child guidance clinics to the disturbed or educationally handicapped child in the schools (Fein, 1974). The need for school psychologists continued to grow. In 1954, the Thayer Conference was held to define the role of the school psychologist and state recommendations for training and functions of school psychological personnel. The school psychologist was defined at this conference as "a psychologist with training and experience in education. He uses his specialized knowledge of assessment, learning and interpersonal relationships to assist school personnel to enrich the experience and growth of all children and to recognize and deal with exceptional children" (Herron et al., 1970, p. 4). The Thayer Conference, in this first delineation of the role of the school psychologist, presented a new aspect of functioning to the school psychologist who, prior to that time, had been generally restricted to testing children, writing reports, and making treatment referrals. The functions of the school psychologist were described as:

1. Measuring and interpreting the intellectual, social and emotional development of children
2. Identifying exceptional children and collaborating in the planning of appropriate educational and social placements and programs
3. Developing ways to facilitate the learning and adjustments of children
4. Diagnosing educational and personal disabilities and collaborating in the planning of re-educational programs (Herron et al, p. 4).

Competencies

The role and functioning of the psychologist in any school system may be determined by the system's specific requirements or its financial constraints; it may also be defined by the individual psychologist and his/her own competencies and interests. The psychologist's function and services will also be determined to a great extent by the attitudes and preferences of those who work with him/her. Competencies are required in individual and group assessment, individual and group intervention procedures, the consultation process, and ecological assessment and intervention. In addition, the psychologist must understand the roles of others with whom he/she will have to work, both in the schools and the community. The psychologist should have knowledge of strategies to assist the school administration and staff in evaluating the effectiveness of the school in meeting the needs of the pupils and the community. The psychologist must be familiar with curricula and with curricular innovations, have a knowledge of instructional methods and materials in basic subject areas, be able to suggest remedial techniques in planning instructional programs, and be able to assist in planning classroom structure (Tennessee State Board of Education, 1975).

Pielstick (1970) defined the truly competent school psychologist of the present as one who is capable of adapting to emerging changes in the field, and who is also capable of influencing the direction of these changes. The doctoral level psychologist serves at a policy making level, may plan curricula, effects behavior change, does research, supervises other psychological personnel, and effects attitude changes in the school staff, parents and the community (Fein, 1974).

Not all states require the highest level degree in psychology or school psychology for state certification as a school psychologist, but the doctoral degree is required by many school systems as a condition for employment in this position. There are eligibility requirements for state licensure that must be met. Duties of the school psychologist typically include the following: supervision of staff (including trainees or interns); individual, group and/or family therapy; consultation on psychological matters with administrative staff, teachers, parents, and personnel from other helping agencies; diagnostic evaluation of referred learning and/or socio-emotional adjustment problems; providing inservice programs; and participation in the development and implementation of preventive mental health activities within the school system (Memphis City Schools, Note 5).

Other positions in the area of school psychological services include those of the psychological examiner and the psychometrist. The psychological examiner, or psychological services worker, is generally required to have a master's degree in psychology or educational psychology, and must meet state eligibility requirements for licensure and/or certification for this position. The psychological services worker will generally work under the supervision of a psychologist to provide psychological services to referred pupils with learning or adjustment problems. His/her duties may include conducting intensive diagnostic work-ups in children with learning or adjustment problems; consulting with teachers, parents, principals, out-of-school agencies, and other psychological and counseling personnel; engaging in psychological counseling with children and parents; participating at the request of other departments in the development of suitable educational programs for pupils with special needs, interpreting and reporting educational and psychological diagnostic findings; participating in pilot programs and/or related research; and participating in inservice training programs (Memphis City Schools, Note 5).

Minimum qualifications for the position of psychometrist include a bachelor's degree in psychology or educational psychology. Advanced degrees and/or experience in related areas such as counseling and special education are desirable. Examples of the duties of the psychometrist are: assessment of children's learning or adjustment problems; administration and scoring of individual intelligence, achievement, and objective personality tests; collection and reporting of observational and test data; under appropriate supervision, conducting individual and group counseling, and participating in inservice training programs (Memphis City Schools, Note 5).

The Psychologist as Consultant

Parents and teachers too often visualize the role of the school psychologist as only that of a "gatekeeper" for special education

(Sabatino, 1972), determining eligibility for special class placement through a brief diagnostic appraisal. Passage of PL 94-142 has given the psychologist a more positive role in the education of the exceptional child. Psychological testing does in most states remain a legal prerequisite to provision of special education services. These tests are administered to help determine whether a child needs special class placement or additional assistance while remaining in the regular classroom. In addition to this function, the psychologist is now recognized as a facilitator of learning by school children, working with teachers in the interests of children (Cartwright, Cartwright, & Ysseldyke, 1973). His/her role is visualized by Tolbert (1978) as being expanded to include "participation in planning programs for special education pupils, and helping make the classroom situation productive for all who can participate in it" (p. 195).

Teachers today are having to cope with a larger variety of behavioral and learning problems. The most advocated role of the school psychologist has therefore become that of a consultant working with those in direct contact with children (Herron et al., 1970; Waters, 1973; Williams, 1972). Findings of one survey on perceptions of school psychologists by school personnel were that 1) psychologists were doing more consultation than individual evaluation of children, and 2) school personnel preferred these consulting activities to psychometric activities (Waters, 1973). The psychologist as a consultant takes the role that increases the teacher's skills and competencies rather than working directly with the children (Lebovitz, 1968). The psychologist is involved in three general types of consultation: interpretation of test scores or of behavior, defining particular action needed in a situation or finding help for the teacher, and, in crisis consultation, helping the teacher who is unable to deal effectively with a child (Herron et al., 1970). Behavior management is one area in which the school psychologist is becoming increasingly involved as a consultant, helping the teacher either to increase desired behaviors in children within the classroom or decrease undesired behaviors. The psychologist may observe in the classroom and help the teacher develop behavioral assessment materials, may assist in development of instructional strategies that relate to the assessment material, and may aid the teacher in implementation of the program (Stephens, 1970).

A Spectrum of Services

The greatly expanded role of school psychological services is demonstrated in the following description of the services provided in a metropolitan school system. The Mental Health Center of the Memphis,

Tennessee, City School System (MCSMHC) also functions as one of the state Mental Health Centers, offering psychological services and other kinds of mental health services. The staff currently includes 69 credentialed and qualified psychologists, psychological service workers, school social workers, alcohol and drug workers, and psychometrists. Reasons for referral to MCSMHC include aberration of intellectual functioning, developmental retardation, giftedness, learning difficulties, school achievement, social-emotional-behavioral adjustment, family conflicts, home and/or community environment, physical disability, alcohol/drug abuse, and others. A wide variety of services are provided by MCSMCH, including:

a) Diagnosis (psychological and social)
b) Individual, group, and family therapy
c) Consultation (principals, teachers, parents, other agencies)
d) Work with board suspended students
e) Alcohol and drug abuse counseling
f) Alcohol and drug abuse prevention programs
g) Behavior management programs
h) Parent study groups (to assist parents in understanding and dealing with their child's special problems in learning disabilities, emotional disturbances, etc.)
i) Staff development activities for Memphis City Schools staff (topics include Behavior Management, Adolescents, Learning Disabilities, Child Abuse, Communications Skills, etc.) (Memphis City Schools, Note 4)

One area of service provision to which MCSMHC devotes considerable time and effort is that of classroom management. In some instances staff works with individual teachers to design a classroom management program which meets their needs. Other strategies may involve staff assuming control of the classroom and demonstrating specific management techniques to the teacher. Workshops for teachers and administrators combine the theoretical basis for classroom management with specific examples of how to apply it. Goals of the programs have been to improve student behaviors and to improve teachers' skills in classroom management. Success of the program has been documented in all grades, kindergarten through twelfth grade, in

1) Providing the teacher with effective methods of dealing with problem situations, thus
   a) reducing and/or eliminating discipline problems
   b) reducing the number of teacher-student conflicts and confrontations
2) Helping to create an environment conducive to
   a) effective teaching and learning
   b) good mental health of students and teachers

3) Increasing the average daily attendance
4) Reducing home and board suspensions (Memphis City Schools, Note 4).

Psychologist-Teacher Relationships

Results of a study conducted by Herron et al., (1970) showed that teachers want more from psychologists than just the scores on psychological tests. Good psychological reports were defined as those that answered the referral questions clearly and concisely, and included a variety of specific suggestions for dealing with the problem. Teachers also felt that the psychologist who had a knowledge of classroom procedures was able to provide more specific and meaningful recommendations.

The psychologist expects the teacher to be able to screen children educationally and behaviorally, to be aware of behavioral and learning problems within the classroom, and to ask for assistance as needed (Sabatino, 1972). The teacher should expect from the psychologist 1) a profile of the child's present functioning, 2) a diagnostic and explanatory summary, and if necessary 3) a method of reinforcement for use in behavior management of the child (Sabatino, 1972). The psychologist may then assist the teacher in developing approaches that will enhance the child's present learning and behavioral strengths and will establish new strengths.

Both the psychologist and the teacher affect the welfare of the individual child. Both have the improvement of the child's abilities as a goal. An additional goal of the psychologist in working with the teacher is to help the teacher develop confidence in his/her own abilities and to increase his/her expertise in the management of children. However, many teachers see the psychologist as someone critical of their ability to manage the classroom. To resolve this problem, the psychologist should communicate acknowledgment of the teacher's role as a competent professional concerned with helping the individual child.

ELEMENTARY GUIDANCE COUNSELOR

Traditional Role

Guidance had its beginnings in the social reform movements of the early 1900s, as part of an effort to "institute and upgrade help for young people . . . wanting to live productive lives and escape from poverty and wretched working-conditions" (Tolbert, 1978, p. 56). The focus of guidance programs for a number of years was on vocational assessment and placement. This strong emphasis on occupational information and guidance continued through the 1930s and into the 1940s. In schools, the dual role of the teacher-counselor was common. There was little agreement as to needed competencies, and professional and personal qualifications of counselors were often minimal.

The National Defense Education Act of 1958 included provision for funds to expand and upgrade guidance personnel training and to improve school guidance programs and facilities (Dimick & Huff, 1970). At this time most of the counseling programs were in secondary schools. There was a growing concern in regard to the preparation and function of the elementary counselor; however, little effort was made to differentiate between elementary and secondary school functions of the counselor in their preparatory programs or in their school roles. The 1965 extension of the National Defense Education Act did provide funding for the training of elementary school counselors. The Elementary and Secondary School Education Act of 1965 also supported the concept of the elementary counselor.

The inappropriateness of the traditional high school counselor role in working with elementary school children had become apparent as soon as counselors began working with this population (Brown, 1977). There was an evident need for identification of goals, functions, skills, and training necessary to effectively meet the needs of elementary school age children. A task force was created in 1965 by the Association for Counselor Educators and Supervisors (ACES) and the American School Counselors Association (ASCA) to define the role of the elementary school counselor. Members of the committee included school counselors, counselor supervisors, and counselor educators. The guidelines for the development of elementary school counseling and guidance programs that were formulated through their efforts became a statement of policy (ACES-ASCA Joint Committee, 1966), which was endorsed by the American Personnel and Guidance Association (APGA) in 1969.

The guidance counselor had been long thought of as a crisis counselor; it has been only since the definition of this role by the ACES-ASCA Task Force (1966) that the guidance counselor has been recognized as a developmental counselor, working with all children, and as a consultant and coordinator as well (Brown, 1977). The functioning of the counselor in these three roles was described in the ACES-ASCA policy statement:

> A. *Counseling*: It is the premise of this statement that counseling both individually and in small group situations can provide assistance to children in the normal process of growing up as they seek to understand themselves, meet the developmental tasks of childhood, learn effectively, and develop

realistic self-concepts. Emphasis is on the child as a learner in the school situation.

1. *Individual counseling* is the process of establishing with the child a relationship which enables him to communicate his needs, to explore his feelings, to learn about himself, to set goals and develop self direction in moving toward these goals. Often the child is trying to communicate his need for help and this provides an opportunity for the counselor to develop a greater understanding of the child and to become more sensitive to the child's needs. Such counseling is not necessarily a communication of words on the part of the child. The content of the counseling process will reflect the developmental level of the child and may be through play media rather than verbal communication. The counselor represents to the child a non-evaluative adult in a helping relationship.

2. *Group counseling* is the process of establishing relationships with a small group of children enabling them to communicate with the counselor and each other certain identified needs. Such counseling is particularly helpful in personal and social growth as children have an opportunity to react and interact and to work out some of their behavioral changes. Group counseling provides a major learning experience in human relations.

B. *Consultation* is the process of sharing with another person or group of persons information and ideas, of combining knowledge into new patterns, and of making mutually agreed upon decisions about the next steps needed. The Counselor as a professional person with a background in child growth and development and the behavioral sciences helps parents to grow in understanding of their children in the school situation. He may provide insight for the parent about the child's potential, his motivation, and his unmet needs. In turn the Counselor learns from parents about their children and offers them a chance to express their feelings about the child and the school.

C. *Coordination* is the process of relating all efforts for helping the child into a meaningful pattern. The Counselor member of the school staff coordinates the organized effort of the school and community for the individual child as a learner in the school situation. Coordination is the method used to bring into focus the school's total effort in the child's behalf, eliminating duplication of effort and ensuring follow-through on decisions made and policies established. This involves close working relationships between the counselor, teacher, parent, and other school and community personnel whose contacts with the child in the school situation are significant. (ACES-ASCA Joint Committee, 1966).

Competencies

All states require that the school counselor be certified, licensed, or hold a counseling endorsement on a teaching certificate (Tolbert, 1978). Certification is obtained through a recognized master's level program. Certification requirements vary from state to state, and standards differ in scope and nature. Competencies needed by the counselor to effectively perform the three functions listed in the ACES-ASCA Statement of Policy are considered by Brown (1977) to be:

1. Depth of knowledge in:
    child growth and development
    theories of counseling
    group dynamics
    interpersonal relations
    psychology of learning
    personality dynamics
    curriculum of the elementary school
2. Background and understanding in:
    community and culture
    elementary school program
    curriculum trends and developments
    basic goals of guidance
    organization of pupil personnel services
    research procedures
    reading program
    world of work
3. Specialized skill in:
    observation and interpretation of behavior, particularly the interpreta-
    tion of feeling from nonverbal behavior
    consultation with parents
    counseling—individually and with groups
    interpretation of the methods by which children communicate their
    needs
    use of toys, art, and other media for communicating with the child
    case conferences and case records
    statistics
    educational measurements
    psychological testing
    organization and administration of guidance services (p. 12)

Bernard and Fullmer (1977) summarized descriptions by other authors of the counselor-consultant in listing five major work areas:

(1) working with children for assessment, placement, and individual and group counseling; (2) working with principals and teachers conducting conferences and inservice courses, and interpreting the objectives of the pupil personnel program; (3) working with other school personnel, such as instructional materials managers, librarians, nurses, reading consultants, and speech therapists; (4) working with parents to consider educational programs and problems, counseling with parents, organizing workshops and discussion groups, and interpreting pupil personnel services; and (5) working with community agencies on referrals, participating in staff conferences, and being active in professional organizations (p. 223).

The role of guidance was also conceptualized in terms of the people for whom services are provided (Bernard & Fullmer, 1977):

Services for *all* pupils:
  (a) Orientation of new pupils (formal)
  (b) Evaluation of potential

(c) Evaluation of past performance
(d) Evaluation of articulation of pupils from school to school and level to level
(e) Group guidance for information-sharing activities

Services for *individual* pupils:

(a) One-to-one counseling or counseling in groups with emphasis on group interaction processes
(b) Individual child study (clinical approach)
(c) Information about the environment
(d) Placement of the individual in groups for instruction
(e) Placement of the individual in job or college

Services for *teachers*:

(a) Deal with referrals from teachers
(b) Participate in classroom with teachers
(c) Cooperate in dealing with parents

Services for *administrators*:

(a) Curriculum development
(b) Community liason (information only)

Research services for *school and community*:

(a) Survey of the community for occupational placement
(b) Follow-up of students to assess effectiveness of guidance program (pp. 8–9)

Teachers, administrators, pupils and parents can and should actively participate in any guidance program. The school, home, and community must work together in many guidance-related activities in order to receive full benefit from such services. Both teachers and parents must understand, accept, and work with any program in order for it to be effective. The counselor will need to actively plan for and promote positive attitudes and cooperation on the part of the school staff, the parents, and the community (Tolbert, 1978).

An Exemplary Program

The following description of a school guidance program, written for distribution to faculty, parents, and interested members of the community in which the school is located, is included as being representative of elementary school guidance services today:

Welcome to the Campus School Guidance Program

At Campus School we believe that an elementary school should provide a wide variety of experiences to meet the total needs of children. No longer can we concentrate only on developing academic potential of children. Now we must work to nourish a multi-dimensional child whose intellectual, social, physical, creative, artistic, and affective needs are met.

Through our Guidance Program we are attempting to provide the affective education component that will work with the other school programs to produce a well-rounded, fully developed child. Our Guidance Program philosophy is based on the following premises:

1. All children have worth and need to feel accepted and productive and that they have control over their lives.
2. Children develop at different rates, and individual differences should be recognized.
3. Children need to try out different roles, and they need to learn how to cope with the negative results of the roles they try.
4. A guidance program should be "prevention-oriented" rather than merely "crisis-centered."

Major Objectives of Campus Guidance Program

1. To help each child develop his/her full potential intellectually, socially, emotionally, and physically.
2. To encourage the development of a positive and realistic self-concept for each child.
3. To provide counseling services to children, parents, and teachers.
4. To consult with parents, school and community personnel regarding the needs of students.
5. To help integrate the resources of the school and the community in order to meet the individual needs of the children.
6. To aid in developing a better understanding of our changing environment and the world of work.
7. To keep accurate records of individual student progress and to make these readily available to qualified school personnel and other appropriate persons.

Implementation of the Guidance Concept

One full-time counselor has the major responsibility for the guidance program. The counselor works with teachers, parents, and staff in assessing student needs and in meeting them through individual counseling, small group counseling, and group guidance meetings. Students also are encouraged to come to the guidance center on a self-referral basis. The counselor also serves as Coordinator of PACE (Positive Affective and Creative Enrichment), which is a program designed to develop positive self-concepts. The Department of Guidance and Personnel at M.S.U. offers a valuable source of materials and consultants to augment the program. They also assist the guidance programs by providing us with exceptionally qualified graduate assistants and practicum students who help increase the quantity and quality of our services. The Guidance Department and the Special Education Department of the Board of Education are additional useful resources in helping meet the needs of children. In addition, a Mental Health Center worker is available to the counselor for regular consultation concerning special student needs.

Typical Problems Handled by the Guidance Counselor

Peer Relationships—The counselor works individually with these children, in small friendship clubs or in larger group settings.

Poor Self-Concept—Through small groups, PACE, Hobby Window, and advisee groups, the counselor works to improve positive feelings about self.

Educational Problems—The counselor consults with the student, his/her teacher, and his/her parents to help assess learning difficulties. These problems include underachievement, overachievement, and special needs for enrichment.

Physical Problems—The counselor works with the administration, teachers, parents, and students to identify physical problems and to help students adjust to them.

Selected Activities of the Guidance Program

Advisor/Advisee Program: A classroom affective education program for all students run by teachers and coordinated by the counselor.

PACE Clubs: Small group activities for development of creativity and positive self-concept.

Friendship Clubs: Small group meetings to develop friendship.

Birthday Card Display: Each child's birthday is publicly recognized.

Hobby Window: Individual recognition of student hobbies.

In conclusion, we at Campus School feel strongly that for children to excel, be productive, and feel fulfilled they must feel good about themselves. Therefore, in many different ways the Guidance Program is trying to offer our students opportunities that will help them feel like saying, "I'm glad I'm me!" (Williamson, Note 7)

Implications of PL 94-142

Aubrey (1978) emphasized the change passage of PL 94-142 is making in the role of the counselor, stating that implementation of its provisions "will challenge and extend the content repertoire of any counselor and require new sources of knowledge and expertise" (p. 353). Implications of the law for the counselor were also pointed out by Sproles, Panther, and Lanier (1978). These authors emphasized that additional training, both in upgrading of skills and in new areas, will be needed for the profession to fully meet the challenge presented in implementing this legislation.

Skills that counselors already possess can help greatly in achieving the goals of PL 94-142. Bernard and Fullmer (1977) gave three ways in which the counselor-consultant may help alleviate problems arising from implementation of PL 94-142: 1) helping special teachers by counseling students, 2) counseling the regular teachers who have exceptional students, and 3) counseling parents of exceptional students.

Tobert (1978) stated that PL 94-194 is of major concern to school counselors, who "will be involved in helping to make the classroom situation as profitable as possible for the handicapped who can be accomodated, in diagnostic and referral services, in planning parent-approved individual special education programs, and other related duties" (p. 39).

One area in which counseling-consulting skills will be especially helpful is that of attitudes toward the mainstreaming program. Sproles et al. (1978) listed important points to consider:

1. The regular teachers' apprehension and resentment of having handicapped children added to their classes;
2. The special education teacher's input into the regular teachers' operation;
3. Resentment toward special education teachers' small classes, abundant materials, and seemingly more flexible schedules;
4. Parents of the handicapped children becoming involved in their children's education (apprehensions for parents, students, and teachers can arise);
5. Apprehensions and resentments about the material, personnel, and extra time required for exceptional students, their parents, and the community;
6. Apprehensions of regular students and handicapped students as they integrate; and
7. Resentment of all adults for the increased paperwork and legal formalities required by PL 94-142 (p. 212)

In the past, counselors and special education teachers have seldom interacted. Mainstreaming of the exceptional child now makes it imperative that the counselor, the special education teacher, and the regular classroom teacher collaborate in helping *every* child develop to his/her potential.

SCHOOL SOCIAL WORKER

Traditional Role

Social work in the schools had its beginnings in the 1900s, in the cities of New York, Boston, and Hartford. During this early period, the social workers were employed by private agencies or civic organizations, rather than by the school system. The first employment by a school system of a social worker was in 1913. Influences which brought about the employment of school social workers were

(1) the passage of the compulsory school attendance laws
(2) new knowledge about individual differences among children and their capacity to respond in improved environments
(3) the realization of the strategic place of school and education in the lives of children and youth (Costin, 1969, p. 440).

One of the early duties of the social worker was directly related to the passage of the compulsory school laws, social workers becoming known as school attendance officers. Many professionals at the time of the compulsory school attendance laws passage felt that nonattendance at school was linked to social ills such as poverty, low wage levels, illiteracy, and ill health. It was felt that the social worker could contribute information about the truant child's environment. The social worker also served as a liaison with the parents, explaining the demands of the school and the difficulties and needs of their child.

The 1920s brought an expansion of the role of the social worker to the field of child maladjustment, including juvenile delinquency. Social workers at this time were often known as visiting teachers because of the increased time spent in the students' homes. Functions of the visiting teacher or social worker involved helping the child's family use resources in the community, working directly with the parents in relationship to the child, and interpreting the child or his/her environment to the school (Oppenheimer, 1925). None of the functions involved working directly with the child. The importance of working with the child and helping him/her deal with emotional reactions to experiences at school was not recognized until the late 1920s, when the social worker was enlisted to work with the diagnosing and treatment of "difficult" children or children with "nervous conditions."

The depression of the 1930s and World War II contributed to the lack of growth in the profession of school social work in the 1930s and 1940s. However, Costin (1969) reported that existing programs changed from "the image of authority or involvement with law enforcement duties such as attendance and emphasis was given to the goal of happy wholesome childhood for all children" (p. 445). Increased interest was shown in the establishment of trusting and accepting relationships between the social worker and the child. Work with parents also continued, with emphasis on helping parents perceive and share the school's concern for the child.

Taber (1954) identified several practices within the school systems at that time which often impeded the establishment of a productive relationship between the social worker, the parent, and the school:

1. The robbing of children of their individuality in the classroom
2. The failure of the school to adapt programs to the individual even though the importance of adapting educational programs to individual needs had been recognized
3. The confusion and vacillation over discipline in the schools, and
4. The lack of parent-teacher relationships in many schools

The utilization in the late 1950s of the social worker as a consultant to the teacher and the school administrator was aimed at remedying some of the ills Taber identified. Knowledge of the child and his/her environment allowed the social worker to play a consultive role both to teachers about children in their classrooms and to the school administrator about school conditions that impinged on the well-being of the student.

The 1960s brought an expansion of services from the field of social work into the schools, and the 1970s produced even more changes in the role of the social worker. The need to establish effective relationships with other pupil personnel services was recognized. Interdisciplinary teams came into being to assist in the coordination of all services to the child. Practitioners were urged to develop new and innovative ways of working with children and their families. The need for establishing child-school-community relationships was recognized as being important in the child's overall functioning. Meyer (1973) summarized the challenge to the social worker by emphasizing that even though the worker had the skills necessary to deal with intrafamily relationships, he/she needed also to learn how to deal with other relationships in the child's environment—the parents' landlord, the parents' employer, the child's teacher, and all significant others.

Competencies

The term *school social worker* may be used in different school systems to describe those with bachelor's degrees in social work, master's degrees in other fields, usually counseling and guidance, or master's degrees in social work (Alderson & Krishef, 1973). Some states require that school social workers have a master's degree in social work plus education courses and practicums (Ellis & Bryant, 1976). In addition to these minimal requirements, many states are now specifying that the degree must be obtained from a college or university with an approved competency-based program in social work. Competencies considered most important for the school social worker are in the areas of intervention skills, problem-solving skills, collaborative skills, consultation skills, and community organization skills (Ellis & Bryant, 1976). A wide range of knowledge is needed to fulfill these competencies, including information about school and community politics and power structures, financial policies within the school system and how they affect the social work program, negative and positive aspects of school subcultures, and sociological issues that affect the equality of education (Costin, 1975).

There is much overlap in the contemporary roles and functions of the guidance counselor and the school social worker, both as described in the professional literature and in actual school situations. In schools having one or the other, functions and responsibilities merge. Many smaller systems have neither. School psychologists, mental health centers, public health departments, social workers from other organizations providing human services, volunteer organizations, and concerned and involved teachers and parents perform, at varying times, the functions of counselor and social worker.

Emerging Role

The emerging role of the social worker encompasses aspects of the traditional role as well as new roles. Costin (1969) surveyed a number of social workers and found that they provided services to teachers, children, administrators, parents, and the community. A similar study in 1975 showed that the services identified by Costin in 1969 were still being provided but with different emphasis (Meares, 1977). The changing emphasis was attributed to:

1. New role definitions for the social worker
2. Increased social work resources with varying levels of competencies
3. New demands on the school systems brought about by integration, inflation, high dropout rates, and urban ghettos, and
4. Increased concern for individualizing programs for children.

The study conducted by Meares pinpointed seven major tasks performed by the social worker of today: 1) preliminary tasks to the provision of school social work services, 2) assessing the child's problems, 3) educational counseling with the child and his parents, 4) clarifying the child's problems to others, 5) facilitating school-community-pupil relations, 6) facilitating the utilization of community resources, and 7) leadership and policy making.

Preliminary Tasks   These would include explaining the nature and scope of social work to the administration. A study done in the late 1960s showed that confusion existed at the administrative level about the role of the social worker (Costin, 1969). Superintendents of schools interviewed saw the social worker as:

(1)   investigating homes and neighborhoods
(2)   assisting in the collection of background material for the psychologist when mental retardation was suspected in the child
(3)   preparing summaries of cases being transferred to other social agencies
(4)   serving on community agencies
(5)   providing information for teachers' meetings
(6)   acquiring social and personal data for principals and teachers to be utilized for increased effectiveness of educational procedures (p. 450)

The superintendents did not view major social work activities as including direct work with pupils, consultation with teachers on improving classroom procedures, changing school policies and procedures, and negotiations with families and agencies to solve certain problems.

The social worker should come to an agreement with the administration prior to the initiation of services as to the goals and objectives of the social work program. Once an agreement is made, appropriate referrals for services can be made and misunderstandings about suitability of referrals can be avoided.

Assessing the Child's Problem   The school social worker is called upon when data concerning home life are needed or when help for the family seems indicated. He/she is usually a member of the interdisciplinary team organized to evaluate, diagnose, and make recommendations for the child's educational program, providing information on the child's relationship with parents and siblings, the parents' relationships with each other and their children, conditions within the home such as financial and employment status, and the family's relationships with other families within the community. As such information may not be available to other members of the assessment team, the social worker is able to help the team see the child's problems in terms of the child's total environment. Once the evaluation has been completed, the social worker's ongoing relationship with the child and his/her parents helps ensure the compliance of the family with the recommendations made by the evaluating team.

Educational Counseling with Child and Parents   Counseling with the parents, with the child, and with the parents and child together is an important role for the school social worker. Prior to the counseling, however, the worker must know what the school expects of the parents and of the student. Open communication with the teachers and the administrators must be maintained throughout the time spent with the child and the child's parents to provide feedback to the worker on the effects of the program.

In the counseling sessions, the social worker must be able to offer support to both parents and child even though they may have different perspectives on topics such as poor performance or misbehavior at school (Moynihan, 1978). Prior conferences with the teacher help the social worker to be familiar with the child's particular strengths and weaknesses. In counseling with the parents, the worker must be able to see the child from their point of view but must also be able to present the child's point of view to the parent.

Clarifying the Child's Problems to Others   The social worker has the responsibility to learn as much as possible from all sources about the student to be served. Sources will include the parents, the school personnel, and people and organizations within the community. The social worker then must synthesize all information into an accurate picture of the child and the child's problem and be able to explain the child to those around him/her. The social worker must act as an advocate for the child in those situations where the child cannot speak for himself/herself. The worker can explain to the teacher those conditions within the child's home and community environment that influence the child's classroom behavior. The social worker can also explain the child's school problems to parents who may be intimidated by their lack of familiarity with the school system.

Consultation with school administrators on pupil welfare and policy formulation is appropriate for the social worker, who is able to provide information to the administrator about environmental and community conditions that will affect policies with the school. The social worker is also becoming more of an advocate for the child in matters of school policy and procedures, being able to view the changes from the child's point of view and respond to the administration on the part of the children being affected by the changes.

Facilitating School-Community-Pupil Relations   Activities involved in this area pertain to the betterment of relationships in the school-community-pupil triad. The social worker must first assess the relationship by studying and evaluating ways in which "pupil characteristics interact with school-community conditions and how they affect educational opportunity for groups of pupils" (Costin, 1975, p. 137). Well planned programs for the improvement of school-community relations can help the teaching staff to better understand factors in this dimension which affect the educational process. Planning for parent education groups can also be done by the social worker. Wayne and Feinstein (1978), in studying parent groups, found that "the cumulative effect of positive experiences with school personnel could certainly change outdated stereotypic attitudes toward the public school system" (p. 351).

Facilitating the Utilization of Community Resources   Meares (1977) explained, "Tasks included in this area are related to encouraging and assisting families and children in utilizing community services and sharing information that contributes to understanding between the family and social agency" (p. 197). The social worker is able to assist the family in locating services in the neighborhood that will aid them in obtaining necessary services such as medical care, supplementary income, and food stamps. The social worker can also assist in obtaining mental health services for the entire family if needed. For students, such as physically handicapped children who need additional services in the community, the worker can aid in locating such services as recreational opportunities and other extracurricular activities.

Knowledge of the community is a must for the social worker if he/she is to assist in meeting the needs of the child and the child's parents. The social worker must know about the power structures within the community, the relationship between the community and the school administrators, and the demographics of the community, as well as resources available either within the community or close to the community, such as recreational facilities and work opportunities for teenage students (Costin, 1975).

Leadership and Policy Making   Tasks included under leadership and policy making are in the areas of research, inservice training for teachers, work with parent groups, consultation with school administrators, and work within the community to bring about new social services.

Social Worker-Teacher Relationships

Traditionally, the social worker's case load in the school was largely determined by the teacher's referral of children. Children who had problems such as withdrawal, aggressiveness, school failure, or school phobia were often referred. The social worker then would investigate the problems as described by the teacher and, if indicated, would work with the child and the child's family. The social worker would maintain a liaison between the teacher and the child and parents during counseling and would help all involved in understanding how a solution could be reached.

More recently, however, the social worker has enlarged his/her relationship with the teacher and is serving not only children referred by the teacher. The social worker can assist the teacher in understanding those social issues that may affect many children within the classroom (Moss, 1976). The social worker can also inform the teacher about conditions within the school district that could influence learning in the classroom, such as the value placed on the educated person within the community, the value placed on recreational activities, and the major issues of concern within the community.

OCCUPATIONAL THERAPY

Traditional Role

Occupational therapy, like physical therapy, is one of the younger medical professions. An early definition of occupational therapy was "any activity, mental or physical, prescribed by a physician and guided by the therapist for the distinct purpose of contributing and hastening recovery from injury" (Wellisch, 1949, p. 33). Occupational therapists were generally employed in hospital settings or clinical facilities and were concerned with acute care. Treatment of psychiatric patients was one of the earliest roles of the occupational therapist. However, in addition to work with the psychiatric patient, the therapist has also traditionally provided care for patients with other acute conditions.

When working with the patient, the therapist first evaluates the patient's skills, work habits and performance, social skills, and behavior. Once the evaluation is completed, the therapist channels the patient into activities that will help the client learn to live with himself/herself and others and also to gain further insight into himself/herself. Activities used include arts, crafts, recreation, and daily living activities. Through treatment, the therapist attempts to demonstrate the value of the patient's involvement in an occupation in improving his overall functioning in society.

Occupational therapy in general is aimed at stimulating independence and enhancing productive functioning. For example, the therapist emphasizes the importance of activities of daily living during the treatment of patients. Skills in areas such as cooking, housekeeping, dressing, bathing, and toileting are taught, using adaptive equipment as needed. Adaptive equipment for use in the patient's vocational area is also prescribed by the occupational therapist after the assessment of the client's needs.

The occupational therapist is also concerned with improving or maintaining the person's overall strengths and range of motion. The fabrication of splints for prevention of contractures has traditionally been a role of the occupational therapist, as well as the use of weights, machines, and crafts for strengthening.

Emerging Role

Johnson (1973) stated that if occupational therapy is to continue to successfully provide services for its patients, more time is needed than is readily available in hospitals. Occupational therapy's greatest contribution may therefore be made in settings other than the hospital. According to Johnson:

> The most ideal marketplace for occupational therapy may be in community health centers, school systems, day care centers, early child-care facilities, institutions for the chronically ill or for persons requiring long term care as a result of either biological, social, cognitive or behavioral problems, industrial settings, environments designed to reverse the cycles of poverty and welfare, vocational settings, or in specified medical settings where

medicine and occupational therapy share or jointly seek common goals (p. 4).

The passage of laws such as PL 94-142 provides the occupational therapist with the opportunity to contribute skills to the habilitation of children with developmental disabilities. Even though occupational therapists have been employed in the public schools since 1942, the passage of the Right to Education laws has allowed the therapist to serve many more children with a greater variety of problems.

To work within the school system, the therapist must be a graduate of an approved curriculum in occupational therapy and have registered status with the American Occupational Therapy Association (AOTA). According to AOTA's (1969) statement on occupational therapy with mental retardation, the therapist should have also done post-graduate work in the areas of growth and development.

The competencies needed to work with children with disabilities were stated by the AOTA Task Force (Note 1):

> . . . evaluate the individual's performance capacities and deficits and select tasks or activity experiences appropriate to the defined needs and goals. The therapist facilitates and influences the client's participation and investment, evaluates responses, assesses and measures changes and development. Finally the occupational therapist validates the assessment, shares her findings and makes appropriate recommendations to the appropriate persons including professionals, sub-professionals and consumers (p. 4).

The Task Force also recommended that the occupational therapist should become an advocate to promote passage of legislation and implementation of programs for the handicapped, and stressed the importance of the occupational therapist engaging in research with other professionals to aid in the understanding of mental retardation and other developmental disabilities.

Functions in the School Setting

The area of clinical functioning includes evaluation, treatment, and provision of follow-up services. After evaluation of the child's performance capabilities and deficits, the therapist selects tasks or activities appropriate to meet the needs of the child.

The occupational therapist working with the pediatric population emphasizes habilitation, or the acquisition of new skills, rather than rehabilitation as with the adult population. Evaluation of the child would include assessment of the developmental level of skill acquisition. Evaluation of postural reflexes, sensory mechanisms, and overall motor responses is also done. If deficits are noted, treatment is implemented by the therapist. Gorga (1976) stated that "the therapist offers many sensory clues through physical manipulation of the child in the desired movement, emphasizing kinesthetic awareness and external stimulation through tactile (rubbing, slapping, tapping), visual and auditory channels" (p. 193). The occupational therapist also evaluates personal-social skills, particularly in the area of feeding skills. In conjunction with the physical therapist, nutritionist, nurse, and other professionals, the occupational therapist plans a program for feeding skill development which might include adaptive seating, adaptive equipment, and activities for stimulating better oral-motor control.

In the preschool-age and school-age child, the occupational therapist again looks at the child's functional abilities in self-help skills, which include manipulation of objects, dressing, toileting, and feeding skills. Some treatment objectives for this age child, according to Anderson, Greer, and McFadden (1976), might include "development of dominance in a hand; development of reach, grasp, and release with a prosthesis, improvement of writing skills, or increase of range of motion in the upper extremities" (p. 144). Evaluation of the perceptual-motor abilities area is also done during this age period. After evaluation a treatment program is developed based upon the child's functional level and ability to control himself/herself and the environment.

For the child in the prevocational stage, the occupational therapist may be involved in the assessment of true vocational skills. The occupational therapist may assess the technical skills and social abilities of the child in a work situation by observing such items as the child's attention span, frustration level, speed, and ability to relate to other persons. The therapist may also examine muscle strength and coordination needed for various tasks.

If the child is in a wheelchair, the therapist alone or with a physical therapist may prescribe or build adaptations for the chair. Accessories such as trays, lap boards, adjustable arm rests, and solid seat inserts may enable the child to function more effectively in the school setting.

In addition to clinical functioning, major roles of the occupational therapist in the school setting include consultation with and training of teachers and parents. As part of the educational team, the occupational therapist may serve as consultant to the special education or regular classroom teacher. The therapist can aid the teacher by supplying pertinent information about the child's abilities and disabilities and by offering suggestions on ways to best stimulate the child in the classroom. The therapist needs to explain any restriction or precaution to the teacher but also needs to stress that the child needs to be as independent as possible. Even though the therapist treats the child directly, he/she should teach the classroom teacher therapeutic skills so that the teacher is prepared to handle the child and is comfortable in teaching the child.

Occupational therapy, as with physical therapy, may not be available on a daily or even weekly basis to all children who need this service. The teacher must therefore be made aware of activities to be done on a daily basis within the classroom. The occupational therapist can impart this knowledge in consultation with the teacher for specific suggestions, or through inservice training programs for many teachers for general suggestions.

The occupational therapist and teacher may also work together as part of a team whose role is to evaluate children prior to their entrance to school to determine if any disability is present. The therapist may possibly work with the teacher in selecting or developing a screening test for the child which would identify developmental delays.

If treatment is initiated with the child, the occupational therapist and teacher must communicate to each other their immediate goals and recommendations for attaining them. The therapist can aid the teacher by suggesting adaptive equipment such as special chairs, pencils, or scissors that would aid the child in classroom work. The occupational therapist might also suggest different positions that the physically handicapped child should be placed in during the day for alleviation of pain or exhaustion. The teacher will need to communicate to the therapist what cognitive skills are being stressed so that the therapist can incorporate these goals into the therapeutic program.

The therapist should also participate in the teaching of parents about environmental stimulation activities and developmental experiences for their child. Frequent interaction with the parents about the progress of their child provides the parents with reassurance and incentive to continue with home-based stimulation or therapeutic programs.

According to Anderson, Greer, and McFadden (1976), mainstreaming trends have helped to foster the idea of the resource occupational therapist. The occupational therapist in this capacity is able to serve a number of schools and provide services to more teachers and children than when based at one school. The resource occupational therapist can aid in the curriculum development for the handicapped, can assist in pupil placement and can consult on transportation and architectural barriers. Therapists acting as consultants can aid in the design of tables and chairs, toilet facilities, drinking fountains, doorways, and play areas that allow the maximum functioning of the handicapped child.

Implications of Mainstreaming for the Occupational Therapist

There is much overlap of skills among occupational and physical therapists and special education teachers. Banus (1971), in describing the role of the occupational therapist, stated, "I believe that our greatest strength lies in our knowledge of early neuromotor, psychosocial and visual perceptual-motor development and dysfunction. With this background, we can work with children in terms of prevention, habilitation or rehabilitation" (p. xii). This statement reveals the similarities in the roles of the occupational therapist and the special educator. However, differences are present. Nelson (Note 6) pointed out that the special educator's strengths are in adapting instructional materials and in individualizing instruction, while the occupational therapist's strength is in the teaching of developmental skills to the child. The two disciplines should therefore be viewed as complementary, not competitive. Anderson, Greer, and McFadden (1976) drew attention to the need for definition of the role of the occupational therapist in the public school in order to complement the roles of the special educator and others working with the handicapped, rather than duplicating efforts.

Other factors affecting the development of public school occupational therapy programs include the scarcity of therapists experienced in working with the more severely involved, certification requirements of some state departments of education, and the issue of whether or not the school-based occupational therapist must have prescriptive referral from a physician before working with a child (Anderson et al., 1976). The American Occupational Therapy Association's Bylaws (1972) stated that "Registered members may accept referrals from qualified physicians and from others seeking occupational therapy services. They shall collaborate with qualified professionals in those instances where collaboration is indicated" (p. xviii). However, some states are requiring that only physicians' referrals may be accepted. This deviation from the AOTA bylaws presents problems to the occupational therapist who is functioning within the educational system rather than within the medical model. These issues are of major concern for the occupational therapist as he/she implements the occupational therapist's role within the public school system and as he/she attempts to elicit the assistance of teachers in identifying the needs of children within the classroom. Their resolution will help in the establishment of the quality occupational therapy programs needed for provision of appropriate services to the handicapped.

PHYSICAL THERAPY

Traditional Role

Physical therapy, one of the youngest of the health professions, had its origin during World War I. The "reconstruction aides," as physical therapists were then known, were usually nurses with specialized training in the rehabilitation of war casualities.

The early physical therapists were involved in the treatment of traumatic injuries such as fractures, amputations, and spinal cord injuries. With the outbreak of poliomyelitis in the 1950s, physical therapists became involved with the treatment of this and other disorders and disabilities.

In the treatment of children, physical therapists have drawn from their backgrounds in orthopedics and their knowledge of techniques for treating acute injuries and diseases. The evaluation of children has traditionally involved manual muscle testing, range of motion measurements, sensory tests, body alignment assessments, and assessments of activities of daily living (Pearson & Williams, 1972). Treatment has included passive or active range of motion and muscle re-education or strengthening. In earlier years, this treatment was usually provided only in special clinics or in self-contained schools for the physically handicapped.

Competencies

The licensed physical therapist must have a bachelor of science degree in PT from an approved school of physical therapy and must have passed an examination for state licensing given by the Professional Examination Service. In 1976, physical therapists from university affiliated facilities and faculty members from these universities formulated competencies for the physical therapist in the developmental disabilities. These competencies included areas of assessment, treatment, consultation, and research (*O/PT Guidelines*, 1976). In the area of assessment, desired competencies include being able to:

1. Identify appropriate clinical assessment tools including limitations and values of the tools as well as the yield of the instrument.
2. Select the evaluation method and/or tools appropriate to the client's age, disability and reason for referral.
3. Identify an appropriate sequence for presenting tools with respect to available data or observations of the client.
4. Select the physical setting for the assessment that is appropriate to the client's age, disability and personality.
5. Establish the optimum climate and direct the evaluation session so as to elicit the client's best performance.
6. Obtain the information needed from parents or other members involved in the care, treatment and education of the client.
7. Analyze and integrate information from his/her evaluation with results from other disciplines into a comprehensive picture (p. 13–14).

Competencies considered necessary for the physical therapist to carry out an effective treatment program were listed as follows:

1. Apply knowledge of etiology, course and/or history of the disability in order to develop a treatment plan for remediation of motor, perceptual, cognitive and/or adaptive dysfunction.
2. Identify the areas assessed and treated by other disciplines, the means by which physical therapy can utilize information from other disciplines, procedures for referring clients to other disciplines and ways to appropriately collaborate with other disciplines in treatment.
3. Initiate and conduct a physical therapy program for a client and evaluate, change, adapt or terminate the program as necessary.
4. Report orally and in writing to other professionals, clients, family members, and non-professional staff, regarding the results of a physical therapy procedure, total management and other relevant information related to the client with mental retardation or handicapping condition (p. 15–16).

The Physical Therapist in the School Setting

Most severely handicapped children served by the physical therapist will probably continue to be educated in self-contained classrooms, with the physical therapist working closely with the classroom teacher. However, with implementation of the concept of the least restrictive environment, some severely physically handicapped children may be served in a regular classroom. If the regular classroom teacher is not aware of what occurs in therapy, he/she may be reinforcing behaviors and postures that the physical therapy program is designed to eradicate (Connolly & Anderson, 1978). In such instances, the physical therapist must impart to the classroom teacher knowledge of proper positioning and handling, simple stimulation techniques, and methods of promoting the child's independence in activities of daily living. Lectures and workshops for teachers and aides, as well as individual conferences, are necessary for the success of the physical therapy program. In the mainstreamed setting, the therapist will not be able to provide all needed services. It is therefore important that the therapist have confidence in the ability of the classroom teacher to handle a role in the therapy program. The therapist must be psychologically able to experience "role release" and allow others to perform some of the tasks usually assumed by the physical therapist.

The physical therapist in a school program will find his/her role as a member of the treatment team much broader than if he/she were in a clinical setting. The physical therapist will probably be working with a wider range of disabilities. Generally, physical therapists have been more involved in the treatment of children with cerebral palsy than with any other of the developmental disabilities. In addition to serving this group, the therapist in the school setting is now treating children with physical handicaps such as spina bifida, hydrocephalus, muscular dystrophy, chromosomal defects, and motor delays due to mental retardation.

Physical therapists have in recent years also become involved in the identification and treatment of children with perceptual-motor and visual-motor problems. Miller and Goldberg (1975), utilizing sensorimotor integration, were able to attain better control of body movements and more accurate perceptions of body and objects in space in a child with perceptual-motor problems. Mathis and Harshman (1977) used a sensorimotor approach with children diagnosed as having learning disabilities. At the end of 8 weeks the children showed significant improvement in identification of body parts, movement in space, gross motor activities, and shape constancy. Montgomery and Richter (1977) carried out a similar study with trainable mentally retarded children, obtaining results showing that such children involved in sensory integrative therapy made greater gains on test batteries after the therapy than did children involved in developmental physical education programs or in adaptive physical education.

The physical therapist is often requested to work with the physical education teacher in providing developmental play activities for retarded children or children with perceptual-motor problems. In these cases, even though there is no need of specialized treatment, the therapist can suggest activities or sources of such that can be beneficial in physical education programs.

Physical therapists may also participate in screening programs. Studies (Cronis & Gleason, 1974) have shown that the physical therapist is able to make early identification of those problems that need treatment. Screening of children for orthopedic problems at the time of their first entry into school would allow early treatment, thus preventing development of many chronic problems. The issue of whether a prescriptive referral by a physician is necessary for the therapist to do such screening, or to work with any child, is a deterrent to more effective use of the therapist in the public school (Connolly & Anderson, 1978).

The classroom teacher can assist the physical therapist by providing an initial liaison with parents. The teacher is usually familiar with the family and any problems in the home that might interfere with the therapy program. This information will be of importance to the physical therapist in the planning of a home program. Parents of children with handicaps are important members of the treatment team and, like the teacher, must learn how to handle the child and understand treatment goals. The teacher will be of help in planning meetings of the parents, the therapist, and himself/herself, for the purpose of discussing the goals of the therapy program, methods used to implement the program, the role of the parents, and the progress of the child. The therapist may continue to act as a consultant for the child who no longer has need of active treatment.

SCHOOL NURSING

Traditional and Changing Role

The school nurse has provided services in our school systems since the early 1900s. Traditionally, the nurse was viewed as the person who served the students only when they were ill, taking temperatures, bandaging cuts, and providing other minor medical services. Health programs in which the nurse was sometimes involved were isolated, not comprehensive in scope, and seldom integrated into the educational program of the child. The nurse's role remained essentially the same, with emphasis primarily on acute care of children, until the thrust of the 1960s involved the school nurse in programs of prevention of social problems as well as medical treatment or prevention of disease.

In 1966, the American Nursing Association described the role of the school nurse: "School nursing is a highly specialized service contributing to the process of education . . . The professional nurse with her experience and knowledge of the changing growth and behavioral patterns of children is in a unique position in the school setting to assist children in acquiring health knowledge, in developing attitudes conducive to healthful living and in meeting their needs resulting from disease, accidents, congenital defects or psychological maladjustments" (Bryan, 1973, p. 1). The school nurse was no longer seen as solely a provider of isolated services but was recognized as playing an important part in the integration and coordination of pupil services.

Competencies Needed

The National Council for School Nurses (1972) recommended that the nurse who wants to function in a school setting be educated in an institution of higher learning. In addition to the basic preparation for nursing, the school nurse needs specialized education in nursing including courses in areas such as physical medicine and rehabilitation, normal and abnormal behavior, growth and development, pediatrics, body chemistry and nutrition, and physical and occupational therapy. The nurse also needs expertise in working with the community. The nurse must be able to integrate skills of counseling, consultation, and teaching, and use these skills effectively with persons of varying ages, cultures, and knowledge.

An understanding of school organization, its purposes and its operation is of extreme importance to the nurse. The nurse must be able to coordinate efforts in health development with a system whose primary purpose is not health, and work with other school personnel and community agencies to promote the health and well-being of all children within the school. As stated by Fricke (1968):

Frequently the child with a problem first finds his way to the nurse's office. Many of these children are faced with varying degrees of social, psychological and emotional problems . . . her awareness of her own role and that of others places her in the position of making professional decisions and initiating action through appropriate measures such as referral or follow through, functioning effectively within the educational model as part of the interdisciplinary team (p. 412).

Functions of the School Nurse

In many instances, school health services are provided through agreements between the school system and local, county, or state health departments. The health department nurse may visit the school at regularly scheduled intervals and/or special services are to be provided. Services provided to schools through health departments may include health appraisal, health education and counseling, and prevention and control of communicable diseases. Nurses "serve as health resource persons; assist in the integration of health instruction into the curriculum; counsel with students, faculty and parents on health related problems; and serve as liaison between the school, community health and welfare agencies, and the medical profession. The school health nurses also implement various screening programs . . . in an effort to identify early symptoms for referral and follow-up" (Memphis-Shelby Co. Health Dept., Note 3). The school nurse of today will at various times assume the roles of evaluator, counselor-consultant, and educator.

Nurse as Evaluator As evaluator, the school nurse may screen children upon their entrance into the school system. Areas of health concern such as auditory and visual acuity, immunization against communicable diseases, and physical condition are checked. Many school systems do annual visual and auditory screening in kindergarten, first, third, and fifth grades yearly. Recent expansion in many states of school immunization laws to include all students through grade twelve has necessitated screening of health records to insure compliance by all students with the law.

The nurse plays an important role in the early identification of potential learning disabilities. The nurse should be able to review the child's developmental history, particularly motor development, since delayed motor development is highly suggestive of potential learning problems (Feriden, 1972). Once the child has been identified as high risk for problems, the nurse uses developmental screening tests to determine the child's ability levels as an aid to the provision of appropriate learning experiences.

For children who have chronic disease or disabilities, the nurse obtains a full past history so that adequate follow-up can be provided in the school. For children with long term disabilities, the nurse can provide the necessary liaison between the child's physician and the school, and supply needed medical information on an ongoing basis.

Nurse as Counselor/Educator   The nurse has an important role as a health counselor and educator. The nurse will find it necessary to establish relationships, not limited to the school setting, with the child and his/her family, other professionals on the school health team, the teacher, the curriculum committee, the school administration, and the community (National Council for School Nurses, 1972).

Counseling can be done with individual children, groups of children, individual parents and teachers, or groups of parents and teachers. To be a counselor the nurse must have both a thorough knowledge of health and adequate skill in performing counseling. The nurse should be able to interpret health findings to both families and teachers in terms that are understandable. In counseling. the nurse must be able to convey the importance of the health needs of the child. If necessary, the nurse visits the child's home to provide health information to the parents. If the child is on medication, the school nurse may need to reinforce or explain the doctor's orders regarding the medication. The nurse should be knowledgeable enough to explain the side effects of any medication to both parents and teachers, thus helping to alleviate some of the anxiety about the administration of drugs (Havercamp, 1970). The nurse may make subsequent visits to assist the parents in the continuing care of their child.

The school nurse in many settings will actually work as a teacher in health education for children. Topics that the nurse is well trained to explain include nutrition, dental care, good health habits, venereal disease, and drug abuse (Bryan, 1973). The nurse may also initiate special projects, such as health fairs, to increase knowledge of the children and school personnel about health. The nurse should utilize every appropriate method to encourage and support meaningful health education.

School personnel should be educated as to the importance of adequate health services within the school, since this may be the only source of health care for some children. The school nurse should serve as a consultant in integration of health instruction into the curriculum, and actively participate in inservice programs for staff development.

School Nurse-Teacher Relationships

The school nurse assumes an even more important role with the increasing numbers of handicapped children being served in the regular classroom. As a member of the placement team, the nurse can provide valuable information as to environmental adaptations and ancillary services needed to accommodate the physically handicapped student in the regular classroom. When a child with a physical or medical handicap is admitted to the class, the nurse can assist in the development of specific plans for modifying the child's program, materials, and/or classroom environment to meet the child's individual needs.

The teacher who has for the first time a child in his/her classroom with a condition such as epilepsy or diabetes may be ignorant of proper procedures in case of a diabetic reaction or a seizure. Reassurance from the nurse can lead to the matter-of-fact acceptance by the teacher of the child and his/her program. If the child is on medication, the nurse can make the teacher aware of any possible side effects, and can interpret medical information on the child's cumulative record which might be unclear to the teacher. If learning problems are suspected by the teacher, the nurse may be able to find implications for identification of the problem in the child's developmental and medical history. If any condition needing treatment is suspected to be present, the nurse can assist the teacher and parents in locating appropriate diagnostic and treatment services.

The school nurse is often the logical supplier of information to the students on such topics as sex education, drug and alcohol abuse, or other teenage concerns. The teacher can aid the nurse in planning content and materials for these courses by providing information about the level of understanding of the children in the class and by helping adapt the materials and presentation to the children's level.

PARAPROFESSIONALS AND VOLUNTEERS IN THE CLASSROOM

Preceding sections of this chapter have described the roles and functions of *professional* ancillary personnel considered to be essential to a high quality continuum of services for handicapped children. This section focuses on the vital contributions currently being made in a growing number of schools by another integral part of the education team: *paraprofessionals* and *volunteers*. Development of the paraprofessional concept has been relatively recent, although the utilization of paraprofessionals and volunteers in special education programs has been a commonly accepted practice for several decades (Cruickshank & Haring, 1957). There has been a more recent trend toward the use of teaching assistants, teaching aides, and volunteer workers in the regular classroom. These support people play important and unique roles as members of the instructional team, functioning effectively as adjuncts to the teaching process.

Paraprofessionals

The paraprofessional concept has been generally adopted because of its instructional and economic advantages. Greer (1978), in a comprehensive and highly recommended article on the use of paraprofessionals and volunteers, pinpointed 1965 as a year that significant numbers of salaried paraprofessionals began to appear in the public schools, under provisions of Title I of the Elementary and Secondary Education Act. Legislation mandating appropriate services to the handicapped has since accelerated the use of these support people.

Willems et al. (1975) listed several advantages, other than the obvious economic saving, which result from increased utilization of teacher aides. The use of aides frees the teacher from a number of tasks that are necessary but that do not require professional expertise. This provides teachers with more time for planning, leading to greater individualization of instruction. The implementation of instructional techniques such as multi-media instruction, team teaching, one-to-one teaching, and the ungraded classroom can be facilitated. Students are not only provided with more individual attention, but also profit from the additional appropriate adult models.

It seems obvious that since the teacher is a trained, skilled professional, his/her instructional time is too valuable to be spent performing tasks that can be as efficiently handled by noncertificated personnel (Anderson, Greer, & Zia, 1978). Such tasks include roll taking, record keeping, preparing materials, supervising the children at rest and play, and monitoring student work. Under the direction of the teacher, the aide can function as an adjunct to the teaching process, listening to the children read, guiding the children in working on assignments and locating materials, and, in general, taking an active role in the instructional process. Blessing (1967) referred to the role of the aide as being that of a parent surrogate, functioning as the parent does at home—listening, reading, explaining, clarifying, encouraging.

Greer (1978) stated that paraprofessionals may be categorized as "teacher assistants" or "teacher aides," making this distinction:

> The *teacher assistant* is responsible for direct support to the teacher and assumes any portion of the professional's responsibilities so designated under the teacher's supervision. Teacher assistants have limited decision making authority regulated by their relationships with the teaching professionals and local school system policies. The *teacher aide*, on the other hand, takes no independent action, and has no decision making authority. This person performs routine tasks assigned by teachers or other specified personnel (pp. 3–4).

The teacher aide is recognized as being less responsible for instructional activities, generally assisting with more personal care activities, such as toileting and feeding needs of more severely handicapped pupils. The following activities were considered by Greer as suitable for teacher assistants. Teacher aide and volunteer responsibilities are also reflected in the list:

1. Reinforcing positive behavior.
2. Assisting in large-group instruction.
3. Tutoring individuals and small groups of children.
4. Correcting home and seat work activities.
5. Checking standardized and informal tests.
6. Observing and recording behavior.
7. Collecting materials and preparing displays, teaching centers, and similar instructional activities.
8. Assisting children with make-up work as a result of absence from school or class.
9. Assisting students with oral and written communication.
10. Participating in reading and story telling activities.
11. Assisting with hands-on activities.
12. Assisting with fine and gross motor activities, physical development, and lifetime physical and recreational activities.
13. Providing a model with whom the children can identify.
14. Recording written materials for children who have visual or other learning disabilities.
15. Assisting children with extended day activities.
16. Helping children solve personal conflicts with other children.
17. Assisting on instructional field trip activities.
18. Assisting children with self-care activities.
19. Assisting with feeding and toileting activities.
20. Working with audio-visual equipment.
21. Assisting the teacher with noninstructional tasks.
22. Assisting in classroom organization and management (p. 4).

Volunteers

While paraprofessionals are required to have a higher level of training or experience, and generally have greater responsibilities, the role of volunteers is equally valued and essential (Greer, 1978). Volunteers may engage in many of the activities for paraprofessionals listed above. The National School Volunteers Program listed these general objectives (Carter & Dapper, 1974) for the volunteer in the school:

1. To relieve the professional staff of nonteaching duties
2. To provide needed services to individual children to supplement the work of the classroom teacher
3. To enrich the experiences of children beyond that normally available in school
4. To build better understanding of school problems among citizens and to stimulate widespread citizen support for public education

Schools without sufficient economic resources to employ para-professionals can initiate a campaign to enlist the assistance of volunteers. Parents, homemakers, semiretired individuals, and concerned citizens can serve effectively under the direction of the teacher. Some school systems have additionally adopted a cross-age tutoring program with high school students serving in the capacity of elementary teaching volunteers.

SUMMARY

Esbensen (1966) stated that the prime role of the effective teacher is to make decisions regarding what is to be taught, what instructional methods are to be utilized, and how to structure the learning environment. The more resources available to the classroom teacher, including competent ancillary personnel, the greater the opportunity for implementing the role described by Esbensen and for providing truly individualized instruction. Obviously, one teacher in a classroom with 30 children is limited in the amount of individualization which can be accomplished. The possibilities suggested in this chapter and throughout the book provide assistance and direction in meeting individual needs.

REFERENCES

ACES-ACEA Joint Committee on the Elementary School Counselor. *Report of the ACES-ASCA joint committee on the elementary school counselor*, April 2, 1966 (Working Paper). Washington, D.C.: American Personnel and Guidance Association, 1966.

ACES-ASCA Joint Committee on the Elementary School Counselor. *The elementary school counselor in today's schools*. Washington, D.C.: American Personnel and Guidance Association, 1969.

Alderson, J. J., & Krishef, C. H. Another perspective on tasks in school social work. *Social Casework*, 1973, *54*, 591–600.

American Occupational Therapy Association. *Occupational therapy with mental retardation*. Rockville, Md.: AOTA, 1969.

American Occupational Therapy Association Yearbook: Bylaws. Rockville, Md.: AOTA, 1972.

Anderson, R. M., Greer, J. G., & McFadden, S. M. Occupational therapy for the severely handicapped in the public schools. In R. M. Anderson & J. G. Greer (Eds.), *Educating the severely and profoundly retarded*. Baltimore: University Park Press, 1976.

Anderson, R. M., Greer, J. G., & Zia, B. Perspectives and overview. In R. M. Anderson, J. G. Greer, & S. J. Odle (Eds.), *Individualizing educational materials for special children in the mainstream*. Baltimore: University Park Press, 1978.

Aubrey, R. F. Consultation, school interventions, and the elementary counselor. *Personnel and Guidance Journal*, 1978, *56*(6), 351–354.

Banus, B. S. *The developmental therapist: A prototype of the pediatric occupational therapist.* Thorofare, N.J.: Charles B. Slack, Inc., 1971.

Bernard, H. W., & Fullmer, D. W. *Principles of guidance* (2nd ed.). New York: Thomas Y. Crowell, 1977.

Blessing, K. R. Use of teacher aides in special education: A review and possible implications. *Exceptional Children*, 1967, *34*, 107–113.

Brown, J. A. *Organizing and evaluating elementary school guidance services: Why, what, and how.* Monterey, Cal.: Brooks/Cole Publishing Co., 1977.

Bryan, D. *School nursing in transition.* St. Louis: C. V. Mosby, 1973.

Carter, B., & Dapper, G. *Organizing school volunteer programs.* New York: Citation Press, 1974.

Cartwright, G. P., Cartwright, C. A., & Ysseldyke, J. E. Identification and diagnostic teaching of handicapped children in the regular classroom. *Psychology in the Schools*, 1973, *10*, 4–11.

Connolly, B., & Anderson, R. M. Severely handicapped children in the public schools: A new frontier for the physical therapist. *Physical Therapy*, 1978, *58*(4), 433–438.

Costin, L. B. A historical review of school social work. *Social Casework*, 1969, *50*, 439–453.

Costin, L. B. School social work practice: A new model. *Social Work*, 1975, *20*, 135–139.

Cronis, S., & Gleason, A. W. Orthopedic screening of school children in Delaware. *Physical Therapy*, 1974, *54*, 1080–1083.

Cruickshank, W. M., & Haring, M. G. *A demonstration: Assistants for teachers of exceptional children.* Syracuse, N.Y.: Syracuse University Press, 1957.

Dimick, K. M., & Huff, V. E. *Child counseling.* Dubuque, Ia.: William C. Brown Co., 1970.

Dublinske, S., & Healey, W. C. PL 94-142: Questions and answers for the speech-language pathologist and audiologist. *Asha*, 1978, *20*(3), 188–205.

Eisenson, J., & Ogilvie, M. *Speech correction in the schools.* New York: Macmillan, 1977.

Ellis, J. A. N., & Bryant, V. E. Competency based certification for school social workers. *Social Work*, 1976, *21*, 381–385.

Esbensen, T. Should teacher aides be more than clerks? *Phi Delta Kappan*, 1966, *44*, 237.

Fein, L. G. *The changing school scene.* New York: John Wiley & Sons, 1974.

Feriden, W. E. The role of the school nurse in the early identification of potential learning disabilities. *Journal of School Health*, 1972, *42*, 86–87.

Fricke, L. B. Comments on a conference report on educational preparation of the nurse for school health work. *Journal of School Health*, 1968, *38*, 412.

Garber, F. E. The speech clinician as a member of the educational team. In R. J. Van Hattum (Ed.), *Clinical speech in the schools.* Springfield, Ill.: Charles C Thomas, 1969.

Gorga, D. I. Occupational therapy. In R. B. Johnston & P. R. Magrab (Eds.), *Developmental disorders.* Baltimore: University Park Press, 1976.

Greer, J. V. Utilizing paraprofessionals and volunteers in special education. *Focus on Exceptional Children*, 1978, *10*(6), 1–15.

Hallahan, D. P., & Kauffman, J. M. *Exceptional children: Introduction to special education.* Englewood Cliffs, N.J.: Prentice-Hall, 1978.

Havercamp, L. J. Brain injured children and the school nurse. *Journal of School Health*, 1970, *40*, 228, 235.

Herron, W. G., Green, M., Guild, M., Smith, A., & Kantor, R. E. *Contemporary school psychology*. Scranton, Pa.: International Textbook Co., 1970.

Johnson, J. Occupational therapy: A model for the future. *American Journal of Occupational Therapy*, 1973, *27*, 1-7.

Lebovitz, L. The present status of school psychology as a major sub-discipline. *Journal of School Psychology*, 1968, *7*, 3-9.

Lilly, M. S. *Children with exceptional needs: A survey of special education*. New York: Holt, Rinehart & Winston, 1979.

Lundeen, D. J. Speech disorders. In B. R. Gearheart (Eds.), *Education of the exceptional child* (Vol. 19). Scranton, Pa.: Intext, 1972.

Mathis, H. J., & Harshman, H. W. Therapeutic program for the learning disabled child. *Physical Therapy*, 1977, *57*, 823-825.

Meares, P. A. Analysis of tasks in school social work. *Social Work*, 1977, *22*, 196-201.

Meyen, E. L. *Exceptional children and youth: An introduction*. Denver: Love Publishing Co., 1978.

Meyer, C. H. Purposes and boundaries: Casework fifty years later. *Social Casework*, 1973, *54*, 268-275.

Miller, T. G., & Goldberg, K. Sensorimotor integration: An interdisciplinary approach. *Physical Therapy*, 1975, *55*, 501-504.

Montgomery, P., & Richter, E. Effect of sensory integrative therapy on the neuromotor development of retarded children. *Physical Therapy*, 1977, *57*, 799-813.

Moss, A. F. Consultation in the inner-city school. *Social Work*, 1976, *21*, 142-146.

Moynihan, S. K. Utilizing the school setting to facilitate family treatment. *Social Casework*, 1978, *59*, 287-294.

National Council for School Nurses. *School nursing for the 70's*. Washington, D.C.: American Association for Health, Physical Education, and Recreation, 1972.

Nichols, A. C. Public school speech and hearing therapy. In R. W. Rieber & R. S. Brubaker (Eds.), *Speech pathology: An international study of the science*. Amsterdam: North Holland Publishing Co., 1966.

Occupational/physical therapy guidelines for training in university affiliated facilities. Washington, D.C.: Maternal and Child Health, Department of Health, Education, and Welfare, 1976.

Oppenheimer, J. J. *The visiting teacher movement with special reference to administrative relationships* (2nd Ed.). New York: Joint Committee on Methods of Preventing Delinquency, 1925.

Pearson, P. H., & Williams, C. E. (Eds.). *Physical therapy services in the developmental disabilities*. Springfield, Ill.: Charles C Thomas, 1972.

Perkins, W. P. *Speech pathology: An applied behavioral science*. St. Louis: C. V. Mosby, 1971.

Pielstick, N. L. The appropriate domain of the school psychologist. *Journal of School Psychology*, 1970, *8*, 317-321.

Sabatino, D. A. School psychology—special education: To acknowledge a relationship. *Journal of School Psychology*, 1972, *10*, 99-105.

Sproles, H. H., Panther, E. E., & Lanier, J. E. PL 94-142 and its impact on the counselor's role. *Personnel and Guidance Journal*, 1978, *57*(4), 210-212.

Stephens, T. M. Psychological consultation to teachers of learning and behaviorally handicapped children using a behavioral model. *Journal of School Psychology*, 1970, *8*, 13–18.

Taber, R. C. Children caught in cross currents: The rights and responsibilities of children and parents. *Bulletin of the National Association of School Social Workers*, 1954, *29*, 12–21.

Tennessee State Board of Education. *Tennessee regulations for certification of teachers*. Nashville, Tenn.: State Department of Education, 1975.

Tolbert, E. L. *An introduction to guidance*. Boston: Little, Brown & Co., 1978.

Van Hattum, R. J. On achieving potential. *Asha*, 1978, *20*, 3–6.

Waters, L. G. School psychologists as perceived by school personnel: Support for a consultant model. *Journal of School Psychology*, 1973, *11*, 40–45.

Wayne, L. L., & Feinstein, B. B. Group work outreach to parents by school social workers. *Social Casework*, 1978, *59*, 345–351.

Wellisch, E. Occupational and physical therapy as adjuncts to child guidance. *Mental Health*, 1949, *11*, 35–39.

West, R. An historical review of the American literature in speech pathology. In R. W. Rieber & R. S. Brubaker (Eds.), *Speech pathology: An international study of the science*. Amsterdam: North Holland Publishing Co., 1966.

Willems, A. L., and others. How should classroom elementary aides be chosen? *Education*, 1975, *96*, 85–88.

Williams, D. Consultation: A broad, flexible role for school psychologists. *Psychology in the Schools*, 1972, *9*, 16–21.

Wilson, B. A. Introduction: Problem and project. *Journal of Speech and Hearing Disorders*, Mono, Suppl., 1961, *8*, 1–9.

REFERENCE NOTES

1. American Occupational Therapy Association, Inc. *Occupational therapy in mental retardation: Report of a task force*. Rockville, Md.: AOTA, April, 1973. Not an official document.

2. American Speech and Hearing Association. *Speech-language pathology and audiology: Career information*. Pamphlet, undated.

3. Memphis and Shelby County Health Department. *1978 Annual Report*. Memphis, Tenn.

4. Memphis City Schools, Mental Health Center. *End of year report*. Mimeographed material, June 30, 1978.

5. Memphis City Schools, Mental Health Center. *Job descriptions*. Mimeographed material.

6. Nelson, C. A. *Occupational therapy and special education*. Unpublished paper, 1974.

7. Williamson, P. *Welcome to the Campus School guidance program*. Memphis State University Campus School, Memphis, Tenn., Mimeographed material, 1979.

13
SUPPORTIVE SERVICES IN THE COMMUNITY

Sara J. Odle and Susan Kelly

New social and developmental perspectives on handicapping conditions are bringing about positive changes in the placement and treatment of handicapped citizens. Results of a recent national opinion survey indicated that "an overwhelming majority of Americans believe the time has come for increased services and expanded rights for persons with physical, mental, and sensory impairments" (Office for Handicapped Individuals, 1979a, p. 4). Seventy-nine percent of the respondents to the survey supported special efforts on behalf of the disabled, almost double the number supporting special efforts on behalf of women, minorities, and exconvicts. This support was evidenced across all segments of the surveyed population, regardless of any demographic characteristics. Seventy-one percent also agreed that advocates for the handicapped were mostly asking for changes which were long overdue.

The affirmation of the rights of the mentally retarded and other handicapped persons through passage of recent legislation (PL 93-516, PL 94-103, PL 94-142, PL 95-602) and through judicial decisions is acknowledgment of the prevailing philosophy in regard to this segment of our population.

THE NORMALIZATION PRINCIPLE

Nirje (1976) defined normalization as the "making available to all mentally retarded people (and those with other handicapping conditions) patterns of life and conditions of everyday living which are as close as possible to the regular circumstances and ways of society" (p. 231). This normalization principle, from which our current philosophy regarding the handicapped was partially derived, was first presented in relation to institutional care and management of the mentally retarded (Kokaska, 1974).

435

It has since been expanded, and practical application of the principle is evident throughout present delivery of services to both retarded persons and those with other handicapping conditions. Examples of its application are the mainstreaming of the handicapped student, the deinstitutionalization of the retarded, and the recent federally legislated provision for independent living services in the community (PL 95-602, 1978).

The normalization principle dictates that the provision of necessary services take place within as normal a social context as possible (Meyen, 1978). Expansion of opportunities and integration of the handicapped into normal community activities is stressed. As Juul (1978) explained, "The normalization principle simply implies that the handicapped ought to be able to live a life as equal as possible to a normal existence and with the same rights and obligations as other people. The handicapped are also to be accepted with their exceptionalities when these cannot be remedied" (p. 326).

The normalization principle applied to regulations, practices and services has resulted in an increased emphasis on community-based services (Bruinicks & Warfield, 1978) and has indeed made the provision of this aid imperative. Such services must be comprehensive, community-centered, and continuous (providing a continuum through the life span). This chapter reviews the needs of the handicapped in reference to the lifestyle of the normal, and describes various community-based services necessary to meet these needs.

DEINSTITUTIONALIZATION AND SERVICE DELIVERY AGENCIES

The federal government, in a 1974 Executive Order (No. 11776), proposed three major goals: 1) reduce the occurrence of mental retardation by half before the end of this century, 2) return one-third of the institutionalized to the community, and 3) assure the retarded full status as citizens under the law (Haring, 1978). Progress has been and continues to be made toward these goals. However, many of the institutionalized have been returned to the community before practical plans were made and put into action to aid in the adjustment of both the handicapped and the community. In a recent study, Conroy (1977) found that while releases from public institutions have increased, readmissions have increased as well. He suggested that such figures reflect the fact that "public pressure to get people out of institutions has far outstripped its essential corollary: pressure to create adequate normalizing community service systems" (p. 46). Addressing the same problem, Juul (1978) stated "One form of neglectful treatment has sometimes replaced another," and added that humanistic ideas are sometimes being used as a rationale for reducing services and thus cutting costs to the community (p. 326).

Successful alternatives to institutional placement require improvement and expansion of community-based support systems. The 1962 President's Panel on Mental Retardation recommended a continuum of care which would coordinate and use in proper sequence and relationship "the medical, educational, and social services required by a retarded person to minimize his disability at every point in his lifespan" (Mayo, 1962, p. 74). A uniform and comprehensive system of service provision would include counseling and preparing the parents for the integration of the person into the community, working with the person in the institution to bridge the transition, and developing school and community services to meet the needs. While some communities have developed such programs, in most areas no such provision exists. Tobin (1978) pointed out, "In contrast to other industrial societies, our lack of articulation between . . . long-term care institutions and community providers of social and health systems is noteworthy" (p. 74). Any thoughtful examination of community residence as a viable alternative to institutional placement must recognize the fact that the success of such deinstitutionalization depends upon the adequacy of the community-based continuum of supportive services, and the degree to which these services can replace those formerly centralized within the institution.

ADVOCACY FOR THE HANDICAPPED

A declaration on the rights of mentally retarded persons was issued in 1968 by the International League of Societies for the Mentally Handicapped. The general and special rights of the mentally retarded which were spelled out in this declaration are equally applicable to all handicapped persons:

ARTICLE I
The mentally retarded person has the same basic rights as other citizens of the same country and same age.

ARTICLE II
The mentally retarded person has a right to proper care and physical restoration and to such education, training, habilitation and guidance as will enable him to develop his ability and potential to the fullest possible extent, no matter how severe his degree of disability. No mentally handicapped person should be deprived of such services by reason of the costs involved.

ARTICLE III
The mentally retarded person has a right to economic security and to a decent standard of living. He has a right to productive work or to other meaningful occupation.

ARTICLE IV

The mentally retarded person has a right to live with his family or with foster parents; to participate in all aspects of community life and to be provided with appropriate leisure time activities. If care in an institution becomes necessary it should be in surroundings and under circumstances as close to normal living as possible.

ARTICLE V

The mentally retarded person has a right to a qualified guardian when this is required to protect his personal well being and interest. No person rendering direct services to the mentally retarded should also serve as his guardian.

ARTICLE VI

The mentally retarded person has a right to protection from exploitation, abuse and degrading treatment. If accused, he has a right to a fair trial with full recognition being given to his degree of responsibility.

ARTICLE VII

Some mentally retarded persons may be unable, due to the severity of their handicap, to exercise for themselves all of their rights in a meaningful way. For others, modification of some or all of these rights is appropriate. The procedure used for modification or denial of rights must contain proper legal safeguards against every form of abuse, must be based on an evaluation of the social capability of the mentally retarded person by qualified experts and must be subject to periodic reviews and to the right of appeal to higher authorities.

ABOVE ALL, THE MENTALLY RETARDED PERSON HAS THE RIGHT TO RESPECT.

(Adopted by the Assembly of the League at the 4th International Congress of the International League of Societies for the Mentally Handicapped, Jerusalem, October 24, 1968.)

Rights of the handicapped which are now directly protected by federal legislation were listed by Meyen (1978):

Rights to a free and appropriate education

Rights to adequate treatment in residential institutions

Rights to appropriate earnings consistent with their level of productivity, in institutions and other settings which provide work opportunities

Rights (of handicapped persons and their parents) to due process and consultation in placement decisions and other areas affecting their well being

Rights of access to employment, transportation, education, and the environment

Rights to reasonable protective services (pp. 207–208)

Unfortunately, as Haring (1978) pointed out, these legislated provisions for meeting the needs of the disabled are too often being ignored, standards are not being upheld, and in many instances mandated services are not yet being provided. Both governmental and local agencies and concerned community members are placing increased emphasis on assuring and protecting the entitled rights of the handicapped. The advocacy approach to improving delivery of services to handicapped children and adults is increasingly being recognized as the quickest and most effective way of ensuring that the disabled receive the services to which they are entitled.

Advocacy may be carried out by formal organizations, informal groups, or by individuals. Advocates function as change agents, working "to speed up the responsiveness of society and of any system in society to the needs of the people" (Dickman, 1976, p. 40). Advocacy "helps define the special needs of the handicapped, points out gaps in existing services, and helps develop programs to fill unmet needs. . . . (It) encourages the developmentally disabled and their families to speak out, individually or through their organizations, when private or tax-supported agencies fail to provide necessary services or make their services inaccessable or difficult to utilize" (United Cerebral Palsy Association, 1977, p. 59). Areas in which advocacy is needed include architectural barriers, housing, transportation, tax benefits and exemptions, Social Security and SSI benefits, education, vocational training and employment, other civil rights, and the participation of the handicapped in community life (Haring, 1978).

Types of Advocacy

Advocacy programs seek to provide handicapped persons with individualized assistance in order to protect their interests and ensure their rights within the community. Larsen (1977) described three major forms of protective services: legal advocacy, operational advocacy, and personal or case advocacy.

Legal advocacy services provide qualified legal assistance, and emphasize litigation, legislation, and the recognition of legal rights. Passage of major state and federal legislation for educational, vocational, and civil rights of the handicapped has been in large part the result of legal advocacy approaches. Legal actions during the past several years have been in the categories of right of treatment, questions of standards (identification, evaluation, placement procedures), and right to education (Haring, 1978). An alphabetized listing by Larsen (1977) of suits filed because of noncompliance with legislative or court directives included "architectural barriers, classification, committment, custody, education, employment, guardianship, protection from harm, sterilization, treatment (institutional), voting, zoning (group home)" (p. 27).

Legal advocacy is considered the single most important form of advocacy. However, the backlog of court cases and the slowness of the judicial process make it imperative that other forms of advocacy be utilized to speed provision of needed services to the disabled. Operational advocacy, as defined by Larsen (1977) is the "presence of a system that focuses on (a) ease of access to services at the local level; (b) delivery of full preventive and remedial services to all who need them; and (c) the provision of consumer-oriented, rather than institutionally-oriented, services" (p. 27). Person or case advocacy is the most common approach to assuring protective services. Features common to various models are that they "(a) serve individual consumers who are unable to represent their own interests; (b) make provisions for meeting the expressive needs of the individuals that they serve; (c) assure that the individual contacts and is served by appropriate services; (d) protect the individual's human and civil rights; and (e) provide the individual with continuity across time and services" (Larsen, 1977, p. 27).

The Citizen Advocate

Citizen advocacy is an alternative protective service which depends on community citizens as volunteers to represent the interests of other less competent persons on a one-to-one basis. These citizen advocates may receive special training and help from public advocacy offices.

Wolfensberger (1973) defined the citizen advocate: "a mature, competent citizen volunteer, representing, as if they were his own, the interests of another citizen who is impaired in his instrumental capacity, or who has major expressive needs which are unmet and which are likely to remain unmet without special intervention" (p. 11). The advocate, as viewed by Wolfensberger, fills two needs of the disabled—instrumental and expressive. The instrumental advocate deals with practical, everyday problems; he/she may be a trustee or a guardian. The expressive advocate meets needs for communication, support, and relationship; he/she will be an advocate-friend. Often a combination of the two roles will be found, perhaps as a foster parent or tutor.

Strichart and Gottlieb (1979) reported findings of a 1976 survey of citizen advocates. The purposes of the study were to discover their reasons for volunteering as advocates, their perception of the effects of the program on their proteges and themselves, and to produce a description of the volunteer advocate. Results of the study showed 54 percent of the citizen advocates carrying out expressive functions exclusively, with 8 percent playing only an instrumental role. The advocates seemed to generally spend their time with the handicapped in social-recreational activities. As a result of the study, the citizen-advocate office for that area suggested these guidelines for the volunteer advocate: That he "(a) provide friendship, guidance and emotional support, (b) monitor programs and services, (c) provide opportunities for socialization and community exposure, and (d) secure legal assistance when necessary;" in short, that he carry out an "instrumental-expressive-guide-advocate role." As the volunteer advocates seemed to be uncomfortable in the instrumental role, it was recommended that they be given additional training, through formal training procedures, in the area of instrumental functioning.

Citizen advocacy provides opportunities for greater exposure of the public to learning experiences with the handicapped. It produces positive changes in attitudes of the advocates themselves, as well as those of the public. "Attitudes and beliefs about the nature of mental retardation (and other handicapping conditions) greatly influence the public policies and private actions that affect and control decisions regarding the scope, characteristics, and quality of services" (Meyen, 1978, p. 191). Advocacy in its various forms is seen as an increasingly necessary and effective aid to service delivery to the handicapped.

Advocacy and the Teacher

Among other findings of a survey in the area of parent education described by Becker, Bender, and Kawabe (1976), 58 percent of the parents of the mildly handicapped and 54 percent of the parents of the severely handicapped went first to the child's teacher for information of any type in regard to the child. The teacher is often the person to whom the parent feels closest, or is perhaps the only source available or known to the parent. Haring (1978) suggested that the study of advocacy is needed in teacher training curricula. The handicapped are often unable to become their own advocates or direct others in advocacy efforts. The teacher should know of resources and be able to direct parents or others to sources of information. Teachers therefore need better preparation in community involvement, especially in advocacy activities.

Educational Advocacy and Due Process

State and federal legislation provides for an appropriate public school education for all handicapped, but this legislation is, in too many instances, not being implemented. Many parents are not aware of the mandated educational rights of their children and the "due process" procedure for assuring appropriate services. The failure of many school systems to provide appropriate services, or in many cases, any services at all, is being addressed by many parent organizations and other citizen advocacy groups across the country. Organized efforts are being made to train individuals in educational advocacy. One such organization is *Education Advocacy for Children with Handicaps* (*EACH*). The primary purposes of this nonprofit, statewide organization are:

a. To educate and promote the education of parents of handicapped children regarding their children's needs, rights, and resources.
b. To provide and assist in the provision of individual advocacy for children with handicaps including, where appropriate, litigation and other legal assistance.
c. To provide training for individuals in order to make them more effective advocates for children with handicaps.
d. To establish evaluation standards by which the effectiveness of advocates for children with handicaps may be evaluated (EACH, Note 1).

SERVICE NEEDS OF THE DEVELOPMENTALLY DISABLED

The definition of *developmental disability* as revised in the 1978 Amendments to the Developmental Disabilities Act (PL 95-602) reads as follows:

"Developmental disability" means a severe, chronic disability of a person which (a) is attributable to a mental or physical impairment or combination of mental and physical impairment; (b) is manifested before the person attains age twenty-two; (c) is likely to continue indefinitely; (d) results in substantial functional limitations in three or more of the following areas of major life activity: (1) self-care; (2) receptive and expressive language; (3) learning; (4) mobility; (5) self-direction; (6) capacity for independent living; and (7) economic self-sufficiency; and (e) reflects the person's need for a combination and sequence of special, interdisciplinary, or generic care, treatment, or other services which are of lifelong or extended duration and are individually planned and coordinated (PL 95-602, 1978, Title V).

Priorities for Services

Four priority service areas were identified in this Act's provision for programs to assist the developmentally disabled:

1. Case management services to assist DD persons in gaining access to needed social, medical, educational and other services, including follow-along and coordination of services.
2. Child development services for the prevention, identification and alleviation of developmental disabilities among children, including: early intervention, counseling and training of parents, early identification of DD and diagnosis and evaluation of such disabilities.
3. Alternative community living arrangement services for assistance in maintaining suitable residential arrangements in the community, including in-house services, family support services, foster care, group living, respite care, and staff training, placement and maintenance.
4. Nonvocational social-development services, for assistance in performing daily living and work activities (Office for Handicapped Individuals, 1979b, pp. 3–4).

Needs Surveys

Professionals, parents of the handicapped, and the handicapped themselves are in general agreement as to components essential to comprehensive service delivery. Larsen (1977) identified areas of needed emphasis in community service to the handicapped: early intervention, public schools, community residential services, family counseling, inhome family support services, and protective services. Smith and Neisworth (1975) placed emphasis on physical, social-personal, vocational, and general support needs, and stated that the range of services to the handicapped should include evaluation/diagnosis, short term provision of rehabilitation/habilitation services, and long term provision of workshops, adult education, counseling, health insurance, community housing, and so forth. Fanning (1973) reported results of a survey of agencies, professionals, and parents to determine priorities for services to the retarded. Areas of greatest need as ranked by the respondents were:

1. Children and adult training services (social, vocational, educational)
2. Group or residential homes
3. Guidance and counseling for families
4. Diagnostic and evaluation services
5. Consultation and education (for community paraprofessionals, professionals, and agencies)
6. Recreational opportunities
7. Temporary (respite) care (p. 46)

A similar survey (United Cerebral Palsy Associations, 1977) had as its goal the identification of general and specific problems faced by the handicapped, their families, and the community. This problem census identified six major community needs: information/awareness, the high risk infant, education, transportation, home help services, and system analysis of complex agencies. System analysis asks "Who does what for whom? What and where are the missing pieces? Who can supply them? What will it take?" (Dickman, 1976, p. 33). The first step in system analysis is to assess the territory, determining the needs, the resources, the make-up of the population, services present, and services needed.

Meyen (1978) summarized material in the Developmental Disabilities Assistance and Bill of Rights Act (PL 94-103) in the following table of essential services (Table 1). In his discussion of the material, Meyen pointed out that while the mildly handicapped may need only some of these services (usually education, training and employment), the more severely involved will probably require them all at some period of life. Their availability in the community is therefore necessary.

AVAILABILITY OF GENERIC SERVICES

One corollary of the normalization principle is the use of generic services whenever possible, instead of providing separate ones (Wolfensberger, 1972). Generic services are those typical services which the public

Table 1.   Essential services for retarded and other handicapped persons[a]

Category	Description

1. Developmental programs
   a. Day activity
   b. Education
   c. Training
	1. Includes a variety of educational and care programs appropriate for a person's age and severity of handicapping conditions.

2. Residential services
   a. Domiciliary
   b. Special living arrangements
	2. Includes out-of-home living quarters: 24-hour lodging and supervision, and less supervised living arrangements for less severely handicapped persons (e.g., supervised apartment).

3. Employment services
   a. Preparation
   b. Sheltered (including work activity)
   c. Competitive
	3. Includes a continuum of vocational evaluation, training, and work opportunity in supervised and independent settings.

4. Identification services
   a. Diagnosis
   b. Evaluation
	4. Includes efforts to identify presence of disabilities and their probable cause(s), and to assess and plan service needs of the disabled person.

5. Facilitating services
   a. Information and referral
   b. Counseling
   c. Protective and socio-legal
   d. Follow-along
   e. Case management
	5. Includes a variety of actions needed to insure that disabled persons are informed of available services, assisted in getting services, provided protection of rights and guardianship if needed, and given continued review of plans to insure that services are appropriately delivered.

6. Treatment services
   a. Medical
   b. Dental
	6. Includes appropriate medical care, prosthetic devices needed for maximum adjustment, and dental care.

7. Transportation	7. Transportation to training, work, and other activities.
8. Leisure and recreation	8. Structured and unstructured leisure opportunities as needed.

Source: *Exceptional Children and Youth: An Introduction* by E. L. Meyen. Love Publishing Co., Denver, 1978, pp. 193–194. Reprinted by permission of the author and publisher.

[a] Much of this material has been adapted from material in the Developmental Disabilities Assistance and Bill of Rights Act. (Public Law 94-103).

receives outright or which are easily available at a standard price. Such services are taken for granted by most families, and considered a necessary part of everyday living. The handicapped person or the family with a handicapped member is denied many such services because they are not accessible or not available; or if available, the cost of the special service is prohibitive. Kenowitz, Gallaher, and Edgar (1977) described the frustrations of the handicapped and their families when attempting to secure medical or dental care, use public transportation, attend the church of their choice, secure insurance, find a babysitter, or locate recreational or social activities in which to participate.

An extensive study was made by Scheerenberger (1970) to obtain information as to the availability of generic services for the retarded and their families. Specific objectives were to study accessibility of generic services, to identify problems encountered by professional persons in providing these services, and to identify problems encountered by parents in obtaining the services. The study involved 504 representatives from four generic service categories (medical, guidance and counseling, religious, and sociorecreational) and 232 parents from the same sociogeographical areas as the service providers. Problems found that were preventing the use of generic services by the retarded and their families included: 1) a scarcity of services, especially in low income areas, 2) lack of coordination between other generic agencies and specialized programs, 3) services having "low visibility" and parents being unaware of their existence, 4) lack of support and guidance from professionals trained in programming for the retarded, 5) inability of parents to pay for services, and 6) lack of specialized programs necessary to supplement and complement generic services. One of Scheerenberger's greatest concerns was that potential consumers of generic services knew little about the availability and accessibility of existing services. He concluded that comprehensive and effective programs for the handicapped should provide for greater utilization of generic services, and stated that "Specialized and generic services must participate in a balanced partnership to meet the needs of the retarded, and their programs must be identifiable, well-publicized, readily accessible, and coordinated" (p. 16).

Results of a less extensive study by Kenowitz, Gallaher, and Edgar (1977) also suggested that generic services are not readily available to the handicapped. These authors emphasized the necessity of sensitizing the providers of generic services to the needs of the handicapped and their families. For optimal use of available services, the community and the handicapped must be brought together. To accomplish this, Kenowitz et al. recommended the development of community action networks in every community. The primary purpose of such networks would be to bring together the families needing services and the agencies responsible for the delivery of such services. In order to do this, the community must recognize its responsibility and provide services, and the handicapped must be trained in using the services. Service deficiencies must be identified, and programs adapted or developed to fill these needs. Personnel in these service programs will need to be trained to promote community integration of the handicapped.

Baroff (1974) provided a comprehensive listing (see Table 2) of the many disciplines and service agents which must be involved in the delivery of essential services to the handicapped throughout their lives. Some aspects of delivery of these services are discussed in the following sections of this chapter.

MEDICAL AND HEALTH SERVICES

New social perspectives on the handicapped have caused changes in the kinds of medical service delivery they require. The recent emphasis on home placement and community services has drawn attention to the role played by the medical profession in community service provision. Prevention of developmental disabilities and early identification of handicapping conditions receive high priority on lists of needed community services. The role of the medical profession within the support system does not end, however, when successful referral of a severely handicapped patient to other services is made. Since most such patients have associated physical disabilities and other health problems, their ongoing health management needs may require increased contact with and dependency upon their physician during all stages of life. Drug therapy is playing an increasingly important role in the treatment of many handicapping conditions, but requires careful medical administration and supervision. In addition to the treatment of any problems amenable to surgical correction, medication, or other physical care, the doctors may also find themselves consulting and referring with dental, orthopedic, and nutritional services. Richardson, Guralnick, and Tupper (1978) stated that, "the majority of pediatric residents now in training will be expected to function . . . not only as consultants and counselors to individual children and their families but will also participate in coordinating the effective delivery of services through a variety of community facilities" (p. 3).

Progress toward Prevention of Developmental Disabilities

Statistics show that one child in 16 may have a birth defect (Dickman, 1976). Monies are being provided by the federal government to encourage research in an attempt to lower this figure. Medical research into the etiology of various handicapping conditions has resulted in a greater awareness of the importance of prenatal factors. Biochemical and genetic research has led to discovery of a number of genetic causes of handicapping conditions, and current research is exploring control of genetic deficiencies. Detection of chromosomal abnormalities and some genetically determined metabolic disorders is being made possible through the prenatal diagnostic technique of amniocentesis. Other recent findings have shown that there is great possibility of damage to the fetus through the mother's use of drugs, alcohol, tobacco, and other commonly ingested substances. Nevertheless, the etiology of most conditions remains a mystery, and much more research will be required before efficient control of prenatal variables is a reality. The public generally does not seem aware of the critical importance of the environment of the unborn child. Greater dissemination of information regarding research findings in this area seems imperative.

The High-Risk Infant

New medical procedures involving improved delivery techniques and paranatal infant screening are aiding in reducing the number of handicapping conditions caused by paranatal factors. The identification of high-risk infants through screening programs has proved a valuable preventive procedure. Simple screening procedures are used to detect phenylketonuria (PKU) and other inborn errors of metabolism causing mental retardation if left untreated. While over 40 states have laws requiring that PKU testing be done, cost problems and scattered population of some states have interfered with their implementation. Concern over failure of communities to make fuller use of genetic counseling, prenatal diagnosis, and screening of the newborn has been voiced by many leaders in medical and scientific research (*Handicapped Americans Reports*, 1978).

Since numerous unknown and complex etiologies make complete prevention of developmental disabilities impossible, early and accurate identification of existing or suspected problems is essential. Determination of a child's condition and prognosis through appropriate examination and testing seems a primary medical responsibility. However, there is often a delay both in early identification and in provision of services to both the child and his/her family. Dickman (1976) suggested possible reasons for this delay:

1. Maldistribution of pediatricians, neonatologists and public health specialists who are qualified to give useful guidance.
2. Lack of knowledge among primary physicians in family practice and pediatrics concerning treatment facilities, pre-school programs and other helpful resources in their geographic area.
3. Lack of universal coordination among medical, allied health and child development specialists for the dissemination of their bodies of knowledge to be used in community based medical services.
4. Lack of a delivery system offering continuity of care, periodic monitoring and reassessment to safeguard the developmental potential of the infant who has been identified as "at risk" (p. 95).

Table 2. Array of services needed by handicapped throughout their lives

Services	Service agents	Service disciplines
	Prenatal	
Prevention Prenatal care, treatment of the fetus, genetic counseling, therapeutic abortion	**Health agents** Primary physician, local health department, hospital clinic, fetology service	Physician, public health nurse, genetic counselor
	Infancy and preschool	
Prevention (medical) Metabolic screening (e.g., PKU), immunization, avoid lead paint ingestion, routine medical care, nutrition	**Health agents** Primary physician, well-baby clinic (local health dept.), hospital	Physician, public health nurse, nutritionist
Prevention (psychological) Stimulation, training, education	**Child care agents** The home, adoptive home (adoptive agency), foster care(social service), child development center	Mother or mother surrogate, teacher and teacher-aide, social worker, volunteer (student, parent, foster "grandparent")
Identification Screening, diagnosis, parent counseling, medical treatment, management	**Health agents** Well-baby clinic (health dept., hospital), primary physician, medical specialist, developmental evaluation clinic, home nursing service, local association for retarded children, mental health service, pastoral counseling, genetic counseling	Public health nurse, pediatrician, psychologist, social worker, physical therapist, speech therapist, dentist
Training and education Self-help (feeding, dressing, toileting); language, cognitive, motor, social-emotional training	**Early childhood education agents** Child development center (generic and specialized)	Teacher, teacher-aide, psychologist, speech therapist

			Parent and parent surrogate, social worker, institutional staff providing special medical and related services

Residential — The home, adoptive home, foster family care, institution — Parent and parent surrogate, social worker, institutional staff providing special medical and related services

School age

Training and education
Self-help (as needed); academic, social, motor, language, recreational, vocational (prevocational, vocational, on-the-job) training; activities of daily living

Education and rehabilitation
Child development center, public school (elementary, junior high, senior high), vocational rehabilitation agency, employer

Teacher, teacher-aide, school psychologist, guidance counselor, speech therapist, rehabilitation counselor, business and industry

Residential — The home, foster care (family, group), group home, short term and long term institutional care — Parent and parent surrogate, social worker, staff of institution (physician, nurse, physical therapist, teacher, psychologist, speech therapist, rehabilitation counselor)

Recreational
Community recreational programs
Generic and special recreational resources; day programs; camping-day and overnight, summer, year-round; scouting

Recreator, group worker, volunteer (student, etc.)

Adulthood

Vocational
Prevocational, vocational (as appropriate), and on-the-job training; competitive employment; sheltered employment (extended employment and work activity)

Semiskilled and unskilled jobs in industry, service, and government; sheltered workshop; vocational rehabilitation agency

Employer, personnel manager, rehabilitation counselor, staff of sheltered workshop (administrator, evaluator, work supervisor, personal adjustment counselor, instructor)

continued

Table 2. (Continued)

Services	Service agents	Service disciplines
Activity program (Primarily for severely and profoundly retarded persons)	Adolescent and adult Activity center—preferably tied to a sheltered workshop	Teacher, teacher-aide
Recreational	(see School age)	
Residential	Community and institutional Home, group home, apartment, long term and short term institutional care	Parent and surrogate parent, counselor, institutional staff (see "School age-Residential")
Advocacy Assuring the rights of retarded persons, especially those who will not achieve independence	Federal, State, and local services as provided by law, e.g., Social Security benefits, Veterans' benefits (children of servicemen), guardianship, legal counsel	"Advocates"

Source: *Mental retardation: Nature, cause and management* by G. S. Baroff, John Wiley & Sons, New York, 1974, pp. 124-125. Reprinted by permission of the author and publisher.

The Physician-Parent Relationship

Rheingold (1975) reported that medical workers seem to limit their interviews with parents to reporting the diagnosis or advising in regard to institutional placement. Parents must go elsewhere for information as to available services. There appears to be a genuine need for increased awareness within the medical profession of the range of alternatives to placement, including early intervention programs. In addition, the doctor should be aware of the degree of emotional impact involved in an informing interview and of the extent to which family needs are informational as well as emotional. These informational needs are important; an improved perspective can often be provided the parent by clear presentation of a realistic prognosis along with some discussion of available options. Some programs are attempting to meet these needs through multidisciplinary support services. A "crisis intervention team" of medical personnel, psychologists, and social workers provides early supportive services to parents, offering information and advice about the child's need and available community resources and services (Soeffing, 1975).

The physician is usually the first professional to identify more serious handicapping conditions, those apparent at birth or shortly thereafter. In most instances, the responsibility for informing the parents of diagnostic results falls on the doctor alone. Odle, Greer, and Anderson (1976) reported that surveys of parental attitudes revealed feelings of dissatisfaction and resentment in regard to the informing interview. Many doctors seem unaware of the many problems of the handicapped and their families, and lack skill in interpersonal communication. Others may not refer parents to needed special services because of lack of knowledge both about developmental defects and about available community resources. Recommendations for elimination of barriers in referral delivery systems include education of physicians and other medical personnel in the following areas:

a. The *relationship* between the concerned family and the primary physician including the emotional impact faced by families and support needed from the primary physicians. The portrayal of family reaction is essential to the future of the parent/child relationship.
b. The involvement of the primary physician in referring the individual and his family to appropriate specialists and early treatment-education programs.
c. The follow-along responsibilities of the primary physician.
d. The research findings that are utilized by the service specialists that are the rationale for early identification and program services.

e. The utilization of medical, allied health, and other professionals in the total service delivery system.
f. Alternative choices for referral to existing programs when there is a lack of a community resource.
g. The partnership that should be formed among physicians, parents, and other agencies when resources need to be developed (Dickman, 1976, pp. 95–96).

DEVELOPMENTAL AND EARLY INTERVENTION SERVICES

The importance of early intervention cannot be overemphasized if the community support service system is to make an optimum contribution to the development of the handicapped child. Early intervention and developmental services are usually those kinds of services needed and/or provided to the handicapped child and his/her family subsequent to diagnosis of the handicap and prior to entrance into some program of formal education at school age. Such service continuums include both infant intervention programs and preschool programs. The degree of success achieved by these early services seems to be dependent to a certain degree upon the age of the child at the time of their introduction (Lacoste, 1978). Within certain limitations, the earlier the services are provided, the better the results in both child development and family adjustment.

Services provided in these programs usually include: 1) further evaluation of the initial diagnosis, and establishment of realistic developmental expectations, 2) parent counseling, both psychological and informational, 3) home training, including practical techniques for management of the child in the home, specialized child training practices, and developmental exercises, and 4) social experiences and exposure to parents and children with similar problems, and to normal children.

Agencies providing early intervention services include medical clinics associated with large hospitals, community child guidance and mental health clinics, clinics that are facets of residential facilities, and early intervention programs associated with universities or with public school systems. Regardless of the provider of such services, the program should be responsive to consumer need instead of professional. Parents should be actively involved in implementation of the program, serving as primary change agents. The primary focus of early intervention efforts should be "development of mutually reinforcing parent-child relationships, by involving the parents in all diagnostic and developmental evaluations; by responding to parental suggestions and wishes in planning intervention programs; and by seeking to develop parental self-sufficiency in caring for and teaching their own children" (Larsen, 1977,

p. 23). A well organized and well executed system of such early intervention services can be a key component of the community service continuum, with proven effectiveness in the past and considerable potential for future aid to handicapped children and their families.

RESIDENTIAL SERVICES

Residential services are among the most essential to normalization since they provide an appropriate alternative to institutional placement. Such services encompass a full range of options, including residence with the immediate family, respite homes for limited stays, foster home or adoptive home placement, and group homes or half-way houses. The half-way house was defined by Meyen (1967) as a supervised housing arrangement "which may include counseling and group activities for small groups of mentally retarded [or otherwise handicapped] individuals capable of relatively independent living or for individuals needing opportunities to become oriented to community life" (p. 19). The range of residential services may also include such lesser-used options as nursing homes, intermediate care facilities, and independent living arrangements, including subsidized supervised apartments.

One great need in this area of services is for alternatives to institutionalization for the handicapped adult whose home placement with his/her family must be discontinued due to the parents' increasing age and their consequent inability to care for him/her, or due to unexpected changes in the home situation. There are basic government funding programs for which many disabled people are eligible that would aid the disabled person in the reach toward more independent living. These programs include income maintenance (SSI), medical assistance (Medicaid), home health aides (Department of Social Services), Housing Assistance Program (providing accessible housing at affordable rentals and subsidized for the handicapped as well as for the elderly), vocational training programs (Vocational Rehabilitation), and civic, voluntary, and philanthropic social and recreational programs (Pagano, 1976). Often the handicapped who are entitled to these services do not know of them or have no way to take advantage of them. Services are needed which will assure or facilitate use of these entitlements. The funding is available, but support services are needed to obtain it.

Independent Living for the Handicapped

In addition to advocacy in securing support services, there must be counseling and training for independence. Pagano (1976) described one small, voluntary nonprofit organization, *Independent Living for the Handicapped, Inc.*, Brooklyn, NY, which provides services designed to help a group of dystrophic disabled adults take the option of independent living. A listing of services provided by this organization is representative of areas in which the disabled may need assistance for community living:

1. Counseling and advocacy services; informing of entitlements and how to get them; assisting directly or supporting the efforts of the handicapped
2. Apartment finding service; evaluating the apartment and the neighborhood for accessibility
3. Holding tenants' meetings, socials; "Training for Independence" (how to find an apartment, be assertive, cope with daily living problems such as budgeting, shopping, using free time creatively, firing someone)
4. Assistance in finding, training, supervising home attendants; emergency aide service
5. Subsidized and specialized van service—for socialization, shopping, and becoming part of the community (p. 9–10).

Federally Sponsored Services

Provisions of the Housing and Community Development Amendments of 1978 (PL 95-557) include funds for the construction and rehabilitation of housing to "serve the unique needs of handicapped individuals between the ages of 18 and 62 or families with a handicapped member or members of any age." The legislated purposes of this funding are to:

1. support innovative methods of meeting the needs of handicapped persons by providing a variety of housing options ranging from small group homes to independent living complexes;
2. provide handicapped occupants with an assured range of services and opportunities for optimal independent living and participation in normal daily activities; and
3. facilitate the access of handicapped persons to the community at large and to suitable employment within the community (Office for Handicapped Individuals, 1979a, p. 5).

A new program of comprehensive independent living services for the disabled was created as part of the 1978 Rehabilitation, Comprehensive Services, and Developmental Disabilities Amendments (PL 95-602). This program provides grants-in-aid to states to encourage establishment and operation of special centers for independent living. Handicapped persons themselves are to be meaningfully and substantially involved in both planning for and management of these centers for comprehensive service delivery. The wide range of services to be provided includes:

intake counseling and evaluation of client need;
referral and counseling for attendant care;
advocacy regarding legal and economic rights;
skills training;

housing and transportation referral and assistance;
health maintenance programs;
community group living arrangements;
individual/group social and recreational activities; and
attendant care and training of personnel to provide such care (Office for
Handicapped Individuals, 1979a, p. 1).

FAMILY SUPPORT SERVICES

Many parents, as well as the disabled themselves, feel that they have no
supportive resources outside of the immediate family. Parents often
become apathetic and disillusioned because of repeated failure to find
needed information or services. Findings of a survey to identify parent
needs (Becker et al., 1976) were that problems of parents included
"inability to receive a reasonable and understandable diagnosis; lack of
information as to services available to the child and the family; and
psychological and emotional problems related to guilt, feelings of inferiority, and financial difficulties" (pp. 4–5).

A support system was defined by Moore and Seashore (1977) as "a
network of individuals, groups, and organizations, with the potential of
supplying resources to a person or family" (p. 4). Relationships in a support system may range from the formal and expert to the companiona-
ble. Sources of support may include close friends, role models, parents of
children with similar problems, persons with like handicaps, skilled
problem solvers, and information agents. A support system is needed so
that the family can better carry out their basic tasks of everyday living,
can cope with any crises that may occur, and can not only maintain
family skills and competencies, but can have the freedom to grow personally, socially, and professionally (Moore & Seashore, 1977).

Some degree of support service is a virtual necessity for the family
which includes a handicapped member. The current trend toward deinstitutionalization brings with it the need for an increase in the quality and
quantity of community-based aid. In the area of practical life services,
this may include home help services, respite care, crisis intervention
services, visiting nurses or other health care sources, some form of day
care service, and aid in transportation. A number of community agencies
and resources will be involved in the provision of necessary services.

Respite Care

An especially vital support service for the family of the severely handicapped is respite care, the short term temporary care of the disabled
family member (Moore & Seashore, 1977). Such care is imperative during times of family crisis or emergency. The provision of a brief period of

relief from the continuous care of the handicapped child can also help in keeping families together. The availability of respite services may be an important factor in the family's decision to keep the handicapped child in the home. Respite care services may also be used to provide short term intensive training in specific skills to the handicapped child (Larsen, 1977), thus increasing the possibility of a positive parent-child relationship.

Counseling and Information Services

Emphasis in the past has been on counseling with parents of the handicapped, and to some degree with other members of the family. There needs to be more provision for such service to the handicapped themselves—to the mentally retarded as well as the physically handicapped; to the child as well as the adult. Various types of counseling services should be available at appropriate times. Needs of both the family and the handicapped member will vary at different ages of the handicapped, and counseling may be carried out by many informed persons in the context of provision of services. Therapeutic counseling or psychiatric therapy is not seen by parents as being as great a need as attention to problem solving and providing answers to their questions. Concrete informational needs seem to outweigh psychological and emotional ones (Matheny & Vernick, 1969), but both are vital to the success of home placement, especially for families of severely involved individuals. Larsen (1977) recommended that family counseling include instruction in child-training procedures, information on available community resources, and counseling about attitudes and psychological needs—their own and those of the handicapped family member. The family may lack understanding of the terminology used by professionals in reporting the diagnosis and recommended treatment and services. Advice may be needed in wise use of financial resources in providing for present or future needs of the handicapped person. There is an ever-changing need for informational services.

Counseling services may be obtained from public or private family service agencies or mental health clinics. While these offer psychological and emotional guidance, the quality and quantity of informational counseling is usually inadequate (Abramson, Gravink, Abramson, & Sommers, 1977). Dean (1975) stated that parents of handicapped children experience an almost universal "lack of information on where to turn for appropriate . . . services after diagnosis, evaluation, and prescription have occurred" (p. 527). Abramson et al. (1977) found that over 50 percent of a large sample of parents surveyed were dissatisfied or uncertain about the information they received. Parents, especially those of the severely handicapped, report discouragement and frustration in their search for help because of misinformation, negative attitudes encountered, lack of services, and improper services (Haring, 1978).

In addition to referral to appropriate agencies, services and programs, parents require help to deal with the increasingly complex and fragmented service delivery system. At the local level, some degree of information and assistance is currently provided by parent organizations, mental retardation agencies, human service centers, mental health centers, or private practice professionals. There is great need for coordinating agencies to serve as depositories of information and agents of communication among providers and users of all services (Smith & Neisworth, 1975). Currently, few such information and coordinating centers exist.

RECREATIONAL SERVICES

Recreation has great potential for normalization. As Luckey and Shapiro (1974) stated, "The constructive and creative use of leisure . . . is becoming generally accepted as an essential segment of training programs intended to prepare mentally retarded persons for life and work in the community" (p. 35). Many handicapped adults have experienced success in their employment settings, but have not been able to fully adjust to and participate in community living because they have not been aware of available recreational resources or have not known how to use them. The broad areas of competence identified by Kokaska (1978) as being essential to the success of handicapped persons in their adult roles included physical development and leisure skills. Brolin (1976) also included "utilizing recreation and leisure" in his career education curriculum designed for total preparation for life.

Many generic recreational services are available to the handicapped. However, professionals in the field of recreation are not fully aware of the recreational needs of the disabled. There are few practical guidelines to follow in program planning to provide for these needs. Other problems include a lack of public awareness regarding needs and availability of existing services, logistical problems (available and accessible transportation for the handicapped), and insufficient financial support from the community.

Recreational services fill important ongoing needs that differ at various stages in life, and thus must offer a range of programs geared to such change. Handicapped children benefit from such community activities as specialized summer camps, noncompetitive sports programs, the Special Olympics, arts and crafts programs, organized outings, and scouting. It is encouraging to note that the Boy Scouts of America have recently lifted the age limits for the handicapped who because of disability may be unable to reach Cub, Eagle, or Explorer status before the prescribed age. In addition, handicapped scouts are now allowed to substitute alternate tests for those tasks they are physically unable to do. All handicapped boys in the United States now have the opportunity to earn awards previously denied them.

Local parks and recreation departments, community centers, service organizations, and parent groups usually concentrate on providing recreational services to children. Many handicapped adults therefore find themselves without postschool leisure time and recreational opportunities. Corcoran and French (1977) stated that handicapped persons may not be aware of adult leisure time opportunities that are available, or that they might not have the social skills that would allow them to feel comfortable in such community settings. Disabled persons may have never had the opportunity to choose and participate in activities or programs based on their personal likes, dislikes, and abilities (Kenowitz et al., 1977). Another deterrent to their use of recreational facilities and programs is the lack of appropriate transportation. A definite need exists for appropriate recreational programs and organized social activities, and for the training of the handicapped in recreational skills and the use of leisure time.

SCHOOL-COMMUNITY INTERACTION FOR NORMALIZATION

Wolfensberger (1972) provided an operative definition of normalization which has implications for the classroom teacher as well as for the community: the "utilization of means which are as culturally normative as possible, in order to establish and/or maintain personal behaviors and characteristics which are as culturally normative as possible" (p. 28). Larsen (1977) pointed out that "If our ultimate goal for the handicapped is normal behavior patterns occurring in normal environments, the former will not be easily obtained in the absence of the latter" (p. 25). Haring (1978), agreeing that special education needs to be more relevant to adult functioning, stated, "Many educational goals for the handicapped . . . can be gained only through actual practice in the community. Once these skills are gained, they may be lost unless he continues to practice them in an accepting community which is oriented to his unique capabilities and needs" (p. 241).

Normalcy and the Teacher

Kokaska cited Perske (1972) in stating that the positive self-concept of the handicapped cannot thrive "under conditions which by their very nature and structure convey the covert message that one is regarded as being incapable of filling a respected role" (p. 49). The teacher who feels that patience, sympathy, acceptance, and tolerance are the most important factors for reaching the handicapped may unwittingly foster immature and deviant behavior which is not a component of the disability itself. Hamalian and Ludwig (1976) emphasized that "community indifference and inadequate preparation for adult life combine to perpetuate social and economic dependence" (p. 173). The teacher may contribute to this inadequate preparation of the handicapped through failure to consider the relationship between process and goals of instructional programming for the handicapped. Kokaska (1974) recommended that the teacher ask when planning an activity, "Does this provide experiences with responsibility and prepare the student to cope?" and teach continually from that frame of reference. His further suggestions to the teacher are summarized:

Visualize future functioning of the student in relation to present time frames and develop methods which would move him toward ability to so function

Appraise attitudes and activities in relation to the long term goal of normalcy

Be an active agent in the coordination of class, home, and community in provision of enabling experiences

Be able to project the student in adult roles

Provide instruction to the family which fosters normalization (knowledge of community agencies and services, and alternatives and techniques to develop appropriate social behavior)

Facilitate the adjustment and success of the student in transfers to educational/living situations

CONCLUSION

Community provision for the handicapped does not minimize the role and responsibility of the parent and the education system, but supports and encourages progress of the disabled toward a more normal existence. However, as Smith and Neisworth (1975) emphasized, "Effective, adequate, and comprehensive community programming for all citizens cannot be expected to occur without commitment" (p. 288). It is not enough for the community to have the expertise, the organizational ability, and the financial resources for development of such a program; more basic for its success is the individual and collective commitment of the members of the community to meeting the needs of *all* its citizens.

REFERENCES

Abramson, P. R., Gravink, M. J., Abramson, L. M., & Sommers, D. Early diagnosis and intervention of retardation: A survey of parental reactions concerning the quality of services rendered. *Mental Retardation*, 1977, *15*(2), 28–31.

Baroff, G. S. *Mental Retardation: Nature, cause and management*. New York: John Wiley & Sons, 1974.

Becker, L. D., Bender, N. N., & Kawabe, K. K. *Exceptional parents: A survey of programs, services and needs*. Sacramento: Division of Special Education, California State Department of Education, 1976. ERIC-ED 148 043.

Brolin, D. E. *Vocational preparation of retarded citizens*. Columbus, Oh.: Charles E. Merrill, 1976.

Bruininks, R. H., & Warfield, G. The mentally retarded. In E. L. Meyen (Ed.), *Exceptional children and youth: An introduction*. Denver: Love Publishing Co., 1978.

Conroy, J. W. Trends in deinstitutionalization of the mentally retarded. *Mental Retardation*, 1977, *15*(4), 44–46.

Corcoran, E. L., & French, R. W. Leisure activity for the retarded adult in the community. *Mental Retardation*, 1977, *15*(2), 21–23.

Dean, D. Closer look: A parent information service. *Exceptional Children*, 1975, *41*(8), 527–530.

Dickman, I. R. (Compiler). *Thinking/learning/doing advocacy*. New York: United Cerebral Palsy Association, 1976.

Fanning, J. W. Coordinating community services. *Mental Retardation*, 1973, *11*(6), 46–47.

Hamalian, C. S., & Ludwig, A. J. Practicum in normalization and advocacy: A neglected component in teacher training. *Education and Training of the Mentally Retarded*, 1976, *11*(2), 172–175.

Handicapped Americans Reports, 1978, *1*(3), 5–6.

Haring, N. G. (Ed.). *Behavior of exceptional children* (2nd ed.). Columbus, Oh.: Charles E. Merrill, 1978.

Juul, K. European approaches and innovations in serving the handicapped. *Exceptional Children*, 1978, *44*(5), 322–330.

Kenowitz, L. A., Gallaher, J., & Edgar, E. Generic services for the severely handicapped and their families: What's available? In E. Sontag (Ed.), *Educational programming for the severely and profoundly handicapped*. Reston, Va.: The Council for Exceptional Children, 1977.

Kokaska, C. Normalization: Implications for teachers of the retarded. *Mental Retardation*, 1974, *12*(4), 49–51.

Kokaska, C. Career awareness for handicapped students in the elementary schools. *Career Development for Exceptional Individuals*, 1978, *1*(1), 25–35.

LaCoste, R. Early intervention: Can it hurt? *Mental Retardation*, 1978, *16*(3), 266–268.

Larsen, L. A. Community services necessary to program effectively for the severely/profoundly handicapped. In E. Sontag, (Ed.), *Educational programming for the severely and profoundly handicapped*. Reston, Va.: The Council for Exceptional Children, 1977.

Luckey, R. E. & Shapiro, I. G. Recreation: An essential aspect of habilitative programming. *Mental Retardation*, 1974, *12*(5), 33–35.

Matheny, A. P., & Vernick, J. Parents of the mentally retarded child: Emotionally overwhelmed or informationally deprived. *Journal of Pediatrics*, 1969, *4*, 953–959.

Mayo, L. W. *A proposed program for national action to combat mental retardation*. Report of the Presidents' Committee on Mental Retardation. Washington, D.C.: U.S. Government Printing Office, 1962.

Meyen, E., Need for planning services and facilities for the mentally retarded. In E. L. Meyen (Ed.), *Planning community services for the mentally retarded*. Scranton, Pa.: International Textbook Company, 1967.

Meyen, E. L. *Exceptional children and youth: An introduction*. Denver: Love Publishing Co., 1978.

Moore, C., & Seashore, C. N. *Why do families need respite care? Building a support system*. Silver Spring, Md.: Montgomery County Association for Retarded Citizens, 1977. ERIC-ED 145 614.

Nirje, B. The normalization principle. In R. B. Kugel & A. Shearer (Eds.), *Changing patterns in residential services for the mentally retarded*. Washington, D.C.: Presidents' Committee on Mental Retardation, 1976.

Odle, S. J., Greer, J. G., & Anderson, R. M. The family of the severely retarded individual. In R. M. Anderson & J. G. Greer (Eds.), *Educating the severely and profoundly retarded*. Baltimore: University Park Press, 1976.

Office for Handicapped Individuals. Key legislation affecting handicapped individuals. *Programs for the Handicapped*, 1979, Jan.–Feb., (1), 5–7. (a)

Office for Handicapped Individuals. Rehabilitation, comprehensive services and developmental disabilities act of 1978. *Programs for the Handicapped*, 1979, Jan.–Feb. (1), 1–4. (b)

Pagano, N. A. *Integrated living for severely disabled people: A radical approach*. Paper presented at the 84th annual meeting of the American Psychological Association, Washington, D.C., Sept. 3–7, 1976. ERIC-ED 143 943.

Perske, R. The dignity of risk and the mentally retarded. *Mental Retardation*, 1972, *10*(1), 24–27.

Rheingold, H. Interpreting mental retardation to parents. In J. J. Dempsey (Ed.), *Community services for retarded children*. Baltimore: University Park Press, 1975.

Richardson, H. B., Guralnick, M. J., & Tupper, D. B. Training pediatricians for effective involvement with handicapped pre-school children and their families. *Mental Retardation*, 1978, *16*(1), 3–7.

Scheerenberger, R. C. Generic services for the mentally retarded and their families. *Mental Retardation*, 1970, *8*(6), 10–16.

Sharing experiences in thinking, learning, doing advocacy. New York: Professional Services Program Dept., United Cerebral Palsy Associations, 1977.

Smith, R. M., & Neisworth, J. T. *The exceptional child: A functional approach*. New York: McGraw-Hill, 1975.

Soeffing, M. Families for handicapped children: Foster and adoptive placement programs. *Exceptional Children*, 1975, *41*(8), 542.

Strichart, S. S., & Gottlieb, J. Advocacy through the eyes of citizens. In J. Gottlieb, (Ed.), *Educating mentally retarded persons*. Baltimore: University Park Press, 1979, in press.

Tobin. S. The mystique of deinstitutionalization. *Society*, 1978, *15*(5), 73–75.

Wolfensberger, W. *The principle of normalization in human services*. Toronto: National Institute on Mental Retardation, 1972.

Wolfensberger, W. Citizen advocacy for the handicapped, impaired and disadvantaged: An overview. In W. Wolfensberger (Ed.), *Citizen advocacy and protective services for the impaired and handicapped.* Toronto, Canada: National Institute of Mental Retardation, 1973.

REFERENCE NOTE

1. Education Advocacy for Children with Handicaps (EACH). *Bylaws of EACH*, Mimeographed material, 1979.

14

SPECIAL EDUCATION, VOCATIONAL EDUCATION, AND VOCATIONAL REHABILITATION
A Spectrum of Services to the Handicapped

William M. Jenkins and Sara J. Odle

NEEDS OF THE HANDICAPPED

Handicapped individuals, especially the mentally retarded, spend more years of their lives as adults in need of vocational services than they do as children in need of educational services (Gelman, 1974). The handicapped usually require special preparation and special services in order to reach their potential in vocational, personal, and social areas. Among the kinds of services needed by the handicapped secondary level student or adult are 1) evaluation and assessment of aptitudes, abilities, and attitudes, 2) vocational counseling and referral to appropriate programs, 3) vocational training, including training in necessary related social and communication skills, 4) job placement, including provisions for various degrees of sheltered employment, and 5) followup services to evaluate job adjustment and changing needs. Agencies currently providing various components of these services include the public school system, whose vocational responsibilities have been increased by recent legislation, state vocational rehabilitation agencies, and public vocational training centers funded by state and federal agencies under the Vocational Rehabilitation

Act of 1973. Private nonprofit rehabilitation facilities provide some programs, as do residential institutions which attempt to prepare residents for employment.

Needs Studies

The community/work adjustment of the handicapped is of special interest because of the current emphasis on normalization and the rights of the handicapped. Deinstitutionalization is also increasing the need for vocational services. Moves toward minimum-competency testing and teacher accountability have implications for vocational training of the handicapped.

Educational systems have in the past generally provided inadequate or inappropriate vocational or career education programs for the handicapped, resulting in their underpreparation and consequent underemployment or unemployment (Halpern, 1979). Post-school programs provided by vocational rehabilitation, other public agencies, and special interest groups have not been able to fully compensate for the lack of early, ongoing sequential development of necessary skills and attitudes. Parents have long felt that their handicapped children have not received the educational services needed for securing employment after leaving school. Vocational rehabilitation counselors have stated that much time must be spent in training clients coming from special education programs in attitudes and skills which could be appropriately taught in the public schools.

Brolin and D'Alonzo (1979) pointed out that a majority of the handicapped fail to adjust satisfactorily in employment and community living. Throughout their educational experiences, a great number of handicapped students fail to acquire adequate social and academic skills, and also suffer from a discontinuity in career development. Work-study programs in high schools have seldom been effective in developing the full potential of the student. Data cited by Martin (1972) showed that only 21 percent of the handicapped leaving secondary schools would be either suitably employed or college-bound. Forty percent would be underemployed; 26 percent unemployed. Ten percent of the handicapped were seen as requiring a sheltered work and home situation; three percent would remain totally dependent. These figures are felt by some to reflect the failure of the educational system to provide the relevant skills necessary for the handicapped to maximize their abilities, both vocational and social.

Brolin, Durand, Kromer, and Muller (1975) carried out a study to determine postschool adjustment of former special education students in the Minneapolis Public Schools. Study results were to be used in planning for curriculum changes in the system's high schools. Results showed that a large percentage of the former students had problems in vocational adjustment after leaving school. Reported problems were "unemployment, low pay, low level jobs, not knowing how to find and apply for jobs, lack of experience, lack of appropriate skills, and lack of job openings" (p. 147). Employers of the former students listed their primary assets as reliability and punctuality, good work and good work habits; greatest problems were undependability, slowness of intelligence, necessity for supervision, and moodiness, lack of self-confidence, and personal problems.

An earlier study was made by Brolin (1973a) as to the needs of secondary level EMR students and needed teacher competencies. The study involved all secondary special education teachers in Wisconsin (N = 251) and 30 administrators. Results of the study supported redirecting curricula and teacher education toward a career development approach. Secondary teachers of the educable should be able to provide instruction in occupational and psychosocial areas and in daily living activities as well as in academic areas. The importance of occupational curriculum competencies was rated significantly higher than the other areas, but was apparently the most neglected in actual practice. Needs for special education prevocational specialists, greater involvement of other school personnel, and more direct service to special education programs by community agencies were also seen as areas for development.

Possible Reasons for Failure to Meet Needs

Educable mentally retarded students do not usually go on to other education after leaving secondary school programs, so it is essential that they receive effective vocational training and career education while in school. One obvious reason for failure of the schools to meet this need has been the inadequate training of special education teachers for competency in providing necessary job related skills, knowledge, and attitudes. Other problems (Brolin, 1973b) include inadequate communication between special education teachers and vocational rehabilitation personnel, no time to develop and supervise work experiences, and insufficient knowledge of mental retardation by personnel outside education (rehabilitation workers, employment services, social services, and so forth).

Brolin (1973b) also gave the lack of systematic vocational evaluation for the students as a primary reason for the failure of secondary school work-study programs. He placed the responsibility for vocational development of the EMR with the secondary school program, pointing out that the vocational rehabilitation agencies are already carrying overloads, and emphasized that a vocational evaluation program should be an integral part of the secondary school curriculum. Such a program should include, according to Brolin, the following components: 1) clinical assessment (medical, social, educational, and psychological), 2) work evaluation (including intake and counseling interviews, vocational tests, standardized tests used with caution, work and job samples, and situational assessment focusing on general work habits and behaviors), 3) work adjustment, and 4) on-the-job tryouts.

Coordination Between Agencies

Special education, vocational education, and vocational rehabilitation in the past have, with rare exceptions, not been coordinated. There have been very few programs combining vocational training resources with special education resources. The necessity for cooperation in developing educational and vocational programs to meet the needs of the handicapped is assuming greater importance as the present normalization philosophy is requiring communities to accept more responsibility for this population. In the last few years there have been encouraging evidences of federal and state awareness of the need for cooperation between agencies providing vocational services to the handicapped. Such interagency cooperation has been described as the "single, most significant factor for service delivery to handicapped persons in vocational education" (Parents Campaign for Handicapped Children and Youth, 1978, p. 9). The close relationship is recognized by the placement of special education and vocational rehabilitation in the Department of Education, under the currently proposed government reorganization of the Department of Health, Education, and Welfare (HEW) which would make Education a Cabinet level post.

Similarities in Philosophy

The separation of special education and vocational rehabilitation has long been viewed by many as an artificial dichotomy. Differences between the provision of services by special education and vocational rehabilitation are primarily due to governmental organizational structure and funding, not in any underlying philosophical differences. Elements in the philosophies and theories behind the provision of services by the two disciplines are mutual and similar. DiMichael (1964) described the spirit and rationale of rehabilitation, and pointed out that its concern is with *all* handicapped, not with any particular subgroups. His delineation of the philosophy of rehabilitation fully reflects the present concern with the rights of all handicapped. Stevens and Reid (Note 4) listed several specific points of mutual concern:

1. There is a mutual concern for identifying conditions of body deformity (or mental handicap) that may tend to interfere with normal problem solving in everyday living.
2. There is a mutual concern for the alleviation, reduction, or removal of a handicapping condition.
3. There is a mutual concern for teaching or training the handicapped person to make adaptations to situations which determine his adjustment.
4. There is a mutual concern for assisting the handicapped person to develop a realistic self-concept that meets the requirements of daily life, to the end that he views himself capable of a useful and happy existence.
5. There is a mutual concern for assisting the individual to develop a broad array of social competencies that will compensate for his mental/physical limitations (Note 4, pp. 3–4).

VOCATIONAL REHABILITATION SERVICES

Vocational rehabilitation programs in the United States were developed in a number of states in the early part of the twentieth century, without any financial aid from the federal government. Federal funding and administrative involvement in vocational rehabilitation began in 1920, with the passage of the Smith–Fess Act (PL 236). Under this act, the federal government provided grants-in-aid to states having approved programs. The states were required to pass enabling legislation and establish state administrative boards. Federal funds were allocated to the states according to population and on a matching basis. At present (1979) the federal government provides funds on an 80-20 basis; the states provide the lesser amount.

Expansion of Vocational Rehabilitation Services

Services under the Smith-Fess Act were limited in scope and were restricted to those persons with physical disabilities. Broader provision of services has been written into succeeding legislation, so that the state-federal vocational rehabilitation program now encompasses a wide range of services for eligible disabled and handicapped persons:

1. comprehensive evaluation;
2. medical, surgical, and hospital care, and related therapy to remove or reduce disability;
3. prosthetic and orthotic devices;
4. counseling, guidance, referral, and placement services;
5. training services;
6. services in comprehensive or specialized rehabilitation facilities;
7. maintenance and transportation during rehabilitation;
8. tools, equipment, and licenses for work on a job or in establishing a small business;

9. initial stock, supplies, and management services for small businesses, including acquisition of vending stands by the state agency;
10. reader services for blind persons and interpreter services for deaf persons;
11. recruitment and training services to provide new careers for handicapped persons in the field of rehabilitation and other public service areas;
12. construction or establishment of rehabilitation facilities;
13. provision of facilities and services which promise to contribute to a group of handicapped persons but which do not relate directly to the rehabilitation plan of any one person;
14. services to families of handicapped persons when the services will contribute to the rehabilitation of the handicapped client;
15. post-employment services, including follow-up and follow-along to help disabled persons hold a job; and
16. other goods and services necessary to render a handicapped person employable (*RSA Programs*, p. 6).

Services to various handicapped populations since 1920 have steadily increased in both quality and quantity, although administrative and financial strictures have prevented full implementation of legislative provisions. Several pieces of legislation are especially noteworthy.

Passage of the Barden-LaFollette Act (PL 113) in 1943 made the mentally retarded eligible for vocational rehabilitation services. Definitions of vocational rehabilitation in the early decades after the beginning of the state-federal program had until this time precluded provision of services to this group.

The Rehabilitation Act Amendments of 1954 (PL 565) greatly increased federal funding of rehabilitation, including awarding of grants to educational institutions for training of vocational rehabilitation personnel. The rehabilitation profession became concerned with the motivation and work personality of their clients, as well as with their physical capabilities for work, and a new type of service, evaluation and work adjustment, became available to clients. This service assesses all aspects of the person's ability to function in an employment setting, and helps him to develop the attitudes, behaviors, and personal habits and relationships necessary for success on the job (Brolin, 1976). Progress was also made during this decade in providing services to the institutionalized mentally ill and mentally retarded, and in placement of the blind in industry.

Another major expansion of services came with the passage of PL 333, the Vocational Rehabilitation Amendments of 1965, which provided for extended evaluation to determine rehabilitation potential. Realistic determination of capacities and limitations of some handicapped clients may involve months of continued evaluation in vocational, social, psychological, medical, and other areas. The extended evaluation provision of this act enabled Vocational Rehabilitation to provide for many such handicapped who formerly would have been quickly rejected (Jenkins, in press).

The Rehabilitation Act of 1973 (PL 93-112) emphasized the rights of all individuals to appropriate services. The rights of the handicapped were not only acknowledged, but mandated. Increased emphasis was placed on serving the severely disabled. There was also a greater stress placed on client participation in the rehabilitation process. The act provided that an individualized written rehabilitation plan should be developed by the counselor and client together, with the client becoming an active and equal participant in making decisions concerning the kinds of services he needs (McLelland, 1976).

Other sections of the 1973 legislation contributed to the greater effectiveness of the rehabilitation program through removal of architectural and transportation barriers and through the establishment of civil rights for the handicapped. Many physically handicapped persons have found themselves unable to obtain employment or avail themselves of services easily accessible to the nonhandicapped because of architectural barriers or lack of appropriate transportation. Employers' attitudes toward hiring the handicapped have formed another kind of barrier—an intangible one. Sections 502, 503, and 504 of the 1973 Act provided legislative impetus to the drive for a barrier-free environment for the handicapped. Progress has continued toward ensuring compliance with these sections of the Act.

Habilitation as Well as Rehabilitation

This early definition of rehabilitation was given by the National Council on Rehabilitation (1942): "Rehabilitation is the restoration of the handicapped to the fullest physical, mental, social, vocational, and economic usefulness of which they are capable" (Obermann, 1967, p. 102). Present concerns of rehabilitation legislation with the developmentally disabled make it clear that current definitions must include "habilitation" (an original development of the person's capabilities) as well as "rehabilitation" (a restoration of former abilities) as objectives of the state-federal program of vocational rehabilitation. Of the 35 million physically and mentally handicapped in the United States, approximately 10 million are categorized as severely disabled and unable to function in regular employment settings (Humphreys, Note 3). Greater emphasis is now being placed on the underdeveloped potential and capabilities of this population, and less on their liabilities.

With the passage of the Rehabilitation Act of 1973 (PL 93-112), Vocational Rehabilitation began the provision of a broad spectrum of services to *all* handicapped, including those for whom vocational placement can never be a reality. However, under this Act, to be eligible for rehabilitation services the applicant was to have "a physical or mental disability which constitutes a substantial handicap to employment, with a reasonable expectation that vocational rehabilitation services will benefit the person in obtaining and sustaining employment." This definition seemed to impede intended provision of services. A revised and more liberal definition of "handicapped individual" was given in the 1974 Rehabilitation Act Amendments (PL 93-516), thus clarifying the intent of Congress to make the Acts applicable to "any person who (a) has a physical or mental impairment which substantially affects one or more of the person's major life activities, (b) has a record of such impairment, or (c) is regarded as having such an impairment" (DeLoach & Greer, in press).

The current normalization movement toward the integration of the handicapped in normal society to the greatest extent possible would also provide special facilities within regular communities for the more severely impaired. The comprehensive Rehabilitation Services Amendments of 1978 (PL 95-602) provide for such services to those handicapped who may never have employment potential, but who can benefit from services to assist them in areas such as independent living, social skills, and more fulfilling use of their time. Persons so severely handicapped that they are unemployable and/or unable to function independently in the family or community are eligible under these 1978 Amendments for a number of comprehensive services (Jenkins, in press).

The Comprehensive Independent Living Services Program authorized and funded under the 1978 Amendments is "designed to meet the needs of individuals whose disabilities are so severe that they do not presently have the potential for employment, but may benefit from vocational rehabilitation and other services which will enable them to live and function independently" (Office for Handicapped Individuals, 1979, p. 1). The capacity of this population for independent living can be enhanced with supportive services and more accommodating environments. The commitment of Vocational Rehabilitation to the provision of services and protection of rights of *all* handicapped is indicated in the title of the 1978 Act, the Rehabilitation, Comprehensive Services, and Developmental Disabilities Amendments (PL 95-602), and clearly delineated in its specific provisions.

Present and Future Directions of Vocational Rehabilitation

In addition to establishment of comprehensive independent living services, major provisions of PL 95-602 include:

1. State protection and advocacy systems for the disabled
2. The establishment of a new National Institute of Handicapped Research
3. Programs of government-industry interaction to increase employment opportunities for the handicapped
4. Establishment of a National Council on the Handicapped
5. Establishment of a central clearinghouse for information and resources available for the handicapped
6. Expansion of enforcement authority for Sections 502, 503, and 504 of the 1973 Amendments
7. Provision of vocational rehabilitation services for American Indians, and
8. Expansion and extension of services to the developmentally disabled

Robert R. Humphreys, Commissioner of the Rehabilitation Services Administration (RSA), described these legislative provisions as the beginning of a "national commitment to provide a continuum of care for our disabled citizens" (Office for Handicapped Individuals, 1978, p. 8). Additional new directions currently being explored were also listed by Humphreys:

Working toward a fully coordinated Head Start-special education-vocational education-vocational rehabilitation program, nationwide

Undertaking a comprehensive national survey of disability and service needs, with consequent development of a national data system on disability

Mounting a major outreach and referral program with respect to disabled individuals who are egregiously underserved—those with multiple handicaps of physical or mental disability combined with cultural and economic deprivation

Creating a coordinated program of deinstitutionalization involving transitional living, group homes, and habilitation and rehabilitation services

Eliminating disincentives to rehabilitation, including the retention of Medicare-Medicaid benefits and food stamps after employment

Supporting legal assistance centers for the disabled to protect their rights under Title V of the Rehabilitation Act

Establishing a nationwide system of client assistance programs so that through omsbudsmen, disabled individuals will be able to "fight the system" to obtain the fullest possible service benefits

Demonstrating new approaches to meet the transportation and residential needs of disabled people

Initiating a cooperative research effort in central nervous system (spinal

cord) regeneration, and in areas of disability prevention, ameliora-
tion, and treatment

Adopting new focus for international rehabilitation interchanges to take
advantage of technological and service delivery innovations of
developed nations

Exploring ways to meet the need for new or renovated rehabilitation
facilities and physical improvement in institutions which house
physically and mentally disabled people

VOCATIONAL EDUCATION FOR THE HANDICAPPED

Vocational education has long been a part of the school curriculum,
traditionally being offered exclusively at secondary or postsecondary
level. This vocational training has been of value to many, but for the
physically, mentally, or educationally handicapped, it has seldom been
enough or too often has been inappropriate. While there have been some
excellent programs, few secondary-school-age handicapped learn the living skills and specific technical skills that are needed to become and
remain employed.

Vocational education services to the handicapped were emphasized
in the Vocational Education Amendments of 1968 (PL 90-576), which
recognized the need for the older handicapped student to have greater
access to vocational training, including a broader range of vocational
opportunities and the modification of vocational educational facilities to
give the handicapped ready access to such facilities. Since 1968,
comprehensive vocational education legislation has been passed in many
states. However, although there has been this greater emphasis on vocational education in the last several years, the charge by Goldstein (1969)
that too much emphasis is placed on academics and too little on development of social/occupational competence is still valid. Reviews and
assessments of vocational education programs for the handicapped, as
summarized by D'Alonzo (1978), show that little has been done to carry
out the intent of the 1968 federal legislation. Halpern (1979), concurring
with these findings, stated that areas of concern include an inappropriate
emphasis on academics, the failure of the mainstreaming movement to
provide adequate secondary level models, and the reluctance of vocational education to finance appropriate services for the handicapped.

Passage of the Education for All Handicapped Children Act (PL
94-142) in 1975 was an important step toward achievement of vocational
goals for handicapped students. The act's definition of special education
included "vocational education . . . organized education programs . . .
directly related to the preparation of individuals for paid or unpaid

employment, or for additional preparations for a career requiring other than a baccalaureate or advanced degree" (*Federal Register*, Tuesday, August 23, 1977, Section 121a). The law also specifically included industrial arts, consumer and homemaking programs as appropriate for handicapped children, as preparation for more advanced vocational education.

The Vocational Education Act Amendments of 1976 (PL 94-482) strengthened the ability of the states to provide increased service to both handicapped children and disabled individuals of all ages who need vocational education. Under this legislation, 10 percent of the federal funds allocated to the states for vocational education must be spent on programs and services for the handicapped. Vocational programs in secondary schools must comply with all requirements of PL 94-142; vocational education plans for a handicapped child must be coordinated with his/her individualized education program (IEP) (Razeghi & Davis, 1979). Such services as vocational instruction, curriculum development and modification, modification of vocational equipment, supportive services such as interpreters for the deaf, guidance and counseling, job placement, and placement follow-up are included under this law. Each state department of education has a coordinator of vocational education for the handicapped within the division of vocational education.

One program illustrating a state department of education's role in improving the quality of vocational services to the handicapped is that developed in Illinois. The Illinois Network of Exemplary Occupational Programs for Handicapped and Disadvantaged Students (Illinois State Board of Education, 1978) consists of eight demonstration centers and one diffusion/coordination center. Intensive assistance to local school districts is provided through consultation services, workshops, inservice and preservice programs, and development and distribution of materials relevant to programming for the handicapped. Workshops on instructional development for special students are held across the state. These workshops focus on materials from the Network and from the State Department of Adult, Vocational, and Technical Education. Each of the eight demonstration centers works with local school districts to upgrade their vocational programs for the handicapped. Service agreements may be developed between these Network sites and local schools, whereby such services as consultation, workshops, and materials will be provided.

Recent Developments in Joint Service Delivery

A joint work group was formed in 1977 by the Bureau of Education for the Handicapped (BEH) and the Rehabilitation Services Administration (RSA) to prepare guidelines for school districts in coordination of services to the handicapped under the Rehabilitation Act of 1973, the Education for All Handicapped Children Act of 1975, and the Vocational Education Amendments of 1976. An October, 1977 federal government administration policy directive from the Commissioners of Education and Rehabilitation to state rehabilitation agencies had as its purpose

> To assure that handicapped persons eligible for services under the Education for All Handicapped Children Act of 1975 (PL 94-142), the Vocational Education Act Amendments (PL 94-482) and the Rehabilitation Act of 1973 (PL 93-112) receive all appropriate services for which they are eligible.
> To assure that all agencies administering these laws understand that eligibility under one law should not, in and of itself, result in a denial of *complementary* services under another of the laws.
> To assure that the Federal agencies involved are fully committed to helping State and local agencies to engage in coordinated service delivery for handicapped persons.
> Further, without restricting the eligibility of any handicapped person, it is the intent of the Commissioners to encourage their constituent State and local agencies to give priority to identifying severely handicapped persons requiring services and to assuring the prompt and effective delivery of services to all those who qualify for them (Boyer & Humphreys, Note 1).

A later communication (Boyer & Humphreys, Note 2) supplemented the 1977 memorandum by providing additional clarifying guidance on cooperative agreements between educational and vocational agencies, and announced a joint national drive toward expansion and improvement of service delivery to handicapped individuals. Immediate priority was given to the development of formal cooperative agreements between special education, vocational rehabilitation, and vocational education programs in order to maximize services to these persons.

One such cooperative agreement, the Michigan Inter-Agency Model and Delivery System of Vocational Education Services for the Handicapped, was first developed in 1971. Michigan's program has resulted in improved and expanded services to secondary and post-secondary students (Parents' Campaign for Handicapped Children and Youth, 1978). The interagency agreement has since served as a model for other states planning for cooperative services delivery. Another example of interagency planning is shown in Table 1, which illustrates the coordination of services resulting from cooperative agreements between agencies in the state of Idaho.

Vocational Development, A Complex Process

Cook and Engleman (1978) called for a coordinated plan through the school experiences of the handicapped:

Table 1. Service agreement between Idaho agencies

Service	Agency		
	State Division of Vocational Rehabilitation	State Division of Vocational Education	State Department of Education, Division of Special Education
Information, consultation	X	X	X
Evaluation of potential, when critical to development of individual plan	X		X
Counselling client/student	X		X
Medical restoration	X		
Vocational training	X	X	X
Maintenance of client	X		
Placement of client/student	X	X	X
Transportation of client/student	X		X
Telecommunications	X		
Salaries of selected personnel involved in delivering special program		X	X
Supplies and instructional materials over and above standard school resources		X	X
Instructional staff travel needed for workshops, prevocational meetings, or work placement coordination		X	
Staff development	X	X	X
Specialized support services contingent on student/client condition, program circumstances, and problem	X	X	X

Source: *Interagency Planning: Special Education and Related Services for Idaho's Handicapped/Exceptional Students* by J. A. Schrag and Robert C. West, Department of Education, Special Education Section, Boise, Id., 1978, p. 6c.

Vocational education plays an important role in the overall plan of education for the handicapped. In order to maximize their potential, the handicapped must be educated and trained for the world of work, and this training must begin at an early age and continue through to successful employment. It is therefore imperative that related agencies share a common understanding of the handicapped population, their characteristics and needs, and cooperatively plan together in order to prepare the handicapped for employment (p. 294).

In 1977, the National Center on Employment of the Handicapped initiated a 5-year program to conduct Programmatic Research on Employment Preparation (PREP) for severely disabled youth, with special emphasis on the transition from school to work (Vandergoot, Jacobsen, & Worrall, 1977). At this Human Resources Center, research and development has been and is being carried out in four major core areas: independent living, career education, job placement, and attitudes toward the disabled. Figure 1 illustrates graphically the need for cooperation and interaction between various persons and professions and with the disabled person through the entire school-work life cycle, for each of the four areas.

CAREER EDUCATION

In the last few years, the concept of career education has emerged as a significant development in the provision of services to the handicapped. The goal of career education for *all* students throughout the nation was first described by Sidney P. Marland, United States Commissioner of Education at that time, in 1971. Commissioner Marland proposed that *every* high school graduate be prepared for either gainful employment or postsecondary education, and career education became a priority for the U.S. Office of Education. Federal support for the career education concept has continued since the inception of the movement in the early 1970s. In 1974 an Office of Career Education was established in the U.S. Office of Education. Research and development funds have been provided through this office for development of career education materials, construction of model programs, and preparation of educators. The federal Career Education Incentive Act (PL 95-207) was passed in 1977. This act, designed to infuse career education into the school curriculum, authorized funding for development of career education models and demonstration of effective career education techniques.

Characteristics of Career Education

The concept of career education as total preparation for life is an educational philosophy, not a single program or a synonym for vocational education. While many do equate this new concept with vocational

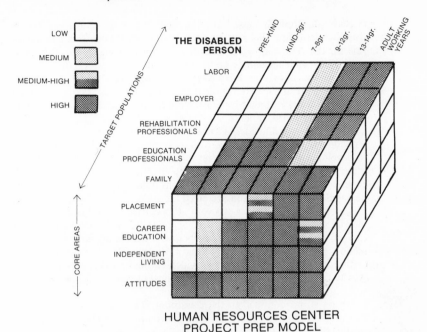

LOW

MEDIUM

MEDIUM-HIGH

HIGH

TARGET POPULATIONS

CORE AREAS

THE DISABLED
PERSON

PRE-KIND. KIND-6gr. 7-8gr. 9-12gr. 13-14gr. ADULT WORKING YEARS

LABOR

EMPLOYER

REHABILITATION
PROFESSIONALS

EDUCATION
PROFESSIONALS

FAMILY

PLACEMENT

CAREER
EDUCATION

INDEPENDENT
LIVING

ATTITUDES

HUMAN RESOURCES CENTER
PROJECT PREP MODEL

Figure 1.   The Human Resources Center Project PREP model. "This PREP (Programmatic Research on Employment Preparation) model has been designed to show the four care areas of our programmatic research and the target audiences of that research. The model is really multidimensional (e.g. Placement is a function of Attitudes, Independent Living, or Self-Sufficiency at Work, Career Education, the Disabled Person, Family Members, Rehabilitation and Education Professionals, Employers, etc.). Although all of the interactions cannot be adequately represented by this graphic device, it does show the intensity of individual interactions between key variables and persons with disabilities at different points in their life cycles. For example, the placement process is highly important in the life of a 20-year-old person with a disability, while the direct impact of an employer on a child with a disability is slight." (Reprinted with permission from Vandergoot, D., Jacobsen, R. J., and Worrall, J. D., *New Directions for Placement—Related Research and Practice in the Rehabilitation Process*, Human Resources Center, 1977, p. 8.)

education, career education is defined as being far broader, encompassing the total curriculum of the school, beginning at kindergarten and continuing through adulthood. It is envisioned as an infusion into the curriculum of experiences which will help students to understand and perform successfully in their varied life roles. The concept includes education for all aspects of community living—as family member, citizen, consumer, participant in avocational activities, and worker.

Banta (1978) reviewed various definitions of career education, and concluded that, regardless of the wording of the definition, most proponents of the concept would agree on these characteristics of career education:

1. Career education is based on the belief that *all education experiences*—curriculum, instruction, counseling—should confer an appreciation for the dignity of work and prepare the individual for a life of economic independence and personal fulfillment.

2. *Every teacher in every subject* can utilize career education as an *instructional strategy* to increase student motivation. Course content may be given additional meaning by illustrating the ways it can be used in pursuit of one or more careers.

3. Career education includes a career development component in which individuals are exposed to a variety of occupations and are encouraged to develop a work ethic and a set of work values; to explore their own interests, values, and aptitudes; to participate in various work experiences; and to make career decisions that are compatible with their personal characteristics and preferred life style.

4. Career education is concerned with *all* occupations, and is designed for individuals of *all* ages. Viewed developmentally, awareness and exploration of various occupations takes place in elementary and junior high school, preparation for occupations takes place in high school, then further specialization may be provided through post-secondary study. Adults continually need to upgrade their skills and/or knowledge, and some must be retrained for new jobs.

5. Learning is not confined to the classroom. The *resources* of the *home and the community* should be used to complement the efforts of the schools in career education.

6. Career education strategies can and should be used in every subject, but career education does not conflict with or detract from the achievement of other legitimate education concerns, such as basic skills, citizenship, culture, and family responsibility. Career education does not demand large expenditures for new materials, buildings, or staff . . . additional funds *are* needed for inservice education of teachers, counselors, and school administrators, for expanded offerings in vocational education, and for some career-related materials (p. 3).

Career Education for the Handicapped

Murphy (1978) related the universally accepted components of career education to the education of the handicapped:

1. *Career education is an educational philosophy rather than a physical entity, or single program.* A philosophical approach to the education of the handicapped is needed which embodies efficacious programs for enhancing their employability. A viable career education plan in the school in conjunction with Public Law 94-142, The Education of All Handicapped Children Act, will mesh nicely with Section 504 of the Vocational Rehabilitation Act of 1973. Section 504 reads: "No otherwise qualified handicapped individual in the United States shall, solely by reason of his handicap, be excluded from the participation in, be denied the benefits of, or be subjected to discrimination under any program or activity receiving federal financial assistance."

2. *Career education begins at grade K and continues through adulthood.* Public Law 94-142 requires educational programs for handicapped

children age 3 through 21; Section 504, through adulthood. The problem remains one of identifying which occupational choices are realistic options for children having various handicapping conditions.

3. *Career education is concerned with learning about work and involves more than preparation for work.* An excellent way for handicapped children to learn about work is through interviews of successful handicapped adults. This contact with handicapped adults will go a long way toward stimulating awareness and attitudes on the part of the children as well as their teachers.

4. *Career education is encompassed in the totality of education.* Career exploration and career awareness are essential ingredients of a total educational program. Teachers need to be aware of handicapped employees in their local communities. These people should be guest speakers in the classrooms emphasizing answers to these kinds of questions: How did you obtain your job? What do you do? What skills do you need? How much are you paid? How can we prepare for work in school?

5. *Career education seeks to prepare all students for successful and rewarding lives by improving their basis for occupational choice.* This concept is the foundation of all laws for the handicapped. Handicapped children have a right to the same opportunities that nonhandicapped children have (pp. 25–26).

Recognition of the importance of career education in the life of the handicapped was shown with the 1976 organization of the Division on Career Development within the Council of Exceptional Children (CEC). The Division is described as an organization for all people concerned with the career development of the exceptional. Career development is defined as "a process that facilitates responsible and satisfying life roles (such as student, worker, consumer, family member, citizen) through the use of teaching, counseling, and community interventions" (Brolin, 1978b, p. 2).

There is much every child should learn about careers and jobs long before secondary school age. This career awareness, important for all children, is especially so for the handicapped, who are deprived of experiences others get normally, such as paper routes, baby sitting, or mowing lawns. The individual educational program (IEP) mandate by PL 94-142 provides the vehicle for implementing a sequential career development program, beginning with the handicapped child's entry into school, so that he/she will have a greater opportunity to reach his potential as a member of society. Murphy (1978) emphasized the importance of sequential planning for the exceptional:

Career education relies on exposure to many different areas of knowledge. It begins with making individuals aware of both "self" and their environment. It means helping them to learn who they are and how they behave. The content of career learning flows from their study of work, work roles, and work relationships. These handicapped children need ideas and concepts that will enhance their ability to understand the present world in which they live and work. It is necessary to reconstruct traditional instructional strategies so that classroom experiences provide career maturational elements as well as subject matter learning (p. 30).

Programs in Career Education

During the past decade, many states have made legislative provision for career education programs. However, financial constraints, as well as lack of administrative guidelines and model programs of demonstrated effectiveness, have hindered implementation at local levels. Some states have made much progress in developing comprehensive career education guides for teachers. A representative example of such a program is the Michigan Model for Career Development. The Model views career education as containing two broad categories, career development and career preparation, and identifies "four basic interrelated knowledge, skills and attitude components: self-awareness and assessment, career awareness and exploration, career decision-making, and career planning and placement" (Michigan Department of Education, 1974, p. 3), all interrelated throughout the individual's life. Career preparation is defined as "the acquiring of academic and vocational knowledge and skills necessary to implement career decisions and plans" (p. 1). The *Reference Guide*, published by the Michigan State Department of Education, identifies desired career development and academic outcomes. A companion publication, *Ideas for Activities* (1976), includes career development goals and activities, developed by teachers, for teachers of secondary level special education students. The format of this book enables the user to easily locate ideas by academic subject area or by disability area.

Other career education instructional materials have been developed through federal grants, efforts of state and local school systems and other agencies, and by commercial publishers. Information on these materials can be secured through the ERIC Clearinghouse on Career Education, the ERIC Clearinghouse on Handicapped and Gifted Children, and the Educational Products Information Exchange (Brolin & D'Alonzo, 1979). Materials for career education are similar in their listings of career education components and desired competencies. Kokaska (1978) included four basic areas of development in the process of career education: career awareness, career exploration, career orientation, and career preparation. Six broad areas of competence were also identified by Kokaska as being essential to the success of the handicapped person in his adult roles: social interaction, work skills, decision making, self-evaluation, a positive self-concept, and physical development and leisure skills. Brolin (1976) described career education as a coordination of school, family, and community components to work toward economic, social, and personal fulfillment for each individual. He identified 22 competencies, falling under three curriculum areas, which he considered most essential to the career development of the handicapped:

DAILY LIVING SKILLS

1. Managing Family Finances
2. Selecting, Managing and Maintaining a Home
3. Caring for Personal Needs
4. Raising Children, Family Living
5. Buying and Preparing Food
6. Buying and Caring for Clothing
7. Engaging in Civic Activities
8. Utilizing Recreation and Leisure
9. Getting Around in the Community

PERSONAL-SOCIAL SKILLS

10. Achieving Self-Awareness
11. Acquiring Self-Confidence
12. Achieving Socially Responsible Behavior
13. Maintaining Good Interpersonal skills
14. Achieving Independence
15. Achieving Problem-Solving Skills
16. Communicating Adequately with Others

OCCUPATIONAL GUIDANCE AND PREPARATION

17. Knowing and Exploring Occupational Possibilities
18. Selecting and Planning Occupational Choices
19. Exhibiting Appropriate Work Habits and Behaviors
20. Exhibiting Sufficient Physical and Manual Skills
21. Obtaining a Specific Occupational Skill
22. Seeking, Securing and Maintaining Employment (p. 202)

A recent CEC publication (Brolin, 1978a) gives behavioral objectives, suggested activities, and suggested personnel responsibilities for each of an expanded 102 specific competencies under the three curriculum areas.

Critical Issues in Career Education for the Handicapped

The Bureau of Education for the Handicapped (BEH) in 1973 too optimistically proposed that by 1977 every handicapped child leaving school would have had career educational training relevant to the job market, meaningful to his career aspirations, and realistic in regard to his fullest potential (Brolin & D'Alonzo, 1979).

Issues which have been and continue to be of importance in the implementation of career education programs are those of 1) teacher attitude toward career education, 2) teacher training in implementing career education programs, and 3) cooperation between school and community and between education and vocational agencies in developing and carrying out such programs. Murphy (1978) cited the recommendations of the 1976 National Advisory Committee on the Handicapped that educators should:

1. recognize that career and vocational opportunities are as important to handicapped persons as to other citizens;
2. assure that handicapped children have access to career and vocational programs;
3. set aside necessary funds to establish and expand vocational education programs for the handicapped;
4. assure that state plans include a section outlining programs in career and vocational education for the handicapped; and
5. assure that the availability of federal support be contingent on inclusion of these provisions (p. 29).

Brolin and D'Alonzo (1979) listed and discussed critical issues in career education for the handicapped, stating that these issues must be resolved if career education is to be effectively implemented. They presented six major issues:

1. Should career education be primarily job centered or life centered?
2. Should career education be taught as a separate program or be infused throughout the curriculum?
3. Will the special education teacher still be primarily responsible for the handicapped student?
4. Will career education aid or impede the mainstreaming process?
5. What will be done with former courses, materials, and teaching processes?
6. How can personnel best be prepared to meet the career development needs of handicapped students?

Gillet (1978) surveyed 125 colleges and universities, both public and private, having degree programs in special education. Results of the questionnaire showed that although the majority of schools felt that career education for the exceptional child is an important area, teacher preparation in this area is still quite inadequate. Respondents to the Gillet questionnaire were asked to list areas of content for a teacher training course in career education for the exceptional child. The following areas were suggested:

1. Sequentially developed objectives, both academic and vocational, for a career education program for grades 1 through 12.
2. Stages of occupational development resulting in occupational choice.
3. Evaluation procedures and techniques for assessing job readiness and work performance on job stations.
4. Materials usable in a career education program for grades 1 through 12.

5. Components of a work-study program: job analysis, task analysis, job placement, types of jobs, kinds of work-study programs.
6. Personnel roles involved in a career education program.
7. Outside agency involvement in the career education program (Gillet, p. 517).

Results of the Brolin and Gillet studies, the emphasis of the Department of Health, Education and Welfare on career education and vocational education, and the mandate of PL 94-142 for education of the exceptional through the age of 21 all highlight the necessity for a greater emphasis on career/vocational education in the curricula for both the exceptional child and his/her teacher.

CONCLUSION

With appropriate guidance and training, most of the handicapped can look forward to paid employment as an important part of their careers. For others, more handicapped, terminal career goals will involve the ability to function adequately within the family unit and to engage in appropriate avocational activities. The focus of career education for each individual will necessarily depend upon his abilities, needs, and interests. There are many and varied resources, human, material, and financial, which must necessarily be involved in application of this broad concept of career development. To properly prepare the handicapped for careers requires cooperation between various disciplines and agencies over a period of years. In the past decade, there has been much progress toward this cooperation, at the federal level, through legislative action, through governmental policy statements, and through intergovernmental agency policy agreements. Effective interagency planning at the state level has implemented improved vocational and career training for the handicapped in some states, although at the local agency level comparatively little has been done in policy writing, program development, or community involvement.

Experimental training programs have fully demonstrated that inadequate or inappropriate instruction is a more formidable barrier to the employment of the handicapped than is any limitation within the handicapped person himself (Halpern, 1979). The legislative mandates of the past decade, the movements toward career education and competency-based teaching, and the growing acceptance of the philosophy of normalization have created an environment in which the handicapped can now be more effectively prepared to reach their employment potential (Razeghi & Davis, 1979). However, this goal of appropriate vocational and avocational training for all can only be reached through the cooperative efforts of the family, regular and special education, agencies involved with the handicapped, and business and industry.

REFERENCES

Banta, T. W. (compiler). *Career education: A framework for teamwork*, Knoxville, Tenn.: Bureau of Educational Research and Services, College of Education, the University of Tennessee, 1978.

Brolin, D. E. Career education needs of secondary educable students. *Exceptional Children*, 1973, *39*(8), 619–624. (a)

Brolin, D. E. Vocational evaluation: Special education's responsibility. *Education and Training of the Mentally Retarded*, 1973, *8*(1), 12–17. (b)

Brolin, D. E. *Vocational preparation of retarded citizens*. Columbus, Oh.: Charles E. Merrill, 1976.

Brolin, D. E. (Ed.). *Life centered career education: A competency based approach*. Reston, Va.: The Council for Exceptional Children, 1978. (a)

Brolin, D. E. President's message. *Career Development for Exceptional Individuals*, 1978, *1*(1), 2–3. (b)

Brolin, D. E., & D'Alonzo, B. J. Critical issues in career education for handicapped students. *Exceptional Children*, 1979, *45*(4), 246–253.

Brolin, D. E., Durand, R., Kromer, K., & Muller, P. Post-school adjustment of educable retarded students. *Education and Training of the Mentally Retarded*, 1975, *1*(3), 144–148.

Cook, I. D., & Engleman, V. Vocational education for the handicapped: Methodology for planning and implementing inservice. *Education and Training of the Mentally Retarded*, 1978, *13*(3), 294–297.

D'Alonzo, B. J. Career education for handicapped youth and adults in the '70's. *Career Development for Exceptional Individuals*, 1978, *1*(1), 4–12.

DeLoach, C., & Greer, B. *Metamorphosis: Adjustment to severe physical disability*. New York: McGraw-Hill, in press.

DiMichael, S. G. Vocational rehabilitation: A major social force. In H. Borow, (Ed.), *Man in a world at work*, Boston: Houghton Mifflin, 1964.

Federal Register. Tuesday, August 23, 1977, Part II (Rules and regulations for amendments to Part B, Education of All Handicapped Children Act of 1975, PL 94-142, Education of handicapped children).

Gelman, S. A system of services. In *New neighbors: The retarded citizen in quest of a home*. Washington, D.C.: Presidents' Committee on Mental Retardation, 1974.

Gillet, P. Career education: A survey of teacher preparation institutions. *Exceptional Children*, 1978, *44*(7), 516–518.

Goldstein, H. Construction of a social learning curriculum. *Focus on Exceptional Children*, 1969, *1*, 1–10.

Halpern, A. S. Adolescents and young adults. *Exceptional Children*, 1979, *45*(7), 518–523.

Higgins, S., & Barresi, J. The changing focus of public policy. *Exceptional Children*, 1979, *45*(4), 246–253.

Illinois State Board of Education. *The Illinois network of exemplary occupational programs for handicapped and disadvantaged students*. Chicago: Illinois Office of Education, 1978.

Jenkins, W. M. History and legislation of the rehabilitation movement. In R. Parker & C. Hansen (Eds.) Rehabilitation and counseling sources for persons with disabilities. Boston: Allyn & Bacon, in press.

Kokaska, C. Career awareness for handicapped students in the elementary schools. *Career Development for Exceptional Individuals*, 1978, *1*(1), 25–35.

McLelland, S. W. Individualized written programs. In W. M. Jenkins, R. M. Anderson, & W. L. Dietrich (Eds.), *Rehabilitation of the severely disabled*. Dubuque, Ia.: Kendall/Hunt, 1976.

Martin, E. W. Individualism and behaviorism as future trends in educating handicapped children. *Exceptional Children*, 1972, *38*(7), 517–525.

Michigan Career Education. *Reference guide: Career development goals and performance indicators*. Lansing, Mich.: Michigan Department of Education, 1974.

Michigan Career Education. *Ideas for Activities*. Lansing, Mich.: Michigan Department of Education, 1976.

Murphy, L. Career education and the handicapped. In T. W. Banta (compiler), *Career education: A framework for teamwork*. Knoxville, Tenn.: Bureau of Educational Research and Service, College of Education, The University of Tennessee, 1978.

Obermann, C. E. *A history of vocational rehabilitation in America*. Minneapolis: T. S. Denison & Co., 1967.

Parents' Campaign for Handicapped Children and Youth. *Closer Look*. Box 1492, Washington, D.C.: Summer 1978.

Programs for the handicapped. Office for Handicapped Individuals, 1978, *3*.

Programs for the handicapped. Office for Handicapped Individuals, 1979, *1*.

Razeghi, J. A., & Davis, S. Federal mandates for the handicapped: Vocational education opportunity and employment. *Exceptional Children*, 1979, *45*(5), 353–359.

RSA programs. Washington, D.C.: U.S. Department of HEW, Office of Human Development, Rehabilitation Services Administration, 1977.

Schrag, J. A., & West, R. C. *Interagency planning: Special education and related services for Idaho's handicapped/exceptional students*. Boise: Department of Education, Special Education Section, 1978.

Vandergoot, D., Jacobsen, R. J., & Worrall, J. D. *New directions for placement—related research and practice in the rehabilitation process*. New York: Human Resources Center, 1977. Washington, D.C.: U.S. Department of HEW, Office of Human Development, Rehabilitation Services Administration.

REFERENCE NOTES

1. Boyer, E., & Humphreys, R. *Policy memorandum*, October 17, 1977.

2. Boyer, E., & Humphreys, R. *Policy memorandum*, November 21, 1978.

3. Humphreys, R. *Testimony presented at Hearings of the Subcommittee on the Handicapped*, Senate Committee on Human Resources, March 14, 1978.

4. Stevens, G. D., & Reid, L. L. *Special education and rehabilitation: An artificial dichotomy*. Paper presented at The International Rehabilitation Seminar, Copenhagen, Denmark, June, 1963.

CONCLUSION

15
MAINSTREAMING
A Decade of Debate and Action

Gail L. Ensher, James F. Winschel, and Burton Blatt

As we approach the end of a decade, the debate over mainstreaming continues to absorb the energies of parents and professionals alike. The discussion that follows states in unequivocal terms three positions on this critical issue. Of course the authors realize that in the final analysis opposing views must of necessity submit to compromise.

The arguments presented are possibly most germane to the education of the mildly handicapped, although their relevance to all disabled children—whether in home, school, or institution—is unmistakable. The debate is written so as to heighten the probability that all positions related to this complex issue will be given adequate hearing, After all, parents, students, and professionals, individually or in mass, are likely to best serve children with special needs as they are informed of the issues and are thereby capable of engaging in debate and action.

MAINSTREAMING: THE IMAGE OF CHANGE

Gail L. Ensher

Challenge is synonymous with mainstreaming,
as are goals worthy of pursuit and teachers
fired by faith and imagination.

A decade of mainstreaming moves swiftly to a close. Surely it is time to forget past arguments and to get on with the task of improving what is already in practice. Mainstreaming stands as a symbol of education's

An earlier version of this paper appeared in *The Exceptional Parent*, 1976, 6, 6–12. Dr. Ensher's and Dr. Winschel's contributions have been completely revised; Dr. Blatt's discussion is reprinted by permission of the author and the publisher.

concern for the rights of all children. Its commitment to the education of the handicapped within the least restrictive environment (compatible with their maximum welfare) offers children of all levels of disability opportunities for training divested of the segregation and labeling which marked an earlier era. Already the critics of change speak with muted voices and in increasing numbers the original detractors of mainstreaming are supporting the new models of service delivery.

In theory, mainstreaming for the handicapped has about it the aura of opportunities made equal and the promise of accomplishment within the purview of regular education. The concept of least restrictive environment presumes the goals of normalization, the individualization of instruction, the reduction of labeling, a zero reject policy, and educational alternatives. These benchmarks of change confirm our commitment to the educability of intelligence, the plasticity of character, and the regeneration of body and spirit. Should mainstreaming succeed, the classroom isolation and the demeaningly low expectations that have been identified with much of special education will be a thing of the past.

What of our progress to date? Mainstreaming has reduced the populations of our institutions and, in the process, has contributed mightily to the alleviation of human suffering. Mainstreaming has given rise to a new awareness of the plight of handicapped children and a new willingness to accommodate differences within the broad expanse of regular education. And for all degrees of impairment, mainstreaming is elevating the conscience of society and is generating new demands for effort on the part of teacher, parent, and child. No longer will we tolerate warmed-over curricula, skills without sequence, or failure as the equal of success. Challenge is synonymous with mainstreaming, as are goals worthy of pursuit and teachers fired by faith and imagination.

Does mainstreaming really work? Yes, mainstreaming works when children make the long trek from institution to special school. It works when grade level teachers individualize instruction to meet the needs of children who might otherwise fail to achieve. It works when typical children in need of remediation seek out the resources of special class and teacher. And mainstreaming is working when the nonacademic activities of schools are fully available to all children without regard to limitations or placement. Indeed, the accommodation of variance is indicative of education at its best. The promise of mainstreaming is that "special" will be the character of all schools and as an adjective need not refer to either programs or children.

Handicapped children have not been the only victims of the segregated settings that flourished under the auspices of special education. Parents of the handicapped have been the misfits of the PTA and special class teachers the outcasts of the faculty lounge. In response, schools have characterized parents as uncaring and have branded teachers as martyrs. The result has been isolation, a lack of influence, and a substandard education for the children we seek to protect and serve.

The scene has changed dramatically since the advent of mainstreaming. Regular class teachers are being trained to meet the needs of children with mild and moderate disabilities, and special educators are assuming new roles as diagnosticians, consultants, and resource personnel. Meanwhile, parents more than ever are manifesting a rightful responsibility as advocates for their own children. Progress has not been made without monumental effort. Still, we have succeeded in rethinking our moral and philosophical commitments and, in a more limited way, have moved to reorder mission and priorities. It is already evident that this awakening holds promise that the ordinary is sufficient to the needs of almost all children when it is delivered with skill, enthusiasm, commitment, and love.

The mainstreaming movement, initially fueled by emotion and unsubstantiated conviction, has remained open to scrutiny. Across the land, qualified investigators are examining its theory and practice. The picture that emerges suggests both the widespread success of our initial efforts and the plethora of questions yet to be answered. Can the mystique of special education be lifted so as to instill in regular classroom teachers a confidence in working with the handicapped? How can we better educate children of diverse abilities to an acceptance of differences and a preference for the heterogeneity of unsegregated settings? How are we to interpret "least restrictive environment" when difficult judgments are to be made and the freedom of one seems the restriction of another? And how are we to prevent the backlash that seems to inevitably accompany the errors of implementation that are the province of all new movements? Answers to these questions are being sought and, whether immediately found or not, the problems to which they are addressed are clearly resolvable. Fortunately, ours has been a field well endowed with patience, persistence, and ingenuity.

The mainstreaming movement has delivered on its promise. The depopulation of institutions proceeds unabated, and service agencies are increasingly committed to integration of the handicapped within the life of the community. The passage of PL 94-142 has confirmed in law our good intentions, while giving us the resources to achieve the parity of educational opportunity long sought for handicapped children.

The 1970s have slowed the practices of abuse, ridicule, and separation that heretofore marked the education and training of the handicapped. In the decade ahead, mainstreaming as a slogan will disappear, while in practice its pedagogy will be routine within school and community.

MAINSTREAMING: A STILL AUDIBLE DISSENT

James F. Winschel

*. . . special educators have romanticized
the efficacy of regular class placement.*

Educators, like politicians, seem destined to repeat the errors of history. A catchword, spawned in passion and nurtured by disillusionment, has gripped our attention and clouded our memory. In the bottom drawer the research and philosophical treatises of yesteryear lie dusty and unheeded, and in the drama of educational change, mainstreaming holds forth on center stage.

There is a faddish quality to mainstreaming. It has grown too quickly and been loved too well. Like hula hoops and Progressive Education, it has captured our imagination and consumed our energies. Mainstreaming like other fads will have its day. In the inevitable tomorrow, special educators will again assume the responsibilities that with fervor they now urge upon general education.

Mainstreaming was born of the frustrations imposed upon special education by mismanagement in the regular school. Special classrooms, in particular, become catchalls for the unwanted and the oppressed, and a structure founded on aid to the handicapped proved insufficient to the awesome burden. With devastating regularity, special settings became the dumping grounds for the black and the poor, the disadvantaged and delinquent, the academically different of every stripe and hue. In this environment, the miseducation of children was common, but society, not special education, was largely to blame.

While the apologists for mainstreaming have tempered their initial demands for integration and have cloaked their intentions in deceptively reasonable language, one needs to understand that the bottom line is an assault on the special class structure of community based schools. Yet, generations of children, limited by physical and mental impairments, have found in special classes a haven from the unbridled competition and special ostracism that was too often their lot in the regular grades. With what conviction can we say that the elimination of these places of refuge will contribute to the welfare of handicapped children? While one acknowledges a certain stigma in special class placement, research has also shown that the attitudes toward program, teachers, and instruction of children so placed is not less positive than that of students in the graded school.

In their zeal to assume new roles and in their desire to be divested of responsibility for the mildly handicapped, special educators have romanticized the efficacy of regular class placement. Reality is something else. The typical graduate of minority group schools in the richest city in the world is reported to be functionally illiterate after 8 years of schooling. And in a prominent Eastern state the requirement of moderate academic competency among high school graduates has been viewed with dismay, first, because of the low standard it implies and second, because many students are presumed incapable of meeting the criterion. This is not to mention the drug addiction that is sweeping schools, the guards that patrol hallways, or the plummeting scholastic achievement scores that embarrass a nation. In a recent appearance before a Congressional committee, the author of a popular text on reading testified that if illiteracy continued to grow at its present pace, we would be faced in the 1990s with the need to import talent to manage the technical and academic structures of our society. One wonders at the folly with which we have ennobled the capacity of regular education to resolve the problems of its ordinary mission, much less the perplexities of children with special needs.

Is it possible that we have been mesmerized by high sounding ideals? *Integration?* It is too often the isolation of a deaf child in a class of hearing children. *Individualization?* Too often it is token attention to a child slow to learn by a teacher spread too thin and accountable overall for grade level achievement. *Normalization?* It was the failure of this principle that first necessitated special education. For a large proportion of handicapped children, the social and academic demands of regular education—simply stated—are abnormal. *Educational alternatives?* It is not a new concept. Special education has always offered special schools and special classes, remedial and resource rooms, itinerant teachers and homebound instruction—a host of alternatives to failure and rejection. What is too seldom understood is that the association of a handicapped child with higher ability groups results in emulation only when the disparity between child and group is sufficiently narrow as to hold hope for bridging the chasm.

The tide of literature on mainstreaming threatens to engulf us. Its selective interpretation by a vast army of proponents runs roughshod over dissent and ignores the disquieting evidence that places in doubt the efficacy of current integration practices. Special class teachers are subjected to a questioning of their motives, parents are goaded to criticize the educational placements of their children, and students themselves are encouraged toward dissatisfaction. A growing disenchantment with these developments will restore a balance to the educational process, and in the aftermath, general and special educators alike will be more temperate in their attitudes toward change.

Mainstreaming, as it is cautiously implemented, can be a positive force in American education. This observation is also true of the wise use of special settings that frequently call for the purposeful separation of children in need of intervention beyond the scope of normal school practice. The substandard settings that housed programs in the 1950s and 1960s are largely a thing of the past, as are the retreads and incompetents who posed as teachers. Only the curriculum—which too often mirrors the content of regular education—is in need of rehabilitation. When reading is secondary to language development, problem solving more important than arithmetic, and helping others more praiseworthy than helping oneself, we will have taken a giant stride toward reformation. Social and cognitive growth are the real business of special education. Indeed, we are in a unique position to modulate academic content which is the staple of general education and to concentrate instead on teaching children *to think* and *to be*.

I was a teacher of children, sometimes retarded, often black, and always poor. I pulled their teeth, wiped their noses, shared their joys and their sorrows. At all times I expected them to achieve and at all times summoned them to a self-concept not less positive than that of the children who were by blood my own. "Children" was the only label by which I knew them and, in an environment geared to the joy of learning, more sought to enter than to leave. It was not mainstreaming, but children who learned thrived in being special and accepted the difference. In this imperfect world, failure and rejection were still possible; they just weren't mandated. Will the advocates of mainstreaming do as well? The question is perhaps premature. For now, the voice of dissent is still justified.

MAINSTREAMING: DOES IT MATTER?

Burton Blatt

With the wisdom and technology of our age, could we teach Helen Keller as Anne Sullivan did . . .

Like most arguments in education, the current mainstreaming debate will soon be forgotten—even by its zealous participants—and its passing will go unlamented, if not entirely unnoticed. Its demise will occur not because "this" was right or "that" was wrong, but rather because it never really mattered. A more genuine problem, often misunderstood by the debaters themselves, is this: Are *teaching* and *learning* more related to process or substance, to interactions or structures? But even that question has a troubling appearance, becoming an embarrassing falsehood when applied to the arts. Among writers, painters, and composers, the question is meaningless. The artist simply creates, knowing that his work is not easily categorized nor subject to the simplicities of thoughtless people in search of easy truths. Just possibly, the mainstreaming debate is also a charade, evolving from simplistic conclusions, drawing our attention from serious problems, and focusing our energies on the trivial, the obvious, and the unimportant.

Teachers have long recognized the inconsequence of administrative rules, unique curricula, or special pedagogies as determiners of behavior. Human beings are seldom so talented as to create environments that elicit desired responses with lawful consistency. It may well be a fortunate imperfection, for out of this "flaw" comes one of the few human traits that offer hope for continued variation among people. (Skinner's dismay is another's joy.) Unfortunately, we find it necessary to deny our inability to order things. There will always be those who would "do something" in pretense of accomplishment and who would "claim much" in pretense of change. Undoubtedly, much of human action is related to the search for order, predictability, and influence. Alas, the work of the alchemist is now the work of the pedagogue.

Conventional research programs have been of little value in providing answers to the mainstreaming-segregation issue. Partially, our empirical failure may be attributed to a misunderstanding of the variables. Belief systems within education would appear to be inflexibly attached to the notion that the pedagogical map (organization, curriculum, and method) composes the most significant factor, contributing most to differences in achievement among otherwise equal groups or individuals. As a consequence, we study the relative effectiveness of diverse methods, unique settings, or one curriculum in relation to another. And, as we proceed in our investigations, the nature of the child or the personality of his/her teacher are presumed peripheral to the comparisons being made. Of course, controls are employed but merely for the purpose of neutralizing the peripheral or "intervening" factors while curriculum, method, or school are examined.

The research approach has not worked. It has not worked precisely because the major goals of the researcher have been at odds with the major objectives of education for the mildly retarded. My assertion deserves explanation: First, special education has sought historically to secure warm and receptive teachers. By contrast, and in order to focus on variables presumed more crucial, researchers have tended to neutralize the effect of teachers. Second, special education has sought to subordinate typical curricular goals to the objectives of social growth and interpersonal relationships; nevertheless, educational researchers have continued to study academic aptitude and school achievement. And third, the objectives of special education have focused on the child, while research has centered on the method, the program, and the organization. Not surprisingly, the proliferation of research and literature on "best approach" programs has done little to solve our problems or settle our debates. What we have finally learned—if we have learned anything—is to reject the dichotomy of special versus regular class attendance as the crucial factor in a child's academic progress. Indeed, the current data consistently suggest that children's experiences are not systematically different from one class to another, from program to program, or curriculum to curriculum.

Is mainstreaming a valid educational issue? I conclude that it is not! The program, the curriculum, the label, the organization—the most obvious components of education—are strangely irrelevant to the relationships we seek to understand. Those educational components which do matter—largely ignored in our research—are the teacher as a human being who teaches and learns, children as learners with potentials and rights, and the environment—rich, flexible and thoughtfully created. (At the same time, one senses the futility of segregation. The environments people need are more often obtainable and more easily created in the heterogeneous "normal world." But that is another debate.)

How far have we come in our ability to educate the child with special needs, the different individual? Would mainstreaming help our cause or harm it, or make no difference? With the wisdom and technology of our age, could we teach Helen Keller as Anne Sullivan did or instruct Victor as Jean Itard once taught that "wild savage"? And if we could, would we not also be marked in history as noble people, kin to those who have glorified human potential and decency?

There was a uniqueness that marked the education of Helen Keller, Victor, and the innumerable others who dot the history of the special education profession. Was it a segregated program, the mainstream, a curriculum or "a something" codified and lawful that caused those people to learn and to change? It was not! There was a human spirit who sought an understanding with itself and with the finite world. And there was a great teacher. Inevitably, there was the interaction. That is what mattered.

INDEX